# AMERICAN SEXUAL POLITICS

ESSAYS FROM THE

*JOURNAL OF THE HISTORY OF SEXUALITY*

# AMERICAN
# SEXUAL
# POLITICS

## Sex, Gender, and Race
## since the Civil War

EDITED BY

## JOHN C. FOUT AND MAURA SHAW TANTILLO

THE UNIVERSITY OF CHICAGO PRESS
*Chicago and London*

The essays in this volume originally appeared in various issues of the
*Journal of the History of Sexuality*. Acknowledgment of the original publication
date may be found on the first page of each essay.

The University of Chicago Press, Chicago, 60637
The University of Chicago Press, Ltd., London
© 1990, 1991, 1992, 1993 by the University of Chicago
All rights reserved. Published 1993
Printed in the United States of America
ISBN (cl.) 0-226-25784-3
ISBN (pa.) 0-226-25785-1

97  96  95  94  93    5  4  3  2  1

Library of Congress Cataloging-in-Publication Data

American sexual politics : sex, gender, and race since the Civil War /
    edited by John C. Fout and Maura Shaw Tantillo.
        p.   cm.
        "Essays from the Journal of the history of sexuality"—Prelim. p.
        Includes bibliographical references and index.
        ISBN 0-226-25784-3 (cloth). — ISBN 0-226-25785-1 (pbk).
        1. Sex customs—United States—History.   2. Sex crimes—United
    States—History.   3. Sex and law—United States—History.   I. Fout,
    John C., 1937-      .   II. Tantillo, Maura Shaw.
    HQ18.U5A46   1993                                              92-47347
    305.3′0973—dc20                                                   CIP

The paper used in this publication meets the minimum requirements of
American National Standard for Information Sciences—Permanence of Paper
for Printed Library Materials, ANSI Z39.48-1984. ∞

# Contents

# Acknowledgments

The publication of this second anthology of essays drawn from the *Journal of the History of Sexuality* has allowed us to accomplish still more of the objectives set during the initial launching phase of the journal four years ago. Through the gracious and unstinting help of our outside reviewers and members of our editorial boards, we can offer readers interested in the history of sexuality access to the resources of an international, multidisciplinary scholarly enterprise, committed to meeting the highest standards of critical and theoretical work. In this volume, especially, we would like to thank the contributors for their truly integrated perspectives on the role of sexuality and sexual politics in America. In addition to the scholars, we would like to acknowledge with gratitude the commitment of the journal staff, particularly Susan F. Rogers, assistant editor, and Professor Michèle D. Dominy, review editor. We also thank the faculty and staff at Bard College who have assisted us. Our appreciation of the support of the Journals Division of the University of Chicago Press remains as strong as ever.

John C. Fout
Maura Shaw Tantillo
Annandale-on-Hudson, New York

# Introduction

AMERICAN HISTORY SINCE the Civil War has been a period of ongoing political, economic, and social transformation almost unparalleled in modern Western culture. Central to that evolution, of course, was the establishment of an urban, industrial society in the latter half of the nineteenth century and the emergence of a technological society in the latter decades of this century, a process still underway in our time—scholars increasingly have referred to these two epochs as the modern and postmodern eras. The expanding political, economic, cultural, and even military roles for the United States in world affairs—the ascent of the United States as a world superpower—have contributed much to shaping the course of twentieth-century American history. Nonetheless, although these developments have had a substantial impact on the lives of all Americans, it is the more direct impact of social and economic change on the everyday lives of individuals that provides the context for the essays presented here. The central issue addressed in this anthology—modifications in sexual behavior and the growing significance of sexual politics—must therefore be understood as a response to the reorganization of society in the many generations since the Civil War. Controversies about sexuality surely have evolved from the alterations in patterns of work, family organization, and gender relations that have been the driving force behind the continuing struggles over "appropriate" sexual behavior for women and men.

For too long historians have underestimated the importance of sexual politics; this anthology is a contribution to what is yet a rather small but rapidly expanding body of literature that will surely assist scholars in reevaluating the formative role that sexual politics has played in the larger scheme of American political life. The essays in this anthology were originally published in the first three volumes of the *Journal of the History of Sexuality*; topically they encompass a broad range of issues in

1

the history of sexual behavior in America since the Civil War. Some of the essays are also comparative and are concerned with sexuality and sexual politics in both Canada and the United States. In putting this collection together, one of the central goals was to provide readers interested in the history of sexuality with a truly "integrated" view, in the sense that the essays examine the experiences of men and women, blacks and whites, straights and gays, and so on. As a result, the authors provide a far more comprehensive picture of the period under study than has been the case in any recent study. The essays in their entirety probe the fascinating intersections between and controversies around gender, sexuality, race, and class. They delineate the myriad complex factors that have shaped American sexual politics in very specific ways in the past hundred and twenty-five years.

Thus readers interested in American social and political history, gender studies, lesbian and gay history, African American history, and multicultural studies will find this collection of considerable interest. These essays also reflect the ever-expanding boundaries of gender studies. While many of the essays are specifically focused on women, a number of others offer new insights on men's issues—strife over sexual behavior, of course, is often a reflection of actual alterations in women's and men's gender roles and the anxiety that results when people have difficulty understanding or adjusting to such changes. Taken in their entirety, the essays in this volume also provide another kind of perspective on American sexual politics because they approach this enigma from a host of disciplinary perspectives. Scholars from the social sciences and literature are represented in the volume, and the essays illustrate the diverse methodologies used in various disciplines by scholars examining sexuality across time. Similarly, this multidisciplinary approach means that the authors have drawn on an enormous variety of primary sources, published and unpublished, which has led to new findings. Important new archival documents have been used and, in other instances, scholars have based their research on personal interviews.

The anthology is organized into two sections, which reflect two distinct periods in the history of sexuality in America: the first eight essays in Part 1 focus on the period from "the Victorians to the Flappers"; and the eight essays in Part 2 are concerned with "Sexual Politics and Sexual Radicals since the 1940s." If the first period under study began somewhere around the 1880s, it was surely preceded by the changes occurring from mid-century onward and speeded up by the impact of the Civil War, emerging industrialization, and the appearance of an organized women's movement. That latter movement naturally grew out of expanding employment and educational opportunities for women, which in turn accelerated women's demands for greater political and economic equality. Moreover, the developments in the latter half of the nineteenth century epitomize the transition away from Victorian values regarding gender roles and appropriate sexual behavior to the new and often contentious lifestyles of the "modern" era. Those changes, to emphasize an earlier point, also coincide with the shift to an urban industrial democracy in the United States in the latter half of the nineteenth century. With the political, economic, and social restructuring of American society, alterations in the dominant sex and gender system gradually evolved as well.

The essays in Part 1 also illuminate why the older Victorian value system was under siege, and how reformers and reactionaries alike fought a bitter struggle to reform or retain the existing system—which, it was widely agreed by all, was in flux. Indeed, by the years immediately preceding the outbreak of World War I, Victorian assumptions about sexuality were largely a thing of the past. In turn, the war itself hastened the adoption of the new ideas about sex, a phenomenon patently obvious in the Roaring Twenties. Although it generally has been assumed that the 1920s was another watershed period in the history of sexuality, the essays presented here question whether sexual behavior and gender roles in that decade were modified all that dramatically. The Depression era may have undercut a process that had been accelerated by World War I, and therefore the ultimate impact may be less than was earlier believed. Rather, the period from the 1880s through the 1930s may well define the chronological limits of a distinct period in the history of sexuality in America.

Many historians, when writing about sexual politics in the decades after World War II, initially tended to emphasize the changes in attitudes toward sexuality reflected in the emergence of the "second women's movement" and the gay rights movement of the late 1960s. However, as new research has shown, the 1960s reform movements did not develop out of a vacuum. Much like the earlier period when the Civil War helped to shape the developments leading to the 1880s, the transformations in American life brought on by World War II had a decided impact on the next generation; rapidly changing patterns of women's work and the transformation of the American family impacted on American society in substantive ways both during the war and in the immediate decades thereafter. Thus, as a number of the essays in Part 2 demonstrate, the explosion of new ideas in the 1960s was preceded by the transformation begun in the 1940s. It is also important to note that, just as the growing concern and the resulting discussion in the late nineteenth century about sexually transmitted diseases played a role in the breakdown of Victorian values, so its contemporary counterpart, AIDS, has been a central issue in contemporary sexual politics since the early

1980s. The AIDS crisis and even the growing abortion debate have forced society to confront a range of issues around sexual politics anew, resulting once again in public discussion of explicit sexual behavior and sexual lifestyles. The two debates over AIDS and abortion have also spawned new activist movements that few would have expected in the 1960s and 1970s.

## PART 1: FROM THE VICTORIANS TO THE FLAPPERS

Scholars generally agree that important developments around issues of sexuality and gender began to surface about the middle of the nineteenth century, but most existing studies have focused on the period from the 1880s onward, often seen as a turning point in the history of sexuality. Although the essays in Part 1 emphasize the importance of the developments beginning in the 1880s, this collection recognizes as well that the Civil War was a pivotal time for American society; with the emancipation of millions of slaves, for example, a troubled new era in race relations was inaugurated. It should not be surprising that these changes had decisive impact on gender relations, sexuality, and sexual politics during the turbulent years that followed. Anthony S. Parent, Jr., and Susan Brown Wallace's essay on "Childhood and Sexual Identity under Slavery" and Martha Hodes's piece on "The Sexualization of Reconstruction Politics: White Women and Black Men in the South after the Civil War," the first two essays in this anthology, introduce this complex problem. They illustrate how racial problems intersected with issues of gender and class, and, as other essays clearly demonstrate as well, those factors have been an ongoing feature of American race relations right up to the present day. Clearly the sexual politics of race were shaped by the legacy of that "peculiar American institution"—slavery—and the burden of that unfortunate history has been an ongoing source of crisis and confrontation between whites and blacks.

Parent and Wallace based their study of "Childhood and Sexual Identity under Slavery" on a remarkable compilation of slave narratives taken down in 1929 and 1930 by Ophelia Settle Egypt and others at the Social Science Institute at Fisk University in Nashville, Tennessee; all the interviewers were also African Americans. This underutilized source was first published in 1941 and has been reexamined by Parent and Wallace to study the impact of slavery on children, but with the specific purpose of scrutinizing how the treatment—all too often, the abuse—by their white masters shaped these individuals' understanding of their sexuality, sexual identity, and even attitudes toward their own bodies long after slavery was ended. These men and women who recalled their brutal childhoods for the Fisk interviewers vividly remembered the day-to-day impact of slavery on their families. The former slaves graphically described how violence, sexual abuse, forced marriages, and the buying and selling of slaves irrespective of family units had a devastating impact on their own sense of self-worth; slaves were forced to accommodate their own personal, sexual, and family needs to this vicious social system. Parent and Wallace's study, therefore, offers significant new insights on the slavery experience from the perspective of sexuality and gender identity. The authors discuss how those degrading experiences were carried with these former slaves into their adulthood as free individuals. Clearly, the memory of slavery for most former slaves continued to affect their attitudes toward their own bodies and their sexual behavior long after Emancipation. Their responses to white culture were similarly influenced.

Martha Hodes traces what she calls the "sexualization of Reconstruction politics" by examining what impact the emancipation of the slaves had on race relations and sexuality. She argues that there was an important shift away from the manner in which society in the antebellum South had regarded sexual relations, primarily between white women and black men. This same issue would be regarded with great anxiety by white Southerners during the period of Reconstruction and long after. The new intolerance after the Civil War, she believes, was played out through the violent actions of the Ku Klux Klan, whose activities enunciated a manifesto of white concerns about the maintenance of a rigid racial hierarchy. Her essay is based on the testimony before an 1871 congressional committee investigating Klan violence in the South and a host of contemporary sources. The major thrust of Klan violence was directed at black men, and it took place in those areas of the South where there was less social and economic inequality between whites and blacks. Black manhood became intertwined with the freeman's newly acquired economic and political power and his goal of equal citizenship. Accusing a black man of the rape of a white woman was a common rationale for Klan attacks. Black men were beaten, maimed, castrated, and even killed. White women who had relationships with black men were also terrorized, because anyone who broke sexual taboos could be a target for Klan attacks. But why were black men often castrated? Obviously, taking away their manhood would serve to subvert political equality between blacks and whites. This brand of sexual violence against black men, as shown in a later essay by Robyn Wiegman, continued well into the twentieth century. Issues of citizenship and masculinity have molded the sexual politics of race for over a hundred years, and this pattern betrays a long history of violence against black men down to the present day.

The next three essays in Part 1, by Kevin J. Mumford, Jesse F. Battan, and Joan Smyth Iversen, examine still other issues in sexual politics in the latter half of the nineteenth century, but from the perspective of the dominant white middle-class cultural perspective. If there had been a prevailing sex and gender paradigm in Victorian America, it was shaped largely by white, middle-class Americans and by the 1880s was under siege. A range of new issues around sexuality had emerged, which were challenging the older value system. These issues reflect the symbiotic relationship between assumptions about appropriate gender behavior and appropriate sexual behavior. It was widely assumed that a biological imperative shaped gender roles, which dictated how men and women were supposed to behave sexually. However, with the roles that women played in society undergoing a transformation—especially the changes in the patterns of women's employment and the emerging women's movement—and with men's roles being reexamined as a result, the debate over sexual behavior reached a new level of intensity by the turn of the century. Although the existing literature on the progressive era has tended to emphasize the role of the state in regulating sexuality (for instance, attempts at control of prostitution and venereal diseases) and the emergence of a moral purity movement, the essays that follow offer new insights by focusing especially on the sexual radicals and sexual reform ideas.

In his essay on " 'Lost Manhood' Found: Male Sexual Impotence and Victorian Culture in the United States," Kevin J. Mumford examines a problem underlying an ongoing crisis in male sexuality, namely, the challenge of impotence. The concern about that predicament, he demonstrates, was actually interconnected with a number of other issues affecting masculinity—factors, his essay suggests, that were also indicative of the shift away from Victorian sexual values in the last decades of the nineteenth century. Mumford sees his research as a corrective of sorts, because recent scholarship has focused largely on women's sexuality or gay male experiences; he aims the spotlight on the male heterosexual. In the early Victorian period, when America was essentially an agricultural and preindustrial society, impotence was perceived as intertwined with reproductive concerns and fear of bodily depletion. Male impotence, however, came to be seen as quite a different problem by the early twentieth century. Mumford explores the complex factors involved in that transformation. In an urban industrial society, impotence was regarded as a problem of repressed desire as well as a sign of the damage done by modern civilization; these factors combined to deplete the sexual energy of the middle-class male, it was believed. Conversely, the white male of the artisan class represented a muscular masculinity unaffected by civilization, while black male sexuality was depicted as hypersexual, similar to that of barbaric, primitive tribal people. The debate over impotence now increasingly mirrored concerns about male sexuality from a racial and class perspective in a threatening big-city environment.

Jesse F. Battan's essay, "'The Word Made Flesh': Language, Authority, and Sexual Desire in Late Nineteenth-Century America," is an excellent companion piece to Mumford's study. Battan focuses on another interesting facet of the debate over sexuality, namely, the controversy over sexual language—particularly the anxiety over the use of explicit Anglo-Saxon words for sexual activities. He profiles those "reformers" who sought to expand the discourse on sexuality and those "reactionaries" who sought to constrict it. Battan, like Mumford, believes his findings also confirm the breakdown of Victorian values by late in the century. The conflict demonstrates the power of language and reveals why issues such as obscenity and censorship are often such a fundamental part of any dispute over sexuality. Battan is especially interested in the Free Love movement, and he examines how its leaders provoked controversy through their promotion of the use of the explicit sexual vernacular to discuss problems that individuals were experiencing in their own sexual lives. The Free Lovers posited that Victorian prudery had had a debilitating and unhealthy impact on people's sexual behavior and that through the liberation of the language, a healthy sexual life could result. Battan scrutinizes the writings of Moses Harman, the editor of *Lucifer, the Light-Bearer,* and Ezra Hervey Heywood, the editor of *The Word,* as well as Heywood's wife, Angela Tilton Heywood, who was an important voice in her own right in the Free Love movement. These activists sought to create a forum where people could discuss their sexual dilemmas without fear of censorship. The Free Love newspapers provoked fierce public controversy and therefore played an overt role in the "liberation" of sexually explicit language.

The focus in Joan Smyth Iversen's essay, "A Debate on the American Home: The Antipolygamy Controversy, 1880–1890," shifts to women and some of the complex misgivings about women's sexuality in the late nineteenth century reflected in the antipolygamy movement. Iversen maintains that the Mormon practice of polygamy, or patriarchal (plural) marriage, which was made public in 1852, developed into a controversial issue in American sexual politics because companionate marriage was in the process of becoming the dominant family ideal. After the Civil War, polygamy became an especially contentious issue because of the Mormons' drive for statehood for Utah. The Supreme Court ruled against polygamy in 1879, and in the same year women in Salt Lake City founded an organization that came to be known as the Woman's National Anti-Polygamy Society. These women had launched a women's crusade, but, as Iversen demonstrates, their movement came into conflict with the movement for women's suffrage; Mormon women had had the right to vote in the Utah Territory since 1870, and they were suffragists. Of the two mainstream women's suffrage organizations, the National Woman Suffrage Association, under the leadership of Susan B. Anthony and Elizabeth Cady Stanton, supported the Mormon women, and the American Woman Suffrage Association took a stand against the polygamous women. The conflict was played out in the 1880s as Congress debated taking the vote away from Utah women, which it indeed did in 1887. In focusing on that suffrage dispute, Iversen shows how the controversy became an argument about the American home. Because of the belief, which flourished in some quarters, that virtuous women were protected by traditional marriage, Mormon women were seen as victims of licentious men who supported polygamy; suffrage and sexual politics became intertwined.

The last essay in Part 1 to focus mainly on the period before World War I is Angus McLaren's "Sex Radicalism in the Canadian Pacific Northwest, 1890–1920." McLaren's findings also establish the radicalization of the debate over sexuality by the late nineteenth century and show how ideas about social reform and sexual reform were played out in Canada. In fact, many of the same controversies over gender and sexuality in North America were being contested all across Western culture at the same time, through a network of sexual radicals. McLaren rightly points out that there have been numerous investigations of the opponents of sexual radicalism in Canada but few studies on the advocates of these ideas, which emanated primarily from the political Left. His essay concentrates on two relatively neglected radical thinkers, Robert Bird Kerr and Dora Forster, who were both born in England but left for Canada in the early 1890s, where they eventually married. They returned to Britain in 1922, and in the following year Kerr became the editor of the *New Generation.* On the surface Kerr, who practiced law in various western Canadian provinces, led a rather mundane bourgeois existence. Nonetheless, during these years in Canada Kerr and Forster were writing for a series of socialist, progressive, and radical sexual reform publications in Canada, the United States, and Great Britain, such as the *Champion,* a suffrage newspaper in British Columbia, *Lucifer, the Light-Bearer,* in Chicago, and the *Malthusian,* an English neo-Malthusian publication (later renamed the *New Generation*). McLaren provides a detailed analysis of Kerr and Forster's sexual radicalism and traces their contacts with other sexual radicals in many countries.

The essay by Pamela S. Haag, "In Search of 'The Real Thing': Ideologies of Love, Modern Romance, and Women's Sexual Subjectivity in the United States," and Ann duCille's essay, "Blues Notes on Black Sexuality: Sex and the Texts of Jessie Fauset and Nella Larsen," are companion pieces that address the question, How liberated was women's sexuality in the 1920s and 1930s? The essays offer contrasting images of black and white women and reflect the similarities and differences between a dominant cultural perspective and the perception of women's sexuality within and outside of African American culture. Both scholars rethink the supposed gains for women in the age of the flappers. Their findings challenge the view that the decade of the 1920s was a positive turning point in the history of sexuality, which supposedly altered gender roles in ways that led to new options for women.

Pamela Haag, for example, questions the widely held assumption that with the modernization or liberalization of sexual mores, especially in the period after World War I, came a transformation of sexuality that brought sexual freedom for women. Was it really a time when society acknowledged that women had sexual desires that could be expressed inside or outside of marriage? Can we assume that women were no longer judged by standards of chastity or virginity, as had been the case in the Victorian period? That age, by contrast, had sought to repress women's sexuality entirely, at least for middle-class women. Haag reinterprets the 1920s and 1930s and argues that many of the views from the nineteenth century were largely replicated in the twentieth; that is, women's sexuality was still seen as unruly and out of control, rather than rational and self-controlled—the attributes of male sexual behavior. She draws upon a broad miscellany of contemporary sources, from popular advice columns for the lovelorn to the social scientific literature, in order to highlight the variety of discourses on women's sexuality, and she stresses that class differences played an important role in differentiation of heterosexual behavior. The sexual mores of working-class women were still highly denigrated, because these women were seen as oversexed and out of control. At the same time, middle-class women found themselves in a position where their sexual behavior was rigidly shaped by standards of conduct that determined how a "nice girl" comported herself. Haag constructs a complex analysis of this phenomenon through her discussion of ideologies about love and romance, which, she maintains, actually inhibited women from exercising proprietary control over their own sexual lives.

Ann duCille also challenges prevailing suppositions about black women's sexuality, which, she argues, largely have been defined through the images of black women blues artists and epitomized by the songs of women such as Ma Rainey and Bessie Smith, who sang of love and sex and longing and loss with the most direct and provocative language. They created a vernacular discourse on sexuality that supposedly was representative of the sexual attitudes and activities of all black women, and they articulated the material ills of a changing society when they spoke for blacks both in the rural South and in northern urban ghettos. By contrast, it has been asserted that black women novelists, who wrote about the lives of middle-class northern black women, enunciated a view of sexuality that was far more conservative and considerably less representative of black women as a whole. DuCille's study of two novelists, Jessie Fauset and Nella Larsen, who published in the 1920s and 1930s, contests these interpretations and argues that Fauset's and Larsen's prose represented in reality a black bourgeois blues. Their novels also focused on sexuality, especially black female desire, and, like the lyrics of the classic blues, addressed erotic and power relationships through their portrayal of male and female characters who experienced the lust and longing of middle-class women—and of their men. DuCille argues for a more comprehensive representation of the African American experience, which has too often been understood as singular and monolithic. Fauset's and Larsen's writings should not be seen as less authentically black because they are not raunchy or sensational. Moreover, they reflect how the lives of the black female bourgeoisie were qualitatively different from an uninhibited urban working class or a rural black peasantry. In fact, Fauset and Larsen confronted a far broader range of sexual problems for black women, duCille suggests, than the lyrics of Ma Rainey could begin to address.

### PART 2: SEXUAL POLITICS AND SEXUAL RADICALS SINCE THE 1940s

The period in American history since the 1940s has witnessed remarkable changes in sexual politics; many scholars in fact have asserted that after World War II a new period in the history of gender relations and sexuality began, an era of sexual reform movements focusing especially on women's reproductive rights and gay liberation. Certainly the second women's movement (or the second wave of feminism) in the 1960s, as well as the lesbian and gay rights movement—first launched, it has been suggested, by the Stonewall riots in New York City in 1969—actually had their origins in the dramatic social changes that came with World War II. That war, as well as the reactionary McCarthy era, had a decisive impact on gender relations and sexuality, and it signaled the emergence of new issues in sexual politics. The essays in Part 2 of this volume are concerned with developments since the 1940s that represent the second major shift in gender relations and sexual behavior in America, the first having occurred in the Victorian era. It is interesting that the sexual politics of the 1880s and 1960s were each an outgrowth of a major war and the development of a women's movement.

The first four essays in Part 2 are concerned, in the main, with sexual politics in the 1940s and 1950s. Many of the circumstances in those years set the scene for the emergence of issues in the 1960s that have dominated the increasingly fierce confrontation over gender and sexuality in our own time. In turn, the AIDS plague and the growing abortion controversy in the 1980s have resulted in the feminist and the lesbian and gay rights movements taking center stage, but, as in earlier periods, gains made by women and gays have prompted a vigorous counterattack from the radical Right and the fundamentalist Christian and orthodox Jewish denominations. Like the moral purity movement of the late nineteenth century, the sexual reformers are trying to advance their agenda through a well-organized effort to reverse the gains achieved in the 1970s and 1980s. The *Roe v. Wade* decision and revisions of the penal codes of most states, which resulted in declining state intervention in sexual activities, have prompted attempts by the Right to reinstate government regulation of the body in order to mandate monogamous reproductive sexuality within the confines of heterosexual marriage. The Moral Majority and prolife advocates epitomize these latter responses.

Robyn Wiegman's essay, "The Anatomy of Lynching," demonstrates the continuity of race as a factor in twentieth-century sexual politics; many of the earlier issues of the nineteenth century have appeared in a not so thinly disguised twentieth-century form. Wiegman, a specialist in African American literature, contrasts Ralph Ellison's response to lynching as expressed in his provocative story entitled "The Birthmark," first published in 1940, with the stark reality of the actual practice of lynching and castration of black males in early twentieth-century America. This approach makes it possible for Wiegman to offer a sophisticated perspective on sexual violence as a form of racial control. She argues, for example, that racism is interconnected with sexual mutilation and questions relating to sexual difference. The control of black males could be accomplished by evoking the image of black male sexual violence being perpetrated against helpless and innocent white women. If society could be convinced that this myth was truly a reality, then sexual mutilation or genocide could be rationalized as a necessary response, since the state was unable to control black male hypermasculinity and hypersexuality. The black male was reincarnated as a sexual villain, and the only effective weapon was excision of that part of the body that was his source of strength. Castration therefore served as a means of effecting white supremacy through the emasculinization of black males. Writers such as Ralph Ellison understood that all too well and sought to unmask the reality behind sexual and racial violence directed at African American males.

Sonya Michel, in her essay on "Danger on the Home Front: Motherhood, Sexuality, and Disabled Veterans in American Postwar Films," draws upon another valuable source for the scholarly evaluation of sexual politics, namely, the medium of film. Michel is one of a growing number of social historians who have turned to film to scrutinize the dominant cultural norms expressed in Hollywood's portrayal of American life. Women had made substantive gains in employment, in the military, and in education during World War II, and Michel's evaluation of postwar films clearly reveals a negative response to such changes—a response that articulated male concern about masculinity and male roles in a postwar world. As her analysis of a group of films demonstrates, anxiety about men's place in the family and society at large resurfaced after the Korean War and the Vietnam conflict as well. It might be argued that the development of a men's movement in our own time is evidence that changing gender roles for women have sustained male concerns and that gender role anxiety has fueled sexual politics since the 1940s. Certainly in the films studied by Michel, the difficult readjustment that veterans returning to civilian life encountered—especially the men who were now physically disabled—raised a problematic issue for women because, as Hollywood saw it, women were now supposed to defer to their men's needs. Women were urged to give up their plans and dreams and, of course, to behave in a sexually submissive manner so that their men could make a successful transition back into the family, where males were still supposed to play a dominant role.

Carole Joffe's essay, "Portraits of Three 'Physicians of Conscience': Abortion before Legalization in the United States," examines the conditions surrounding abortion in the period before the *Roe v. Wade* decision in 1973. But if the images that most often survive from that era are those of coat hangers and "back alley butchers," they are only one piece of a complex history. Joffe turns to a group of individuals whose story has not been told—the "physicians of conscience," as she calls them—licensed medical doctors who risked their own careers because they felt personally obligated to provide women in need with safe abortions. She emphasizes, of course, that many doctors performed these illegal procedures, but the group of physicians she studied were well-established and highly qualified mainstream professionals who had a great deal to lose if they were discovered. They functioned in a climate where abortion was criminalized and where the highly negative image of the back-alley abortionist was pervasive. However, the number of women seeking abortion was on the rise and therefore the medical imperative was ever greater. Joffe offers fascinating insights on the way in which three physicians negotiated such treacherous incongruities. Her case studies are drawn from a sample of more than forty physicians whom she interviewed. Readers are given the opportunity to understand how a variety of professional and ethical dilemmas shaped the response of physicians of conscience when they practiced medicine against the law.

In "Disclosure and Secrecy among Gay Men in the United States and Canada: A Shift in Views," Roy Cain studies the reversal of a process begun in the last decades of the nineteenth century, namely, the medicalization of sexuality—which, in terms of homosexuality, had led to the establishment of a pathology of illness for same-sex activities. Cain explores the rationale behind what he calls demedicalization, the abandonment by the scientific community of that nineteenth-century medical model in the period between the 1950s and the 1970s. Cain's essay, along with those by Lillian Faderman, Katherine Cummings, and Arthur Flannigan-Saint-Aubin, are the four contributions in the anthology that address issues around the lesbian and gay experience. It is not surprising that chronologically they come at the end of this volume, since the modern gay rights movement in the United States and Canada has been a product of the period since World War II (by comparison, the movement in Germany is already a hundred years old). The movement away from a medical model was a crucial part of lesbian and gay self-liberation, just as it was a lifting of the scientific condemnation of same-sex activities. Cain also provides an interesting perspective on these issues by examining the patterns of secrecy and disclosure among gay people. He begins with the 1950s and early 1960s, when secrecy among gay people prevailed—a response that seemed appropriate, given the negative views of homosexuality then common. In contrast, with the emerging gay rights movements in the 1970s and gradual demedicalization, openness and disclosure were seen as the desirable response and secrecy was disdained. Cain discusses why both approaches were at times problematic for gay people.

Joshua Gamson's essay, "Rubber Wars: Struggles over the Condom in the United States," bridges the gap chronologically between the first four essays in Part 2 and the last essays in this anthology, because he compares two periods in the history of the condom debate, the 1930s and 1940s with the 1980s. He explains how the contexts for the two debates were quite different and how each era shaped a contrary response to the meaning of the condom. In the earlier period, while there were those who saw the condom as a reliable method of preventing the spread of venereal disease, much of the debate focused on the condom as a means of preventing contraception, and it was widely condemned by the Catholic church. As a result, a series of legal battles over the condom were carried on in the courts in the 1930s, 1940s, and beyond. As late as 1965, for example, the U.S. Supreme Court ended the ban on the use of condoms by married people. Moreover, with the development of an effective birth control pill in 1960 and increased use of IUDs, condom use declined dramatically. It was, of course, the AIDS epidemic that quickly revived condom use, and their sales have increased dramatically since the early 1980s. But in the 1980s the condom debate was being fought in the public media, and the controversy was being shaped by the role played by media advertising executives and the television networks. Gamson employs a complex theoretical argument to understand the shift in the meaning of the condom and the contentious disputes that have swirled around its use.

Lillian Faderman focuses on the lesbian subculture in the United States over the past dozen years in her essay, "The Return of Butch and Femme: A Phenomenon in Lesbian Sexuality of the 1980s and 1990s." In so doing she demonstrates once again how very different the lesbian experience is from that of the gay male. She bases her study on an array of lesbian publications and many personal interviews with lesbians from across the country. She focuses on a shift in attitudes that took place around issues of sexuality, relationships, gender roles, and the perceived differences between lesbians and heterosexual women. Faderman questions the prevailing belief that the 1980s were a conservative backlash to the radicalism of the 1970s, informed by the conviction that the revival of butch and femme roles was a throwback to the 1950s. She argues that the return of neo-butch/femme in its 1980s guise was quite different from the form it had taken thirty or forty years earlier. Rather, it was an attempt on the part of lesbians to resist cultural assimilation. Given that many of the earlier taboos against lesbians were no longer in force, the radical lesbian was not easily differentiated from other women. In the 1970s butch/femme roles still survived, but largely, Faderman believes, in a politically "incorrect" underground. In the 1980s and even into the 1990s, butch/femme relationships were now increasingly idealized, even romanticized, and unlike the earlier period when these relationships were limited mainly to working-class women, middle-class lesbian intellectuals saw butch/femme roles as a new means of establishing a unique lesbian identity. Moreover, the neo-butch/femme revival has been far more open-ended and less doctrinaire in its approach to lesbian roles, even in sexual activities, and a broader range of lifestyles and greater flexibility for lesbians has resulted.

In her essay, "Of Purebreds and Hybrids: The Politics of Teaching AIDS in the United States," Katherine Cummings investigates how AIDS currently is being taught in the classroom, since originally it was seen as a gay male disease. To do so she analyzes the literature on AIDS since the disease was first reported, in order to establish how much that literature has changed in the past decade. She examines a highly regarded scientific textbook on AIDS published in 1988, as well as a selection of recent educational videos produced between 1987 and 1990; the text and the videos were prepared for use in the classroom at the high school and college levels. Like the text, the videos have been widely used and often praised for their objectivity. Cummings reveals that even these recent representations of the disease and its "victims" are problematic—stereotypes still abound and little real progress has been made in getting beyond old biases about AIDS. This is terribly unfortunate, Cummings argues, because the way that the disease is perceived affects how scientists carry out their research, how people with AIDS are treated by society at large, and, very significantly, how the medical profession responds in its treatment of AIDS patients. Continued misinterpretation of the disease also has an impact on education, especially in which individuals are perceived as being at risk and in how research is financed. Cummings's analysis shows us just how far we have to go before society really understands the social and medical dimensions of AIDS.

The last essay in the anthology brings the reader back to where the collection began, in one sense—the subject of race. Arthur Flannigan-Saint-Aubin, in "'Black Gay Male' Discourse: Reading Race and Sexuality between the Lines," not only focuses on one of the most recent developments in the gay rights movement, the establishment of an African American movement (now with its own discourse on male homosexuality), but he also seeks to interpret the meaning behind and the message in a recent anthology of writings by men who are themselves gay African Americans. Essex Hemphill, a black gay cultural activist and poet, edited the collection entitled *Brother to Brother: New Writings by Black Gay Men,* which was published in Boston in 1991. Essex credits Joseph Beam for conceiving the anthology; Beam himself, who died of AIDS in 1988 at the age of thirty-three, edited the first such anthology, *In the Life,* which was published in Boston in 1986. *Brother to Brother* is a collection of essays, poems, and short stories that seek to articulate what has heretofore been unspoken and hidden, black gay male desire. The authors sought to establish their own voice in a culture that is both homophobic and racist. Flannigan-Saint-Aubin also seeks to understand for whom these texts were written and why. Interestingly, he suggests that while other black gay male readers will find much that speaks to their own experiences, the collection as a whole is rather pointedly addressed to white gay male and black heterosexual male readers.

From this very brief overview, it should be clear that this anthology introduces a broad range of topics, which illustrate the diversity of issues and controversies that have dominated sexual politics in the United States from the Civil War to the present. For those readers who are not very familiar with this history, the collection will serve to introduce the complexities of this vast subject. At the same time, specialists in the field can anticipate much new material drawn from sources that have been underutilized or not previously examined. These essays illustrate just how important the debate over sexual politics has been in America, and the information contained here fills a large gap in our knowledge of this troubling feature of modern life. Finally, although the authors of these essays represent a variety of disciplines, all of them have written for a multidisciplinary audience, leaving behind the jargon that often makes for difficult reading when essays are narrowly written for specialists in a single field. Thus readers can anticipate a collection that is accessible to undergraduate and graduate students, specialists in the field, and general readers as well.

PART 1

_____

# FROM THE VICTORIANS

# TO THE FLAPPERS

# Childhood and Sexual Identity under Slavery

ANTHONY S. PARENT, JR.

*Department of History*
*Wake Forest University*

and

SUSAN BROWN WALLACE

*Psychologist*
*Fairfax County, Virginia, Public School District*

Students of history continue to ignore the simple fact that all individuals are born by mothers; that everybody was once a child; that people and peoples begin in their nurseries; and that society consists of individuals in the process of developing from children into parents. [Erik Erikson, 1959][1]

ALTHOUGH CHILDREN WERE present in substantial numbers during late antebellum slavery, little scholarly attention has been paid to them. Even less concern has been directed toward their development.[2] Remarking upon slavery studies in 1986, Leslie Howard Owens points out that "children are often so closely connected with the behavior of adults and parents that the historical record needs considerable maturing." When childhood is discussed, children's lives are often seen as distinct from that of their parents and separate from the brutalities that they suffered. When evidence is presented from the slave autobiographies and slave interviews, one is led to believe that adults conveyed

---

[1] Erik H. Erikson, "Ego Development and Historical Change: Identity and the Life Cycle," *Psychological Issues* 1 (1959): 18.

[2] Slave children, fourteen years old and younger, were 45.5 percent of the slave population, according to a sample based on the 1850 census (James Oakes, *The Ruling Race: A History of American Slaveholders* [New York, 1982], p. 249). For discussions of children under slavery, see Willie Lee Rose, "Childhood in Bondage," in *Slavery and Freedom*, ed. William W. Freehling (New York, 1982), pp. 37–48; Paul D. Escott, *Slavery Remembered: A Record of Twentieth-Century Slave Narratives* (Chapel Hill, NC, 1979), pp. 30–31, 34; John W. Blassingame, *The Slave Community: Plantation Life in the Antebellum South*, 2d ed. (New York, 1979), pp. 179–91; Eugene D. Genovese, *Roll, Jordan, Roll: The World the Slaves Made* (New York, 1974), pp. 502–18.

This essay originally appeared in the *Journal of the History of Sexuality* 1993, vol. 3, no. 3.

little of their own suffering to their carefree children.[3] For example, John Blassingame writes in a study on the slave community, based on slave autobiographies and memoirs, that "black children played in promiscuous equality with white children. Together they roamed the plantation or went hunting, fishing, berry picking, or raiding watermelon and potato patches. Indeed, at first, bondage weighed lightly on the shoulders of the black child."[4] Owens suggests, on the other hand, that slavery at its best was comprehended by the mothers, fathers, and children as the "great compromiser."[5]

For this study we are defining childhood as that period under age fifteen or occurring anytime an individual defines an experience as happening during childhood. Erik H. Erikson writes that childhood proper ends with the advent of puberty.[6] The age of menarche of slave girls has been approximated at age fifteen. Eugene D. Genovese believes that the lives of boys changed dramatically at the age of twelve, when they (often eagerly, because of its connotation of manhood) went behind the plow. Deborah Gray White writes that girls entered the workforce at the same time as boys, between twelve and sixteen years old, joining them in the "trash gangs," picking up stubble and weeds during the growing season and picking cotton during the harvest. It was here in this three-generational mix of pregnant women, nursing mothers, and elderly women, White speculates, that young girls emerging from an asexual childhood learned about men, marriage, and sex. Like Blassingame, both White and Genovese find that children before age twelve were vir-

---

[3]Leslie Howard Owens, "The African in the Garden: Reflections about New World Slavery and Its Lifelines," in *The State of Afro-American History Past, Present, and Future,* ed. Darlene Clark Hines (Baton Rouge, LA, 1986), pp. 33–34.

[4]Blassingame, *Slave Community,* pp. 183–84. For a similar conclusion drawn from an analysis of the WPA interviews, see Genovese, p. 505. Deborah Gray White, *Ar'n't I a Woman? Female Slaves in the Plantation South* (New York, 1985), pp. 92, 98, 184 n. 3. On the other hand Escott, working with twentieth-century interviews, suggests that "the happy child of plantation fable was far less common than southern whites supposed. Masters and mistresses frequently misunderstood the feelings and actions of slave children" (p. 31).

[5]Owens, pp. 33–34.

[6]Erik H. Erikson, "The Human Life Cycle," in Erik H. Erikson, *A Way of Looking at Things: Selected Papers from 1930 to 1980,* ed. Stephen Schlein (New York, 1987), p. 605; James Trussell and Richard Steckel, "The Age of Slaves at Menarche and Their First Birth," *Journal of Interdisciplinary History* 8 (1978): 504; White, p. 94. Philippe Ariès, on the other hand, has found that the appellation of "child" was indifferent to biological phenomenon but instead tied to dependency, such that a worker of twenty-five could still be a "boy" in sixteenth-century France, yet as soon as children were weaned they mingled with adults in everyday life. At the same time, the privileged classes were discovering childhood as a separate and distinct stage of development (Philippe Ariès, *Centuries of Childhood: A Social History of Family Life,* trans. Robert Baldick [New York, 1962], pp. 25–27).

tually segregated from their parents because of the work regimen on the antebellum southern plantation. Paul Escott finds that at age fifteen boys and girls left childhood activities and chores and took on adult work tasks.[7]

Twentieth-century interviews of African Americans who had experienced slavery as children open a window into the developmental lives of slave children.[8] For this study we are using the more than one hundred narratives or interviews of former slaves collected in 1929 and 1930 by Ophelia Settle Egypt, a member of the research staff of the Social Science Institute at Fisk University in Nashville, Tennessee. The Fisk University interviewers were themselves African Americans. Escott in his analysis of twentieth-century slave narratives has observed that in these interviews "there was more honesty in the all-black interviews and less obeisance to social rituals [of contemporary racial etiquette]. . . . This ritual was wholly lacking in the Fisk collections."[9] In the narratives, the former slaves spoke of their experiences as children. We have focused upon those events that are primarily sexual or that have impact upon the individual's development of sexual identity. These narratives give evidence of how the slaves developed their sense of sexual identity and show how they viewed sexuality and issues of a sexual nature. The Fisk University editors of the published narratives noted that these narratives document "how the slaves met their basic needs of sex, hunger and rest, within the narrow confines of the system. They represent essentially the memories of childhood experiences, and provide, in a measure, a personal history of the social world as recreated and dramatized by these slaves in the course of the telling. Taken as a whole these autobiographies constitute a fabric of individual memories, which sheds interesting light on the mentality of the slave."[10] Since we are concerned not only with the accuracy of the events but also with how the perception of the events influenced the individual, we see the narratives as a rich source of knowledge about the concerns of the slave children.

[7]Genovese, p. 505; White, pp. 94–95; Escott, pp. 16–17, 31–32.

[8]Escott, pp. 3–16; George P. Rawick, *From Sundown to Sunup: The Making of the Black Community* (Westport, CT, 1972), pp. xv–xxi. Blassingame, thoroughly critical of the former slave narratives, nevertheless concedes that "given the average age of the informants when they were freed, their stories contain a great deal of information about the childhood experiences of slaves" (John W. Blassingame, ed., *Slave Testimony: Two Centuries of Letters, Speeches, Interviews, and Autobiographies* [Baton Rouge, LA, 1977], pp. iii–iv, xlvii.

[9]Escott, pp. 9–10.

[10]Ophelia Settle Egypt, *Unwritten History of Slavery: Autobiographic Account of Negro Ex-Slaves* (Nashville, TN, 1941), reprinted in *The American Slave: A Composite Autobiography*, vol. 18, ed. George P. Rawick (Westport, CT, 1972), p. iii. All further citations to Egypt's work (in the Rawick volume) will be given in parentheses in the text.

The narratives were prompted by a series of questions that the informants were asked to consider. However, each former slave brought to the encounter not only his own personal memory of the event, but also the effect that time and experience had upon the individual. In many cases, the events had been repressed until the interviewer spoke of them. In one case, a former slave told the interviewers that he thought it was against the race to speak about slavery. In other cases, many events may have been embellished in their retelling. In all cases, the narratives are a valuable recollection of the individuals' lives as children under slavery, which one former female slave born in 1855 anticipated in saying, "I don't know anything [about slavery] 'cept what happened when I was a child" (p. 276).[11]

Although these memories may have been affected by the years after slavery, the experiences point to issues that concerned these individuals during childhood. Roy Shafer has written:

> Each account of the past is a reconstruction that is controlled by a narrative strategy. The narrative strategy dictates how one is to select, from a plenitude of possible details, those that may be reorganized into another narrative which is both followable and expresses the desired point of view of the past. Accordingly, this reconstruction, like its narrative predecessor, is always subject to change. For whenever new explanatory aims are set and new questions raised, new slants on the past will be developed and new evidence concerning the events of the past will become available. Change of this sort typifies historical narratives of every kind.[12]

We began with many questions about how slave children viewed their circumstances. It is important to note that in some cases, there were few if any direct references to our questions. We were concerned with the number and quality of references to sexual issues. We wanted to know how much knowledge slave children had about sexual functions and events. What did slave children know about breeding? How did they see the relationship between their owners, their parents, and themselves? What effect did sale of family members have? What opportunities were present for children to develop a sense of identity? Were there common

[11]Our use of oral interviews here should not be construed to mean that we favor this type of documentation to the exclusion of others. Written autobiographies and memoirs, contemporary interviews, plantation records, traveler's accounts, and folklore also shed light on childhood and slavery. We are using all the above types of evidence in our history of childhood under slavery, which is in progress.

[12]Roy Schafer, *The Analytic Attitude* (New York, 1983), p. 193.

themes, wishes, and desires evident in the slave narratives? Were sexual fantasies present? Did children fantasize ideal situations when they were faced with conflict? What role did violence play in the sexual identities of slave children?

Twentieth-century psychoanalytic theory helps us to understand notions of authority and dependence in identity development. Sigmund Freud and others believed that this development was influenced by sexual knowledge, thoughts, and conditioning. Freud was the first psychological theorist to focus on the developmental aspects of personality and on the importance of childhood experiences in its formation. In doing so, he developed stages of psychosexual development and stressed the importance of childhood sexuality. Freud believed that the unconscious held the key to personality and that many problems stem from unresolved conflicts at a previous stage of psychosexual development. Erik Erikson, while not abandoning Freud's concept of development or the role of the unconscious, did not dwell upon the importance of unconscious sexual forces. He developed instead a theory that focused upon the psychosocial stages of development, and on the development of ego identity and one's sense of self. Both theorists stressed the importance of relationships with parents and primary caregivers in developing a sense of self. Erikson believed that as a result of the individual's interaction with others, his personality developed through a series of predictable life crises. One of these crises occurs at the stage of what he termed "identity development versus role confusion," which occurs around the time of adolescence. Before adolescence, the first cultural problems of identity occur when the individual attempts to negotiate through five epigenetic sequential stages: "trust versus mistrust"; "autonomy versus shame and doubt"; "initiative versus guilt"; "industry versus inferiority"; and "identity versus role confusion." Each stage must be mastered, for the social problems are fraught with danger for the individual. Erikson believed that how an individual felt about himself influenced his interactions with others and determined how he developed from that stage on; Erikson used his theories in writing psychohistories of Mohandas Gandhi, Martin Luther, and others.[13]

---

[13]Although psychoanalytic theory is Eurocentric in origins and was developed after slavery, Erikson used it to analyze other cultures. It serves as a heuristic tool to analyze slave children, who, like any other children, seem to go through epigenetic stages. See Erik Erikson, *Childhood and Society,* 2d ed. (New York, 1963), pp. 65, 247–74. See also Sigmund Freud, "Three Essays on the Theory of Sexuality" (1905), in vol. 7 of *The Standard Edition of the Complete Psychological Works of Sigmund Freud,* ed. James Strachey (London, 1963), pp. 125–245.

## I

What did the slave children know about sexual functions? Surprisingly, we learn from their testimony, they knew very little. Their parents, perhaps in an effort to shield them from slavery's most invasive feature—sexual exploitation—or in an effort, however difficult, to protect their innocence, revealed little to their children about sexual functions or procreation.[14] One woman remembered that "When [menstruation] happened, mother didn't tell us. I didn't know what had happened to me. I went running to the branch and washed myself. I come on up the road just naked; done been to the branch washing. It never did hurt me, though" (p. 137). Most of the former slave women made no reference to menstruation at all. Slave children sleeping in trundle beds knew nothing that went on at night. A former slave to Dr. Gale remembered in Tennessee that "children never knew anything went on at night; all of their play was in the day" (p. 15). Another said, "We had a little trundle bed, and when we was put in it we didn't see no more till the next morning, and we had better keep quiet, too. We never did see daylight after we was put in that bed until the next morning. Their [parents'] beds was high enough to roll their [children's beds] under their's. They had [a] hemp rope across their bed to keep from falling in on us" (p. 293).[15] Although the children were not consciously aware of events during childhood, the concerns with the "goings-on in the night" suggested that sexual concerns for these children were unconscious but nonetheless influencing their identities.

Although reared on farms, apparently privy to the sexual behavior of farm animals, slave children knew remarkably little about where babies came from. When queried by children, parents told them that either the doctor or the midwife brought babies. Unsatisfied with this response, children eavesdropped, hid under houses during childbirth, and looked in hollow logs and in parsley patches for babies. "They wouldn't tell me nothing about babies. I heard them say one day—somebody said, 'Don't tell Anne, [anything] but the doctor brings these babies.' I heard her talking to one of her daughters who had a baby. They wouldn't tell

[14]Escott finds this pattern pervasive in the slave narratives (Escott, pp. 52–53). See also Genovese, pp. 462–63; White, pp. 96, 105. Gutman finds this pattern of withholding sexual knowledge to be evidence of sociosexual choice made in child-rearing by African American parents (Herbert G. Gutman, *The Black Family in Slavery and Freedom, 1750–1925* [New York, 1976], pp. 82–83).

[15]In these interviews, not one of the former slaves mentioned seeing parents show affection. Genovese gives one example and suggests that the children did see affection displayed between husband and wife within the quarter. One heard his mother singing to her husband, "Sleepy creature, sleepy creature / There's something to do 'sides sleeping" (Genovese, p. 463).

me 'cause I wouldn't know no better than to blab it out; but I did not tell this" (p. 187). A woman who was a child on Dr. Gale's plantation agreed: "No, they didn't tell you a thing. I was a great big girl twelve or thirteen years old, I reckon, and a girl two or three years older than that and we'd be going 'round to the parsley bed looking for babies; and looking in hollow logs. It's a wonder a snake hadn't bitten us. The woman that would wait on my mother would come back and tell us here's her baby; and that was all we knew. We thought she brought it because it was hers. I was twenty years old when my first baby came, and I didn't know nothing then. I didn't know how long I had to carry my baby. We never saw nothing when we were children" (p. 10). "They used to tell us that Aunt Sarah brought babies," recollected another woman, "and I didn't know no better. It was a long time after the Civil War 'fore I knowed where babies come from" (p. 295). Another former slave girl recalled that "one day I asked my mother where babies come from; she said the doctor brought it. One day I crawled up under the house when a girl was fixing to have a baby; I heard her holler and after a while I heard the baby crying. I asked my mother why the girl hollered if the doctor brought the baby; she told me to get out of there or she would kill me" (p. 138).

Most of the former slaves who spoke of their childhood under slavery agreed that their parents felt they did not need to know much about sexual matters. This lack of knowledge was probably present in much of the nonslave population as well. Interestingly, psychoanalytic theory would suggest that by attempting to suppress sexual knowledge, conflicts and crises were more likely to occur.

Slave children were ignorant, the informants believed, because their parents did not trust them to keep secret the goings-on in the slave quarters, not only with regard to the intimacy of sexual relations but also to the clandestine thefts of hogs or chickens or the harboring of fugitives. Elderly ex-slaves recollecting their ignorance not only lamented their lack of knowledge but also commented upon the carnal knowledge of the then contemporary youth. One woman remembered that "whenever white women had babies they would make us stay out. I never did know then where the babies would come from. First thing I would know the baby would start to holler. We never seed nothing. People was very particular in them days. They wouldn't let children know anything like they do now. The children now know everything" (p. 303). Another female informant said, "Children then wasn't like they is now. Little girls know more now than I did after I got grown. I work all one day and a half in a hollow stump trying to find me a baby. When the doctor come around with the saddlebags I told him to bring me a baby. I never knowed where they come from. They know now where they come from. I hear these little girls talking about their beaus now. They know more than I know" (p. 156).

Should children be given information about the facts of sexual life? In a 1907 letter to a colleague, Freud wrote about this question, noting a letter written by a child to her aunt, regarding where the aunt got her babies. "Explanations about the specific circumstances of human sexuality and some understanding of its social significance should be provided before the child is eleven years old."[16] Freud believed that the fantasy stories that adults told children about their sexuality actually increased their desire to know, rather than reducing it. Infantile theories about the nature of marriage or sexuality were often not retained in the individual's conscious memory. Freud believed, however, that they were manifest in childish games, and later the wish to be married (or sexual) could manifest itself in a phobia or other form of infantile expression.[17] Less than the question of where babies came from, the child concerned himself with the nature of marriage and of being married. This resulted, according to Freud, from the child's observations of his parents and his own sexual impulses, which were invested with pleasurable feeling.[18] Freud also emphasized the importance of how the child behaved when he finally received the correct sexual information.[19] He noted that in some children sexual repression had gone so far that they did not hear any information. This repression could result from the message the child had received that such information was dirty or negative. Erikson, likewise, saw the withholding of information from the child in a negative way, as interfering with the sense of ego development. His stage of "identity development" began at around age twelve and was concerned with the individual's ability to control his destiny. Consciousness of adult sexual roles began to emerge at this time.

Although the former slaves said that they knew little about sexual functions and procreation, it is evident that many of the slave children nevertheless had concepts of courtship and of marriage. (In the psychoanalytic sense, this is related to concern about sexuality and sex role.) They had rules about who was available to whom and looked down on slaves who did not follow these rules.[20] The Fisk University interviewers

---

[16]Sigmund Freud, "The Sexual Enlightenment of Children," in *Sigmund Freud: Collected Papers*, ed. Ernest Jones, 5 vols. (New York, 1959), 2:43.

[17]Sigmund Freud, "On the Sexual Theories of Children," in ibid., 1:72.

[18]Ibid., p. 69.

[19]Ibid., p. 74.

[20]Beth Bailey has defined courtship broadly, encompassing "a wide variety of conditions, intentions, and actions, for men and women woo each other in many ways, not all of which lead to marriage." Bailey also looks at the convention of courtship as the system of rules and understandings that provide a context, both culturally constructed and histori-

asked the former slaves: "Did they have many love affairs on the plantation? How did they court then?" Although the responses varied, the former slaves were quick to point out that they were more restrained in
their behavior than contemporary youth. "They just laffed and talked.
Didn't let the boys get around the gals like they do now. He sat over
there and you sat over here and do your courting. I never said 'No,'
honey" (p. 252). One woman, fifteen years old when slavery ended, said:
"We would just sit and talk with each other. I told him once I didn't
love him, I hated him, and then I told him again that I loved him so
much I just loved to see him walk" (p. 275). A former slave from Henry
County, Tennessee, said, "Boys wasn't like these now. We didn't pay no
'tention to people courtin'" (p. 293). "They courted then just like they
do now. Only they wasn't fast like they are now. I never in all my born
days went out at night by myself and stayed out like these young folks do
now. When I went out I always had company" (p. 136). "They would let
us have company, but they couldn't stay no longer than ten o'clock" (p.
140). The following man, who had been enslaved in Christian County,
Kentucky, was the only informant to hint of casual sexual liaisons in the
Fisk University interviews. "Did you court the girls?" "Nope, I would
just laugh at them sometime." "How did you court the girls?" "Me, I
didn't court them. I didn't court them a'tall. All of them loved me; I
didn't court. You see, they didn't do like they might do now. They
would call one another 'Hon,' and I would say 'Sweet.' And they would
say, 'Let's go home' and there would be something going on like a quilt-
ing, and I would go and take a gal home. They didn't do like they do
now" (pp. 145–46).[21]

---

cally specific, for concrete acts and individual experience. Although Bailey's work is concerned with middle-class white America, she does note the change in courtship before
1930 when the lower class, prompted by pressure to escape from cramped and crowded
housing and the opportunity that hard cash afforded in the new city living, introduced
"dating" (Beth L. Bailey, *From Front Porch to Back Seat: Courtship in Twentieth-Century
America* [Baltimore, 1988], pp. 6, 19). Blassingame has found courtship within the quarters to be "a highly formalized ritual involving a series of questions to determine one's
availability as a sexual partner." The courtship ritual of "riddles, poetic boasting, sexual
innuendos, figurative speech, circumlocution," initiated by the man but controlled by the
woman in her ability to say no, was taught to the young by the old (Blassingame, *Slave
Community*, pp. 158–60). In addition, Genovese has found signs, charms, love potions,
and improvised songs (pp. 469–71). The courtship rituals described by Blassingame and
Genovese appear to reflect the actual experience of adults rather than the conventions of
courtship learned by slave children.
    [21]This is the only response that suggests casual sexual liaisons. Herbert Gutman be-
lieves that adolescent girls involved themselves in casual sexual liaisons shortly after
menarche at about age sixteen until the birth of the first child at about age eighteen. On the

The mores of the community and parental control played a role in who courted and when they began. Seventeen for boys and twenty-one for girls were not uncommon ages that these former slaves associated with courting. Courting was then a supervised activity on the girl's plantation.[22] "Well, they courted nicer than they do now," remembered one woman. "They would come and see the girl they liked, and talked to them at night after the work was done; and sometimes they would ask them to marry; and sometimes they wouldn't. The white folks married you then" (p. 204). Another woman recalled that her mother blocked her courting. "No'm," she responded, "not when I was with her. When we left there I was eleven years old [a year after slavery ended] and I was not old enough to have a big time, and after we got big enough to have a big time mother wouldn't let us go nowhere 'thout an old woman was with us. I didn't have no good time till I married, and I married when I was fourteen years and six months old. I was going to have a good time anyway" (p. 280). Her youthful marriage seems to be an exception, for "girls didn't marry so fast in those days," said one informant (p. 226). One girl who began courting at fourteen courted for seven years, believing that she had to turn twenty-one before she married, when her beau "stole her from mother," who had said, "I will never give all the gal I have to a black nigger like you" (pp. 195–96). Note the negative racial image associated with the marriage and the separation from the mother.

Boys, too, understood that mothers and community pressure delayed courtship for them. "We didn't court much in them days. A boy had to be near 'bout grown. The fust girl I went with I was nearly eighteen years old. When you got ready to marry all you had to do was for the girl to ask her mother and you had to get permission from the master and that was just about all to it. . . . If a boy went with a girl and said things that he shouldn't he could get a whipping for that. If you fooled a girl up and

---

other hand, the evidence presented by Trussell and Steckel suggests greater abstention from sexual activity. They suggest the age of first birth to be twenty-one, although they estimate the age of menarche to be earlier, at fourteen and a half. The slaves interviewed by the Fisk University group are more in line with Trussell and Steckel. At the same time, the "most important" informants about female adolescent sexual behavior used by Gutman were two former *male* slaves. Gutman's discussion of sexual abstention of southern urban women in their twenties during the 1880s and his theory of the persistence of slave-held values into freedom appear to support greater sexual abstention during slavery (Gutman, pp. 63, 559 n. 15, 636 n. 13; Trussell and Steckel, p. 504). For a discussion of the literature, see Robert W. Fogel, *Without Consent or Contract: The Rise and Fall of American Slavery* (New York, 1989), pp. 180–84.

[22]White notes that "the slow pace of courtship dictated by anxious mothers" is an example of African American culture, denying the owners' desire for early reproduction (pp. 97, 98, 104–5).

got her with an armful you had to take care of her" (pp. 306–7). "I wasn't big enough to court; I had to slip. I knowed the road she'd come, and I could slip off and meet her sometimes, but we had to dodge the old folks 'cause they would whip me sho'. I'd walk a little piece with her, but I didn't know what to say. Young folks then wasn't like they are now.... I would just ask her (girl) what was the news, and I thought I was doing big courting then; I would brag to the boys about it" (p. 260). An ex-slave from Christian County, Kentucky, vividly remembered that "one time I seen a girl have her hand up in the collar of a boy, and she take a small switch off a tree—a black gum tree—and give that boy a whipping. He wasn't no account. He had asked for her company and she granted it. He was too young. They [females] weren't allowed to have company before they was 21 years old, and for a boy when he was just about 17 years old he was just about the right age to be considered a man" (p. 146).

Yet here as elsewhere children recalled that the owners' control and plantation discipline interfered with courting.[23] "I'd go down to my sister's house and do my courting down there. I could go down there and stay till nine o'clock. He'd [master] make 'em marry who he wanted 'em to marry. You couldn't marry who you wanted to" (p. 273). "The master would do all the courting for you, yes sir he saw to that, he, he, he. Once married [you] would stay at one of [the] parent's homes" (p. 222). Permission was not forthcoming for slaves to date free Negroes. One ex-slave remembered that "it wasn't but one family of free niggers up here. White people didn't recognize them, and they didn't 'low niggers to go around them. If they knowed they went around them they would cut their backs off nearly. The men woulda noticed the slave girls if the white folks woulda let them. Then they wouldn't let the girls go with a free Negro" (p. 133). In another instance, a free man, a barber who showed deep emotional commitment despite the personal cost, gave himself to his sweetheart's master to marry her. It made a lasting impression upon the informant's young mind: "That love is an awful thing, I tell you. I don't know if I would give my freedom away to marry anybody" (p. 296).

Former slave children remembered the violence associated with courtship and marital visitation. Such images created a sense of anxiety about the development of adult sexual roles. The cultural trait of exogamy retained from West Africa encouraged romances across

---

[23]White suggests that an owner's permission for visitation in the hopes of early childbirth and reproduction of the labor force was "an insidious kind of breeding," which eroded the parental and community desires for slower-paced courtship (p. 98).

plantations.[24] Boys or young men had to risk paddy rollers on the road unless they had permission from their owners to visit. Without a pass, a slave was at risk of a beating by the paddy rollers, "whose business it was to see that niggers would not rove around at night without the master's knowing about it" (p. 32). One woman, fifteen years old when slavery ended, said: "You had to court right there on the place 'cause they had padder rollers, and if you went out without a pass they would whip you" (p. 275). One man recalled the story of a slave named Brown who "had a wife at my place, and he came every night to see her, so he came that night and he didn't get back as early as he [master] thought he ought to. Brown was a strong man and this white man that was the son of my master attempted to whip him; so Brown threw him and ran to the woods. He pursued and found him sleep on a sand bar out in the river; so he killed him in his sleep and threw him in the river" (p. 54). The murder of a strong man like Brown, who had the audacity to visit his wife nightly, certainly gave pause to young boys projecting their own marital futures.

Visitation became more restricted during the war in an attempt to stop men from running to Union lines. "During the War, the colored men that had wives at other places, they wouldn't let them go to visit them at all; they said they'd get to talking, and they threatened to shoot any who tried to go" (p. 4). During the war the consequence of a girl going out at night was fatal. "We had a girl on the place running out at all times of night. I knowed something bad was gonna follow her. You could hear the soldiers after her, and you could hear her scream. They just killed her" (p. 137).[25] Many frightening images were associated with courting among the former slave children.

As with most other areas of daily life, there was a range among the former slave children of activities where they could see their parents and other slaves in recreational roles and where they could meet possible mates. Parties and social events had to be granted by the owner (pp. 106–7). "Niggers didn't have time to do much courting in them days. White folks would let them have suppers 'round Christmas time, then after that it was all over and no more gatherings till the next summer; then they would let them set out under the shade trees sometimes on Sunday evening, and all like that" (pp. 132–33). Many of the parties were related to weddings. One ex-slave from Nashville recalled that "they wouldn't marry 'less they could have a dance" (p. 260). Some-

[24]Gutman points to the contrasting traditions of exogamy of slaves and endogamy of slaveowners to prove persisting social memory and cultural choice in African American society (Gutman, pp. 87–93). See also Escott, pp. 50–52.

[25]See Gutman (pp. 386–87) on the rape of girls and women by Union soldiers during the war.

times the slaves would have parties after the white people had finished theirs. "Jimmie Baxter's was a place that we could go and have a good time," recalled one of Dr. Gale's former slaves. "There, the white folks would have a party and when they finished eating, they would set the things out on the table for the colored to eat" (p. 9). Usually, around the Christmas holidays, slaves had some time to have social gatherings. Some were able to sit outside in the summer and converse with other slaves. This was unheard of on other plantations.

The most common social events were corn-shuckings, quiltings, and dances.[26] Another event was a candy-pulling. One former slave, remembering his childhood, noted that they had dances and parties, but they "would be sho' 'nuf parties," unlike the ones he witnessed as an adult (p. 222). Another former slave, fifteen years old when the war began, was a corn general at a corn-shucking social, who would call out the songs. At the corn-shucking men competed on two sides. The masters provided whiskey and the paddy rollers did not bother the slaves. He recalled a fight when a fence rail was torn down at a corn-shucking. "The ladies would wait on us and give us cakes and pies and all kind of good things to eat. That was the only enjoyment we had, but we sure had a good time then" (p. 106). Another former slave remembered hearing at a corn-shucking, "Rock me Julie, rock me, hey, hey, I'm going way to leave you" (p. 295).[27]

When asked whether there were dances on the plantation, the corn general remembered that "when we wanted to have a dance, we had to ask the master. They would have a fiddler, and we would tromp around mighty" (p. 107). Another slave vividly recalled, "Lord, yes, they'd pick banjoes, and have big dances. . . . Oh, they would have dances at a different house every week, on Saturday nights. No'm, we wouldn't dress up so much; girls come in clean cotton dresses; we thought we was dressed up enough. . . . [We] jest dance and skip and hop ourselves to death" (p. 215). Another woman, fifteen years old when slavery ended, remembered that "sometimes way back there they had big dances and would dance against each other with a glass of water on their head" (p. 195). Another woman added, "We had good times. . . . I danced a pattillion. Vernon, he played everything. They had a bass fiddle and a big fiddle, and a little boy played it, and he had on a ruffled shirt and a scissor or hammer tail coat" (p. 251). This reference is important, not only for the individual's memory of the dances, but because of the specific role that

[26]Blassingame, *Slave Community*, pp. 160–61.

[27]Blassingame has written that the songs at the parties were "lusty songs about courting and love, they were filled with metaphoric references to sexual intercourse" (ibid., p. 161).

was designated to a slave child at the particular function. She noted his special clothing and ability to play the bass fiddle.

The former slaves noted that Christian folks did not go to dances. Some recounted that once they accepted Christianity, they no longer danced.[28] "I was a wild thing when I was young. Why I was more on dancing than my Ole Missy, and she taught me to dance, too." After this former slave joined the church she stopped dancing and observed, "Dancing was an injury to me, I see it now" (p. 25). Another slave noted that the Christian folks would have suppers, but they wouldn't dance. These Christian slave gatherings were viewed as more threatening by whites than the dances. "White people were very hard on colored for being religious. They liked to see you fiddling and dancing all the time. They were hard on them for preaching. . . . As for me, I went where I wanted to go, but I had to have a pass. Some of them didn't get passes and they would get caught and be sent out to jail, beat up and made come on back. They used to tell you sometimes that they would send you down the river and they would send you to Mississippi, Georgia, and Alabama or Louisiana" (p. 121). These former slaves were located in the Nashville, Tennessee, area and believed that being sent further south was worse than death. How confusing, though, to the slave child to perceive that such an awful punishment could befall a slave for making a moral choice about his religious life.

Slave children were called upon to entertain themselves and their owners. "We would play them plays." "Sugar Tea," "Goosey," "Frog in the Middle and Can't Get Out," and "The Americans Are Gaining the Day" were mentioned. Slave children had little idea of who Americans were at that time, although the 1850s was a period when American nationalism and nativism were at a high point. "For games when we'd go to parties and get tired of dancing, then we played songs like that." This slave of Dr. Gale's also noted that they sang rebel songs for the white people but would never sing spirituals for them. She also recalled: "You know white folks always did like to hear niggers sing, 'I'll court Miss Millie Simmons on a long summer's day'" (pp. 15, 16). Contrast this with the songs that slave children sang for themselves. One ex-slave noted that the children sang "Old Black Joe" and "Ring a ring a Rineo." It contained the lyrics "Ain't seen a nigger in a mile or more / You take Sal and I take Sue / Ain't no difference between the two"—songs that did not portray positive images of black people (p. 84). Indeed such songs more likely contributed to a sense of negative identity for the slave

---

[28]Blassingame suggests over time, with Christianization, parents taught their children that premarital sex and shame were synonymous. These children learned little from their parents about sex except to abstain before marriage (ibid., pp. 162–63).

child. There were few opportunities for the slave children to project healthy images of black people in their play, particularly if the play was viewed by whites. For slave children, even social behavior such as singing songs was regulated. Their imitation of whites and blacks was carefully scrutinized by the masters, but also by their parents, who were trying to protect them from chastisement and harm. Those who repressed the urges to dance and party, in favor of religion, found an even harsher situation in some cases, although in so doing they appeared to be developing a more autonomous self-identity.[29]

If their parents proffered naïveté, their owners rejoiced in promiscuity. Slaves and owners viewed bastardy differently. Even if a slave girl who was an unwed mother was ostracized from other girls, their owners took pride in bastards. "When I was a girl if you walked with a girl who had had a baby we would be cut all to pieces. We wouldn't be allowed to speak to her. Now they ain't folks if they ain't got babies" (p. 160). This ostracism apparently reflected an African American female rite of passage, an attempt to alter the behavior of the slave girl, who now as a parent should no longer involve herself in casual prenuptial liaisons. It had less to do with the child, for the slaves recognized no shame or illegitimacy in childbearing.[30] The slaveowners, influenced by market considerations and the necessary reproduction of the labor force, benefited from the fecundity of prenuptial females. Otherwise, they were insensitive to the cultural implications of childbirth in the slave community. "Whenever a girl had a baby in slavery they [slaveowners] never paid no 'tention to it, 'cause they knowed they would have more slaves the more babies they got" (p. 137). "Yes, some of them had children for them what wasn't married to you. No, they [slaveowners] wouldn't do noth-

---

[29]Erikson wrote that play was the "royal road" to the young ego's effort to make sense of its experience. Erikson felt that in play children revealed their concerns more clearly than they did in words (see Erikson, *Childhood and Society,* p. 98). However, play was often restricted for slave children, under the scrutiny of owners and parents. Of this behavior, Hussein Abdilahi Bulhan writes that "the slaves, the oppressed depend on and share the paranoia and false beliefs of their oppressors. But since they ordinarily lack safe and convenient objects on which to project these beliefs, they project on themselves the negative attributes cast on them and those emanating from their condition, and an inferiority complex. It also reinforces and 'validates' the false beliefs and narcissism of the dominant group" (Hussein Abdilahi Bulhan, *Frantz Fanon and the Psychology of Oppression* [New York, 1985], pp. 151–52). See also Charles Pinderhughes, "Managing Paranoia in Violent Relationships," in *Perspectives on Violence,* ed. Gene Usdin (New York, 1972), p. 111. The games and songs of the slave children are a conduit because, Fanon wrote, "in every society in every collectivity, exists—must exist—a channel, an outlet through which the forces accumulated in the form of aggression can be released" (Frantz Fanon, *Black Skin White Masks* [New York, 1952; rpt. 1968], pp. 145–46).

[30]Gutman, pp. 63, 74, 557 n. 6.

ing; they was glad of it. They would be glad to have them little bastards; brag about it" (p. 251). "Old Miss would be setting there just knitting and watching the babies; they had a horn and every woman could tell when it was time to come and nurse her baby by the way they would blow the horn. The white folks was crazy 'bout their nigger babies, 'cause that's where they got their profit. A old white woman would come there and look after them" (p. 117).

Former slaves remembered as children the ceremony, or the lack of it, associated with slave marriages. These ceremonies informed the children of the commitment and the importance of the relationship. No clear pattern emerges except that slaves attempted to legitimize their relationships publicly to the community at large.[31] As in courtship, children saw that the master often interfered, coupling slaves, giving permission, or unceremoniously breaking the bond. The important decision about whether and whom to marry was often made by the owner and was not made by the slave. The slave children distinguished between the white owners' control over their marital choices and their own. One ex-slave explained: "That was the reason my mother had to marry again, because they would carry their husband off to one state or another. White folks when they [their] children married they just give them all [that] they wanted to have and let them go" (p. 141). Anne, a slave in Wilson County, Tennessee, could not "remember seeing any of them marry on the place" (p. 183). "Ten to one, they didn't marry at all," said one informant (p. 217). Yet another remembered, "Sometimes they would slip there and sleep with the women and wouldn't marry at all. They would slip just like they do now" (p. 140). There were times when the owner simply coupled the slaves without ceremony. A female ex-slave of Dr. Gale remembered that "my mother was born in Mississippi and brought here. My father was born in Maryland. He was an old man when he come here, but they just bought them and put them together. My mother was young—just fifteen or sixteen years old. She had fourteen chillen and you know that meant a lots of wealth" (p. 5). Another ex-slave also believed that the owner's desire for increasing wealth accounted for the coupling of slaves: "They would have women that been married long time, two or three years, and didn't have no children; white folks would take them and make 'em marry somebody else, or sell 'em. Wonder what make 'em want so many children like that, make 'em rich, I guess" (p. 207). Another woman recalled that "most of the time the ole marster jest told them they was man and wife; and they was. . . . Well, they didn't act much different after they was married; they knowed they was man and wife; she knowed he was her husband; and the white

---

[31]Ibid., pp. 274–77.

folks would built them a little hut to live in; and we would give them a big party; and give 'em some dishes and things to put in the one room cabin, you know" (p. 214).

In other instances the informants recalled "irregular" weddings, which were not officiated by a minister.[32] One former slave, talking about irregular weddings, distinguished between big ones and little ones. "It was considered a big wedding to jump over the broomstick, but when you just asked for them and go on to bed after getting the permission, then that was a little wedding. . . . I never saw a wedding until I was a great big gal," she said. "They said they use to hold a broom and make them jump over it. At one time a man wanted a wife and all he had to do was ask old master for the gal, and then if he said 'yes' all they had to do was to go on and go to bed. One old Mistiss by the name of Fletcher would sometimes go and make them get up and tell them that married life was too good for them; and tell them to get up and get out and go to work" (p. 195).[33] Another woman remembered that they "joined their right hands. That's all they did and they said they was married" (p. 249). An ex-slave remembered: "When they got ready to marry, they would just come to the marster and tell him that he wanted one of his women, and he could just take her. They didn't have no ceremony. . . . They jump over the broom stick in them days. I never seed nobody marry until I was free. Niggers never knowed about marriage, because they couldn't read" (p. 300). "People marry different now from what they use to back in those old days. When people married they had to get an order from one master to the other master, and then set a time. I saw them jump over the broom stick many times. The man use to jump over the broom stick and the woman would stand still" (p. 174).

A preacher- or squire-officiated wedding often followed by a supper or a dance would also be considered a "regular" wedding.[34] In these weddings the young slaves observed a more formal control of the services. If the broomstick ceremony reflected retention of earlier magical rituals of Africans, the preacher-officiated wedding reflected the growing institutional strength of Christianity in the community. "Sometimes Uncle Square [Squire?] Wallace would go through some sort of cere-

---

[32]Ibid., p. 275.

[33]Blassingame denies the existence of the broomstick ceremony except as a metaphor that parents used or as a ritual that followed a preacher-officiated ceremony. He believes that "looking back on bondage from the 1930s, blacks who had been children watching such ceremonies often conflated the wedding ritual and the post-nuptial jumping of the broom. Either they had not seen or had forgotten the wedding ceremony" (Blassingame, *Slave Community*, p. 167). Gutman, on the other hand, has confirmed the existence of the broomstick ceremony but recommends further study of its origins (Gutman, pp. 276–77).

[34]Gutman, p. 275.

mony. But he didn't know a letter in the book. Sometimes Square would marry them on Saturday night" (p. 217). "When they wanted to marry they just ask old master, and the squire would marry them" (p. 140). "I never went to but one wedding while I was little, I slipped off and went to that one. My father whipped the fire out of me, too. The preacher said some kind of ceremony out of the Bible, but they didn't have no license" (p. 293). "The slaves married like they do now. If you wanted your preacher to marry you, they would but if you didn't they would have a white preacher. Sometime the white people would give one of the biggest *to-do*'s you ever heard of. They would dance and eat and so on. Yes, they would join right hands and the matrimony was said like they do now" (p. 149). One informant remembered that a preacher married the slaves in front of the boss's front gate and a supper and a big dance followed (p. 260). "Two of my sisters married right where I am living now. A preacher married them, just like they do now, only they didn't have a license like they do now. White folks would give them a rooster and an old hen for supper sometimes" (p. 132).

The war helped to impose contractual legitimacy in the minds of African American youth. Securing rights to their children, civil rights, army pensions, and land ownership had more consideration than the legally sanctioned moral and sexual restraint implicit in the marriage contract in encouraging partners to formalize their marriages, Leon Litwack has observed.[35] For the children, then, full participation in their newly won freed status was associated with contractual and state-recognized marriages. "In those times people married just like we marry now, only they didn't get a license but they would get permission from their owner first and then from the girl's parents. Sometimes they got a preacher to marry them, and sometimes they jumped over the broom stick. When they were married by a preacher, they called that a lawful marriage, and when the War come up if a soldier died the wife could get a pension; but if they married by jumping over the broomstick, they didn't recognize that if a soldier died, and his wife could get nothing" (pp. 124–25). A man who was fourteen years old when the war ended remembered that "in the [army] camps they was teaching them about their citizenship. I remember well when the people had to marry over. They all come together, and the magistrate would meet them and marry them. I remember my mother and father went and got married but some slaves wouldn't do it" (pp. 58–59).

[35]Leon F. Litwack, *Been in the Storm So Long: The Aftermath of Slavery* (New York, 1979), pp. 240–41.

## II

Although slave children were often deprived of sexual knowledge, it is not necessarily true that they were shielded from the social realities evident in slavery. Testimony in the slave narratives reveals systematic and deliberate degradation and discipline designed to prepare the youth for a life of perpetual slavery. This pattern of abuse had implications for issues of development, autonomy, individuality, identity, personality, and sense of self. Na'im Akbar writes, "The shrewd slave-makers were fully aware that people who still respected themselves as human beings would resist to the death the dehumanizing process of slavery. Therefore, a systematic process of creating a sense of inferiority in the proud African was necessary in order to maintain them as slaves. This was done by humiliating and dehumanizing acts such as public beatings, parading them on slave blocks unclothed, and inspecting them as though they were cattle or horses."[36] Much of the degradation that Akbar writes about involves manipulating any sense of positive regard related to sexuality. Some of the manipulation involved repressing information. Children for the most part were not told their birthdays; even when the information was available they felt that their owners deliberately refused to tell them. The degrading practices included having children eat from troughs, as if they were animals. Slaveowners also controlled terms of endearment by not allowing children to define who their parents were or to use the same terms as whites used with their parents. A former slave on Dr. Gale's plantation remembered that in slavery the children could not call their father "papa" because the whites said "papa" but had to say "daddy" and "mammy"; when freed they called their father "papa" (p. 5).

Historians and psychologists have applied a psychoanalytic theory to the history of slavery. Orlando Patterson defines the process of slavery as "social death"—"the permanent violent domination of natally alienated and generally dishonored persons." In every slave society he finds that slaves are ritually humiliated, dishonored, and estranged from their birthright and tradition.[37] On the sexual content of violence, Frantz Fanon earlier reminded us that "we know how much sexuality there is in all cruelties, tortures, [and] beatings."[38] Hussein Abdilahi Bulhan states that "slavery in fact reeked with violence in its crudest forms. A society founded on the exploitation of slaves was the crudest form of structural

---

[36]Na'im Akbar, *Chains and Images of Psychological Slavery* (Jersey City, NJ, 1984), pp. 20–21.

[37]Orlando Patterson, *Slavery and Social Death: A Comparative Study* (Cambridge, MA, 1982), pp. 1–14.

[38]Fanon, p. 159.

violence."[39] David Brion Davis writes: "This general [psychoanalytic] orientation helps one to understand the paradox of the slave who is given an important role within a family's domestic economy but stands outside the delicate dynamics of kinship psychology. Deracinated from his own kinship group, the slave discovers that his own fate depends on adventitious circumstance. No brethren can protect him from arbitrary oppression or avert his murder or sexual violation."[40]

The attempts at control through ritualized humiliation and institutionalized violence, often sexual in content, sought to reinforce in the children the view that they were not human. Leonard Shengold has written extensively about the effects of childhood sexual abuse and deprivation, which he conceptualizes as "soul murder." He defines soul murder as "the deliberate attempt to eradicate or compromise the separate identity of another person."[41] Slaves would have understood this term; they referred to their owners as "soul drivers."[42] This "soul" or "psychic" murder involves killing the instinct for love in human beings. Children are more vulnerable to soul murder because they desperately need to maintain the image of a loving, rescuing parent or caretaker. The double bind of slavery—the parental authority informed by community mores and the owners' authority informed by market considerations—at once compounded the ignorance and the confusion of children. Children oftentimes did not have consistent parenting from their natural parents, both because of slavery and forced separation and because the owner instead of the parent might be seen as a caretaker. Genovese points out that slaveowners, as part of the strategy of paternalism, deliberately manipulated and exaggerated their role as caretaker during the childhood years by pampering slave children and by imposing themselves between parents and children, with dangerous consequences for the children's personal adjustment.[43] In Eriksonian theory, betrayal by a parental figure could lead to an inability to trust other persons. There is evidence of this in the narratives. Blacks did not trust whites at all. Within the black community there was mistrust of some members, but there is more evidence that the slaves developed trusting, close kinship relation-

---

[39]Bulhan, p. 156.

[40]David Brion Davis, *Slavery and Human Progress* (New York, 1984), p. 16.

[41]Leonard Shengold, *Soul Murder: The Effects of Childhood Abuse and Deprivation* (New Haven, CT, 1989), p. 2. In his discussion of the term, Shengold states that August Strindberg in 1887 wrote an article entitled "Soul Murder" on Henrik Ibsen's play *Rosmersholm*, to describe the taking away of a person's reason for living (p. 19).

[42]For example, see a letter from Henry Bibb to Mr. Albert G. Sibley, November 4, 1852 (in Blassingame, *Slave Testimony*, p. 55).

[43]Genovese, pp. 513–14.

ships. Shengold points out that abuse, deprivation, and neglect under conditions of dependency elicit a situation of helplessness and rage. Both of these feelings must be suppressed in order for the child to survive. These conditions were present for slave children. In many cases the person who has experienced events that contribute to soul murder will identify with the aggressor, a situation that sometimes occurs during brainwashing. Some former slaves even referred to their owners as their white families. The appropriate and expected emotions are denied or deadened. Survivors of attempted soul murder often muster considerable ego strength and, although scarred, proceed with psychological development.[44]

Gutman reminds us that the double bind of slavery at the same time encouraged a biculturalism that posed a contradiction for most slave-owners, whose social and economic livelihood required slaves to reproduce themselves. Child-rearing by encouraging kinship and familial ties, which shaped slave behavior from one generation to another, also encouraged the development of an alternative, even oppositional culture to that of their masters. As Gutman writes, "What a slave child learned always depended upon how that child was taught and who taught that child. . . . A bicultural analysis of slave socialization together with an awareness of the relationship between the slave family and the enlarged kin group allows us to view the slave family as more than an owner-sponsored device to reproduce the labor force and to maintain 'social control.' . . . Passageways for a developing slave culture shaped the interior fabric of the developing slave communities, and also served to socia-

---

[44]It is clear from the narratives that despite the similarities in the slavery experience, there were indeed variations in the former slaves' responses to their experiences. There was clearly not one identifiable internalized slave personality, as suggested by Stanley Elkins's early work, despite the fact that many slaves were observed to behave in stereotyped ways; see Stanley Elkins, *Slavery: A Problem in American Institutional and Intellectual Life* (Chicago, 1959). Charles Pinderhughes, in taking issue with the simplicity of Elkins's 1959 work, focused on Elkins's perception that blacks were infantilized and whites internalized. He noted that in American and western European cultures, active mastery and competition were valued as traditionally masculine roles, while female roles were devalued. He argued that "controlling, demanding, self-centered, self-entitling, narcissistic, infantile roles were idealized and assumed by white masters while parental roles of feeding, cleaning, and serving were demeaned and pressed upon black slaves and servants. In this sense, whites were infantilized toward the omnipotent controlling role of infants and blacks were paternalized toward the feeding, cleaning, service-on-demand role of mothers." Pinderhughes pointed to not only the complexity of the condition of slavery, but also the shared, demeaning effects on both blacks and whites. See Charles A. Pinderhughes, "Questions of Content and Process in the Perception of Slavery," in *The Debate over Slavery*, ed. Ann J. Lane (Urbana, IL, 1971), pp. 102–8.

lize the slave child."[45] This cultural adaptation and family formation more than anything else allowed the slave to contend with the abuse, degradation, and humiliation of slavery.

An institutionalized practice that degraded and humiliated slave children was their owners' deliberate disallowance of underwear. Forcing children to advance into puberty without underpants shamed them. It is clear that slave children wanted appropriate clothing and that they had a sense of shame regarding their lack of it. Children became painfully aware of this as they began their adult sexual development. Possessing real clothing was often related to a change in status, such as growth into the adult workforce or marriage.[46] Boys and girls wore nothing but gender-undifferentiated shirts or "shimmys" and only received breeches or dresses once they began adult-level chores or moved into the house or to town. Winger Vanhook remembered, "All de black chillun wore a long shirt. It come down to de middle ob de legs, an' you couldn't tell a gal from a boy."[47] "Colored children didn't wear drawers, and you'd knit your own stockings," recalled a Tennessee woman (p. 5). Another woman confirmed that children had to knit socks themselves, adding, "I never want to see no more brown stockings and things; I never did like brown, looks so dirty, just like mud" (p. 205). A former slave from Henry County, Tennessee, said that "when boys got pretty large they wore body breeches. They wore a shirt and nothing else until they got a certain age" (p. 294). One former slave, who described himself as "quite a small boy about fourteen years old," said, "[We] never did know what a undershirt was in them days, and no underwear of any kind, summer nor winter. Sometimes we would get some old summer breeches that was wore out, and we would wear them for underwear in the winter" (p. 216). A woman ex-slave from Arrington, Tennessee, remembered that "we had red flannel clothes in the winter. In the summer we went about with not a God's thing on but a 'shimmy.' We always went in our 'shimmy tails' in the summer" (p. 136). One male ex-slave from Hardeman County, Tennessee, remembered that "we wore great long shirts until we was great big boys" (p. 76); another ex-slave remembered that on their planta-

[45]Gutman, pp. 261–62; see also Escott, pp. 18–35.

[46]Eugene Genovese writes that the child's embarrassment at the exposure of private parts by wearing slips without underpants requires no explanation. On the other hand, he excuses the owners' culpability as a blind spot, for "the sexual prudery of the whites always went along with a failure to notice blacks, so that naked children, not always small, romped everywhere" (Genovese, p. 505). Yet the treatment here seems to fit a pattern that Orlando Patterson describes as ritual humiliation designed by the slaveowners deliberately to degrade and shame the slaves (Patterson, pp. 1–14).

[47]James Mellon, ed., *Bullwhip Days: The Slaves Remember* (New York, 1988), p. 38.

tion the women, including his mother, wove cloths, four cuts each night before bed; nevertheless the "boys until they got up large enough to work wore little slips. We called them shirts; they'd sew it up like a sack and cut a whole in the neck for your head to go through, and you wore that until you were ten or twelve years old. There was not much difference in the dress of girls and boys" (p. 56). Although dress was gender-undifferentiated, the slave child was painfully aware of gender differences and the degradation caused by the lack of appropriate clothing. "In the summer time we would go around half naked," one individual, "Massa's slave son," recalled. He remembered that "we didn't wear nothing but one piece—a shirt that come down below your knees" (p. 82). Another woman remembered that when her black-as-satin grandfather married her black-as-satin grandmother, "he didn't have on nothing but a shirt, that's all they give them to wear then" (pp. 309–10). It is no wonder that a former slave recalled, "Why the darkies thought they couldn't do without their underwear in them days" (p. 213).

Girls aware of their sexual vulnerability developed a sense of modesty, covering up their bodies. They recalled that their dresses often did not fit. "The white gingham dresses would be so narrow they would split them" (pp. 5–6). "The women wore theirs straight too, and they called them sacks. Sometimes it would fit and sometimes it wouldn't" (p. 56). "We wore hoop skirts on Sundays jest like the white folks. I never did like them things; if you didn't sit down this-a-way, that old hoop skirt would shoot up like this. We did not wear short dresses. Then we wore white waists, and a real long skirt. The, you know, the style come in of wearing these here long things that warn't 'xactly no drawers—come way down to yo' ankles, and we wore them, too, jest like the white folks" (p. 205). "The clothes resembled them Sister Sutton [an elderly informant also present at the interview] had on. You would never see a grown woman with a dress on shorter than hers, and sometimes they would be longer. When they dressed up on Sunday their dresses would drag on the ground" (p. 37). There is little doubt that a sense of modesty and decency was evident in slave girls.

Boys too wanted pants, for having clothing made them feel more like persons, more human. One man recalled that he was seven years or older when he got his first pair of pants—when he moved from the countryside to Bowling Green (p. 92). Frederick Douglass likewise was about seven or eight years old, preparing for his trip to Baltimore, when he got his first pair of pants. He wrote that he washed in the creek for three days, for Miss Lucretia had promised him a pair of trousers if he got all the dirt and dead skin off. "The thought of owning a pair of trousers was great indeed! It was almost sufficient motive, not only to make me take off what would be called by the pig drovers the mange, but the skin itself."[48]

Slaveowners were persistent in equating and treating the children and their parents as stock or domestic animals, and in some instances as pets. Family members were separated from one another, sold, or given away indiscriminately. It was very difficult for slaves to develop a positive self-esteem and self-image when they were treated as if they were animals. Their worth was related by their owners to physical size, to how much money a slave would sell for, to how many children a slave could breed. Ego strength ultimately came from their ability to recognize the cruelty and mean-spiritedness of their owners and to develop, in contradistinction, their own set of values and sense of body-ego. In doing so they recognized the absurdity of treating people like stock and criticized their owners for degrading people thus.

The informants associated their owners' buying and selling of slaves as equating them with animals. Mules, horses, hogs, pigs, and dogs were common terms used by slaves when discussing their owners' sale of slaves. Slave children saw people sold from the public square—put on the block like stock. "Back there they bought and sold colored people just like they do horses and mules now. Many husbands, wives and children were separated then and never met again" (p. 121). One man recalled that "I never have seen my mother since I left, or my sister or brother. Diana was my mother's only girl," and he said that "the man who sold me was a speculator in slaves. Buy them just like mules" (pp. 104–6). "[The owner] was mean to them, even if he was going with them. If his wife find it out he would have to sell her (Negro concubine). He would sell his own children by slave women just like he would any others. Just since he was making money. In slavery, niggers and mules was white folks' living. They would sell for $500 and $1,000. My mother sold for $1,000" (p. 298). "They would drive slaves off just like they do hogs now" (p. 305). When "old Charlie Merrill, the nigger trader, come along they sold my daddy [who had killed his overseer] to him, and he carried him way down in Mississippi. Ole Merrill would buy all the time, buy and sell niggers just like hogs. They sold him Aunt Phoebe's little baby that was just toddling long, and Uncle Dick—that was my mammy's brother" (p. 116).

The intrapersonal violence of slavebreeding cannot be underestimated, for the equation of slaves with domestic animals and market value was not lost upon slave children. Slaves were depicted by their

---

[48]Frederick Douglass, *Narrative of the Life of Frederick Douglass* [1845], in Michael Meyer, ed., *Frederick Douglass: The Narrative and Selected Writings* (New York, 1984), p. 42.

owners as cattle and without human morals; breeding was an important aspect of this. Informants remembered slaveowners calling a man "nigger buck and a woman a nigger winch," whom they would buy and carry down to a Mississippi cotton plantation, where suckling babies could be sold from their mothers (pp. 44–45). "I've seen droves of 'em come through, all chained together. And I laughed; I didn't know no better. . . . I was just a little motherless child, kicked and knocked about" (p. 254). "In Lexington, Kentucky, between Bowling Green and Louisville, was a great place for tobacco and flax. They would raise darkies there and place them in droves along the road having a rope between them like these big cable ropes. They would have the left hands of two people tied to the same rope so they could not run away. A mother would walk along with a child, a suckling, and they would take her and sell her from that child like taking a mother from her pigs" (p. 169). In selling mothers from their children, slaveowners "thought Negroes were cattle and stock" (p. 173). Dr. Gale's ex-slave, whose own parents had been coupled, remembered: "They would buy a fine girl and a fine man and just put them together like cattle; they would not stop to marry them. If she was a good breeder, they was proud of her." Dr. Gale "had a regular farm of slaves he'd just raise them to sell" either to his Louisiana plantation or to hire out locally (p. 1). "Some of the ole marsas used to have the colored folks; and they would take women away from their children just like you would sell a hog or something. Aw, Chile, you better be glad you warn't here in them days. You couldn't do nothin' but cry; better not say you didn't want to go, er nothin'. Sho' was awful" (pp. 204–5). Mrs. Sutton believed that "whenever they'd get overstocked with niggers, like cattle, now-a-days, they would gather up all the niggers and have a big block and stan' them up there, and there was a man to cry them off. He would put up a girl, and say, 'How much am I offered for her?' Someone would say 'Five Hundred dollars'; then maybe someone else would say 'Five Hundred and fifty dollars' till they disposed of all of them" (p. 31). "It is very seldom you can get a colored person to tell you anything about slavery. The white folks ain't gonna tell you. Women wasn't anything but cattle" (p. 92).

If slave children did not know where babies came from, they did know where the value of the babies went—to the owner. Slaveowners were quick to speak of their slave children within their earshot as potential breeders. One woman, an ex-slave of Dr. Gale, said: "I was stout and they were saving me for a breeding woman but by the time I was big enough I was free. . . . I'd hear them saying, 'She's got a fine shape; she'll make a good breeder,' but I didn't know what they were talking about" (p. 1). She may not have known what they were talking about but her life script was being written for her. Her mother, who had been coupled with her father, had fourteen children; her aunt in Mississippi had twenty children. Another woman, only four years old when slavery ended, related that her mistress "used to say I wouldn't sell her for nothing. I wouldn't take less than a thousand dollars for him [her brother] and I wouldn't take two thousand for her; 'that's my little breeder.' Mother said I cussed and said, 'Damn you, I won't never be no breeder for you.' I don't know how I learned to cuss" (p. 156). Willie Williams recalled in the same vein his master coming into the nursery: "De marster lots ob times looks dem over an' points out an' says, 'Dat one will be wo'th a thousan' dollars,' an' he points to anudder an' says, 'Dat one will be a whopper.' You see, twas jus' lak raisin' de mules: if you don't hurts dem when dey am young, you gits good strong niggers when dey am big."[49] Still another ex-slave recalled that they kept her grandmother as a house girl because she was "young and supple and could have lots of children. Ain't that hard? . . . You see, their object was to raise her and sell her so she would make a lot of money for them" (p. 309). An elderly ex-slave, fifteen years old when the war began, recalled that "they would see children and give them candy; if they looked healthy they would buy them and raise them up. They would look at them and say, 'that's a mighty fine nigger'" (p. 105).

In some cases, the children believed that marriages were not granted to male slaves who were not big and healthy, because the owners did not feel these men would sire healthy slaves for them. For males, sexual rights were related to size and ability to add income to the slaveowners. Identity was, then, much concerned with size and strength. The message was that puny men were denied wives and sexual rights. They also brought less income if sold by their masters. Girls too were appraised early as potential breeders for the masters: fertile women were prized; barren women were devalued.[50] One man, who was ten years old when slavery ended, recalled that his crippled "mother [was] put on the block three times, and they couldn't sell her. They tried to bid her off for a

---

[49]Mellon, ed., p. 39.

[50]At the same time the black male was more disenfranchised from his sexual status than was the female. Women were valued for their procreative functions, while males were feared for their sexuality. Apart from the female slave's value as a breeder, "she often played a critical maternal role in the lives of white children," serving as wet nurse and primary caretaking figure. She was a valued figure, and yet in slavery the white child was often separated from this treasured person. This painful loss led to an unconscious love-hate attitude on the part of southern whites toward their black nurses and blacks in general. "The importance of blacks was unconsciously disavowed by whites; however this repressed grief was an important factor in race relations during slavery" (Stephen M. Weissman, "Frederick Douglass, Portrait of a Black Militant: A Study in the Family Romance," *Psychoanalytic Study of the Child* 30 [1975]: 750).

dime, but nobody would give it. . . . Why, in them days, they would sell a baby from its mother and a mother from her baby, like cows and calves, and think no more of it" (p. 278). Men and women might be coupled with one another to promote fecundity. Mr. Huddleston, a former slave, stated: "A woman who bore children fast, they would sell her for as much as a man. A woman who was barren, they wouldn't sell her for so much. . . . Maybe a woman would sell, a woman and her baby would be put up. Maybe someone wouldn't want the baby, but they would want the mother; then the baby would be sold to someone else. That's the reason niggers are so scattered out, 'cause they never would sell them as family, but as individuals. . . . Maybe if a scrubby looking nigger like me would ask the girl's mass'r, he wouldn't let her marry; but take a sturdy stock of niggers, he would be glad to have him" (pp. 31, 33, 41–42). A former slave, twelve years old when slavery ended, remembered that "when they got ready to marry, they would just come to the marster and tell him that he wanted one of his women, and he could just take her. They didn't have no ceremony. They wouldn't let a scrubby man come in among them; but if he was healthy he could just take her and start living with her. They jump over the broom stick in them days. I never see nobody marry until I was free. Niggers never knowed about marriage, because they couldn't read" (p. 300). One ex-slave, whose father was a member of the master's family, related that "I would ask him [a girl's master], if I wanted his girl; and if I was a Negro that was profitable and would increase other families, I could marry. Then I would ask my master, and if he gave his consent too, I could marry, but without it I couldn't" (p. 101). He also remembered it being said by Mary, the black overseer at a plantation in Texas, that his fingers were too short to pick cotton. What, in his boyhood mind, would be his likely prospects for marriage? On the other hand, an ex-slave, eight years old when slavery ended, believed that "a great big nigger like me would bring four or five thousand dollars but a little nigger wouldn't bring nothing hardly. Nobody didn't want a little puny nigger" (p. 305).

Childhood memories of sexual violence recall whites exaggerating the slaves' sexual or carnal natures, seeking to dehumanize them. Such violence serves as a stumbling block toward the development of healthy sexuality and an integrated personality. At the same time the whites around them offered few healthy developmental role models, for healthy people do not degrade, sell, rape, and torture people.[51] The be-

---

[51]Herbert Gutman suggests that such sexual punishments were more than simply personal idiosyncrasies; rather, they are demonstrative of ritualistic cruelties. He recommends further study of southern white sexual mores to understand this pattern of punishment (Gutman, pp. 395–96).

havior of whites made growing into maturity as a slave a depressing and frightening prospect. One ex-slave recollected the habitual hazing of bathing blacks for no reason other than to harass and humiliate them in their nakedness. "Slaves would be in the river washing sometimes, and the paddie rollers would come along and see them, and they would throw their clothes up in the trees; and I have seen them running with not a string around them. They wouldn't have time to put nothing on if they had their clothes, 'cause they was running them so close" (pp. 132–33). One former slave girl, ten years old when slavery ended, recalled that "when we was little, she [the mistress] use to whip us and then make us kiss the switch. She was the meanest one of the daughters" (p. 280). This may be the only reference to kissing in these narratives. Either the children did not see their parents kiss or they did not speak of it. Usually a kiss is presented as a gentle, positive action, but here it is coupled with the sadistic whip. The slave must kiss it. The message is, "I know that you have been bad, even though that may not be so, and you should be thankful to me for correcting you." In another instance a former slave recalled that her mistress had led women around by their ears with hot tongs, saying to them that these were their earrings (p. 194). Women for the most part were deprived of the adornment of earrings, which are usually used to make one attractive; yet here the accessory of cruelty and painful disfigurement is called an earring. The same mistress once threatened to cut out the baby from a pregnant woman's belly, a further reminder that the fruit of a woman's sexuality could be destroyed. It was not her own.

From the point of view of the child, sadistic punishment distorted the sexuality of the master, but the violation was particularly frightening if a parent was the target. If not, the child easily projected this possibility onto a parent.[52] "I seed one of our young marsters take an old colored woman and pull her clothes down to her waist and whip her with a cowhide," said one former slave girl. "It's a strange thing to me that they would never try to whip my mammy, but I think that old Marster Jack was the cause of that." She rationalized, equating her mother fully with her mistress, that "she just had trouble with mistress, and he said he wished they might try to help her out, cause she was a woman and Nancy [the slave] was a woman." This is one of the few references in which whites are remembered as referring to a female slave as a woman, a term usually reserved for the white female. In this case the slave and the white woman are both equated as women (p. 282). One former slave remembered that Old Bufford, whose "darkies had chillen by him," tried to force her mother sexually, "and Mammy wouldn't do it; and I've seen

[52]Fanon, p. 145.

him take a paddle with holes in it and beat her, and everywhere it hit it raised a blister; then he would take a switch and break them blisters" (p. 118).

In slavery, the message was that the woman's body was not her own; if she exercised a personal right she was not simply punished but publicly humiliated and dehumanized. The stripping of clothing meant that the violent act cut down to the primal essence of the victim and the slave community at large, revealing to the child her elemental vulnerability. A former woman slave remembered that "when they commenced selling the niggers they would have to strip naked" to be examined. "It was awful to see the condition of some of the women, especially. Some of them were pregnant" (pp. 193–94). A former slave named Martha Harrison remembered that "the way they would whip you was like they done my oldest sister. They tied her, and they had a place just like they're gonna barbecue a hog; and they would strip you and tie you and lay you down" (pp. 116–17). "When they would whip you they would tear your back all to pieces," remembered one ex-slave, who described himself as a fifteen-year-old boy when the war began. "Child, they didn't care for you. We had to stand in fear of them, we had no protection. They would take your clothes off and whip you like you was no more than mules" (p. 105). Yet another recalled an incident when "they beat us till the blood run down our legs. When we left here we was naked; my sister was the weaver and she was weaving some clothes for us, and old mistress took that stuff off the loom and took it upstairs and hid it. We went away naked. . . . Yes, when we left there we had our dresses pulled round in front to hide our nakedness" (pp. 276, 279).

In developing a sense of sexual identity the prospect of sexually inspired physical violence was omnipresent. Children not only learned that white men commonly forced themselves upon black women but that the consequences of resisting could be fatal (p. 51). Slave children learned that if women resisted they could be sold south, separated from their babies, and beaten. A slave woman remembered when she was a child on Dr. Gale's plantation that not all women had sexual relations with white men; of those who did, some went willingly but others were forced: "They had a horror of going to Mississippi and they would do anything to keep from it" (p. 2). At that time, Mississippi was seen as the worst place for a slave to be held. She recalled that her master allowed Aunt Mary Jane to marry a "yellow man" because he knew he could have her anytime he wanted. "He dressed her up in red—red dress, red band and rosette around her head, and a red sash with a big red bow." Her dark-skinned aunt "had two yellow girls to wait on her!" A dance followed the wedding, but the churched couple did not dance. The whites watched (p. 8). A former slave from Hardeman County, Tennessee, recalled a slave named John, "a big double-jointed man," who confronted his owner for making advances to his wife. "John run old man Chapman, for some of the hands told him that Chapman had been after his wife, and John got after him about it. Old Chapman had a gun and John tried to take it away from him and Old Chapman shot him in the arm. . . . He taken his wife and went to Mississippi, and carried John's wife too. John kept on disputing with master and master tapped him over the head with his walking cane" (p. 76). Black men who resisted the rape of their wives and loved ones were choosing death. A slaveowner named Sam Watkins "would ship their husbands (slaves) out of bed and get in with their wives." One man killed Watkins, although "he knew it was death" (p. 2). According to Stephen M. Weissman, "The frequent disruptions of the black family unit were partially related to unconscious retaliatory envy. The white man's need to repress his childhood emotional tie to blacks often took the extreme form of seeing them as subhuman or nonhuman. Tenderness was replaced by cruelty in what could be described as a cultural reaction formation. The power and intensity of the white man's exaggerated sexual fear of the black man was probably related to the power and intensity of his own unconsciously determined incestuous wishes toward black women and its accompanying retaliatory fears."[53] Boys and girls observed that the owners did not respect the sanctity of the marriage bed and that resistance had dire consequences.

In most cases, the children observed that slave women had little choice but to be involved in the liaisons that produced mixed-race children. In some cases, slave women might have sought the relationships, but the cost was great. These children were sometimes not trusted by the other slaves, because of their biological and social relationships with whites. The miscegenation added further confusion to a slave's sense of self-worth. Was it better to be half white, since being black was despised? Yet in many cases the offspring were treated just the same as blacks or were despised by the whites whom they resembled, and who feared them. Sometimes, slave children of owners and their mothers had special privileges. Most continued their status as slaves, although after slavery ended, some were deeded land and given some support by their white families.[54] One woman whose husband's father was the master re-

[53]Weissman, p. 750.

[54]Frederick Douglass was born of a slave mother and an unknown white man. He was separated from his mother at birth and raised by his maternal grandparents, who raised other grandchildren as well. Douglass was sent away for a time and then returned to live in his (presumably) master/father's home, where he received some affection. Douglass rejected the idea of slavery early in his life and met his hero William Lloyd Garrison, according to Weissman, at an abolitionist meeting in Nantucket. A strong bond of friendship

membered that "marsa had a brother to have a child by one of the slaves. 'Course he wouldn't own him, but everybody knowed it, he would give it things, but they treated him (the baby boy) like they did all the other slaves, no'm, didn't make no difference toward him. Well, some of them thought it was an honor to have the marsa, but I didn't want no white man foolin' with me" (pp. 207–8). Another recalled, "I know plenty of slaves (women) who went with the old marster. They had to do it or get a killing. They couldn't help it. Some of them would raise large families by their owner. I know an old banker in Lebanon who gave one of his children a home after they come free" (p. 51). "Aunt Millie" who had master's son lived on a plantation but was free, paid for by a white person. They called her "widow woman" because she lived alone (p. 55). A woman from Nashville remembered a man on the Pike. "I know when I went off he bought a woman, and this woman came from Arkansas, and this here man got with her and got this boy and she got him, and then she turned round and had a black one, and he turned around and sold it. He bought her from Miss Porter and she got jealous and she turned round and had a dark child and he sold [it]" (p. 252).

Issues of identity and sexuality were complicated further when the child was a blood relative of the slaveowner or his white employee. Some of the former slaves pointed out that the slaveowners tried not to show any favoritism. In some cases, they were sold by their relatives. What did it mean to be sold by your father? What did it mean to be seen as less than human by your relatives?[55] One ex-slave remembered that "some of them would treat these [mixed-blood] children better, and some of them wouldn't" (p. 34). Another ex-slave remembered that when he was twelve years old he was sold by his half-brother, "mighty near like Joseph" (p. 86). On the Gale plantation, a woman remembered, her "grandfather was an Irishman and he was a foreman, but he had to whip his children and grandchildren just like the others." Gale, himself, had his children work the same as other slaves and call him "marster," and

---

ensued, and they traveled the abolitionist circuit, with Douglass emotionally recounting his life under slavery and Garrison eloquently denouncing slavery in a manner that left the audience spellbound (ibid., pp. 729–50).

[55]Weissman emphasizes the inconsistent, disguised threads of positive feelings that Douglass had for his white family, saying "These relations were intimate with deep, unconscious, incestuous undercurrents. Douglass was raised as a second-class member of his master's family and received a great deal of special attention and consideration compared to the standard treatment of slave children." Weissman believes that this ambivalent form of black-white interaction was common during slavery and had some of its unconscious roots in early childhood experiences. Indeed for the slave with a white parent, the potential for the ambivalent feelings was great (Weissman, p. 749).

the overseer whipped them like the others. "The only advantage they had was that Marster Gale wouldn't sell them" (p. 3). A witness, a fifteen-year-old boy when the war began, recalled that "they wouldn't make no difference in the half-white slaves. They would get whippings just like we would" (p. 106). Another remembered that the whites treated their children the same as other slaves. "They mighta liked them a little better, but they didn't want to show it" (p. 217). Still another recalled that the children were whipped the same as the others and sold from the block. "They would take them to town and put them on the block, and he was the father of them" (p. 252). The commingling of race with sex and with the violent separations and whippings illustrate the sexual content of the violence about which Fanon wrote.

Often mistresses who felt threatened by the relationships that their husbands had with black women took out their frustration and anger on the resulting children. Dr. Gale's ex-slave remembered a practice that when whites married, the husband would be given a slave cook as a gift, by whom he then had children. They "sometimes favored him so much that the wife would be mean to them and make him sell them. If they had nice long hair she would cut it off and wouldn't let them wear it long like white children" (p. 1). Another informant recalled one family of half-white children of the master on the plantation. "The old lady would be meaner to them than she was to the black ones." She "would not have one of them for a house servant. She would get one right black and wouldn't have none of them in there looking as white as her" (p. 261). In another narrative, an ex-slave recounted the killing of a slave who was presumably half white. One can assume that because of the attention paid to her hair, it was not to her advantage that she bore some resemblance to a white woman. "A woman named Charlotte had real long hair and they cut one side of her hair off and left the other side long. They whipped her one evening for the longest, and told her to get over the barb wire fence, and she said she couldn't, and he jerked her through by the hair, and she never did come to. She was a corpse in ten minutes after they jerked her through" (p. 135).

In yet another case, a mistress was haunted by her slave grandson's similarity to her own son and, like Charlotte, his hair became the object of ridicule and torture. This child lived in the house with the family but was accorded a special status. In this case the mistress would ask him what he had on his head. When he would answer "hair" she would tell him that it was wool. He told interviewers that she used to pull his hair out by the handfuls when he was a child. Again, the slave was subject to conflicting thoughts about his parentage, his bondage, and his physical appearance. In this case the slave grandson was given property at the war's end, but his memory of his grandmother's cruelty remained clear

for many years. Yet his memory of his father turned vitriolic. "I was rid-
ing on a streetcar long after freedom and I passed the cemetery where
my father was buried. I started cussing—'let me get off this damn car
and go see where my God damn father is buried, so I can spit on his
grave, a God damn son-of-a-bitch.' I got no mercy on nobody who bring
up their children like dogs. How could any father treat their child like
that? Bring them up to be ignorant like they did us. If I had my way with
them all I would like to have a chopping block and chop every one of
their heads off" (pp. 83–84). This man clearly had anger at his treatment by his master/father that had survived for decades.

Slave children, especially those of mixed race, might create in fantasy
a family romance. The "family romance" is a psychoanalytic concept
wherein the individual, in recalling events of his life, sometimes modi-
fies and fantasizes a better scenario. An abused child, for instance, might
fantasize that the abusing natural parent is really a step-parent, and
when the powerful real parent realizes that he exists, he will be rescued.
Weissman studied three biographies written by Douglass. He stresses
that, in his opinion, Douglass develops a family romance, a set of fictional parents who create an idealized "good." This mental novel of
early childhood is capable of being revised and rewritten at different
stages of one's life. Like many mythological stories of birth, the hero is a
secret, unacknowledged issue of parents of high station. The hero is
raised by surrogate parents and in time comes to know the identity of his
true parents.[56] Margaret Lavine's family romance contained a grandmother who was stolen from Spain and made a slave and a mother who
had driven away the Indians. This former slave said that her mother, for
whom she was named, was half Indian and half Spanish. Her father was
white, "of course." Her mother was the overseer, hired the hands, and
was "kind of the boss around there about things about the house. . . . I
remember mother crying and mistress got in bed with her. She slept
right with mother. We had trundle beds then." Concerning Margaret
and her siblings, the Yankees said to her mistress, "Goddamn, these
must be your grandchildren the way you are carrying on about them"
(pp. 198–99). They very likely were.

In other instances, the children had fantasies about white women
having close relationships with slaves who might have been biologically
related to them. In some instances the relationships had a confusing
mixture of love and degradation. In one case, the mistress was reported
to have "saved" a pretty slave girl for her son. "A white woman would
have a maid sometimes who was nice looking, and she would keep her

---

[56]Weissman, p. 729. For another example of a family romance, see the autobiography
of Sella Martin written in 1867 (Blassingame, *Slave Testimony*, pp. 703–4).

and her son would have children by her" (p. 2). What was the message then? To be chosen as the pretty slave had advantages, but costs as well. Here, the man was not choosing the slave woman, but she was being chosen for him by another woman, who would be related to any progeny.

In some cases, slave children were treated as treasured pets of their white owners. Often the child was the pet of the mistress, given to her as a gift. In at least one instance, however, the child was also the valued pet of the master. An informant named Mrs. Moore, eleven years old when slavery ended, remembered that her mistress cried "'cause we were the same as her children" after her children were grown. She also remembered that "when I lived with the white folks, I stayed in the house most of the time," but unlike the white children "they fed me right there in the room, on the floor" (pp. 39–40). One former slave noted that, from the time she was a baby, "I slept with ole mistiss till I was too big and used to kick her and they made me a pallet on the floor, and I never stayed in her bed anymore" (p. 182). Another former slave said that his mistress "mothered and raised" slave children (p. 221). One woman remembered that when she was a child they sometimes paired children as companions when a slave and the mistress had children the same age. She recollected about her own situation: "I never called ole Miss nothing but 'mother' in my life" (p. 249). She slept in a trundle bed in the mistress's room as a child. This woman grew up to become a special maid to the mistress, and she traveled extensively with the mistress, unlike other slaves on the plantation. Like others, she spoke of the mistress's family as her "white family" when asked to describe the family of her childhood. Indeed, the relationship between the slave children and the white owners was complex in such situations.

Like the woman who traveled with her mistress, another woman described her life as a special maid or nurse to her mistress. She described herself as being mulatto, having a Quaker father. This fact did not keep her from being given away as a gift to her mistress when she was five years old. She describes a case when she was put on display and revered by her owners. "My young master would have had a fit if I had married. I wasn't thinking about no marriage. I had my company to come to see me. They dressed me awfully nice. My mistress, she would say, 'Go wash,' meaning take a bath, and 'then I will come and dress you.' She would dress me in her clothes, from skin out. The boys just thought some of the girls were doll babies. That's what they thought about me, with my curls and dressed up so nice." She continued, "Yes, I went to parties and danced all night on Saturday night, dressed to death. I used to go to parties, and they all treated me nice. I never had a young man white or colored to say an ugly word to me, because my young master was very strict with me" (pp. 243, 227).

This passage indicates that in these situations the child, as her master's watch and ward, clearly had a status different from the other slaves, since her master would have been upset by either her mistreatment or sexual advances toward her. She was valued for her attractiveness to the "boys." One wonders, however, who the boys were, and what treatment the boys gave to her. In some ways, it sounds as if this attractive child might have been being prepared by her surrogate father to give sexual favors to the company, or for the master himself. She noted her curls. She also made reference to being dressed to death and dressed from the "skin out."

She was obviously aware of her similarity to and differences from whites and other slaves, as was an ex-slave named Lucy, who watched her mistress apply rouge to herself to "make her cheeks real nice and rosy; 'course me, smart, would go right behind her and rub my cheeks, too; and 'course I wasn't the right color. I would say, 'My cheeks don't git red as your'n,' and she would say, 'Lucy, you have to rub 'em harder,' he, he, he. I didn't know, I was so silly and young, but smart. Chile, I was sharp as a tack" (p. 20). For both slave girls described above, their developing sense of identity included incorporating aspects of both worlds, when indeed they did not fit comfortably into either. Similarly, another former slave vividly remembered that after being given to her new mistress at age six, the mistress washed her and made her new clothes—"a dress and some drawers and a drawer body." She said: "I was never dressed so fine in my life, and I just thought everybody was looking at me because I was dressed so fine. . . . The dress had some red in it and some big flowers in it, and I was looking at myself in the glass and I would pull up my dress and look at my pretty clean drawers and things, and when I went in the room where my mistress was I pulled it up again and started looking and saying to myself, 'Don't I look nice and clean under here,' and my mistress said, 'You mustn't do that, that's ugly,' and so then I went out in the woods where there was lots of cedars thick around, and I got down there and pulled up my dress and just looked and danced and danced" (p. 264).

Another woman was raised by her white mistress with her older brother when their mother died in childbirth. She noted that her mistress made an effort to "keep me from messing and mixing with everybody." The mistress was not happy if she played with slaves or poor white children. She went on to note that as a free adult, she continued to discriminate with regard to the persons with whom she interacted. Her father, who lived on another farm, continued to visit the children after the mother's death, every other week. After the war, her father came to retrieve her from the mistress, but she refused to leave with him. The mistress threatened to whip the girl if she showed any interest in leaving with her father. Finally the father, after several trips, told the child how the mistress had mistreated her own mother. She then left with her father but returned many times to visit. This narrative accurately describes the ambivalence of the slaves, particularly those who felt favored by their owners. Despite the fact that they were mistreated, they often identified with whites (pp. 60–69). Likewise, another woman remembered that after the death of her mistress (whom she thought of as a mother), she told her master when asked if she would stay, "I'll go home" to Mississippi. Her master cried that it was her mistress's wish for her to stay with the white children. "I had a little boy [beau] down there I was crazy about, and I wanted to go back to him," yet she remained in Tennessee (p. 266). The loss of parents (through absence or death) combined with living in the master's household was a confusing situation for a slave child. When racial origins were unknown, or racial identity was ambiguous, it often presented an even more confusing picture.

When slave children spoke of grooming, they often compared their physical features to those of white children. Invariably, the slave child did not benefit from the comparison. As noted earlier, the slave child was at both an advantage and a disadvantage if he had some characteristics in common with whites. Although skin color was often mentioned, hair was also a particular area of focus. White people resented slave children who had hair like that of whites, as shown in the cases above, where the former slaves remembered the mistress cutting off their hair and not letting them wear it like white children; the slave child's white grandmother pulling out his hair, referring to it as wool; the slave woman being jerked through the fence by her hair, resulting in her death. Children made references to the care of their hair during slavery. "Chillen was just as lousy as pigs. They had these combs that was just like cards you 'card' cotton with, and they would comb your head with them. They wouldn't get the lice out, but it would make it feel better. They had to use larkspur to get 'em out; that would always get lice out of your head" (p. 115). Another slave who was raised in Virginia noted, "In them days they made me comb my hair with an old kyard (card) what we used for spinning" (p. 110).

In a particular narrative, a slave noted that his hair was cared for by another species. "Me and my brother was in the trading yard before the Civil War. We stayed in there three or four weeks. They would fix us up and carry us in a great big old room and circle us all around every morning and every evening. They would have us up in a showroom to show us to the people. They would hit us in the breast to see if we was strong and sound. Monkeys would play with us and see if any boogies was in our heads. They would do pretty well if they found any, but if they didn't they would slap us. They had the monkeys there to keep our heads clean" (p. 75). This must have been a particularly confusing and humiliating experience for these two slave boys. Again, they were valued for their strength but humiliated by people and by monkeys.

In other cases, slave children were allowed to bathe nightly, and these children combed and wrapped their hair in cotton strings (p. 307). Another slave noted the difference in her grooming when staying with two different families. "I had never been clean like that before, and staying with them po' white folks I had had a time with those body lice. They would get so bad I would take my dress off and rub it in the suds and rinse it out in the branch; and sometimes I would be rinsing it and Mistress would call me, and I would be so scared I would put it on wet and run to her. I had a time, I tell you; they might nigh eat me up when I was staying there, and I was so glad to be clean" (p. 270). It was not important to many owners that slaves were groomed. Indeed, grooming was one of the indicators that a slave had a privileged status. For the slaves treated as pets, cleanliness was emphasized. Lucy remembered, "We had to [be] always nice and clean and everything" (p. 28). Elsewhere slave children were seen as stock animals, not in need of special grooming. Certainly, no one took time to help the slave child make his or her hair attractive, because parents had little time and owners understood this lack of grooming as one of the many ways slave children learned their slave role.

It is obvious that slave children's sexuality was developing as they became more concerned with dress, dance, and courting relationships. Despite practices occurring in slavery, there is evidence of ego strength and identity formation. Margaret Lawrence has suggested that it is with turmoil that ego strength is tested. Slaves remained individuals despite their owners' efforts to depersonalize them, and only through being individuals could they develop identity. Even among slave children there was a range of experiences and level of acceptance. They were presented with many barriers to the development of a sense of identity. What it meant to become a man or a woman was compounded by the times and the condition of servitude. However tragic and noxious the events recalled, it should be observed that most of the former slaves did go on to be productive men and women.[57] Leonard Shengold notes that he has

---

[57]In her work with poor inner-city families in Harlem, Margaret Lawrence found that, despite obstacles, children in these families have the same developmental tasks to perform as any other children. Each child is affected by nature, nurture, and noxia, according to Lawrence. Nature is described as the constitutional makeup influenced by genetics. Nurture is the care or love the child receives from a parent or parental figure. Lawrence de-

treated people who were able to survive their attempted childhood soul murder with considerable intactness and psychic strength; many other people with similar experience are often devastated by the experience or are unmotivated for a variety of reasons to seek treatment. A number of those untreated persons grow up to be soul murderers themselves. Shengold, however, suggests that in spite of and sometimes because of traumatic early experiences, some individuals are able to make important contributions to their cultures.[58]

Although there were slaves whose souls were murdered, there is evidence that most sought to develop their own identities. In doing so they passed through epigenetic stages of development. Despite the separation and betrayal that occurred in the first stage of "trust versus mistrust" in infancy and childhood, many slave children went on to develop a sense of trust. There is evidence in the narrative that some of the slaves genuinely cared for each other and sometimes for whites and did not develop pervasive mistrust. Erikson felt distrust occurred if this first-stage crisis was not resolved. The ritual degradations of slavery made the second stage, "autonomy versus shame and doubt," a difficult period for slave children. Despite many efforts to shame the children because of their slave status, their lack of manners and education, their "blackness," their association as chattel, or their alleged inferiority, many were able to develop a sense of autonomy and were freed of the pervasive shame and doubt that would occur if Erikson's second stage was not successfully negotiated. Indeed slave children learned modesty and decency despite being stripped and being made to live without underwear. Many developed strong religious commitments, in part related to the degrading practices that occurred. The third stage of "initiative versus guilt" was fraught with peril for many slave children. Erikson felt that as the child gave up fantasies, he might suppress an inner "powerhouse of rage."[59] In slavery, desire to develop individual thought and initiative was usually thwarted or discouraged. Few slave children were able to pursue goals with confidence, without fear of punishment. Many were

---

scribes noxia as trauma or severe injury, either physical or mental. She goes on to say that despite trauma, many of the poor, primarily black, children in Harlem and elsewhere survive and do well. "Nature, nurture, and noxia do not exist alone in Harlem. They are intertwined, interlarded, soaked through and through, and mixed with strength, ego strength. Strength abounds in Harlem. Three hundred years of oppression and it survives. . . . Even anger may show strength. It can sustain a child and protect him until he is helped to find more suitable vehicles for his ability to love and to act" (Margaret M. Lawrence, *Young Inner-City Families: Development of Ego Strength under Stress* [New York, 1975], p. 35).
    [58]Shengold, p. 7.
    [59]Erikson, *Childhood and Society*, p. 257.

forced into work that was done for their owners' profit, with little regard for their individual sense of accomplishment. Even then productive work was undervalued. Evidence of rage exists in the narratives. During this stage the children became painfully aware that they were slaves.

In the next stage of identity development, "industry versus inferiority," the latency-age child developed a sense of competence in his ability to perform both physically and intellectually—if the initiative stage was not completed earlier, industry could not be properly developed. Because so many negative identity issues are referenced in the narratives, it seems that many slave children developed a sense of inferiority as opposed to competence. The next stage, according to Erikson, brought concerns of "identity versus role confusion." Here a desire for uniqueness and wholeness as a valued individual brought with it a sense of fidelity to others, which resulted from and strengthened a sense of identity. Despite insecurity in family life, individuals were faithful to their families and to individuals that they cared about. These informants also had a major adjustment to make in childhood or early adulthood, from slave to freedperson. This is a unique situation common to few individuals and cultures. Deprived of decency, modesty, religion, consistent relationships, and sexual rights, many of these slaves developed a keen sense of morality. Their sexuality was often exploited because of its advantage to the slaveowner. The sense of extended family (not always related to biological heritage) existed in slavery because of the harsh conditions of permanent and temporary separation. This sense of family was in rare cases extended to whites who the slaves felt had been important to them. The destruction of slavery would afford a collective catharsis, a healthy resolution, a redemption, for the ex-slaves, but it offered no comparable resolution to the former owners. Gutman writes: "Neither the coming of the Union Army nor the general emancipation altered the sexual beliefs of southern ex-slaves, southern whites, and northern whites. But the social upheaval associated with the war and the emancipation allowed ex-slaves to act upon their beliefs in a changed setting and even—for some—to try to reverse sexual and social practices that violated prevalent slave moral and social norms. The task proved difficult."[60] As a people the bond of family and cultural values may have compensated for the travail of slavery, but as individuals nothing could compensate for the wrong childhood.

[60]Gutman, pp. 385–86.

# The Sexualization of Reconstruction Politics: White Women and Black Men in the South after the Civil War

MARTHA HODES

*Department of History*
*University of California, Santa Cruz*

IN THE ANTEBELLUM SOUTH, sexual liaisons between white women and black men threatened the institution of racial slavery in a way that sex between white men and black women did not. A child's legal status as slave or free followed the mother; therefore, when white women had children by black men not only were racial categories eroded, but boundaries of slavery and freedom were eroded too, as free people of African ancestry endangered racial slavery. At the same time, however, as long as the institution of slavery remained in place, so too did a mostly satisfactory, if at times unreliable, system of stratification.

Although whites invoked ideology about the sexual ardor of black men in the colonial and antebellum periods,[1] antebellum documents reveal that communities of white Southerners displayed some degree of toleration for liaisons between white women and black men under the institution of racial slavery. Black men could be acquitted or pardoned on charges of raping white women; white husbands could be denied divorces even if their wives had committed adultery with black men; and the black men in such adultery cases could go without retribution.[2]

---

[1]See Winthrop Jordan, *White over Black: American Attitudes toward the Negro, 1550–1812* (Chapel Hill, NC, 1968; rpt. New York, 1977), pp. 32–43, 151–62, 398–99, 579; George Fredrickson, *White Supremacy: A Comparative Study in American and South African History* (New York, 1981), pp. 104–5; Elizabeth Fox-Genovese, *Within the Plantation Household: Black and White Women of the Old South* (Chapel Hill, NC, 1988), p. 291; Eugene Genovese, *Roll, Jordan, Roll: The World the Slaves Made* (New York, 1972), pp. 461–62.

[2]Martha Hodes, "Sex across the Color Line: White Women and Black Men in the Nineteenth-Century American South" (Ph.D diss., Princeton University, 1991), pp. 70–79, 86–101.

This essay originally appeared in the *Journal of the History of Sexuality* 1993, vol. 3, no. 3.

This toleration was due, in part, to white ideology about the sexual depravity of white women outside the planter classes. Those who held authority in antebellum Southern communities were likely to consider poorer white women to be the depraved agents of illicit liaisons, including liaisons with black men. Thus could white ideology about lower-class female sexuality overshadow ideas about the dangers of black male sexuality.[3]

The shift away from white toleration for sex between white women and black men accompanied the political transformations that came with the demise of racial slavery. The separation of blacks and whites was essential to Southern whites who were determined to retain supremacy after the Civil War; consequently, the "mixture" of people of European ancestry and people of African ancestry became a much more serious taboo. Because it was the men among the former slave population who gained suffrage rights and a measure of political power—and who therefore had the potential to destroy the racial caste system—whites focused on the taboo of sex between white women and black men with a new urgency.

Following the war, white anxiety and alarm about black male sexuality reached an unprecedented level of intensity. During the Reconstruction era black male sexuality first became a major theme in white Southern politics, thereby commencing an era of terrorism and lynching.[4] As part of the same process, white ideology about white female sexuality changed as well, though not as rapidly and never as completely.

This essay examines the white Southern response to sexual liaisons between white women and black men in the years following the Civil War. The intertwining of sex and politics in the minds of white Southerners in the postemancipation South was betrayed throughout testimony taken for the congressional investigation of the Ku Klux Klan in 1871. In these years, the Klan's actions represented the common concerns of Southern whites who wished to retain a racial hierarchy.[5] In jus-

[3]This toleration was never as great as that displayed for liaisons between white men and black women, not only because of the inheritance laws of slavery, but also because the antebellum South was a patriarchal society in which the transgressions of white women were graver than those of white men. For a study of sexual liaisons between white women and black men prior to Reconstruction, see Martha Hodes, "Wartime Dialogues on Illicit Sex: White Women and Black Men," in *Divided Houses: Gender and the Civil War*, ed. Catherine Clinton and Nina Silber (New York, 1992).

[4]Nell Irvin Painter points out the crucial need to study sexuality in Reconstruction politics in her article, "A Prize-Winning Book Revisited," *Journal of Women's History* 2 (1991): 126–34.

[5]Eric Foner writes: "In effect, the Klan was a military force serving the interests of the Democratic party, the planter class, and all those who desired the restoration of white supremacy." See Eric Foner, *Reconstruction: America's Unfinished Revolution, 1863–1877*

tifying their acts of violence, Klansmen and their supporters often conflated the newly won political and economic power of black men with alleged sexual liaisons with white women. White women accused of participating in such liaisons were, in turn, abused and assaulted by the Klan. Ultimately, the Klan offered white Southerners a new language of sexualized politics; this language moved away from the white-only rhetoric of democracy and republicanism that had justified the coexistence of black slavery and white liberty, to issue ominous warnings about the perils of racial equality.

Politics and sexuality were inextricably entwined at this moment in the history of the American South. Joseph Rainey, a black Republican from South Carolina in the House of Representatives, unmasked the connection between political rights and black manhood in an 1873 congressional debate. Southern white men, Rainey declared, wished to withhold citizenship rights from the black man because actions such as suffrage "had a tendency to make him feel his manhood," which in the eyes of white men "is asking too much."[6] James Rapier, a black Republican representative from Alabama, took his white opponents on their own terms, equating manhood with the right to vote and announcing that "nothing short of a complete acknowledgment of my manhood will satisfy me."[7]

It was precisely this equation of political rights and black manhood that became so central in the wars of the Reconstruction South. The idea of manhood, which had long implied the rights and responsibilities of citizenship in American political thought, now took on connotations, in white minds, of black male sexual agency, and specifically of sexual transgressions with white women. The Reconstruction-era discourse among white Southerners about black political participation and black male sexuality was characterized by a language of sexual alarm. One arena in which this discourse took place was in discussions by and about the Ku Klux Klan.

## THE TERRORIZATION OF BLACK MEN

Although black women and whites who supported the rights of the freedpeople were also victims of Klan terror during Reconstruction, the greatest violence was reserved for black men. The Klan was most active in areas of the South where the economic disparity and social inequality

---

(New York, 1988), p. 425.

[6]*Congressional Record,* 43d Cong., 1st sess., December 19, 1873, p. 344.

[7]*Congressional Record,* 43d Cong., 1st sess., June 9, 1874, p. 4784.

between blacks and whites was least remarkable. Members preferred to gather in areas with smaller black populations such as the Piedmont and upland regions, for the most part ignoring cities, the plantation heartland, most tidewater, coastal, and delta areas, and areas in which white Republicans were a significant presence.[8]

Six young returning Confederate officers had organized the Klan as a secret social club in Pulaski, Tennessee, in 1865 or 1866, creating their name from the Greek word for circle, *kuklos*.[9] The activities of their club soon encompassed the harassment of freedpeople, and by 1868 branches of the organization were established, at least for some time, in all Southern states. Although lacking central control, the Klan's methods were consistent. The majority report filed by congressional investigators in 1871 concluded that "we see from Maryland to Mexico, the same general spirit of spite against the freedman, and determination to keep him down and use his labor without compensation."[10] Tactics ranged from the destruction of property to whipping and maiming, castration, rape, and murder. Because Klan participants early on realized the power of operating as an underground organization, there were few public signs of their existence. Moreover, attacks generally took place in isolated rural areas at night. Attackers disguised themselves, and one group might number about a dozen, although mobs of fifty or a hundred also launched attacks.

Klan membership included all classes of white Southerners, but leaders usually were drawn from among the more well-to-do.[11] The former Confederate general Nathan Bedford Forrest became the Klan's leader, or Grand Wizard, and state leaders included lawyers, businessmen, journalists, former governors, and future U.S. senators among their ranks. Klansmen were motivated by the goal of white supremacy, most con-

[8]On the geography of the Klan, see Allen Trelease, *White Terror: The Ku Klux Klan Conspiracy and Southern Reconstruction* (Westport, CT, 1971), p. 64; Wyn Craig Wade, *The Fiery Cross: The Ku Klux Klan in America* (New York, 1987), p. 57; David Chalmers, *Hooded Americanism: The First Century of the Ku Klux Klan, 1865–1965* (New York, 1965), pp. 10, 16; John Hope Franklin, *Reconstruction: After the Civil War* (Chicago, 1961), p. 155.

[9]On the nineteenth-century Klan, the most thorough work has been done by Trelease; see also E. Foner, pp. 425–44, 454–59; Wade, pp. 31–111; Chalmers, pp. 8–21; Franklin, pp. 152–73; George Rable, *But There Was No Peace: The Role of Violence in the Politics of Reconstruction* (Athens, GA, 1984); Leon Litwack, *Been in the Storm So Long: The Aftermath of Slavery* (New York, 1979), pp. 274–82; John Carpenter, "Atrocities during the Reconstruction Period," *Journal of Negro History* 47 (1962): 234–47.

[10]*Report of the Joint Select Committee to Inquire into the Condition of Affairs in the Late Insurrectionary States* (13 vols.), 42d Cong., 2d sess., 22 (Washington, DC, 1872) (hereafter cited as *KKK Report*), pt. 1:270.

[11]On the participation of all white classes, see Rable, p. 30.

cretely manifested in white control of formal politics. Members claimed to guard against insurrection by freedpeople, deter crime, punish corruption, and protect against "lawlessness."

Klan victims had no effective legal recourse until as late as 1871.[12] Anti-Klan laws passed by state governments proved nearly impossible to enforce; the use of military power was slightly more effective. On the national level, President Ulysses S. Grant's determination to control the Klan in 1868 (the year in which the violence reached its zenith) did not succeed in arrests and convictions until 1871. White Southerners who disagreed with Klan tactics for the most part remained silent, and for blacks to defend themselves in any organized fashion would have meant taking up arms; the retaliations, they knew, would be more than they could withstand.[13]

In April 1871, a committee of twenty-one members from both houses of Congress embarked on an investigation of Klan violence.[14] Republicans, the party of Abraham Lincoln and of virtually all blacks in the Reconstruction South, outnumbered Democrats, the party of most white Southerners. For months, testimony was taken in Washington as well as in North Carolina, South Carolina, Georgia, Mississippi, Alabama, and Florida. The committee discovered that those in greatest danger of attack were black men who defied white efforts to retain a racial hierarchy: voting Republicans, especially political leaders; labor activists; those who displayed economic independence (landowners, for example); and those who crossed boundaries of the color line, ranging from talking back to forming sexual liaisons. Among whites, Republican officials and teachers of the freedpeople suffered, as did Northerners ("carpetbaggers") and white Southern Republicans ("scalawags").

Congressmen listened to both victims and perpetrators, though Klansmen and their sympathizers were evasive and claimed ignorance (aided immeasurably by the organization's underground nature). When asked about an organization of disguised harassers in his Mississippi community, for example, one witness said: "If there is, I don't know it, and never heard of it, sir; that is, to know it to be a fact, or ever to have heard of its being a fact."[15]

---

[12]Trelease writes: "Within the traditional federal system, the crimes of the Ku Klux Klan were offenses against state and local law; the central government lacked jurisdiction over murder, assault, robbery, and trespass, and but for the Klan most Republicans would have kept it that way" (p. 383).

[13]On this point, see E. Foner, p. 437.

[14]On the committee, see Trelease, pp. 391–98. Although the congressional proceedings did break the organization, few Klansmen were brought to justice; see Trelease, pp. 399–418; Rable, pp. 106–10.

[15]*KKK Report*, pt. 12:623. In Alabama, a white man similarly said: "I will state my

The victims, black and white, male and female, had much more to say, although they could not always speak forthrightly. Notably, stories about white women and black men were usually told by white witnesses, some of whom sympathized with Klan victims and some of whom did not. Because even sympathizers often relayed secondhand accounts, it is impossible to separate fabricated accusations from observed transgressions, or false admissions given under threat from truthful confessions. Yet whether true or untrue, what comes through consistently in the testimony is the way in which extreme white anxiety over sexual liaisons between white women and black men was linked to fears of black men's political and economic independence. Indeed, oscillating between silence and cautious articulation in the congressional testimony, black men who were themselves victims of the Klan did not hesitate to make this connection.

The ordeal of Henry Lowther, a married freedman in central Georgia, illustrates the ways in which white anger at black male political power merged with sexual accusations.[16] Twenty disguised Klansmen had come to the Lowther home on horseback one night, but Lowther had managed to elude them. "They said I had taken too great a stand against them in the republican party," Lowther recalled. "I worked for my money and carried on a shop. They all got broke and did not pay me, and I sued them." Lowther concluded: "They have been working at me ever since I have been free. I had too much money." Lowther was jailed on charges of conspiring to murder another black man but was denied a trial. A white man came to warn Lowther of trouble and asked whether Lowther was "willing to give up your stones to save your life," indicating castration. As Lowther remembered the scene, almost two hundred Klansmen arrived in the middle of the night, and twenty of them carried him away to a swamp. "The moon was shining bright, and I could see them," Lowther recalled; all the men were Democrats. There the Klansmen castrated him.

Did Lowther know the reason for the attack? "Any offense against the law, any breach of the peace, any violence, any insult to any white woman, or anything of that kind?" asked one of the congressional investigators. "No, sir; I never insulted any white woman," Lowther said. "They said I was getting to have too much influence in the republican party there." When pressed, however, Lowther admitted that the attackers "said I was going to see a white lady," but he pointed out that the

---

theory about the Ku-Klux organization. Of course I know no Ku-Klux; I never consciously saw one in my life" (pt. 8:431).

[16]For Lowther's narrative, see *KKK Report*, pt. 6:356–63; see also pp. 430–31.

charge was untrue. The white woman in question had hired Lowther to tend her land, but this charge had not been made when Klansmen had first come for him. According to a Southern white Republican judge, once Lowther had been assured that "he would not be compelled to incriminate himself before the court," he had admitted "that he had sexual intercourse with a white woman."

This judge denied that formal politics had prompted the assault on Henry Lowther. "It was a very unusual thing to proceed to that kind of punishment for political opinions," he said. "I do not believe, and I cannot believe, that the maltreatment of Henry Lowther was owing to his politics."[17] Yet in the castration of Henry Lowther, and in cases throughout the congressional testimony, white Southerners invoked charges of illicit sexual behavior toward or with white women together with accusations of Republican activism or the de facto crime of successful crops—that is, of political or economic authority and independence. When a man named Jourdan Ware was murdered, for example, his attackers told him it was "on account of his politics" and his economic security and warned him that he must "not vote the radical ticket any more." Afterward, whites testified that Ware had insulted and frightened a white woman.[18] When John Walthall was accused of sleeping with white women and murdered, a black neighbor felt sure the accusation was the consequence of a labor dispute between Walthall and his white employers.[19]

Klansmen could also resort to sexual mutilation for any act that struck them as demonstrating political or economic power on the part of black men, whether or not they tacked on an accusation of sexual misconduct. In North Carolina, for example, a black man was forced to mutilate his sexual organs with a knife due to a labor dispute.[20] In 1871, Robert Elliott, a black representative from South Carolina, spoke for "nearly every Southern state" when he described Klansmen as seeking "revenge for political power lost" in all their violence toward black men.[21]

## THE PROTECTION AND ABUSE OF WHITE WOMEN

Although the Reconstruction-era Klan excluded white women from membership, there is scattered evidence that white women played a part

---

[17]Ibid., pp. 426, 443. The judge could not say why Klansmen had visited Lowther the first time, before his alleged encounter with a white woman (p. 426).

[18]Ibid., pp. 44–45, 74–75, 405; pt. 7:885, 900.

[19]*KKK Report*, pt. 6:474, 476.

[20]Testimony of John W. Long, Ku Klux Klan Papers, William Perkins Library, Duke University, Durham, NC (hereafter cited as WPL); see also *KKK Report*, pt. 6:359.

[21]*Congressional Globe*, 42d Cong., 1st sess., April 1, 1871, p. 392.

in Klan activities.[22] Some female relatives sewed Klansmen's costumes, either voluntarily or on orders, while others lent their own clothing as disguises.[23] Other women, however, urged their husbands not to participate in raids, and a few expressed direct apprehension. One white woman in North Carolina "thought when the 'Yankees' came in and whipped them, she saw a heap of trouble; but she said the 'Yankees' were gentlemen compared to these Ku-Klux." This woman "had seen more trouble lately since these men had been there than the Yankees ever made." And a white woman in Alabama was whipped and thrown into a ravine (and later died of the injuries) for informing on Klansmen.[24]

As a specifically male-only organization, one of the Klan's stated purposes was that "females, friends, widows, and their households shall ever be special objects of our regard and protection."[25] The Klan's intention to protect women applied, of course, to white women only. As part of their violent rampages, Klansmen also assaulted and raped black women.[26]

Klansmen took offense when a black man acted in a manner they judged even mildly insulting to a white woman.[27] In the minds of Klansmen and their sympathizers, the rape of white women was the logical extreme to which black men would go without the institution of slavery to restrain them.[28] A white judge from Georgia thought that the rape of white women by black men was "vastly more frequent now" than during slavery, though he could not cite any actual cases.[29] In another instance, Grand Wizard Nathan Forrest said: "Ladies were being ravished by some of these negroes, who were tried and put in the penitentiary, but were turned out in a few days afterward." When pressed for details, Forrest admitted only hearsay and claimed lack of recollection.[30]

Nonetheless, a black man merely accused of raping a white woman

[22]Kathleen Blee, *Women of the Klan: Racism and Gender in the 1920s* (Berkeley, 1991), pp. 12, 13. For one instance of violence by a white woman, see *KKK Report*, pt. 1:264.

[23]On costumes, see Trelease, pp. 53–54; and, for example, *KKK Report*, pt. 2:87; pt. 6:519; pt. 7:955; pt. 9:813.

[24]See testimony of John W. Long, Ku Klux Klan Papers, WPL; *KKK Report*, pt. 2:100; pt. 8:157–58.

[25]*KKK Report*, pt. 2:364, repeated or paraphrased on pp. 366, 399, 422, 507, 524, 530, 555, 561, 572–73; pt. 13:9.

[26]See *KKK Report*, pt. 2:36–37, 49, 99–100, 148; pt. 6:75, 375–77, 387; pt. 7:914, 1004; pt. 8:80, 547, 553; pt. 9:930, 1188, 1189; pt. 12:1084.

[27]See, for example, pt. 6:86 (for "saucy expression to a white lady"); pt. 7:1166 (for being "abusive to ladies"). See also testimony of Sandy Sellers and John W. Long, Ku Klux Klan Papers, WPL.

[28]See *KKK Report*, pt. 7:833, 835–36, 842, 845; pt. 9:1260.

[29]*KKK Report*, pt. 6:124.

[30]*KKK Report*, pt. 13:7, 14–15.

could be lynched.[31] Charles Clarke of Georgia was charged with raping the white daughter of a Methodist preacher. The judge found insufficient evidence for conviction, and Clarke was returned to jail, supposedly pending further investigation. Thirty-six undisguised Klansmen shot Clarke dead at the jail.[32] Similarly, a white businessman in Georgia described an 1866 case in which a black man was accused of raping a sixteen-year-old white girl. "They caught that negro, tied him to a stake, and burned him in the day time before, I suppose, a thousand people," he recalled. "They never had any trial, or proof, or anything of that sort, and they never gave the name of this girl, so far as I ever knew."[33] By these means did the Klan claim to fulfill the purpose of protecting white women.

Their protection of women was circumscribed not only by race, but by class as well. White women of the lower classes could not count upon white ideology about white female purity and black male aggression to absolve them of illicit sexual activity. White women whom Klansmen and their sympathizers judged to be lacking in virtue were subject to abuse ranging from insulting language to rape.[34] Georgia Klansmen, for example, "'shot five balls through Rice Heath, a negro who was living in adultery with a white woman named Griffin. They then strapped the woman across a log, and whipped her so severely that she could not sit up yesterday.'"[35]

Klansmen also practiced the sexual mutilation of white women who lived outside particular boundaries of sexual propriety. In a Georgia case of cohabitation in which the accused black man was castrated, a witness recounted that Klansmen "took the woman, laid her down on the ground, then cut a slit on each side of her orifice, put a large padlock in it, locked it up, and threw away the key, and then turned her loose."[36] In North Carolina, a white girl with a bad reputation was assaulted by the Klan; one witness testified that "they took her clothes off, whipped her very severely, and then lit a match and burned her hair off,

---

[31]See Richard Brown, *Strain of Violence: Historical Studies of American Violence and Vigilantism* (New York, 1975), p. 323; statistics for lynchings due to the alleged rape of white women by black men do not exist. See also Rable, p. 98.

[32]*KKK Report,* pt. 7:655–66, 723–27.

[33]*KKK Report,* pt. 6:214. See also pt. 2:8, 142, 268–69, 310, 315; pt. 6:275, 574, 575, 577–78; pt. 7:611, 1061, 1097, 1190–93; pt. 8:242, 446; pt. 11:364; pt. 12:879.

[34]See, for example, *KKK Report,* pt. 7:1007 (insulting language); pt. 2:4; pt. 8:550–51; pt. 12:652 (physical abuse); pt. 8:549 (rape).

[35]*KKK Report,* pt. 7:1096; the quotation was reprinted in the report from the *Savannah News,* n.d.

[36]*KKK Report,* pt. 7:1120.

and made her cut off herself the part that they did not burn off with the match."[37]

In the testimony, the reputations and characters of white women were continually evaluated by white Southerners, and the congressional committee participated in this discourse. When questioned about the reputation of the white woman with whom Henry Lowther allegedly had had sexual relations, for example, a white judge called her "one of those low-down tramps which are scattered about the country."[38]

Similar descriptions of "bad" white women abounded. A white farmer who testified about the murder of Jourdan Ware had heard that Klansmen were on the lookout for "a sort of low character of a white woman" who "harbored about his house."[39] In another case, a white man testified that Klansmen beat a black man who had asked a white woman "to have connection with him." The woman had refused, and, when questioned as to her character, the witness said: "I suppose it was fair, because if she had been a common whore or strumpet, I do not suppose they would have paid any attention to it."[40] When a black Georgian accused of attempting to rape a white woman was not terrorized, the committee asked a white witness: "What was there about that case that mitigated it; was the woman of bad character?" The man answered that the alleged victim was "a woman of low position in society, and such a proceeding would not have been so great a shock to her, perhaps, as to one of higher refinement."[41]

Black men and women spoke in the same language when they described white women to the congressional investigators. Henry Lowther echoed the judgments of the white witnesses, calling the white woman in his narrative a "bad character."[42] In the murder of John Walthall, a black neighbor named Maria Carter identified four white sisters with whom, she said, Walthall had had sexual liaisons before his marriage. When the committee inquired whether these were "women of bad character," Carter replied, "Yes, sir; worst kind."[43]

Party politics could also be a motive for Klan assaults on white women, despite women's lack of formal political power. Again, the congressional investigators participated in this discourse. A conversation between a white North Carolina man and the congressional committee

---

[37]*KKK Report,* pt. 2:37.
[38]*KKK Report,* pt. 6:431.
[39]*KKK Report,* pt. 7:920.
[40]*KKK Report,* pt. 6:108, 125.
[41]Ibid., pp. 291–92.
[42]Ibid., p. 362.
[43]Ibid., p. 413.

illustrates the intertwining of the moral reputations and political leanings of white women:

*Q:* Were the women whipped because they were republicans?

*A:* That I cannot answer; I can only make the statement that in every instance— [the man at the house had voted for the republican ticket]

*Q:* You said they were women of low character.

*A:* Some of them were; others were of good character.

*Q:* The most of them were women of low character?

*A:* Yes, sir.

*Q:* What do you mean by women of low character?

*A:* I mean base women.

*Q:* Do you mean strumpets and unchaste women?

*A:* Yes, sir; of course women have been whipped who were not of that character. . . .

*Q:* I understood you to say that men were whipped at the same time?

*A:* I said this, that when women were whipped the men who lived at the place were republicans. They have whipped one woman where there was no man at all."

*Q:* That was a woman of bad character?

*A:* Yes, sir.[44]

A former North Carolina Klansman likewise testified that a white widow had been harassed because "she believed with the radical party" and at the same time "had been accused of having black men lying around there and staying."[45] Alabama Klansmen whipped a white woman, "a loose character," because "it was thought she wasn't keeping a nice house." The committee then asked a witness whether the woman was "a radical" or a "Union woman."[46] For white Southern men, then, the threat of black men's political power and its link to sexual transgressions with white women indicates the conflation, in the minds of Klansmen and their supporters, of sexual immorality and party politics.

## THE SEXUALIZATION OF RECONSTRUCTION POLITICS

The terrorization of black men, the abuse of white women of the lower classes, and the conflation of politics and sex were interlocking elements in the broader sexualization of politics in the Reconstruction South. De-

[44]*KKK Report*, pt. 2:195–96.
[45]Ibid., p. 233.
[46]*KKK Report*, pt. 9:733, 772–73.

spite their own violent actions, both sexual and otherwise, Klansmen took upon themselves the policing of sexual conduct beyond transgressions between white women and black men, indicating the retrenchment of authority on the part of Southern white men dismayed at the outcome of the war. White men whose politics were in accord with the Klan were left alone if they were sexually engaged with black women; indeed, Klansmen themselves were guilty of such transgressions.[47] But Klansmen searched out white men who were their political enemies and whom they suspected, or purportedly suspected, of sexual liaisons with black women.[48] In Georgia, for example, a white Republican sheriff and a black woman who had been living together were drowned.[49] Further, white men were also described by other whites as "bad" or "low" for committing offenses ranging from running houses of prostitution to having children with black women.[50]

Klansmen also targeted those who formed sexual liaisons across the Mason-Dixon line (a white Northerner who worked for the Freedmen's Bureau was punished for marrying a white Southern woman by having his horse disfigured);[51] and there were numerous Klan assaults for adultery and fornication between whites and between blacks.[52] The Klan and their supporters, in fact, policed a whole range of sexual and social behaviors, responding with violence to accusations or rumors of abortion, incest, wife or child abuse, and drinking.[53]

All such transgressions—not only liaisons between white women and black men—were bound up with politics in discourses about Klan violence. A white man in Georgia, for example, when asked why a particular "mulatto" man was whipped, said: "I heard some people allege that there was a feeling against Colby for living with a near relative of his, I think his daughter, as his wife." When the committee asked if this had been an "incestuous connection," the witness replied: "Yes, sir; I heard that alleged against him; I also heard other people, white men, say that

[47]See *KKK Report*, pt. 6:79, 172; pt. 9:1390–91.

[48]See *KKK Report*, pt. 2:229; pt. 6:82–83, 184, 187, 274; pt. 7:696, 972, 1204; pt. 8:429, 445–46; pt. 9:1297–98; pt. 10:1440–41, 1485, 1523–24; pt. 11:226–27; pt. 12:623–24, 632, 701.

[49]*KKK Report*, pt. 6:362–63.

[50]See *KKK Report*, pt. 2:78; pt. 6:280; pt. 9:1070, 1107; pt. 12:849.

[51]*KKK Report*, pt. 9:926–27. In another case, a Southern woman was whipped, possibly for "marrying a Union man" (pt. 9:947).

[52]See *KKK Report*, pt. 2:270, 539, 546–47; pt. 6:310, 422; pt. 7:642, 875, 1044; pt. 9:1143, 1361.

[53]See, for example, *KKK Report*, pt. 11:126 (abortion); pt. 7:1075–76; pt. 9:916; pt. 12:849, 921 (incest); pt. 2:502, 556; pt. 8:611; pt. 9:987; pt. 10:1808; pt. 11:361; pt. 13:13, 48 (wife or child abuse); pt. 7:1126; pt. 11:330 (drinking).

there was nothing against Colby except his politics. Both of these things were stated to me."[54]

Grand Wizard Nathan Forrest claimed that the Klan "had no political purpose,"[55] and the minority members of the committee agreed, denying "any political significance" to the organization.[56] Others, however, linked Klan assaults for sexual misconduct to Reconstruction politics, whether that misconduct was fabricated, rumored, or real.[57] When the investigating committee asked a North Carolina Klansman about the purpose of the organization, he said: "It was to keep down the colored un's from mixing with the whites." And in what way could this be done? "To keep them from marrying, and to keep them from voting," he answered.[58]

Witnesses also offered theoretical interpretations about the connections between politics and sex in Klan violence. A white North Carolina man said: "The common white people of the country are at times very much enraged against the negro population. They think that this universal political and civil equality will finally bring about social equality. . . . There are already instances . . . in which poor white girls are having negro children."[59] The white postmaster of Meridian, Mississippi, a Democrat, thought the Republicans took "the position that putting colored men into office, in positions of prominence, will gradually lead them to demand social equality, and to intermingle by marriage with the whites."[60] A white lawyer in Mississippi thought poor whites were "induced to believe that republicanism means social equality; that, if a man is a republican, he must necessarily be in favor of white people and

[54]*KKK Report*, pt. 7:1114.

[55]*KKK Report*, pt. 13:6. In 1868, Forrest had described the organization as "a protective, political, military organization" that supported the Democratic party and opposed black suffrage; see ibid., pp. 32–35, reprinted from the *Cincinnati Commercial*, August 28, 1868.

[56]*KKK Report*, pt. 1:292.

[57]Trelease writes: "The Klan's purpose was political in the broadest sense. It sprang up in opposition to every aspect of Radical Reconstruction: the whole idea of racial equality or 'Negro domination,' as white Southerners chose to regard it, economic and social as well as narrowly political" (Trelease, p. 49). Elsewhere in the book, however, Trelease employs a narrower definition of politics, for example, when he writes: "Much of the Klan's activity was purely racist in inspiration, with little or no political overtone" (p. 35); "Klan raiding was less political in motivation by 1871" (p. 319); and "As always, raids were made for nonpolitical reasons too, although the victims were virtually all Republican" (p. 360). See also E. Foner, pp. 425, 428–30.

[58]*KKK Report*, pt. 2:434.

[59]Ibid., p. 318.

[60]*KKK Report*, pt. 11:76.

negroes marrying and associating on terms of perfect equality in the social circle."[61]

The violence of the Reconstruction years can be explained only by a definition of politics that is broad enough to encompass traditional acts of citizenship and authority such as voting and economic independence, and, at the same time, the power of sexual agency. With the end of racial slavery, black men were granted rights—and seized opportunities—never before available to them. Every form of power exercised by black men, whether in the political arena of state conventions concerned with suffrage and legal equality or in the domestic sphere over black women, meant a parallel loss of power for white men.[62]

The end of racial slavery also meant the potential end of a racial hierarchy. At least some blacks in the Reconstruction South had thought that, with the end of slavery, distinctions of color would no longer be made. One black Republican warned in 1871 that for blacks to speak in terms of color even among themselves was dangerous, for, as he heard freedpeople saying, "We are all one color now."[63] Whites, of course, resisted. For Southern whites, racial hierarchy could be maintained primarily through the development of a rigid color line: if blacks and whites did not have children together, then racial categories could be preserved. Obviously, white men had been largely responsible for the blurring of racial categories throughout the era of slavery; their power of sexual coercion had stemmed from their political, economic, and social authority in Southern society. Now, for the first time, black men possessed political power, as well as opportunities for greater economic and social power. White Southerners thus conflated those powers with a newly alarmist ideology about black male sexuality. Armed with such an ideology, they hoped to halt the disintegration of their racial caste system, as well as the potential political, economic, and social power within communities of freedpeople.

White fears of political and sexual agency on the part of black men intensified through the next decades; lynching reached its height in 1892 and continued into the early twentieth century.[64] From the 1890s on,

[61]Ibid., p. 310.

[62]E. Foner, pp. 79–81, 84–110, 281–91. On changes in black families, see Jacqueline Jones, *Labor of Love, Labor of Sorrow: Black Women, Work, and the Family from Slavery to the Present* (New York, 1985), pp. 58–68; Litwack, pp. 244–47.

[63]*New National Era,* August 31, 1871, cited in E. Foner, p. 288.

[64]Brown, pp. 323–25. See also Edward Ayers, *Vengeance and Justice: Crime and Punishment in the Nineteenth-Century American South* (New York, 1984), pp. 238–55; Joel Williamson, *The Crucible of Race: Black-White Relations in the American South since Emancipation* (New York, 1984), pp. 306–10, 464–75; Jacquelyn Dowd Hall, "'The Mind That Burns in Each Body': Women, Rape, and Racial Violence," in *Powers of Desire: The Politics*

black activists began to expose these connections between politics and sex. In 1892, Ida B. Wells argued that lynching could be "explained" by white Southern resentment at "giving the Afro-American his freedom, the ballot box and the Civil Rights Law." Wells connected these rights to black manhood, declaring that white Southerners were "wedded to any method however revolting, any measure however extreme, for the subjugation of the young manhood of the race."[65]

Both Wells and Frederick Douglass maintained that accusations of the rape of white women had been unknown to black men prior to emancipation.[66] Douglass explicitly located such accusations with the advent of black political power. "It is only since the Negro has become a citizen and a voter," he wrote in 1892, "that this charge has been made."[67] This charge, Douglass observed two years later, "was intended to blast and ruin the Negro's character as a man and a citizen."[68] Although convictions for the rape of white women were not, in fact, unknown to black men before and during the Civil War,[69] Wells and Douglass were correct in their belief that from the Reconstruction era on, white ideas about the dangers of black male sexuality reached an un-

---

*of Sexuality,* ed. Ann Snitow, Christine Stansell, and Sharon Thompson (New York, 1983).

[65]Ida B. Wells, "Southern Horrors: Lynch Law in All Its Phases," in *Selected Works of Ida B. Wells-Barnett,* ed. Trudier Harris (New York, 1991), pp. 28, 37. See also Gail Bederman, "'Civilization,' the Decline of Middle-Class Manliness, and Ida B. Wells's Antilynching Campaign (1892–94)," *Radical History Review* 52 (1992): 5–30; Paula Giddings, *When and Where I Enter: The Impact of Black Women on Race and Sex in America* (New York, 1984), pp. 17–31, 85–94.

[66]Frederick Douglass, "Why Is the Negro Lynched?" in *The Life and Writings of Frederick Douglass,* ed. Philip Foner, 4 vols. (New York, 1955), 4:493, 498–99, 501–2; Wells, "Southern Horrors," p. 18.

[67]Frederick Douglass, "Introduction to the Reason Why the Colored American Is Not in the World's Columbian Exposition," in P. Foner, ed., 4:474; see also Douglass, "Why Is the Negro Lynched?" pp. 501–2.

[68]Douglass, "Why Is the Negro Lynched?" p. 503. See also Ida B. Wells, "A Red Record: Tabulated Statistics and Alleged Causes of Lynchings in the United States, 1892–1893–1894," in Harris, ed., p. 146. Similarly, in 1919, W.E.B. Du Bois wrote: "The charge of rape against colored Americans was invented by the white South after Reconstruction to excuse mob violence. No such wholesale charge was dreamed of in slavery days and during the war black men were often the sole protection of white women" (*Writings in Periodicals Edited by W.E.B. Du Bois, Selections from "The Crisis,"* ed. Herbert Aptheker, 2 vols. [Millwood, NY, 1983], 1:193).

[69]See, for example, Donna Spindel, *Crime and Society in North Carolina, 1663–1776* (Baton Rouge, LA, 1989), p. 109; Philip Schwarz, *Twice Condemned: Slaves and the Criminal Laws of Virginia* (Baton Rouge, LA, 1988), pp. 22, 72, 82–84, 150–52, 155–64, 205–10, 291–95; *Columbus Daily Sun,* February 22, March 2, March 29, and December 5, 1861; *Athens Southern Banner,* July 16 and July 23, 1862.

precedented level of virulence and brought with them, for the first time, near-inevitable white violence.

White ideology about the purity of white women also intensified after emancipation, but it never cut thoroughly across class lines or took on the same ironclad quality as ideology about black male sexuality.[70] Ideas about the sexual depravity and agency of poor white women no longer overshadowed ideas about the dangers of black male sexuality; the twin ideologies now bore more equal weight.

A modern example illuminates the ongoing legacy, in both North and South, of white ideologies about black male and white female sexuality. In the summer of 1989 in New York City, a young black man named Yusuf Hawkins was shot and killed by a group of young white men, who thought Hawkins was going to visit a white girlfriend. The white woman, who was from a lower-class Italian American family and known in the neighborhood to fraternize with black and dark-skinned Hispanic men, had previously been subject to abuse from her white friends. "I should spit in your face, you nigger-lover," one of the white men had said to her on the very afternoon of the murder. Some of the woman's white neighbors later blamed her for the murder. The *New York Times* reported that on the day after the murder, "both men and women volunteered more criticism for the young woman than for any of the suspects, faulting her choice of boyfriends." One neighbor said: "She provoked everybody. It's a sin." The *New York Post* ran a front-page photograph of the woman, with a caption that read, in part: "A photographer caught the pensive 18-year-old—clad in a leopard skin top and black miniskirt—sitting quietly on a friend's car." During the trial, one of the defense lawyers asked the jurors to "keep an open mind" and consider the possibility that "maybe this woman caused this whole thing." Only one white man was convicted for the murder of Yusuf Hawkins; the others were convicted of lesser charges or acquitted.[71]

This case encapsulates the legacy of the history told here: white men accused a black man of a sexual liaison with a white woman and killed him; white neighbors and their legal allies censured the white woman for her sexual behavior; and the criminal justice system treaded lightly on the white men who had committed the murder.

---

[70]One illustration of this is the Scottsboro case in the 1930s; see Dan Carter, *Scottsboro: A Tragedy of the American South* (Baton Rouge, LA, 1969); James Goodman, "Stories of Scottsboro" (Ph.D. diss., Princeton University, 1990).

[71]*New York Times,* September 1, 1989; April 3 and 23, 1990; May 18, 1990; March 13 and 14, 1991; April 24, 1991; and *New York Post,* September 2, 1989.

# "Lost Manhood" Found: Male Sexual Impotence and Victorian Culture in the United States

KEVIN J. MUMFORD

*Department of History*
*Stanford University*

IN ANY GIVEN edition of a popular late nineteenth-century tabloid, the *National Police Gazette,* located between boxing results, bizarre crime stories, and revealing photos of showgirls, one could usually find two or three pages of sexual advertising. Alongside advertisements for "rubber safes" and "female illustrations," there were notices addressed to "Sufferers from Nervous Debility, Youthful Indiscretions, [and] Lost Manhood," promising to restore a "nerveless condition to one of renewed vigor."[1] The condition that these products purported to cure was male sexual impotence. Whatever the efficacy of the products, the advertisements themselves offer some intriguing clues about late Victorian understandings of sexual disorders. A survey of comparable texts indicates that both earlier in the preindustrial era and later in the twentieth century the dominant conceptions of impotence substantively differed from the conception that prevailed in Victorian culture. This essay maps the changing conceptions of male impotence and analyzes these conceptual changes within the context of the histories of sexuality and masculinity in the United States.

The topic of impotence seems particularly ripe for historical investigation, in part because an analysis of male sexual disorders might provide a corrective to the scholarship on sexuality and also help to develop

I would like to thank Estelle Freedman for her seminar on "Women's, Family, and Sexual History" and for theoretical and practical suggestions. I would also like to thank John D'Emilio, Steve Epstein, David Halperin, Peggy Pascoe, Mary Louise Roberts, and Chris Waters for helpful suggestions on earlier versions of this essay.

[1] *National Police Gazette,* October 29, 1887, p. 15.

This essay originally appeared in the *Journal of the History of Sexuality* 1992, vol. 3, no. 1.

a critical perspective on contemporary sexual politics. In general, historians have focused more on female sexuality than male sexuality, and
when they did turn to men, they designed research on either homosexuality or masculinity but never directly investigated the history of men
and heterosexuality. These trends are perfectly understandable but, unless balanced by a broader inquiry, they can also be misleading. For example, scholarly debates over the content and significance of the
Victorian sexual ideology of female "passionlessness" have yielded important insights into the historical subordination of women, but they
also have given the impression that male sexuality was a transhistorical
given.[2] The history of sexual politics itself belies this conclusion.
Whether in the antebellum female moral reform critique of male licentiousness, the late nineteenth-century social purity critique of prostitution, or the 1970s radical-feminist critique of patriarchy, sexual activists
questioned the dominant belief that men were naturally lustful, driven
by either God-given, biological, or essential sexual impulses.[3] This essay
can be read as part of that reform tradition. An analysis of impotence
not only exposes the historical contingency of male sexual behavior, but
it also reveals with particular clarity the relations of power that determined a specific sexual system.[4]

To explore both the contours of conceptual change and systems of
social inequality, this essay analyzes two paradigmatic shifts in impotence discourse, one roughly in the 1830s and another in the 1920s. The
first shift occurred in the social context of the separation of sexuality

[2]On the tendency in the historiography to overlook male sexuality, see John D'Emilio
and Estelle B. Freedman, *Intimate Matters: A History of Sexuality in America* (New York,
1988), p. xiv. On the importance of studying homosexuality in relation to heterosexuality,
see Eve Kosofsky Sedgwick, *Epistemology of the Closet* (Berkeley, 1990). Important work on
heterosexuality has recently emerged, including Jonathan Ned Katz, "The Invention of
Heterosexuality," *Socialist Review* 20 (January–March 1990): 7–34. On female sexuality
see Nancy F. Cott, "'Passionlessness': An Interpretation of Victorian Sexual Ideology,
1790–1850," *Signs* 4 (1978): 219–36; Carl Degler, "What Ought to Be and What Was:
Women's Sexuality in the Nineteenth Century," *American Historical Review* 79 (1974):
1467–90; and Carroll Smith-Rosenberg, *Disorderly Conduct: Visions of Gender in Victorian
America* (New York, 1985), especially pp. 167–216.

[3]Smith-Rosenberg, *Disorderly Conduct*, p. 116; David Pivar, *Purity Crusade: Sexual
Morality and Social Control, 1868–1900* (Westport, CT, 1973), p. 53; Robin Morgan, ed.,
*Sisterhood Is Powerful: An Anthology of Writings from the Women's Liberation Movement*
(New York, 1970), pp. 219–27, 245–56.

[4]It is probably worth reiterating the point—this essay represents a narrative of the history of the dominant sexuality and does not include direct analysis of the subaltern. But if
this narrative reads as hegemonic, that seems to me inevitable, for it centers on the hegemony of white male heterosexual ideology in order to interrogate systems of inequality. To
deny the historical reality of these power relations seems to me not only intellectually
wrong but politically dangerous.

from reproduction, the rise of sexual reform movements, and the elaboration of a new model of sex difference. By the 1830s the dominant understanding of the disorder had evolved from a belief that impotence represented a divine curse of infertility that struck both men and women to the belief that impotence was a predominantly male disorder that impaired sexual performance. By the 1880s, largely in response to modernization, physicians and reformers drew a connection between impotence and "overcivilization" and argued that civilized men, although superior to other groups of men, were particularly susceptible to sexual impotence. It was this contradiction between civilized superiority and sexual vulnerability, I believe, that generated a crisis in late Victorian masculinity. By the 1890s at least some middle-class men proclaimed that, in effect, they had lost their manhood.[5]

The second paradigmatic shift in impotence discourse occurred in the early twentieth century, as sexual scientists helped to replace the Victorian nervous system theory of impotence with what might be called a psychological one. Underlying this shift in scientific theory was a more fundamental transformation of the sex/gender system: sexual standards, gender conventions, and ideals of marriage were redefined in the early twentieth century.[6] Consequently, by the 1920s male sexual impotence was understood as a problem of repressed desire rather than bodily depletion, for which experts prescribed a therapy not of continence but of sexual release. Taken together, these dramatic developments seemed to sophisticated moderns to signal the coming of a sexual revolution.[7] But it might better be characterized as a counterrevolution, for the emergent sex/gender system supported a theory of male impotence that had the

---

[5]Clyde Griffen recently has suggested that historians move away from the "crisis of masculinity" thesis, because it overgeneralizes, and instead research case studies of men. Still, detailed social histories of masculinity, if placed in their cultural context, could help to refine rather than refute the crisis thesis. See Clyde Griffen, "Reconstructing Masculinity from the Evangelical Revival to the Waning of Progressivism: A Speculative Synthesis," in *Meanings for Manhood: Constructions of Masculinity in Victorian America,* ed. Mark C. Carnes and Clyde Griffen (Chicago, 1990), pp. 183–204.

[6]My use of the concept of a sex/gender system derives from Gayle Rubin's classic article, "The Traffic in Women: Notes on the 'Political Economy' of Sex," in *Toward an Anthropology of Women,* ed. Rayna R. Reiter (New York, 1975).

[7]Daniel Scott Smith, "The Dating of the American Sexual Revolution: Evidence and Interpretation," in *The American Family in Social Historical Perspective,* ed. Michael Gordon (New York, 1973), pp. 321–35. An emergent interpretation emphasizes the "counterrevolutionary" character of the 1920s (Christina Simmons, "Modern Sexuality and the Myth of Victorian Repression," in *Passion and Power: Sexuality in History,* ed. Kathy Peiss and Christina Simmons [Philadelphia, 1989], pp. 157–77). See D'Emilio and Freedman, pp. 233–35.

dual effect of undermining women's sexual authority and reinforcing inequalities of difference.

In early American society, colonists typically defined impotence as a fertility problem. They organized intimate relations within what John D'Emilio and Estelle Freedman term the "reproductive matrix," a family-centered system that encouraged sexual relations within marriage and treated nonprocreative acts as sins against God (which if committed by men were termed "onanism").[8] Given that the socially acceptable goal of sexual relations was procreation, it is not surprising that reproductive authorities—clergy, physicians, and midwives—blurred any distinction between sterility and the inability to perform sexually. They tended to conceive of impotence in men as comparable with barrenness in women. One entry in the Oxford English Dictionary (under the heading "Impotence") suggests that in discussing impotence, some authorities did not emphasize gender difference, claiming that "impotence may exist in either sex." Speculation about the causes of impotence usually focused on divine providence, rather than on individual physiology. As one authority put it, impotence was "some mysterious interference of heaven."[9]

Sexual norms in early America not only supported this definition of impotence but also linked impotence with diminished manhood. Colonists believed female orgasm was necessary for conception and held husbands responsible for both impregnating and giving erotic pleasure to their wives.[10] A husband who failed at either task would likely be considered impotent, as one colonial court case suggests. Anna Maria Miller petitioned the court of Philadelphia to restrain her husband, George, from forcing them to leave the province. She alleged that her husband had failed to consummate their marriage and that therefore he wanted to leave for "Parts remote and unknown where he may be free from the reproach and scandal of Impotency." The couple had married two years earlier, when Anna believed George to be a "perfect Man." But George had proven to be "impotent in his virility" and "[un]qualified for the Procreation of Children." To verify Anna's claims, an investigative body was convened to discover if George was in fact impotent, which they did by inspecting both his "organs of Seed" and the quality of his erections. They declared that although George had one deformed testicle, he pos-

[8]D'Emilio and Freedman, pp. xvii–xx, 16–27.

[9]Robert Ericson, "The Books of Generation: Some Observations on the Style of English Midwife Books, 1671–1764," in Sexuality in Eighteenth-Century Britain, ed. Paul-Gabriel Boucé (Manchester, 1987), pp. 48–77; Angus McLaren, Reproductive Rituals: The Perception of Fertility from the Sixteenth to the Nineteenth Century (New York, 1984); Thomas Malthus, quoted in Oxford English Dictionary, s.v. "Impotence."

[10]See McLaren, pp. 53–70.

sessed "sufficient Erection and length of penis." Thus George was declared fit to perform his duties as husband, and his reputation as a man was saved.[11]

Over the course of the next century, in response to both cultural and structural developments, the prevailing conception of impotence gradually shifted. A comparison of preindustrial and late Victorian impotence remedies suggests the extent and direction of change. In the preindustrial era, some infertile couples resorted to consuming aphrodisiacs, including red meats or certain seeds and berries, supposedly endowed with fecundity.[12] Others may have purchased specially prepared substances that were advertised in eighteenth-century advice manuals such as *Onania* and *Aristotle's Masterpiece*. The advertisements that appeared there contrasted sharply with those in the *National Police Gazette:* while the former promoted cures for infertility such as "Elixir of Life" and "Prolific Powder," the late nineteenth-century notices emphasized male sexual performance in promoting substances that promised to "cure sexual weakness," "increase desire," and "develop parts."[13] More than a change in marketing strategies for aphrodisiacs, this contrast suggests that between roughly the middle of the eighteenth century and the middle of the nineteenth century, the dominant conception of impotence shifted from predominantly a problem of infertility to a problem of diminished sexual capacity, while the associated construction of masculinity shifted from emphasizing male reproductive duty to emphasizing male sexual self-control.

The origins of this conceptual change (and of the first paradigmatic shift in impotence discourse) can be located in the historical separation of sexuality from reproduction. During the nineteenth century, through abstinence, contraception, and abortion, northern middle-class white couples cut their rate of fertility by half. Simultaneously, northern Protestants revised the sexual traditions of their Puritan forerunners and elaborated a new moral distinction—between sex for reproduction and sex as an expression of specific cultural ideals, such as romantic love or

[11]Martin Duberman, "Male Impotence in Colonial Pennsylvania," *Signs* 4 (1978): 395–401. For a similar case, in which a Plymouth wife petitioned the court for a divorce because of her husband's inability to "perform the act of generation," see D'Emilio and Freedman, p. 25.

[12]McLaren, p. 73.

[13]Both *Onania* and *Aristotle's Masterpiece* are discussed in "Some Sexual Beliefs and Myths in Eighteenth-Century Britain," in Boucé, ed. For their impact on early America see D'Emilio and Freedman, pp. 19–20; *National Police Gazette,* October 18, 1889, p. 15. McLaren draws a similar distinction between preindustrial aphrodisiacs and contemporary ones (pp. 76, 79–80).

spiritual fulfillment.[14] One effect of this emergent distinction between sexuality and reproduction was the increase in prescriptive literature and popular reform movements that discussed nonprocreative sexual behavior. From the prominent physician Benjamin Rush to the health reformer Sylvester Graham, early nineteenth-century authorities focused particularly on the theme of male licentiousness, or what Rush characterized as "the wanton dalliance with women." At first glance, however, their work seems to suggest continuity with earlier religious prohibitions of onanism. In his *Medical Inquiries and Observations, Upon the Diseases of the Mind,* for example, Rush characterized all nonprocreative behavior as the "futile attempt of indolence that cheats the intentions of nature and God." But a closer look reveals that these and other writers had combined the traditional moral injunctions against nonreproductive sexual activity with a new concern about the somatic consequences. Rush argued that the "sexual appetite, which was implanted in our natures for the purpose of propagating our species, when excessive, becomes a disease of both the body and the mind."[15] Termed debility, this disease depleted the nervous system, leaving the sufferer vulnerable to a variety of related disorders. In Rush's controversial formulation, debility was caused not only by too little stimulation (as his mentor William Cullen had argued) but also by too much.[16]

As scientists further explored the connection between mental or physical stimulation and somatic disorders, they began to focus on sexually related cases of debility. French physician Claude-François Lallemand combined the theory of debility with the conception of body fluids as limited resources to diagnose the sexual disorder called spermatorrhea. Appearing in the United States in 1853, Lallemand's *A Practical Treatise on the Causes, Symptoms, and Treatment of Spermatorrhoea* reported that masturbation, foreplay, illicit thoughts, and extramarital sexual relations could trigger spermatorrhea, resulting in (among other things) continual and involuntary genital secretions. Medical textbooks

---

[14]D'Emilio and Freedman, pp. 55–84. On fertility rates, see Carl Degler, *At Odds: Women and the Family in America from the Revolution to the Present* (New York, 1980), pp. 210–27. See also Nancy F. Cott, *The Bonds of Womanhood: "Woman's Sphere" in New England, 1780–1835* (New Haven, CT, 1977); Katherine Kish Sklar, *Catherine Beecher: A Study in American Domesticity* (New York, 1977); and Mary Ryan, *Cradle of the Middle Class: The Family in Oneida County, New York, 1790–1865* (New York, 1982).

[15]Quotations from Benjamin Rush in Ronald Walters, ed., *Primers for Prudery: Sexual Advice to Victorian America* (Englewood Cliffs, NJ, 1974), p. 27.

[16]My discussion of debility draws heavily on Stephen Nissenbaum, *Sex, Diet, and Debility in Jacksonian America* (Westport, CT, 1980), pp. 55–60; see also Lester S. King, *Transformations in American Medicine: From Benjamin Rush to William Osler* (Baltimore, 1991), pp. 52–54.

and articles included discussions of spermatorrhea, and popular tracts advised young men on how to avoid the disorder. The growth in advice literature probably heightened concern about the loss of bodily fluids among men and helped to make spermatorrhea "a household word."[17]

Thus between roughly 1810 and the 1850s, several prominent physicians and reformers had formulated a new scientific conception of impotence. The writings of Rush, Graham, and Lallemand contributed to the novel theory that licentiousness could diminish the individual's bodily energy. The resulting depletion, they reasoned, induced the state of debility, which in turn adversely affected male sexual performance. Rather than viewing impotence as a curse from heaven that impeded procreation, nineteenth-century authorities promoted the theory that it was predominantly a male disorder, caused by insufficient self-control, that resulted in the inability to perform sexually.

The development of this etiology of impotence corresponded to a growing movement of male youth to the city. The few published tracts reveal that physicians targeted the cohort of young men who in the early nineteenth century had been pushed from rural household economies and pulled toward the urban northeast. In his popular *Young Men's Guide* (1846), for example, William Alcott warned his readership about the disastrous potential of urban vice: "A whole race of young men in our cities, of the present generation, will be ruined."[18] Young, enfranchised, geographically and socially mobile, these men were a powerful symbol of autonomy and potential sexual disorder. Impotence discourse shifted in ways that addressed these symbolic concerns, perhaps reflecting a deeper anxiety among reformers about authority in an era when independent self-made men challenged traditional social hierarchies.[19] But although reformers warned disorderly men about the risks of impotence (and advised them on how to regain their virility), they generally treated disorderly women, whom they termed "fallen," as beyond reform. The fallen woman symbolized a challenge to the cult of domesticity, particularly to the idea that innately pure women were responsible for restraining men's lust. By the 1830s, it was widely believed that lost womanhood—unlike lost manhood—could not be redeemed.[20]

---

[17]John S. Haller and Robin M. Haller, *The Physician and Sexuality in Victorian America* (New York, 1974), pp. 212–25.

[18]Quotations from Alcott in Walters, ed., p. 35.

[19]Paul Johnson, *A Shopkeeper's Millennium: Society and Revivals in Rochester, New York, 1818–1837* (New York, 1978), pp. 137–41; Smith-Rosenberg, *Disorderly Conduct* (n. 2 above), pp. 77–79, 90–109; Ryan, pp. 165–79.

[20]Estelle B. Freedman, *Their Sister's Keepers: Women's Prison Reform in America, 1830–1930* (Ann Arbor, MI, 1981), pp. 15–21.

Toward the goal of redemption, reformers and scientists advocated continence, holding up impotence as one extreme consequence of male sexual misconduct. Graham advised young men to restrain from "self-pollution," "illicit commerce between the sexes," and "unnatural commerce with each other."[21] Continent men saved their masculinity through "preserving their bodily chastity" and avoiding "adultery of the mind."[22] Incontinent men were likely to be found wanting in virtually all manly endeavors, especially in the pursuit of profit. According to one physician, "Everyday employment should be . . . a necessity. A man who is lazy . . . is nearly always a licentious man."[23] Moral rectitude, productivity, and self-restraint were the characteristics or behaviors that saved manhood.

The new emphasis on manly chastity reflected not only shifts in scientific thought but also a broader emphasis on the individual, and particularly the body, in antebellum culture.[24] Inspired by the reform activity of the Second Great Awakening, especially by perfectionism, authorities on male sexual health such as Graham argued that "the millennium, the near approach of which is by many so confidently predicted, can never reasonably be expected to arrive until those laws . . . which God has implanted in the physical nature of man are . . . universally known and obeyed."[25] Thus in the burgeoning health reform movement, dietary faddists, water-cure specialists, animal magnetizers, and physical educators focused attention on the disciplining of the body as a route to moral perfection.[26] So too did temperance reformers and antislavery activists (who contrasted southern licentiousness, as exemplified by the incidence of interracial sex, with a northern ideal of self-control). Finally,

---

[21]Sylvester Graham, *Lectures to Young Men, on Chastity,* 4th ed. (Boston, 1838), pp. 38, 74, 94.

[22]Graham emphasizes the mental excitement caused by "convulsive paroxysms" as the cause of debility and impotence more than he emphasizes the loss of semen, as did later theorists of impotence (ibid., pp. 58–61).

[23]Walters, ed., p. 42. Mary Ryan hints at the connection between the rise of merchant capitalism, market culture, and "economic manhood" (Ryan, pp. 167, 173).

[24]See Bryan Turner, *The Body and Society* (Oxford, 1984); Michel Foucault, *The Use of Pleasure,* vol. 2 of *The History of Sexuality,* trans. Robert Hurley (New York, 1985), pp. 15–32; Thomas Laqueur, "Amore Veneris, vel Dulcedo Appeleteur," in *Zone: Fragments for a History of the Human Body,* part 3, ed. Michel Feher, Ramona Naddaff, and Nadia Tazi (Boston, 1989), pp. 334–43; Peter Wagner, "The Discourse on Sex—or Sex as Discourse: Eighteenth-Century Medical and Paramedical Erotica," in *Sexual Underworlds of the Enlightenment,* ed. Roy Porter and G. S. Rousseau (Manchester, 1988).

[25]Graham, quoted in Harvey Green, *Fit for America: Health, Fitness, Sport, and American Society* (Baltimore, 1986), p. 11.

[26]The convergence among perfectionism, fitness, and the body is discussed in Green, pp. 9–29.

Charles Rosenberg and Anthony Rotundo each have suggested that the construction of masculinity increasingly emphasized the body: they argue that the eighteenth-century ideal of "publik Usefulness" gradually gave way to a more individualized "physical ideal of manliness."[27]

This analysis of changing conceptions of the body suggests the extent to which gender relations had influenced impotence discourse. The new etiology of impotence was predicated on an emergent model of sex difference that counterpoised the irrational and uncontrollable female body with the rational male body. The new conception imposed certain burdens on men, to be sure, and one tenet of impotence theory held that man's loss of will resulted in a loss of bodily energy and ultimately in his loss of control over erection. But this conception nevertheless presumed that, by virtue of their sex, men possessed the will to exercise that control in the first place. In sharp contrast, women were viewed as driven by, rather than actively controlling, their bodies. As Carroll Smith-Rosenberg has argued, woman was "seen as a higher, more sensitive, more spiritual creature—and as a prisoner of tidal current of an animal and uncontrollable nature."[28] Of the several most significant developments—a new concern with the erotic apart from reproduction, the growth of scientific literature about impotence after 1830, reformers' anxiety about young men in the city—it was the attribution of sexuality and rationality to the male body and of reproduction and irrationality to the female body that decisively shaped the first paradigmatic shift in impotence discourse.

Throughout the nineteenth century, physicians continued to rely on the opposition between male and female bodies to define the etiology of impotence. By the 1870s, however, physicians not only focused on differences between men and women, but discussed class and racial differences among men. At the same time, they also refined the prevailing definition of impotence by shifting the emphasis away from immorality

---

[27]Clyde S. Griffen, *Their Brother's Keepers: Moral Stewardship in the United States, 1800–1865* (New Brunswick, NJ, 1965); Carroll Smith-Rosenberg, *Religion and the Rise of the American City: The New York Mission Movement, 1821–1870* (Ithaca, NY, 1971); Jayme Solokow, *Eros and Modernization: Sylvester Graham, Health Reform, and the Origins of Victorian Sexuality in America* (Westport, CT, 1983); Ronald Walters, *The Antislavery Appeal: American Abolitionism after 1830* (New York, 1978), pp. 67–79; Ronald Walters, "The Erotic South: Civilization and Sexuality in American Abolitionism," *American Quarterly* 25 (May 1973): 177–201; Anthony Rotundo, "Body and Soul: Changing Ideals of American Middle-Class Manhood, 1770–1920," *Journal of Social History* 18 (Winter 1985): 22; and Charles Rosenberg, "Sexuality, Class, and Role in Nineteenth-Century America," in *No Other Gods: On Science and American Social Thought,* ed. Charles Rosenberg (Baltimore, 1987), pp. 72, 76–78.

[28]Smith-Rosenberg, *Disorderly Conduct* (n. 2 above), pp. 195–96.

or individual licentiousness and toward external social pressures—that is, overcivilization—as the cause of impotence.

These and other implicit developments in impotence discourse surfaced in the diagnosis of neurasthenia. New York City neurologist George M. Beard popularized the disorder, introducing its general etiology to his colleagues in 1869. Beard connected the increasing number of cases of neurasthenia with what today we would term modernization; he argued that it resulted from overcivilization—from the "necessity of punctuality," "railway travel," and the "disorderly city." Although some physicians initially expressed skepticism, more agreed that neurasthenia was a serious problem, and Beard's 1881 treatise, *American Nervousness,* became the standard textbook.[29]

Historians have focused more on general neurasthenia than on Beard's subsequent discussion of sexual neurasthenia. He began researching *Sexual Neurasthenia* soon after completing *American Nervousness;* but Beard died in 1882, before the volume was completed. His long-time colleague, A. D. Rockwell, published the book in 1884, which outlined the variety of types of neurasthenia—including cerebral, digestive, and spinal—though it maintained that the sexual type was most prevalent. Like general neurasthenia, sexual neurasthenia stemmed from the depletion of nervous energy, caused by overcivilization and the stifling quality of rationalized culture.[30] To a greater extent than earlier theories of impotence, sexual neurasthenia relied on the conception of the body as a closed-energy system, or what G. J. Barker-Benfield has termed the "spermatic economy." Hence physicians tended to conceive of nervous energy as scarce and finite, in much the same way as a financier might conceive of economic resources in a market economy.[31]

While physicians treated both men and women who suffered from neurasthenia, their formulation of sexual neurasthenia emphasized the difference between male and female bodies. Given that sexual neurasthenia was a disorder of diminished sexual energy, and that most physicians conceived of women more as reproductive than as sexual beings, it is

---

[29]George Beard, "Neurasthenia, or Nervous Exhaustion" *Boston Medical and Surgical Journal* 3 (1869): 217–27; George Beard, *American Nervousness* (New York, 1881), pp. 97–133. For general biographical information on Beard, see Charles Rosenberg, "George Beard: A Profile," in Rosenberg, ed., pp. 24–27; Barbara Sicherman, "Paradox of Prudence: Mental Health in the Gilded Age," *Journal of American History* 62 (1976): 890–912.

[30]George Beard, *Sexual Neurasthenia* (New York, 1883).

[31]Beard, *American Nervousness,* pp. 9–11; G. J. Barker-Benfield, *Horrors of the Half-Known Life: Male Attitudes toward Women and Sexuality in Nineteenth-Century America* (New York, 1976), pp. 175–88.

not surprising that they tended to associate diminished sexual energy with the male variety of neurasthenia. Sexual authorities saw the female body as a closed-energy system, much the same as the male body, but they conceptualized the female system as a cycle of fertility, driven by the womb. Beard and other sexual authorities worried about the effects of overcivilization on women; but, again, they primarily focused on women's reproductive capacity, pointing to the deleterious consequences of the civilizing process for the womb and menstrual cycle.[32] Indeed, one best-selling remedy for female disorders, Lydia Pinkham's all-vegetable elixir, promised to counteract overcivilization by fortifying the reproductive organs. In short, although physicians disagreed over whether women possessed sexual urges (engaging in debates rarely conducted about men), they emphasized the importance of the womb to women's psychic and physical health.[33]

While Victorian physicians continued to center sex difference in their definitions of impotence, by the 1880s dramatic social change—the end of slavery and worker-capital conflict—prompted some physicians to discuss racial or class differences. This shift reflected a key trend in late nineteenth-century thought—the rise of evolutionary naturalism. Indeed, social Darwinism (specifically, the doctrines that there exist immutable laws of human development and that a natural hierarchy of groups determined social inequalities) had gained a strong following among nineteenth-century sexual authorities. Beard relied on several aspects of social Darwinism, which he learned about from his "close friend Herbert Spencer," to understand the relationship between society and the etiology of neurasthenia.[34] One connection between Beardian sci-

[32]Beard's discussion of women acknowledges some sexual energy, but he focuses on reproductive disorders and emphasizes the womb. This is in sharp contrast to cases of nymphomania or female masturbation, explicitly sexual disorders, in which doctors performed clitoridectomies. See Beard, *Sexual Neurasthenia,* pp. 200–206; on clitoridectomies see Elaine Showalter, *Sexual Anarchy: Gender and Culture at the Fin de Siècle* (New York, 1990), pp. 130–31. For the argument that in treating disorders physicians emphasized female sexuality, see Degler, *At Odds* (n. 14 above), pp. 252–57.

[33]For women and neurasthenia, see Cynthia Russett, *Sexual Science: The Victorian Construction of Womanhood* (Cambridge, MA, 1989), pp. 111–13, 115–19; for overcivilization and reproduction, see Judith Walzer Leavitt, *Brought to Bed: Childbearing in America, 1750–1950* (New York, 1986), pp. 64–86; Sarah Stage, *Female Complaints: Lydia Pinkham and the Business of Women's Medicine* (New York, 1979); Thomas Laqueur, *Making Sex: Body and Gender from the Greeks to Freud* (Cambridge, MA, 1990), pp. 175–81; also see Lawson Tait, *The Pathology and Treatment of Diseases of the Ovaries,* 4th ed. (New York, 1883).

[34]Paul Boller, Jr., *American Thought in Transition, 1865–1900* (Lanham, MD, 1981), pp. 27–56, 59–60; Stephen J. Gould, *The Mismeasure of Man* (New York, 1985), pp. 113–45; and Beard, *Sexual Neurasthenia,* p. 67.

ence and Spencerism was the evolutionary concept of arrested develop-ment. In this theory individuals or groups developed in stages, becom-ing more civilized and fit as time passed. At certain stages, however, some groups ceased to evolve—and development was arrested. The con-sequences of arrested development included criminal behavior, lower intelligence, and diminished inhibitions. Individuals or groups evincing arrested development therefore lacked the capacity to control their im-pulses, particularly their sexual instincts.[35]

Beard and other sexual scientists employed these evolutionary con-cepts to explain the incidence of impotence among different groups of men. In brief, they argued that white middle-class men were highly sus-ceptible to sexual neurasthenia, that working-class men were largely im-mune from the disorder, and that black men represented what might be called hyperpotency. Thus in the late nineteenth century, there emerged at least two primary sexual boundaries—drawn along class and race lines—which, if they wished to avoid both impotence and primitive sex-ual excess, white middle-class men had to negotiate. By the 1890s these negotiations seemed to require more and more vigilance, leaving some men weak and debilitated, and late Victorians proclaimed they were in the midst of a crisis.

The importance of class in late nineteenth-century definitions of manhood can be seen in Beard's discussion of impotence among com-mon laborers and rural men. In Beard's view, workers were "constitu-tionally different" from urban professionals, possessing a kind of natural immunity from the enervating influences of civilization. In drawing the distinction between the "highly organized brainworker" and the "muscle worker," Beard classified the latter as "persons who have very strong, old-fashioned constitutions and are rarely or never in-jured in the nervous system." Robust and constitutionally resistant to overcivilization, the muscle worker was immune from neurasthenia in general and from impotence in particular.[36]

Physicians and reformers incorporated this ideal of artisan virility into their medical practices and reform movements. Beard, for example, treated one sexual neurasthenic, a man who expressed dissatisfaction with his routinized life as an urban professional, by advising him to take more exercise. Thus by selectively following the routines of workers and farmers, this mid-level manager in burgeoning industrial America might defend himself from the deleterious effects of civilization that had

---

[35]On arrested development and Darwinism see Russett, pp. 50–78; also see Gould, pp. 122–35.

[36]Beard, *Sexual Neurasthenia*, pp. 113, 149–50.

drained his nervous resources.[37] For others Beard would more likely prescribe rest, because in certain cases strenuous activity could compound "nervelessness." Most reformers of manhood, however, addressed the problem of a "flaccid bourgeoisie" by promoting physical exercise or manly work.[38] In effect they romanticized the artisan—as a symbol of a bygone era, not only of republican virtue and evangelical morality but also of authentic manhood.[39] It remains difficult to determine how current among middle-class men the artisan ideal had become, or how its popularization influenced workers themselves, but one conclusion can be drawn: in contrast to the discussion of impotence in the 1830s, when authorities emphasized the value of self-control for upwardly mobile men, late nineteenth-century conceptions of impotence emphasized sexual distinctions drawn along class lines. Thus some middle-class men idealized (or parodied) the artisan, even as they became more and more enmeshed in corporate bureaucracies that eroded the autonomy and appropriated the skills of craftsmen.[40]

A comparable contradiction can be seen in the increasing emphasis on racial difference in late nineteenth-century discussions of impotence.[41] In the lexicon of evolutionary science, the black man was

[37]Beard, *Sexual Neurasthenia;* George Beard, "Nervous Diseases Connected with the Male Genital Function," *Medical Record,* June 2, 1882, pp. 617–20. Many physicians prescribed similar therapies (see Haller and Haller [n. 17 above], pp. 174–87). Medical texts linked idleness with diminished sexual energy, as in cases of men who experienced frequent nocturnal emissions; active men avoided these problems. See, for example, a pamphlet from the popular Physician's Leisure Library series by Edward Martin, *Sexual Weakness and Impotence* (Detroit, 1893), pp. 86–88.

[38]Green (n. 25 above), chap. 5; James C. Whorton, *Crusade for Fitness: The History of American Health Reformers* (Princeton, NJ, 1982). Similar efforts to restore young manhood can be seen later in the Boy Scouts movement. For a discussion of Boy Scouts and the "crisis of masculinity," see Peter Filene, *Him/Her/Self: Sex Roles in Modern America* (New York, 1974), pp. 105–7; also see David I. MacLeod, *Building Character in the American Boy: The Boy Scouts, YMCA, and Their Forerunners* (Madison, WI, 1983), pp. 49–59.

[39]While Jackson Lears does not explicitly refer to sexuality, his discussion of patricians in the Gilded Age suggests that not only spiritual emptiness but also anxiety about lost manhood launched antimodernism. See T. J. Jackson Lears, *No Place of Grace: Anti-Modernism and the Transformation of American Culture, 1880–1920* (New York, 1981), pp. 74–83.

[40]Sean Wilentz, *Chants Democratic: The Rise of the Working Class in New York City, 1780–1850* (New York, 1985), pp. 61–103; on the decline of artisan republicanism, see David Montgomery, *Workers' Control in America: Studies in the History of Work, Technology, and Labor Struggles* (Cambridge, MA, 1979), pp. 9–27.

[41]A different example of racial difference and sexual scientific thought (which initially interested me in the topic of impotence) can be found in the discourse on black people of mixed race. In the 1840s Josiah Nott argued that the "mulatto" was impotent (by which he meant sterile), reflecting both the prevailing view of racial mixture as species-

termed a reversionary type, who exhibited criminal tendencies, inferior intelligence, and immorality.[42] According to G. Frank Lydston, the supposedly higher rate of perpetration of rape by black men than by white men could be attributed to the fact that "inhibitory influences such as ordinary self-control are more effective in the white than in the Negro race." Lydston explained that "when a race of a low type is subjected to an emotionally intellectual strain, inhibitory or restraining ideas and impulses are affected." The slightest provocation was enough to destroy the Negroes' self-control and bring "the primitive instincts to the surface"—a "reversion manifest in the direction of sexual proclivities."[43]

This racial discourse played a dual role in Victorian culture—as a justification for white domination and as a negative reference for the dominant group—which can be seen in the medical literature about impotence.[44] In Beard's view, for example, "there [was] almost no insanity among Negroes . . . nor [was] there functional nervous disease." Because Beard believed that black people were "not very much in advance of their African ancestors," he argued that they possessed a "supernatural constitution."[45] Like the muscle worker, the Negro was considered to be immune from general neurasthenia and from impotence in particular. Beard, upon returning from a trip to the Sea Islands, argued that Negroes' "indulgence of passions was severalfold greater, at least, than is the habit of whites." According to Beard, their sexual prowess was such that "if you would find a virgin among them, it is said you must go to the cradle."[46] While physicians advised their patients to emulate the artisan, they emphasized a sharp opposition between black and white male sexuality, holding up the black man as a "bit of barbarism at our

---

crossing and the U.S. conception of the mulatto that frequently invoked comparison to a mule. In the 1930s E. Franklin Frazier scientifically refuted the mulatto-impotence thesis. For Nott's thesis see George Fredrickson, *Black Image in the White Mind: The Debate on Afro-American Character and Destiny, 1817–1914* (Middletown, CT, 1971), pp. 76–77.

[42]Ibid., pp. 228–56.

[43]G. Frank Lydston, *Diseases of Society and Degeneracy (The Vice and Crime Problem)* (Philadelphia, 1904), pp. 337, 381; also see G. Frank Lydston and Hunter McGuire, *Sexual Crimes: Among the Negroes, Scientifically Considered* (Atlanta, 1893). Lydston also studied male impotence; see his *Impotence and Sterility: Aberrations of the Sexual Function and Sex-Gland Implantation* (Chicago, 1917).

[44]See Winthrop Jordan, *White over Black: American Attitudes toward the Negro, 1550–1812* (New York, 1967), pp. 32–44.

[45]Beard, *American Nervousness,* pp. 188–91.

[46]Ibid., p. 188. Beard also discusses the sexuality of Native Americans (*Sexual Neurasthenia,* pp. 102–4, 261–63).

door-step" and contrasting his primitive lack of sexual will with "the restraint of the Anglo-Saxon."[47]

In diagnosing the black man as hyperpotent, scientists and reformers
stigmatized him as morally inferior by divesting him of sexual self-
control. But the stigmatization served ulterior purposes. In mapping
hyperpotency on black men and then furthering among white men a regime of continence as its antithesis, scientists and reformers helped to
transform sexual self-restraint into a social practice through which middle-class men not only avoided sexual disorders but also distinguished
themselves as white. Impotence was a white man's problem; unlike
black men (and Victorian women), white men possessed the capacity to
exercise enough rational self-control to avoid the disorder.[48]

In the final analysis, the rise of Beardian science represented a complex transitional era in the history of impotence. Older ideas about impotence operated alongside novel theories, reflecting the variety of
conceptions of male sexuality that circulated in late nineteenth-century
society. One advertisement in an 1893 edition of the *National Police
Gazette* pitched a remedy, "Brown's capsules," that targeted the
antebellum disorder of spermatorrhea by "stopping drains within 48
hours," while another pitched a cure for neurasthenia that purported to
"restore perfect vigor and Nerve force to small Shrunken and Weak Sexual Organs." The etiology of neurasthenia itself reflected sexual scientific thought in transition. Thus Beardian science can be seen as the
fullest development of the antebellum theory of debility—or, perhaps
as persuasively, as the harbinger of the second major transformation of
impotence discourse in the twentieth century. Beard had identified a
contradiction implicit in Victorian impotence discourse that would
come to be seen as the root of the modern sexual crisis: the rise of civilization was inevitable and widely believed to be a sign of progress, and
yet the civilizing process engendered deleterious sexual consequences
for the civilized man. By the 1890s some civilized men sounded the
alarm of a crisis in masculinity.

Several historians have analyzed the content of these proclamations
and have argued that the crisis reflected men's response to the first wave
of New Womanism, which symbolized middle-class women's increasing
encroachment into traditionally male spheres of power, such as higher
education and the professions.[49] But my analysis of shifts in impotence

[47]Beard, *American Nervousness,* pp. 268–69.

[48]Ibid., pp. 188–91.

[49]For the differences between the New Womanism of the 1890s and of the 1920s, see
Smith-Rosenberg, *Disorderly Conduct* (n. 2 above), pp. 245–96. John Higham's article,
"The Reorientation of American Culture in the 1890s," in *Writing American History,* ed.

discourse suggests a sexual—more than a gender—crisis. By the late nineteenth century, the regime of male continence had become part and parcel of late Victorian respectability. But middle-class men's achievement of civilized self-restraint seemed to signify more their social superiority than their attainment of manhood. Moreover, the advertising pitches for impotence remedies suggest that a new standard of male sexuality—"giant strength and power," "enlarged organs," and "sexual power"—was gradually emerging and becoming more and more central to constructions of masculinity. Yet white middle-class men (at least the men who visited their doctors for sexual advice or sent away for impotence cures) were less and less confident about their ability to rise to the new standard.[50] Just beneath the surface of Victorian civility lurked, I believe, the fear that respectable middle-class men were assiduously conserving their sexual energy but losing their manhood.

Some thirty years later, Wilhelm Stekel opened his two-volume treatise on male impotence with the declaration that "in men love-inadequacy is increasing to an alarming degree, and impotence has come to be associated with modern civilization."[51] Stekel believed the crisis to be as acute in the 1920s as many had believed it to be in the 1890s. But although the origins can be located in the late Victorian era, by the 1920s the solution to the crisis had changed dramatically—and so had the conception of male impotence. Scientists, physicians, and psychologists increasingly concerned themselves with the problem of male impotence, publishing their research in medical journals and books, and much of their work refined Beard's theory of sexual neurasthenia. Beginning in 1910, however, something of a reaction against Beardian science developed. A survey of the medical literature on male sexual disorders published between 1910 and 1930 reveals that the sci-

---

John Higham (Bloomington, IN, 1970), first argued for a crisis in American culture; later studies refined Higham's argument by adding gender as a category of analysis and arguing for a crisis in masculinity. See Joe Dubbert, "Progressivism and the Masculinity Crisis," in *The American Man*, ed. Elizabeth Pleck and Joseph Pleck (Englewood Cliffs, NJ, 1980), pp. 309–15; Filene, pp. 69–93; and Michael Kimmel, "The Contemporary Crisis in Masculinity in Historical Perspective," in *The Making of Masculinities: The New Men's Studies*, ed. Harry Brod (Boston, 1987), pp. 121–54. Elaine Showalter (n. 32 above) has refined the masculinity thesis by adding sexuality as a category of analysis (see especially chaps. 3 and 9).

[50] These phrases appear again and again in *National Police Gazette* advertising. See *National Police Gazette*, September 30, 1892, p. 13; November 11, 1892, p. 15; and June 2, 1894, p. 15. For the increase in medical literature and for the suggestion of the growing incidence of neurasthenia in general, see F. G. Gosling, *Before Freud: Neurasthenia and the American Medical Community, 1870–1910* (Urbana, IL, 1987), especially chap. 5.

[51] Wilhelm Stekel, *Impotence in the Male*, 2 vols. (New York, 1927), 1:1.

entific consensus on what caused impotence and how to treat it was shifting gradually away from a Beardian model of scarcity, depletion, and saving toward a psychological model of abundance, repression, and spending.

Although scientists continued to employ Beardian theories of impotence, they refined the concept of sexual neurasthenia, in part by distinguishing bodily depletion from bodily defect or injury. They divided cases of impotence into at least three categories: symptomatic, structural, and psychic. Within the category of symptomatic impotence, general practitioners included cases that appeared to derive from underlying disease, such as diabetes or influenza. Surgeons dealt with what they termed structural impotence as a physical deformity. They treated it by surgically enlarging the arteries leading to the penis or testicles; others applied electricity to the genital area, in order to "re-vitalize the sexual system."[52]

Turn-of-the-century medical articles discussed psychic impotence more than symptomatic or structural impotence. Physicians continued to draw from the Beardian tradition, exploring the ways that incontinence and civilization influenced the disorder and drawing social distinctions between groups of men based on their susceptibility to psychic impotence. Some physicians primarily targeted promiscuity, while others identified overcivilization as the cause of impotence. Dr. John Lewis argued that the lack "of sexual capacity" was in part the result of "masturbation, excessive sexual indulgence." In a narrative of the history of impotence, Dr. P. C. Remondino stated that "city dwellers among Europeans and Americans, in comparison to those who lead a country life, enjoy a shorter sexual life and are highly susceptible to psychic impotence." Accordingly, some physicians advanced the Beardian corollary of the overcivilization theory: that "psychic impotence is found mostly in the highly organized society, among *superior* men."[53] Between 1890 and 1910, scientists and physicians generally continued to view impotence as a problem of civilized sexuality and to conceptualize the body as a closed-energy system in which sexual resources were scarce and conservation was required.

As impotence research and therapy continued, however, medical

[52]Henry I. Raymond, "Treatment of Loss of Sexual Power by Ligation of Veins," *Medical News* 66 (1895): 580.

[53]John Lewis, "Materialistic View of Impotence," *Medical News* 1 (1892): 571; P. C. Remondino, "Some Observations on the History, Psychology, and Therapeutics of Impotence," *Pacific Medical Journal* 42 (September 1899): 522; B. S. Talmey, "Impotence in the Male," *New York Medical Journal* 116 (November 1922): 502; Samuel Wesel Gross, *A Practical Treatise on Impotence, Sterility, and Allied Disorders of the Male Sexual Organs* (Philadelphia, 1890).

opinion on the causes of impotence began to change. The shift reflected trends within and outside of science. A new conception of disease filtered through the still nascent medical profession, transforming scientific research methods in particular and health care in general.[54] Concomitantly, some physicians rejected the concept of neurasthenia because it was predicated on what seemed an unscientific theory of nervous exhaustion.[55] Additionally, as psychologists followed physicians in cultivating a culture of professionalism, they too studied the problem of sexual impotence, shifting the object of scientific enquiry from nervous systems to psyches.[56] Finally, these developments in medical theory and practices coincided with two broad shifts—one in capitalism, from producerism to consumerism, and another in gender ideology, from separate and incommensurable spheres to overlapping compatibility.[57] By the 1920s a fully developed psychological theory of impotence had overtaken the theory of neurasthenia. Sexual experts increasingly stressed repressed desire instead of the depletion of bodily resources; accordingly, they were more likely to prescribe therapies of sexual release, rather than restraint, while some psychologists went so far as to argue that restraint itself caused impotence.

The about-face in physician's attitudes toward masturbation illustrates the shift from a Beardian model to a psychological one. In the 1920s, much of the medical literature focused on the problem of male masturbation to the same, if not greater, extent than had both preindustrial and Victorian medical texts and advice manuals. But many physicians now targeted the psychological guilt arising from masturbation rather than the physically depleting effects. As one physician summarized this new view of the solitary vice: "Masturbation as a rule does not much harm beyond that which we believe it to be wrong." Influenced by this "revision of the unfortunate attitudes towards onanism," experts such as Dr. Irwin Koll even argued that "the orthodox notion which the laity had deeply ground onto its moral make up as the bad ef-

---

[54]On changes in the hospitals related to the rise of the germ theory of disease, see Charles Rosenberg, *The Care of Strangers: The Rise of America's Hospital System* (New York, 1987), pp. 151–54.

[55]J. L. Tracey, "That Neurasthenia Foolishness," *Journal of the American Medical Association* 42 (1904): 78. As one authority put it, "To diagnose neurasthenia is to beg the question."

[56]Hamilton Cravens, *The Triumph of Evolution: American Scientists and the Heredity-Environment Controversy, 1900–1941* (New York, 1978), pp. 57–71.

[57]See Jackson Lears, "From Salvation to Self-Realization: Advertising and the Therapeutic Roots of the Consumer Culture, 1880–1930," in *The Culture of Consumption*, ed. T. J. Jackson Lears and Richard Wightman Fox (New York, 1983); Lawrence Birken, *Consuming Desire: Sexual Science and the Emergence of a Culture of Abundance, 1871–1914* (Ithaca, NY, 1988), pp. 114–27.

fects of masturbation is the most prevalent factor in the production of psychic impotence."[58]

In lifting the traditional prohibition on masturbation, sexual experts revealed the extent to which, in the conflict between civilization and nature, the modern phase of the battle was turning against the forces of self-restraint and in favor of sexual release. In certain ways, Freudian psychology would provide the margin of victory. In his influential 1908 essay, "Sexual Morality and Modern Nervousness," Freud acknowledged the importance of Beard's work, specifically its correlation between civilization and nervousness.[59] But Freud invoked Beard more to critique than sustain his work. Whereas Beard's solution to the problem of overcivilization emphasized self-control, Freud questioned the assumptions of civilized morality and prescribed a shift from inhibition to expression as a way to avoid neurosis.[60] As he argued, "The benefit, for a young man, of abstinence beyond his twentieth year cannot be taken for granted."[61] Increasingly, it seemed to many experts that, like the specific Victorian prohibition against masturbation, the overall regime of continence probably induced more sexual problems than it solved. Thus by the late 1920s, the Freudian psychoanalyst Wilhelm Stekel rejected male continence and argued that "whoever shows a strong sexuality at an early age, in spite of masturbation and so-called sexual excess, will preserve it to advanced age."[62]

As they reevaluated the tenets of civilized morality, sexual authorities sparked debates about sexuality across several academic disciplines. Criminologists concerned with the sexual basis of crime reversed the Victorian formula that nonprocreative activity led to mental exhaustion and argued instead that "sexual excesses are usually the result, rather than the cause, of nervous disorder." The New Psychologists, Progressive-era behaviorists, adopted a similar view of male sexuality; they saw human behavior as guided by a cluster of inherited but nonetheless malleable impulses, one of the most powerful of which was the

[58]Irwin S. Koll, "Sexual Impotence: Etiology, Pathology, Treatment," *New York Medical Journal* 101 (1915): 236; R. W. Shufeldt, "Impotence, Medically and Legally Considered," *Pacific Medical Journal* 49 (January 1905): 26.

[59]Sigmund Freud, "Civilized Morality and Modern Nervousness," in *Sexuality and the Psychology of Love,* ed. Phillip Rieff (New York, 1977), pp. 33–34. Also see Phillip Weiner, "G. M. Beard and Freud on 'American Nervousness,'" *Journal of the History of Ideas* 17 (1956): 269–72.

[60]Nathan G. Hale, Jr., *Freud and the Americans: The Beginning of Psychoanalysis in the United States, 1876–1917* (New York, 1971); on the institutionalization of some aspects of Freudianism, see Gerald Grob, *Mental Illness and American Society, 1875–1940* (Princeton, NJ, 1983).

[61]Freud, p. 33.

[62]Stekel, *Impotence in the Male,* 1:111.

sexual impulse. In addition, many sexologists expressed the view that innate instincts or drives determined sexual behavior.[63] As John Burnham has argued, by the 1920s "whatever the author's ethical social stance or the psychological theory, the sexual instinct was admitted to be general, inherited, and human as well as animal."[64]

Sexual authorities now argued that, theoretically, male sexual desire was powerful and abundant but among civilized men the sexual instinct had been damaged by years of internalized repression. Hence experts who treated impotence replaced therapies designed to restore sexual energy with therapies designed to lift inhibitions. Physicians experimented with a variety of aphrodisiacs to draw out sexual desire, including "canine semen" and "cannabis indica [marijuana]."[65] In one particular case, in which the physician had "reached the end of his therapeutic rope," none of the usual treatments had proven effective. The situation was serious because, according to the physician, the patient was "becoming a wild-eyed paranoiac." Finally, in a last-ditch effort to cure the impotent man, the physician inquired whether the patient knew of a "voluptuously developed girl, young and good looking and of sufficient elastic morality," who "would of necessity be highly magnetic." The physician proposed that the patient and the woman spend the night together, on a bed "positioned precisely two feet from the wall," though they were to be separated by a thick glass partition, ensuring that "the treatment was to be platonically moral." The impotent man was instructed to keep a diary detailing the effects of electrical exchange. But the notebook was "utterly forgotten," apparently because the patient "had no time for clerical work." According to the physician, "the patient turned up at my office the next morning with his former lacklusterless eyes beaming like two shiny jet beads, a flushed nose and an expansive smile." As it turned out, the patient "had within ten minutes after the initiation of the treatment thrown all stipulation and technical direction to the four winds and undertaken his own cure."[66]

Whatever its rate of success, the new therapy reflected a decisive shift

[63]See Charles Flint, "Sexual Crimes," *New York Medical Record,* August 3, 1912, pp. 210–15; on the influence of sexology, see G. Alder Blamer, "A Case of Perverted Sexual Instinct," *American Journal of Insanity* 39 (1892–93): 23–28; for similar views in periodicals, see Bemis J. Pauley, "The Feeble-Minded as Criminals," *New Republic,* August 16, 1916, pp. 66–68. See John O'Donnell, *The Origins of Behaviorism: American Psychology, 1870–1920* (New York, 1985), pp. 13–15; Birken, chaps. 2 and 6.

[64]John C. Burnham, *Paths into American Culture: Psychology, Medicine, and Morals* (Philadelphia, 1988), p. 58.

[65]Koll, p. 236; Talmey, p. 502.

[66]Remondino (n. 53 above), pp. 517–18; Stekel provides dozens of such cases (see Stekel, *Impotence in the Male,* 1:235–62).

in impotence theory from emphasizing the male nervous system to emphasizing the object of male desire, a shift that can be seen in medical discussions of homosexuality and impotence. Before about 1910, authorities on impotence avoided the issue of sex perversion; when they did discuss the relationship between impotence and homosexuality, their analyses seem confused. Beard argued that cases of perversion were "very much more frequent than supposed," which he had learned from observing homosexuals in New York City.[67] He attributed perversion to men who suffered from extreme nervelessness and who had lost their "attributes of virility": "Their genital organs atrophy . . . their body loses its force and energy and at last they come to a condition where they partake of feminine costume, and assimilate to women."[68] But on the whole Beard strained to link bodily depletion with homosexuality, largely because he was working with an undeveloped psychological concept of perversion that was incongruous with his general theory of nervelessness. By the 1920s, however, some psychologists devoted large sections of their books to answering the question, "Why is the homosexual impotent with women?" Stekel identified two general cases of homosexual impotence. The first case concerned the "passive ones," the feminine homosexual, whom Stekel contrasted with "the 'active ones' who overcome the inhibitions and evinced their potency through all sorts of homosexual acts." The second, and more common, case concerned the latent homosexual, who was impotent because of sexual inhibitions: he could not admit his homosexual tendency, but he was terrified by "his lack of interest in the opposite sex."[69] In either case, some physicians argued that internalized inhibitions and anxiety about the object of sexual desire caused male impotence.

One solution both to the particular case of homosexual impotence and to the general problem of male inhibitions was to refortify the sexual aim toward women by encouraging wives and girlfriends to become more sexually responsive. Increasingly, physicians not only treated impotent husbands but also counseled wives on how to be more sensitive to their spouse's sexual problems. B. S. Talmey reported the case of one patient, a thirty-five-year-old professional man, "burdened with many responsibilities" and "happily married," who complained that he was unable to achieve an erection. He did report, however, that he experi-

[67]Beard, *Sexual Neurasthenia,* pp. 99–106.

[68]Ibid., p. 91.

[69]Stekel is unusual because he discussed the homosexual more than did most authorities on impotence. See Stekel, *Impotence in the Male,* 1:46–50; 2:274–75. For a full discussion of his complex views on homosexual impotence, see *Impotence in the Male,* vol. 2, especially chaps. 18 and 20.

enced "healthy erections" while asleep. Talmey advised the wife to "watch her husband and if she notices a strong erection in his sleep, she should suddenly wake him and cause him to effect conjugation." Talmey also advised that, in every way possible, the wife should humor her husband, "Mr. X," who claimed that "he found conjunction was only possible if his wife was attired in Tyrolean peasant costume and assumed the same posture as his pretty dairy maid years ago had taken when she first taught him the arts of Venus." In another case, Stekel advised a wife to fulfill her husband's sexual fantasies—which required that during intercourse "she had to treat him like a dog and call him Caro." In short, the burden of male impotence seemed to be shifting to women.[70]

Of the growing number of experts who studied marital relations and male impotence, perhaps none was as influential as Dr. William Robinson, president of more than ten medical societies and chief of genitourinary surgery at Bronx Hospital. Robinson published fifteen books dealing with sexual matters; his *Sexual Impotence,* published in 1912, went through thirteen editions.[71] In contrasting Victorian with modern approaches to sexual disorders, Robinson argued that the "older doctors" had overlooked the role of women in exacerbating, and in some instances causing, male sexual impotence. He employed the term "frigidity" to describe the sexually unresponsive wife. Found primarily among the middle class, the frigid woman had "absolutely no desire and no pleasure." According to Robinson, "a man is to them an indifferent object." An early formulation of frigidity classified it as a pathological disorder: "With the cases of sexual perversion may be classed those women in whom such intensely modest ideas have been acquired by education that the sexual act not only gives no pleasure, but actually gives rise to feelings of disgust." Others expressed the view that, rather than a discrete malady, frigidity was symptomatic of a more serious disorder, prevalent among women who were "probably in most cases homosexual."[72]

---

[70]Talmey, pp. 501–2; Stekel, *Impotence in the Male,* 1:74. Some of the social hygiene literature also seemed to engage in blaming women for male impotence; see Max von Gruber, *Hygiene of Sex* (Baltimore, 1926), pp. 106–9.

[71]William Robinson, *Sexual Impotence: A Practical Treatise on the Causes, Symptoms, and Treatment of Impotence and Other Sexual Disorders in Men and Women* (1912; New York, 1930).

[72]Robinson appears to be the first authority to use the term "frigidity," but I did not systematically survey the literature on female sexual disorders. See Robinson, p. 241; Arthur Conkin Brush, "Neurological Causes of Impotence," *New York Medical Journal* 58 (1893): 147. For a Freudian interpretation, see Wilhelm Stekel, *Frigidity in Women* (New York, 1926); more research on frigidity might show that the classification of frigidity coin-

Although they contested the precise meaning of frigidity, sexual experts agreed that sexually repressed women increased the incidence of sexual impotence in men. As one expert commented, "Sanctimonious frigidity will not call out his virility." Robinson, however, conceded that "the woman's virginal reserve attracts men"; but he advised wives that they "must not continue this reserve throughout [their] entire married life."[73] Yet even as they criticized women for failing to elicit sexual responses from their husbands, male experts instructed wives to modify their sexual behavior in subtle and particular ways. Further research on frigidity may reveal that these women, whom physicians classified as ill, were in fact clinging to the earlier ideal of passionlessness as a way to resist both sexually demanding husbands and increasingly powerful sexual scientists.[74]

Whether or not they were actually resisting remains to be seen, but clearly women were being held to a new standard of sexuality. Throughout the nineteenth century, many physicians had pronounced women to be devoid of sexual feeling, providing their social roles as paragons of virtue with a measure of scientific legitimacy. Within the Victorian sex/gender system, through voluntary motherhood and maintenance of the purity ideal, women could claim the authority to restrain male lust, both within and outside the home.[75] By the 1920s this was dramatically changing. The New Woman—liberated, citizen, worker—openly flirted with men in public and displayed an erotic sensibility. As Christina Simmons has argued, modern "women were supposed to desire and enjoy sexual relations but they were considered less lustful than men."[76]

As experts manipulated the ideology of passionlessness, they helped to revise the Victorian conception of the successful marriage. Psychologists and physicians not only encouraged wives to become more erotically stimulating, but in some cases they advised husbands of

---

cided with the classification of the lesbian. On sexology and lesbians, see Lillian Faderman, *Odd Girls and Twilight Lovers: A History of Lesbian Life in Twentieth-Century America* (New York, 1991), pp. 45–54.

[73]Talmey, p. 502; Robinson, p. 114.

[74]This might suggest a sexual version of Linda Gordon's argument about reproduction and voluntary motherhood; see Linda Gordon, "Voluntary Motherhood: The Beginnings of Feminist Birth Control Ideology in the United States," in *Clio's Consciousness Raised,* ed. Mary Hartman and Lois Banner (New York, 1974), and *Woman's Body, Woman's Right: A Social History of Birth Control in America* (New York, 1976).

[75]Cott, "'Passionlessness'" (n. 2 above).

[76]On the rise of the New Woman, see Smith-Rosenberg, *Disorderly Conduct* (n. 2 above), pp. 197–219; Nancy Cott, *The Grounding of Modern Feminism* (New Haven, CT, 1988), pp. 143–74. My interpretation of the social consequences follows closely the work of Christina Simmons (n. 7 above), quotation on p. 170.

unresponsive wives to take drastic steps to overcome their impotence and even advocated adultery. One physician, for example, said that there was "but one cure in cases of this class [in which the wife was frigid] and that is for the husband to set aside all mores and social and marital restrictions and have his sexual needs ministered to." Another suggested to his patient that he "locate a young woman, possessed of strong desires for sexual gratification."[77] Although exceptional, such cases illustrate the extent to which experts, and presumably some married couples, increasingly judged marital success by a new model of companionate marriage that emphasized sexual fulfillment.[78]

Scientific revision of sexual standards, gender conventions, and marriage occurred within the context of a popular debate over a new modern morality.[79] As working-class and middle-class women entered the public sphere in increasing numbers, as immigrants and African-Americans formed subcultures that included distinctive sexual values, and as an emergent youth culture experimented with premarital sex in the context of dating, sophisticated moderns declared a sexual revolution. They encouraged display of the erotic and of sexual expression and emphasized the appeal of sexual "others."[80] Modern impotence discourse corresponded with the revolution, encouraging male sexual release and highlighting sexual satisfaction as an important part of middle-class marriage. But the new view of impotence also shifted the balance of power in gender relations. By sexualizing women and stigmatizing those who resisted as frigid, and by then making performance of this normative sex role critical not only to a good marriage but also to male sexual health, modern impotence discourse could serve to legitimate men's sexual claims on women.

From the eighteenth to the early twentieth centuries, the changing conceptions of impotence reveal broad trends in the history of male sexuality. The two paradigmatic shifts in impotence discourse—from a problem of infertility to a problem of depleted sexual energy, and then from bodily depletion to a psychological complex of repressed desire—

[77]Shufeldt (n. 58 above), p. 8; Talmey, p. 500. Such cases recur throughout Stekel's discussion of impotence and marriage; see Stekel, *Impotence in the Male*, 1:235–62.

[78]Judge Benjamin Lindsey, *The Companionate Marriage* (New York, 1920); Regina Lois Wolkoff, "The Ethics of Sex: Individuality and Social Order in Early Twentieth-Century American Advice Literature" (Ph.D. diss., University of Michigan, 1974), pp. 24–70.

[79]The contours of the debate can be seen in the exchange between William Jennings Bryan, "Morals for Men and Women," *New Republic*, August 16, 1923, pp. 68–71, and Clement Wood, "Modern Sex Morality," *New Republic*, September 12, 1923, pp. 32–35.

[80]On the social origins of the modern sexual revolution, see D'Emilio and Freedman (n. 2 above), pp. 172–73.

mark both the 1830s and the 1920s as periods of decisive change in male sexual ideology. An analysis of these contexts points up the historical forces—social structure, sexual science, the politics of difference—that combined to reshape not only male sexuality but heterosexuality in general. Moreover, historical analysis of impotence discourse reveals that, although the incidence of impotence in men consistently signified diminished manhood, the prevailing standard of masculine sexual behavior changed over time: from the preindustrial era, when manhood depended on the successful reproduction of the family, to the antebellum era, when manhood was achieved by controlling sexual impulses, to the early twentieth century, when to be a man required the display of sexual strength.

Historical investigation of impotence not only illuminates the direction and forces of sexual change, but it also suggests certain recurrent motifs: from the preindustrial to the modern era, definitions of male sexuality were shaped by, and in turn reinforced, systems of social inequality. For example, the first paradigmatic shift in impotence discourse turned on a model of sex difference that privileged contradistinctions between the female body and the male body and reinforced a gender system that endowed men with the power of rational self-control and attributed irrationality to women. Late Victorian reformulations of impotence relied similarly on a model of racial difference by attributing sexual uncontrollability to black men. At the same time, impotence discourse actually helped to launch a revolt from Victorian sexual restraint that facilitated the emergence of a modern system of sexual satisfaction in marriage. "Lost manhood" had been found, but its recovery may have both reinforced inequalities of difference and eroded ideological constraints on male heterosexual desire.[81]

[81]Racial difference shaped modern views of impotence. Margaret Mead's study of "primitive sexuality" argues that Samoan men were not impotent and Samoan women were not frigid. See Margaret Mead, *Coming of Age in Samoa: A Study of Adolescence and Sex in Primitive Societies* (New York, 1928), pp. 169–71. On the decline of the innate female purity model, see Estelle B. Freedman, "'Uncontrolled Desires': The Response to the Sexual Psychopath, 1920–1960," in Peiss and Simmons, eds., pp. 211–13.

# "The Word Made Flesh": Language, Authority, and Sexual Desire in Late Nineteenth-Century America

JESSE F. BATTAN

*Department of American Studies*
*California State University, Fullerton*

In a letter written to Ezra Heywood, editor of an obscure monthly newspaper called *The Word*, a reader described an experience she had had with her daughter. "The other day," she wrote in 1881, "my little girl, who is in her twelfth year, came to me and said, 'Mama, what does "fuck" mean?'" The girl's mother quickly asked her where she had heard such a word. "Why, today at school, Willie ———— said to me, 'Mamie, won't you fuck me?'" her daughter breezily replied. Rather than express shock or condemn her child's youthful inquiry, the woman responded by telling her "exactly what it meant." In doing so she described the act in "plain English words of four letters" and used her own body, as well as "a well-executed photograph of the male organ in [a] state of erection," to demonstrate the physiological issues involved in sexual intercourse.[1]

On the face of it, the writing and publication of this letter is startling. In an age that has been characterized by its prudery, reticence, and censorship, such sentiments and such language seem quite out of place. This reaction, however, is primarily the result of a gap in our understanding of the diversity of the sexual culture of nineteenth-century America. Although recent scholarship has done much to supplant the traditional view of the monolithic power of the repressive sexual moral-

I would like to thank Leila Zenderland and the journal's anonymous reviewers for their helpful comments and criticism. The initial research for this essay was funded by a faculty research grant from California State University, Fullerton.
[1]"Mother," "Correspondence," *The Word*, March 1890, p. 3.

This essay originally appeared in the *Journal of the History of Sexuality* 1992, vol. 3, no. 2.

ity that emerged by the 1830s,[2] we still know much more about Victorian efforts to shape sexual ideology and behavior than we do about those who opposed them.[3] Little is known, for example, of the activities of nineteenth-century sexual radicals—the self-described "Free Lovers"—who rejected the ideas advocated in Victorian "primers for prudery." Studies that have been done on these reformers have concentrated primarily on the legal struggles that accompanied their efforts to disseminate birth control information or to defend First Amendment freedoms.[4] These studies, however, have not paid sufficient attention to the battles over words—the politics of language—that were central to the conflicts that occurred between competing sexual ideologies. The goal of this essay is to examine these struggles to define the nature of public language from the perspective of those who attempted to expand the limits of sexual discourse as well as from the point of view of those who sought to constrict it.

## WORDS OF CONTENTION

Throughout the nineteenth century, heated debates occurred over the meaning of words and their proper usage.[5] These linguistic contro-

[2]See, for example, Peter Gay, "Victorian Sexuality: Old Texts and New Insights," *American Scholar* 49 (1980): 376, and *The Bourgeois Experience: Victoria to Freud—Volume I, Education of the Senses* (New York, 1984); Jeffrey Weeks, *Sex, Politics, and Society: The Regulation of Sexuality since 1800* (London, 1981), pp. 15–16; Anita Clair and Michael Fellman, *Making Sense of Self: Medical Advice Literature in Late Nineteenth-Century America* (Philadelphia, 1981), pp. 91–112; David Cannadine, "The Victorian Sex Wars," *New York Review of Books,* February 2, 1984, pp. 19–22; Carroll Smith-Rosenberg, *Disorderly Conduct: Visions of Gender in Victorian America* (New York, 1985), pp. 86–87.

[3]For discussions of these efforts in England and America, see Walter E. Houghton, *The Victorian Frame of Mind, 1830–1870* (New Haven, CT, 1973), pp. 353, 356–58, 367–68, 408–9, 419–21; Nathan G. Hale, Jr., *Freud and the Americans: The Beginnings of Psychoanalysis in the United States, 1876–1917* (New York, 1971), pp. 24–46, 465, 475; Ronald G. Walters, ed., *Primers for Prudery: Sexual Advice to Victorian America* (Englewood Cliffs, NJ, 1974); John S. Haller, Jr., and Robin M. Haller, *The Physician and Sexuality in Victorian America* (Urbana, IL, 1974); Charles E. Rosenberg, "Sexuality, Class, and Role," *American Quarterly* 25 (1973): 131–53; Nancy F. Cott, "'Passionlessness': An Interpretation of Victorian Sexual Ideology, 1790–1850," *Signs* 4 (1978): 219–36; Linda Gordon, *Woman's Body, Woman's Right: A Social History of Birth Control in America* (New York, 1983), pp. 12, 16–24, 110–11.

[4]Hal D. Sears, *The Sex Radicals: Free Love in High Victorian America* (Lawrence, KS, 1977), pp. 68–79, 96, 111, 273; Gordon, pp. 65–66, 107–8; Taylor Stoehr, ed., *Free Love in America: A Documentary History* (New York, 1979), p. 45; Martin Henry Blatt, *Free Love and Anarchism: The Biography of Ezra Heywood* (Urbana, IL, 1989), pp. 142–71.

[5]Kenneth Cmiel, *Democratic Eloquence: The Fight over Popular Speech in Nineteenth-Century America* (New York, 1990); Leo Marx, "The Uncivil Response of American Writers to Civil Religion in America," in *American Civil Religion,* ed. Russell E. Richey and

versies took a variety of forms and reflected large-scale changes in the structure of American life. Urbanization, industrialization, social and geographic mobility, and the emergence of a democratic culture all worked to undermine stable patterns of deference by multiplying the ways in which all forms of knowledge were communicated. The number of voices making themselves heard, as well as the linguistic styles they used, was expanding. Preexisting boundaries, based on gender and class distinctions, that had served to limit access to the public domain of expression and expertise were being destroyed.[6] As a result, the question of who could speak and write and the context in which this would occur became politically divisive issues. These battles over language were an outgrowth of the struggles between competing groups who strongly believed that words could shape the new social world that was emerging.

Waging war against the growing use of vernacular forms of speech, for example, linguistic conservatives argued that diction, syntax, and word choice reflected the essential character of men and women and determined the nature of society itself.[7] The sensuality aroused by the use of slang undermined the internalized hierarchy of reason over desire. Further, colloquialisms and informal language created a false intimacy that destroyed the "natural" hierarchy between the refined and the vulgar, which was the basis of a stable social order. These linguistic purists—whose numbers included journalists, clergymen, and educators—insisted that the proper use of words would promote reticence and reserve, rather than garrulity and familiarity, and would recreate a social world in which proper deference would reign over an unchecked egalitarianism.[8]

Nowhere was the struggle between linguistic purity and vulgarity more evident than in the conflict over words used to describe sexuality. Although the contending voices in this dialogue supported diametrically opposed ideas on the nature of sexuality and the role it should play in the creation of their vision of the ideal society, all were convinced of its power and sought to monitor and guide it. Linking consciousness to conduct, the participants in this struggle believed that the erotic imagination and the behavior it inspired could be controlled if the words used

---

Donald G. Jones (New York, 1974), pp. 222–51; Daniel T. Rodgers, *Contested Truths: Keywords in American Politics since Independence* (New York, 1987), p. 4.

[6]Cmiel, pp. 15, 61; Richard D. Brown, *Knowledge Is Power: The Diffusion of Information in Early America, 1700–1865* (New York, 1989), pp. 11–13, 292–96.

[7]Cmiel, p. 14.

[8]Ibid., pp. 123–29, 134, 138–39.

to describe sexuality were carefully chosen. They all believed, in short, that language could be used to regulate the expression of sexual desires.

Efforts to use language to control erotic images and impulses escalated throughout the nineteenth century. In fact, they played a central role in the development of Victorian sexual ideology. Motivated by their distrust of sensual desires, Victorian moralists worked to inculcate a sense of shame in response to erotic stirrings and promoted chastity in thought and speech as well as in conduct. Convinced that individual health and social stability required the strict regulation of sexual desires, they correspondingly attempted to circumscribe the social geography of sexual discussions by sharply distinguishing between language that was appropriate for public and for private life.[9] Their attempts to eradicate linguistic and artistic forms of "obscenity" that began with local, extralegal actions of vice societies in the 1830s and culminated in the enactment of the Postal Act of 1873 (known as the Comstock Act) grew out of this desire to restrict sexuality to the private arena.[10]

By severely limiting what could be said, where it could be said, and who could say it, Victorian moralists attempted to suppress any discussion of sexuality that had not been carefully neutered. Those empowered to discuss this topic—clergymen, physicians, and moral reformers—engaged in conversations filled with biblical images of sin and redemption, medical metaphors of sickness and health, and obtuse euphemistic references that carefully filtered out any hint of sensuality.

[9]Norbert Elias, *The Civilizing Process: The History of Manners,* 2 vols., trans. Edmund Jephcott (New York, 1978), 1:180–81, 186, 189–90; Karen Halttunen, *Confidence Men and Painted Women: A Study of Middle-Class Culture in America, 1830-1870* (New Haven, CT, 1982), pp. 56–57, 104–5, 107–10; John Kasson, *Rudeness and Civility: Manners in Nineteenth-Century Urban America* (New York, 1990), pp. 11, 114–17, 123, 161–62, 169–73; Michel Foucault, *The History of Sexuality: An Introduction,* vol. 1 of *The History of Sexuality,* trans. Robert Hurley (New York, 1978), pp. 17–18; Karen Lystra, *Searching the Heart: Women, Men, and Romantic Love in Nineteenth-Century America* (New York, 1989), pp. 17–18, 90–100, 106–7.

[10]For discussions on the efforts of moral reformers in the nineteenth century to control sexual thought and conduct, see Smith-Rosenberg, pp. 109–28; David J. Pivar, *Purity Crusade: Sexual Morality and Social Control, 1868-1900* (Westport, CT, 1973); Barbara Leslie Epstein, *The Politics of Domesticity: Women, Evangelism, and Temperance in Nineteenth-Century America* (Middletown, CT, 1981), pp. 125–37; Lori D. Ginzberg, *Women and the Work of Benevolence: Morality, Politics, and Class in the Nineteenth-Century United States* (New Haven, CT, 1990), pp. 19–23, 202–9; John D'Emilio and Estelle B. Freedman, *Intimate Matters: A History of Sexuality in America* (New York, 1988), pp. 156–60, 203–15. Anthony Comstock's attempts to enforce the Postal Act of 1873 are explored in Heywood Broun and Margaret Leech, *Anthony Comstock: Roundsman of the Lord* (New York, 1927); James C. N. Paul and Murray L. Schwartz, *Federal Censorship: Obscenity in the Mail* (New York, 1961); Paul S. Boyer, *Purity in Print: The Vice-Society Movement and Book Censorship in America* (New York, 1968), pp. 1–22.

Fearful of the stark imagery connoted by vulgar language, they condemned words that incited forms of sexual behavior threatening to the institutions and relationships they had created to control erotic desires. Rather than reflect a conspiracy of silence that sought to eliminate all discussions of sexual issues, the goal of Victorian prudery was to use language to properly socialize desire.

Within the expanding terrain of public language in the nineteenth century, however, there were also many attempts to create alternative ways of writing about sexuality. The most radical attempts were made by the Free Lovers. The Free Lovers first appeared in the 1850s, when the term "free love" became more than a derisive epithet used to describe any form of sexual behavior that deviated from prescribed norms. It instead denoted a system of ideas that challenged Victorian sexual ideology. During this time the term "Free Lover" was also capitalized and used as a descriptive noun to indicate membership in a loosely knit but highly self-conscious group of politically and socially active men and women. Drawing on the ideas of utopian reformers of the early nineteenth century, the Free Lovers sought to regenerate society by reconstructing the relationships that regulated the expression of human emotions.[11]

One of the most important ways in which the Free Lovers sought to achieve their goals centered on their use of "obscene" language. Their use of such language to promote their radical ideas, they claimed, was not motivated by a desire to titillate their audience. Rather, it reflected their fundamental desire to eradicate a sexual culture they saw as corrupt and corrupting. Much more was at stake here than simply free speech: the Free Lovers' war against Victorian prudery was an attempt to fundamentally transform American society through the revitalization of language.

Like their orthodox counterparts, the Free Lovers believed that what was said in public influenced what was performed in private. In contrast to conservative moralists, however, they argued that the unwillingness to candidly discuss every aspect of human physiology led not to purity and health but to vulgarity and disease. By exercising their right to investigate the "sexual question" and to communicate their findings, they tried to create an alternative sexual discourse. Sexual health could be achieved, they maintained, only after "the prudishness, the false mod-

---

[11]The Free Lovers came from a wide range of social and economic backgrounds, were geographically dispersed, ranged in age from eighteen to eighty-five, and could be found in provincial outposts as well as in urban centers. For a more in-depth discussion of these reformers, see Sears; John Spurlock, *Free Love: Marriage and Middle-Class Radicalism in America, 1825–1860* (New York, 1988); and Blatt.

esty that shrinks from open and fearless discussion of everything pertaining to the sexual nature of men and women" had been overcome.[12] Not denial but confrontation, not euphemisms but direct expression, not "suppression or prohibition, but education and enlightenment" would destroy unhealthy behavior and return the sexual appetites of men and women to their "natural" condition.[13] In their reform ideology, the purification of the physical body as well as the body politic depended on the open examination of human sexuality.

In order to use language to transform consciousness and behavior, the editors of Free Love newspapers published materials that challenged the fundamental tenets of Victorian sexual ideology. Among the most influential were Moses Harman, editor of *Lucifer, the Light-Bearer,* and Ezra Hervey Heywood, editor of *The Word.*[14] These newspapers provided a forum in which they and their audience could describe their sexual experiences without fear of censorship. For example, they published articles that rejected the image of childhood as a state of sexual innocence and argued for an education that would expose children to the "facts" of human sexuality rather than the "soothing-syrup of legalized duplicity and fashionable deceit!"[15] Defending their right to disseminate birth control information, these editors also printed advertisements and articles that described a variety of contraceptive practices, and they initiated a series of debates on the benefits and problems created by their use.

Heywood and Harman also paraded before the eyes of their readers striking examples of "aberrant" sexual behavior. Their newspapers were filled with vivid accounts of wives driven to illness or early graves by the unbridled lusts of their husbands. Sadie Magoon of Los Angeles, for ex-

[12]Moses Harman, "Heywood Again under Arrest," *Kansas Liberal,* June 8, 1883, p. 3.

[13]Moses Harman, editorial response to N. C. Mitter Pleade, "Various Voices," *Lucifer,* March 10, 1897, p. 79. The Free Lovers did not live in an unrestricted world in which all sexual practices were of equal value. They clearly identified some—homosexuality, for example—as deleterious to the health of the individual and the stability of society. In fact, they shared many of the presumptions regarding "normal" or "healthy" sexuality held by their conservative Victorian counterparts. Their understanding of the etiology of sexual deviance, however, was quite distinct. Influenced by the radical naturalists of the eighteenth-century Enlightenment, the Free Lovers argued that, in the state of nature, human sexual energy was benign. It emerged as a destructive force only after the rise of civilization and subsequent efforts to repress it.

[14]*Lucifer* (Valley Falls, Topeka, and Chicago), which succeeded the *Valley Falls Liberal* (1880–81) and the *Kansas Liberal* (1881–83), was published from 1883 until 1907, when it was succeeded by the *American Journal of Eugenics* (Chicago and Los Angeles, 1907–10). *The Word* (Princeton, MA) was published from 1872 until Ezra Heywood's death in 1893.

[15]Angela Heywood, "Evolution of Morals in Youth," *The Word,* June 1884, p. 2.

ample, related a typical case of one woman who had married what most considered to be "a good man." His constant sexual demands, however, soon destroyed her health. "The sparkle left her eye, and the bloom her cheeks. She grew thin and had a peculiar gait, and at last could no longer walk at all, and was confined to her bed and in time became partially paralyzed." But the horror continued. Even while bedridden and placed under a nurse's care, when her day nurse left she was at the total mercy of her husband, a "human brute," who continued to gratify his desires. "Through his constant nightly abuses she was, to quote from her nurse and my informant," wrote Magoon, "'raw as beef steak.'"[16] The plight of this woman, as well as the experiences of countless others who were similarly treated, were publicized as examples of "the hidden mysteries of the marriage institution." Since the "secrets of the inner temple of home" were guarded more closely than "those of the cloister," the Free Lovers insisted that the conspiracy of silence had to be broken for the liberation of the enslaved to begin.[17]

In addition to these stories of "women who slowly perished" as a result of the "sexual excesses forced on them" by their husbands, the editors of Free Love newspapers also published accounts of other forms of sexual "perversion." In a letter that found its way into the columns of *Lucifer* in 1890, for example, Dr. Richard V. O'Neill, a New York physician, described his treatment of a woman whose mouth and throat were filled with "venereal ulcers" as a result of her husband "putting his private organ into his wife's mouth," as well as his contact with a man who sought a cure for his "*insatiable* appetite for *human semen* [emphasis in original]." The patient, who claimed to have inherited this disease from his father, complained that he had traveled far and wide in order "to find men to allow him to 'suck them off' as he says." Further, the patient confessed that he had often engaged in oral sex with members of his family, men as well as women, who would "*suck* each other's *private parts* in the presence of each other."[18]

In the hands of the Free Lovers, deviant behavior was neither celebrated nor condemned. Rather, they believed that only by publicly acknowledging these acts of perversion in clear language could they be understood and eliminated. As Harman argued, the "cancers that are eating the life out of our social system can never be cured by the cover-

[16]Sadie Athena Magoon, "Another Instance of Inhuman Cruelty," *Lucifer,* February 14, 1890, p. 3.

[17]Lily White, "Sexual Abuse in Marriage," *Social Revolutionist,* March 1857, p. 85; May Huntley, "A Common Story Seldom Told," *Our New Humanity,* September 1895, p. 66.

[18]Richard V. O'Neill, M.D., "A Physician's Testimony," *Lucifer,* February 14, 1890, p. 3.

ing up or plastering over process. The evil must be laid bare in all its native hideousness. The healing influences of nature's air and sunshine must be allowed to do their work if ever the patient is to be cured."[19] Straining against the conspiracy of silence that confined the discussion of these "hidden crimes" to "private circles," these sexual muckrakers publicized them in order to create a groundswell of public outrage and inspire political action that would effectively meliorate the conditions they described.[20]

## "NAUGHTY WORDS" AND "FOUL-MOUTHED WOMEN"

The very words the Free Lovers used to express their ideas also provided a significant source of conflict with orthodox moralists. To create alternative forms of sexual behavior, they discussed tabooed subjects in "terms peculiarly direct, and liable to offend fastidious public sentiment."[21] It is here—in their efforts to revitalize the vocabulary of sexual knowledge—that we gain the clearest insight into the Free Lovers' ideas on linguistic reform.

By far the most radical nineteenth-century critique of linguistic prudery was carried on by Angela Fiducia Tilton Heywood and her husband and comrade, Ezra Heywood. Together, they achieved considerable notoriety in the 1870s and 1880s by using words that offended almost everyone, including some Free Lovers. While the Free Lovers regarded themselves as supporters of "the most unpopular of all unpopular reforms," the Heywoods' ideas on the power of words to effect changes in consciousness and behavior placed them at the cutting edge of even this most radical of movements.[22] Stephen Pearl Andrews, an ardent critic of many aspects of Victorian society, observed in 1883 that the "boldness of speech" in which they expressed their views on marriage and sexuality "frightened and repelled the conservatives on the one hand, and even more their own associates in the reformatory world, who were not ready to be committed to so much." In the important struggle for the freedom to speak openly about the "sex question," Andrews concluded, they were "the extreme case; if they can be endured, anybody can."[23]

As the publisher of unorthodox notions and obscene language, it was

[19]Moses Harman, "Horrors upon Horrors," *Lucifer*, February 14, 1890, p. 2.

[20]W. F. Barnard, "Love and Progress," *Free Society*, November 22, 1903, p. 1; Voltairine de Cleyre, "The Gates of Freedom," *Lucifer*, May 8, 1891, p. 4; White, p. 85.

[21]Stephen Pearl Andrews, "Where and When to Meet the Issue," *Lucifer*, July 26, 1889, p. 1.

[22]Sara Crist Campbell, "Lucifer Club Column," *Lucifer*, March 27, 1891, p. 3.

[23]Stephen Pearl Andrews, "Co-operation," *The Word*, October 1883, p. 1.

Ezra Heywood who faced the wrath of the censors and the judicial system empowered to impose their will. It was Angela Heywood, however, who provided the most outspoken defense of their "habit of saying naughty words, and shocking the whole world by saying them."[24] Such words, she argued, effectively exposed the gap between private behavior and public language. The use of "naughty words," however, would do more than illuminate the hypocrisy of the old moral order. The language of sexual candor also held the power to transform social relationships. For Angela Heywood, words were symbols of vibrant truths, the expression of which would destroy the artificial inhibitions that sustained all forms of inequality. By enabling men and women to communicate their emotions in a more direct way, words could liberate them from destructive forms of consciousness and behavior.

Angela Heywood's desire to openly discuss every aspect of human sexuality developed at an early age. "As a girl," she recalled in 1889, "I used to say, in myself, 'When I grow up I shall deal with men's penises, write books about them; I mean to and I will do it.'"[25] An odd goal for a nineteenth-century woman, yet it was one that she realized nonetheless. Her ambitions were in part inspired by her intellectual heritage. Born in Deerfield, New Hampshire, she traced her lineage on her mother's side to John Locke. From her mother, Lucy M. Tilton, Angela inherited her distaste for the prudery of "'learned' men and 'refined' women" as well as the corresponding view that sexuality was worthy of "respect and study." Raised on a farm and alerted to the natural processes of animal reproduction, she early learned to regard human sexuality with reverence. "From babyhood," she wrote in 1884, "I was taught to have sacred regard for the human body-form and all its belongings, to call penis 'penis' and womb 'womb'; it never occurred to me that it could be considered indelicate or 'vulgar' to speak, orally or writtenly, of sex organs by their proper names."[26]

Moreover, as a young woman she was drawn to the ideas of a circle of abolitionists and transcendentalists whom she regarded as her "immediate teachers," which included William Lloyd Garrison, Wendell Phillips, Thomas Wentworth Higginson, Bronson Alcott, Theodore Parker, Ralph Waldo Emerson, and Walt Whitman.[27] As a result of her

[24]Ibid.

[25]Angela Heywood, "Sex Service—Ethics of Trust," *The Word,* October 1889, p. 2.

[26]Angela Heywood, "The Woman's View of It—No. 2," *The Word,* February 1883, p. 2; Ezra H. Heywood, "From a Cell in States Prison," *Lucifer,* February 19, 1892, p. 3; Angela Heywood, "Creative Dualism—Motherhood," *The Word,* November 1888, p. 3, and "Penis Literature—Onanism or Health?" *The Word,* April 1884, p. 2.

[27]Angela Heywood, "The Woman's View of It—No. 2," p. 2. In 1893 Angela proudly recalled that when she was a young girl, Bronson Alcott would pat her on the head and de-

contact with what Stephen Pearl Andrews described as "the old antislavery ranks," when she began to explore the sex question she "carried their
*Abolitionist* boldness of speech into that subject."[28] While the antislavery
radicals may have inspired her willingness to speak out, the essential element of Angela Heywood's critique of linguistic prudery—the belief in
the redemptive power of words themselves—was most influenced by
what F. O. Matthiessen has described as the "transcendental conception
of language."[29]

By the mid-nineteenth century, writers such as Emerson, Parker,
Alcott, and Whitman had developed a sharp critique of the linguistic
shifts that accompanied the development of Victorianism as a cultural
system. Modern civilization, with its emphasis on "respectability," conformity, and materialism, had alienated man from his natural environment. Reflecting this fall from grace, the essential link between words
and the physical and spiritual realities they represented had been destroyed. As Emerson argued in 1836, the "corruption of man is followed by the corruption of language." Losing their power to "stand for
things" as they are, words no longer signified their essential meanings.
Instead, reflecting the artificiality of a spiritually bankrupt civilization,
the language of genteel culture had become rarefied, capable only of
stimulating "duplicity and falsehood."[30]

For these transcendentalists, the solution to both forms of corruption lay in the redemptive power of language. By reconnecting words to
things, language would be revitalized. It could then provide men and
women with a clear, coherent, and ultimately harmonizing vision of
their physical desires, the natural world, and the spiritual truths they
symbolized.[31] Influenced by German idealism and English romanti-
cism, the transcendentalists looked to the language of the "folk"—in

---

clare: "She is a metaphysical prodigy." See Angela Heywood, "Dance of Ideas in Sex-Ethic
Forces," *The Word,* April 1893, p. 3.

[28]Andrews, "Co-operation," p. 1.

[29]F. O. Matthiessen, *American Renaissance: Art and Expression in the Age of Emerson
and Whitman* (New York, 1970), p. 32. See also John T. Irwin, *American Hieroglyphics:
The Symbol of the Egyptian Hieroglyphics in the American Renaissance* (New Haven, CT,
1980), pp. 3–40; Philip F. Gura, *The Wisdom of Words: Language, Theology, and Literature
in the New England Renaissance* (Middletown, CT, 1981); David Simpson, *The Politics of
American English, 1776–1850* (New York, 1986), pp. 230–59.

[30]Reginald L. Cook, ed., *Ralph Waldo Emerson: Selected Prose and Poetry,* 2d ed. (San
Francisco, 1969), p. 15; Matthiessen, pp. 30–40, 517–32.

[31]Catherine L. Albanese, *Corresponding Motion: Transcendental Religion and the New
America* (Philadelphia, 1977), pp. 53, 97; Simpson, pp. 251–62; Mary Kupiec Cayton,
*Emerson's Emergence: Self and Society in the Transformation of New England, 1800–1845*
(Chapel Hill, NC, 1989), pp. 179–80.

this case, the earthiness of Elizabethan Saxon English—as the source for authentic forms of communication.[32] The rehabilitation of language and society, they argued, would only occur when the words and phrases spoken in fields and streets replaced the language found in dictionaries and literature. In search of the "mother-tongue," writers such as Bronson Alcott insisted that it was better to study the speech of the "simple countryman amidst the scenes of nature" than to "commune with [the] citizen amidst his conventions, or read with [the] professor in college or hall, the tomes of a library."[33]

In addition to democratizing the sources of language, the transcendentalists expanded the perimeters of what it could describe. All experiences, ranging from cooking and cleaning to courting and loving, were worthy of discussion. Moreover, as Emerson argued, such discussions should include words—even "obscene" words—normally "excluded from polite conversation."[34] Carrying this idea further, Whitman insisted that the reconnection of words to things would only occur after the "forbidden voices . . . of sexes and lusts" had been freed from the censor's grip. Once men and women had learned to "publicly accept, and publicly name, with specific words" every aspect of human sexuality without resorting to the euphemisms of genteel society, that which had formerly been "indecent" would be "clarified and transfigur'd."[35] In the transcendentalists' program for the creation of a language "true to nature," the reticence as well as the elitism of linguistic conservatives would be eliminated.[36]

Along with ideas imbued by her mother or learned from radical

[32]Matthiessen, pp. 30, 33–37, 39; Simpson, pp. 251–52; Cmiel (n. 5 above), pp. 94–122.

[33]Odell Shepard, ed., *The Journals of Bronson Alcott* (Boston, 1938), p. 95.

[34]Cook, p. 128.

[35]John Kouwenhoven, ed., *Leaves of Grass and Selected Prose by Walt Whitman* (New York, 1950), p. 44; Walt Whitman, *Leaves of Grass: Comprehensive Readers Edition*, ed. Harold W. Blodgett and Sculley Bradley (New York, 1965), p. 737. Even though Whitman has often been described as the most outspoken critic of the prudery and reticence characteristic of the "genteel tradition" in American literature (Douglas L. Wilson, ed., *The Genteel Tradition: Nine Essays by George Santayana* [Cambridge, MA, 1967], p. 52; Matthiessen, p. 523; Marx [n. 5 above], pp. 234, 245), when placed alongside Angela Heywood's tirades against linguistic prudery his lyrical challenges appear quite tame. The Free Lovers were so outspoken in their attacks on Victorian reticence that Whitman, in a letter to William D. O'Connor (November 12, 1882), expressed his desire to distance himself from the "Free religious and lover folk" who challenged Comstock's attempts to imprison the publishers of his poetry. Rejecting their offers of assistance as well as their flagrant violations of the Comstock Act, Whitman refused to "do any thing to identify myself specially with free love." See Edwin H. Miller, ed., *Walt Whitman: The Correspondence*, 6 vols. (New York, 1964), 3:314–15, 335.

[36]Shepard, p. 95.

thinkers, Angela Heywood's desire to challenge the linguistic purity created by what she referred to as "the compound of silks, insinuation, laces, and mincing called society" was also driven by her own experiences as a working woman. Taught the value of work at an early age, Angela engaged in a variety of occupations, ranging from domestic servant, seamstress, farmhand, and innkeeper to librarian, writer, and platform speaker.[37] As one who maintained a lifelong sympathy for the plight of working women, Angela always resented the fact that "shopgirls, mill-girls, and house-girls [are] regarded below par in social life simply because they work and have not means accumulated from others' earnings."[38] Moreover, as Stephen Pearl Andrews observed in 1883, her contempt for "the superciliousness and pretension of superiority by the rich and 'cultured'" was influenced by the ways in which working girls were verbally and physically treated by the men and women of the professional and leisured classes. In a short biographical sketch, Andrews perceptively noted that Angela Heywood and "others of her order were constantly approached and tempted or insulted by men of the so-called superior classes." From such contacts she early learned that the "private language and lives" of these men were "utterly corrupt," but in public their words and deeds "were delicate and refined to the last degree." Angela Heywood's firsthand experience with the "organized hypocrisy" of genteel society, combined with her "natural and inherited revolt against a pretended sanctity, propriety and culture on the part of the polished hypocrites," led to her firm "determination that folks shall hear openly talked about what in secret they dwell on as the staple of their lives; that the hypocrisy shall be exposed; that the inflated pretense of virtue which does not exist shall be punctured and collapsed."[39]

As a self-described "word painter," Angela attempted to use words to reveal the brutality and unhappiness bred by Victorian sexual ideology. Her goal was to communicate the inner truths obscured by genteel language and reintroduce men and women to what she referred to as a transcendent "throbbing" or vitalistic "rhythmic Reality."[40] By enunciating "words of fire and power," connections could be drawn between the symbol and the truth it represented, dissipating the foggy mists spun by Victorian prudery. In pursuit of what she called "Fleshed Realism," she sought to make the word flesh, a transforming force that would draw its

[37]Angela Heywood, "Men's Laws and Love's Laws," *The Word*, September 1876, p. 1, and "The Woman's View of It—No. 2," p. 2.

[38]Angela Heywood, "Woman's Love: Its Relations to Man and Society," *The Word*, July 1876, p. 1.

[39]Andrews, "Co-operation," p. 1.

[40]Angela Heywood, "Personal Attitudes—Plain Facts," *The Word*, October 1887, p. 2, and "Essential Being—Ethical Expression," *The Word*, January 1885, p. 2.

power for change from the essential truths it reflected.[41] The radical alteration of the sexual lives of men and women—the rehabilitation of desire—would result from the revitalization of the language used to describe sexuality.

Angela Heywood's efforts to revise what she termed "sex-nomenclature" extended even to the very names of the sexual organs and their functions. This became a cause célèbre when she began advocating the use of the "Anglo-Saxon" designation for "two well known objects and their associative use"—namely, "c[ock], c[unt] and f[uck]."[42] Her use of the infamous "three words" created quite a stir, not only among genteel moralists, but within the Free Love movement itself. Notoriety, however, was not her goal. Her defense of the use of these words grew out of her earlier attempts in the 1870s to include the word "penis" in her lectures. Angela's insistence that this word be used in public discourse was inspired by her belief that a new language would equalize the relationship between men and women. Since women did not possess "formulas of expression concerning the male generative organ," she insisted, "woman's generative organ has, for ages, been a foot-ball in men's talk." Because of this gap in women's vocabulary, "no companionable exchange in dialect" had been possible. The dialogue between men and women thus had always been lopsided, in favor of men.[43]

Seeking to realign the balance of power, Angela Heywood argued that in *The Word,* as well as in nature, "Penis goes with Womb," and she warned that their "'cultured' readers" would have to get over their distaste for it. "If man says 'womb' without rising heat or dishonest purpose," she argued, "why should not woman say 'penis' without blushing squirm or sheepish looks." "Penis and Womb," she announced, "have arrived in Literature" and should become permanent fixtures in any discussion of the intimate lives of men and women.[44]

Eventually, however, Angela grew dissatisfied with the Latinate designations of the sexual organs. For her, the term "penis" no longer adequately described the male organ's power and vigor. "What mother can look in the face of her welcome child and not religiously respect the rigid, erect, ready-for-service, persistent male-organ that sired it?" she

[41]Angela Heywood, "Woman's Love," p. 1, and "Human Sex-Power—Fleshed Realism," *The Word,* December 1892, p. 3.

[42]Angela Heywood, "Sex-Nomenclature—Plain English," *The Word,* April 1887, pp. 2–3; "Editorial Notes," *The Word,* July 1884, p. 2.

[43]Angela Heywood, "Sex-Nomenclature—Plain English," p. 2, and "Sex Service—Ethics of Trust," p. 2.

[44]Angela Heywood, "Men, Women, and Things," *The Word,* December 1883, p. 3, and "Men, Women, and Things," *The Word,* June 1883, p. 3.

mused in 1887. "Penis is a smooth, musical, almost feminine word," she argued, and should be replaced by the word "cock" as the symbolic designation of the male organ. "Built projective, carrying the seed of Life, ordained to propose what woman may accept, man is instinctively true to nature in coining the word cock to define creative power," she insisted. Preferring Saxon words, she maintained that they "exactly define sex-organs and their mutual use." Why should people be afraid of such words, she wondered. "In literature we have cocks as weathervanes, cocks as faucets, cocks as fowls, cocked hats, cocked rifles and cocks as leading gentlemen members of clubs." This word would have more power, and be truer to its function, if it were used to describe the male reproductive organ.[45] Even though "Latin names and devious phrases prevail in literary and scientific discourse," she urged Americans to incorporate "plain English" designations of the "sexual organs and their use" into their everyday speech and writing. Only then, she insisted, would "predatory penis-commerce" cease to exist.[46]

For Angela Heywood, it was "not the pen only, but the penis" that was "mightier than the sword."[47] Or rather, it was the penis guided by the pen and what it represented—conscious thought, discussion and choice—that would lead to the regeneration of public and private life. As long as sexual desire is not *spoken out about,* in the mental, social, and literary world, so long will disaster mar sex-experience." While in the past the improper use of man's sexuality had transformed it into a powerful force of destruction, by discussing its nature and the consequences of its expression men could learn to control their desires and redeem themselves by treating women with respect. "An *irresponsible* penis manufactures 'prostitutes,' 'harlots,' 'whores,' 'strumpets,'" she stated, but "a conscientious penis *glorifies* woman."[48]

Stressing the importance of "intelligent, natural, honest, plain-speaking," Angela emphasized her belief that communication should precede physical contact. When men and women speak honestly to one another, the "light beam of thought" creates cooperation through understanding. "Such graceful terms as hearing, seeing, smelling, tasting, fucking, throbbing, kissing, and kin words, are telephone expressions," Angela argued, "lighthouses of intercourse centrally immutable to the situation." While feelings can be communicated through touch, a more

[45]Angela Heywood, "Sex-Nomenclature—Plain English," pp. 2–3.

[46]Angela Heywood, "Penis Literature," p. 2, and "Men, Women, and Things," *The Word,* December 1883, p. 3.

[47]Angela Heywood, "Sex-Symbolism—The Attucks Shaft," *The Word,* December 1888, p. 3.

[48]Angela Heywood, "Personal Attitudes—Plain Facts," p. 2, and "Sex-Symbolism—The Attucks Shaft," p. 3.

intimate form of contact would be established if men and women demonstrated a "spontaneous, expressive candor."[49] Once they "think" about each other as well as "feel" one another, once they place "man's penis under scrutiny of day-light Thinking as well as in test of physical, mid-night Feeling," the unhealthy images fostered by the prudery of orthodox morality would be erased and the dark side of sexuality would disappear.[50]

Through her creation of a new "human grammar," Angela sought to realize "Sex-Unity," or the harmonious relation between the sexes.[51] Such a "natural mode" of expression would free women from forms of communication that reinforced their powerlessness. Orthodox definitions of obscenity led to "slavish phraseologies," which had maintained the unequal relationship between the sexes. By controlling language and "keeping the mysteries of Sex, the secrets of coition, the momentous potencies of Love and Parentage deep *hidden* in dark places" beyond their reach, men maintained their control over women.[52] Autonomy for women would be achieved only after a revolution in the ways in which affectional relationships are discussed, envisioned, and experienced. And the agent of revolution, Angela asserted, will be "the force of woman's tongue" calling men's "penises, over-loaded with white, child-making blood . . . to order." In the past, she concluded, women had been "ears and men mouths; now *we* must speak also."[53]

By eliminating the artificial boundaries that separated public life from private life and exposing the hypocrisy of social elites, Angela sought to inaugurate a revolution in class as well as in gender relationships. The liberation of women from their bondage to men was part of a larger struggle to free both women and men from a system of economic and political domination. Striking out at the oppression bred by the centralized control of knowledge, Angela argued that those in power were fearful of the circulation of ideas. The "church-state grip" on sexual knowledge, she wrote, keeps "women and labor" in a condition of "subjected destitution." The power of elites, she contended, was maintained by their "usurpation of the means of education, legalized censorship of

[49]Angela Heywood, "The Ethics of Touch—Sex-Unity," *The Word*, June 1889, p. 3.

[50]Angela Heywood, "Personal Attitudes—Plain Facts," p. 2, and "The Religion of Sexuality," *The Word*, January 1884, p. 2.

[51]Angela Heywood, "Essential Being—Ethical Expression," p. 2, and "The Ethics of Touch—Sex-Unity," p. 3.

[52]Angela Heywood, "Essential Being—Ethical Expression," p. 2, and "The Woman's View of It—No. 4," *The Word*, April 1883, p. 3.

[53]Angela Heywood, "Love and Labor," *The Word*, October 1876, p. 1, and "Men, Women, and Things," *The Word*, October 1883, p. 3, and "The Ethics of Touch—Sex-Unity," p. 3.

the press, of behavior and morals." As a result, "propertyless workers" were rendered the "helpless slaves of privileged robbers."[54] Economic and political equality would only be realized after the power that ortho-dox moralists gained by "falsifying words" had been destroyed.[55]

Just as women, properly armed with an expressive sexual vocabulary, were to be responsible for their own liberation in private life, the eco-nomically downtrodden and politically powerless were to be revolution-ary agents for change in public life.[56] By challenging the "arrogant 'cultured' pretense" and prudery of the wealthy, "respectable" members of society who hid behind their "arrogant aristocracy of 'tastes,'" the outcasts of genteel society—"publicans and harlots, 'slums' and 'mudsills'"—would expose "the superstitious hypocrisy" of "'ladies' in parlors who call man's penis his 'teapot,' his 'thing.'"[57] The raw lan-guage used by the "girls and boys of the street," who described their bodies without the affectation of restraint, would redeem society. True civilization, she concluded, "comes *up* from the masses, not down from the classes."[58]

For Angela Heywood, the reconstruction of gender and class rela-tionships awaited the revitalization of the language of sexual discourse. "When fit words please the ear as physical-human beauty pleases the eye, when sentences are quick with warm, throbbing life; when LANGUAGE, in original power and charming surprise, is the perennial miracle Sponta-neity allows it to be; when souls know bodies, and mind informs matter well-enough to help us meet and work in the realm of ethical possibil-ity," the millennium will be at hand. A "new literature," she argued, would create "new social harmonies, a new heaven and a new earth."[59] Reconnecting words to things, obscene language would inaugurate the social and emotional transformations that Victorian moralists were struggling to forestall. As a result of her linguistic innovations, class and gender hierarchies would be destroyed, and equality and intimacy

[54]Angela Heywood, "Dance of Ideas in Sex-Ethic Forces," p. 3, and "Evolution of Morals in Youth," *The Word*, June 1884, p. 2.

[55]Angela Heywood, "Sex-Nomenclature—Plain English," p. 2.

[56]Angela Heywood, "Dance of Ideas in Sex-Ethic Forces," p. 3, and "Personal Health—Social Propriety," *The Word*, September 1887, p. 3, and "Body Housekeeping—Home Thrift," *The Word*, March 1893, p. 3.

[57]Angela Heywood, "Sex Service—Ethics of Trust," p. 2, and "Personal Attitudes—Plain Facts," p. 3, and "Sex-Nomenclature—Plain English," p. 3.

[58]Angela Heywood, "Sex-Nomenclature—Plain English," p. 3, and "Personal Attitudes—Plain Facts," p. 3.

[59]Angela Heywood, "Essential Being—Ethical Expression," p. 2, and "The Grace and Use of Sex Life," *The Word*, June 1890, p. 3.

would replace inequality and formality in *public* as well as in *private* relationships.

## CONSEQUENCES OF THE "WAR OF WORDS"

From the perspective of both the Free Lovers and those who tried to censor their efforts, the restriction or expansion of sexual discourse held the key to the structure and character of the social order itself. While both groups celebrated a common vision of an ideal world in which health and virtue flourished, each was convinced that the ideas and patterns of behavior advocated by their opposing faction led only to disease and immorality.

Anthony Comstock, for example, who spent his professional career putting gamblers, pornographers, and quack doctors behind bars, claimed that he knew of "nothing more offensive to decency, or more revolting to good morals" than the publications of Free Lovers such as Angela and Ezra Heywood. He found them to be "foul of speech, shameless in their lives, and corrupting in their influence," and he warned of certain "ruin and death" awaiting those entranced by their doctrines. Their goal, he argued, was to destroy the moral "restraints" that ensured premarital chastity and marital fidelity. In pursuit of this end, they held "public meetings where foul-mouthed women" lectured to audiences who were reduced to an "enervated, lazy, shiftless, corrupt breed of human beings, devoid of common decency, not fit companions, in many cases, to run with swine."[60]

In their struggles "to protect the morals of the community" and prevent "the libertine and rake from poisoning the minds" of the young, moralists such as Anthony Comstock underscored the power of words to unleash or restrain "the baser passions."[61] This is clearly demonstrated in Comstock's description of a young man confronting a piece of "obscene literature." At first, before he examines his forbidden prize, he is troubled by pangs of conscience. A "sense of guilt and shame" conjured by an image of a disapproving teacher or mother overwhelms him, and he hesitates. Willpower and conscience, however, are no match for curiosity aroused. As he casts aside these forces of restraint and eagerly feasts on the images contained within the offending volume, a "mighty force from within is let loose." The "passions that had slumbered or lain dormant are awakened," and the young man is ruined. In the conserva-

---

[60]Anthony Comstock, *Traps for the Young,* ed. Robert Bremner (Cambridge, MA, 1967), pp. 158–59, 163.

[61]Anthony Comstock, *Frauds Exposed; or, How the People Are Deceived and Robbed, and Youth Corrupted* (1880; rpt. Montclair, NJ, 1969), pp. 513, 512.

tive Victorian imagination, mental purity was maintained only by avoiding words and images that elicited sensual thoughts. "Good reading refines, elevates, ennobles, and stimulates the ambition to lofty purposes," Comstock concluded, while "evil reading debases, degrades, perverts, and turns away from lofty aims to follow examples of corruption and criminality."[62]

In contrast, the Free Lovers envisioned themselves as sexual scientists pursuing knowledge that would liberate men and women from the corrupting influences of orthodox morality. Moses Harman clearly expressed this in his response to a reader's request for aid in obtaining "obscene books and pictures." "Lasciviousness and salacity are signs of abnormality or perversion, due primarily to ignorance," he wrote, "and the pure minded will make use of these symptoms as the physician does the symptoms of disease, and guided by these symptoms try to assist the sufferer to health or sanity."[63]

For the Free Lovers, mental purity was gained through education. They explained away the heightened prudishness displayed by censors like Comstock as a manifestation of the guilt they felt toward their own overheated sexual imaginations. "If Anthony Comstock will seriously and carefully examine into his own emotional condition," wrote one of Angela Heywood's supporters in 1890, "he will find himself troubled, and seriously so, with perverted and depraved emotions, which he should immediately try to correct, by a scientific course of hygiene." As Angela herself argued, the "pretense that English words, which so exactly define sex-organs and their mutual use, are indelicate, is a part of that *mental* disease which, insisting that ignorance guarantees social purity, enacts 'obscenity statutes' to *hinder increase of physiological knowledge!*"[64] Rather than an effort to maintain moral purity, the Free Lovers viewed the activities of these censors as a conspiracy on the part of church, state, and genteel society to perpetuate economic and emotional slavery.

While they shared a common goal—mental purity—orthodox moralists and sexual radicals were thus divided by their differing views on how to realize it. In contrast to genteel efforts to avoid discussing unsavory topics, the Free Lovers fought to expand the dimensions of public discourse to include the exploration of private issues. This difference

[62]Comstock, *Traps for the Young*, pp. 133, 135–36, 5; Hale (n. 3 above), pp. 24–25, 41, 43–44.

[63]Moses Harman, editorial comment on N. C. Mitter Pleade, "Various Voices," *Lucifer*, March 10, 1897, p. 79.

[64]F. H. Marsh, "Correspondence," *The Word*, June 1890, p. 4; Angela Heywood, "Sex Nomenclature—Plain English," p. 2.

cost the Free Lovers dearly. The "war of words," wrote David W. Hull after the arrest of his brother Moses Hull in 1876, often led to "actual battles" fought by men and women who were willing to "come forward and face the danger."[65]

In rural areas and in small towns, for example, linguistic prudery was enforced primarily by community leaders who controlled access to knowledge, as well as through more informal controls, such as gossip, social ostracism, and the ever present "scarecrow" of respectability, Mrs. Grundy.[66] In these village environments, the Free Lovers also faced mobs of local citizens, who torched their homes and printing offices and confiscated and burned their publications. Further, it was not uncommon for those on the lecture circuit to be attacked by armed toughs who threatened, and frequently delivered, violence against their persons as well as their property.[67]

In urban centers, where knowledge was more easily disseminated and a consensus on moral issues was more difficult to maintain, efforts to censor language relied on more formal controls.[68] With the passage of the Postal Act, which empowered Comstock and his agents to examine letters, newspapers, journals, and books sent through the mails for "obscene" content, the federal government joined ranks with the growing number of local reform societies after the Civil War who used the police and courts to prosecute sexual radicals.[69] Ezra Heywood, for example (whose experience was far from unique), was arrested and convicted in

[65]David W. Hull, "The Revolution," *Hull's Crucible,* July 1, 1876, p. 6.

[66]Mrs. Grundy, a minor character in Thomas Morton's play *Speed the Plough* (1800), personified in nineteenth-century England and America the prying, prudish scold forever concerned with the behavior of others. See Peter Fryer, *Mrs. Grundy: Studies in English Prudery* (London, 1963), especially pp. 15–16, 18, 19. For a nineteenth-century description of this phenomenon, see Victoria C. Woodhull, "The Scare-Crows of Sexual Slavery," *Woodhull and Claflin's Weekly,* September 27, 1873, pp. 3–7, 14.

[67]Hull, "The Revolution," p. 6; Leo Miller, "Correspondence," *The Word,* May 1877, p. 3; J. H. Cook, "A Few Way-Marks," *Lucifer,* April 9, 1886, p. 7, and "A Tribute to Cora Barry," *Lucifer,* July 10, 1891, p. 3; Alvin Warren, "Reminiscences of Berlin Heights," *Our New Humanity,* June 1896, pp. 37–40. See also Spurlock (n. 11 above), pp. 160–61, 226–27.

[68]Richard S. Randall, *Freedom and Taboo: Pornography and the Politics of a Self Divided* (Berkeley, 1989), pp. 167–75; Brown (n. 6 above), pp. 292–96.

[69]The legal conflicts between Anthony Comstock and the Free Lovers and civil libertarians who challenged the boundaries established by the Postal Act of 1873 are thoroughly explored in Broun and Leech (n. 10 above), pp. 170–93; Sears (n. 4 above), pp. 67–80, 107–17, 165–74, 179–81, 199–201, 216–19, 232–33, 273; Blatt (n. 4 above), pp. 78–79, 110–19, 162–63, 166; D'Emilio and Freedman (n. 10 above), pp. 160–67; Lawrence B. Goodheart, *Abolitionist, Actuary, Atheist: Elizur Wright and the Reform Impulse* (Kent, OH, 1990), pp. 179–80, 183–92.

1890 for publishing the letter quoted at the beginning of this essay. At the age of sixty-one, he was sentenced to two years in prison.[70]

Even though, as Walt Whitman observed in 1882, the linguistic prudery of "good folks" found in "good print everywhere" seemed to "lingeringly pervade all modern literature, conversation and manners," it is important to remember that it did not go unchallenged.[71] It is equally important to note that this challenge provoked an intense reaction. Throughout the last three decades of the nineteenth century, the Free Lovers were confronted by a wide range of enemies. "Mobs from the streets, local and national 'government,' 'religious' intolerance, lascivious superstition, the Pharisees of 'morality' and the Pharisees of 'culture' have all in turn wrestled with the Free Love Idea," Ezra Heywood defiantly proclaimed, "and all have been thrown by it."[72]

## CONCLUSION

While Ezra Heywood's views on the Free Lovers' ability to circumvent the forces that sought to silence them were overly optimistic, the hardships they endured as a consequence of their battles with censorship were essential to shaping sexual discourse in the nineteenth century.[73] Unlike pornographers and abortionists, whose acts were clothed in secrecy until exposed by Comstock and his agents, the Free Lovers courted prosecution in order to uncover the duplicity of genteel society. "Called to public discourse on sex-issues" in response to the efforts of orthodox moralists "to suppress [the] investigation of [sexual] questions by invasive 'statutes,'" as Angela Heywood observed in an article tellingly entitled "Penis Literature," they met the forces of censorship head on and openly challenged their power to place controls on sexual discourse.[74] In consequence, the Free Lovers faced the full wrath of their censors and continually tested the limits of their authority. As one of their contemporaries argued, by publishing "words morally certain to provoke arrest," the Free Lovers expanded the margins of free speech

---

[70]Sears, pp. 178–81; Blatt, pp. 163–66.

[71]Walt Whitman, "A Memorandum at a Venture," *North American Review* 134 (1882): 546–47.

[72]Ezra Heywood, "The Free Love Movement," *The Word*, July 1879, p. 4.

[73]D'Emilio and Freedman, pp. 156–66; Gordon (n. 3 above), pp. 55–56, 96; William Leach, *True Love and Perfect Union: The Feminist Reform of Sex and Society* (New York, 1980), p. 82; Lewis Perry, *Childhood, Marriage, and Reform: Henry Clarke Wright, 1797–1870* (Chicago, 1980), pp. 254–55.

[74]Angela Heywood, "Penis Literature," p. 2.

and provided a buffer that "marked the limits of safety" in which more moderate critics of Victorian society and culture could operate.[75]

Moreover, by bringing to light the "wail of suffering" and the "cries of distress" of those ill served by Victorian sexual ideology, the Free Lovers showed many people that their discomfort was not unique and emboldened them to speak out against Victorian ideas and institutions.[76] By revealing the private experiences hidden by public discourse, they were able to criticize Victorian moralists for not living up to the very values they espoused. "Virtue, Chastity, Rectitude allwise suffer by *conventional falsehood;* so Gentlemen and Ladies, the sooner 'pure' hypocrisy ceases, the whole truth is out and afloat," Angela Heywood concluded, "the better for all Humankind."[77]

Even though Comstock's forays into a thriving sexual underworld that found expression in pulp fiction and the sensationalist press did uncover a literature that used words to incite untamed erotic desires, this language did not pose a threat to the logic and power of Victorian notions of sexual propriety. In fact, these two linguistic styles mutually reinforced one another. The Free Lovers exposed the connection between the language used by the "'upper' ten" and the "'lower' million" in order to eliminate the destructive consequences of the hypocrisy bred by the separation of public and private life and by the rift between words and things. To accomplish this, they liberated sexual discourse from the mincing words of prudes and from the sniggering vulgarity of back-street conversations and promoted a vocabulary that allowed men and women to regain control over their erotic and emotional lives. By rescuing the "proper English words from the slums and filth where the obscenists had placed them," declared one of Angela Heywood's supporters, the Free Lovers had successfully "scoured" them of their taint of vulgarity and transformed them into a force capable of creating the

---

[75]George E. Macdonald, *Fifty Years of Freethought,* 2 vols. (New York, 1929), 1:531.

[76]Stephen Pearl Andrews, "Correspondence," *Woodhull and Claflin's Weekly,* May 27, 1871, p. 6.

[77]Angela Heywood, "Penis Literature," p. 2. Victoria Woodhull, for example, published the details of the extramarital liaison between Henry Ward Beecher and Elizabeth Tilton because she felt it her duty to bring to light the discrepancy between the public pronouncements and the private indiscretions of this well-respected clergyman. Her goal in unmasking their affair, she claimed, was to eliminate the hatred, jealousy, debauchery, dishonesty, and immorality bred by a moral system at odds with itself. See Victoria Woodhull, *Complete and Detailed Version of the Beecher-Tilton Affair* (Washington, DC, 1872), p. 10, and "Naked Truth; or, The Situation Reviewed!" (1873), in Madeleine B. Stern, ed., *The Victoria Woodhull Reader* (Weston, MA, 1974), p. 11. For a fascinating discussion of the Beecher-Tilton scandal, see Altina L. Waller, *Reverend Beecher and Mrs. Tilton* (Amherst, MA, 1982).

physical and spiritual purity envisioned but never realized by Victorian moralists.[78]

While their willingness to shock "public sensibilities" by exploring issues previously "tabooed or held to be improper for public discussion" was the source of their strength as reformers, it was also responsible for the unsavory reputation the Free Lovers gained at the hands of conservative moralists.[79] Held up as symbols of depravity, they were relegated to the margins of social discourse, both in their own day and in the decades that followed. Zacariah Chafee, Jr., for example, while researching an entry on Ezra Heywood for the *Dictionary of American Biography*, noted in 1929 that because Heywood had "strayed so far from the paths of orthodoxy," no other biographical dictionary had been "willing to soil its pages with any mention of him." More than sixty years later, the radical ideas and activities of Free Lovers such as Moses Harman and Angela and Ezra Heywood still remain largely unexplored.[80] Nonetheless, in order to understand the battles that shaped the sexual culture of nineteenth-century America, it is necessary to restore their efforts to redefine the limits of public language to the historical record.

Seeking to understand the relationship between language, authority, and desire, the Free Lovers used words to bring subconscious ideas into the arena of conscious thought and rational control, celebrated their power to regenerate the individual and transform society, and explored the relationship between language and the construction of the gendered self, the social self, and, in ways that intertwined the two, the sexual self. Only by viewing these activities within the framework of the broader nineteenth-century concern with the power of words to shape consciousness and behavior—as well as with the powers that words represent and serve—can we fully understand the reasons why the Free Lovers risked so much to expand the discourse of desire.

[78]Angela Heywood, "Morality of Free Love," *The Word,* August 1876, p. 3; F. H. Marsh, "Correspondence," *The Word,* June 1890, p. 4.

[79]Woodhull, *Beecher-Tilton Affair,* p. 5, and "Naked Truth," p. 23.

[80]Zacariah Chafee, Jr., to H. L. Koopman, Esq., May 15, 1929, Heywood Papers, John Hay Library, Brown University. The Free Lovers occupied the fringes of even the most radical reform movements in the nineteenth century. Many of those who attacked fundamental aspects of Victorian society—feminists, moral purity crusaders, free thinkers, socialists, and anarchists, for example—struggled to disown the Free Lovers in their ranks and to disavow their pronouncements. In many respects, historians of these reform movements have carried on the tradition and relegated the Free Lovers to the periphery of historical activity in the nineteenth century. For recent efforts to counter this, see Sears (n. 4 above); Spurlock (n. 11 above); and Blatt (n. 4 above).

# A Debate on the American Home: The Antipolygamy Controversy, 1880–1890

JOAN SMYTH IVERSEN

*Department of History*
*State University of New York College at Oneonta*

F OR MORE THAN half a century, the Church of Jesus Christ of the Latter-day Saints (LDS), known as the Mormons, was engaged in a conflict with the larger United States society over its adherence to the religious tenet of patriarchal (plural) marriage, which encouraged leading Mormon men to marry more than one wife. After denying rumors of its practice, the church officially proclaimed its belief in 1852, scandalizing Gentile, that is, non-Mormon, America and eliciting a response from the newly formed Republican party, which condemned the practice of polygamy and slavery as the "twin relics of barbarism" in its 1856 platform. Following the Civil War, the polygamy issue became central to the Mormons' long and protracted struggle with the federal government to obtain statehood for the Utah territory.[1]

American outrage over Mormon polygamy often expressed itself in images of the Utah "Saints" as licentious and lustful Turks. The irony of these accusations was that Mormons were both proponents of Victorian propriety and sexually conservative. Noting this, scholars have described the Mormon practice as "puritan polygamy," observing that plural marriage was an attempt to restore the biblical patriarchal family and that, while the

[1] The classic study of the Utah struggle for statehood and its conflict with the federal government has been Gustive O. Larsen, *The Americanization of Utah for Statehood* (San Marino, CA, 1971). The most recent monograph dealing with this topic is Edward Leo Lyman, *Political Deliverance: The Mormon Quest for Utah Statehood* (Urbana, IL, 1986). Whereas Mormon historians once held that polygamy was only a diversionary issue raised by anti-Mormons who really opposed the power of the LDS church, recent interpretations by Lyman and historian Jan Shipps have found the polygamy issue to be critical to the anti-Mormon struggles. Note that while this marital practice is correctly termed "polygyny," contemporaries referred to it as "polygamy," and that term will be used in this article.

This essay originally appeared in the *Journal of the History of Sexuality* 1991, vol. 1, no. 4.

rest of nineteenth-century America was in transition toward the ideal of companionate marriage, Mormons held to the earlier notion of sex primarily for the purpose of procreation.[2] The principle of plural marriage was rooted in the theology of the LDS church, which held both that souls were awaiting procreation in order to find salvation and that marriages would endure in the afterlife. An upright Saint could anticipate experiencing heaven surrounded by his wives and children. A Mormon woman earned her place in the afterlife by fulfilling her noble mission to propagate, providing life for waiting souls. Consequently, religious conviction provided the primary motivation for the practice, although in the ensuing debate over polygamy, as we shall see, Mormons justified the practice with many other arguments.

Despite a continuing historical interest in Mormon polygamy there is still a great deal unknown.[3] The difficulty is that the practice of polygamy was undertaken mostly while under attack by the larger society, at times in Utah, under surveillance by federal marshals. For some periods, plural wives were forced to take to an "underground" society to hide pregnancy. Understandably, church leaders would not disclose marital records. Thus, in the study of Mormon polygamy it is difficult to ascertain the actual numbers of polygamists. Additionally, the absence of stable, consistent patterns of plural living make generalization difficult.

During the height of the antipolygamy controversy estimates of the actual number of Mormons practicing polygamy varied from 3 percent to 80 percent. The first objective studies estimated that 12.6 percent of Mormon males actually practiced polygamy. Later scholars revised this estimate to 8.8 percent.[4] However, very recent scholarship indicates that these per-

---

[2]This description is quoted in Klaus J. Hansen, "Mormon Sexuality and American Culture," *Dialogue: A Journal of Mormon Thought* 10 (Autumn 1976): 51; John D. D'Emilio and Estelle B. Freedman, *Intimate Matters: A History of Sexuality in America* (New York, 1988), pp. 117–18.

[3]For many years the major source for the study of polygamy was the popularized account by Kimball Young, *Isn't One Wife Enough?* (New York, 1954; reprint, Westport, CT, 1970), which was based upon interviews collected in the 1930s but omitted formal documentation. A very important recent study, Jessie L. Embry, *Mormon Polygamous Families: Life in the Principle,* Publications in Mormon Studies, vol. 1 (Salt Lake City, UT, 1987), has attempted a more empirical survey by utilizing the Kimball Young interviews as well as new interviews with descendants of plural homes conducted by the Charles Redd Center for Western Studies at Brigham Young University. Social historians have also studied Mormon polygamy in the context of other utopian experiments of the time, for instance, Oneida and the Shakers. The two major works of this genre have been Lawrence Foster, *Religion and Sexuality: Three American Communal Experiments of the Nineteenth Century* (New York, 1981); and Louis J. Kern, *An Ordered Love: Sex Roles and Sexuality in Victorian Utopias* (Chapel Hill, NC, 1981). Foster has made greater use of primary source material in LDS archives, while Kern has attempted a more multidisciplinary analysis.

[4]James E. Smith and Phillip R. Kunz, "Polygyny and Fertility in Nineteenth-Century America," *Population Studies* 30 (1976): 470–71.

centages are underestimates. Working closely with census data for specific localities, counting children from plural homes and widows, researchers now estimate that in some localities as many as 50 percent or more of the population would have been involved in polygamy.[5]

However, the myth that Mormon men collected harems has been dispelled. Studies indicate that 60 percent of the Mormon male polygamists married only one plural wife. When choosing a plural wife, a man tended to select a woman who was the age that his first wife had been at the time of their marriage, even though he was by then ten to thirty years older. This pattern and its restraints caused Sir Richard Burton, noted English traveler, to observe upon visiting Utah that what one found was not a harem but rather what appeared like a man living with his wife and mother.[6]

Mormon polygamy never operated freely enough to establish definite rules or institutions. There were myriad arrangements and adjustments, often varying over life spans. But, in reality, the Mormons tended to follow the pattern of monogamy in the organization and dynamics of family living.[7] Studies reveal that perhaps 60 percent of the plural wives had separate residences at some point in the marriage, with husbands visiting each wife at regular intervals. There is no evidence that polygamy was concentrated more in urban or rural areas. A high incidence of men actually married sisters, perhaps hoping to ensure ease of adjustments. And, most important, it should be noted that Utah made divorce more available than other states.[8]

Anthropologically, Mormon polygamy can be seen as serving the functions of linking the families of church elites through the sharing of women, controlling the sexuality of women, and ensuring the loyalty of group members.[9] For Mormons, however, the practice was tied, first and foremost, to religious loyalty. There is ample evidence that men were asked by church leaders to take additional wives, and clearly a preponderance of church leaders were polygamists. Loyalty also meant that monogamous

[5]Lowell "Ben" Bennion, "The Incidence of Mormon Polygamy in 1880: 'Dixie' versus Davis Stake," *Journal of Mormon History* 11 (1984): 27–42, finds larger towns in Utah's southern region with as much as 40 percent of the population practicing polygamy. A similar study with a lucid explanation of the difficulties in arriving at the demographics of polygamy is Larry Logue, "A Time of Marriage: Monogamy and Polygamy in a Utah Town," *Journal of Mormon History* 11 (1984): 3–26.

[6]Embry, p. 34; Burton is quoted in James L. Clayton, "The Supreme Court, Polygamy and the Enforcement of Morals in Nineteenth-Century America: An Analysis of Reynolds v. United States," *Dialogue: A Journal of Mormon Thought* 12 (Winter 1979): 52.

[7]James Edward Hulett, Jr., "The Sociological and Social Psychological Aspects of the Mormon Polygamous Family" (Ph.D. diss., University of Wisconsin—Madison, 1939), p. 10; Vicky Burgess Olson, "Family Structures and Dynamics in Early Utah Mormon Families, 1847–1885" (Ph.D. diss., Northwestern University, 1975), p. 59.

[8]Embry, pp. 40, 149; Foster, pp. 399–400.

[9]Kern, pp. 153 ff.

Mormons did not openly speak against plural marriage. In fact, belief in the institution became a touchstone of loyalty to one's religion, especially as the antipolygamy crusade intensified.[10]

Although there had been attempts to legislate against Mormon polygamy before 1879, when the antipolygamy crusade originated, this legislation had not been rigorously enforced, and the Mormons were convinced it violated constitutional guarantees of freedom of religion. They instigated a test case but were disappointed when Chief Justice Waite ruled in that case, *Reynolds v. United States,* that Mormon polygamy was disruptive of peace and good order, threatening the foundations of the country. In a decision that articulated dominant contemporary discourse, Waite explained that society was founded upon marriage, and the practice and form of that institution was critical to the state. Further, democracy rested upon monogamy, whereas polygamy was based upon patriarchy, and its toleration would lead to despotism and the destruction of our Republic.[11]

The same year as the *Reynolds* decision, events in Salt Lake City led to a mass meeting of antipolygamous women who sent a petition to Lucy Hayes, wife of the president, and to Congress, asking to be delivered from the evils of polygamy and the power of the LDS church. This meeting had been organized by the newly formed Anti-Polygamy Society, which in April 1880 began publication of a national newspaper, the *Anti-Polygamy Standard.*[12]

The women of the Anti-Polygamy Society of Salt Lake City wasted no time in reaching out to the rest of the country. Their petition to Lucy Hayes called upon "the Christian women of the United States" to help them, and the first issue of their paper printed an appeal from Harriet Beecher Stowe to the "Women of America."[13] *Anti-Polygamy Standard* editor Jennie Froiseth went on a lecture tour east, enlisting women in Brooklyn and New England to the cause.[14] By August 1880 the women had changed their name to the Woman's National Anti-Polygamy Society and included directions in their paper for women to organize chapters.

The antipolygamy women and their congressional allies had immediate victories. They were successful in unseating George Q. Cannon, polygamist, as Utah's territorial representative to Congress in 1882. The culmination of their efforts came with the passage, in the same year, of the Edmunds Bill which criminalized polygamy and established the Utah

[10]Leonard Arrington and Davis Bitton, *The Mormon Experience: A History of the Latter-day Saints* (New York, 1979), pp. 199–200; Stanley S. Ivins, "Notes on Mormon Polygamy," *Western Humanities Review* 10 (1956): 232.

[11]Clayton, p. 51.

[12]Barbara Hayward, "Utah's Anti-Polygamy Society, 1878–1884" (M.A. thesis, Brigham Young University, 1980), pp. 14–21.

[13]Harriet Beecher Stowe, *The Anti-Polygamy Standard* 1 (April 1880): 1.

[14]*Journal History* (LDS church) (November 10, 1880), p. 9.

Commission to enforce federal rulings in the territory. Since plural marriage could be hidden from civil marriage records, the law provided for prosecution for "unlawful cohabitation." Federal marshals were given the authority to hunt down polygamists and to force wives and children to testify. The harassment of Mormon families that followed only increased the defiance and resistance of the polygamous Saints, and hundreds of Mormon men were sent to the penitentiary as "cohabs." The campaign was not without some humorous moments. When asked, on a witness stand, to explain why her alleged husband was visiting each week if not to cohabit, a plural wife responded that he came to "wind the clock."[15]

In retrospect, the antipolygamy women of Salt Lake City had clearly launched a woman's crusade. Lucy Hayes became president of the Woman's Home Missionary Society of the Methodist Episcopal Church, founded in 1880, declaring as part of its mission the aid of "suffering sisters in Utah."[16] By 1883 this society elected Angie Newman of Nebraska secretary of its newly formed Mormon Bureau. She worked with the antipolygamy women of Salt Lake City to set up the Industrial Christian Home for the rescue of polygamous wives. This effort, described in a recent study, was part of a larger effort for home rescue by Protestant women in the American West that reflected a covert struggle to increase the power of female moral authority in nineteenth-century America and the churches.[17] Antipolygamy women reached out to the national temperance women, enlisting the help of Frances Willard to write the introduction to Jennie Froiseth's book, *The Women of Mormonism* (1882), which published in book format some of the stories, "heart histories," of the victims of polygamy that had appeared in the *Anti-Polygamy Standard*.

This woman's crusade, however, was on a collision course with the larger issue of woman suffrage in the country because of the ironic fact that the Mormon women were suffragists. Utah women had been granted the vote as early as 1870 by the Mormon-dominated legislature and, nine years later, had affiliated themselves with the National Woman Suffrage Association (NWSA) under the leadership of Susan B. Anthony and Elizabeth Cady Stanton.[18]

[15]William McKay to Attorney General Benjamin Brewster, March 23, 1885, box 93, Department of Justice Files, DOJ 1885, National Archives, Washington, DC.

[16]"Memorial of the Woman's Home Missionary Society to the General Conference of the Methodist Episcopal Church" (Philadelphia, May 1, 1884).

[17]Peggy Ann Pascoe, "The Search for Female Moral Authority: Protestant Women and Rescue Homes in the American West, 1874–1939" (Ph.D. diss., Stanford University, 1986), p. 123.

[18]Utah woman suffrage is explained in Beverly Beeton, *Women Vote in the West: The Woman Suffrage Movement, 1869–1896* (New York, 1986); and Thomas G. Alexander, "An Experiment in Progressive Legislation: The Granting of Woman Suffrage in Utah in 1870," *Utah Historical Quarterly* 38 (Winter 1970): 20–30.

This Mormon-suffrage alliance had exacerbated controversies within the suffrage ranks, split since 1869 into rival organizations—the NWSA (Anthony and Stanton) and the American Woman Suffrage Association (AWSA) (Lucy Stone and Henry Blackwell). When debate in Congress suggested removing the vote from the Utah women, the NWSA invited the Mormon women to attend their 1879 Washington, D.C., convention. Lucy Stone was scandalized.[19] She printed an article in her newspaper, the *Woman's Journal,* criticizing the women of the NWSA for affiliating with the polygamous women, which elicited an angry response by Elizabeth Cady Stanton and Matilda Joslyn Gage in the *National Citizen and Ballot Box.*

Anthony and Stanton had already demonstrated that their organization was more willing to take on controversial issues such as divorce, avoided by the AWSA, which generally adhered to a more "conservative," suffrage-only platform. Moreover, Anthony was anxious to make her association as national as its name. She proudly referred, in a letter to Harriet Robinson, to "all our friends in the West," adding, "You see Mrs. Stanton and I have *personally helped* the women all over the west . . . they know and believe in us."[20]

Not surprisingly, the antipolygamy women initially found a more sympathetic response in the pages of the *Woman's Journal* since leading women of the AWSA, such as Harriet B. Stowe and Julia Ward Howe, had openly aligned themselves with the antipolygamy movement. Soon the antipolygamy women addressed their appeal to all the suffragists of America in an "Open Letter," explaining that they were in favor of the "general principle of woman suffrage . . . [but] suffrage, as it exists in Utah, is an entirely different matter from what the suffragists in the East are working for."[21] Antipolygamy women soon received recognition from suffrage women. By 1883, Sarah A. Cooke, officer of the National Anti-Polygamy Society and former Mormon, was acknowledged as an honorary vice president for Utah in the NWSA. Within two years, two other antipolygamy leaders, Jennie Froiseth and Cornelia Paddock, held office in the organization as well.[22]

The stage was now set for what was to be a struggle throughout the de-

---

[19]Lucy Stone to Harriet Hanson Robinson, March 4, 1879, Robinson-Shattuck Papers, Schlesinger Library, Radcliffe College (microfilm); Joan Iversen, "The Mormon-Suffrage Relationship: Personal and Political Quandaries," *Frontiers: A Journal of Women's Studies* 11 (Fall 1990): 8–16 is a more detailed study of the Mormon-suffrage alliance.

[20]Susan B. Anthony to Harriet Hanson Robinson, n.d. (?December 1882), Robinson-Shattuck Papers; italics in the original quotation.

[21]"Open Letter to the Suffragists of the United States," *Anti-Polygamy Standard* 3 (April 1882): 1; "Polygamy and Woman Suffrage," *Anti-Polygamy Standard* 1 (June 1880): 20.

[22]"Scrapbooks," Robinson-Shattuck Papers.

cade, played out in the suffrage movement as well, as forces in Congress worked to eradicate polygamy, the power of the LDS church, and Utah woman suffrage. In 1887 the Edmunds-Tucker Act disenfranchised all the women of Utah.

Suffragists could not support any action that took the vote from any group of women. But the antipolygamy movement had enjoined American women to enter a struggle to end a system associated with the degradation of woman. The problem was that the suffrage alliance with Mormon women presented an ideological dilemma. How could one argue for the vote as a vehicle to advance the status of woman, when these Mormon women had not used the ballot to cast off a marital system seen by all as backward and degrading to their sex? Even more basic to the controversy was the underlying, unstated question—which road best led to the advancement of woman, pursuit of status and moral authority in the home or insistence upon complete political equality?

Emerging from this interaction of antipolygamy with the question of Mormon woman suffrage came an interesting clash of views—a three-cornered debate over the position of woman and the American home, advanced by the antipolygamy movement, Mormon women, and the suffrage allies of the Mormon women. From its inception, the outrage toward Mormon polygamy had spawned a popular literature, well within the mainstream of nineteenth-century popular fiction. The Mormons provided "a new set of exotic themes" to be presented as fact with such "stock characters as the brutal husband, the suffering wife, and the innocent child."[23] Blameless heroines, duped by evil Mormon elders, were subjected to various kinds of humiliation and torture. Leave aside the Mormon setting of most of these books, and one finds the familiar plots of duplicity, mesmerism, jeopardized virtue, and flight. Similar stories were circulated about other groups that contemporary America saw as subversive, such as Catholics and Masons. Scholars have noted the proto-pornographic elements of this literature and speculated on what it revealed about Victorian readers' sexual anxieties. Polygamy was especially offensive because it put no restraints on men's sexual impulses.[24] Women's historians have demonstrated that the efforts of nineteenth-century women to control male sexuality and to safeguard the family were vital to the struggle for the protection of women. While antipolygamy attacks might appear at first to be in defense of the status quo and conservative Victorian family values, a closer

[23]Karen Lynn, "Sensational Virtue: Nineteenth-Century Mormon Fiction and American Popular Taste," *Dialogue: A Journal of Mormon Thought* 14 (Autumn 1981): 102.

[24]David Brion Davis, "Some Themes of Counter-Subversion: An Analysis of Anti-Masonic, Anti-Catholic, and Anti-Mormon Literature," *Mississippi Valley Historical Review* 47 (September 1960): 205–24; Charles A. Cannon, "The Awesome Power of Sex: The Polemical Campaign against Mormon Polygamy," *Pacific Historical Review* 43 (February 1974): 82.

glance reveals an underlying battle, a "domestic politics" to advance woman's power.[25]

The attack on polygamy borrowed heavily from the polemical tactics used in the debate over slavery, which had linked that institution with a threat to the home. It was no accident that Harriet Beecher Stowe endorsed the first issue of the *Anti-Polygamy Standard,* urging American women to "free her sisters from this degrading bondage." Stowe had very effectively employed the tactics of "domestic politics" in the cause of abolition and now turned to polygamy as her field of battle.[26]

The writings of the antipolygamy women employed the melodrama of contemporary popular fiction. However, underlying these melodramatic trappings, antipolygamy tracts reveal a rhetorical consistency, attesting to a genuine struggle—moral reform women's search for power and authority in home and nation. While the stories are placed in the familiar context of wronged, true womanhood, the struggle is for the power of woman, and the message sounds an alarm to the nation that the very Republic is in jeopardy from polygamy, not simply because the home is threatened but because of woman's position in it. As Angie Newman declared to Congress: "Homes are the rock on which this Republic is built. Homes where one woman reigns as queen sitting upon a throne whose honor knows neither compromise nor division."[27]

Newman's statement is a refrain of Chief Justice Waite's decision in the *Reynolds* case, echoing the truism that the Republic rested upon the monogamous home. But Newman carried the argument further, defining this home in terms of the position of woman in the home. We see here the strategy of the moral reform women—utilizing the discourse to argue that the strength of the nation rests upon a monogamy that restricts male power while not directly attacking male power. Rather, they identify the enemy of the ideal American home as Mormon patriarchy—an alien notion that contains "elements of the harem idea."[28] Thus, the antipolygamy women used the "Orientalist" threat and the dominant view of the national superiority

[25]The seminal articles that signaled the interpretation of Victorian propriety as part of a struggle for woman's status were Daniel Scott Smith, "Family Limitation, Sexual Control, and Domestic Feminism in Victorian America," *Feminist Studies* 1 (1973): 40–57; and Nancy F. Cott, "Passionless: An Interpretation of Victorian Sexual Ideology, 1790–1850," *Signs* 4 (1978): 219–36.

[26]Gillian Brown, "Getting in the Kitchen with Dinah: Domestic Politics in Uncle Tom's Cabin," *American Quarterly* 36 (1984): 512.

[27]Jeannette H. Ferry, "The Industrial Christian Home," Utah Territorial Papers, National Archives, Washington, DC (microfilm), p. 13.

[28]Jesse H. Jones, "The Harem Idea," *Woman's Journal* 2 (May 1871): 139; Waite had also compared Mormon polygamy to the Indian practice of suttee. Clayton (n. 6 above), p. 52.

of the American home to garner support for woman's moral authority in that home.[29]

While the antipolygamy writing often returned to this refrain of polygamy as alien, Asiatic, and un-American, it also played on other Victorian fears. A common theme of this literature was that of true womanhood betrayed, portraying woman as victim. Since the established belief held that woman was morally superior to man, Mormon polygamous women must be explained as the "helpless victims of the male priesthood."[30] Stories told of young women deceived about the actual truth of polygamy until they arrived in Utah. Some, as plural wives, were subjected to dreadful treatment by the first wife—one is described as having been left alone in a garret to give birth. The first wives, often portrayed as martyrs, deteriorate in character from the travails of polygamy, losing delicacy and refinement.[31] The literature decried the economic exploitation of polygamous wives, and pictorial representations of the Mormon women often used the imagery of slavery—a husband wielding a whip or a wife shown as "all-purpose slave."[32]

These horror stories carried a subliminal warning to the "gentle reader"—she too was in jeopardy from the unchecked Mormon lust. One anti-Mormon lecturer stressed that all women in Mormon country had to be on guard and told of a Mormon's proposal to her to become his plural wife.[33] The same woman reported being propagandized by the prominent Mormon Ruth Fox. Mormon women, like Fox, who advocated polygamy presented a special problem for antipolygamy crusaders, who viewed the polygamous woman as victim, and thus had to be explained as "fanatics and hypocrites"—"the most degraded of all the women of Mormonism."[34] Participating as they did in this practice, they became "coarse and unrefined." This denigration was so widely accepted that one of the leading Mormon women, on a lecture trip east, reported a woman's observation to her that she didn't "look degraded."[35]

Another important antipolygamy contention was that there were de-

[29]I am indebted to Dr. Kathleen O'Mara for pointing me to the significance of this aspect of antipolygamy discourse as it is described in the important work of Edward W. Said, *Orientalism* (New York, 1978).

[30]Gail Farr Casterline, "'In the Toils' or 'Onward for Zion': Images of the Mormon Women" (M.A. thesis, Utah State University, 1974), p. 3.

[31]Jennie A. Froiseth, *Women of Mormonism* (Detroit, 1882), pp. 90–98, 74–89.

[32]Davis Bitton and Gary L. Bunker, "Double Jeopardy: Visual Images of Mormon Women to 1914," *Utah Historical Quarterly* 46 (1978): 189–90.

[33]Lulu Loveland Shepard, "Notebook, 1917–21," Historical Department of LDS church, Salt Lake City, UT.

[34]Froiseth, p. 131.

[35]"Romania Pratt Letter," *Woman's Exponent* 10 (March 1882): 146.

leterious effects on progeny of plural homes. A popular notion of genetics held that moral depravity led to inherited physical degeneracy. Angie Newman reported to Congress that there was "a physical deterioration" observable in the children of polygamy as well as mental inferiority. "They do not begin to measure up to the standard of American children of the same age."[36] Jennie Froiseth explained the degeneracy of Mormon youth as caused by the unfortunate prenatal influence of polygamy, describing one boy who became a sadistic "desperado" because his father had entered polygamy when his mother was pregnant. In general, she stated, children developed observably "depraved tastes" and lost the innocence of childhood from being raised in polygamous homes.[37]

It is interesting that many illustrations in the antipolygamy literature were provided by formerly polygamous women. One of the founders of the Anti-Polygamy Society in Salt Lake City was Sarah Cooke, an apostate of the LDS church. Although polygamy was not the original cause for the nineteenth-century "Goodbeite" schism (a substantial split in the church membership), some of these women became antipolygamy members. Cornelia Paddock described the membership of the Anti-Polygamy Society as only one-third Gentiles, that is, non-Mormons. These prominent non-Mormons came from the ranks of the mine owners, Protestant clergy, and the army post in Utah. Paddock also claimed that many of the characters in her best-selling antipolygamy novel, *The Fate of Madame La Tour,* were personal friends, some of whom she named.[38] There is a need for research uncovering the extent of membership of former LDS members in antipolygamy ranks as well as an assessment of the antipolygamy sentiment among the monogamous Mormons of the period. Perhaps these groups have been neglected by historians because of the more accessible record left by prominent polygamous Mormon women, who defied contemporary expectations and argued articulately for the practice of plural marriage.

Elite Mormon women, often reflecting the same values as their critics, offered a strong defense of polygamy. Emmeline B. Wells, plural wife and editor of the first woman's newspaper in the West, the *Woman's Exponent,* was an outspoken defender of polygamy from her earliest associations with

---

[36]Lester E. Bush, Jr., "Mormon 'Physiology,' 1850–1875," *Bulletin of the History of Medicine* 56 (1982): 218–39; Hearing on Industrial Home Petition, Committee on Education and Labor, U.S. Senate, May 7, 1886, Utah Territorial Papers, National Archives, Washington, DC (microfilm).

[37]Froiseth, pp. 196, 193.

[38]Cornelia Paddock to Thomas Gregg, March 3, 1882, Miscellaneous Mormon Documents, Chicago Historical Society (microfilm, Utah Historical Society); a very important study showing the influence of one of these apostate women is Richard Van Wagoner, "Sarah Pratt: The Shaping of an Apostate," *Dialogue: A Journal of Mormon Thought* 19 (Summer 1986): 69–99.

the suffrage leadership. This "degraded" plural wife justified polygamy in the same terms of true womanhood offered by the antipolygamy women, as she and other Mormon women shared the contemporary belief of woman's moral superiority. Writing to the NWSA in 1879, Wells predicted that "woman" would become "the power that will work out and solve the problems which now vex the people of the nation" and that men would come to acknowledge the "moral influence of woman in politics."[39]

Wells, a devout Saint, saw her woman's rights in the context of her religion—characterized by millennial promise. Mormons believed in both the Father and the Mother godhead. Wells further believed that her church offered institutional support for the expansion of woman's sphere because of the recorded promise of Joseph Smith, the founder of the church, that he would "turn the key" for Mormon women to empower them for further development.[40] Wells's faith in Smith's promise is reflected in her earliest published letter to the national suffragists, where she explains that Utah woman suffrage will provide the expanded responsibilities and knowledge to develop woman's character.[41]

Mormon women did not see the ballot as a weapon to overthrow polygamy; indeed, they saw it as inextricably bound to the defense and mission of their church. The paradox was noted at the time: "But even more staggering is the fact that Mormon women base their indignation against their persecuting saviours on women's rights, the very ground upon which their saviours have based their crusade."[42]

Fundamental to the Mormon woman's adherence to polygamy was her belief in its divine origin. The practice seemed suited to the verities of human nature, that is, man's sexual proclivities and woman's moral superiority. Woman, stated Susa Y. Gates, Mormon leader Brigham Young's daughter, is "the purer, the better part of humanity."[43] Since there were not enough good men for women to marry, monogamy would deny woman her sacred right to motherhood. Gates regarded motherhood in a visionary and romantic way. She was, for example, very impressed with a cover illustration on Charlotte Perkins Gilman's magazine, the *Forerunner*, which showed mother and baby supporting the earth.[44]

[39]"Emmeline B. Wells Letter," *National Citizen and Ballot Box* 4 (July 1879): 6.

[40]Jill Mulvay Derr, "Woman's Place in Brigham Young's World," *Brigham Young University Studies* 18 (1978): 379; Carol Cornwall Madsen, "A Mormon Woman in Victorian America" (Ph.D. diss., University of Utah, 1985), pp. 173–74.

[41]"Letter from Emmeline B. Wells," *National Citizen and Ballot Box* 3 (August 1878): 6.

[42]Quoted in Larsen (n. 1 above), p. 57.

[43]Susa Young Gates, "Family Life among the Mormons," *North American Review* (March 1980), p. 348.

[44]Susa Young Gates, "Woman in History," Historical Department of LDS church, Salt Lake City, UT, typescript (microfilm, Utah Historical Society).

Men are not by nature monogamous, Mormon women argued. Look at the Gentile world, where one found infanticide, prostitution, and adultery because of the differences in male/female nature. On the other hand, the "plural order" offered "delicacy, modesty and refinement."[45] These latter claims were euphemisms for the fact that intercourse was forbidden during pregnancy and lactation.

The innate logic of polygamy, Mormons often stated, could be demonstrated by the hypocrisy and evils seen in the larger society. A Mormon cleaning woman expressed this view to one of the men of the Utah Commission who had come to enforce antipolygamy laws, when she told members of the commission that they "lived in polygamy but they won't own up to it and marry the women."[46] Of course, underlying this reasoning lay the issue that most divided the defenders of Mormon polygamy from antipolygamy women—acceptance of the double sexual standard. Both groups of women agreed that women were the "potential victims of male sexuality" and that control of that sexuality was a woman's issue. But for Mormon women the answer was the practice of plural marriage, not insistence upon a single sexual standard. In short, they believed that "polygamy meant male responsibility for the consequences of male sexuality."[47]

Mormon women such as Emmeline Wells really hoped, in their initial contacts with women's rights leaders, that they could advocate plural marriage within the context of women's rights. As a male Mormon historian expressed the hope, "The women of Mormondom, and the women of America, have a common cause, in this all-vital marriage question, which is destined to receive some very decided and peculiar solution before the end of the century."[48]

For these and other reasons, Mormon women saw themselves as women's rights women. The articles in the *Woman's Exponent* reported the activities of women's rights leaders, praised coeducation and independence for women, and recorded the advancement of women. The magazine's masthead read "The Rights of the Women of Zion, and the Rights of Women of All Nations." Utah was noteworthy in its early education of women; the University of Deseret in Salt Lake City had been coeducational from its founding in 1850. The Saints also opened careers to women, and Mormons were among the first of the country's women doctors.

[45]Helen Mar Whitney, *Why We Practice Plural Marriage* (Salt Lake City, UT, 1884), pp. 50–51, 25–29.

[46]Florence Violet Miles Sterling interview, Kimball Young Collection, Huntington Library, San Marino, CA, typescript.

[47]Julie Dunfey, "'Living the Principle' of Plural Marriage: Mormon Women, Utopia, and Female Sexuality in the Nineteenth Century," *Feminist Studies* 10 (1984): 530.

[48]Edward W. Tullidge, *The Women of Mormondom* (New York, 1877; reprint, Salt Lake City, UT, 1975), p. 515.

Moreover, Mormon women related these achievements to the practice of polygamy. They insisted, in what was especially difficult for critics to grasp, that their marital system was key to their liberation.[49] While some of this can be dismissed as defensiveness under attack, there is some validity to their position. Although the institution of polygamy was based upon a patriarchal order, the realities of the system were often quite different. The separate households established for plural wives, the absence of husbands, and the economic needs of the larger families created conditions that fostered independence. Thus, Mormon women could and did argue that polygamy "freed" them to develop individually.[50]

Perhaps because of their Mormon confidence in having the practice of polygamy accepted by contemporary America, the Mormon women were dismayed as the antipolygamy crusade increased in vehemence. Emmeline Wells observed the "prejudice and bitterness" of the outside world and bitterly asked, "If there is so much certitude on the side of monogamy . . . then why trouble about the matter [polygamy] at all?"[51]

Although elite Mormon women thought of themselves as united with the cause of women's rights, they did not see themselves in conflict with male authority or their church. Emmeline Wells went to suffrage meetings with the permission and blessing of church leaders and saw women's rights as part of her identification as a devoted Mormon. It is interesting to note that the year before the Mormon women went to the Washington convention of the NWSA, the Mormon-published *Deseret Evening News* criticized the prospectus of the organization's newspaper, the *National Citizen and Ballot Box*, for stating as one of its principal aims "to make those women discontented who are now content."[52]

The Mormon women as members of the suffrage associations did not share all of the values of their suffrage allies, many of whom defended them during the antipolygamy crusade. These differences emerge as one examines the position of the suffrage allies in the antipolygamy debate.

Over the years, a group of suffrage leaders consistently supported the Mormon women. Susan B. Anthony, Lillie Devereaux Blake, Clara Colby, Matilda Joslyn Gage, Belva Lockwood, Mrs. Saxon, Sara Spencer, and Elizabeth Cady Stanton were all, in various ways, supportive of the Mormon-suffrage alliance. While no prominent suffrage women supported disfranchising the women of Utah, these women, all early members of the

---

[49]Judith Rasmussen Dushku, "Feminists," in *Mormon Sisters,* ed. Claudia L. Bushman (Cambridge, MA, 1976), p. 193.

[50]Marybeth Raynes, "Mormon Marriages in an American Context," in *Sisters in Spirit,* ed. Maureen Ursenbach Beecher and Lavina Fielding Anderson (Urbana, IL, 1987), pp. 233–36; Joan Iversen, "Feminist Implications of Mormon Polygyny," *Feminist Studies* 10 (1984): 505–23.

[51]Emmeline B. Wells, "Home Again," *Woman's Exponent* 15 (June 1886): 4.

[52]"Prospectus," *National Citizen and Ballot Box* 2 (June 1878): 8.

NWSA, did more. Some accompanied the Mormon women when they lobbied in Washington to stop anti-Mormon legislation.[53] None of these suffragists, obviously, advocated the practice of polygamy. However, in defending the Mormon-suffrage alliance, these allies defied contemporary conventionality, sometimes adding a different perspective to the anti-polygamy debate.

Elizabeth Cady Stanton's defense of the Mormon-suffrage alliance was rooted in her devotion to a wide and tolerant platform for woman's rights and to her commitment to the secularization of American culture. These principles and, more important, Stanton's vision of the equality of the sexes and the future restructuring of marriage and family shaped her response to the Mormon debate.

Stanton, alone of her contemporaries, actually discussed polygamy with a large audience of Mormon women. She and Anthony visited Salt Lake City shortly after the women of Utah were granted the vote. Although they had been invited by a schismatic group, they had received an invitation as well from Brigham Young to speak to the Mormon women. Stanton grasped this opportunity, intending "to say all we had to say at the first session," as both she and Anthony did not believe that the Mormon women would be allowed back again.[54] After describing her views about the history of marriage, the early matriarchate, and the origins of monogamy, she engaged in a dialogue with the women. She approved the sexual strictures of polygamy described by the Mormon women that protected the "sacredness of motherhood." But, she noted, they had agreed with her that women "were still far from having reached the ideal position . . . in marriage."[55]

Her tolerance for some of the Mormon women's views reflected the fact that Stanton, unlike the antipolygamy women, was not horrified or outraged by the "immorality" of polygamy or its "degradation of woman." Her historical perspective on marriage, that monogamy had only come to civilization through pagan Rome, and her rejection of the conservative acceptance of the "divine truth" of religion, made her more accepting of the differing customs of the Mormons, though she disapproved of polygamy. Stanton's opposition to polygamy was matched by her criticism of conventional marriage. She did not see the Mormon woman as any more deluded than any woman who accepted the biblical view of woman's inferiority and patriarchal marriage. The Mormon women, adhering to polygamy, were victims of "religious delusion," but then again, all women had to recognize

---

[53]"Letter from Miss Grundy," *National Citizen and Ballot Box* 3 (January 1879): 7.

[54]Theodore Stanton and Harriot Stanton Blatch, *Elizabeth Cady Stanton: As Revealed in Her Letters, Diary and Reminiscences* (1922; reprint, New York, 1969), 2:132–33.

[55]Elizabeth Cady Stanton, *Eighty Years and More: Reminiscences, 1815–1897* (1898; reprint, New York, 1969), pp. 283–85.

that governments and religions were "human inventions."[56] Thus, Stanton's condemnation of polygamy differed from that of the antipolygamy reformers.

While she shared the antipolygamy women's and Mormon women's view that woman was morally superior, Stanton differed from both groups in her critique of contemporary marriage, which she derogatorily labeled "the Man Marriage." Marriage, in its present state, she viewed as unsatisfactory—a one-sided, distorted institution, based upon the subjugation of woman. Only when woman achieved full equality, independence, and self-respect and the conditions of "moral health existed" would ideal marriage be possible. In this companionate marriage of equals, both partners would continue to grow, develop, and share interests.[57] For Stanton, ideal marriage could only come with the achievement of woman's full equality.

While she believed that ideal marriage would be monogamous, Stanton did not believe this could be achieved until society accepted a single sexual standard of behavior. Contemporary marriage did not meet this standard, and she labeled it, also, as polygamy—the "well known form of marriage of a man with many mistresses." "How," she asked, "can we have a monogamic relation with only one party true to its requirements?"[58] In contrast to the antipolygamy women and the Mormon women, Stanton directly challenged the unequal power relations and double sexual standard of the era. The ideal American home could not be realized, she believed, until women were lifted from all religious superstition and social revolution had transformed the very foundations of society.

From this evolutionary perspective, Stanton was consistently supportive of the Mormon women. She defended the Mormon women's affiliation with the NWSA, saying that when "any class of women suffer whether in the home, the Church, the Courts . . . a voice in their behalf should be heard in our conventions."[59] Although she was out of the country during the height of the antipolygamy crusade, Stanton later expressed her disapproval of the federal enforcement of the antipolygamy laws and its interference with Mormon religious freedom. She felt about this crusade as she did about congressional efforts to restrict easy divorce laws—that legislation on marriage and divorce should not occur until woman had a voice in government.[60]

[56]Ibid., p. 285.

[57]Elizabeth Cady Stanton, "The Man Marriage," *Revolution* (April 8, 1869), pp. 217–18, Elizabeth Cady Stanton Papers, Library of Congress, Washington, DC (microfilm).

[58]Elizabeth Cady Stanton, "Home Life," August 1878, Stanton Papers.

[59]Elizabeth Cady Stanton, "Change Is the Law of Progress," February 23, 1890, Stanton Papers.

[60]Stanton, *Eighty Years and More,* p. 285, and "Change Is the Law of Progress."

Stanton saw the struggle for woman's rights as primary. She urged woman's identification with her sex and regarded the early critics of the Mormon-suffrage alliance as male identified. Unlike the antipolygamy women and Mormon women, Stanton directly confronted male power and established religion. While these two groups argued their differing views of home and marriage, Stanton concluded that "until men and women view each other as equals . . . marriage will be in most cases, a long hard struggle to make the best of a bad bargain."[61]

While undoubtedly appreciative of Stanton's support, the Mormon women could hardly acquiesce in her view of them as women deluded by religion. The irony is that they more shared the values of the antipolygamy women.

Susan B. Anthony did not demonstrate Stanton's equanimity in facing polygamy in 1871. She privately recorded her repugnance to it during that visit and even confronted her Goodbeite hosts publicly about the practice.[62] Yet, because of her single-minded and pragmatic commitment to organization building, Anthony was closely allied with the Mormon women leaders over the next thirty years. The Mormon women respected Stanton but were closer in association and sympathy to Anthony.

When the antipolygamy crusade grew nationally and became intertwined with the suffrage movement, Anthony never spoke out publicly about the issue. Rather, she took steps to differentiate her support for Utah woman suffrage from the polygamy issue. Privately, Anthony explained to two Mormon women that the suffrage association could not allow itself to become identified with the polygamy issue, and when Belva Lockwood spoke out in protest at the federal attack on Mormon homes at the 1884 NWSA Convention, Anthony publicly opposed her.[63]

In spite of this, Anthony never wavered in her support of the Mormon-suffrage relationship and, on occasion, spoke out against the hypocrisy of anti-Mormon critics. When various women's groups sought Anthony's support in 1899 to publicly condemn the elected polygamist congressman, B. H. Roberts, Anthony refused. "Why should we go away out to Utah to seek a man to punish?" She spoke out later, not in defense of polygamy, but in criticism of the double standard of morality in most of America. Men in Congress could hardly condemn Roberts for immorality because, she observed, "people who live in glass houses should not throw stones."[64]

---

[61]Stanton, "The Man Marriage."

[62]Ida Husted Harper, *The Life and Work of Susan B. Anthony*, 3 vols. (1908; reprint, New York, 1969), 1:390–91.

[63]Romania Pratt, "Woman Suffrage Convention," *Woman's Exponent* 10 (March 1882): 143–46; Emmeline B. Wells, "Washington Convention," *Woman's Exponent* 13 (March 1884): 156.

[64]"Miss Anthony on Roberts," *Woman's Exponent* 28 (November/December 1899): 80; Harper, 3:1153.

But, for Anthony, endorsing the Mormon-suffrage alliance was very different from endorsing polygamy, and she wanted her official biography to record that she hated the practice and its subjugation of woman. She further added, in a letter to a Mormon woman, that she disapproved of polygamy especially when it was justified "as a requirement of religious faith" because, she noted, it made the detested practice "entirely too respectable."[65] The vehemence of Anthony's observation led her correspondent to observe that "Miss Anthony had the natural Puritanic horror of what she deemed promiscuous marriage . . . [and] did not . . . comprehend the spiritual principle which differentiated a religious sacrament from loose marital custom."[66]

While the term "Puritanic horror" might not be an accurate description of Anthony's view of polygamy, her response to the practice is more visceral and different from Stanton's abstract tolerance and was probably related to her personal rejection of marriage. Like Stanton, Anthony was critical of the subjugation of woman in contemporary marriage. When a man in Salt Lake City suggested to her that perhaps the future might bring polyandry, she indignantly responded, "Away with your man-visions! Women propose to reject them all, and begin to dream dreams for themselves."[67] While Anthony never fully elaborated on this concept of a woman-defined marriage, she often spoke of the necessity for equality in marriage, as did Stanton. However, unlike Stanton, she always expressed this hope for equality in economic terms. "What women most need," she believed, was self-respect, which could only come when she "scorn[ed] to eat the bread of dependence." Similarly, when she first confronted polygamy in Utah she condemned it in economic terms, stating that it was "even more dreadful than [the dependence of] monogamy, for here it is two, six, a dozen women . . . dependent on the one man."[68]

This emphasis by Anthony on woman's need for economic independence before companionate marriage would be possible is unique to her and reflects her overall awareness of the unequal contemporary power relationships. Kathleen Barry, her recent biographer, believes that implicit in Anthony's critique of marriage was her unstated "awareness of sex as domination," critical to her choice of spinsterhood.[69] Thus, Anthony's position on polygamy, intertwined with her personal choice of life-style, is subtly different from that of Stanton and the antipolygamy women, based upon a rejection of the sexual domination existing in nineteenth-century heterosexual relations.

[65]Harper, 3:1153.

[66]Gates, "Woman in History" (n. 44 above).

[67]Harper, 1:388.

[68]Quoted in Lee Virginia Chambers-Schiller, *Liberty, a Better Husband: Single Women in America: The Generations of 1740–1840* (New Haven, CT, 1984), p. 68; Harper, 1:390.

[69]Kathleen Barry, *Susan B. Anthony: A Biography of a Singular Feminist* (New York, 1988), p. 124.

While Anthony never endorsed the antipolygamy movement, in her efforts to strengthen the suffrage struggle she welcomed the addition of moral reform and temperance women to its ranks. For the same reason she agreed to the merger of the NWSA with its rival organization. From 1888 to 1890, as steps were taken by a select committee to plan the merger, the antipolygamy crusade was at its peak in Utah, and antipolygamy suffragists worked to prevent the Mormon women from being affiliated with the new organization. These efforts failed, and the Mormon women remained in the merged organization.[70] Of course, by then, the church had replaced its suffrage representatives with nonpolygamous women and, in 1890, publicly abandoned its stand on plural marriage with the Woodruff Manifesto.

After the abandonment of plural marriage the Mormons became even more conservative in family values, and one scholar speculates that "having been branded sexual outcasts, the Saints may well have felt that they had to 'out-Victorian' the Victorians."[71] The Mormon women, having regained the franchise with statehood, gradually became less identified with the woman's rights struggle nationally. By the time that American society was in its postsuffrage period, bringing greater legal and social emancipation to all women, the Mormon women actually had less autonomy in their own culture.[72]

The polygamy issue did not disappear with the manifesto, and women's groups rose again to demand an antipolygamy amendment to the Constitution by the end of the century. But with the official end of polygamy in 1890 and the merger of the suffrage organizations completed, the three-way debate on the American home was ended. The issue of polygamy and constitutional guarantees of religious freedom continues as a concern to civil libertarians.[73] Significantly, antipolygamy's victory was achieved by the reformers' turning to the federal government and the methods of moral coercion. After Utah achieved statehood, efforts were directed toward obtaining an antipolygamy amendment and later toward preventing easy divorce. The early efforts of the home rescue women to advance woman's power disappeared in these new crusades, replaced by more insistence upon community morality. The arguments on the family, woman's rights, and the nation moved into new phases.

[70]Iversen, "The Mormon-Suffrage Relationship" (n. 19 above).

[71]Hansen (n. 2 above), p. 53.

[72]Anne Firor Scott, "Mormon Women, Other Women: Paradoxes and Challenges," *Journal of Mormon History* 13 (1986–87): 14.

[73]Michele Parish-Pixler, "Polygamy: Practicing What They Preach," *Civil Liberties* (Summer 1990), p. 6.

# Sex Radicalism in the Canadian Pacific Northwest, 1890–1920

ANGUS McLAREN
*Department of History*
*University of Victoria*

WHAT IS WRONG with monogamy? Some pertinent comments on the question were made in a 1901 article entitled "The Wanderings of the Spirit," published in the Chicago-based libertarian journal *Lucifer: The Light-Bearer.* The author conjured up the image of another world where music, not love, was the most treasured possession. In this society young people were not allowed to sing until they came of age. And even then they were allowed only one song, which was to last them a lifetime. It was a sin to hanker after another melody or be caught humming a foreign refrain. What happened? If one were stone deaf it did not really matter, but most people eventually became bored with the same old song. Illicit music-making reached such proportions that ultimately the state passed legislation to allow people to change their tunes. But, asked the author, what kind of progress was it when you simply exchanged one song for another? The conventional assumption was still being made that once you had found the right tune you should never be attracted to any other. Society chose to regard as most virtuous those who, spurning adventure and creativity, restricted their repertoire to a lifelong solo.[1]

Perhaps the most interesting fact about this witty little parable on the limitations of monogamy is that it was written in Canada. Canada is not usually associated with the history of sexual radicalism. In the "true North strong and free," such exotic strains of social criticism appear to have rarely flourished.[2] But in Britain at the turn of the century socialists

---

[1] Robert Bird Kerr, "The Wanderings of the Spirit," *Lucifer,* August 17, 1901, p. 242.
[2] But for Finnish sex radicals in Canada, see J. Donald Wilson, "Matti Kurikka and A. B.

This essay originally appeared in the *Journal of the History of Sexuality* 1992, vol. 2, no. 4.

such as George Bernard Shaw, H. G. Wells, and Havelock Ellis added such critiques of current sexual mores to their intellectual arsenals. To the horror of conservative hereditarians, these mavericks used the assertion of the importance of childbearing to argue for the creation of extensive welfare provisions and against the restrictions of traditional bourgeois morality.[3]

In Canada, hereditarian thinking was very much dominated by social conservatives, but a few daring individuals on the political Left were attracted by the sexually subversive potential of eugenics. Historians have told us much about the enemies of sexual radicalism in Canada and next to nothing about its proponents.[4] To remedy this oversight, this essay focuses on two of the country's least known but most provocative thinkers, Robert Bird Kerr and Dora Forster. These two writers attempted in Canada, as did like-minded radicals in Britain, France, and America, to link the campaigns for sexual reform and social reform. An analysis of their arguments and of the similar musings found in the contemporary progressive press provides an indication of the role that eugenics played in advanced circles in the discussion of sexuality, discussions to which even Canada was not immune.

Robert Bird Kerr, the author of "The Wanderings of the Spirit," was born in 1867, the son of the parish minister of Yester, located south of Edinburgh.[5] He attended Edinburgh University, where he lost whatever

---

Makela: Socialist Thought among the Finns in Canada, 1900–1932," *Canadian Ethnic Studies* 20 (1978): 13; "Matti Kurikka: Finnish Canadian Intellectual," *BC Studies* 10 (1973): 60–61.

[3]George Bernard Shaw, *The Revolutionist's Handbook* (1903), vol. 10 of *Collected Works* (London, 1930); H. G. Wells, *Socialism and the Family* (London, 1906); Havelock Ellis, *The Task of Social Hygiene* (London, 1912); Eden Paul, *Socialism and Eugenics* (London, 1911); Eden Paul and Cedar Paul, eds., *Population and Birth Control: A Symposium* (New York, 1917).

[4]Michael Bliss, " 'Pure Books on Avoided Subjects': Pre-Freudian Sexual Ideas in Canada," *Historical Papers* (1970), pp. 89–108; James G. Snell, " 'The White Life for Two': The Defense of Marriage and Sexual Morality in Canada, 1890–1914," *Histoire sociale/ Social History* 16 (1983): 111–28. For the larger context, see Ronald G. Walters, *Primers for Prudery: Sexual Advice to Victorians* (Englewood Cliffs, NJ, 1974); Anita Claire Fellman and Michael Fellman, *Making Sense of Self: Medical Advice Literature in Late Nineteenth-Century America* (Philadelphia, 1981); Neil Sutherland, *Children in English Canadian Society* (Toronto, 1976); and Andrew Jones and Leonard Rutman, *In the Children's Aid: J. J. Kelson and Child Welfare in Ontario* (Toronto, 1980).

[5]On Kerr's life, see the accounts in *New Generation*, January 1927, pp. 1, 6; Hilda D. Romanes, "Robert Bird Kerr," ibid., May–June 1951, pp. 4–5; Rosanna Ledbetter, *A History of the Malthusian League* (Columbus, OH, 1976), pp. 239–40; Richard A. Soloway, *Birth Control and the Population Question in England, 1877–1930* (Chapel Hill, NC, 1982), pp. 195–96, 202–4.

religious beliefs he might have once harbored and, during further study in Germany at the University of Bonn, was converted by reading George Drysdale's *Natural Religion* to neo-Malthusianism. Kerr was trained as a barrister, but what he did upon his return to Britain is unclear. He later was reported to have been associated at the time of the founding of the Fabian Society in the late 1880s with Sidney and Beatrice Webb and George Bernard Shaw.[6] The Webbs did visit Kerr in 1911 at the time of their cross-country tour of Canada.[7] Kerr's most important relationship, however, was with Dora Forster, who ultimately became his wife. In 1893 the twenty-six-year-old lawyer set sail for Canada; Forster, already committed to Kerr, soon followed. Kerr practiced law in a number of small towns in British Columbia—Phoenix, Victoria, and Kelowna— and by all reports led an apparently unremarkable existence. At Phoenix, a copper-mining boom town controlled by Granby Mines, he served as city solicitor and auditor.[8] He and Forster left Phoenix for Victoria in 1905 and three years later moved on to Kelowna, where they remained until 1922. Kerr, one of the few barristers and solicitors in the Okanagan Valley, served as secretary of the Kelowna Board of Trade.[9]

But at the same time that Kerr and Forster were playing the role of a middle-class, respectable couple in a series of provincial towns, they were contributing inflammatory articles on sexuality to advanced publications in Canada, Britain, and the United States. We know little about their day-to-day existence, but in any event they must have hid from their neighbors their writing on sexual radicalism. From 1898 to 1906 they wrote for *Lucifer,* the Chicago-based libertarian journal; from 1903 to 1909 for such Canadian progressive papers as *Western Clarion, Western Socialist,* and *Cotton's Weekly;* from 1906 through World War I for the *Malthusian,* the English neo-Malthusian periodical; and in 1912 for the British Columbian suffragist paper, the *Champion.* We will follow their activities until 1922, when they returned to England and Kerr assumed the editorship of *New Generation,* which in 1923 replaced the *Malthusian* as the mouthpiece for the English neo-Malthusian movement.

To place Kerr and Forster in context something first has to be said of

[6]Kerr stated that he was with Shaw in Bradford in 1893; see Robert Bird Kerr, "George Bernard Shaw," *Lucifer,* January 4, 1906, pp. 437–38.

[7]G. Feaver, "'Self Respect and Hopefulness': The Webbs in the Canadian West," *BC Studies* 43 (1979): 57.

[8]On Kerr in Phoenix, see Gregory Neil Fraser, "Phoenix: British Columbia's 'Copper Camp,' 1891–1920" (B.A. thesis, University of Victoria, 1972); *Henderson's B.C. Gazetteer and Directory* (1893–1902); *Phoenix Pioneer,* March 5, 1904, p. 1.

[9]On Kerr in Kelowna, see *Wrigley's B.C. Directory* (1918); *Kelowna Daily Courier,* February 2, 1922, p. 1.

the nineteenth-century discussion of sexuality in Britain and America. Attacks in Britain on the existing form of marriage were associated with the Owenite Socialists of the first half of the century and the free thinkers of the latter half. The most influential of the mid-Victorian sexual radicals was George Drysdale. This Scottish physician was an active campaigner for fertility control and a vehement supporter of the women's movement. His anonymously authored *Physical, Sexual, and Natural Religion* (1855), in addition to being a major work on contraception, contained attacks on existing marriage relationships as forms of "legal prostitution" and defenses of prostitutes as the victims of both a double sexual standard and the restriction of women's employment.[10] But when his brother, Charles Drysdale, launched the Malthusian League in 1877 to campaign for a restriction of the birthrate, the sexual radicalism of George Drysdale found no place in the league's pronouncements. To make neo-Malthusianism respectable, the league based its defense of birth control solely on the conservative teachings of Robert Malthus. Only by the restriction of fertility, it argued, could the poor improve their lot. But the employment of contraceptives, the league implied, would not in any serious way change the relationship of the sexes.[11]

The Fabian Society, which began in the 1880s as the Fellowship of the New Life, aspiring as it did to change England both socially and morally, included members such as Annie Besant, H. G. Wells, and George Bernard Shaw, who felt that birth control could play a more positive role than that envisaged by the Malthusian League. Indeed, Shaw and Wells went on to sketch out portrayals of future societies in which the state, in its pursuit of efficiency, would actively intervene in childbearing.[12] Kerr and Forster were on the fringes of the Fabian Society in its early years and advanced similar arguments.

Kerr was also involved in the 1890s in some way with the English Legitimation League.[13] The *Adult,* the league's journal, edited by George Bedborough and Henry Seymour, appeared in June 1897 with

---

[10]On the Owenites, see Barbara Taylor, *Eve and the New Jerusalem: Socialism and Feminism in the Nineteenth Century* (London, 1984). On Drysdale's views, see his "A Doctor of Medicine," *The Elements of Social Science; or, Physical, Sexual, and Natural Religion: An Exposition of the True Cause and Only Cure of the Three Primary Social Evils: Poverty, Prostitution, and Celibacy,* 26th ed. (London, 1887).

[11]Ledbetter, pp. 57–121; Soloway, *Birth Control,* pp. 55–133.

[12]Angus McLaren, *Birth Control in Nineteenth-Century England* (London, 1978), pp. 174–97; Samuel Hynes, *The Edwardian Turn of Mind* (Princeton, NJ, 1968), pp. 87–172; Peter Kemp, *H. G. Wells and the Culminating Ape: Biological Themes and Imaginative Obsessions* (London, 1982), pp. 73–78.

[13]On the Legitimation League, see Phyllis Grosskurth, *Havelock Ellis: A Biography* (New York, 1980), pp. 191–94.

the avowed aim of securing the rights of the illegitimate and campaigning for sex education and immediately drew the support of writers interested in sexuality, such as Grant Allen, Edward Carpenter, and Mona Caird.[14] Further notoriety was won by the league's involvement in the Edith Lanchester affair. This young Battersea woman, having fallen in love with a socialist, was committed by her father to an asylum. Although successful in campaigning for her release, the league and its journal both soon disappeared, after Bedborough was found guilty of selling Havelock Ellis's *Sexual Inversion,* which the court judged "an obscene and filthy work." The prosecution was in part motivated by the belief of the police that the league was a front for anarchist activities.[15]

In their attempts to wed political and sexual concerns, Kerr and Forster were following a course already set by the English Left.[16] A central question was whether restriction of fertility, which was associated with Malthus's conservative doctrines, could somehow be turned to the purposes of the working class. Henry Seymour, who edited the *Adult* when Bedborough was first jailed, was an active anarchist. Like other libertarians, he was not at first enthusiastic about birth control. In 1886 he provided an introduction to P. J. Proudhon's *The Malthusians,* in which the French author asserted, "The theory of Malthus is the theory of political murder . . . an organization of suicide."[17] But after Annie Besant attacked such moralizing, Seymour backtracked: "We Anarchists, while not urging the slightest objection to the limitation of offspring where necessary or advisable,—nevertheless do flatly deny that the increase of poverty and population *necessarily go hand in hand.*"[18]

Thomas Shore, an active freethinker, went on in the *Anarchist* to endorse the neo-Malthusian Henry Allbutt's *A Wife's Handbook* as full of "solid practical information."[19] Seymour continued to argue, however, that if Malthusianism were linked to the faction of the Left, it was to that which supported state socialism. Collectivists, who were not hypocrites, he argued, would see "the necessary correlative in the sovereignty of the syringe."[20] He extended his thinking somewhat in *Anarchy of Love* (1888), espousing the vague doctrine that since so many marriages de-

[14]*Adult: A Journal for the Advancement of Freedom in Sexual Relations* (published 1897–99).

[15]Hermia Oliver, *The International Anarchist Movement in Late Victorian London* (London, 1983), p. 145.

[16]McLaren, *Birth Control,* pp. 43–78, 157–74.

[17]P. J. Proudhon, *The Malthusians* (London, 1880), pp. 6–7; see also Henry Seymour, *The Malthusian Theory* (London, 1889), pp. 9–10.

[18]*Anarchist,* June 1, 1886.

[19]Ibid., June 1 and July 1, 1886.

[20]"The Malthusian Theology," ibid., September 1, 1886.

stroyed love, sexual liberty was required.[21] And in *The Physiology of Love: A Study on Stirpiculture* (1898) Seymour tried to wed psychological and physiological concerns. Drawing on the once popular science of phrenology, he argued that sexual activity was a necessary safety valve for the body's electrical build-up. Contraception he now implicitly condoned, stating in passing that, thanks to chemistry, women had contraceptives and so did not have to become mothers unless they so desired.[22] Seymour went about as far as any English anarchist could in embracing sex radicalism. Robert Kerr reported that he attended the meetings of the Legitimation League and found most of the anarchists morally conservative. He singled out Peter Kropotkin, who, sneered Kerr, "shuns the sex question as a cat shuns water."[23]

Much closer to Forster and Kerr's views were those of the American libertarians associated with Moses Harman and his journal, *Lucifer*.[24] From 1898 to 1907 Kerr and Forster were *Lucifer*'s constant contributors and financial supporters, as it continued a long American tradition of combining social and sex radicalism. For the previous seventy years, the United States had experienced intermittent flurries of sexual debate, which frequently accompanied religious revivals.[25] Abner Kneeland's *Boston Investigator* provided a forum for free thought, sex radicalism, and working-class agitation in the 1830s, while in the 1850s the Mormon and Oneida experiments in communal living paralleled surges in discussions of feminism, free love, and spiritualism. And in the last decades of the century, Ezra Heywood's *The Word* in Boston and Moses Harman's *Lucifer*—first in Kansas and later in Chicago—provided outlets for discussions of sex reform. Late nineteenth-century spiritualism and free thought were not always as far apart as one might think.

[21]Henry Seymour, *Anarchy of Love; or, The Science of the Sexes* (London, 1888), p. 15.

[22]Henry Seymour, *The Physiology of Love* (London, 1898), pp. 33, 97.

[23]"The Truth," *Lucifer*, January 23, 1902, p. 434. Kerr claimed to have crossed the Atlantic with Kropotkin. See *New Generation*, November 1922, p. 1; Paul Avrich, "Kropotkin in America," *International Review of Social History* 25 (1980): 1–34.

[24]On Harman, see Hal D. Sears, *The Sex Radicals: Free Love in High Victorian America* (Lawrence, KS, 1977). The Legitimation League and *Lucifer* were linked, inasmuch as Lillian Harman, daughter of Moses Harman, was honorary president of the Legitimation League. Some of the league's members, such as George Bedborough, wrote for *Lucifer*. See also Edward Royle, *Radicals, Secularists, and Republicans: Popular Freethought in Britain, 1866–1915* (Manchester, 1980), pp. 182, 248, 252–53.

[25]See Louis J. Kern, *An Ordered Love: Sex Roles and Sexuality in Victorian Utopias: The Shakers, the Mormons, and the Oneida Community* (Chapel Hill, NC, 1981); R. L. Muncy, *Sex and Marriage in Utopian Communities* (Bloomington, IN, 1973). For responses, see David J. Pivar, *Purity Crusade: Sexual Morality and Social Control, 1868–1900* (Westport, CT, 1974).

A perusal of these radical papers reveals the heady brew that could be concocted by combining scientism, free thought, sex radicalism, and libertarianism. "Free love" usually meant no more than marriage that could be entered and ended without coercion. "Free motherhood" similarly signified a situation in which the woman had the right to determine whether or not to bear children. The more mystical assumed that limitation of fertility would be achieved by continence; the more scientific envisaged recourse to contraception. The common goal of freedom attracted a variety of adherents. Anarchists such as Victoria Woodhull were drawn to the defense of free love, while spiritualists such as Lois Waisbrooker were led via mysticism into anarchism.[26] It was in response to these challenges that nervous American financiers such as J. P. Morgan and Samuel Colgate supported the Comstock Act of 1873, which was employed not just to make the sale of contraceptives illegal but to silence the supporters of sex radicalism and free thought.

What drew Kerr and Forster to the Harman group was its espousal of free love eugenics based on the early stirpiculture writings of John Humphrey Noyes and Henry C. Wright.[27] Anarchist eugenics—not to be confused with the later coercive eugenics of Francis Galton and Karl Pearson—asserted that only by freeing women could the race be improved.

Kerr played a key role in contributing to *Lucifer*'s attack on traditional morality and its dysgenic results. Moses Harman referred to him as "our constant and faithful helper," while Lillian Harman asserted that he was "one of *Lucifer*'s best friends, and a personal friend of my own as well."[28] Kerr and Forster sent the Harmans articles and financial support but had little direct contact with the Americans. In 1906, though, they met in San Francisco with such supporters of free love as Lydia Todd and Lois Waisbrooker. Kerr later jokingly attributed the city's famous earthquake and fire of the same year to God's displeasure at this conference of sex radicals.[29]

[26]Martin Henry Blatt, *Free Love and Anarchism: The Biography of Ezra Heywood* (Urbana, IL, 1989); Taylor Stoehr, ed., *Free Love in America: A Documentary History* (New York, 1979); Margaret S. March, *Anarchist Women, 1870–1920* (Philadelphia, 1981), pp. 72–76.

[27]Sears, p. 121; Lewis Perry, *Childhood, Marriage, and Reform: Henry Clark Wright, 1797–1880* (Chicago, 1980), pp. 171–256. For a continuation of this strand of thinking in the twentieth century, see Scott Nearing, *The Super Race: An American Problem* (New York, 1919), pp. 24, 52–53, 80.

[28]"The Truth," *Lucifer*, January 23, 1902, p. 436; Lillian Harman, letter to editor, ibid., December 26, 1901, p. 407.

[29]Ibid., May 10, 1906, p. 512; August 2, 1906, pp. 558–59. Lois Waisbrooker spent some time at the turn of the century at the Home Colony on Puget Sound in the state of Washington; it is possible she was in contact with Kerr and Forster in British Columbia.

Kerr's contributions to *Lucifer* dealt with three main topics: sexuality, politics, and eugenics. He was critical, as his comments on monogamy in "The Wanderings of the Spirit" suggest, of the repressive aspects of Victorian sexuality.[30] Indeed he argued, as did other radicals from the time of Owen and Fourier, that the moral constraints of society were the actual cause of sexual excesses and immorality.[31] Monogamy perhaps had been required at one time for the protection of offspring, but now, insisted Kerr, contraceptive protection offered the possibility of separating love from parenthood. All could be lovers, but only some could or should be parents. Those who led a free sexual life Kerr referred to as the "varietists," and he claimed to know several women of this persuasion.[32] He was presumably thinking of the participants of what was, in effect, the "free love conference" held in San Francisco in 1906.

Kerr extended his critique of sexual relationships from monogamy to existing sex roles. In "A Strange Custom," he developed a Shavian parable concerning the planet Ceres, where the men were forced to wear dresses and always keep covered the most shameful part of their anatomy—their noses. Accordingly, they were reduced to being helpless, decorative creatures. Only with rational dress reform and equitable sharing of responsibilities could progress take place.[33]

But if Kerr was a critic of existing sex roles, he reserved much of his most biting criticism for the suffragists. As his own references to writers such as August Bebel, Grant Allen, Charlotte Perkins Gilman, Havelock Ellis, Edward Carpenter, Karl Pearson, William Morris, E. Belfort Bax, Edward Bellamy, and George Bernard Shaw suggest, he was preoccupied by the question of how feminism could be related to the issues of sex and socialism.[34] He was impatient with those feminists who on the one hand demanded political reforms, but on the other refused to come

---

The *Agitator* (later to appear as the *Syndicalist*), the Home Colony's journal, carried articles that sound remarkably like the works of Kerr and Forster; see, for example, the issues of October 1, 1911, August 15, 1912, and July 1, 1913. For helpful leads on this, I have to thank Charles Pierce LeWarne, author of *Utopias on Puget Sound, 1885–1915* (Seattle, 1975).

[30]Collections of Kerr's articles, including "The Strasburg Geese," "The Rights of Children," and "Up to Date Fables," were advertised and sold by *Lucifer*.

[31]*Lucifer*, February 26, 1903, pp. 49–50; October 29, 1905, pp. 397–98.

[32]Ibid., April 9, 1903, pp. 98–99.

[33]"A Strange Custom," ibid., March 20, 1902, p. 73.

[34]Ibid., January 23, 1902, p. 434. Kerr followed Grant Allen's line: "Whether we have wives or not—and that is a minor point about which I, for one, am supremely unprejudiced—we must have at least mothers" (Edward Clodd, *Grant Allen* [London, 1900], p. 162).

down from their pedestals to deal with the practical problems of changing sex roles.[35]

Politicians, of course, had shown even less sensitivity to sexual issues. Kerr concluded, however, that the Fabian socialists had gone furthest in attempting to place sexuality in a social and political context. In defending Sidney Webb, Beatrice Webb, and George Bernard Shaw in a libertarian journal, Kerr was leaving himself open to attack.[36] C. L. James charged that Kerr was blind to the coercive aspects of collectivism; Moses Harman pointed out that anarchists had always shown themselves more liberal than socialists on the sexual question.[37] In a spirited retort Kerr replied that "anarchistic voluntarism," as much as it promised in the abstract, simply did not work in reality. In the United States, he pointed out, whites were "voluntarily" burning and lynching blacks, and it was the state that was trying to stop them.[38] As for the sex issue, Kerr reiterated his argument that anarchists such as Benjamin Tucker, Wordsworth Donisthorpe, J. C. Spence, and J. Greeve Fisher had continually skirted the subject while the Fabians sought to come to grips with it.[39]

What underlay Kerr's concern for some sort of collectivist response to the challenge of changing sexual norms was his interest in eugenics. In an article entitled "Darwin, Weismann, and Harman," he spelled out his argument.[40] Darwin, he argued, had revealed how evolution necessarily led in the natural state to the survival of the fittest. What Darwin had not taken into account, but what the German zoologist August Weismann had noted, was that the practice of birth control reversed evolution and led to racial degeneration rather than progress. Kerr be-

---

[35]*Lucifer,* September 13, 1906, pp. 581–82. Kerr did go out of his way to praise Voltairine de Clayre; see *Lucifer,* May 1, 1902, p. 125. For assistance on this subject I would like to thank Paul Avrich, author of *An American Anarchist: The Life of Voltairine de Clayre* (Princeton, NJ, 1978).

[36]*Lucifer,* June 12, 1902, pp. 169–70. One of the rare clergymen whom Kerr praised was the American Social Gospeller G. D. Herron, who took up something very similar to a Fabian socialist stance. See G. D. Herron, *Social Meaning of Religious Experiences* (New York, 1896; rpt. New York, 1969).

[37]*Lucifer,* May 22, 1902, pp. 145–46; January 23, 1902, pp. 436–38.

[38]Ibid., April 24, 1902, pp. 113–14; December 5, 1901, pp. 377–78; "A Rose by Any Other Name," ibid., January 9, 1902, p. 418.

[39]"The Truth," ibid., January 23, 1902, p. 434. But Kerr overlooked the fact that anarchist publications did carry radical critiques of existing sexual mores; see, for example, Alexander Cohen's remarkable defense of abortion reprinted in a Boston periodical ("The Case of Mrs. Eden," *Rebel,* February 1896, p. 56).

[40]This article, which appeared in *Lucifer,* March 4, 1899, was also carried as an addenda to Forster's *Sex Radicalism,* discussed below. See also *Lucifer,* June 12, 1902, pp. 169–70; January 28, 1904, pp. 25–26.

lieved, however, that Jane H. Clapperton and Moses Harman had the answer—it was necessary to throw off the restraints of economic dependence and monogamy.[41] "Let every mother who wishes to have a child be absolutely free to select its father, then the problem is solved." If women were economically provided for by the state, the healthy would want children and would naturally choose as fathers for their children not the wealthy or powerful, but the most fit. The collective maintenance of children, the endowment of motherhood, and the sexual freedom of women would, asserted Kerr, result in the improvement of the race.[42]

Kerr's works were marked by inherent tensions. He declared himself in favor of the absolute sexual freedom of women; he also stated that everyone did *not* have the right to bear children. He cited the American eugenicist arguments of the evils spawned by the uncontrolled breeding of the infamously unhealthy Jukes family and the assertions of Fabians such as H. G. Wells that breeding was too important to be ignored by the state.[43] Francis Galton—coiner of the term "eugenics"—voiced the new concern that the Darwinian struggle was being reversed as a result of the employment of contraceptives by the fit. His antifeminism was explicit. Kerr and many progressives hoped that while the rights of women could be extended, they would also be complemented by an enunciation of the "rights" of children—the rights of being born and brought up as well as possible.[44]

The women contributors to *Lucifer* were not all convinced. Lizzie M. Holmes put Kerr in his place by wearily commenting: "I have been so

---

[41]On Clapperton, see McLaren (n. 12 above), pp. 204–5; on Harman's views, see Moses Harman, *The Right to Be Born Well* (Chicago, 1905).

[42]*Lucifer,* July 9, 1903, pp. 202–3; February 1, 1906, p. 459. For a similar line of argument followed by feminists such as Olive Schreiner and Charlotte Perkins Gilman, see Jane Lewis, "Motherhood Issues during the Late Nineteenth and Early Twentieth Centuries: Some Recent Viewpoints," *Ontario History* 75 (1983): 15–16; Rosaleen Love, "Darwinism and Feminism: The 'Woman Question,' in the Life and Work of Olive Schreiner and Charlotte Perkins Gilman," in David Oldroyd and Ian Langham, eds., *The Wider Domain of Evolutionary Thought* (London, 1983), pp. 113–31.

[43]*Lucifer,* June 11, 1903, pp. 169–70; May 21, 1903, p. 145. Richard Dugdale's *The Jukes: A Study in Crime, Pauperism, Disease, and Heredity* (New York, 1877) carried the assertion that in seven generations one family had cost society over a million dollars in relief, imprisonment, and medical care. See Sears (n. 24 above), p. 124.

[44]"The Rights of Children," *Lucifer,* September 7, 1901, pp. 274–75; "How to Be Born Well," ibid., October 22, 1903, p. 321. Edward Bellamy's *Looking Backward* (New York, 1888) impressed the biologist Alfred Russell Wallace with the notion that female choice was crucial for healthy human selection. Grant Allen, best known for his portrayal of "bachelor motherhood" in *The Woman Who Did* (London, 1895), popularized such ideas in *Falling in Love* (London, 1891); and see also Martin Fichman, *Alfred Russell Wallace* (Boston, 1981), pp. 139–50; Donald C. Bellamy, "'Social Darwinism'"

many times exasperated since I took an interest in social questions—which is about forty years ago—at the assurance with which so many radical men have presumed to tell free women what they ought to do."[45] Holmes pointed out that there was as yet no real understanding of heredity; in any event, no one had the right to ask a mother to sacrifice herself for the unborn. Lillie D. White agreed that it was peculiar that so many "old men grannies" should be morbidly preoccupied by the issue of women's ability to breed.[46] In reality Kerr was treating women, Carrie Austin protested, not as equals, but as livestock.[47] Kerr was not without his defenders. Amy Linnett and Adeline Champney argued that at the very least Kerr was serving a useful purpose in pointing out that women should not reproduce unthinkingly.[48] Kerr's main support, however, came from his companion Dora Forster.

Dora Forster contributed articles to *Lucifer* between 1899 and 1905.[49] Those that appeared between 1904 and 1905 she reissued as a pamphlet entitled *Sex Radicalism as Seen by an Emancipated Woman of the New Time*.[50] The main thrust of her writings was to call for a rational reappraisal of sex. She optimistically believed that doctors would play a key role in creating a new science or sociology of sexuality and in so doing circumvent the churches' longstanding taboos against such discussions. Women, she noted, traditionally had been praised for their ignorance or what was more politely termed their "innocence," but the new demand for sex and marriage manuals revealed a growing desire for physiological knowledge. At the moment the available books, like those of Dr. Thomas Low Groves and Dr. Alice Stockham, were replete with

Revisited," *Perspectives in American History* 1 (1984): 96–97; Peter Norton, *The Vital Science: Biology and the Literary Imagination* (London, 1984), pp. 136–40; Daniel Kevles, *In the Name of Eugenics: Genetics and the Use of Human Heredity* (Berkeley, CA, 1985), pp. 3–40.

[45]Lizzie M. Holmes, letter to editor, *Lucifer,* May 14, 1903, p. 138.

[46]Lillie D. White, letter to editor, ibid., August 8, 1903, p. 234.

[47]Carrie Austin, letter to editor, ibid., August 20, 1903, pp. 249–50.

[48]Adeline Champney, letter to editor, ibid., August 27, 1903, pp. 257–58; Amy Linnette, letter to editor, ibid., September 3, 1903, p. 268. For the context of this debate see John C. Spurlock, *Free Love: Marriage and Middle-Class Radicalism in America, 1825–1860* (New York, 1988).

[49]Little is known of Dora Forster. She claimed that she was active in the English campaign for women's education and appears to have been acquainted with the English feminist Lady Florence Dixie. See *Lucifer,* April 9, 1903, p. 94; Lady Florence Dixie to Dora Forster, ibid., April 27, 1905, p. 294. In Kerr's obituaries there is no reference to Forster other than mention of the fact that she followed him to Canada.

[50]Dora Forster, *Sex Radicalism as Seen by an Emancipated Woman of the New Time* (Chicago, 1905).

"goodly nonsense." The growth of "secularism, spiritualism, and economic reform (socialism and anarchism)" gave Forster confidence that the sort of studies she envisaged, and of which her own tract was an example, would provide more accurate portrayals of sexual needs and practices.[51] Forster reported that "in the frank-spoken west," by which she presumably meant British Columbia, candid conversations on such subjects were already taking place.[52]

The tragedy of the existing moral system, according to Forster, was that it doomed thousands to unnecessarily unhappy lives. Conservatives like Tolstoy, who defended chastity, monogamy, and the ascetic ideal, pessimistically believed that self-control could be based only on fear of disease or damnation.[53] As a result the natural sexual interest of children and young women was denied. Brides ignorantly entered marriages that soon resulted in "depleted magnetism" and lost love.[54] The wife found herself tied to her husband and legally subjected to the most immoral demands. As the Chinese bound the feet of their women, so westerners employed the institution of marriage to restrict women's freedom.[55] The irony was that while puritans scorned the prostitute, they supported a system of marriage in which women effectively were bought and sold. The only difference between the married woman and the whore was, according to Forster, that "the honest woman like the honest politician is the one who stays bought."[56]

The fact that women were not free was Forster's proof that a sex war, complementing the class war, was being fought.[57] Men categorized women according to whether they were married, single and celibate, or prostitutes. The single woman was prevented from achieving economic independence and offered no meaningful option but marriage. The husband gained from marriage a housekeeper, a sex slave, and a nurse. The woman received, according to Forster's grim calculations, only the negative benefits of not being childless and not remaining a spinster. Religion, as the creation of men, sanctified this inequitable situation: "The church, with the keen eye for the material side of things which characterize it, formerly insisted on the wife promising to be 'buxom (bowsome,

[51]Ibid., pp. 9, 10; see also Jayme A. Sokolow, *Eros and Modernization: Sylvester Graham, Health Reform, and the Origins of Victorian Sexuality in America* (London, 1983), pp. 127–43.
[52]Forster, *Sex Radicalism*, p. 11.
[53]Ibid., p. 19.
[54]Ibid., p. 21.
[55]Ibid., p. 22.
[56]"Sex Morality," *Lucifer,* December 3, 1903, p. 369.
[57]Forster, *Sex Radicalism*, p. 26.

obedient) in bedde and at borde.'"[58] And even in the sex act itself, noted Forster, men received sexual satisfaction; few women did.

Forster traced the campaign against sexual oppression from Mary Wollstonecraft, Percy Shelley, John Stuart Mill, George Drysdale, and Edward Carpenter, to George Bernard Shaw. Each had in her or his own way shown the disastrous consequences of "exclusive sex possession" and the preoccupation with "sin."[59] But as far as Forster was concerned, the findings of historians and anthropologists such as Friedrich Engels, Johann Bachofen, Lewis Morgan, J. F. McLennan, John Lubbock, Henry Maine, and J. S. Mill on the pernicious evolutionary effects of the subjection of women were even more impressive.[60] If the race is to be improved, she argued, women should be free to select their mates on the grounds of "sound heredity, both physical and mental."[61] At the moment women were not free but sold to those who could afford to keep them and then subjected to careers of unthinking propagation. Women, in revolting against such a fate, were now refusing to reproduce, much to the horror of a white male supremacist like Teddy Roosevelt. "The men would now teach the women a different lesson, in the name of patriotism. But we will not help them do it. I hope the scarcity of children will go on till maternity is honored at least as much as the trials and hardships of soldiers campaigning in wartime. It will then be worthwhile to supply the nation with a sufficiency of children."[62] This "birth strike," according to Forster, was women's way of signaling their refusal to tolerate a life of mindless propagation.[63] Her chief concern, which she shared with Kerr, was how the control of reproduction could be turned to positive purposes.

Forster declared that the two most important problems of the twentieth century were, first, how to use the power of sex, and second, "how to encourage and reward women in the reproductive function so that they may be willing to bear more than two children each."[64] Her conclusion was that both issues could be answered and a friendship of the sexes made possible by sex education. Such an education would begin by accepting the naturalness of children's sex play. For Forster, masturbation

[58]Ibid., p. 35.

[59]Ibid., p. 38; see also "The Passing Ideal and the Coming Ideal," *Lucifer,* January 22, 1903, pp. 9–10.

[60]"Jealousy," *Lucifer,* March 4, 1903, p. 57; also Carrie Austin to Dora Forster, ibid., April 2, 1903, p. 91.

[61]Forster, *Sex Radicalism,* p. 24.

[62]Ibid., pp. 20, 39.

[63]See also George Noyes Miller, *The Strike of Sex* (London, 1895); William J. Robinson, "The Birth Strike," *International Socialist Review* 14 (1914): 404–6.

[64]Forster, *Sex Radicalism,* p. 42.

was only a danger if indulged in to excess and usually only when marriage was delayed or prevented.[65] She wanted all youths from the age of fourteen to receive some sex education. Drawing on accounts of the Oneida colony, she suggested that it would be wise for the young woman of sixteen to be sexually initiated by an older man and prepared by "surgical skill" to lose her virginity.[66] The mature woman would be free to choose first her lover and then the father of her children. Between the ages of twenty and thirty, the support of the community freeing her from economic worries, she would devote herself to childbearing. The desire for children, asserted Forster, would be recognized as distinctly different from the desire for passionate fulfillment. She cited the Oneida colonists and Lois Waisbrooker as having already spelled out the differences between amorous and reproductive love; she referred her readers to the works of Dr. E. B. Foote, Dr. Alice Stockham, and Ida Craddock to explain how fertility control made such a distinction possible.[67]

At the age of thirty, the woman would leave behind her childbearing career and enter a "home partnership" with a spouse.[68] It would not always be a monogamous relationship. Unhappiness resulting from sexual exclusiveness was to be shunned; happiness based on either constancy or variety were to be pursued. In contemporary society, Forster declared, most women were robbed of all sexual feelings; the joys of maternity provided only partial compensation.[69] In the future, "compulsory motherhood" would be replaced by "free motherhood," in which the "sex freedom" of the woman would be the basis for healthy relationships. The result would be not a world of promiscuity, but one in which self-control replaced social coercion.

Women needed economic and mental independence, asserted Forster; these in turn would ensure women the right to their own persons.[70] But she recognized that if women were to change, men would have to change as well. The male had to be sexually reeducated if the woman were to gain the same sort of sexual pleasure: "He loves in the same manner as some of our northern barbarians drink,—he tosses off the wine of life in one fierce draught, caring only that it quenches thirsts, instead of sipping its delicious fragrance. More complete knowledge of

[65]Ibid., p. 11.

[66]Ibid., p. 44.

[67]Ibid., p. 41. On the works of Foote, Stockham, and Craddock, see Norman E. Himes, *Medical History of Contraception* (New York, 1936), pp. 260–85. On the circulation of such works in Canada, see Angus McLaren, "Birth Control and Abortion in Canada, 1870–1920," *Canadian Historical Review* 59 (1978): 323–27.

[68]Forster, *Sex Radicalism*, p. 47.

[69]Ibid., p. 13.

[70]"Real and Ideal," *Lucifer*, September 10, 1903, p. 275.

both sexes, and more worthy experiences and training will do much to adjust this discrepancy."[71] This notion of sex "training" necessarily complementing "sex freedom" had a characteristically early twentieth-century progressive ring to it. Similarly ambiguous was Forster's presentation of procreation in which motherhood would be "free," yet rewarded and encouraged.[72]

*Lucifer* disappeared in 1906, falling victim to a wave of antilibertarian sentiment that swept America. Harman was arrested in 1905 for using obscenities in *Lucifer,* although the initial target of the police was Dora Forster's *Sex Radicalism.* In 1906 the seventy-five-year-old editor was sentenced to a year of hard labor at Joliet State Prison.[73] *Lucifer,* combining as it did an interest in sex, eugenics, feminism, and radical politics, was a perfect vehicle for Kerr and Forster's work. In the Canadian and British publications, to which they turned, they could never be quite as outspoken.

Kerr and Forster were especially circumspect in their propagandistic activities in British Columbia. They supported the Socialist party of Canada but were not as candid in their contributions to its journals as they were in *Lucifer.*[74] Dora Forster was prompted to write to the *Western Socialist* in 1902, however, after the editor of the women's page, Dorothy Drew, expressed interest in the works of Edward Carpenter and Lois Waisbrooker.[75] She sent Drew the following letter:

Dear Comrade: I see that you recommend Edward Carpenter's admirable little book, "Love's Coming of Age," and I think you may be interested to have the names of some other books on the sex question. I send you the last two numbers of Lucifer—the only periodical devoted to this immensely important subject.

[71]Forster, *Sex Radicalism,* pp. 46–47. Forster elsewhere called on lovers to become "sexual artists" ("Sex Domination," *Lucifer,* May 7, 1903, pp. 129–30).

[72]Forster's work was both applauded and attacked by libertarians. See Lizzie Holmes to Dora Forster, *Lucifer,* April 27, 1905, p. 299; Carrie Austin to Dora Forster, ibid., July 2, 1903, pp. 193–94.

[73]Harman survived to publish the *American Journal of Eugenics* (1907–10); see Sears (n. 24 above), p. 264.

[74]Phoenix was an active center of the Socialist party of Canada. On the radicalism in the Kootenay region of British Columbia, see Ronald Grantham, "Some Aspects of the Socialist Movement in British Columbia, 1898–1933" (M.A. thesis, University of British Columbia, 1942); Paul A. Phillips, *No Power Greater: A Century of Labour in British Columbia* (Vancouver, 1967); Ross Alfred Johnson, "No Compromise—No Political Trading: The Marxian Socialist Tradition in British Columbia" (Ph.D. diss., University of British Columbia, 1975); Cole Harris, "Industry and the Good Life around Idaho Peak," *Canadian Historical Review* 66 (1985): 315–44.

[75]"We Women," *Western Socialist,* November 8, 1902, p. 3.

I would especially recommend the following all mentioned in Lucifer's advertisements.

1. Women in the Past, Present and Future by August Bebel, leader of the German Socialist Party.

2. "What the Young Need to Know," by Edwin C. Walker.

3. The British Barbarians, by Grant Allen.

4. Motherhood in Freedom, by Moses Harman.

5. Origins of the Family, by Frederick [sic] Engels, one of the founders of scientific socialism.

It is to be regretted that American socialists shirk this subject, which has been frankly and so well dealt with by European socialist leaders—such as Marx, Engels, Bebel, Carpenter, Grant Allen and Bernard Shaw. In America nearly all the advanced thinkers on the sex question have been driven into the anarchist movement.[76]

Kerr similarly attempted to convince the readers of the *Western Clarion* of the need to include a discussion of sexuality in the socialist program.

My information has been gained chiefly from talking to wage earners so my ideas are very practical. I have especially talked to women wage earners who are even more practical than men, and differ surprisingly from male wage earners in their ideas of what things are wrong. As nearly all American and Canadian socialists have confined themselves to preaching to women, it may interest you to hear the experience of one who has spent a good deal of his life learning from women. Such knowledge is very important because women suffrage is a thing of the immediate future, and there is not the ghost of a chance of getting socialism unless men and women alike cordially support the Socialist party.[77]

Kerr then proceeded to give accounts of women who suffered the tyranny of males and the disinterest of socialists. But the fact that Kerr could cite European socialist luminaries such as Karl Kautsky as being sympathetic to women's immediate demands did not impress many Canadian readers. "Stonehenge" wrote in reply that the sex question was so

[76]Dora Forster to Dorothy Drew, ibid., November 29, 1902, p. 3. See also later discussions along similar lines in the *Western Clarion*, August 13, 1904, p. 1; December 14, 1907, p. 2. Mrs. Dora Kerr was reported as having been nominated, though not elected, to the 1903 provincial executive committee of the Socialist party of Canada. See *Western Socialist*, November 15, 1902, p. 4; November 22, 1902, p. 4; January 17, 1903, p. 4.

[77]*Western Clarion*, October 13, 1906, p. 2. Kerr was also aroused by the misogyny of E. Belfort Bax to write to *Justice*, the organ of the Social Democratic Federation, to protest that it was ignoring the International's own policy on the woman question, in particular the support of the endowment of motherhood; see *Justice*, December 29, 1906.

complicated that it could only be broached after economic inequalities had been dealt with.[78]

In addition to contributing to the British Columbia socialist press, Kerr and Forster also sent letters to *Cotton's Weekly,* a socialist paper published in Quebec's eastern townships by William Ulric Cotton. In 1908 and 1909 his sister, Mary Cotton Wisdom, editor of the women's page, defended the suffragist movement and castigated the sexual double standard.[79] Kerr confined his contributions to *Cotton's Weekly* to comments on the British scene; Forster continued to hammer away at the necessity of socialism explicitly speaking to the needs of women, as argued by the Webbs, Wells, and Gilman: "No woman," asserted Forster, "who is mentally worth anything will support a socialism which aims at securing systematized work and livelihood for men while leaving women in their present position of political and social slavery."[80]

When the Political Equality League was formed in British Columbia just prior to the First World War to campaign for women's suffrage, Kerr and Forster threw themselves into the movement.[81] Both spoke on behalf of the league, and Forster became its Kelowna organizer. At this level of political involvement they chose to cloak their socialist and neo-Malthusian interests. Eugenic concerns, however, received a good deal of attention in the mouthpiece of the league, the *Champion.* It advertised Frances Swiney's *The Responsibilities of Fatherhood,* reprinted Florence Woolston's "The Eugenics of Suffrage," applauded American laws on the "sterilization of degenerates," and insisted on feminists' concern for "racial progress." British Columbia suffragists wanted the vote, declared the *Champion,* "because they believe that a greater development of mind and heart will make them better fitted for the responsibilities of

[78]*Western Clarion,* October 13, 1906, p. 2. See Karl Kautsky, *Vermehrung und Entwicklung in Natur und Gesellschaft* (Stuttgart, 1910), pp. 243–52; and on the United States, see also Mari-Jo Buhle, *Women and American Socialism, 1870–1920* (Urbana, IL, 1981); Bruce Dancis, "Socialism and Women in the United States, 1900–1920," *Socialist Revolution* 27 (1976): 122–23.

[79]Janice Newton, "Women and *Cotton's Weekly:* A Study of Women and Socialism in Canada, 1901," *Resources for Feminist Research* (Fall 1980), pp. 58–60. I owe special thanks to Janice Newton who, in the course of her own research, uncovered information on Forster and Kerr, which she generously shared with me.

[80]*Cotton's Weekly,* December 30, 1909, p. 2; February 17, 1910, p. 2; March 11, 1909, p. 7; April 15, 1900, p. 7; April 22, 1909, p. 7; May 27, 1909, p. 7; and see also Janice Newton, "From Wage Slave to White Slave: The Prostitution Controversy and the Early Canadian Left," in Linda Kealey and Joan Sangster, eds., *Beyond the Vote: Canadian Women and Politics* (Toronto, 1989), pp. 217–36.

[81]See *Kelowna Daily Courier,* October 10, 1912, pp. 1, 6; October 17, 1912, p. 3; and *Champion,* August 1912, p. 14; November 1912, p. 12; January 1913, p. 7; May 1913, p. 6.

motherhood."[82] The suffragists expressed enough of a concern for the issue of breeding to draw the support of Kerr and Forster. The eugenic preoccupations of the Canadian feminists, however, tended to be aimed at securing a more disciplined, orderly society, not the libertarian utopia envisioned by the contributors of *Lucifer*.[83]

With the disappearance of *Lucifer*, Kerr also began to send letters and articles on the sex issue to the *Malthusian,* published in London, England. This journal, thought to be the first in the English-speaking world to defend consistently the morality of family limitation, was far less liberal than *Lucifer*. As the mouthpiece of the Malthusian League, it argued ad nauseam that only by a restriction of fertility could the working class improve its standard of living. A defender of socialism, free love, and eugenics, Kerr was very much in a minority position, but he persisted in his attempts to enlighten his fellow contributors.

His first goal was to soften the harshly deterministic line of the league. Family restriction would only be acceptable, he argued, if it were discussed in personal, not class, terms. "It is useless to tell a man that if he and ten million others will have small families, he will gain something. The thing to do is to show him how he will gain by *having a small family himself;* no matter what the others do."[84] He attacked the idea floated in the *Malthusian* that large families be fined; all the state should do is provide sex education and free "preventatives." "A knowledge of preventatives," he argued, "is an important part of popular education and should be furnished by the state."[85] Once individuals had the knowledge—and even the Malthusian League, for all its abstract discussion of neo-Malthusianism, did not give practical advice on contraception until 1913—it was up to them how they used it.

Kerr's second goal was to maintain the links between fertility restriction and the radical counterculture in which it found its most outspoken defenders. Neo-Malthusians, he protested, in their eagerness to win respectability were hastily turning their backs on the spokespersons of such embarrassing causes as free love, socialism, and libertarian eugenics.[86] To make it clear that he had not given up the role of social critic,

---

[82]*Champion,* August 1912, p. 13; November 1912, p. 6; January 1914, pp. 11–12; February 1914, p. 16; September 1913, p. 7. See also Carol Bacchi, "Race Regeneration and Social Purity: A Study of the Social Attitudes of Canada's English-Speaking Suffragettes," *Histoire sociale/Social History* 11 (1978): 460–73.

[83]For attacks on the state of Washington's sterilization law, see *Agitator,* October 1, 1912, p. 1.

[84]*Malthusian,* September 1906, p. 65.

[85]Ibid., October 1907, pp. 74–75.

[86]Ibid., December 1908, p. 95; June 1917, p. 45; December 1917, pp. 98–99. On attacks on Kerr for his defense of free love, see ibid., January 1909, p. 6.

Kerr defended these movements while attacking the puritan police state of America for its persecution of Margaret Sanger and castigating English racism and "all the superstitions of an imperial and patriotic nature."[87]

Kerr's writings were presumably accepted by the editors of the *Malthusian* because he did fulfill one valuable function—that of an expert reporter on conditions in the overseas empire. With his account of the hard times that Canada was enduring, they could shore up the Malthusian argument that immigration offered no escape from the inevitable population problem; restriction of fertility was as necessary on the North American plains as in the slums of Newcastle.[88] The Malthusian League was also becoming aware by the end of the First World War of how little impact it was having on English society. To take advantage of the postwar interest in birth control, a more flexible approach was required. As a result the dour *Malthusian* was ended by the Drysdale family in 1922, and *New Generation* was established as the voice of neo-Malthusianism. Kerr, who with Forster returned to England the same year, became the journal's editor in 1923; he only relinquished its direction a short time before his death in 1951.[89]

It is possible to interpret Kerr and Forster's leaving Canada as an indication that the country simply was not receptive to their mix of socialist and eugenic ideas. They certainly were not "typical" Canadian radicals, but one could just as easily say that Moses Harman was not a typical American or Havelock Ellis a typical Englishman. Obviously Kerr and Forster were so atypical that they only found friendly responses to their proposals in that small, cosmopolitan coterie of sex radicals scattered throughout the world.[90]

But though they felt isolated in Canada, they were not entirely alone in believing that aspects of sex radicalism could be incorporated in a socialist program. Echoes of such concerns were intermittently sounded in the left-wing press. During the First World War, the *B.C.*

[87]Ibid., April 1915, p. 29; July 1912, p. 51.

[88]Ibid., August 1910, p. 67; December 1910, pp. 103–4; May 1914, p. 39; June 1915, p. 44; September 1915, p. 72.

[89]*New Generation*, February 1923, p. 1; May–June 1951, pp. 4–5. On Kerr's later views, see his *Our Prophets* (Croyden, 1932); *Is Britain Over Populated?* (Croyden, 1927); "The Sexual Rights of Spinsters," in *World League for Sexual Reform: Proceedings of the Third Congress, London 1929* (London, 1930), pp. 91–94.

[90]See Leslie Fishbein, *Rebels in Bohemia: The Radicals of the Masses, 1911–1917* (Chapel Hill, NC, 1982); Judith R. Walkowitz, "Science, Feminism, and Romance: The Men and Women's Club, 1885–1889," *History Workshop* 21 (1986): 37–59; Lucy Bland, "Marriage Laid Bare: Middle-Class Women and Marital Sex c. 1880–1914," in Jane Lewis, ed., *Labour and Love: Women's Experiences of Home and Family, 1850–1940* (Oxford, 1986), pp. 123–46.

*Federationist* carried letters from readers calling for "eugenic babies" rather than sickly ones and reported J. S. Woodsworth's support of sex education and companionate marriage. Ada Muir wrote in the *Voice* of her admiration for Lillian Harman, while Florence Rowe provided the *One Big Union Bulletin* with articles on "Better and Fewer Babies." Violet McNaughton's opening of her column in the *Western Producer* in 1927 to the discussion of family limitation elicited a flurry of letters from prairie progressives interested in eugenics. "I hold," wrote Carl Axelson of Bingville, Alberta, "that it is essential for every person to study physiology to the extent of securing correct knowledge of our bodies and the relation and interdependence of sex and especially information regarding reproduction." Another writer upbraided those who were fearful that "the effort to improve the human family by using more commonsense and knowledge in the choosing of a life-mate would eliminate sentiment and love." Sophia H. Dixon of Unity, Saskatchewan, a future founder of the Co-operative Commonwealth Federation, cited Russia as an example of a society in which such improvements of the race were being pursued.[91]

What all these individuals imagined was a better, future world in which a rational, scientific, but noncoercive approach would be taken to the sex question. Access to sex education, contraceptives, divorce, and the endowment of motherhood would, they hoped, free women from the trap of loveless marriages and mindless breeding. The evils spawned by the Victorian marriage system—illegitimacy, prostitution, venereal disease—would disappear. The sex radicals' understanding of the laws of heredity were slim, to say the least. But their better-qualified opponents who supported conservative Galtonian eugenics would turn their "science" to even more transparently self-serving purposes.[92]

---

[91]*B.C. Federationist,* February 6, 1914, p. 5; March 21, 1919, p. 3; *The Voice,* May 12, 1911, p. 3; *One Big Union Bulletin,* November 6, 1924, p. 2; *Western Producer,* January 6, 1927, p. 12; February 10, 1927, p. 12; March 3, 1927, p. 12. Further letters on the subject ran through November 1927. For the personal journal of a Canadian woman drawn during the years 1906–19 to the ideas of Edward Carpenter, Emma Goldman, and Charlotte Perkins Gilman, see Alice A. Chown, *The Stairway* (1921; rpt. Toronto, 1988).

[92]On the continuing interest of the British Left in eugenics, see Michael Freeden, "Eugenics and Progressive Thought: A Study in Ideological Affinity," *Historical Journal* 22 (1979): 645–71; Greta Jones, "Eugenics and Social Policy between the Wars," *History Journal* 25 (1982): 717–28; Diane Paul, "Eugenics and the Left," *Journal of the History of Ideas* 45 (1984): 567–90; Richard A. Soloway, *Demography and Degeneration: Eugenics and the Declining Birth Rate in Twentieth-Century Britain* (Chapel Hill, NC, 1990), pp. 199–202. On Canada see Angus McLaren, *Our Own Master Race: Eugenics in Canada, 1885–1945* (Toronto, 1990).

# In Search of "The Real Thing": Ideologies of Love, Modern Romance, and Women's Sexual Subjectivity in the United States, 1920–40

PAMELA S. HAAG

*Department of History*
*Yale University*

IN 1913 THE MARYLAND Vice Commission and its national counterparts observed that women they labeled charity girls "like[d] to have a good time. 'S.C.Y.' goes with young men who are studying law; while on vacation from the telephone exchange, they used to have parties each night at which they would drink a great deal and have promiscuous immorality. . . . They would all leave the next morning thinking they had had a glorious time." S.C.Y.'s good times, however, would invariably lead her to the red-light district, the commission concluded: young wage-earning women who allowed men to treat them to "a glass of beer, an ice cream, a dance" would "drift quickly into prostitution," insofar as they had already practiced a less lucrative form of barter in permitting men to buy their companionship, if not their sexual labors.[1] Yet as middle-class girls increasingly socialized and entertained men in public venues rather than in the home, attended college, worked for wages, and insisted on distinguishing their youthful, modern values from those of their Victorian predecessors, dating emerged as a whitewashed description of heterosexual customs not unlike those earlier consigned to the demiprostitute charity girl. Indeed by the 1940s the young woman who attended petting parties and insisted, "If a girl has to pay her own way on a date, she may as well go alone," would be judged, however be-

---

[1] Kathy Peiss, *Cheap Amusements: Working Women and Leisure in Turn-of-the-Century New York* (Philadelphia, 1986); Maryland Vice Commission, Report (1913), 3:25, Enoch Pratt Free Library Archives, Baltimore, MD. Forty-seven municipal vice crusades were launched between 1900 and 1917. Barbara Meil Hobson cites one estimate that over one billion pages were published on "vice" between 1900 and 1920 (*Uneasy Virtue: The Politics of Prostitution and the American Reform Tradition* [New York, 1987], p. 140).

This essay originally appeared in the *Journal of the History of Sexuality* 1992, vol. 2, no. 4.

grudgingly, as a prototypical participant in youth and leisure culture. In this transformed, sexualized world, according to one observer, "All of 'em pet. Good women. Poor women. All of 'em."[2]

This essay will reappraise the transformation in sexual mores—described as liberalization or modernization—suggested in the above quotes. Sexual modernity, as understood by historians and historical actors, encompassed several transformations, including, first, an acknowledgment—facilitated by psychoanalysis and sexology—of female sexual desire prior to or outside of marriage, couched by flappers as defiance of the purportedly repressive habits of Victorian predecessors. Second, as nice girls were acknowledged to have sexual desires, virginity and chastity declined as rigid barometers of female sexual virtue, and advocates of anti-Victorian sensuality explicitly championed eradication of the sexual double standard that had denied women their desires. Challenges to the double standard, in turn, rendered increasingly deviant or suspicious women's resistance to heterosexual companionability, which by the 1900s—as I will describe in Section 1—was identified as the principal route to emotional intimacy and self-realization.

A few historians have critiqued the liberatory pretensions of heterosexual relations in the "modern manner." Christina Simmons, particularly, persuasively argues that the modern companionate idea of hetersexual relations developed as a conservative response to threats posed to the patriarchal marital institution by feminism and the decline of the household as a center of economic activity and achieved popularity only by the eclipse of lesbian sexuality. Sheila Jeffreys argues, similarly, that the liberatory idealization of companionate heterosexuality as the "normal" expression of female sexuality prohibitively and repressively stigmatized emotionally intimate relations between women.[3]

---

[2]As quoted in Paula Fass, *The Damned and the Beautiful: American Youth in the 1920s* (New York, 1977), p. 309. On leisure see Roy Rosenzweig, *Eight Hours for What We Will: Workers and Leisure in an Industrial City, 1870–1920* (Cambridge, 1983); John Modell, *Into One's Own: From Youth to Adulthood in the United States* (Berkeley, CA, 1989); and Lewis Erenberg, *Steppin' Out: New York Night Life and the Transformation of American Culture, 1890–1930* (Westport, CT, 1981). On adolescence see Joseph Kett, *Rites of Passage: Adolescence in America* (New York, 1977); Harvey Graff, *Growing Up in America* (Detroit, MI, 1987). On consumer culture see Richard Wightman Fox, ed., *The Culture of Consumption* (New York, 1981); Colin Campbell, *The Romantic Ethic and the Spirit of Modern Capitalism* (London, 1987) for a revised periodization; Lisabeth Cohen, *Making a New Deal* (New York, 1989). Modernization is discussed by Peter Filene, *Him/Her/Self: Sex Roles in Modern America* (New York, 1974); Elaine Tyler May, *Great Expectations: Divorce in Twentieth-Century America* (Chicago, 1980). Lawrence Stone, *The Family, Sex, and Marriage in England, 1500–1800* (New York, 1979), provides a larger history of individualism and the modern family.

[3]Christina Simmons, "Modern Sexuality and the Myth of Victorian Repression," in

These studies generally leave intact the assumption that women regained their sexual desires with modernity. Simmons judges that despite its heterosexual imperative, modernity established sexuality as "a basic expression of personal rights in the 1920s." Karen Lystra similarly describes a progression from the nineteenth to the twentieth century "away from [sexuality] as something that a woman's father owned, and then her husband, toward something that only she possessed." This reasoning, however, assumes that if no discrete outside party such as the husband, the male head of a household, or, more broadly, the patriarchal state, possesses a woman's sexual identity, then the woman, by elimination, must own it herself. Indisputably, the entrenchment of psychoanalysis—with its popularized lesson that all individuals possess sexual instincts—sculpted the modern sexual sensibility that Simmons and Lystra describe.[4] According to Howard Gadlin, the historical accident of psychoanalysis "updated the female personality" by affirming that "women were passive and irrational, sexually bound"; it granted women freedoms to seek fulfillment but only within the "boundaries of their sexuality." In her study of lesbianism Lillian Faderman similarly argues that in the 1920s, and largely in response to Freudianism, "the sex drive was identified, perhaps for the first time in history, as being the foremost instinct—in women as well as men—inescapable and all but uncontrollable." Faderman usefully identifies legitimized female desire as "permanently intertwined with real love," yet like Gadlin she upholds the ruling assumption of modernization—that women regained their desire in the fascination with sexology that began in the 1920s.[5]

Yet who really "possessed" the female sexuality so central to modern discourses on romance and love? It seems that in a culture that constructs the self as property and subjectivity as self-ownership, sexual rights derive from an acknowledgment of women's sexual sovereignty rather than simply an acknowledgment of women's sexual desire.[6]

---

*Passion and Power: Sexuality and History,* ed. Christina Simmons and Kathy Peiss (Philadelphia, 1989), pp. 157–78; Sheila Jeffreys, *The Spinster and Her Enemies: Feminism and Sexuality, 1880–1930* (London, 1985).

[4]Simmons, p. 73; Karen Lystra, *Searching the Heart: Women, Men, and Romantic Love in Nineteenth-Century America* (New York, 1989), pp. 81, 235. See also Michael Grossberg, *Governing the Hearth: Law and the Family in Nineteenth-Century America* (Chapel Hill, NC, 1988).

[5]Howard Gadlin, "Private Lives and Public Order: A Review of Intimate Relations in America," *Massachusetts Review* 17 (1976): 323; Lillian Faderman, *Surpassing the Love of Men: Romantic Friendship and Love between Women from the Renaissance to the Present* (New York, 1981), p. 304.

[6]On the proprietary self, see Walter Benn Michaels, *The Gold Standard and the Logic of*

The governing ideologies of sexual modernity—framed by psychoanalytic theories of the self—in fact replicated rather than transcended nineteenth-century assumptions of a proprietary male self and an unruly, sexually dispossessed female self. Although ideologies of modernization seemingly restored to women their sexual desires, I will argue in Section 2 that they in fact posited a bifurcated female self, whose sexuality belonged to the elusive subconscious rather than to the proprietary, rational female self capable of claiming and acting upon desires.

Because historians have assumed the general sexualization of all women through twentieth-century cultural and intellectual transformations, they have been comparatively less interested in the interaction of class identities and female sexuality in the "modern manner." Whereas the oversexualization of the working-class woman—as opposed to the assumed "passionlessness" of the middle-class woman—informs most analyses of nineteenth-century sexual identities, studies of sexuality in the 1900s tend to tacitly uphold, through their occlusion of class, the notion of a national, hegemonically "classless middle-class" American culture.[7] The relation between class and sexual identities deserves more sustained attention for several reasons.

First, the aggregate identity of the sexually modern—and presumably liberated—middle-class girl initially was negotiated in the crucible of class and finally secured, I would argue, through the demarcation of prostitution (or sexual profiteering) from premarital sensual expression legitimized by an idealized, all-consuming love. The immediate historical context of sexual modernity included a dominant—although by no means ubiquitous—middle-class ideology that had upheld a dichotomy between public women who, de facto, performed sexual labor and wives whose sexuality was safely inscribed in the private realm, if acknowledged at all. As middle-class girls trespassed into the morally dangerous world of urban leisure, catering to the often economically redundant adolescent, newly drawn class territories dictated revised sexual codes as

---

*Naturalism* (Berkeley, CA, 1989); Wai Chi Dimock, *Empires for Liberty: Melville and the Poetics of Individualism* (Princeton, NJ, 1990); both are what might be described as histories of subjectivity.

[7] See George Chauncey, Jr., "From Sexual Inversion to Homosexuality: The Changing Medical Conceptualization of Female 'Deviance,'" in Simmons and Peiss, eds., pp. 87–118; Carroll Smith-Rosenberg, *Disorderly Conduct: Visions of Gender in Victorian America* (New York, 1985); Nancy Cott, "'Passionlessness': An Interpretation of Victorian Sexual Ideology," *Signs* 4 (1978): 219–36; Ellen Rothman, "Sex and Self Control: Middle-Class Courtship in America," *Journal of Social History* 15 (1981): 409–26; Charles Rosenberg, "Sexuality, Class, and Role in Nineteenth-Century America," *American Quarterly* 25 (1973): 131–53.

well. As the idea of romantic love grew to legitimize a female sexuality that was not, strictly speaking, commercially contracted but not necessarily linked to the realization of a marital contract either, a woman's commodification of her sexuality became the prohibited, and presumably class-specific, avenue by which she claimed her sexuality as her own.

Second, insofar as Americans of disparate income levels increasingly identified themselves as "middle-class," sexuality became not only reflective of materially based class differences, but also a constitutive component of class as a cultural category.[8] The gradual, modern shift from a phenomenological idea of sexual vice based on physical chastity to an expressive taxonomy of vice based, in the words of one college student, on *"how* [a woman] is not a virgin" demanded that a girl tell the right kind of story to authorize her sexuality. If an alienation from desires characterized the "natural" young woman, the unnatural and class-specific artifices of narration and self-stylization emerged as tools by which a woman might invent or earn her sexual subjectivity, by distinguishing it both from the commodified sexuality of the prostitute or the gold digger and from the "unconscious" sexuality increasingly ascribed to the "vulgar" classes. A properly fashioned self-invention or narrative demonstrated the integrity of consciousness and sexual instinct assumed for the male subject. Conversely, the working-class girl—as defined by material status as well as by personal style—appears in a variety of discourses as the girl who cannot properly own her sexuality because she either cannot master her instincts or because she alienates and relinquishes her sexuality according to the rules of the market and economic pragmatism.[9] Hence, the interdependency of heterosexual definition and class differentiation persisted in the 1920s and 1930s in subtler form.

The crucial importance of narrations, both verbal and symbolic, to modern ideas of legitimate female sexuality highlights an additional revision, implicit throughout this essay, concerning the meaning of "ideology." Methodologically, this essay draws on an array of discourses from the 1920s and 1930s—from the social scientific literature to popular "advice to the lovelorn" columns. Obviously, as social historians

[8]Beth Bailey, *From Front Porch to Back Seat: Courtship in Twentieth-Century America* (Baltimore, MD, 1988), p. 11. Bailey cites a Purdue poll from 1952 in which 47 percent of all high school students whose fathers were unskilled laborers defined themselves as middle class, as did 59 percent of those whose fathers held "mid-level jobs working with tools." As Bailey concludes, "These responses seem to show that young people had a sense that class lines were flexible and not primarily determined by income" (p. 11).

[9]Dorothy Bromley, *Youth and Sex* (New York, 1934), p. 106; Elinor Glyn, *It* (New York, 1927), p. 195; James Bridges, *The Meanings and Varieties of Love: A Psychological Analysis* (New York, 1935), p. 15.

underscore, prescriptive, scientific, and popular literature bear nebulous relations to lived experience. Yet it is my contention that the relation between ideology and experience in and of itself has a history: the meaning and relative importance of discourses—both verbal and symbolic—vary according to historical setting. Particularly in the modern context, when structures of prohibition and repression are heavily dependent on objective, scientific formulations of truth—the "normal" and the "deviant," for example—it is crucial that historians read ideological material with an eye to what Foucault labels the micropolitical operations of power: that is, the extent to which individuals and groups rely on and inevitably reproduce hegemonic ideologies in their historically specific conceptions of self—the meaning of "I" carried to ostensibly private, politically impervious experiences. In this light, I will juxtapose widely diverse sources in order to disclose the deeply lodged, commonsense definitions of women's sexual subjectivity that bridged discursive idiosyncrasies. In other words, I will view ideology and discourse as tools by which a new female subjectivity was constructed, rather than as imperfect reflections of a female sexual subject who existed beyond or prior to discursive invention.[10]

I

In 1924 the publisher Bernarr MacFadden christened *Dream World* magazine, a chronicle of "true love and romance" stories, with a promise to animate the "stern and uncompromising realities of life" through "soft, hazy dramas" of love that can "carry you outside of yourself." Enter the "theater of the imagination!" MacFadden urged, and "no matter how dull and prosaic your environment, . . . you can build castles in the air; you can construct your whole career." Despite his unapologetically ethereal vision, MacFadden and his *Dream World* readers saw themselves as engaged in a project subversive to the grinding demands of modern life: they were fashioning—or justifying—an idealized vision of selfhood that fused the separate worlds of work, leisure, and family life in the early twentieth century. The repertoire of romantic love stories, as well as prolific professional and prescriptive commentaries on young love, apotheosized romance as an unruly and by some accounts transcendent alchemy, one that reintegrated and transformed the self,

[10]Michel Foucault, *The History of Sexuality: An Introduction,* vol. 1 of *The History of Sexuality,* trans. Robert Hurley (New York, 1978); see Judith Butler, *Gender Trouble: Feminism and the Subversion of Identity* (New York, 1990); and Denise Riley, *Am I That Name? Feminism and the Category of "Women" in History* (Minneapolis, MN, 1988) for examples of poststructuralist revisions of the sex/gender dichotomy.

restored integrity, and, MacFadden concluded, gave us "something to live for."[11]

The belief in a philosophy of love as "the most divine thing we are allowed to know about on earth," while not lacking in precedents, gained velocity and popular currency in the early 1900s, probably because imperatives of socioeconomic modernity leveled particularly dramatic assaults on nineteenth-century attributes of class and gender identity.[12] In her history of courtship Ellen Rothman observes that "1910 and 1920 were separated by as wide a gulf as that between any two American generations." One of the most dramatic developments of the early 1900s, which coincided with the entrenchment of leisure time and mass entertainment, was the cultural invention of adolescence and youth as a prolonged—and potentially dangerous—period for education and social interaction. Collectively these transformations brought young women into relatively unstructured public contact with men in amusement resorts, increasingly sex-integrated workplaces, and college campuses, which demanded new rules for sexual conduct. As T. J. Jackson Lears has observed, the erosion of nineteenth-century communal and religious networks encouraged a vision of the self as fragmented and "somehow 'unreal,'" comprised only of a series of manipulable social masks. Social worker William Thomas articulated such a fear in 1924 when he wrote, exasperated, "The world has become large, alluring and confusing. . . . There is no universally accepted body of doctrines."[13]

Perhaps in response to the fragmentation of social roles and identities, both popular and sociological discourses on romance and sexuality depicted love as impervious to the splintering interventions or interests of the market and distinct from the rationalistic, functional relations of work or sexual barter. America, one writer noted, "appears to be the only country in the world where love is the national problem. To admit

[11]Editorial in *Dream World*, February 1924. *Dream World*, after 1924 renamed *True Love and Romance* (hereafter cited as *True Love*), is available only at the Library of Congress and the offices of the MacFadden Publishing Company. It published issues continuously from 1924 to the early 1950s. (Another MacFadden publication, *True Story*, had a circulation of two million.) For this research, I read two or three of the cover stories for every third year of the magazine from 1924 to 1945.

[12]May, *Great Expectations*, p. 47. May's study of divorce suggests that even though the bourgeois household fulfilled few necessary economic functions, middle-class marriages in the late nineteenth century remained loyal to a system of "duties and sacrifices," rather than personal satisfaction, as the basis of marriage. See also Sandra Herman, "Loving Courtship or the Marriage Market?" *American Quarterly* 25 (1973): 235–55, for a discussion of late nineteenth-century advocates and challengers of pragmatic courtship.

[13]Ellen K. Rothman, *Hands and Hearts: A History of Courtship in America* (New York, 1984); T. J. Jackson Lears, "From Salvation to Self Realization," in Fox, ed., p. 9; and William Thomas, *The Unadjusted Girl* (New York, 1923), p. 73.

the desire to marry for any other motive than 'true love' is to risk being considered mercenary and materialist. . . . Our present American culture is the only one which has attempted to capitalize on violent emotional attachments and make them a basis for marriage."[14] Elinor Glyn, a popular author of romance novels, explained her philosophy of love in a 1923 treatise: "Being in love is the only time that two human beings can rise beyond this material world of ours into a sphere whose atmosphere seems to envelop them with transcendent happiness." Yet such happiness, Glyn cautioned, never envelops couples "who do not expect joy. He will secure the pleasure her money can give him, or whatever it was he desired and calculated upon—and vice versa—but how ugly all that is!"[15]

The person who plunged heedlessly into romantic love defied rational economic interests—the "shackles of wealth and poverty"—and thereby transcended socioeconomic identities. Emmanuel Berl in *The Nature of Love* (1924) identified love as "the desire to belong to the self no longer. . . . Love destroys the personal self and reaches out to the substantial self. . . . Love saves us from our self." *True Love* confirmed Berl's distinction between the substantial self and the dreary rituals of the personal self in presenting love as the vital spark that allows people to "really touch your inner life. . . . You can live in a crowded city, and loneliness may be eating your heart out. [People] are just a neutral something" until love awakens the meaningful "inner life."[16]

In keeping with the imperative that true love transcend the bleak nexus of class hatred and "shackles of wealth and poverty," MacFadden defended another of his profitable magazine enterprises from charges of commercialism: "It is the purpose of *True Story* magazine to present, not the highly colored, imaginative plots of those who make story writing a business . . . but to take unvarnished stories of people who are giving their memories to the world. Love stories are lived." MacFadden's insistence on the similar veracity of *Dream World* and *True Love* narratives served as a partial justification, it seems, for allying the ostensibly incompatible aims of the market and true love.[17]

At the same time, a burgeoning population of professional social workers attempted to codify standards of normal adolescent sexuality on a transformed urban landscape. By acknowledging female desire yet endorsing sexual expression only after "the consecration of real love," a social hygienist who wrote a prizewinning handbook for high school

---

[14]Oliver Butterfield, *Love Problems of Adolescence* (New York, 1939), p. 14.
[15]Elinor Glyn, *The Philosophy of Love* (New York, 1923), foreword.
[16]Emmanuel Berl, *The Nature of Love* (New York, 1924), p. 15; *True Love,* March 1927.
[17]*True Love,* March 1924; February 1927; and June 1924.

students echoed the popular wisdom of love as personally transformative. "When the wonder and beauty of the higher force of love is won," she wrote, "it leads to service, to each other and the world." In this example the careful allocation or preservation of a girl's sexuality sets in motion a chain reaction, eventually enabling the realization of a heroic self who serves her mate and, indeed, the entire world.[18]

Advice columns, as capillaries between individual experiences, professional expertise, and the mass culture that distilled love out of the confusing and alluring conditions of modern life, hint at the extent to which a philosophy of love framed adolescents' tentative encounters with romance. Letters from the 1920s published in Doris Blake's *New York Daily News* column are filled with references to "love" stirred by momentary encounters in dance halls. In a fairly typical letter from 1925, "Worried" tells Blake, "I am very fond of a girl. In the class room she is always staring and smiling at me and when I meet her in the street she smiles. Do you think this girl loves me?" Although Blake delivered a sober prognosis to "Worried," she more often magnanimously nurtured her readers' ideas of love as the authentic feeling rewarded by diligent dating. Her readers, in turn, envisioned love as ennobling risks and, occasionally, excusing moral lapses: it sanctioned dating the poor man over the rich man and often served as a talisman against accusations of sexual promiscuity. Blake, who thought herself an "old fogy" for refusing to condone petting, could nevertheless forgive the young woman who had "loved well but not too wisely" in "forfeiting [her] self-respect" to an untrustworthy man. The imperative of finding "the real thing" apparently influenced tremendously the expectations and lived experiences of modern adolescents. Sociologists Robert and Helen Lynd discovered, for example, that teenagers—who devoured *True Love* magazines—"demanded love as the only valid basis for marriage. [They] regard romance in marriage as something which, like their religion, must be believed in to hold society together. Love is the mystery—it just happens."[19]

Rhapsodic accounts of the frog-to-prince alchemy of love responded to the fragmenting realities of 1920s culture. By their vehement disavowal of materialism, adherents of the therapeutic value of love boasted

[18]Quoted in Paul Achilles, *The Effects of Sex Literature on High School Students* (New York, 1923).

[19]See John Modell, "Dating Becomes a Way of American Life," in *The American Family in Sociohistorical Perspective,* ed. Michael Gordon (New York, 1973); Robert Lynd and Helen Lynd, *Middletown: A Study in Modern American Culture* (New York, 1956); Doris Blake's advice column, *New York Daily News,* September 22, 1925. Blake's column ran from 1921 to at least 1951. I read approximately one hundred letters per year for every fifth year from 1920 to 1945, about six hundred letters in all.

that it erased class hierarchies and nurtured an energized, vital self that transcended the model of an alienable, fragmented self intrinsic to economic definitions of selfhood. If men sold their labor to perform machine-like work, broken into ever more discrete productive tasks, love made them self-possessed subjects again. As a 1935 study observed, "Love has actually a transforming power. There is some truth in the fairy tale: the dragon is changed to a prince. . . . Such is the magic power of love."[20]

According to its promoters, romance transcended the sexual double standard as well: it legitimized—or at least naturalized—women's sexual desires if they were awakened and exercised in the nebulous context of love. While very few social workers or popular commentators sanctioned young women's promiscuity, they often underscored (and tacitly endorsed) the lawless virtues of romantic love in generally lawless adolescence, and they consequently demarcated a tenuous territory between absolute vice and absolute virtue, in which women might claim their sexuality as neither a coin of economic exchange nor a possession to be claimed only in marriage. Women could deploy the ideology that "anything was alright as long as you were in love" to repudiate social barriers and customs. Furthermore, love's insular predilections created possibilities for individually executed protests against sexual hierarchy. As Emmanuel Berl noted, love constructed "lofty walls against outside influences. Love avoids society: it is a separating influence." Presumably, true love's scorn for regulatory social rituals or laws, as well as women's freedoms from capture or compulsory motherhood, would facilitate their self-realization and liberation through sexuality and love.[21]

The equation of self-possession, love, and sexuality has also enticed several feminist historians to appraise the companionate heterosexual ideal as a comparatively liberating swing in the history of sexuality. Yet as I will discuss in Section 2, sexual modernization, while it conceded that women might be sexual beings, never established that women were sexual subjects, in unconditional possession even of their heterosexual desire. The ideology of love and consecrated desire that promised to "carry you outside of yourself," beyond the particularities of social identity, thus also ensured that you were carried back.

## II

Freud first visited America in 1909, dispersing a quickly popularized vocabulary of sexual modernity and fulfillment. As early as the mid-

[20]Bridges, p. 87.
[21]Berl, p. 2; Rothman, *Hands and Hearts*, p. 186.

1920s, terms such as the "unconscious," "drives," "narcissism," and "instincts," among others, emerged as keywords for understanding and categorizing sexuality. The boy who dated a sexually reluctant girl might complain in an advice column that she had "unconsciously" led him on, while advice literature aimed at middle-class young women consistently urged the cultivation of an unneurotic "personality." In its widely disseminated—and distorted—form, Freudianism fixed the coordinates of modern self-identity: the "conscious" and the sexualized domain of the "subconscious."[22] Yet the ideological legitimation of female sexual pleasure enabled by this new concept of selfhood invariably replicated older, gendered paradigms of the female self as irrational, unruly, and generally dispossessed from both desire and judgment. Whereas popular psychoanalytic theories tended to affirm the male subject's self-possession, assuming an alliance between his conscious action and unconscious instincts, the same theories when applied to female subjects tended to replicate and exaggerate their *lack* of self-possession—a woman's alienation from sexual desires claimed by an internally alien unconscious. As benefactors of the integrated, vital self promised by myths of love, young men possessed their ostensibly uncontrollable instincts inasmuch as these instincts were seen as inextricably and legitimately linked to conscious actions, including some degree of aggression toward women and, plausibly, more overtly violent assaults. The crucial difference, then, between being a sovereign sexual subject—with its attendant rights—and being able to do sexual things remained a gendered one.

Literature that sought to orient young heterosexual sociability amplified gender-specific theories of sexual subjectivity because turbulent adolescence aggravated generally destabilized sexual mores. Winifred Richmond's *The Adolescent Girl* (1929), a study of "normal" adolescent sexuality and its "psychopathic," "neurotic," and "narcissistic" variants, illustrates the assumed relation between female desire and consciousness. After dismissing the psychopathic girl as a "law unto herself," Richmond confidently outlined the simple maxims of a normal girl's sexual identity: "We must expect an interest in the opposite sex to take precedence over everything else, whether she admits it or no. . . . Consciously or unconsciously, the instinctive drive is there, coloring her thoughts, shaping her ambitions, prompting her actions." Richmond later paradoxically asserted that although girls may not understand their sexuality, they in fact control sexual encounters with boys even if they accomplish this control through subconscious predispositions they do

---

[22]Nathan Hale, *Freud in America* (New York, 1971); Doris Blake's correspondents, even as early as the 1920s, frequently refer to the unconscious.

not apprehend. "Girls have no more need to be afraid of boys than boys of girls. Every girl who is honest with herself knows that it is she who sets the key for her relationship with men. Consciously or unconsciously she attracts them or repels them . . . and they but play up to her lead."[23]

Although her exposition of female sexual desire appears dangerously distanced from a young girl's rational possession, Richmond envisioned herself as a spokesperson for an enlightened sexual modernity that restored to women their sexual desire. "All forms of delinquency, even when the features are something else such as stealing . . . are linked to the instinctive [sexual] urge," Richmond contended, and "the girl who indulges in sex relations around the time of puberty is but obeying a natural impulse and is no more to be regarded as inherently depraved or vicious than a young animal." Thus Richmond acknowledged—and caricatured—a female sex instinct yet alienated this instinct from the rational deliberateness of conscious experience: the delinquent girl cannot be held responsible because she does not possess her desire. Rather, it possesses her. Delinquency, in fact, by Richmond's logic transpired precisely after a girl has had her sexual desires awakened like "a sleeping tiger" and then embarks on a rational, "conscious search for experiences." Because only the delinquent girl entertains a dialogue between conscious and subconscious desire, Richmond admonished society to "impose restraints upon [female] instinctive forces." Richmond imparted a confusing and not particularly optimistic message: if following an animalistic instinct relieved women of responsibility, but at the cost of their subjectivity, then following a deliberate, consciously chosen sexual trajectory similarly imperiled their claims to rational self-sovereignty (or at least to respectability) by stigmatizing them as deviant or delinquent. Because woman cannot rationally claim her desire, she achieves none of the rights granted by self-ownership. Although clichés of insatiable female desire both preceded and extend beyond the discovery of the unconscious, it is important to recognize that the very ideology of sexual modernity, with its replication of the bifurcated female self, perpetuated hierarchical and patriarchal paradigms that feminists hoped a companionate ideal would countermand.[24]

Sanford Read's 1928 sociological study of the struggles of male ado-

---

[23]Winifred Richmond, *The Adolescent Girl: A Book for Parents and Teachers* (New York, 1929), pp. 117, 194. See also Phyllis Blanchard, *The Adolescent Girl: A Study from the Psychoanalytic Viewpoint* (New York, 1920); Bridges (n. 9 above); Howard Wooston, *Prostitution in the United States* (New York, 1921); Dan McCown, *Love and Life: The Sex Urge and Its Consequences* (Chicago, 1928); Bernard Talmay, *Woman: A Treatise on the Normal and Pathological Emotions of Feminine Love* (New York, 1913); Andre Tridon, *Psychoanalysis and Love* (New York, 1922); Grace Elliot, *The Sex Life of Youth* (New York, 1929).

[24]Richmond, p. 112.

lescence pays explicit homage to Freud's "highly humanistic" theories of sexuality. Compared to Richmond's study of female adolescence, however, Read's humanistic reading of Freudian theory appears notably gender-specific. Read endorses Freud's view that "our psychological reactions are just as rigidly determined as our physical ones" and thereby acknowledges the general existence of uncontrolled sexual instinct, yet he proceeds to craft a specifically masculine relation between conscious and unconscious. The normal male will refine and master his "old impulses and instincts during adolescence," Read contends, greatly developing some "while others are subordinated. In connection with the reproductive function, love is born with all its attendant passions—jealousy, rivalry, and all the phenomena of human courtship." The interface of male rationality and subconscious desires (a threshold of delinquency for girls) produces a law-abiding subject in properly trained boys, according to Read. The productive activity here described—the transmutation of unruly desires into conscious, civil elaborations such as love and courtship—presupposes a healthy, self-possessive, and self-mediating relation between two planes of human experience. If the adolescent male goes wrong, Read suggests, it is not because he cannot possess his desires; on the contrary, delinquency transpires if forces that "the law cannot recognize" are "perverted by the correctional taboos of society. These tend in many instances to lead to undue individual repression, with the result that [perversions] are engendered." Hence, while society represented the only effective, rational regulatory agent in the girl's sexual development, it paradoxically represented the disruptive force for the boy, who, individually possessing the rational faculties to produce an integrated, functional subjectivity out of his instincts, was better left alone.[25]

MacFadden, in *The Virile Powers of Superb Manhood,* celebrated the male sex instinct as the generative "nervous energy" that "supplies the power of sex, the power of manhood. . . . Sexuality has been strongly marked in all the great men of eminence," MacFadden said, and it generated the "fiery ardor of a patriot, the intense ambition and noble deeds of the warrior." Although ostensibly MacFadden underscores the raw power of the sex instinct, he crucially links this power to male consciousness—specifically, to the greatest accomplishments and heroics of

[25]Sanford Read, *The Struggles of Male Adolescence* (New York, 1928), pp. 200, 317, 46, 11, 54. See also William Fielding, *Sex and the Love Life* (New York, 1927); Edith Hooker, *The Laws of Sex* (Boston, 1920); Francis Bernard, *Women's Mysterious Influence over Men* (San Francisco, 1920). For later examples, see Bromley (n. 9 above); Jeannette Brill, *The Adolescent Court and Crime Prevention* (New York, 1938); and Lewis Doshey, *The Boy Sex Offender* (New York, 1943).

masculinity. Whereas the sexual, reproductive energy in the adolescent girl, as Phyllis Blanchard described in 1920, "take[s] possession of her being," the young men that MacFadden describes took possession of their unconscious sexual energy and marshaled it for the causes of "civilization."[26]

Although few authors mention fantasies as dominant or normative components of male sexual development, Sanford Read endorsed the young man's "make-believe world" as generating blueprints for actual production: "There are no limitations of time or space, and all wishes become actualized. . . . The pictures he sees vividly in his imagination stimulate him to set about life's tasks in such a way that castles in the air become reality." The conversion of dreams to material aspirations and accomplishments assumes an integral relation between unconscious imaging and conscious applications. The assumed fragmentation of desire and consciousness in the female, however, rendered problematic or at best superfluous any products generated by her subconscious longings. The Judge Baker Foundation, a private organization for reform of juvenile delinquents, analyzed several cases of female sexual delinquency in 1925 and tended to relegate the often elaborate and clever fantasies of adolescent girls to the detached realm of "wish fulfillment fancies." Tillie, for example, a thirteen-year-old who came before the foundation because she had left home and had an affair with a sailor, composed richly detailed letters to boys whose names she culled from the newspaper. She "engaged in a great deal of fantasy," the foundation remarked, that "need not be regarded as other than wish fulfillment." Neither productive nor inevitably psychopathic, young girls' fantasies of sexual individuation appeared just as ethereal and distant from their selves as from their subconscious.[27]

Psychoanalytic principles, with similar gender modifications, permeated more widely popularized discourses on dating and sexual relations as well. Elinor Glyn, "talking from a commonsense point of view," floridly explained the philosophy of love to a "general audience of young men and maidens" with reference to male instinctual prerogatives that "no laws can alter . . . or really control, [because] a natural force is prompting him." The "unconscious desire to re-create his species" sanctioned man's deliberate, conscious aggression in hunting his woman: "Man is a hunter. . . . A man can only lead while he remains a man, with a man's passion . . . so that this particular branch of moral re-

[26]Bernarr MacFadden, *The Virile Powers of Superb Manhood* (New York, 1924), pp. 81, 12; Blanchard, p. 46.

[27]Read, p. 312; Judge Baker Foundation, *Case Studies from 1925* (Boston, 1925), case 17.

sponsibility [that is, sexuality] cannot be measured, judged or criticized from the same standpoint as any other." According to Glyn, the young man's aggressive sexuality derived from an admittedly mysterious and unruly subconscious force but bore a distinct, rationalized, and crucially productive/procreative relation to his conscious actions. Man "was not designed in the scheme of things to be the soft, silky-voiced [female] creature" engendered by the alienation of unconscious instinct from conscious action.[28]

Judging from her effusive promotional campaigns and her often-mentioned romantic novels, Glyn's hyperbolic depiction of the species-preserving hunter and his willingly dominated unselfish mistress struck a responsive chord with young readers. Ideas of the unconscious, even in the 1920s, had an influence that surpassed professional boundaries and definitions. In 1922 Doris Blake printed a letter from a young girl who was "hurt, angry and disillusioned" by her date's improper sexual advances, to which one male reader responded, "I claim no normal, sane young man would dare to make such a request of a girl if her conduct had not given him reason to believe she was loose. Either purposefully or unconsciously, she led him up to such a request." Another man echoed, "Do you think for one moment any boy, except a degenerate, would venture to make such a request of a girl who had courageously denied him her lips? . . . The girl—perhaps without realizing that she was doing wrong—gave him the impression she was 'that sort of girl.'" Thus the modern genealogy of "she says no but means yes" includes the idea of an unconscious that is filtered through gendered concepts of rationality. If women do not consciously rationalize or know their desires, they have only a circumscribed and precarious claim to sexual sovereignty, or even to the genuine possession of their sexuality, in a culture that defines rights and identity by self-ownership.[29]

As the cinematic icon of sexual modernity, the "It Girl" illustrated the assumed bifurcation of a woman's sexuality from her consciousness. The film star Clara Bow and her contemporaries had "it"—sexual magnetism and charm—yet as suggested by the coy choice of pronoun, sexual magnetism did not constitute a consciously recognized or rationally mediated component of their selves. Rather, according to Glyn, "it" was the internal "other," the magical gift of "entire un-self-consciousness, an indifference to the effects she is producing. . . . Conceit or self-consciousness destroys 'it' immediately. 'It' demonstrates in tigers and

[28]Glyn, *Philosophy of Love,* pp. 107, foreword, 113.

[29]Doris Blake, *New York Daily News,* May 10, 1922; and September 14, 1925. On the idea of self-ownership as the basis of personal rights, see Carole Pateman, *The Sexual Contract* (Stanford, CA, 1989).

cats . . . both being mysterious and unbiddable!" The concept duplicated in popular parlance some of the assumptions of selfhood that
appeared in social scientific literature: awareness of sexuality, or "self-
consciousness," destroys its legitimacy, yet "un-self-consciousness" re-
duces one's sexuality to an animalistic mysteriousness or instinct that
effectively erases subjectivity. Although men also might possess "it,"
they avert the double bind of self-consciousness or selflessness by their
assumed capacity to own, master, and deploy "it" as a tool for actively
seeking sexual adventure. For the young girl, however, the capricious
"it" might "bring joy or trouble" because "it attracts against her will."[30]

The possibility that "it" might bring joy cannot be overlooked: if the
internally alien subconscious might give a young woman exactly what
she does not want, it might just as whimsically and unpredictably give
her the world she longs for—an optimistic, popular love story of the
1920s *True Love* magazine. "My Unknown Lover" promises in a clever
plot of hidden identities that "the hero of young Vida's dreams" can ma-
terialize, though assuredly not through any rational choices or tactics on
the heroine's part. After Vida enters the social whirl of New York society, she disappointingly discovers that male admirers such as Howard
Giles lack the magical qualities of her vividly imaged childhood dream
lovers. Then a mysterious suitor begins sending verses and hyacinths,
and her "dream lover and the writer of the verse had become one; instead of talking to me in words of my own invention, my hero spoke to
me in the fragrance of hyacinths." Vida continues her secret correspondence with the admirer until her father suffers a business failure and
pressures her to marry the uninspired Howard to allay his financial difficulties. At this impasse, her admirer arranges a rendezvous, to which
Vida "would have been afraid to go, to put my beautiful dream to the
daylight test," if not for the threat of having to marry Howard. The story
ends with Vida "idiotically happy" because Howard had been her secret
admirer all along.[31]

Some theorists of romantic fiction would contend that "My Unknown Lover" promises the realization of desires to women who follow
rules of sexual circumspection and fidelity to their romantic dreams.[32]

[30]Glyn, *It* (n. 9 above), p. 53; Elinor Glyn, *Three Weeks* (New York, 1909). Lois W.
Banner, *American Beauty* (New York, 1983), discusses sex appeal as well.

[31]"My Unknown Lover," *True Love*, February 1925. Numerous other stories from the
1920s duplicated the plot of hidden identity.

[32]Tanya Modleski, *Loving with a Vengeance: Mass-Produced Fantasies* (Westport, CT,
1982); and Kay Mussell, *Fantasies and Reconciliation: Contemporary Formulas of Women's
Romance Fiction* (Westport, CT, 1984), emphasize the educative role that romances fulfill
in teaching women how to "read" men and how to conceptualize the threats of sexual violence that surround their lives in more emotionally manageable terms. Both authors dis-

Yet these stories must also be read in relation to the popularly assumed disjunction between sexual desire and the domain of women's conscious agency: the conflation of Vida's dream lover with the scorned Howard, for example, complicates the reward thesis in that it vitiates Vida's skills to consciously choose one "right" man over another. If Vida had betrayed her chivalrous dreams she would have ended up with the wrong man (Howard), yet her loyalty to romantic dreams delivers her the "wrong" man (Howard), too. I do not mean to suggest that the happy ending is irrelevant, but simply that it foils, manipulates, and finally discredits the attempted union of conscious action or rational design with chaotic female desires: whether or not Vida makes a deliberate choice to own her fantasies and try to fulfill them, the capricious hand of Fate will in either case fortuitously give her the man she consciously reasoned to be an inappropriate lover. True love in this paradigmatic plot, then, defies self-determination in ways reflective of the assumed bifurcation of female self and subconscious desire.

As the sedimentation of psychoanalytic concepts continued through the 1930s, sociologists referred with increasing casualness to an essentially gendered relation between conscious and unconscious sexual identities. The hazy persona of a young girl dangerously dispossessed from her subconscious desires took sharper form as a more psychologically complicated, and less sympathetic, figure in Dorothy Bromley's study of *Youth and Sex* (1933). Codifying male instinctual desires into a rubric of "normal," rational behavioral expectations, Bromley portrayed "Pragmatic" male virgins as "undersexed, cold, ambitious." "A man sufficiently aroused to indulge might, after one or two experiences, be expected to seek more complete satisfaction," she speculated, and thus "the instinct for the hunt" differentiated the undersexed from their more pleasant, albeit less obeisant, "Hot Blooded" foils. If the Pragmatic man boorishly calculated his sexual goals, "Virginal" girls, in contrast, floated in an equally condemned haze of unconscious expectations that rendered them abnormally reticent. "Unawakened and in a few instances inhibited," the Virginal girl "consciously or unconsciously awaits marriage as the sesame to a whole world of experience and privilege. . . . What they want is to be 'really in love.' They have romantic notions of what that happy state would be like, but the physical side is a Pandora's box." The naive fantasies and "unquestionable ac-

---

cuss contemporary fiction, and few studies have been undertaken of romance literature in a historical context. See also Janice Radway, *Reading the Romance: Women, Patriarchy, and Popular Literature* (Chapel Hill, NC, 1984), for a reader-response analysis of romance fiction.

ceptance of parental standards" made the Virginal girl a dreary subject for investigation, yet Bromley reserved her venom for the female "Experimenter," who deliberately claimed and mastered her fantasies. "A girl decided to have an affair with a man she had known for two years. Since they were 'sufficiently attracted to each other'—whatever she meant by sufficiently . . . it is pathetic that young people should expect to find Paradise by invoking a biologic factor, even though they will often claim it was 'all to the good.'"[33]

Bromley's condemnation of the girl who rationally claimed and acted on her sexual desires and curiosity illustrates the inflection of sexual modernity as one paradoxically fused with older traditions of self-possession as a gendered privilege and right. Bromley condemns the female Experimenter's deliberateness, just as she does the male Pragmatist's coldness, because they both contradict myths of lawless romance and true love, the assumed goals of sexual experimentation. Yet the condemnations denote opposite assumptions of how the unconscious normally functions in relation to conscious subjectivity: the Pragmatist fails because he has inadequately embraced the rational trajectory of the sexual hunt dictated by his vital instinct, whereas the female Experimenter fails precisely because she *has* laid claim to instincts distorted, Bromley supposes, when rationally acted upon by a female subject. The nuanced distinction between the flaws of the female and male types in this example partially explains the enduring custom of men seeking and women waiting: acting requires a cognizance of interests and desires enabled only by the (man's) self-possession of sexuality. Emmanuel Berl, for example, explained that "the man in love endeavors to possess the object he loves, to appropriate to himself an object which is distinct from him, and which, rightly or wrongly, he regards as suitable for himself."[34] The capacity to appropriate an object and to deem it as distinct from the self assumes that the man in question has a self capable of such deliberations and conscious of the boundaries between self and other.

Bromley's scorn for rationalized female desire dovetailed with a general contempt for women's "selfish" sexual behavior in the 1930s. Because it destabilized social bastions of male prerogative—economic independence and the opportunity to sell one's labor and become a head

[33]Bromley, pp. 84–91. See also Butterfield (n. 14 above); Edwin Clarke, *Petting: Wise or Otherwise?* (New York, 1938); J. Francis Flynn, *Love and Sex Life of Woman* (California, 1931); Maurice Chicdeckel, M.D., *Female Sexual Perversion* (New York, 1935); I. M. Hotep [pseud.], *Love and Happiness: Intimate Problems of the Modern Woman* (New York, 1935).

[34]Berl (n. 16 above), p. 2.

of household—the Depression magnified contradictory claims to the ownership of female sexuality embedded in modern discourses on romance. The "war between the sexes," an assumed adversarial stance between the interests of men and women, accelerated in the economic crisis. Plausibly, an overemphasis on "natural" sex hierarchies comfortingly eclipsed painfully mutable economic hierarchies and also enforced, through its magnified intolerance of the "un-self-conscious" woman, the idea that all men at least owned themselves and their desires, even if they did not properly own their labor in a time when they could not sell it. Sexual ownership or mastery, in turn, when contrasted with women's lack of possession, buttressed otherwise imperiled patriarchal privileges and institutions. A contemptuous, suspicious attitude toward claims of coercion and rape, for instance, appears noticeably more often in Depression-era discourses on sexuality. In a rigid explication of women's inarticulate longings, a 1932 treatise against sex censorship in the movies argued,

> What is the psychoanalytic import of a young woman who says, "I should be afraid to be alone with that fellow?" Of course it is possible that the man is a "white slaver." However it is more likely that even with such a man her virginity would be as safe against *unwelcome* violence as with her 80-year-old grandfather; what she is really revealing, as to her own psychology, perhaps might be more accurately expressed in this way: "By some unconscious association within myself and my own abnormally intense passions, I fear that I would give that man some indiscreet encouragement or provocation if we were left alone" [italics in original].

The idea that young girls unwittingly participate in sexual assaults, as one social worker observed in 1934, hinges on the apparent non sequitur that an individual might have unwitting agency in the first place. Women's claims to sexual ownership probably appeared especially pernicious in the Depression context of heightened anxiety concerning proprietary masculinity and the socioeconomic viability of the male-breadwinner household. Hence they were often discredited by the decidedly traditional charge of female irrationality imparted in the modern, ostensibly liberatory vocabulary of subconscious instinct.[35]

Men's rights to interpret or appropriate female sexuality surfaced par-

[35]Theodore Schroeder, *A Challenge to the Sex Censors* (New York, 1938), p. 78; Brill; Estelle Freedman, "Uncontrolled Desires: The Response to the Sexual Psychopath, 1920–1960," *Journal of American History* 74 (June 1987): 83–106; Assembly of California, *Subcommittee on Sex Crimes* (Sacramento, CA, 1950); Blake, *New York Daily News*, April 13, 1931.

ticularly in *True Love* plots, which often instructed that a woman's failure to recognize her sexual seductiveness and then give herself to the
proper man, however economically enfeebled he might be, would result
in violent appropriation. The hero of "Passion Is Not Enough" provided an exaggerated but not atypical statement of anger against a
woman who did not heed the call of love and sacrifice herself to a poor
man: "He loved her, and yet a feeling of madness drove him on. He
wanted to hurt her. He wanted to take that small body . . . and snap it
in two."[36]

How, then, could young women, perceived as naturally alienated from
their sexuality, claim desire as part of a culturally legitimate identity? The
presumably class-specific skills of narration and self-invention in the modern context increasingly assumed burdens of moral differentiation. As the
phenomenological taxonomy of virtue based on virginity deferred to less
precise moral codes, and as Freudianism presented women as enigmati-
cally sexual yet sexually dispossessed, self-presentations and expressiveness reified a woman's integration of reason and desire, conscious action
and unconscious instinct not assumed to be integral to her self. Furthermore, the capacity to experience and display properly the authorizing sentiments of true love functioned, somewhat paradoxically, as a reflection
of material class differences as well as a constitutive attribute of cultural
definitions of class, a hallmark of the inalienable female subject.

## III

Several middle-class commentators construed the class of vulgar or
common women as collectively lacking a legitimate sexual persona: discourses in the 1920s and 1930s perpetuated the historic oversexualization of working-class women by insisting that they most uniformly
exemplified the disjunction between unconscious sexual instinct and
conscious self-possession. William Thomas endorsed Havelock Ellis's
conclusion that "no sentiment, no calculation pushes [the young
working-class girl] into a man's arms. They let themselves go without reflection and without motive, in an almost animalistic manner, from in-

[36]"Passion Is Not Enough," *True Love*, April 1933. Other typical examples of such stories in *True Love* include "Playboy," December 1932; "The Power of a Madman," July
1932; "The Girl Who Hated Men," 1932; and "Furious Flirtation," July 1936. Incidentally, as Estelle Freedman has argued in "Uncontrolled Desires," deviant male sexual psy-
chopaths, who were assumed to have "uncontrolled" sexual drives in the criminological
and popular obsession with crimes of passion during the 1940s, were most often (errone-
ously) identified as homosexuals. Such an "accusation" perhaps indirectly attests to the
fundamentally gendered construction of the unconscious: because, like a woman, the sex
offender does not actually control or possess his desires, he is not actually a "man" either,
by popular conceptions of the homosexual as pejoratively "feminine."

difference and without pleasure. . . . They lost their virginity as they lost their milk-teeth, and could give no plausible account of the loss." In applying Ellis's theory to his own cases Thomas concluded that a young waitress who "met boyfriends on the street . . . was wholly natural. . . . Religion is as remote to her as a personal experience. . . . Many girls of this kind do not realize motherhood. It is a misery remote from their consciousness, not a part of their being." Significantly, Thomas characterized the wholly natural state of "un-self-reflectiveness" as "one hundred percent feminine"—the waitress described here differed only in that "with a little help she could understand herself, which few women do."[37]

Robert Dickinson's *The Single Woman* (1933) provides the most explicit and sustained analysis of the working-class woman's inability to narrate, and thereby possess, her instincts. "Desire for men appears but no love story" in the "aberrant cases" of heterosexuality that Dickinson relegates to the "popular sexual body." Clerical and domestic workers, who appear in Dickinson's study primarily to illustrate "the seamy side of sex experience," do not discuss "morality, questions of conscience, pleasures or needs. . . . That heterosexual expression . . . affords [only] an illustration of ignorance, and perhaps of instinct."[38]

The working girl and the prostitute that she was always in danger of becoming were both generally perceived to lack an integrated, sexualized subjectivity because they either unwittingly, instinctively, gave their sexuality away without a love story or, more insidiously, they deliberately alienated their sexuality by commodifying it. "Poor women," in short, "[could] not afford to be fanciful."[39]

The middle-class woman, however, did possess the material capacities to craft a refined, legitimizing sexual identity. Emily Hahn's manual of effective seduction techniques, *Seductio ad Absurdum* (1930), humorously described the inhibiting moral categories that once kept the seductress from perfecting her art:

> In former times, our women were divided into two main categories: (a) professionals (those who make a vocation of being seduced) and (b) amateurs (those to whom the process of being seduced was a sideline). However, in late years there has grown up among us a third class, designated as (c). The only familiar term which has yet been applied was coined by Dr. Ethel Waters, who invented for them the descriptive term "freebies" in recognition of

[37]Ellis quoted in Thomas, p. 100.

[38]Robert Latou Dickinson, *The Single Woman: A Medical Study in Sex Education* (Baltimore, MD, 1933), pp. 77, 275, 278, 287.

[39]Ibid., pp. 164, 162.

their independent stand in the matter of economics and convention. . . . To be a freebie, seduction is neither a means of livelihood, as in the case of class (a), or inevitable disgrace, as with (b).

Because seduction constituted a "silly little sin," it lacked "imagination
[and] finesse. . . . The seduction of the middle classes was a monotonous
business," Hahn concluded, "so it has remained for our modern world
to raise it to a place of dignity." Elevating seduction to a middle-class
sport, Hahn implied, required distinguishing it from the grasp of the
sexual marketplace and the tedium of the marital contract—which required imagination.[40]

More serious commentators, too, linked the distinctiveness of middle-class love as an art to the social imperative of cultivating a style or
story, yet some argued as well that only the middle-class girl had the
leisure time to craft a persona in the first place. A 1924 history of the
customs of mankind, which has as its frontispiece a Cro-Magnon man
walking arm in arm with his "wife," argues that "romance and civilization mark time together." The refinement of mere existence and subconscious instincts into romance could only occur, the author speculates,
after mankind had the leisure to weave narratives, "when [they] began to
daydream." William Thomas argued from a sociological perspective
that although "virginity and purity have almost a magical value," the
young girl "does not know she has any particular value" (that is, she has
no consciousness of her sexual worth) until she learns it from others.
The educative task, Thomas warns, "goes on best when life is economically secure, and there are whole strata of society whose life affords no
investment. . . . The girl [from this strata] cannot be said to fall because
she has never risen. She is not immoral, because this implies a lack of
morality, but amoral—never having had a moral code." In some respects Thomas's claim predicts Foucault's idealized description of peasant cultures as "prediscursive": for Thomas, the working-class girl
whose family cannot make leisure investments had poor odds of ever
achieving consciousness of her sexual instincts, yet only by realizing her
value through acquiring a moral or sentient discourse does she become a
personally accountable subject with rights and privileges.[41]

Love, as Emmanuel Berl described it in 1924, "presupposes a steady
income. . . . Elective feelings take for granted that the stage of pure need
is a thing of the past. . . . A feeling can attain a certain degree of subtlety
only if it has at its disposal a habit and a language from which it is impos-

[40]Emily Hahn, *Seductio ad Absurdum: The Principles and Practices of Seduction* (New
York, 1930), p. xvii.

[41]Lillian Euchler, *Customs of Mankind* (New York, 1924), p. 182; Thomas, p. 98;
Foucault (n. 10 above).

sible to separate it." In a revealingly exaggerated description of this dynamic, Berl posits that the productive, creative work of the (male) lover upon the object of his sentiments actually creates or transforms that object into a subject: as "empty canvasses on which our aspirations happen to be painted," the "sentimental will . . . makes us feel that feverish anxiety of the man who is about—like a new Adam—to draw a woman out of his own substance."[42]

If economically secure men created a female subject out of love and its inseparable language, young women had the more daunting task of generating an authoritative sexual identity or subjectivity through tools of narration, style, and self-embellishment: because they were not assumed to be persons in whom sexuality was integral to identity or, more accurately, to consciousness, women integrated sexuality with self through proper narration. While such a claim may sound distant from the realm of social experience, symbolic resources such as narration or personal style performed central roles in demarcating modern sexual exchanges such as dating, for example, from those characteristic of prostitution and from the unreflective, instinctive behaviors of the vulgar class. In this light, it bears emphasis that a girl's failure to craft a heterosexual persona out of the often confused and internally paradoxical discourses on sexuality could have had grave consequences. As evidenced by the juggernaut of legal, political, and, of course, psychoanalytic institutions that emerged from 1920 to the 1940s to regulate the lawless impulses of adolescent desire, an "immoral" young girl who could not properly present herself in court might suffer draconian punishments such as being sent to a workhouse, training school, or foster home, depending on the whims of judicial machinery. In a thoroughly unironic gesture at the assumed dangers of modern female sexuality, New York City founded a Woman's Court in the 1930s—as well as a Wayward Minor's Court—to adjudicate such nebulous offenses as "habitual associations with dissolute persons, . . . willful disobedience to the lawful commands of parents . . . or moral depravity or [danger of becoming] morally depraved."[43] At best, she relinquished status in the middle class,

---

[42]Berl, pp. 23, 24, 98, 109.

[43]Paul Tappan, *Delinquent Girls in Court* (New York, 1945), on the Wayward Minor's Act (Title VII-4), p. 33. See Mabel Wiley, *Girl Delinquency* (New Haven, CT, 1915); Stephanie Wallach, "Sexual Delinquency in the Progressive Era," *Harvard Educational Review* 48 (February 1978): 65–94; Elizabeth Lunbeck, "A New Generation of Women: Progressive Psychiatrists and the Hypersexual Female," *Feminist Studies* 13 (1987): 513–43; Diane Long, "Biology, Sex Hormones, and Sexism in the 1920s," *Philosophical Forum* 5 (1973/74): 81–97; Judy Brumberg, "Ruined Girls: Changing Community Responses to Illegitimacy in Upstate New York, 1890–1920," *Journal of Social History* 18 (1984): 247–72.

as that category increasingly came to be defined by cultural rather than simply economic terms.[44] Although alienation from unconscious instincts constituted the dominant—and by most accounts natural— model of female sexuality and selfhood, it encoded a specific class difference as well: the learned capacity to be unnatural, to embellish the self or tell a narrative that exhibited subjectivity, increasingly distinguished the middle-class girl, who had personality, style, and a line, from the instinctively unaware common girl. If no female naturally possessed a sexually integral self, she could earn—or lose—class status by mastering the artifice of self-invention. By appropriating love and sentiment, the authorizing ideologies of premarital sexual expression, young women cultivated sexual identities. Their self-narrations, both verbal and symbolic, strengthened the attenuated boundary between illicit and legitimate sexuality and might earn them the sexual self-ownership claimed as a general right for men.

A "Hot Blood" interviewed by Bromley emphasized the importance of the distinction between romance and vulgarity in commenting that he (along with 90 percent of Bromley's male interviewees) would marry a nonvirgin, contingent on "*how* she is not a virgin. Am against whores." The apparently oxymoronic yet frequent invocation that "nice girls pet" shifted the burden of moral proof to the qualitative account girls provided concerning their sexual encounters. As long as a girl succeeded in appropriating love as the predecided fate that spurred her to give her virginity to a man (in sharp contrast to selling it as discrete capital), she could claim the moral authority of the lawless, albeit noble, history of love: "The Heloises believe, as ardent women always have," that "when in love, [virginity] is the only thing they have to give."[45]

Insofar as self-narration emerged by the 1920s as a method by which young women might claim sexual entitlements, MacFadden's fleet of popular magazines (catering to a predominantly working-class, female audience between the ages of eighteen and twenty-four) made readily accessible the expressive—and culturally legitimizing—resources of self-invention. Indeed, they suggested that the ostensibly unreflective and unnarratable working class had its own narratives to tell. The typical 1920s *True Love* plot charted a working girl's fitful progress from instinct to a sexual consciousness sanctioned by the talisman of true love. Betty, for example, the heroine of "The Boatbuilder's Daughter" (1927), engaged in the "dangerous experiment" of making love to boatbuilder Joe Bossert, although she does not experiment so much as she instinctively follows. In Joe's presence Betty first feels "strangely

[44]Bailey (n. 8 above), p. 11.
[45]Bromley, pp. 106, 70; Butterfield, pp. 49, 89.

confused . . . I don't know why, but my face felt hot." As Joe "laugh-ingly" seized her arm, promising to "turn her loose" if she allowed him to see her, Betty "wasn't exactly afraid, but something like it. I just wanted to get away." When Joe finally succeeds in kissing her she feels thrilled at her power of attraction. "Joe remained a mystery to me. I had no real love for him. Not as I learned the meaning of love later." A few weeks later Betty discovers her true love, Ted, and confronts the vio-lently jealous Joe with the news: "He caught my arm and pulled me down roughly. 'Listen, if you're old enough to go around with . . .' I couldn't move, I couldn't call to Dad for help." Paralyzed and unable to make any response because she has unknowingly, shamefully, given her sexual favors—and has thus relinquished rights to protection of her sex-uality—Betty is saved only by a fortuitous call from her mother. She later marries Ted, whose physical relation to her is "right and proper be-cause our mutual feeling for each other was love." Hoping that Joe has permanently left town, Betty moves aboard her husband's boat, only to discover that Ted is apparently harboring stolen jewelry. In an act that affirms both the appropriate ownership or meaning of property and the appropriate gift of self dictated by love, Betty falsely confesses to the crime in order to save her husband. In a cruel turn of events, however, Joe reveals himself to have been the thief and visits Ted's boat to retrieve his "stolen goods"—both the jewelry and Betty. Ennobled because she has freely given her self to her husband and because she believes in the proper transmission of property, Betty defends both the jewelry and her virtue by spinning a tale that she had been pining for Joe's love and had eagerly awaited his return. She submits to Joe's kisses to extract informa-tion from him about the burglary and then locks him in the closet for Ted to complete the arrest.

Betty's story contextualizes the moral implications of sexuality. The parallel sexual encounters framing the story, for instance, achieve oppo-site meanings through Betty's narration, her capacity to illustrate her love. When Joe "violently makes love" to her in the first scene, Betty's response "can hardly be called a sin" because she has merely "led a man to make love to her" in accordance with as yet unnamed instincts and unconscious urges. The last scene, which contains similarly eroticized violence, acquires an opposite meaning. Having claimed and legiti-mized her sexuality through true love and marriage, Betty has gained au-thority: she scripts a sexual persona and stages a seduction scene as a noble and legitimate ruse to protect her true love. Betty's inability to know and thereby mediate her sexuality in the first scene exonerates her "sin," whereas love—as properly reified through the various self-sacrifices and stories she produces to protect Ted—empowers her sexual disguise in the last scene, a phenomenologically identical sexual encounter. Betty's moral absolution depends on her skills at narrating her love story, and, ironically, only Betty's giving of her self to Ted enables her to distinguish the use of sexuality as a ruse to capture Joe from her earlier peccadillo.[46]

Becoming a person with a morally legitimate sexuality demanded an expressiveness radically distinct from pragmatic commercialism. The proper story, in fact, could magically convert even the professional prostitute into a character. Winifred Richmond's study of the adolescent girl, for instance, depicts the prostitute as "anesthetic": she has "no natural desire for the opposite sex and is incapable of real love or friendships." The prostitute Richmond describes has won the battle and lost the war. She can sell her labor as a part of her self yet only at the cost of her self: she has no claim to sexual subjectivity or feeling unless she can author an integrative love story defiant of the sexual market.[47]

Vehement disavowal of material interests, however, only partially masked the underlying social truth that for the middle-class girl, at least, dating *did* involve economic exchanges and dependencies that presumably would culminate in a marital relationship in which she "worked" through displaying commodities purchased with her husband's money.[48] How did middle-class commentators distinguish between forms of sexual-economic exchange that, decades earlier, had been viewed as forms of prostitution? Some writers on romance responded to women's economic dependency by encouraging girls to date men who could support families, yet these advisors, because they linked women's sexuality, marriage, and economic need in a more rigorous and traditional fashion, consistently maintained that girls should not pet or accept gifts from men outside a marital commitment. Doris Blake, for instance, contended that girls should choose financially promising men and view heterosexual relations as an economic as well as romantic arrangement; consequently, she asserted that gifts still constituted payment. More modern observers disagreed and upheld the value of snaring a financially secure man, yet they distinguished between sexual barter, gold digging, and dating by relying on another form of symbolic self-narration: the girl who accepted gifts from her lover had to promote material commodities as valuable or desirable to her only inasmuch as they encoded the priceless passion of their commitment to one another.

---

[46]"The Boatbuilder's Daughter," *True Love*, September 1927. For other examples in *True Love*, see "A Woman of That Sort," April 1924; "Why Can't a Girl Forget?" January 1930; and "The Jazz Age," 1925.

[47]Richmond (n. 23 above), p. 123.

[48]Elaine Tyler May, *Homeward Bound* (New York, 1988); Lois Scharf, *To Work and To Wed* (Westport, CT, 1984); Maureen Honey, *Creating Rosie the Riveter* (Amherst, MA, 1984).

By embracing goods as the punctuation marks of a love story or, perhaps, alternative symbolic representations of love, girls ennobled economically necessary material exchanges as integral components of the self that loves, rather than their being the discrete rewards of alienable sexuality commodified.

The specter of sexual commerce that haunted ambiguous heterosexual relationships became more pronounced in the context of economic crisis. Virtually all studies of Depression-era adolescence commented on the weakening boundaries between types. "Stopping halfway between the girl of [a college man's] own class and the paid prostitute," Bromley wrote, the "townie . . . looked for a good time. In exchange for an evening's fun" she would give sexual favors. Pickup dates, the flirtatious encounters that vice reformers viewed as preparatory to full-blown prostitution, receive indifferent mention in Oliver Butterfield's *Love Problems of Adolescence,* as cases in which "presumably neither party knows much of the other and each assumes he is able to take care of himself." As the Depression threatened to expose the economic imperatives and fault-lines of heterosexual relations that had been more gracefully masked in a decade of prosperity, commentators affirmed a dichotomy between love and all other forms of (commercialized) romantic exchanges. Frederick Rossiter, in observing that "the only time when coitus is not a love act on the part of a woman is when she is a gold digger, or selling herself for a price," denied the possibility of a sexual exchange that was not based on love yet was also not economic in nature. In short, most women affirmed the inextricability of culturally legitimate female sexuality from a true love unrelated to economic exchange or gain. Floyd Dell's unusual critique of patriarchy, *Love in the Machine Age* (1930), suggests a similar opposition between a love by which a woman makes sexuality her own—and gives her whole self to its cause—and a commodification of sex: "Love has its own kind of truth which it must follow if it is love," Dell exhorted. "The teaching of purity to girls trains them only for a prostitute-like bargaining for social security with their bodies. . . . To the extent that purity is still inculcated, it trains girls to be neurotic prostitutes, gold diggers or alimony hunters." Patrolling the borders of alien unconscious female sexuality, alienated commercialized sex, and "the real thing"—an all-subsuming true love—these commentators vehemently stigmatized, in a decade of economic crisis, the financial imperatives that might prompt a girl either to marry for money or, conversely, not to marry her true love due to financial hardship.[49]

[49]Bromley, p. 188; Butterfield (n. 14 above), p. 23; Frederick Rossiter, *The Torch of Life: A Key to Sex Harmony* (New York, 1932), p. 207; Floyd Dell, *Love in the Machine Age* (New York, 1930), p. 65.

The ambiguities of heterosexual encounters exacerbated by the Depression, as well as the entrenchment of dating in the middle class, produced a prolific industry of advice literature. Because women were not viewed as essentially or naturally in possession of a sexual subjectivity, prescriptive literature enthusiastically instructed women on the proper invention of their selves in the context of heterosexual relations. They could then claim the privileges accorded to refined class status. "Good breeding is free to anyone who wants it," stated Juliet Farnham, author of a dating etiquette book, and entailed learning the difference between "promiscuity (that is, petting for petting's sake) and slight romantic lapses." In a remarkably serious tone, advisers such as Lucy Brown urged the young woman who wanted to get her man to "be a *person*": "Find out what you're like . . . then proceed to be yourself, to give outward expression to your real self." Although ostensibly a plea for authenticity, Brown's book, like others of the genre, proceeded to script proper lines—stories and self-presentations for various sexual encounters confronting the modern girl. Speech itself, for instance, "is a dead giveaway. It reveals not only your thoughts, but your background. It can more than anything else create the impression that you're a lady." How-to literature consistently decried any displays of female intellect: "Warning!" Brown exclaimed. "Don't appear to be too argumentative, or smarter than [your date]." Dating guides imparted paradoxical messages: they urged naturalness yet authored the master-narrative of self guaranteed to spark romance and exhibit female sexuality properly. The argumentative self, then, comprised an unacceptable natural self and hence required embellishment or renarration. Farnham urged her readers lacking in "really lovable natures" to "appear to have a nice character. . . . This is a desirable technique for getting results in the marriage market." By 1954 Mary Frank would simply title her manual *How to Be a Woman.*[50]

Dating manuals also developed elaborate scripts for how a young woman should act under adversarial—and potentially violent—circumstances. Farnham advised her readers to artfully dodge excessive petting on the first date by striking "a silent, but shocked pose . . . before you allow him to continue." If this tactic failed, Farnham recommended, "go dead emotionally when being kissed. . . . Camouflage your intentions until he likes you tremendously. The first few dates, he sees

[50]Juliet Farnham, *How to Meet Men and Marry* (New York, 1941), p. 130; Lucy Brown, *How to Get Your Man and Hold Him* (New York, 1943), p. 26; Mary Frank, *How to Be a Woman* (New York, 1954); Elizabeth Eldridge, *Co-Ediquette* (New York, 1936). See other examples in Doris Webster, *Mrs. Grundy Is Dead* (New York, 1935); Alice Moats, *No Nice Girl Swears* (New York, 1933), p. 13.

you only as an abstract female. In time, he will like you for yourself if your refusal technique is clever." Significantly, Farnham argues that a man's recognizing and finally loving a girl's true self hinged on her adept execution of a series of camouflaged, appropriately coded messages that perhaps bore little resemblance to the real self's predilections. Becoming a person by specified rules of self-presentation ensured class status and cultural authority; despite the dangers lodged in nuanced expressions that obscured a girl's interests (Farnham advises, for example, that a girl should resist mauling gaily since "laughter leaves no social scars"), only skillful self-narration and stylization created or authorized a culturally legitimate sexual subjectivity in the first place.[51] In an ironic twist, the fiction of naturalness, promoted as a refined woman's sexual persona, presumably ensured that she would not be treated as the *truly* natural—instinctive, unconscious, unreflective—woman timelessly inscribed in the vulgar class. The cult of naturalness also prescribed a clever disguise of pragmatic economic aspirations, for the woman who disclosed her manhunting mission through stylistic lapses such as "glittering like a Woolworth jewelry counter in an obvious attempt to be a siren" returned full circle to the sexual barter of prostitution.

Farnham's guide provided an object lesson against gold digging—an issue that would be made all the more problematic by postwar prosperity and idealized domesticity. In her book Farnham applauded "Bettina, a mousy little individual," who blossomed under Clarence's love, taking delight in "sodas as much as concerts." Bettina's oblivion to hierarchies of monetary value earned her Clarence's name—and, incidentally, a mink coat and diamond bracelet. Marion, in contrast, who had always "felt dead inside," married the equally wealthy Eric in a loveless marriage buttressed by chic commodities. "She looked around the living room with almost sensuous pleasure when the lamps gleamed," Farnham contemptuously noted, "and every piece of furniture was a part of her." Claiming the furniture as hers, an objective source of sensuous pleasure, Marion had failed to justify her acquisitiveness on the grounds of an expressive love that surpassed commercialized sexuality for gain.[52]

After a young woman had discovered her self through the guidance of advice literature and various treatises on love, she had to efface the inter-

---

[51]Farnham, p. 78.

[52]Farnham, pp. 61, 170, 72; Bridges (n. 9 above); Emily Post, *Etiquette* (New York, 1932); Euchler. There are numerous, often comical, examples of the importance of commodities in relationships. A letter to Doris Blake in 1944 read, "I never, never will be happy again [after the young woman's engagement was broken]. Everything is gone out of my life. I never dreamed there'd be such a finis to our romance. . . . What can be wrong? Should I ask for my gifts back?" The strange juxtaposition of heartrending emotionalism

ests that developed out of a subjective stance by learning what Emily
Post labeled "an unconsciousness of self." Another advice book described it as a capacity to "forget the self . . . simply force yourself to
some conversation in which 'I' figures lightly, if at all." A woman's self-
narrative, then, ideally should erase the fact of its authorship, to appear
as something that was always there—a timeless self rather than the construction demanded by ideologies of female sexuality.[53]

By way of brief comparison, men's sexual subjectivities are assumed
to be continuous and integrated, derived from instincts that the rational
male conscious acts upon and possesses as its own; the construction of
self does not appear as a prerequisite to male sexual interests or expression. Doris Blake, for instance, castigated her female reader for her
"unholy passion for taking the gift the gods have laid at her feet [a
boyfriend] and trying to reform it," when "his best act is being himself,"
yet she consistently maintained the importance of a young girl's crafted
expressions: "a look in the eye and a charming suggestive" comment,
she recommended, better communicated a girl's feelings or sexual desires than "cheap familiarities" or other actions. Advisers urged young
men, of course, to honor codes of decorous conduct appropriate to
women who had properly constructed their identity as nice girls. The
more relevant point here, however, is that male sexual identity was not
viewed as authored, and thus their sexual rights or interests were conceptualized as prior to rather than contingent on the effectiveness of
their self-invention. Because men are viewed as sexualized subjects, even
when not engaged in explicit sexual activity, they have only to act upon
and fulfill their sexual drives.[54] Men were assumed initially to be in rational possession of their sexual identity and thus relinquished rights
thereafter according to their conduct; women were assumed initially to
be alienated from sexual identity and acquired rights thereafter, also according to their conduct.

The logic that posited a bifurcation between the conscious, self-
possessed female subject and lawless female sexuality inevitably created
an ideological climate in which a third possibility, the taking of sex

---

with the question of gift exchange suggests the extent to which gifts were imperative aspects of any relationship, which generated anxiety after the emotional attachment to the
giver was disrupted.

[53]Post, p. 591.

[54]Doris Blake's columns, particularly, enforced rigid standards of conduct for men,
given that the women adhered to rules of refined self-presentation. Yet underlying such advice was the timeless assumption that women should act as moral arbiters for male sexuality. In the modern context, the double standard is articulated as based on the naturally
aggressive and instinctive male nature easily driven mad by love passion.

through violence by men, could be viewed as excusable—as a man's misreading of woman (who cannot know herself)—or even eroticized as the means by which a woman first discovers sexuality as her own.

Popular discourses on sexual liberalization in the 1920s and 1930s tantalized society with the possibilities of a lawless, individualistic romantic love that would dismantle repressive patriarchal governance. Love promoted itself as a vitalizing corrective—for both men and women—to the increasingly disjunct arenas of work, leisure, and family life and the essentially fragmentary relations perpetuated by functional contractual relations. Yet fictions of heterosexual companionability and women's possession of their sexual desires masked the older, gendered assumptions concerning self-mastery and rationality, which undergirded the deceptively liberatory notion of sexual instincts generated by modern concepts of the unconscious. In affirming gender-specific structural relations between the unconscious and the conscious, modern discourses on premarital sexuality and love replicated the assumption of a proprietary male self and an unruly and bifurcated female self. While no particular male figure regulated sexuality in the modern manner, this did not result in female ownership of sexuality either. Young women therefore had to earn their sexual subjectivity and status through various means. The prostitute and the working-class girl generally represented alienated sexuality, because they had either commodified or given their sexual favors for material reward or because they lacked the rationality to reflectively comprehend their actions. In either case, they had failed at the act of narration or self-presentation that provided the only evidence of female sexual desires integrated, or fastened, by the female conscious. Finally, the ideology of liberated sexuality dictated that women tell a particular story, one in which they implicate—and ideally give—their selves to the cause of their love.

Although sexual modernization thus inflected (and in some respects obfuscated) the meanings of virtue and vice from phenomenological facts of sexual experience to the expressive meanings attached to these experiences, it maintained, even on an ideological level, the dispossessing notion that women's sexuality constituted an unruly and internally alien entity. Hence women's sexual rights, even in a modern context, remained contingent upon their sexual personae and behavior. Inspired second-wave feminist protests against sexual objectification and imperiled sexual rights today expose the persistence of systemically exploitative sexual relations even in the liberalized modern context.

# Blues Notes on Black Sexuality: Sex and the Texts of Jessie Fauset and Nella Larsen

ANN DUCILLE

*Department of English*
*Wesleyan University*

Because there was a man somewhere in a candystripe silk shirt,
gracile and dangerous as a jaguar and because a woman moaned
for him in sixty-watt gloom and mourned him Faithless Love
Twotiming Love Oh Love Oh Careless Aggravating Love,

   She came out on the stage in yards of pearls, emerging like
   a favorite scenic view, flashed her golden smile and sang.
      [Robert Hayden, "Homage to the Empress of the Blues"]

JAZZ. BLUES. BOOGIE-WOOGIE, black bottom, shimmy, shake, and mess around. Black bodies moving by the millions from southern shacks to northern slums, moving to the beat of the New Negro in a new world. Freud. Sex. Speakeasies and bootlegged gin. Marcus Garvey. Victory in Europe. Bread lines. Unemployment. Race riots and mob violence. Rent parties and literary salons. Detroit. Chicago. *Home to Harlem. Nigger Heaven.* The "authentic," "real colored thing." Josephine Baker. Ma Rainey. Bessie Smith. "Love Oh Love Oh Careless Aggravating Love."

For many students of the 1920s and 1930s, few icons represent the "truth" of a moment at once the best of times and the worst of times as dramatically as the image of the black women blues artists who sang of

This essay is drawn from my longer work, *Coupling and Convention: Black Women Novelists and the Marriage Plot, 1853–1948* (Oxford University Press, forthcoming). I wish to thank the many friends and colleagues whose insights helped to shape this essay, especially Thadious Davis, Indira Karamcheti, Paula Rabinowitz, and Laura Santigian, as well as the Journal's anonymous reviewers.

This essay originally appeared in the *Journal of the History of Sexuality* 1993, vol. 3, no. 3.

sex and love, loss and longing. For black poet Robert Hayden, who grew up in the slums of Detroit in the 1920s and 1930s, the blues were black truth, and blues artists like Bessie Smith, whom he memorialized in the poem excerpted above, were lifelines reaching back through northern ghettos into the rural reaches of the Deep South. Smith, as Hayden heard her, sang "about the uncertainties and sorrows of life as poor Negro people knew them—especially those who had not been out of the South very long."[1] While blues women such as Bessie Smith and Ma Rainey perhaps most often sang of erotic encounters, their songs captured as well the material conditions of a society in flux.

For Hayden and for millions of his contemporaries, the blues—"folk" blues, "classic" blues, "race-record" blues—are signifying art forms that grew out of and speak to the emotional, social, and cultural dimensions of both southern rural and northern urban black American historical experiences. For cultural critic Hazel Carby, reading the period more than half a century later, blues singers of bygone days are an "empowered presence," pioneers who claimed their sexual subjectivity through their songs and produced a black women's discourse on black sexuality.[2] For literary theorist Houston Baker, the blues constitute "a vibrant network"—the "'always already' of Afro-American culture, . . . [the] multiplex, enabling *script* in which Afro-American cultural discourse is inscribed."[3]

Carby's observation reflects the efforts of contemporary feminist criticism to establish black women as active agents within history rather than as helpless victims of history. Her words also demonstrate the leadership role she has played in moving African American cultural studies out of the realm of the intellectual, where the written words of the literati have been privileged, into the world of the material, where other cultural forms such as the blues await analysis. Baker's assertion, on the other hand, reflects the extent to which contemporary literary and cultural theory has already made the blues—and the kind and quality of black life the form depicts—the metonym for authentic blackness. As Carby has argued elsewhere, contemporary African American cultural criticism is actively engaged in "recreating a romantic discourse of a

[1]Robert Hayden, "Homage to the Empress of the Blues," in *Selected Poems* (New York, 1966), p. 44; Robert Hayden, *Collected Prose,* ed. Frederick Glaysher, with a foreword by William Meredith (Ann Arbor, MI, 1984), pp. 144–45.

[2]Hazel Carby, "'It Jus Be's Dat Way Sometime': The Sexual Politics of Black Women's Blues," in *Unequal Sisters: A Multicultural Reader in U.S. Women's History,* ed. Ellen Carol DuBois and Vicki L. Ruiz (New York, 1990), p. 239.

[3]Houston A. Baker, Jr., *Blues, Ideology, and Afro-American Literature: A Vernacular Theory* (Chicago, 1984), pp. 3–4.

rural black folk in which to situate the source of an Afro-American culture."[4] And the quintessential sign of the folk source is the blues.

In *Blues, Ideology, and Afro-American Literature: A Vernacular Theory*, Baker not only situates the southern rural folk experience as the
source of African American culture; he also makes such sitings an intellectual imperative, arguing that the blues should be privileged in the
study of American culture as a way of remapping "expressive geographies" in the United States. "My own ludic uses of the blues are various," he maintains, "and each refiguration implies the valorization of
vernacular facets of American culture."[5] Demonstrating just how broad
and varied his claims for the blues are, Baker goes on to suggest that
"blues energy" may be found in "unlikely expressive spaces in Afro-
America." Of these spaces and those who would map them, he writes:

> A properly trained critic—one versed in the vernacular and uncon-
> strained by traditional historical determinants—may well be able
> to discover blues inscriptions and liberating rhythms even in some
> familiarly neglected works of Afro-American expressive culture.
> Who, after all, has dismissed such works? Normally, they have
> been written off by commentators (black and white alike) con-
> strained by a single standard of criticism. Who is to decipher such
> neglected expressive instances? Surely, the blues critic is the most
> likely agent.[6]

Ironically, Baker's vernacular theory of a "blues matrix" and a germi-
nal black folk culture is itself in danger of becoming a constraining "single standard of criticism"—a contemporary convention that too often
dismisses rather then deciphers, excludes rather than explores. Claiming
the blues as the grand signifier of *the* black experience leaves the blues
critic little room to decipher other inscriptions and liberating rhythms.
Too often writers whose expressive geographies are perceived as lying
outside the blues space are not remapped, but *de*mapped. Black women
novelists, for example, whose settings are the urban North and whose
subjects are middle-class black women are not only dismissed in the
name of the vernacular; they are condemned (along with the critics who
read them) for "historical conservativism"—for, as Baker asserts in his
recent study of black female expressivity, "willfully refus[ing] to conceptualize a southern, vernacular ancestry as a site of both consuming vio-

---

[4]Hazel Carby, "Reinventing History/Imagining the Future," review of *Specifying: Black
Women Writing the American Experience* by Susan Willis, *Black American Literature Forum*
23 (1989): 381–87. The quotation appears on p. 384.

[5]Baker, *Blues, Ideology, and Afro-American Literature*, p. 11.

[6]Ibid., p. 115.

lence and discrete value."[7] In this critical construction, no other site has black cultural currency. Moreover, the complex and often uniquely female psychic and physical violence that propels many "familiarly neglected" women's novels remains undeciphered: the numerous, lifesapping pregnancies of Helga Crane Green in Nella Larsen's *Quicksand* (1928), for example, or the rabid racial self-hatred and class pretensions of white-skinned Olivia Blanchard Cary, whose heartless rejection of her brown-skinned son drives him to suicide in Jessie Fauset's *Comedy: American Style* (1933).

However attractive and culturally affirming, the valorization of the vernacular has yielded what I would argue is an inherently exclusionary literary practice that filters a wide range of complex and often contradictory impulses and energies into a single modality: the blues. In this essay, I call into question the utopian trend in contemporary cultural criticism that readily reads resistance in such privileged, so-called authentically black discourses as the classic blues of the 1920s, while denigrating other cultural forms for their perceived adherence to and promotion of traditional (white) values. Raising questions about the "primitivism" and "racialism" of the early twentieth century, I argue in the first part of this essay that much of the discourse that champions the sexual "self-invention" and "authenticity" of blues queens such as Bessie Smith does so without examining the reflexive nature of the invention—without interrogating the role of ideology in shaping the period, its artists, and its attention to black female sexuality.

While much of my own work argues against merely replacing traditional determinants of intellectual and literary history with vernacular theories of cultural production built primarily on the blues, I attempt in the second section of this essay to take up Baker's challenge—to identify what might be called "blues inscriptions" in the works of two black women novelists of the 1920s and 1930s, Jessie Fauset and Nella Larsen. Though by no means as risqué and ripe with sexual innuendo as the lyrics sung by Bessie Smith, the often parodic prose of Fauset and Larsen—what I call their "bourgeois blues"—also takes as its principal subject the concern with black female desire and erotic relationships that occupies the classic blues. And here, too, the theme is not only men and women in love, lust, and longing, but societies in transition and power relations in flux.

Yet, if it is possible to decipher blues inscriptions in the prose of Fauset and Larsen, it is also possible to trace *anti*-blues inscriptions in their novels. As I read them, their texts are unique in their attention to

[7]Houston A. Baker, Jr., *Workings of the Spirit: The Poetics of Afro-American Women's Writing* (Chicago, 1991), p. 23.

the extremes of their historical moment and the powers of competing ideologies and colliding material conditions. While Hazel Carby argues, quite convincingly, that "different cultural forms negotiate and resolve different sets of social contradictions,"[8] I hope to show that Fauset and Larsen were finely aware of and fully engaged with a wider range of social conditions and ideological apparatuses than many critics have acknowledged. They both wrote within and defined themselves against what Carby has described as the romanticization and elevation to "mythic proportions" of "the discursive category of the folk."[9] Far from merely denigrating the folk and championing the black middle class, however, Fauset and Larsen actually critiqued both the pretensions of the black bourgeoisie and the primitivism assigned the transplanted urban masses. Because of its double vision, their fiction offers a potentially more complex critique of a changing society than the classic blues of their contemporaries.

## IDEOLOGY AS THE MOTHER OF INVENTION

While black blues queens such as Bessie Smith and Ma Rainey sang of sex and sexuality—heterosexuality, homosexuality, bisexuality—with startling explicitness, black women writers of the 1920s and 1930s such as Jessie Fauset and Nella Larsen were in most instances considerably more reticent in their attentions to the black female body. Literary historians and feminist critics have often judged these writers harshly for what black scholar Gloria Hull calls "their restrained treatment of sex," which she says "helped to place them outside the sensational mainstream" of their era.[10] Black feminist critics such as Cheryl Wall and Barbara Christian reflect a widely held critical opinion when they argue that (like their nineteenth-century counterparts) Larsen and Fauset, along with most black women poets of the period, tried to rebut racist imaging of black women as morally loose by presenting a class of black women as prim, as proper, and as bourgeois as middle-class white ladies. In inventing sophisticated, light-skinned, middle-class heroines, the argument goes, these writers adhered to traditional notions of womanhood and made themselves and their characters slaves to the conventions of an "alien tradition." The "genuine," "more honest" poetry of

[8]Carby, "'It Jus Be's Dat Way Sometime,'" p. 238.

[9]Carby, "Reinventing History," p. 384.

[10]While Hull's remark is somewhat ambiguous, by "sensational mainstream" she appears to mean what she sees as the dominant (licentious) discourse of the black Harlem moment, rather than the cultural production of the period in general. See Gloria T. Hull, *Color, Sex, and Poetry: Three Women Writers of the Harlem Renaissance* (Bloomington, IN, 1987), p. 25.

the period, these critics insist, were the lyrics of blues singers such as Bessie Smith and Ma Rainey, whose artistic integrity and racial authenticity are confirmed by their displays of what Hull calls a "raunchy, woman-proud sexuality that echoed the explicitness of this licentious era."[11]

While these readings of Fauset's and Larsen's work seem to me to miss the finer, parodic points of what I would argue are often scathing critiques of so-called middle-class values—of convention, pretension, genteel femininity, and sexual commodification—what I want to challenge here is the implicit definition of what "genuine," "authentic" African American art is. I want to point out some of the problems that arise when African American expressive culture is viewed through the lens of vernacular theories of cultural production and the master narrative of the blues as sexual signifier.

First, such evaluations often erase the contexts and complexities of a wide range of African American historical experiences and replace them with a single, monolithic, if valorized, construction: authentic blacks are southern, rural, and sexually uninhibited. Middle-class, when applied to black artists and their subjects, becomes a pejorative, a sign of having mortgaged one's black aesthetic to the alien conventions of the dominant culture. An era marked by the divergent value systems and colliding imperatives of such internally stratified constituencies as the black bourgeoisie, black bohemia, the working masses, black nationalists, the Harlem-centered literati, and the so-called Talented Tenth is narrowly characterized as "licentious" and sexually "sensational."

A second irony lies in the implication that Fauset's and Larsen's novels are somehow less than authentically black, where *black* is taken to mean sensational, licentious, raunchy. It is, I would argue, an internally dysfunctional reading of the racial subject and the semiotics of the black body that categorizes moral value by color and by class and defines "authentic blackness" as the absence thereof. Such evaluations, in effect, make class, culture, and morality linear concepts in which the genuine, honest, authentic black experience is that of a unilaterally permissive rural peasantry or a homogeneously uninhibited urban proletariat.

Third, such folk-rooted, hierarchical readings of Bessie's blues and Jessie's fiction ironically privilege what is ultimately a narrow represen-

---

[11]Barbara Christian, "Afro-American Women Poets: A Historical Introduction," in her *Black Feminist Criticism: Perspectives on Black Women Writers* (New York, 1985), p. 122; Cheryl Wall, "Poets and Versifiers, Singers and Signifiers: Women of the Harlem Renaissance," in *Women, the Arts, and the 1920s in Paris and New York,* ed. Kenneth W. Wheeler and Virginia Lee Lussier (New Brunswick, NJ, 1982), p. 75. Hull quotes essentially the same passages from Christian and Wall.

tation of women's experiences. As a black feminist discourse or as a narrative theory of the black female subject, the fiction of Fauset and Larsen
might actually be said to attend to a much wider array of women's issues
than the woman-proud lyrics of their blues-singing sisters. Cultural
critic Sandra Lieb notes, for example, that missing thematically from the
repertoires of blues artists like Ma Rainey are such feminized subjects as
motherhood, reproduction, children, and family relations.[12] The omission of this "typically female" subject matter can, and I think should, be
read as part of the particular, counter-conventional politics of the classic
blues, which necessarily transcends the image of archetypal earth
mother. What is of interest to me here, however, is not the thematic silences of the classic blues, but the fact that these silences have gone
largely unnoted by the same feminist critics who chide Fauset and
Larsen for *their* sins of omission—for their alleged inattention to the actual human conditions of the masses of black women of their era.

Addressing the limited view of "women's reality" offered by what she
calls the "daughters of the Black middle class," Cheryl Wall argues that
to "discover the broader dimensions of Black women's reality, one must
turn to an art born from folk culture and perfected by women who had
liberated their creative powers"—the blues. This "folk art equals real
life" equation is as problematic for the blues as expressive realism is for
the novel. There is little evidence to support the assumption that the
majority of black women or even many of them—including poor,
southern, rural black women—lived the kind of sexually liberated lives
or held the kind of freewheeling values *refracted* in the blues. Like other
expressive modalities, the blues invoke the fantastic. They, too, create
what I call an *unreal* estate, a surreal realm that even theorists who argue
against expressive realism still claim as the authentic. Such readings of
literary and social history place blues women outside ideology and bourgeois women in the midst of it. Fauset and Larsen are identified as
daughters of the black middle class, manipulated by the moral and aesthetic dictates of white patriarchal order and governed by white standards of womanhood, beauty, femininity, and the like. Bessie Smith, Ma
Rainey, and Zora Neale Hurston, on the other hand, are invented by
their audiences as signifying sisters, sexually and artistically liberated
and unapologetically black, beyond the pale of white social influences.
What does it mean, then, that Ma Rainey reportedly used lightening
creams and heavy greasepaint to whiten her dark skin? One of her biog-
raphers suggests it means that Rainey, too, was not unaffected by ideology and "conform[ed] to the prejudice against dark skin (shared at the

[12]Sandra Lieb, *Mother of the Blues: A Study of Ma Rainey* (Amherst, MA, 1981), p. 81.

time by many blacks as well as whites)."[13] Perhaps it merely means, however, that Rainey had a fondness for the smell of the greasepaint, as well as for the roar of the crowd. That is to say, whether written by Hurston or sung by Rainey, what Wall calls black women's reality is still *representation,* textual invention that the audience generates as real. Realism, in other words, is as much a code as romance, as much artifice as lightening creams and greasepaint.

The final irony I want to address lies in the choice of the classic blues of Bessie Smith as the privileged signifier of the genuine, authentic, pure black experience. This particular manifestation of the blues is, arguably, an appropriative art form that blends the material and techniques of traditional African American music with the presentational modes of popular *white* American musical theater, most specifically minstrelsy and vaudeville.[14] Some cultural historians maintain, in fact, that the music popularly called classic blues would be more appropriately labeled "vaudeville blues," to reflect the degree to which the form was influenced by the American music hall and the vaudeville stage.[15]

As Ralph Ellison has argued, classic blues were both public entertainment and private ritual,[16] but the fact that what was once local lore could be packaged and distributed, I would argue, altered and institutionalized the form irrevocably, as video technology and mass production have altered reggae and rap. The classic blues, the variety of blues

[13]Lieb, p. 8.

[14]Originally, white minstrel shows and blackface vaudeville acts, which gained almost phenomenal popularity in the 1840s, were attempts on the part of white entertainers to represent authentic black plantation life—to imitate blacks in their "natural habitat," as it were. Black minstrels began to appear a decade later, and a number of black troupes toured the South in the 1860s. Many of the more successful groups, however, were eventually forced out of the business or taken over by significantly more successful and resourceful white companies. A number of blues stars, including Ma Rainey and Bessie Smith, began their careers touring in minstrel shows and tent performances that followed black migrant workers from harvest to harvest. See, for example, Lieb, pp. 4–5; LeRoi Jones [Amiri Baraka], *Blues People: The Negro Experience in White America and the Music That Developed from It* (New York, 1963), pp. 81–94.

[15]Lawrence W. Levine, *Black Culture and Black Consciousness: Afro-American Thought from Slavery to Freedom* (New York, 1977), p. 225.

[16]Ralph Ellison, "Blues People," in *Shadow and Act* (New York, 1972), pp. 256–57. There are many differing opinions on the nature of both traditional and classic blues. In *Blues People,* for example, LeRoi Jones distinguishes between classic blues as public entertainment and traditional or "primitive" blues as folklore. Ralph Ellison argues, however, that Jones's distinction is a false one—that classic blues were both entertainment *and* folklore. "When they were sung professionally in theatres, they were entertainment," Ellison writes, "when danced to in the form of recordings or used as a means of transmitting the traditional verses and their wisdom, they were folklore" (pp. 256–57).

sung and recorded by professional performers such as Bessie Smith and Ma Rainey, are so called both because they standardized and universalized particular, recurrent lyrics, themes, and techniques, and because they re-formed the ritualistic elements of a once private or communal African American folk modality into public entertainment available for mass consumption. Although blues originally were recorded only by white women performers such as Sophie Tucker, black women stage and recording artists became the principal instruments through which the sexually explicit lyrics of the classic blues began to reach the ears of white America as well as black in the early 1920s.[17] But the whys of the commercialization and the *feminization* of the blues—that is to say, how mass production mass-produced the black female as sexual subject—is a complex question that is often eclipsed by the stellar proportions of the phenomenon's whos.

At least part of the "why" of the popularization and the feminization of the blues must be located in the primitivist proclivities of the historical moment. Primitivism, as a prevalent ideology of the early twentieth century, is characterized by an exuberant enthusiasm for the simple, the at-once innocent and sexually uninhibited—qualities the primitivist ascribes to the racially othered, whose alterity is fetishized. Primitivism thrives on icons. In the early twentieth century, no single icon combined the erotic, the exotic, and the innocent to the extent that the new Negro was thought to; for the newly discovered African American was not new at all, but ancient, primal, and primitive—a panacea for an overindustrialized society dying from an acute case of modernity. Such notions were fostered by the work of Sigmund Freud, who endowed "races at a low level of civilization" with an untrammeled sexuality, which he claimed both shielded them from neuroses and inhibited their cultural development. Civilization, Freud argued, advances at the expense of human sexuality. His "dark continent" metaphor for female sexuality was, as Mary Ann Doane has argued brilliantly, a deliberate attempt to link the unknowable female sexual self with the unknown, dark-skinned, "infantile" inhabitants of the African continent.[18]

Such linkages were not invented by Freud, however. For centuries, the black body had functioned as a sign of both the assumed excessive sexuality and the racial primitivism of the African. According to Sander

---

[17]Race records, as recordings of jazz, blues, ragtime, spirituals, gospel, and sermons were called, were marketed almost exclusively in black neighborhoods.

[18]See Mary Ann Doane's chapter entitled "Dark Continents: Epistemologies of Racial and Sexual Difference in Psychoanalysis and the Cinema," in her *Femmes Fatales: Feminism, Film Theory, Psychoanalysis* (New York, 1991), pp. 209–48.

Gilman, by the eighteenth century the sexuality of the black male and female had become an icon for deviant sexuality in general.[19] In the nineteenth century, the fascination with the black female body, in particular, and the primitive sexual anatomy and appetite attributed to the African woman increased the degree to which the black female functioned as an erotic icon in the racial and sexual ideology of western civilization. It is this iconography that Nella Larsen critiques in *Quicksand,* for example, where a white Danish painter, Axel Olsen, propositions the novel's mulatto heroine, Helga Crane, assuming that "the warm impulsive nature of the women of Africa" will make her eager to become his mistress.[20] It is this iconography that helped make a barebreasted Josephine Baker the rage in Paris in the 1920s. And it is this same iconography that, at least in part, accounts for the hegemony of black women in the record industry throughout the decade.[21]

Under what might be called the cult of true primitivism, sex—the quintessential subject matter of the blues—was precisely what hotblooded African women were assumed to have always in mind and body. Blues such as Mary Dixon's "All Around Mama" complemented that already established image:

> I've had men of all sizes, had 'em tall and lean
> Had 'em short, had 'em flabby, had 'em in between,

[19]Sander L. Gilman, "Black Bodies, White Bodies: Toward an Iconography of Female Sexuality in Late Nineteenth-Century Art, Medicine, and Literature," in *"Race," Writing, and Difference,* ed. Henry Louis Gates, Jr. (Chicago, 1986), pp. 223, 228, 232.

[20]Nella Larsen, *"Quicksand" and "Passing"* (in one volume), edited and with an introduction by Deborah E. McDowell (New Brunswick, NJ, 1986), p. 87. Of the racial mythology that propels Olsen, Cheryl Wall writes: "Olsen knows nothing of African women, but that does not shake his belief in their exotic primitivism. Black women, he feels, are completely sentient, sexual beings. Helga Crane should confirm that belief. When she does not, it proves she has been contaminated by the West, has suffered the primordial female corruption." See Cheryl Wall, "Passing for What? Aspects of Identity in Nella Larsen's Novels," *Black American Literature Forum* 20 (1986): 104.

[21]It is interesting to note that black men sang raunchy, man-proud folk and traditional blues long before black women began to record what came to be called classic blues for such major production companies as Columbia, Paramount, and Okeh. In the early 1920s, black composer Perry Bradford finally succeeded in convincing General Phonograph to permit black vocalist Mamie Smith, a veteran of the minstrel circuit, to record his "Crazy Blues" on the Okeh label. The commercial success of "Crazy Blues" spawned other recordings and the signing of other blues women throughout the music industry. By 1922, both race records and the race for records were on; the blues was big business, and blues women quickly became a prized commodity over which phonograph companies fought, at times bitterly, while blues men remained largely unrecorded, perhaps because sex, the quintessential theme of the blues, was a subject more safely sung by black women than by black men.

I'm an all around mama, I'm an all around mama,
I'm an all around mama, with an all around mind.[22]

Out of the mouths of black women, such lyrics spoke boldly to sexual freedom and personal choice, but they also spoke to the racial and sexual iconography that cast African women as hypersexual primitives. In singing the "Copulating Blues," "Courting Blues," "Empty Bed Blues," black women artists seemed to claim that image as their own, chew it up and spit it out in the faces of their accusers. Whether self-affirming or self-deprecating (and many in the black community argued that it was the latter), the move fit the primitivism and exoticism of the thoroughly modern moment.

Men, they call me oven, they say that I'm red-hot,
Men, they call me oven, they say that I'm red-hot,
I can strut my pudding, spread my grease with ease,
'Cause I know my onions, that's why I always please.[23]

With such songs, red-hot mamas punned, parodied, and played with black female desire. They in effect plumbed and inverted their positions as long-exploited, fetishized commodities. But identifying women blues artists as the site of a struggle for black female subjectivity necessarily raises complex questions about agency and interpellation, self and subject, person and persona. Problematizing Hazel Carby's observation that these blues women invented themselves as sexual subjects, I want to suggest that the many colliding ideologies, colluding imperatives, and conflicting agendas of the era make it difficult to determine definitively who constructed whom in the cultural kaleidoscope of the 1920s and 1930s. If black women blues singers claimed their sexual subjectivity through their songs, did they also on some level objectify, exoticize, and eroticize the female body in the process? Did these infinitely inventive blues women create the moment through their songs and exploit that moment? Or did the moment create and exploit them? It was after all their potential to sell records that made black women so essential to the race-record industry in the 1920s. They were abandoned by the industry as quickly as they had been taken up when the increasing popularity of dance bands in the late 1920s and early 1930s created a new market and a new source of profit.[24] Perhaps the answer to the question of agency

---

[22]Paul Oliver, *Screening the Blues: Aspects of the Blues Tradition* (London, 1968); quoted in Daphne Duval Harrison, *Black Pearls: Blues Queens of the 1920s* (New Brunswick, NJ, 1988), p. 105.

[23]Eric Sackheim, comp., *The Blues Line: A Collection of Blues Lyrics* (New York, 1969); quoted in Harrison, p. 106.

[24]Harrison, p. 8.

and interpellation lies somewhere between the two possibilities—in exploring the reflexive nature of ideology and invention, in examining critically the ideological aspects of the epoch that made possible the invention of both the explicitly sexual black female subjects sung in the songs of blues women like Bessie Smith and Ma Rainey and the often more covertly sexual subjects written in the fiction of Jessie Fauset and Nella Larsen.

Interestingly enough, despite their dismissal as "vapidly genteel lace-curtain romances,"[25] several of Fauset's and Larsen's novels seem to me to lay the groundwork for such an ideologically charged analysis. Their fiction tackles some of the most significant social contradictions of the emerging modern era, including the questions of black female agency, cultural authenticity, and racial and sexual iconography. Joanna Marshall, for example, the colored heroine of Fauset's first novel, *There Is Confusion* (1924), is fiercely determined to have a career as a classical dance and music performer at a time when both her race and her gender limit her personal and professional options to marriage, on the one hand, and exotic dancing, on the other. "Couldn't make any money out of you," a white agent tells her, as he refuses to represent her. "America doesn't want to see a colored dancer in the role of a *premiere danseuse*. . . . She wants you to be absurd, grotesque."[26]

In her representation of the racism and racialism that affect her heroine's career, Fauset implicitly challenges the very notion of the real and the authentic; she questions the possibility of the production of a "real" black art in a white-controlled cultural market. For not only do white culture-keepers (in this case, the board of directors of a Greenwich Village theater) determine what authentic black art is, they control the who, how, where, and when of public cultural production and consumption as well. In the next section, I turn to the "familiarly neglected" texts of Fauset and Larsen to explore some of their inscriptions of and challenges to the dominant social and cultural modalities of their time.

## THE BOURGEOIS BLUES OF JESSIE FAUSET AND NELLA LARSEN

> She came out on the stage in ostrich feathers, beaded satin,
> and shone that smile on us and sang.
> [Robert Hayden, "Homage to the Empress of the Blues"]

---

[25]David Littlejohn, *Black on White: A Critical Survey of Writing by American Negroes* (New York, 1966), pp. 50–51.

[26]Jessie Fauset, *There Is Confusion,* with an introduction by Thadious M. Davis (Boston, 1989), p. 148.

Ostrich feathers, beaded satin, yards of pearls, hats, headdresses, furs. These are among the accoutrements that black women blues singers donned in constructing their performance personas. In the novels of Jessie Fauset and Nella Larsen, such accessories not only construct the woman character herself but also help to tell her story. Silks and satins, capes and coats, dresses and lounging pajamas are as central to the bourgeois brand of "somebody done somebody wrong" songs that these texts sing as paints and powders were to the classic blues performance. Tremendous attention is paid in these novels to what women put on their bodies; the characters are acutely aware of how their bodies look in what they put on them. It is important to understand, however, that all this dressing and draping, primping and preening is not merely the frivolous fluff of which novels of manners are made—the affectations and petty preoccupations of bourgeois domesticity, as many critics have suggested. Rather, clothes function semiotically as sexual and racial signifiers. As part of the texts' signifying systems, the dressed or, in Harlem slang, the "draped down" body is the literary equivalent of the woman-proud blues lyric—one of the not always so subtle instruments through which both Fauset and Larsen sing and sign female sexuality.

Helga Crane, for example, the heroine of Larsen's first novel, *Quicksand* (1928), is a studied and deliberate dresser, whose relationship to her wardrobe is a recurrent theme in the text. Throughout the novel, Helga, the daughter of a white Danish mother and a black father, struggles to define and declare her sexual self in the face of iconographies that objectify, exoticize, "ladify," and otherwise oppress her. Clothes (putting them on the body, rather than taking them off) are part of the stuff of Helga's bourgeois blues. They signal both her sexuality and her tenuous relationship to the moral and behavioral codes of the two disparate societies she stands among but not of. As a teacher at Naxos, a southern school for upwardly mobile Negroes, Helga is immediately established as a person apart from the white-worshipping "great [black] community" around her. "A slight girl of twenty-two" with "skin like yellow satin," Helga, we learn in the early pages of the novel, is too fond of vivid green and of gold negligees and glistening brocaded mules to be a proper Naxos Negro. Rather, her taste in colorful clothes links her to that other life whose bodacious blues rhythms will not be entirely repressed, no matter how bourgeois her surroundings. A Naxos Negro's knowledge of place is confirmed by conservatism, "good taste," and moderation in all things, including proper attire. Helga's distinctive dark purples, deep reds, clinging silks, and luxurious woolens signify the pride, vanity, and "uppity" otherness that bring her into disfavor at Naxos. "Clothes," as Larsen writes, "had been one of [Helga's] difficulties at Naxos," with its "intolerant dislike of difference." Larsen continues: "Helga Crane loved clothes, elaborate ones. Nevertheless she had tried not to offend. But with small success, for, although she had affected the deceptively simple variety, the hawk eyes of dean and matrons had detected the subtle difference from their own irreproachably conventional garments."[27]

Perhaps even more than her yellow skin, Helga Crane's clothes mark her racial and sexual alterity. In a later scene, Helga, draped in a stunning red dress, wanders dazed into a storefront church in Harlem. When her bare arms and neck and her clinging red dress are revealed under her coat, the erotic spectacle causes the man next to her to shudder and a sanctified sister to label her a scarlet woman. Helga need not sing the blues to be claimed as a red-hot mama; even just a glimpse of her bare flesh and red dress are enough to earn her the label of Jezebel.

At the end of the novel, taste in clothes again becomes the great *un*equalizer that distinguishes the now married and perpetually pregnant Helga from the folk—the tiny, rural Alabama community around which she has wrapped her life and to which she is trying desperately to belong. Fatally (as opposed to fatefully) married to a grandiloquent Baptist preacher, Mrs. Reverend Pleasant Green immediately makes herself unpopular with the women of her husband's "primitive flock" by trying to "help them with their clothes," tactfully pointing out that aprons and sunbonnets are not proper Sunday church attire.[28]

The final pages of the novel not only return Helga Crane Green to the South (as a site of psychic and physical violence), but they also place her in the ill-fitting and doubly ironic role of *matron*, helpmate, race woman. Like the dean and matrons at Naxos who judged her wardrobe harshly, Helga sets herself up as the standard-bearer of proper dress, "gentler deportment," and home beautification. In other words, here in the backwoods of Alabama, it is Helga who comes to represent the convention, prescription, and smug self-satisfaction she so despised in her Naxos colleagues. Her sense of style and propriety make her even more a misfit among her husband's poor parishioners than her fondness for the unconventional had made her at Naxos. To the women she tries to instruct, she is an "uppity, meddlin' No'the'nah." Even as she is devoured and diminished by too many children too quickly come, even as the body she once thought of only as "something on which to hang lovely fabrics" becomes constantly swollen with child and racked with pain, the women around her pity not Helga but her husband.

We hear no more talk of satin gowns and brocaded mules. But as the story closes, like a lid on a casket, I cannot help wondering if the next

[27]Larsen, *"Quicksand" and "Passing,"* p. 18.
[28]Ibid., pp. 118–19.

garment that will drape the perhaps terminally pregnant Helga is a shroud. Yet, it is not childbirth or motherhood, or even patriarchy, that overcomes Helga, as much as it is the irreconcilable social, psycho-sexual, and racial contradictions that become her quicksand. Helga is unable to fashion an individual identity against the competing ideological and iconographical forces that ultimately render her invisible. Unlike her blues-singing contemporaries, she does not have the luxury of donning a woman-proud persona and acting out the days of her life as a performer on a stage. Yet, Helga too has sung the blues. It is just that no one has listened.

If beads and boas and brocades helped to empower black women blues performers, a decided deliberateness in dressing is one of the ways in which the women characters of Fauset's and Larsen's novels are sexually empowered to attract and seduce—to do business in and around the marriage market. But the empowerment, as both authors explore, is for the most part illusory. In their novels, lace and satin are as constricting and confining as gender roles and colored skin, as the "draped down" would-be seducer becomes not only the seduced, but the fetishized commodity. Two of Fauset's novels, *The Chinaberry Tree* (1931) and *Plum Bun* (1928), provide a fitting forum for exploring both the issue of dressing for social success and the relationship between racial iconography and sexual commodification.

Metaphorically reminiscent of Charles Chesnutt's *The House behind the Cedars* (1900), *The Chinaberry Tree* is concerned with the consequences of miscegenation, adultery, and confining social and sexual values—the "Thou shalt nots," as Fauset calls them in her foreword—of a people who, by virtue of their history as "victims of many phases of immorality," can ill afford to judge others of their race, but who do so nevertheless.[29] Like Chesnutt's white-skinned heroine Rena Walden, Fauset's central female figure, Laurentine Strange, is the illegitimate daughter of a white gentleman and his long-time colored mistress.[30] Unlike Rena, however, Laurentine does not attempt to escape the burdens of her mixed heritage by passing for white. She hopes instead to *pass* into the welcoming arms of bourgeois black society through marriage to a colored man of means and property.

---

[29]Jessie Fauset, *The Chinaberry Tree* (New York, 1931; rpt. New York, 1969), p. x.

[30]Significantly, while critics such as Barbara Christian have assumed that Laurentine's mother, Sal Strange, is an ex-slave once owned by Captain Halloway, Laurentine's father, Fauset takes pains to establish otherwise. We are told explicitly that Sal was born in Mississippi *after* slavery and came north to work for Halloway's mother at the urging of a relative. Fauset, in fact, makes quite a point of romanticizing Halloway and Sal's affair as a "true love match, the kind you read about—Heloise and Abelard and all that kind of thing. She wasn't a slave—she didn't have to yield to him" (pp. 72, 160). While the power

Because of her family history, Laurentine is a social outcast, believed by the colored people of her hometown (Red Brook, New Jersey) to possess bad blood. To a certain extent, Laurentine's quarantine is self-imposed, for she has internalized the value system that blames the victim and holds the child responsible for the sins of the father—and the mother. She has bought the myth of her own bad mixed blood. Scandalized by her illegitimate birth, she is obsessed with being, acting, and appearing decent. Her exemplary life, her successful, white-clients-only dressmaking business (in which she employs two assistants), and her financial independence are not enough decency, however. Her personal prayer is for "peace and security, a home life like other women, a name, protection."[31] As she assesses her own particular human condition, her only hope for legitimacy, respectability, acceptance, and safety is through marriage to the right colored man. Dressing the parts of woman/wife/mother are essential aspects of the coupling process. With one eye on the mirror and the other on marriage, Laurentine chooses her attire like a blues queen preparing for performance: "She would wear the red dress . . . a shallow, round neck, not too low . . . not too elaborate either as though one were deliberately dressing up, as it were."[32] Fauset's irony is clear, for, of course, Laurentine very deliberately is dressing up.

On the off chance that her well-to-do colored suitor, Phil Hackett, might pop in to see her unexpectedly, Laurentine armors herself in a red house dress, "trim and snug and perfect, a little dressier than usual" for the time of day.[33] Later, as she prepares for an evening date she expects to end in a marriage proposal, Laurentine dresses "feverishly" in a "ravishing" red gown and thin smoky stockings. She lets down her long straight hair, because, as Fauset tells us, "she who knew so little of men knew that colored men liked their wives to have straight hair, 'good' hair." Yet, even as Laurentine reckons her womanly wiles, even as she primps and plots and powders, even as she dresses for subtle seduction, "her face hot and flushed" with excitement, she contemplates her own purity: her family life might not be blameless, but she herself has been

---

dynamics between a wealthy white college boy and a poor colored housemaid hardly suggest easy refusal, to read Halloway as master and Sal as slave denies the latter the degree of agency with which the text endows her and robs Fauset of the credit due her for her counter-conventional representation of other than coercive sex between white men and black women.

[31]Fauset, *The Chinaberry Tree*, p. 21.
[32]Ibid., p. 52.
[33]Ibid.

"as pure as snow, as chaste as a nun"—in a ravishing red, figure-hugging habit.[34]

Taken inside Laurentine's consciousness as well as her bedroom, the reader sees the character doubly exposed. In Fauset's work, dressing scenes such as the one above (her novels are full of such scenes) often unfold in the form of double-edged, revealing details that cut through to the underside of the garments, leaving the characters exposed, vulnerable—almost as if the very act of dressing the body is an undressing of the soul. Such scenes reveal both the psychosexual contradictions with which Fauset is concerned and her critique of the historical conditions that produce what might be called a trauma of pretense and hypocrisy. Critics, however, have often missed Fauset's irony, mistaking parody for praise. Historically, black women like Laurentine Strange are as "always-already-sexual" as the blues women against whom they define themselves. What we see exposed, if we read between the lines of Fauset's fiction, is the hypocrisy of the historical moment.

> I need a little sugar in my bowl,
> I need a little hotdog between my roll.
> [Bessie Smith, "Put a Little Sugar in My Bowl"]

While hardly as overtly erotic as "Put a Little Sugar in My Bowl," *Plum Bun* (1928), Fauset's second novel, is nevertheless profoundly concerned with sex and sexuality—a bourgeois version of the copulating blues. In fact, the entire novel can be read as an extended sexual metaphor that raises critical questions about the relationship between power and passion, dollars and desire, and offers an implicit critique of the would-be blues moment and folk modality. The text takes its title and central metaphor from a nursery rhyme: "To market, to market, to buy a plum bun. Home again, home again, market is done." (In the version I grew up on, the item to be purchased at market was a "fat hen.") A plum bun, in the blues idiom with which Fauset plays brilliantly, is, as one of her male characters remarks, "a particularly attractive piece" (of ass). The title, in its metaphorical connection to both the nursery rhyme and the sexual vernacular, announces the text's concern with the mature blues themes of sex as a consumable commodity and the female body as a bargaining chip in a high-stakes game of strip poker, which lays the characters bare without the textual removal of a single piece of clothing. There is no nudity in *Plum Bun,* no sexually explicit love scenes, no groping, petting, or fondling. Yet, as Deborah McDowell points out in her introduction to the Pandora edition, the novel "brims with sexual

[34]Ibid., pp. 58–59.

winks and innuendos,"[35] from its lewdly suggestive title to the tightly conceived formal structures that track the heroine's growth and development through rites of passage—sections of the novel significantly named "Home," "Market," "Plum Bun," "Home Again," and "Market Is Done."

Angela Murray, the not-always-sympathetic mulatto heroine of *Plum Bun,* is another of Fauset's sexually embodied beings. Angela's aim is to beg, borrow, or steal for herself the happily-ever-after fantasy marriage of which fairy tales are made. As models of such marriages, she holds before her the tales of perfect love read to her at bedtime by her light-skinned mother, whose own marriage to a much darker man would seem to Angela blissfully happy, were it not for the differences in her parents' skin colors—a difference of far greater concern to her than to them. Light like her mother but colorstruck to a degree her mother is not, Angela believes that "being coloured in America . . . [is] nothing short of a curse."[36]

While Angela has a painfully well-honed understanding of race relations in the United States, she does not seem to understand that fairy tales, as any aficionado of the blues knows, are not the stuff of which real erotic relations are made. After her parents' deaths, she leaves both her Philadelphia "home" and her dark-skinned sister behind and goes to "market," to New York City, where she intends to rid herself of the burdens of racial prejudice once and for all by passing for white and marrying herself off to a wealthy, influential white man. Finding such a man and making such a marriage become her goals. Ironically, she is detoured from the one by finding the other. She is, in effect, diverted from matrimony by her own desires—material and sexual—even as she thinks she is closing in on the diamond ring. She finds a plum-bun prince easily enough—wealthy, white Roger Fielding. But Fielding does not quite play the marriage market by the rules of Angela's fairy tales. As Deborah McDowell explains: "Angela's and Roger's trips to the market are for two different plum buns. For her the plum bun is power and influence attainable only through marriage to a wealthy white man. For him, the plum bun is sex, a consumable to be bought, used up, and expended. Put still another way, Angela's game play for marriage is Roger's foreplay for sex."[37]

Their "his and hers" shopping lists make the market at once a pas-

[35]Jessie Fauset, *Plum Bun,* with an introduction by Deborah McDowell (Boston, 1985), p. xx. McDowell's introduction includes a particularly provocative, insightful reading of this much misunderstood text.

[36]Ibid., p. 53.

[37]Ibid., p. xiv.

sionate and a perilous place for Angela, as her relationship with Roger becomes a contest of wills and won'ts. In over her head, Angela seeks advice from a friend, Martha Burden, who schools her in the conventions of coupling and the ABCs of trading in the flesh: "It is a game, and the hardest game in the world for a woman, but the most fascinating; the hardest in which to strike a happy medium. You see, you have to be careful not to withhold too much and yet to give very little. If we don't give enough we lose them. If we give too much we lose ourselves."[38]

Angela attempts to play the love game on Martha's terms rather than Roger's, but Roger's trump card turns out to be her own sexual desire, as his constant proximity leaves her "appalled by her thoughts and longings."[39] On the proverbial terrible night, too cold and rainy for Angela to drive him from the "leaping, golden flames" of her fire, Roger presses his advantage, and, with a kiss, "her very bones turned to water." Her panting "Oh, Roger, must it be like this? Can't it be any other way?" is no match for the arms around her and the voice she hears only from a great distance "breaking, pleading, promising: 'Everything will be all right, darling, darling. I swear it. Only trust me, trust me!'"[40]

Thus, even in the guise of a white woman, Angela gets caught in the same trap Alex Olsen attempted to spring on Helga Crane in *Quicksand*. The victim of her own passion, she becomes not the willing wife of Roger Fielding, but his reluctant mistress. The man she hoped to maneuver into marriage maneuvers her into bed. Completing her risqué play with nursery rhyme and adult blues themes, Fauset sends Angela "to market" to buy a "plum bun" and brings her "home again" with an empty basket (or perhaps with a "hotdog for her roll"). Angela gambles her most valuable stock—her virginity—in what the novel, in splendid signification, constructs as a commodities exchange, and she loses, quite literally, her pants. But market is not done . . . yet. And Angela, who, like any good blues woman, has a backdoor man waiting, will have her turn to send Roger packing.

While *Plum Bun*, like much of Fauset's work, has been rejected by many critics as just another novel of manners, its structurally complex and sexually sophisticated mannerisms, as feminist scholars such as Deborah McDowell have demonstrated, defy such easy dismissals. If Bessie Smith and Ma Rainey made being woman-proud and sexually active seem easy, Fauset showed how complex and complicated womanhood and virginity could be in the Roaring Twenties. Long before critics talked in terms of dialectics, Fauset explored the disparities of de-

---

[38]Ibid., p. 145.
[39]Ibid., p. 200.
[40]Ibid., pp. 201–3.

sire and danger and the complications of identity and ideology in the lives of women across class and racial lines.

However concerned with authenticity, ideology, sexuality, and the social contradictions of the day may be *There Is Confusion, Quicksand, The Chinaberry Tree,* and *Plum Bun,* perhaps no novel of the era attends to the iconography of the black female body and the dialectics of desire more dramatically than Nella Larsen's second novel, *Passing* (1929). In fact, in *Passing,* the degree of notice Irene Redfield takes of her friend Clare Kendry's draped down body has led Deborah McDowell to argue that Larsen establishes (if only by implication) the possibility of a sexual attraction between the two women characters. To support her claim, McDowell reads carefully the body language of the text. Steeped as it is in double entendres, red dresses, bare shoulders, and fire imagery, the novel indeed presents a plethora of erotic figures to be read. Irene is ever aware of Clare's "tempting mouth," her "seductive caressing smile," her "arresting eyes," her "incredibly beautiful face," which sends a "slight shiver" over the spectator. As seen through Irene's eyes, Clare is "a lovely creature," "really almost too good-looking," whose gaze leaves her feeling "petted and caressed."

McDowell takes as additional evidence of an erotic attraction between the two women the text's opening image: an envelope containing a letter from the long-lost Clare, who has been passing for white. McDowell views this envelope as a metaphoric vagina and argues that Irene, to whom the envelope is addressed, is justified in her reluctance to open it, given the sexual overtones of the letter it contains:

> For I am lonely . . . cannot help longing to be with you again, as I have never longed for anything before; and I have wanted many things in my life. . . . It's like an ache, a pain that never ceases . . . and it's your fault, 'Rene dear. At least partly. For I wouldn't now, perhaps, have this terrible, this wild desire if I hadn't seen you that time in Chicago.[41]

The letter leaves Irene with flaming cheeks and a rush of feeling for which she can find no name. The eroticism of this and other sexually loaded passages is textually confirmed, according to McDowell, by Larsen's use of fire imagery, "the conventional representation of sexual desire."[42]

McDowell's reading is an enabling one. It redirects our long-diverted critical attention to the treatment of female sexuality not only in

---

[41]Larsen, *"Quicksand" and "Passing,"* pp. xxvi–xxvii. This passage is as quoted by McDowell. I will return to the actual letter a little later.

[42]Ibid., p. xxvii.

Larsen's work, but in that of her contemporaries as well, and it raises important questions about the homoerotic undertones and overtones of this and other texts. Who owns the gaze? Is the gaze inherently masculine or essentially sexual? What happens when women gaze upon each other? Is the very act of gazing upon the female body an appropriation of the masculine and an invocation of the erotic? Is there a grammar of the female gaze? These are among the questions occasioned by McDowell's reading of a lesbian subtext in *Passing.* I am not certain, however, that this provocative interpretation, despite its attention to the figurative language of the text, ultimately supports its own thesis or answers its own questions about what McDowell describes tentatively as Larsen's ability to "flirt, if only by suggestion, with the idea of a lesbian relationship" between Irene and Clare.[43]

What happens, for example, if we historicize Larsen's grammar, placing it within the blues/bohemian/bourgeois moment? Does such a placement give the text's linguistic figures a different face value altogether? Viewed in historical perspective, the looking, touching, and caressing that McDowell reads as signs of lesbian attraction may have more to do with homosociability than with either homo- or heterosexuality, with the nature of both women's culture and the social and linguistic conventions at the time. That is to say, the interaction between Clare and Irene may reflect the moment's preoccupation with the always-already-sexual black female body, or it may suggest a not necessarily sexual way of being women together, which the spread of Freudian thought recoded and perhaps destroyed. It may also reflect a woman's way of talking through the body—of expressing material or experiential desire in bodily terms. As Lauren Berlant has argued, "There may be a difference between wanting someone sexually and wanting someone's body." What Irene wants, Berlant suggests, is not to make love to Clare, but "to occupy, to experience the privileges of Clare's body . . . to wear [Clare's] way of wearing her body, like a prosthesis, or a fetish."[44] "Fetish" seems to me very much the right trope. But if Irene wants to wear the experiences of Clare's fetishized body, Clare wants to don Irene's as well, including, perhaps, Irene's husband, Dr. Brian Redfield.

Here I think we come to the crux of Larsen's complex social and psychosexual critique. Clare and Irene—the exotic and the elite—may represent the dialectics of the renaissance moment itself. Written as part vamp, part flapper, and part femme fatale, Clare reflects the bohemian

[43]Ibid., p. xxiii.

[44]Lauren Berlant, "National Brands/National Body: *Imitation of Life,*" in *Comparative American Identities: Race, Sex, and Nationality in the Modern Text,* ed. Hortense Spillers (New York, 1991), p. 111.

fascination with sexuality, the Greenwich Village high life, the glamorous, the risqué, the foreign, and the forbidden. Irene, on the other hand, with her race work, literary salons, and house parties, signifies the propriety, the manners, the social and racial uplift, and especially the security with which the black bourgeoisie of the 1920s was preoccupied. Viewed in this light, the text's actual sexual preference may be for the autoerotic: Clare and Irene may be read as body doubles or, perhaps more precisely, as halved selves through whom Larsen explores a host of dialectics, not the least of which are desire and danger, woman-proud promiscuity and repression, freedom and confinement.

Larsen has given us something more than just another simple doubling or dividing, however, for Clare is less Irene's alter ego than her alter libido, the buried, long-denied sexual self, whose absence in his wife has led Irene's husband Brian to conclude, with some bitterness, that sex (with Irene?) is a joke. To Irene's concerns that their older son is picking up "some queer ideas about things—some things—from older boys," Brian responds scornfully: "D'you mean ideas about sex, Irene? . . . Well, what of it? . . . The sooner and the more he learns about sex, the better for him. And most certainly if he learns that it's a grand joke, the greatest in the world. It'll keep him from lots of disappointments later on." The fact that Irene cannot bring herself to say the word sex, even to her husband, suggests that she may be the source of Brian's own sexual disappointments. The Redfields' marriage, we know, is largely passionless. The couple sleep in separate bedrooms, and there is a general chill in the air between them, which only warms up in the (sensual) presence of Clare, who Irene suspects is "capable of heights and depths of feeling that she, Irene Redfield, had never known. Indeed, never cared to know." This "suspicion" (Larsen's word) will later be linked to another: that Brian has found in Clare Kendry the "heights and depths of feeling" missing in his wife.[45]

But if Clare is Irene's alter libido, then Irene is Clare's as well, a connection to the "primitive" Negro past, gone but too *instinctual* to be forgotten. This instinctive need to rejoin—the need of the exotic sexual other (Clare) to reconnect with its equally (but differently) exotic racial self (Irene, though perhaps more with what Irene represents than with what she is)—may be the source of the longing, the ache, the unceasing pain, and the wild desire Clare writes of in her letter to Irene. A closer look at the letter, with the phrases McDowell *omits*, lends support to this possible interpretation. (Italics indicate the omitted phrases; the ellipses are Larsen's.)

---

[45]Larsen, *"Quicksand" and "Passing,"* pp. 188–89, 195.

For I am lonely, so lonely . . . cannot help longing to be with you again, as I have never longed for anything before; and I have wanted many things in my life. . . . *You can't know how in this pale life of mine I am all the time seeing the bright pictures of that other that I once thought I was glad to be free of.* . . . It's like an ache, a pain that never ceases. . . . *Sheets upon thin sheets of it. And ending with,* and it's your fault.[46]

While McDowell's edited version of the letter situates Irene as the absolute object of Clare's desire, the actual letter directs the bulk of that "wild desire" to the *other* Negro life Irene represents—the black life Clare shed like a dead skin some time ago and now wants to reclaim, it seems, by appropriating the experiences of Irene's skin, a bit like any other primitivist. (Clare, in fact, can be read as a comment on primitivists who enjoy the privileges of white skin by day but flock to Harlem by night to enjoy the pleasures they associate with black flesh.) The threat to Irene in this configuration is the threat of the displaced other attempting to reclaim its racial self through the absorption of its alternate subjectivity. In other words, the object of desire for both Irene and Clare is a total subjectivity, a whole self—coded in both racial and sexual terms, repressed in Irene and expressed in Clare. The problem is that two halves only make one whole; therefore, the completeness Clare is so intent on pursuing can only be attained at the expense of Irene's subjectivity. In such a reading, the danger Irene senses but cannot name is a fear of a loss of self, and the attraction—the "inexplicable onrush of affectionate feeling"—is love for lost self.

This reading of possible autoerotic signification in *Passing* is by no means a denial of McDowell's homoerotic theory, however, but a possible expansion of it. For there is no essential sexual self; homosexuality is often encoded textually as self-love or narcissism. Through her "unseeing eyes," Irene comes to view Clare as the intruding, insinuating other she loves to hate, but Clare may actually be the threatening, disruptive, daring, sexual self—with "a having way"—that Irene hates to love. Hates enough and fears enough to kill, if we assume that it is Irene who pushes Clare out a sixth-floor window to her death. If we pursue the doubling line and view Clare as Irene's repressed other, her death at Irene's hands is not only murder but suicide.

Many critics read Clare's death at the end of the novel as yet another concession to convention. Once again, a high-spirited, defiant heroine is confined to either the deathbed of marriage or the graveyard. McDowell, for example, maintains that Larsen's ending seems to "pun-

[46]Ibid., p. 145.

ish the very values the novel implicitly affirms, to honor the very value system the text implicitly satirizes."[47] I would argue that the text ultimately affirms neither Irene's values nor Clare's; rather, it holds both up to scrutiny, if not ridicule, as signs of the times. But as Thadious Davis, Claudia Tate, and others have argued, how one views the ending of *Passing* may depend on whom one holds to be the novel's central figure. As my own abbreviated reading no doubt reveals, *Passing* seems to me to be very much Irene's story. Clare, however central to the unraveling of the plot, is a foil against whom Irene's middle-class consciousness develops, or, more correctly, deteriorates in demonic degrees. When Irene instead of Clare is taken to be the central figure and when murder rather than suicide or accident is viewed as the cause of Clare's death, the text's heroine ceases to be a typical, passive, conventional tragic mulatto, who pales beside the powerful image of woman-proud blues performers. She becomes instead a protector of the precious domestic realm—defender of middle-class marriage, bourgeois home, family, fidelity, and, above all, security (Irene is convinced, after all, that Clare is having an affair with her husband and is about to break up her marriage).[48] She gives new meaning to the term "home protection." As a wife, betrayed by friend and husband alike, fighting for her marriage, Irene gains what Houston Baker might call "blues force" as a heroine. She becomes, in such a reading, at once an active agent in the ordering of her own life and a grotesque, which may be precisely the point.

The infinite possibilities of Larsen's fictive invention, in my view, make *Passing* artistically complex beyond the limits of any particular reading or any single rhythm. Perhaps this is why I want not to discredit Deborah McDowell's inspired and empowering interpretation, but to disrupt the fixity of the reading—to wrest it from the assumption that Larsen's sexual signifying *necessarily* suggests lesbian attraction, particularly where no "definition" is offered for "lesbian." Ironically, while she has elsewhere chided Barbara Smith for her "vague and imprecise" definition of lesbianism, McDowell offers no clarification of her own usage of the term.[49] She appears to take "lesbian relationship" to mean a

---

[47]Ibid., pp. xxx–xxxi.

[48]For McDowell, an affair between friend and husband exists only in Irene's imagination, as a projection "of her own developing passion for Clare onto Brian" (ibid., p. xxviii). The novel itself, it seems to me, leaves wonderfully ambiguous the question of an affair between Brian and Clare. Even in a conservative reading, however, Irene is not irrationally out of line to be suspicious of a friend who warns: "I haven't any proper morals or sense of duty, as you have, that makes me act as I do. . . . Why, to get the things I want badly enough, I'd do anything, hurt anybody, throw anything away. Really, Rene, I'm not safe" (ibid., p. 201).

[49]Deborah E. McDowell, "New Directions for Black Feminist Criticism," in *The New*

necessarily physical attraction of female body to female body for seizure of erotic pleasure and sexual satisfaction. *Passing* seems to me, however, to transcend such limited definitions. What is most engaging about the text is the multiplicity of meanings Larsen's brilliant use of the body and her manipulation of both metaphor and materiality inspire. Larsen accomplishes in *Passing* that "surplus of signifiers"—the superabundance of interpretability—which, according to Frank Kermode, makes a work a classic.[50] In both *Quicksand* and *Passing,* Larsen creates that unreal estate I spoke of earlier, a fantastic realm we as critics seem to need to ground in a particular reality. McDowell's reading opens windows into the text, to be sure, but it also seems to me to hinge precisely what Larsen, in splendid ambiguity, has so cleverly unhinged.

In my reading of the 1920s and 1930s, it is only through a disturbing twist of literary fate and intellectual history that Fauset and Larsen have been criticized for not measuring up to the sexual and textual liberation of their blues-singing sisters. At another time, in another context, these two women authors might have been praised for their roles in advancing literary discourse toward a moment where black female desire could be boldly sung on the printed page as well as on the nightclub stage. Perpetually measured against Bessie Smith, on the one hand, and Zora Neale Hurston, on the other, however, Fauset and Larsen have rarely been read in terms of their particular contributions to modernism, to American and African American literature, and to the development of the woman's novel.

Far from silent on the topic of sexuality, these artists are more rightly claimed, I believe, as the first black women novelists to depict openly sensual black female subjects, the first black writers to explore the dialectics of female desire and to address what having children can mean to a woman's physical and mental health, as well as to her independence.

---

*Feminist Criticism: Essays on Women, Literature, and Theory,* ed. Elaine Showalter (New York, 1985), p. 190. In "Toward a Black Feminist Criticism," in the same volume, Barbara Smith suggests that "if in a woman writer's work a sentence refuses to do what it is supposed to do, if there are strong images of women and if there is a refusal to be linear, the result is innately lesbian literature" (p. 175). Smith takes Toni Morrison's *Sula* (New York, 1973) as a case in point, arguing that *Sula* works as a lesbian text "because of Morrison's consistently critical stance toward the heterosexual institutions of male-female relationships, marriage, and the family" (p. 168). McDowell criticizes this definition, arguing that Smith has "simultaneously oversimplified and obscured the issue of lesbianism" (p. 190). The definition of lesbianism that is implied in McDowell's reading of *Passing* seems to me the greater oversimplification.

[50]Frank Kermode, *The Classic: Literary Images of Permanence and Change* (New York, 1975), p. 140.

They were the first black women artists to depict successful, independent, single black professional and working-class women—not all of whom ultimately surrender their careers to male-dominated, bourgeois marriages, as many critics have claimed. Their heroines are by no means passionless decorations, adorning the pristine pages of immaculately conceived "lace-curtain romances." They are, on the contrary, implicitly sexual beings, finely tuned to both the power and the vulnerability of their own female bodies. At a moment when black female sexuality was either completely unwritten to avoid endorsing sexual stereotypes or sensationally overwritten to both defy and exploit those stereotypes, Fauset and Larsen edged the discourse into another realm: a realm precariously balanced on the cusp of the respectable and the risqué; a realm that is at times *neutral,* perhaps, but never *neuter*; a realm in which they, too, participated in reclaiming the black body and in defining African American expressive culture.

What I have tried to do in this essay is to unhinge the fixity with which the blues have come to be claimed as the master narrative of *the* black experience, narrowly defined. While I do not want to deny the importance of the blues as a cultural index, I do want to argue for other indices, for wider analytical angles that allow us to plot African American expressive geographies in inclusive rather than exclusive terms. I have argued as well for the importance of historical specificity and attention to ideology and iconography in decoding and remapping African American cultural cartography—in retheorizing such expansive, explosive, ideologically charged spaces as "the folk," "the bourgeois," "the authentic," and "the real." The novels of Jessie Fauset and Nella Larsen are only two examples of familiarly neglected works whose representations of the 1920s and 1930s can serve to remind contemporary cultural critics and theorists that the era known as the Harlem renaissance was not a monolithic, one-dimensional blues moment.

Fauset and Larsen's fictions are important to literary and cultural theory, then, not just because of what they tell us about the sexual, social, aesthetic, and intellectual codes of their time, but because of what our responses to them can tell us about our own. Our moment echoes theirs in its romanticization of the folk and its preoccupation with cultural authenticity. That Fauset and Larsen are often left out or pushed to the margins in contemporary mappings of African American expressive geographies suggests that we have learned little about the elusive (if not the illusive) nature of "the real colored thing" from the battles fought over the bodies of black female sexual icons such as Bessie Smith and Josephine Baker in the 1920s.

While I do not mean to diminish the significance of these artists or their accomplishments, I am left wondering what it is about *our* moment that has made us turn to theirs. What, for example, accounts for the current resurgence of interest in Josephine Baker's life and art, which has once again made of her a spectacle?[51] Are we, in our attempts at cultural criticism, modern-day primitivists? Are our Afrocentric interests and our vernacular theories and our feminist concerns for female agency colluding with primitivist proclivities like those that helped to bring the black "other" into vogue in the 1920s? Are we, paralleling the moments in which they lived and worked, inventing these artists as icons? Insisting on this question—debating who (or what) invented whom—is more than a little like arguing which came first, chicken or egg? Perhaps what is most important is our own awareness of just how complex and ideologically charged are both the question and our attempts at answers.

[51]I am thinking in particular of recent film representations of Baker's life, which include a 1987 British documentary, *Chasing a Rainbow*; a 1991 made-for-cable television movie, *The Josephine Baker Story*; and a second television movie and a feature film, both in the planning stage. In addition, two of Baker's French films from the 1930s, *Princess Tam-Tam* and *Zou-Zou,* have been rereleased with subtitles and shown to capacity crowds in theaters throughout the United States, as well as marketed on videocassette. See Phyllis Rose, "Josephine Baker: Exactly What Is It," *New York Times,* March 10, 1991.

# PART 2

---

# SEXUAL POLITICS AND SEXUAL

# RADICALS SINCE THE 1940s

# The Anatomy of Lynching

ROBYN WIEGMAN

*Department of English and Women's Studies*
*Indiana University*

When Matt lowered his eyes he noticed the ribs had been caved in. The flesh was bruised and torn. [The birthmark] was just below [Willie's] navel, he thought. Then he gave a start: where it should have been was only a bloody mound of torn flesh and hair. Matt went weak. He felt as though he had been castrated himself. He thought he would fall when Clara stepped up beside him. Swiftly, he tried to push her back. . . . Then Clara was screaming. . . . Matt pushed [her] to go, feeling hot breath against the hand he held over her mouth.

"Just remember that a car hit 'im, and you'll be all right," the patrolman said. "We don't allow no lynching round here no more."

Matt felt Clara's fingers digging into his arm as his eyes flashed swiftly over the face of the towering patrolman, over the badge against the blue shirt, the fingers crooked in the belt above the gun butt. He swallowed hard . . . catching sight of Willie between the white men's legs.

"I'll remember," he said bitterly, "he was hit by a car." [Ralph Ellison, "The Birthmark," in *New Masses,* July 2, 1940]

ABOVE ALL, LYNCHING IS about the law: both the towering patrolman who renarrates the body and sadistically claims it as sign of his own power, and the symbolic as law, the site of normativity and sanctioned desire, prohibition and taboo. In the circuit of relations that governs lynching in the United States, the law as legal discourse and disciplinary practice subtends the symbolic arena, marking out a topos of bodies and identities that gives order to generation, defines and circumscribes social and political behavior, and punishes transgression, from its wildest possibility to its most benign threat. Operating accord-

This essay originally appeared in the *Journal of the History of Sexuality* 1993, vol. 3, no. 3.

ing to a logic of borders—racial, sexual, national, psychological, biological, as well as gendered—lynching figures its victims as the culturally abject, monstrosities of excess whose limp and hanging bodies function as the specular assurance that the threat has not simply been averted, but thoroughly negated, dehumanized, and rendered incapable of return. The overdetermination of punishment in the lynching scenario demonstrates its profoundly psychological function, reinforcing the asymmetry of empowerment that initiates and sustains the disciplinary mechanism in all of its violent complexity. How we understand this complexity—how we can approach the tableau of torture, dismemberment, and death that shapes lynching's specifically racialized deployment—provides the locus around which this essay is organized and makes possible a theoretical foray into the intersecting relations of race and sexual difference in nineteenth- and twentieth-century United States culture.

In particular, I focus on the sexual economy that underlies lynching's emergence as a disciplinary practice for racial control at the end of the nineteenth century, when the threat of ritualized death provided the means for (re)articulating white masculine supremacy within the social and economic specificities of slavery's abolition. As I hope to show, the decommodification of the African American body that accompanies the transformation from chattel to citizenry is mediated through a complicated process of sexualization and engendering: not only does lynching enact a grotesquely symbolic—if not literal—sexual encounter between the white mob and its victim, but the increasing utilization of castration as a preferred form of mutilation for African American men demonstrates lynching's connection to the sociosymbolic realm of sexual difference. In the disciplinary fusion of castration with lynching, the mob severs the black male from the masculine, interrupting the privilege of the phallus, and thereby reclaiming, through the perversity of dismemberment, his (masculine) potentiality for citizenship.[1] While this imposition of feminization works to align the black male, at the symbolic level of the body, with those still unenfranchised, it is significant that the narrative means for inciting and explaining the mob's

---

[1] In focusing on black men in the lynch scenario, I am interested in the overlay of sexual difference as witnessed in castration as the ultimate denouement of the mob's violence. Such a focus, however, is not meant to suggest that black women were not lynched, burned, and summarily mutilated in ways that would also speak to the race/gender axis. As I will discuss later, the inscription of the black male as rapist, that "necessary" narrativity that propels the white mob to violence, carries an inherent negation of the African American woman through the very absence of her significatory role in the psychosexual drama of masculinity that underwrites the lynching and castration of black men. But while black women may be absent from the cultural narrativity that defines and sanctions lynching,

violence takes the form of an intense masculinization in the figure of the black male as mythically endowed rapist. Through this double staging of gender—where the hypermasculinized rapist must "become" the feminine through ritualized castration—lynching inhabits and performs the border crossings of race, sex, and sexual difference.

## MARKING THE BODY

Readers familiar with nineteenth-century United States literature will no doubt recognize that the epigraph from Ellison's exploration of the body politic involved in relations between black and white men bears the same title, "The Birthmark," as Nathaniel Hawthorne's 1843 allegory of sexual difference. In each story, the figure of the birthmark establishes a system of corporeal inscription that links the body to cultural hierarchies of power: Hawthorne's birthmark being the "crimson stain upon the snow" of the beautiful Georgiana, while Ellison's is the mark below the navel of a young black man, Willie.[2] Significantly, both marks evoke castration, Georgiana's "bloody hand" functioning as symbol of her feminine lack,[3] and Willie's mark, through its disappearance into the "bloody mound of torn flesh and hair," evincing his literal castration.[4] While the antebellum story depicts the white female body *as* sexual difference, Ellison's piece rearticulates the symbolics of gender and castration at the site of the black male body. Such a rearticulation is made possible by the shifting relations of race and sexual difference in the late nineteenth century, where Emancipation's theoretical effect—the black male's social sameness—is symbolically mediated by a disciplinary prac-

---

their intellectual and political work against mob violence during the late nineteenth and early twentieth centuries in particular was crucial to African American communal resistance on a broad scale. On this last note, see Hazel Carby, "'On the Threshold of Woman's Era': Lynching, Empire, and Sexuality in Black Feminist Theory," in *"Race," Writing, and Difference,* ed. Henry Louis Gates, Jr. (Chicago, 1986), pp. 301–16. On white women's antilynching struggle, see Jacquelyn Dowd Hall, *Revolt against Chivalry: Jessie Daniel Ames and the Women's Campaign against Lynching* (New York, 1979).

[2]Nathaniel Hawthorne, "The Birthmark," in *The Scarlet Letter and Other Tales of the Puritans,* ed. Harry Levin (Boston, 1961), p. 369.

[3]Ibid., p. 370.

[4]In the final stages of revising this essay for publication, I encountered James R. McGovern's *Anatomy of a Lynching: The Killing of Claude Neal* (Baton Rouge, LA, 1982). While similarly interested in the practice of lynching, McGovern focuses on the specificities of the Neal case and his book is therefore more singularly historical and factual than my discussion here. But I think it significant—and certainly not coincidental—that the concept of anatomy figures centrally in his discussion as well, even as my analysis differs drastically in its deployment of both feminist and poststructuralist theoretical discourses.

tice that literalizes his affinity to the feminine. A brief look at the intertextual connections between these two figurations of the birthmark offers an initial locus for tracing the highly sexual and gendered dimensions of difference that inhabit the anatomy of lynching.[5]

In Hawthorne's parable of sexual difference,[6] a man deeply committed to science marries a beautiful woman only to find that a small birthmark on her left cheek drives him mad. This "visible mark of earthly imperfection"[7] symbolizes in his mind Georgiana's "liability to sin, sorrow, decay, and death,"[8] which aligns her, as emblem of the feminine, with materiality, the body, and the culturally abject. It evinces, in short, her castrated and castrating difference from the male. As the "frightful object"[9] that is the cause of Aylmer's "horror and disgust,"[10] the birthmark takes over his life, becoming, as Teresa de Lauretis might put it, the very ground of his representation, "the looking-glass held up to man."[11] But while Georgiana's imperfect image grants Aylmer the fantasy of his own unbounded power and sets him in struggle with "our great creative Mother,"[12] she remains throughout the story the objectified spectacle of his desire, forever tied, in Laura Mulvey's terms, "to her place as bearer of meaning, not maker of meaning."[13] This position of alienation and negation is so powerful, in fact, that we can hardly be surprised to learn that "not even Aylmer . . . hated [the birthmark] so much as she."[14] When the enigma represented by woman and linked to the secrets of the natural world seems finally overcome, when "the last crimson tint of the birthmark—that sole token of human imperfection —faded from her cheek," Georgiana exhales her last breath, leaving Aylmer with a dead but now perfect woman.[15]

In the project of restoring woman to perfection, Hawthorne's story serves as a paradigm for the relations of sexual difference that underlie nineteenth-century scientific discourses on the feminine, where cultural

[5]Ralph Ellison, "The Birthmark," *New Masses* 36 (July 2, 1940), p. 16.

[6]See also Judith Fetterley, *The Resisting Reader: A Feminist Approach to American Fiction* (Bloomington, IN, 1978), pp. 22–33, for a discussion of the story's tie to sexual difference.

[7]Hawthorne, p. 369.

[8]Ibid., p. 370.

[9]Ibid., p. 371.

[10]Ibid., p. 372.

[11]Teresa de Lauretis, *Alice Doesn't: Feminism, Semiotics, Cinema* (Bloomington, IN, 1984), p. 15.

[12]Hawthorne, p. 374.

[13]Laura Mulvey, "Visual Pleasure and Narrative Cinema," in *Feminism and Film Theory,* ed. Constance Penley (New York, 1988), p. 58.

[14]Hawthorne, p. 379.

[15]Ibid., p. 386.

anxieties about (white) women's place in the emergent public sphere are mediated by returning her to the body and its ascribed inferiorities. Placed there, in the landscape of her anatomy, woman provides the nexus against which masculine *disembodiment* can be achieved: where the rationality of the mind surpasses, even as it appropriates, the physical limitations of the body. In deferring masculine castration by becoming its embodiment, in functioning as the displaced locus of mutation, loss, and death, the female body in Hawthorne's story shares more than a coincidental affinity to the castrated body of the black male in Ellison's piece written nearly a century later. For the literalization of castration pursues the logic of sexual difference from the seemingly self-contained realm of masculine and feminine to that of racial difference and its inscription of corporeal and social division. By depicting the black male within a symbolic system contingent on the discursivity of gender, Ellison's "The Birthmark" articulates the way lynching and castration stages the black male's relationship to masculine power itself.

Published the same year as Richard Wright's *Native Son,* Ellison's little-known story opens at the scene of an accident, as Matt and Clara prepare to identify a body that purportedly has been hit by a car. But their brother, Willie, has been beaten and lynched, his face so thoroughly disfigured they must seek his birthmark, located beneath the navel, for positive recognition. In searching for the mark, Matt discovers castration instead: "where it should have been was only a bloody mound of torn flesh and hair."[16] This discovery establishes the interplay between birthmark and penis that activates the narrative's symbolic structure, allowing us to read castration as the remedy for the symbolic birthmark—the penis—that "flaws" black men. Such a remedy becomes necessary in the social transformation from enslavement to freedom, where the measure of the African American's claim to citizenship is precisely his status as man—a status evinced by the penis, but ultimately rewarded in the symbolic exchange between penis and phallus. Castration circumvents this process of exchange, consigning the black male to the fragmented and decidedly feminized realm of the body. As in Faulkner's *Light in August,* castration literalizes the association of "womanshenegro" that binds together the racial, sexual, and gendered not only in Joe Christmas's psyche, but in the sociosymbolic of United States culture that both the novel and Ellison's story inhabit.[17]

But while the affinity between the castrating marks in Hawthorne's and Ellison's stories demonstrates the dynamic of sexual difference at work in each, such a reading can only partially account for the political

[16]Ellison, p. 17.
[17]William Faulkner, *Light in August* (New York, 1968), p. 147.

and ideological investments underlying lynching and castration. Indeed, by ascribing the black male fully to the feminine, one runs the risk of reiterating the lynch scenario's cultural effect without further illuminating the historical and ideological mappings of race and sexual difference through which this effect has been achieved. For while United States culture has rather routinely posited the black male in relation to the feminine (as in the emasculated icons of nineteenth-century minstrelsy and their twentieth-century comic counterparts), race and sexual difference are not the same. If the phallic lack characteristic of the feminine must be physically and psychologically inscribed—thereby denying the black male the primary sign of power in patriarchal culture—then his threat to white masculine power arises not simply from a perceived racial difference, but from the potential for gender sameness. Within the context of white supremacy, we must understand this threat of a masculine sameness as so terrifying that only the reassertion of a sexual and gendered difference can provide the necessary disavowal. It is this that lynching and castration offer in their ritualized deployment, functioning as both a refusal and a negation of the possibility of extending the privileges of patriarchy to the black man.

In Ellison's "The Birthmark," this refusal is graphically depicted in the story's final image of the body of the castrated black man lying, bloody and brutalized, "between the white men's legs."[18] For it is here that black male castration is figured in its relation to the power and privilege of white masculinity, and the body of the dismembered "other" takes its place as bearer of the white phallus's meaning, deprived of subjective boundaries, and thoroughly objectified and negated. Through the gendered positionalities of castration and its relation to the patriarchal symbolic, then, the conflict presented by the African American's masculine sameness is violently arbitrated in favor of the continued primacy of white masculine supremacy. In this way, the symbolic transposition of the birthmark from the stain of femininity in Hawthorne's tale to the threatening black phallus in Ellison's demonstrates not simply the powerful disciplinary function of race and sexual difference, but their historically contingent production.

## BIRTH OF A NATION

The political effect of the lynch scenario presented by Ralph Ellison in his brief but evocative story relies on the reader's awareness of the broader cultural context of "race relations" in the late nineteenth and early twentieth centuries—a context in which the system of economic,

[18]Ellison, p. 17.

social, and political organization was profoundly altered, as I have suggested, by the African American's emergence from slavery to citizenry. As a response to the ideological incommensurability between white supremacy and black enfranchisement, lynching marks the excess of discourses of race and rights, serving as a chief mechanism for defining relations of power in the postwar years. For the emancipation of five million slaves was neither a widespread cultural recognition of black humanity nor the proud achievement of the democratic ethos. As the late nineteenth century's turn toward the Ku Klux Klan and mob violence makes clear, the transformation from slavery to "freedom" was characterized by a rearticulation of cultural hierarchies in which terrorism provided the means for defining and securing the continuity of white supremacy.[19] The rise of black lynchings in the years following the war—10,000 by 1895, according to one source[20]—is indicative of a broader attitude in the United States toward African American entrance into the cultural order: greeted by a few as the manifestation of a liberal ideal, "freedom" was far from the reigning social reality.

For the *New Masses* reader in 1940, the narrative of dismemberment and murder, overseen by the figure of the law, marked the repetitiousness of white supremacist discipline that greeted the "free" black subject in the 1860s and continued to reiterate his or her secondary social position throughout the twentieth century, including the present day.[21] Both mainstream and alternative newspapers regularly ran stories documenting the scenes of violence, often offering graphic detail of the

[19]On mob violence and the Ku Klux Klan, see National Association for the Advancement of Colored People, *Thirty Years of Lynching in the United States, 1889–1918* (New York, 1919); James E. Cutler, *Lynch-Law: An Investigation into the History of Lynching in the United States* (New York, 1905); Allen W. Trelease, *White Terror: The Ku Klux Klan Conspiracy and Southern Reconstruction* (New York, 1971); Joel Williamson, *The Crucible of Race: Black-White Relations in the American South since Emancipation* (New York, 1984); and C. Vann Woodward, *The Strange Career of Jim Crow* (New York, 1957).

[20]Ida B. Wells-Barnett, *On Lynchings: Southern Horrors; A Red Record; Mob Rule in New Orleans* (New York, 1969), p. 8. Much like statistics on rape, numerical accounts of lynching vary widely, most obviously because of the way the legal apparatus ignored violent crimes against African Americans. Trudier Harris, *Exorcising Blackness: Historical and Literary Lynching and Burning Rituals* (Bloomington, IN, 1984), for instance, cites 4,951 lynchings in the United States between 1882 and 1927, using figures provided by Cutler, who tends to rely on "official" statistics. Wells-Barnett's figure, on the other hand, is an estimation that seeks to account for those violent acts not documented within the larger U.S. community. See also Dowd Hall.

[21]As I write this in the aftermath of the April 1992 acquittals of the white Los Angeles police officers who beat a black male suspect, Rodney King, unconscious, it is apparent that the figuration of the law Ellison depicts in 1940 continues to function as the disciplinary mechanism for instantiating and perpetuating white supremacy. One might even venture to say that the decline of the lynch mob in the second half of the twentieth century has less

practices of torture through which the entire African American population could be defined and policed as innately, if no longer legally, inferior.[22] Such accounts extended the function of lynching as a mode of surveillance by reiterating its performative qualities, carving up the black citizen body in the specular recreation of the initial, dismembering scene. For Trudier Harris, who has studied the legacy of lynching for African American writers of the nineteenth and twentieth centuries, the imposition of a violent, bodily destruction works "to keep Blacks contained politically and socially during the years of Reconstruction . . . convey[ing] to [them] that there was always someone watching over their shoulders ready to punish them for the slightest offense or the least deviation from acceptable lines of action."[23] What constituted "acceptable lines of action" for the newly emancipated slave depended, of course, on whose perspective was being articulated. In the conflict between a South deeply shocked by its lost hegemony and the slave's euphoric desire to grasp the rights and privileges of citizenry, the full panorama of racist violence emerges as the defining conditions of "America" (as ideological trope and national body) itself.

In this regard, we might understand the end of slavery as marking in fuller and more complex ways the birth of the nation, where one of the questions that divided the delegates at the Continental Congress in 1776 was finally settled in favor of a rhetorical and legal, though not altogether economic or political, equality. But as the rise of lynching in the postwar years indicates, this birth brings into crisis the definitional boundaries of nation implicit in the early constitutional documents: here, issues of generation, inheritance, and property rights are theoretically wrenched from their singular association with the white masculine and made available, at least in the abstract, to a new body of citizens. The effect of this transformation is the dissolution of a particular kind of patriarchal order, for while the slave system ensured a propertied relation between laborer and master, and discursively and legally bound the African American to the white father through the surname, Emancipation represents the literal and symbolic loss of the security of the white patronym and an attendant displacement of the primacy of the white male. The many documented reports of slaves changing their names in the first moments of their freedom—and the thematic value of naming

---

to do with real advancements in white supremacy's abatement than with the incorporation of the mob's tenor and function within the legal and law enforcement systems themselves.

[22] For discussion of various newspaper accounts of lynching, see Harris, *Exorcising Blackness*, pp. 1–19.

[23] Ibid., p. 19.

itself in the African American cultural tradition—are indicative of the significance of the material and metaphorical eclipse of the white father's patronymic embrace.[24]

For the nonpropertied white male, the Civil War and Reconstruction represented important transformations in the historical articulation of a white underclass consciousness, offering on one hand the recognition of specific class-bound political interests, while often positing free men and women as competitors to their own economic survival. One of the most prominent national figures embodying this position was Lincoln's successor to the White House, Andrew Johnson. As Eric Foner discusses in his important reconsideration of the Reconstruction era, Johnson, having grown up in poverty himself, identified with the Southern yeomanry. "He seems to have assumed that the Confederacy's defeat had shattered the power of the 'slaveocracy' and made possible the political ascendancy of loyal white yeomen. The freedmen had no role to play in his vision of a reconstructed South."[25] Like other poor whites, Johnson saw slaves as complicit with their masters in maintaining economic and political power over nonslaveholding whites. In this scenario, Foner writes, "the most likely result of black enfranchisement would therefore be an alliance of blacks and planters, restoring the Slave Power's hegemony and effectively excluding the yeomanry from political power."[26] Johnson's inability to read the class interests of poor whites as aligned with the emergent black citizen—as in fact a multiracial underclass exploited by a feudalistic agrarian or developing free market system—demonstrates the contradiction between a class-conscious and white supremacist social vision. Such a contradiction contributed to the political fragmentation of the postwar years, producing violent reprisals toward the emancipated slave from the white yeoman as well as from the planter class.

In these reprisals for offenses more often imagined than real, lynching becomes a primary disciplinary tool, and it takes on over time a narrativizing context that both propels the white crowd to action and defines the methods of torture subsequently imposed. The narrative I refer to features the African American male in the role of mythically en-

---

[24]The most famous name change, of course, is Malcolm Little's shift to X. On the significance of naming to the African American literary tradition, see especially Kimberly W. Benston, "I Yam What I Am: The Topos of Un(naming) in Afro-American Literature," in *Black Literature and Literary Theory,* ed. Henry Louis Gates, Jr. (New York, 1984), pp. 151–72; and Michael Cooke, "Naming, Being, and Black Experience," *Yale Review* 68 (1978): 167–86.

[25]Eric Foner, *Reconstruction: America's Unfinished Revolution 1863–1877* (New York, 1988), p. 181.

[26]Ibid.

dowed rapist, with the white woman as the flower of civilization he intends to violently pluck, and the white male as the heroic interceptor who restores order by thwarting this black phallic insurgence.[27] But in the early decades of the nineteenth century, lynching does not function within this constellation of racial and sexual encodements. Instead, as Trudier Harris discusses, it is a component of the system of frontier justice, operating in lieu of a legally sanctioned trial and consisting of a variety of punishments—most often whippings—without the final denouement of death.[28] In fact, before 1840, writes James E. Cutler in his study of the history of lynching in the United States, "the verb lynch was occasionally used to include capital punishment, but . . . 'to lynch' had not then undergone a change in meaning and acquired the sense of 'to put to death.' . . . It was not until a time subsequent to the Civil War that the verb lynch came to carry the idea of putting to death."[29] And it is not until that time as well that lynching becomes associated almost exclusively with acts of retribution against the legally free citizenry of African American subjects.[30]

The turn toward lynching as a racially coded practice owes its existence, as I have suggested, to the transformations attending Emancipation, from the threat to white economic security presented by the loss of a free labor force to the competitive inclusion of African Americans into the open market's laboring class. But the significance of lynching as coterminous with violence against African Americans in the Recon-

---

[27]D. W. Griffith's 1915 *The Birth of a Nation* is perhaps the classic example of the hysterical tie between the African American's social participation and the discourse of the black rapist. Here, in a film that literally transformed the technical achievements of American filmmaking, the glory and order of the Old South are contrasted with the devastation and ruin wrought by the Civil War and its aftermath. The picturesque racial harmony of the slave system gives way to massive black corruption, as the seemingly innate bestiality of the ex-slave wends its way to the surface. As blacks descend into laziness and drunkenness, they seize the polls and disenfranchise white citizens, before finally laying sexual claim to white women. In the film's finale, as Donald Bogle writes, "a group of stalwart, upright white males, wearing sheets and hoods, no less . . . [defend] white womanhood, white honor and white glory . . . restor[ing] to the South everything it has lost, including white supremacy. Thus we have the birth of a nation." See Donald Bogle, *Blacks in American Films and Television* (New York, 1988), p. 20; Alan Casty, "The Films of D. W. Griffith: A Style for the Times," *Journal of Popular Film* 1, no. 2 (1972): 67–79; and Michael Rogin, "'The Sword Became a Flashing Vision': D. W. Griffith's *The Birth of a Nation*," *Representations* 9 (1985): 150–95.

[28]See Harris, *Exorcising Blackness*, pp. 6–7.

[29]Cutler, p. 116.

[30]See also Dowd Hall, who writes that "the proportion of lynchings taking place in the South increased from 82% of the total [of executions] in the 1890s to 95% in the 1920s; over the same periods the proportion of lynch victims who were white decreased from 32% to 9%. Lynching had become virtually a Southern phenomenon and a racial one" (p. 133).

struction era emerges as well from the historical configuration of citizenry as part of a broader economy of the body in United States culture. As feminist political theorists have discussed, the white male citizen of Enlightenment thought draws his particular suit of rights and privileges from the rhetorical disembodiment of the citizen as a social category, where in Lauren Berlant's words, "the generic 'person'" provides the abstraction necessary for replacing the historically located body with the discursivity of national identity.[31] As she explains: "The American subject is privileged to suppress the fact of his historical situation in the abstract 'person': but then, in return, the nation provides a kind of prophylaxis for the person, as it promises to protect his privileges and his local body in return for loyalty to the state. . . . The implicit whiteness and maleness of the original American citizen is thus itself protected by national identity."[32] In constituting the citizen through the value system of disembodied abstraction, the white male is "freed" from the corporeality that might otherwise impede his insertion into the larger body of national identity.

For the African American subject, on the other hand, it is precisely the imposition of an extreme corporeality that defines his or her distance from the privileged ranks of (potential or actual) citizenry. With the advent of Emancipation and its attendant loss of the slave system's marking of the African American body as property, lynching emerges to reclaim and reassert the centrality of black corporeality, deterring the now theoretically possible move toward citizenry and disembodied abstraction. Through the lynching scenario, "blackness" is cast as a subversive (and most often sexual) threat, an incontrovertible chaos whose challenge to the economic and social coherency of the nation can be psychologically, if not wholly politically, averted by corporeal abjection and death. That lynching becomes during Reconstruction and its aftermath an increasingly routine response to black attempts at education, personal and communal government, suffrage, and other indicators of cultural inclusion and equality attests to its powerful disciplinary function. As the most extreme deterritorialization of the body and its subjective boundaries, lynching guarantees the white mob's privilege of physical and psychic penetration, grants it a definitional authority over social space, and embodies the vigilant and violent system of surveillance that underwrites late nineteenth- and early twentieth-century negotiations over race and cultural power.

---

[31]Lauren Berlant, "National Brands/National Body: *Imitation of Life,*" in *Comparative American Identities: Race, Sex, and Nationality in the Modern Text,* ed. Hortense Spillers (New York, 1991), p. 112.
[32]Ibid., p. 113.

## White Beauty, Black Beast

But why the charge of rape as the consolidating moment of lynching's justification? Why this sexualization of blackness as the precondition not only for mob action, but for lynching's broad cultural acceptance and appeal? The answer to this, like any accounting of the historical, is less apparent than the many contexts in which the evidence of lynching's sexualization appears.* But if we begin where I have suggested, with the narrative of rape (and its culmination in lynching) translating the crisis of Emancipation from economic to sexual and gendered terms, we encounter a very powerful means through which not only black men but the entire black community could be psychologically and physically contained. Most important, we witness the way the rape narrative simultaneously recognizes and subverts the African American male's theoretical equality in the sexual as well as political and economic spheres. On a level less abstract, the rape mythos, as an overwhelmingly southern re-

*The rise of black lynchings in the late nineteenth century and the attendant articulation of the mythology of the black male as rapist demonstrates an increasing reliance on the discourse of sexual difference to negotiate race within the newly emergent economic structures of the twentieth century. This shift and its implications for reading gender and race emerge most fully in Richard Wright's *Native Son* (1940), our literature's most compelling story of the black man caught in the mythology of the rapist—that death, as Bigger Thomas says, "before death came."[a] Revolving around the fated life of Bigger, his employment by a liberal white family, his accidental murder of their daughter, Mary, and his subsequent flight and trial, the novel demonstrates what Wright considers the definitive pattern of race relations in the United States. As he writes in "How 'Bigger' Was Born," "any Negro . . . knows that times without number he has heard of some Negro boy being picked up . . . and carted off to jail and charged with 'rape.' This thing happens so often that to my mind it had become a representative symbol of the Negro's uncertain position in America" (p. xxviii). In Wright's novel, such uncertainty is explicitly linked to masculinity and to the competitive dimensions of black male and white male relations.

The significance of masculinity for Wright's central character is apparent from the opening scene where Bigger's mother describes his failure: "We wouldn't have to live in this garbage dump if you had any manhood in you" (p. 12). Her words fill Bigger with shame and hatred, a deep alienating guilt repeatedly evoked throughout the text and expressly linked to emasculation. When his mother visits him in prison at the novel's end and begs on her knees before Mrs. Dalton for Bigger's life, he is described as "paralyzed with shame; he felt violated" (p. 280). This violation, this symbolic emasculation, functions as a central metaphor in the novel, defining the black man's status in a racist culture, which,

[a]Richard Wright, *Native Son* (1940; rpt. New York, 1966), p. 228. Further citations appear in the text.

sponse to enfranchisement, also challenges the work of the Freedman's Bureau, where the patriarchal logic of the dominant culture became the defining mechanism for organizing the newly freed slave: not only did the bureau appoint the husband as head of the household, assigning to him sole power to enter into contractual labor agreements for the entire family, but it fought for the allotment of land for every freed "male," while granting only unmarried women access to this domain.[33]

In these pronouncements—as in the routine gender segregation attending voting, jury duty, the holding of political and Republican party office—the official program of Reconstruction understood the freedom of black men to entail a "natural" judicial and social superiority over African American women. The nineteenth century's determination of public and private along strict gender lines thus provided a definitional structure through which social space and familial roles were shaped for a population no longer denied the right (and privilege) of maintaining family bonds.[34] But while the patriarchalization of the black family served to institutionalize it within the gender codes prevalent in white

---

as Wright says in his autobiography *Black Boy*, "could recognize but a part of a man."[b] The partiality of masculinity serves to signify black alienation in United States society in general. As Bigger tells his friends: "Every time I think about it I feel like somebody's poking a red-hot iron down my throat. . . . We live here and they live there. . . . They got things we ain't. They do things and we can't. It's just like living in jail" (p. 23). In the figure of the red-hot iron, Wright casts Bigger's oppression in highly sexual and phallic terms, marking segregation, racism, and poverty as the symbolic phalluses of white masculine power burning in Bigger's throat. "You ain't a man no more," Bigger finally says, "[White folks] . . . after you so hot and hard . . . they kill you before you die" (pp. 326–27). Equating being a "man" with access to freedom and power, Bigger posits the white world, so "hot and hard" against him, as castrating.

---

[33]Foner, p. 87.

[34]Because of this articulation of the public/private split in the postwar years—and its contrast to gendered relations within the slave community—Angela Davis, among others, has argued that "the salient theme emerging from domestic life in the slave quarters is one of sexual equality." See Angela Davis, *Women, Race, and Class* (New York, 1981), p. 18. Michele Wallace, *Black Macho and the Myth of the Superwoman* (New York, 1979), concurs with this, finding that through Emancipation, black men were encouraged to adopt white patriarchal roles and practices. On the particular impact on black family structure in the transition from slavery to sharecropping, see Susan A. Mann, "Slavery, Sharecropping, and Sexual Inequality," in *Black Women in America: Social Science Perspectives,* ed. Micheline R. Malson, Elisabeth Mudimbe-Boyi, Jean F. O'Barr, and Mary Wyer (Chicago, 1990), pp. 133–58.

[b]Richard Wright, *Black Boy* (New York, 1945), p. 284.

bourgeois ideology, thereby securing the black family to the formal dimensions of white social behavior, many whites were decidedly threatened by the definitional sameness accorded former slaves. The loss of one patriarchal organization of social life—that of slavery—and its replacement by the seeming egalitarianism of a male-dominated black family, then, has the effect of broadening the competitive dimensions of interracial masculine relations, especially as the black male's new property governance of black women threatens to extend to women of the dominant group as well.

It is in this climate that the mythology of the black male as rapist emerges, working the faultline of the slave's newly institutionalized masculinization by framing this masculinity as the bestial excess of an overly phallicized primitivity. In the contours of Western racial discourse, of course, the primitive sexual appetite associated with blackness is not a new articulation at the end of the nineteenth century, but its crafting in the highly stylized and overdetermined narrative structure of the rape mythos—along with the sheer frequency of its deployment—marks a particular historical configuration of the sexual and gendered in their relation to issues of race and nation. For while the slavery period in

But importantly, this castration is also an inverted sexual encounter between black men and white men, as evinced in the elaborate scene of chase and capture that accompanies the charge of rape against Bigger. Hiding on the roof of a building, Bigger is entrapped by white men wielding a fire hose, "the rushing stream jerked this way and that. . . . Then the water hit him. . . . He gasped, his mouth open. . . . The water left him; he lay gasping, spent. . . . The icy water clutched again at his body like a giant hand; the chill of it squeezed him like the circling coils of a monstrous boa constrictor" (p. 251). The passage that depicts Bigger's subsequent conquest by this monstrous phallic image extends the horrific sexual encounter: "He wanted to hold on but could not. His body teetered on the edge; his legs dangled in the air. Then he was falling. He landed on the roof, on his face, in snow, dazed" (p. 252). Finally brought down by the monstrosity of white masculine desire for and hatred of the black man, Bigger loses consciousness, his strength gone as the violent parody of romantic coupling ends.

In capturing Bigger, the white men—nearly eight thousand searching the city—believe they have made the world safe again for white women. As the prosecutor, Buckley, says in his plea for the imposition of the death penalty: "The law is strong and gracious enough to allow all of us to sit here . . . and not tremble with fear that at this very moment some half-human black ape may be climbing through the windows of our homes to rape, murder, and burn our daughters! . . . Every decent white man in America ought to swoon with joy for the opportunity to crush with his heel the woolly head of this black lizard" (p. 373). While Bigger's murder of the white woman is accidental and the subsequent destruction of her body makes it impossible to garner physical evidence of sexual abuse,

the United States often envisioned the Uncle Tom figure as the signification of the "positive good" of a system that protected and cared for its
black "children," once emancipated, these children became virile men
who wanted for themselves the ultimate symbol of white civilization:
the white woman.[35] The transformation of the image of the black man
from simple, docile Uncle Tom to violent sex offender characterizes the
oppositional logic underwriting the representational structure of black
male images in nineteenth- and twentieth-century United States culture,
a logic in which the discourse of sexual difference—from feminized
docility to hypermasculinized phallicity—comes to play a primary
significatory role.[36]

South Carolina Senator Ben Tillman demonstrates this logic in his
1907 speech before Congress, when he argues for the abandonment of
due process for blacks accused of sex crimes against white women:

> The white women of the South are in a state of seige. . . . Some
> lurking demon who has watched for the opportunity seizes her;
> she is choked or beaten into insensibility and ravished, her body

the central crime, as Buckley claims, "is *rape*" (p. 377). It is for the rape of Mary
Dalton that Bigger must die, as his trespass of white masculine property makes
him the symbol of all that the white world must protect itself from: an "infernal
monster," a "treacherous beast" and "worthless ape" (p. 377).

Given the intensity of the taboo against black men and white women, Bigger
accepts Mary's death as a conscious act: "Though he had killed by accident, not
once did he feel the need to tell himself that it had been an accident. He was
black and he had been alone in a room where a white girl had been killed; therefore he had killed her" (p. 101). In accepting responsibility for Mary's death,
Bigger sees himself not only as refuting white masculine authority, but as gaining an advantage that had eluded him before: "The knowledge that he had killed
a white girl they loved and regarded as their symbol of beauty made him feel the
equal of them, like a man who had been somehow cheated, but had now evened
the score" (p. 155). Through his destruction of the objectified symbol of white
patriarchal rule, Bigger claims his right to masculine selfhood; no longer does he
need the knife and gun, traditional symbols of masculinity, that initially accompanied him to the Dalton home: "What his knife and gun had once meant to
him, his knowledge of having secretly murdered Mary now meant" (p. 141).

Bigger's acceptance of Mary's murder and his consequent sense of freedom
are particularly meaningful when viewed in terms of an earlier and seemingly in-

---

[35]As Dowd Hall writes, "The ideology of racism reached a virulent crescendo, as the
dominant image of blacks in the white mind shifted from inferior child to aggressive and
dangerous animal" (p. 133).

[36]On the Uncle Tom figure in Harriet Beecher Stowe's novel and its impact on
rethinking race and gender in the nineteenth century, see Robyn Wiegman, "Toward a Political Economy of Race and Gender," *Bucknell Review* (Fall 1992).

prostituted, her purity destroyed, her chastity taken from her. . . .
Shall men . . . demand for [the demon] the right to have a fair trial
and be punished in the regular course of justice? So far as I am concerned he has put himself outside the pale of the law, human and
divine. . . . Civilization peels off us . . . and we revert to the . . . impulses . . . to "kill! kill! kill!"[37]

In proposing mob retaliation against the defilers of white womanhood,
Tillman assures his listeners that he does not hate blacks by recalling
"the negroes of the old slave days . . . the negroes who knew they were
inferior and who never presumed to assert equality."[38] These blacks,
with minds like "those of children," posed no sexual threat, as was witnessed, according to Tillman, by the fact that during the Civil War, with
white men away fighting, "there is not of record a solitary instance of
one white woman having been wronged" by the nearly 800,000 black
men left on plantation land.[39] Only with Emancipation and the "return
to barbarism" does rape follow; "the negro becomes a fiend in human
form."[40]

significant event in the novel. Before setting out for the Dalton home on the day
of Mary's accidental death, Bigger gathers with friends at Doc's poolroom to discuss plans for robbing Blum's Delicatessen. While the men had pulled other
"jobs," this was to be their first robbery of a white man. "For months they had
talked of robbing Blum's, but had not been able to bring themselves to do it.
They had the feeling that the robbing of Blum's would be a violation of ultimate
taboo; it would be trespassing into territory where the full wrath of an alien
white world would be turned loose upon them; in short, it would be a symbolic
challenge of the white world's rule over them; a challenge which they yearned to
make, but were afraid to" (pp. 17–18). The language here of "violation,"
"taboo," and "symbolic challenge" significantly scripts the robbing of Blum in
the same terms as the mythic encounter between a black man and a white
woman. This scene and a later one in which Bigger purposely argues with Gus as
a way to avoid going through with the plan indicate the more fundamental conflict that lies at the heart of the mythology of the black male rapist: the struggle
over social, political, and sexual power between black men and white men.

More important perhaps, the incident surrounding Blum clarifies the role of
the white woman in the negotiation of power among men. While white women
have been complicit in the lynching and burning of black men, at times using the
charge of rape themselves in order to protect their positions in the racial hierarchy, the mythology of the black rapist sets them up as the displaced site of a mas-

---

[37]Ben Tillman, "The Black Peril," in *Justice Denied: The Black Man in White America,*
ed. William Chace and Peter Collier (New York, 1970), p. 182.
[38]Ibid., p. 183.
[39]Ibid., pp. 181, 184.
[40]Ibid., p. 185.

As Tillman's rhetoric indicates, the white woman serves, in the ethos of nineteenth-century racialism, as a pivotal rhetorical figure for shaping the mythology of the black rapist. Using her emblem as the keeper of the purity of the race, white men cast themselves as protectors of civilization, reaffirming not only their role as social and familial "heads," but their paternal property rights as well. In this way, as Trudier Harris observes, the white male maintains a position of "superiority not only in assigning a place to his women, but especially in keeping black people, particularly black men, in the place he had assigned for them."[41] In this dual role, the mythology of the black male rapist simultaneously engineers race and gender hierarchies, masking the white male's own historical participation in "miscegenating" sexual activities and ensuring his disciplinary control over potential sexual—and, one must add, political—liaisons between black men and white women. Within the culine struggle, the embodiments of white masculine desire and hence the emblems of a thwarted masculinity for black men. Instead of robbing Blum or challenging Mr. Dalton, who makes his wealth from the overpriced rentals in the "Black Belt," Bigger lives out a drama crafted by the intersecting hierarchies of race and gender, a drama that raises the white woman to the pedestal only to make her bear the burden of the racist patriarchal structure by having her symbolize its hierarchical construction. This does not absolve the white woman from her complicity in maintaining racial oppression, though it does point to the broader pattern in U.S. culture where differences between men are played out within a highly charged configuration of gender.

Within this configuration, the role and status of the black woman takes on a particular cultural negativity as she symbolizes the excess of white womanhood. In *Native Son,* for instance, the raped and murdered body of Bessie Mears, Bigger's girlfriend, is wheeled into the courtroom as graphic display of Bigger's violent criminality. As he puts it, "Though he had killed a black girl and a white girl, he knew that it would be for the death of the white girl that he would be punished. The black girl was merely 'evidence'" (p. 307). But while Bigger recognizes the asymmetrical value placed on black women and white women, he nonetheless understands Bessie's murder within the same contextual framework as that governing Mary's, finding both acts "the most meaningful things that had ever happened to him. He was living, truly and deeply. . . . Never had his will been so free" (p. 225). In tying Bessie to the symbolic act of the white woman's murder—and in marking his violation of her as an equally cathartic trespass—Bigger redefines rape itself: "Rape was not what one did to women. Rape was what one felt when one's back was against a wall and one had to strike out, whether one wanted to or not. . . . It was rape when he cried out in hate deep in his heart as he felt the strain of living day by day" (p. 214). This displacement of the gendered dimensions of sexual violence casts the mythology of the black male rapist as itself a cultural rape, one defined by the materiality of black

[41]Harris, *Exorcising Blackness,* p. 19.

context of nineteenth-century abolitionist and feminist movements, the necessity for disrupting such potential bonds seems important indeed.

And yet, the central figuration of the white woman's sexuality in the rape mythos must be understood as a displacement of the deeper and more culturally complex relation between black men and white men and their claims to the patriarchal province of masculine power. As Harris writes, "The issue really boils down to one between white men and black men and the mythic conception the former have of the latter."[42] Such a mythic conception—in which, as Frantz Fanon says, "the Negro . . . has been fixated [at the genital]"[43]—works through the discourse of the biological, figuring blackness as the corporeal, and thereby equating the colonized laboring body with an extensive, uncontrollable sexuality. In reducing the black male to the body, and further to the penis itself, the

oppression. Such a transformation of the metaphorics of rape simultaneously points to the gendered inscriptions of black male oppression, while crafting the African American woman's death as the ricochet effect of the white woman's pedestaled superiority.

From a feminist perspective, there is something deeply disturbing about the novel's rearticulation of rape as "not what one did to women" and Bigger's subsequent insertion into the position of *sexual*—and not simply racial—victim. In the evacuation of the body of woman, particularly the black woman, from the terrain of sexual violence, Wright seems to hierarchicalize African American oppression in such a way that the thwarting of black masculinity, through literalized castration, outreaches and indeed negates the historical problem of the black woman's routinely violated sexuality. To find it necessary to deny the gendered dimensions of rape, then, to see only the black male as rape's social and sexual victim, serves not only to establish the black male's difference from the feminine, but to displace the category of woman altogether.[c] In this way, the black woman is expelled beyond the narrative's critical gaze as Bigger becomes the universalized emblem of black oppression—a universalization clearly predicated on the framework of masculinity and differences among men.

But while Wright's method of foregrounding the masculine stakes at work in the rapist mythos is defined at the expense of black women, his novel refuses the more traditional structure of male bonding that Eve Kosofsky Sedgwick has defined, in which "the spectacle of the ruin of woman . . . is just the right lubricant for an adjustment of differentials of power [among men]."[d] This we witness in

[42]Ibid.

[43]Frantz Fanon, *Black Skin, White Masks* (New York, 1967), p. 165.

[c]For a discussion of the role of black women in *Native Son,* see Trudier Harris, "Native Sons and Foreign Daughters," in *New Essays on "Native Son,"* ed. Keneth Kinnamon (New York, 1990), pp. 63–84.

[d]Eve Kosofsky Sedgwick, *Between Men: English Literature and Male Homosocial Desire* (New York, 1985), p. 66.

psychic drama of masculinity as it is played out in the colonial scenario of United States culture hinges on the simultaneous desire and disavowal attending the black male's mythic phallic inscription. In *White Hero, Black Beast,* Paul Hoch reads this process of desire and disavowal as constitutive of the unconscious formation of white masculinity, where the overdetermination of the black male's mythic phallicism—as evinced in the proliferation of discourses proclaiming, describing, or denying it—represents "a projection of those aspects of [the white male's] *own* sexuality which society has made taboo."[44] Under such conditions, as Hoch writes, "abandon[ing] control over the bestial supermasculinity he has projected outward on to the black male would threaten the racist's control over his *own* repressed sexuality."[45]

Hoch draws this conclusion not simply from the Freudian psychoanalytic framework he employs, but from the context of the relationship

the final moments of the novel, when Bigger makes a failed attempt to emerge from his alienation to connect with Jan, the white boyfriend of Mary Dalton. "Tell . . . Tell Mister . . . Tell Jan hello" (p. 392), Bigger says to his lawyer, Boris Max, shifting as he does from the servile address of "Mister" to Jan's first name. But the contrast between this hesitant and rather hopeless attempt and the image of utopian masculine bonds offered earlier in the novel—"an image of a strong blinding sun sending hot rays down . . . in the midst of a vast crowd of men, white men and black men and all men, [with] the sun's rays melt[ing] away the many differences, the colors, the clothes, and [drawing] what was common and good upward toward the sun" (p. 335)—demonstrates the deep abyss of color and caste that will accompany the many Biggers to their graves.

In the seeming impossibility of the utopian image to extend to Bigger any hope within the narrative scenario of the black male as rapist, Wright's novel purposely counters the rhetoric of 1930s progressive politics (most obviously that of the Communist party) that offers the image of interracial male bonds as socially transgressive. Instead, his narrative marks the extremity of hatred and violence that ushers the black male into the patriarchal province of the masculine, that province where he is simultaneously endowed with masculine prowess and defiantly deprived of the ability to pursue sexual (as well as social) autonomy. But in exploring the complexities of the rape mythos, Wright cannot wend his way out of the ideological trap of gender that exerts so much power within the disciplinary practice of lynching and castration. Instead, he reiterates the binary inscriptions of sexual difference by positioning the black male's social freedom—as well as the critical reading of his victimization—as oppositional to women. As such, *Native Son* compellingly and disturbingly captures Bigger in the definitional nexus of race, sexuality, and gender that Wright so defiantly sets out to explore.

---

[44]Paul Hoch, *White Hero, Black Beast: Racism, Sexism, and the Mask of Masculinity* (London, 1979), p. 54.
[45]Ibid., p. 55.

between conquest and masculinity in Western cultures. Here, the nature of conquest within the realm of the sexual underwrites the commodity status attached to the female body, helping to produce, through the formation of the feminine as masculine property, the contradictory logic of virgin/whore that subtends "woman" in her various cultural guises. In the bifurcation of the feminine into idealized and non-sexualized virginity on the one hand and defiled and fully sexualized promiscuity on the other, the conquestatory narrative of masculine sexuality is caught between a necessary restraint and a licensed rein. But because conquest is preeminently motivated by the inaccessible, by the taboos orchestrated around restraint, it is ultimately the defilement of the feminine in its ideal state that activates the conquestatory dimensions of "normative" masculine heterosexuality. For Hoch, this means that the phantasm of the black beast conquering the white goddess offers the most impressive demonstration of virility, as it is the greatest violation of the boundaries of restraint. At a fundamental psychic level, he claims, the white male "bitterly resents the black male for the greater opportunities for conquest and defilement his debased standing apparently affords him."[46]

Such resentment literally engenders a complicated process of creation and negation in which the white male invests the black male with definitive masculine powers as the precondition for violently denying and withdrawing such powers from him. In this regard, the white male creates the image he must castrate, and it is precisely through the mythology of the black male as rapist that he effectively does this. In the process, the creation of a narrative of black male sexual excess simultaneously exposes and redirects the fear of castration from the white male to the black male body. And it is in the lynch scene that this transfer moves from the realm of the psychosexual to the material. Harris's descriptive account of the sexual undercurrent of lynching and castration is telling in this regard: "For the white males . . . there is a symbolic transfer of sexual power at the point of the executions. The black man is stripped of his prowess, but the very act of stripping brings symbolic power to the white man. His actions suggest that, subconsciously, he craves the very thing he is forced to destroy. Yet he destroys it as an indication of the political (sexual) power he has."[47] In this destruction of the phallic black beast, the white male reclaims the hypermasculinity that his own mythology of black sexual excess has denied him, finding in sexual violence the sexual pleasure necessary to uphold both his tenuous masculine and white racial identities.

[46]Ibid.
[47]Harris, *Exorcising Blackness*, p. 23.

In negating the black male's most visible claim to masculine power, Harris describes lynching as a "communal rape," a description that inscribes within the lynching and castration scene the relations of power and disempowerment at work in the disciplinary practice most associated with sexual difference: male sexual violence toward women.[48] Through the rape metaphor, the emasculation of the black male undertaken in lynching and castration emerges as the imposition of the binary figuration of gender, with the white male retaining hegemony over the entire field of masculine entitlements, while the black male is confined to the corporeal excess of a racial feminization. But as I have suggested throughout my discussion, and as my reading of *Native Son* in particular demonstrates, it is important to maintain the distinction between the imposition of feminization onto male bodies and the historical framework of the feminine as part and parcel of being born female. Such a distinction enables us to understand the force of the discourse of sexual difference as it constructs and contains hierarchical relations among men without negating the specific materiality of gender oppression that accompanies women's variously raced positions in United States culture. In other words, the imposition of feminization onto male and female bodies is not—politically, theoretically, or historically—the same.

But while castration may function as a means for enacting a gendered difference at the site of the black male body, it is also the case that such a practice of dismemberment enables a perverse level of physical intimacy between the white male aggressor and his captive ex-slave, pointing to an underlying obsession with sexual (as opposed to gender) sameness. Harris's report that "in some historical accounts, the lynchers were reputed to have divided pieces of the black man's genitals among themselves" allows us to envision the castration scene as more than the perverse sexual encounter offered by the rape metaphor.[49] In the image of white men embracing—with hate, fear, and a chilling form of empowered delight—the very penis they were so overdeterminedly driven to destroy, one encounters a sadistic enactment of the homoerotic, indeed its most extreme disavowal. As Eve Kosofsky Sedgwick has discussed in *Between Men,* the male bonding relations that characterize patriarchal structures are dependent in nineteenth- and twentieth-century Anglo-American cultures on the panic image of the homosexual, whose very visibility of same-sex desire provides the disciplinary terms for normalizing heterosexuality in its compulsory formation. From this perspective, we might understand the lynching scenario and its obsession with the sexual dismemberment of black men to mark the

[48] Ibid.
[49] Ibid.

limit of the homosexual/heterosexual binary: that point at which the oppositional relation reveals its inherent and mutual dependence, and the heterosexuality of the black male "rapist" is transformed into a violently homoerotic exchange. "The homosociality of this world," Sedgwick writes in a discussion of the late Renaissance, which holds true for the history of Anglo and African men in the United States, "is not that of brotherhood, but of extreme, compulsory, and intensely volatile mastery and subordination."[50]

In such a volatile and sexually charged realm, the mythology of the black male as rapist functions to script the deeply disturbing transformations in United States racial relations in the late nineteenth century within the double registers of sexuality and gender, thereby granting to the white mob that captures and controls the black body the psychological power of arbitrating life and death. In choosing death—and accompanying it with the most extreme practices of corporeal abuse—whiteness enhances its significatory lack, filling the absence of meaning that defines it with the fully corporeal presence of a hated, feared, and now conquered blackness. The extremity of punishment in the lynching and castration scenario thus provides the necessary illusion of returning to the lost moment of complete mastery—a moment never actually "full," though yearned for, indeed frantically sought after, through the disciplinarity of random mob violence.

## ANOTHER WILLIE

The enduring power of the black male rapist mythos is perhaps best witnessed in the contemporary era in the specter of Willie Horton, the convicted black male rapist used in George Bush's 1988 presidential campaign to signify the potential danger of Democratic party control. Through the figure of Willie Horton, Bush challenged the toughness of his opponent, Michael Dukakis, whose penal reform program in Massachusetts reportedly was responsible for putting a rapist back on the streets. Bush's "get-tough" discourse, deployed here in the context of a test of masculine strength between white men, functioned to align racism with the broader and perhaps more nebulous fear of national decline—that fear so well orchestrated by David Duke and other political spokesmen for white supremacy.[51] That Bush had to quickly disaffiliate himself, in the 1992 presidential campaign, from race-baiting in light of both Duke's tactics and his popular support (which are not un-

---

[50]Eve Kosofsky Sedgwick, *Between Men: English Literature and Male Homosocial Desire* (New York, 1985), p. 76.
[51]See Nina Burleigh, "David Duke," *Z Magazine,* December 1991, pp. 47–51.

connected) is one of the more enriching ironies of contemporary politics. But it also points to the historically aphasic conundrum in which we live: where the narrative scenario of black disempowerment following Reconstruction can be eternally renewed as the fear-invoking context for organizing various levels of white supremacist activity. In this sense, the image offered by Ralph Ellison in "The Birthmark"—where the body of that seemingly fictional Willie lies dismembered between white male legs—occupies a symbolic range quite arresting in its historical diversity. For Bush, in fact, the representation of the black male as sexual threat functioned as the phantasm of his own phallic potential, providing the framework for escaping the limitations of corporeality, and thereby making possible his ascension into the highest position the disembodied abstraction of citizenry in the United States can offer.

Such a figuration of interracial male contestations has important implications for our understanding of the relationship between race and gender, necessitating as it does a rearticulation of the assumption, as Mervat Hatem writes, "that there is an automatic and natural patriarchal alliance among men (of different classes and cultures) against women."[52] The history of patriarchal organizations within the African American community—as well as the definitional relation that reads race through the binary of gender—points to the specificities of social and economic transformation and therefore cannot be assumed under a transhistorical model of masculine domination. In this regard, the equation of women with sexual difference that often accompanies feminist theory's interrogations into the meaning of gender within the social must necessarily be suspended in order to read the multiplicity of ways in which the discourse of sexual difference has been, and continues to be, deployed.[53] As the anatomy of lynching demonstrates, it is precisely through the discourse of a sexual and sexualized difference that racial hierarchies among men have been historically mediated in U.S. culture— the threat posed by black men to white masculine hegemony defined and recuperated by positioning that body as the site where gender and race converge. In such processes of cultural production, all writing of the black male body traverses the discursive terrain of race, sex, and gender.

[52]Mervat Hatem, "The Politics of Sexuality and Gender in Segregated Patriarchal Systems: The Case of Eighteenth- and Nineteenth-Century Egypt," *Feminist Studies* 12 (1986): 252.

[53]For a more extended discussion of the way in which feminist film theory in particular has confined the meaning of sexual difference to the body of woman, see Robyn Wiegman, "Feminism, the *Boyz*, and Other Matters Regarding the Male," in *Screening the Male: Exploring Masculinities in Hollywood Cinema*, ed. Steven Cohan and Ina Rae Hark (New York, 1992).

# Danger on the Home Front:
# Motherhood, Sexuality, and Disabled Veterans
# in American Postwar Films

SONYA MICHEL

*Department of History*
*University of Illinois at Urbana-Champaign*

ONE OF THE IRONIES of the wars of the twentieth century is that as weaponry became more deadly and efficient, medical science and the ability of the military to manage and treat casualties also improved. As a result, a lower proportion of casualties proved fatal, while the numbers of permanently disabled veterans increased.[1] The sight of veterans with missing limbs, in wheelchairs, walking with the aid of canes, crutches, and prosthetics, became relatively commonplace in all of the belligerent nations. At least one, France, visibly singled out wounded veterans for special treatment, reserving certain seats on public transportation for *les mutilés de guerre* (and even granting them priority over pregnant women).

Injuries—scars—disabilities serve as permanent reminders of war. In Elaine Scarry's words, they "memorialize [the fact] that the war occurred and that the cessation of its occurrence was agreed to." Yet, she contends, injuries memorialize without specifying winner or loser, and, as

I would like to thank the members of the Dartmouth Institute on Gender and War for their provocative comments on an early draft of this paper. Wini Breines, Ramona Curry, Tom Doherty, Stephanie Engel, Lynne Layton, Kathleen McHugh, Sarah Minden, and Andrea Walsh offered many helpful comments and suggestions along the way. Working on the final version in the spring of 1991, I had the benefit of weekly discussions of wars past and present with the undergraduates in my seminar on gender and war at the University of Illinois. I am also grateful to Miriam Cooke and Angela Woollacott, editors of *Collateral Damage: Gender and War* (the collected volume for which the present essay was written), forthcoming from Princeton University Press.

[1]On World War I, see John Keegan, *The Face of Battle* (New York, 1976), pp. 268–74. On American casualties during World War II, see Joseph C. Goulden, *The Best Years, 1945–50* (New York, 1976), ch. 2. More than 400,000 American men died during this war, while more than 500,000 returned with serious levels of disability.

This essay originally appeared in the *Journal of the History of Sexuality* 1992, vol. 3, no. 1.

the war and especially its final outcome recede in time, wounds lose their power as political symbols, becoming almost banal.[2] I want to suggest that political meanings do not, in fact, disappear but shift from a specifically nationalist register to one of gender.[3] Injuries, scars, and disabilities, once easily readable emblems of patriotic sacrifice, become signs of masculinity that indirectly evoke service to country by referring to a mode of sacrifice ostensibly available (until the War in the Persian Gulf) only to men.

As signs of either patriotism or masculinity, war injuries are unstable, particularly when soldiers have suffered permanent disability. On the level of the individual, handicaps can be read as signs of weakness or failure, implying feminization and emasculation.[4] On the national level, such handicaps threaten to expose the entire political system, for they point to its vulnerability, its inability to protect all of its citizens. Even on the winning side, disabilities can signify the nation's betrayal of its most loyal adherents. Insofar as political skepticism and opposition are linked with feminization, postwar "normalization" requires a restoration of the veteran's masculinity so that his signification of national triumph does not simultaneously constitute an affront to hegemonic political values.[5]

[2]Elaine Scarry, *The Body in Pain: The Making and Unmaking of the World* (New York, 1985), p. 114.

[3]George L. Mosse discusses the mutual reinforcement between symbols of masculinity and of nationalism in *Nationalism and Sexuality: Middle-Class Morality and Sexual Norms in Modern Europe* (New York, 1985). He stresses that national ideologies incorporate only images of "respectable," correct sexuality—namely, heterosexuality—to represent the nation's goals and spirit.

[4]According to Richard Holmes, emasculating wounds have been among those most feared by soldiers; see his *Acts of War: The Behavior of Men in Battle* (New York, 1985), p. 182. These fears came to be expressed culturally; as Sandra M. Gilbert and Susan Gubar point out, literary representations of the devastating psychological and emotional effects of World War I frequently took gendered forms. A common figure in these texts is "that twentieth-century Everyman . . . [who] is not just publicly powerless, [but also] privately impotent. . . . Such effects of the Great War were gender-specific problems that only men could have," since women, "still struggling to attain public power, . . . could hardly worry about the loss of an authority they had not yet fully achieved" (Sandra M. Gilbert and Susan Gubar, *No Man's Land: The Place of the Woman Writer in the Twentieth Century,* vol. 2, *Sexchanges* [New Haven, CT, 1989], p. 260). As I shall discuss below, the gender anxieties created by World War II were greater for both men and women, for by then women *had* achieved a certain amount of power, which simply compounded male anxieties.

[5]On the postwar reconstruction of gender systems in general, see Margaret R. Higonnet and Patrice L.-R. Higonnet, "The Double Helix," in *Behind the Lines: Gender and the Two World Wars,* ed. Margaret R. Higonnet, Jane Jenson, Sonya Michel, and Margaret Weitz (New Haven, CT, 1987), pp. 31–47; for the United States after Vietnam, see Susan Jeffords, *The Remasculinization of America: Gender and the Vietnam War* (Bloomington, IN, 1989).

The veterans' physical and psychological rehabilitation is carried on in home and hospital, but the work of cultural translation and restoration occurs in many sites. In modern times, popular novels and films have figured importantly in the process. The drama of disabilities—their troubling persistence and resistance to normalization—makes the disabled veteran a common character in the texts of war,[6] so much so that postwar novels and films of recuperation have become distinctive subgenres. Many such novels emerged from post–World War I Britain, France, Germany, and the United States.[7] During the same period the Europeans and, to a lesser extent, the Americans also produced a number of films, several based on novels;[8] in the United States, two of the best-known were *The Four Horsemen of the Apocalypse* (1921), with Rudolf Valentino, and King Vidor's *The Big Parade* (1927).[9] After World War II, American films of recuperation appeared even more regularly.[10]

America's post-1945 films emerged in—and reflected—an intellectual and cultural climate that made women's role in the recovery of disabled veterans especially problematic. "Experts" generally instructed American women to defer to the men returning from war. Using a discourse suffused with popularized Freudian notions, journalists, coun-

[6]According to Sandra M. Gilbert and Susan Gubar, "maimed, unmanned, victimized characters are obsessively created by early twentieth-century literary men" (*No Man's Land: The Place of the Woman Writer in the Twentieth Century,* vol. 1, *The War of the Words* [New Haven, CT, 1988], p. 36).

[7]I am not including texts whose protagonists suffer *only* from psychological disabilities, though their themes—and my interpretation—closely parallel those of texts of physical disability. In the latter category are novels such as Arthur Stuart-Menteth Hutchinson, *If Winter Comes* (Boston, 1921); Warwick Deeping, *Sorrell and Son* (London, 1925); Robert Keable, *Simon Called Peter* (New York, 1921); Jean Giraudoux, *Siegfried et le limousin* (Paris, 1922); Leonhard Frank, *Karl und Anna* (1932); Rebecca West, *The Return of the Soldier* (Garden City, NY, 1925); Jacob Wassermann, *Faber; or, The Lost Years* (New York, 1925); Pierre Drieu La Rochelle, *Gilles* (Paris, 1939); and of course Ernest Hemingway's classic, *The Sun Also Rises* (New York, 1926).

[8]Those based on novels include *As You Desire Me* (based on *Karl und Anna*, 1932); *If Winter Comes* (1923; remake, 1947); and *Sorrell and Son* (1927; remake, 1934).

[9]These two films set up themes that will persist in later postwar films. In *The Four Horsemen,* Valentino plays a French soldier who returns blind from the war; his wife, who has been consorting with a German in his absence, is "punished" by being compelled to care for her disabled husband. In *The Big Parade,* the hero (played by John Gilbert) loses a leg while fighting overseas. After briefly returning to his family in America, he goes back to France to find his sweetheart, who readily embraces him, seemingly without concern about—or at least accepting of—his disability.

[10]Kaja Silverman includes some of these films in the larger category of postwar films of historical trauma, in which "the male subject is constituted . . . [through] castration"; see her "Historical Trauma and Male Subjectivity," in *Psychoanalysis and Cinema,* ed. E. Ann Kaplan (New York, 1990), p. 114.

selors, and psychologists advised women to be tolerant and understanding in order to make their men feel secure.[11] Women were not only to surrender their jobs, but also to subordinate their own dreams, ambitions, and desires to those of the veterans.

These instructions unquestioningly assumed that all men would have difficulty in adjusting to civilian life, whether or not they had seen action or were visibly wounded or psychologically distressed. At the same time the advice betrayed a nagging fear that women would not—or perhaps could not—readily yield their newfound freedom and sense of identity.[12] The war had disrupted gender roles, especially for women, which would have to be reconstructed if postwar social order were to be established.

Nowhere was this more evident than in the realm of sexuality. Though the soldiers' sexual longing was a persistent theme in wartime popular culture, most blatantly in the ubiquitous pinups,[13] women were instructed to temper expressions of their own sexual needs and behave submissively, at least during the early stages of postwar reunions. One military psychiatrist, Herbert I. Kupper, advised women to "submerge [their own] feelings and drives" and "attempt to conform to [their men's wishes]."[14] As historian Susan Hartmann notes, this advice "reflected a recognition of female sexuality as well as a perception of the threat it held for men."[15]

Kupper also suggested that some returning veterans might require mothering, but this, too, was problematic.[16] American mothers were already under attack for overpowering their children. The "pathology of maternal overprotection" was first identified in 1939 by another psychi-

---

[11]For a comprehensive discussion of these instructions, see Susan M. Hartmann, "Prescriptions for Penelope: Literature on Women's Obligations to Returning World War II Veterans," *Women's Studies* 5 (1978): 223–39.

[12]In a fascinating study of Australian women, Marilyn Lake argues that wartime conditions allowed women to express for the first time the latent sexuality and subjectivity that had begun developing before the war, shaped, in large part, by the emphasis on "sex appeal" in advertising and film in the 1930s. See "Female Desires: The Meaning of World War II," *Australian Historical Studies* 24 (October 1990): 267–84. A similar phenomenon could no doubt easily be documented in the United States.

[13]See Susan Gubar, "'This Is My Rifle, This Is My Gun': World War II and the Blitz on Women," in Higonnet et al., eds., pp. 227–59.

[14]Herbert I. Kupper, *Back to Life: The Emotional Adjustment of Our Veterans* (New York, 1945), p. 183.

[15]Hartmann, "Prescriptions," p. 228.

[16]The veteran "needs affection and mothering: not in a demonstrative and apparent way which threatens to overwhelm him but in an assured, very real manner of an intelligent wife. . . . He may appear to be too much of a 'man' on the surface, but within him he has the needs of a love-starved adolescent" (Kupper, p. 184).

atrist, David Levy;[17] in its popular form, the disease became known as "Momism." As social commentator Philip Wylie described it in *A Generation of Vipers* (1942), Momism was an exaggeration of the maternal role that allowed women to dominate their children, especially their sons, rendering them dependent and effeminate.[18] Wylie's indictment of mothers gained renewed scientific legitimacy in 1946 when psychiatrist Edward Strecker published the results of a study of the army's psychiatric rejects. He claimed that in a majority of cases, overprotective mothers were responsible for their sons' immaturity.[19]

Altogether, the experts' "prescriptions for Penelope" (to use Hartmann's phrase) presented an ambiguous and contradictory message. In terms of sexuality, women were to be responsive, but not assertive. In terms of mothering, they were to be nurturing and accepting, but not domineering. And somehow they were to embody the qualities of both sexual partner and mother,[20] even though the combination was obviously fraught with social and psychological taboos. The wealth of articles, pamphlets, and books thus presented conflicting messages for women seeking to aid veterans' readjustment.

[17]Levy's work, in turn, had its roots in the theories of Helene Deutsch, Karen Horney, and Melanie Klein. For an excellent discussion of these theories and their impact on popular culture, especially film, see E. Ann Kaplan, "Motherhood and Representation: From Postwar Freudian Figurations to Postmodernism," in Kaplan, ed., pp. 128–42.

[18]Wylie attributed specifically to mothers a charge that had been made earlier in more general terms by journalist Roy Helton. In "The Inner Threat: Our Own Softness," Helton had contended, "For twenty-five years the feminine influence on Western life has mounted into a dominance in every area but that of politics, and even there its power is absolute as to the direction of our purposes" (*Harpers Magazine* 181 [September 1940]: 338).

[19]Edward A. Strecker, *Their Mothers' Sons: The Psychiatrist Examines an American Problem* (Philadelphia, 1946). Kupper also alludes to this pattern in *Back to Life*. Strecker's charge gained added scientific legitimacy throughout the 1940s and early 1950s in the writings of Erik Erikson, Margaret Mead, and Geoffrey Gorer. On Levy, Wylie, and Erikson, see Barbara Ehrenreich and Deirdre English, *For Her Own Good: 150 Years of the Experts' Advice to Women* (Garden City, NY, 1978), pp. 208–14; on Strecker, see Susan M. Hartmann, *The Home Front and Beyond* (Boston, 1982), pp. 176–77; on Gorer and Mead, see Christopher Lasch, *Haven in a Heartless World: The Family Besieged* (New York, 1977), pp. 72–73; and on Levy, see Lasch, p. 109. Lasch notes that Ernest Groves and Gladys Groves had referred to "the dangerous mother" even earlier, in their 1928 volume, *Parents and Children* (Lasch, p. 209, n. 43).

[20]Robert Westbrook has shown that this combination also appeared in pinups. Betty Grable, the GI's favorite, was explicitly sexual and seductive, but, well known as the wife of trumpeter Harry James, she also evoked marital loyalty and even motherhood. See Westbrook's "'I Want a Girl, Just Like the Girl That Married Harry James': American Women and the Problem of Political Obligation in World War II," *American Quarterly* 42 (1990): 587–614.

Postwar movies, on the other hand, seemed to clarify the situation. Fiction films, particularly those that loosely fit the genre of the "woman's film,"[21] afforded screenwriters and directors space in which to dramatize the tensions of reunions and readjustment. They created characters whose motivation made psychological sense, at least according to the theories then current.[22] Like the prescriptive literature, the films showed that veterans needed both sexual and maternal attention. While depicting the dangers of excesses of either, they simultaneously tried to mitigate the contradiction between the two female roles.[23] Resolution frequently took the form of ministrations by wives and sweethearts who knew how to balance loyalty, deference, and support with a discreet sensuality.

In the case of disabled veterans, contradictions were heightened and the possibility for satisfactory resolution might have seemed remote. Yet filmmakers willingly took on the task of bringing their lives to the screen, for they recognized their rich dramatic possibilities. This was exactly the sort of impossible situation on which the melodramatic "Hollywood film" thrived.[24] Moreover, such films would have universal appeal, for disabled veterans rendered visible (and thus all the more cinematic) the battle scars other soldiers carried hidden.

One of the most highly acclaimed and now classic examples of postwar films of veteran readjustment and disability is William Wyler's 1946 production, *The Best Years of Our Lives*. In a carefully balanced, closely woven narrative, three men return from war, each with certain problems that prevent him from readjusting smoothly. But the film allows these problems to be played out and apparently resolved. The men and their families—and, by extension, America at large—could now put the

---

[21]Interpretations of this genre vary; see, for example, Andrea S. Walsh, *Women's Film and Female Experience, 1940–1950* (New York, 1984), especially ch. 1; and Mary Ann Doane, "The 'Woman's Film': Possession and Address," in *Re-Vision: Essays in Feminist Film Criticism*, ed. Mary Ann Doane, Patricia Mellencamp, and Linda Williams (Los Angeles, 1984), pp. 67–82.

[22]In comparing the films *Now, Voyager* (1942) and *Marnie* (1964), Kaplan makes an important distinction between texts that use "psychoanalysis as a narrative discourse, as a means for producing character-change and explaining [in this case] mother-daughter interactions," and those that "*embody* the level of the psychoanalytic" (p. 129). The postwar films I am discussing would fall into the first category.

[23]Mary Ann Doane notes that wartime and postwar films not only frequently present both excessive mothering and promiscuous sexuality as "dangerous aspects of femininity," but also link them to unpatriotic politics, specifically isolationism; see her *The Desire to Desire* (Bloomington, IN, 1987), p. 81.

[24]See Robert Ray, *A Certain Tendency of Hollywood Cinema* (Princeton, NJ, 1985).

harrowing war years behind them and enjoy the fruits of postwar prosperity.[25]

Throughout the film, recurring triptychs of the three men throw into sharp relief the special difficulties faced by the disabled veteran. Al (Fredric March), a banker turned sergeant, cannot reconcile his cushy postwar life with the memory of his horrific wartime experiences; moreover, he and his wife, Millie (Myrna Loy), must overcome their mutual suspicions before they can resume a trusting relationship.[26] Fred (Dana Andrews), a glamorous flyer who is unable to find a decent job as a civilian, discovers that his hastily contracted wartime marriage will not survive in the peacetime doldrums. These problems are troublesome, but they can be worked out over time.

Homer's difficulties, however, are more intractable. A sailor who was maimed in a ship fire, he has lost both his hands. Homer is played by Harold Russell, a veteran who actually suffered such a loss and wears two prosthetic hooks. The realization that Russell's amputations are authentic, not a clever special effect, produces a double frisson in the spectator that garners even more sympathy for the character he plays.[27] Homer's sacrifice falls just short of the ultimate one. He has not given his life, but he has given his future—as a worker, as a lover, as a "normal" man. His disability is permanent and undeniable; he has been practically, if not literally, emasculated. How can the film possibly recuperate this?

Early on, it becomes apparent that Homer's girl, Wilma, will be the key. Homer can be redeemed only if Wilma—who is literally the girl next door—accepts him as he is and makes good on her prewar promise to marry him. She must match his sacrifice with one of her own. Neither Homer nor the film makes this easy for her. Homer repeatedly tests her loyalty in an effort to provoke her into rescinding her vow. The camera constantly monitors her reactions to his body. In the homecoming scene, for example, Homer's mother is allowed to shudder when she sees his hooks, but Wilma must keep her eyes on his face, fling her arms around his neck, and kiss him as though nothing has happened. Wilma must express the unquestioning acceptance of the ideal mother for her

[25]For a rather different, but compelling, reading of this film, see Silverman, pp. 110–27. Using a Lacanian framework, Silverman argues that the film does not succeed in resolving the postwar traumas it exposes. Below I will detail the ways in which my interpretation differs from Silverman's.

[26]Sexual mistrust and jealousy on the part of both men and women were common themes in wartime and postwar "women's films"; see Walsh, pp. 98–103 and ch. 5.

[27]The use of nonprofessional actors was typical in American postwar films whose directors had been influenced by Italian neorealism. Here Wyler takes the gesture one step further by using a veteran who had actually suffered the loss he depicts.

child and at the same time convey continuing erotic interest in Homer. She must somehow transcend the madonna/whore split in order simultaneously to restore him to wholeness and affirm his masculinity—to "resexualize" him.[28]

Because of the parallel structure of the film—the three couples, each struggling to renegotiate their relationships—the bond between Homer and Wilma will inevitably be compared with those between the other couples. For them, too, the war has created gender imbalances, which must be corrected before order can be restored. Al's return to his all too civilized life clearly gives him the jitters. Still, he lets his glamorous wife know that although she has served as both father and mother in his absence, she must now step aside and allow him to resume his rightful place as head of the family. Like Wilma, Millie tolerantly "mothers" Al as he acts out his anxieties in repeated drinking bouts. But she also allows their old erotic relationship to be rekindled. (The bedroom scenes between the two, a suggestive mix of humor and low-key erotic play, fell well within the bounds of the Hollywood Production Code then in force and also adhered to prevailing sexual mores and marital expertise, which condoned sexual satisfaction within marriage, even encouraging it as an antidote to maternal overinvolvement.)[29] Al and Millie's mutual suspicions of infidelity cancel each other out when both hint that they may have been unfaithful during the war but still love one another.

The dashing Fred finds no such staying power in his marriage. A good-looking working-class fellow, he left a dead-end job as a soda jerk to join the air force, serving as a bombadier. While in training, he met and hastily married Marie, a flashy blonde played by Virginia Mayo. But, like many wartime unions, this one turns out to be a mismatch. Fred discovers that Marie is really a floozie who was only attracted to his uniform and whose loyalty quickly evaporates when he takes off his medals

---

[28]For a fascinating, psychologically astute treatment of another split, see Rebecca West's *The Return of the Soldier* (n. 7 above). In this novel, a shell-shocked veteran suffering from amnesia has forgotten his marriage to a cool, selfish, upper-class woman and insists on being reunited with the sweetheart of his youth, a work-roughened but kind and generous lower-class housewife. The split here is not precisely along the madonna/whore line, but along the lines of class and respectability, for the sweetheart embodies both sensual and maternal qualities in an exquisite balance that restores the veteran's memory but, ironically, compels him to renounce her and accept his socially correct marriage. On the restoration of masculinity in post-Vietnam culture, see Jeffords (n. 5 above).

[29]On the Production Code, see Walsh, pp. 32–34, 206–17. On marital advice and sexual mores, see John D'Emilio and Estelle B. Freedman, *Intimate Matters: A History of Sexuality in America* (New York, 1988), pp. 266–68; Ehrenreich and English (n. 19 above); and Elaine Tyler May, *Homeward Bound: American Families in the Cold War Era* (New York, 1988), ch. 4.

and returns to his humble job in the drugstore.[30] Fred's masculinity is jeopardized not only by his humiliating work but also by Marie's flamboyant philandering.

Their marriage reaches the breaking point on a night when Marie wants to go out on the town and Fred must tell her they are broke. Marie offers to pay for their spree out of her own savings, but Fred tells her to keep her money and insists that she stay home and eat the meal he prepares in their tiny kitchenette. She threatens to go out by herself. Fred's masculinity is on the line in this scene, but he manages to reassert it, even amidst the pots and pans, by strong-arming Marie and telling her, "You're going to stay right here and eat what I cook and like it." His triumph is short-lived, however, for Marie soon leaves for good. The antithesis of the ideal postwar woman, she refuses to rein in her own sexuality and has no compunction about using it to get what she wants. Within the value structure of the film (and according to most contemporary prescriptive literature), her poor showing as a wife results directly from the imbalance between her maternal and sexual qualities.

Fred, meanwhile, has fallen in love with Peggy (Teresa Wright), Al and Millie's daughter. Unlike Marie, Peggy does not attempt to unman Fred, but rather treats him with a combination of respect for his wartime bravery and sensitivity to his plight—both as a drugstore clerk and as the husband of the heedless Marie. Though Peggy clearly returns his love, Fred is reluctant to act on his feelings for her, at first because he feels obliged to try to work things out with Marie, and, when that proves futile, because he believes that he must make something of himself before approaching her. At the end of the film, Fred has finally found a job that looks promising—salvaging old air force bombers—and he allows himself to express his passion for Peggy, who responds with equal intensity.

Though both Al and Millie and Fred and Peggy must make adjustments, not all of them minor, both couples appear in harmonious cameo by the end of the film, constituting an intergenerational model of ideal marriage. Peggy and Fred radiate a progenitive sexuality, while Al and Millie offer contented testimonial to loyalty and endurance. Against this backdrop, Wilma and Homer are married.

On the surface, the wedding scene is all charm and tradition, as relatives and friends gather in the home of Wilma's parents while Homer's cousin Butch plays the wedding march on the family spinet. When the minister tells them to "join hands," Wilma takes Homer's hook and Homer, clearly well practiced, manages to slip the ring on her finger.

---

[30]In the typical mode of the Hollywood film, Fred's problem, dictated chiefly by his class position, is expressed—and resolved—at the level of the individual.

But the image of hook and hand jars against the conventional prettiness of the scene. How can this marriage succeed? By what means will it be consummated?

The delicate psychological balance in their relationship has been established in a crucial scene between Wilma and Homer midway in the film. Until this point, Homer has been avoiding Wilma in the hope that she will finally give up on him. But Wilma persists. In this scene, she confronts him late at night in his family's kitchen. She asks him what his intentions are, parrying his charge that she does not want to spend her life with a disabled man. Finally, he challenges her to come upstairs with him and see for herself "what it's like." She watches while he removes his hooks and shoulder harness and struggles into his pajama jacket. Then she buttons it up and helps him into bed, folding the prosthetic apparatus and placing it neatly on a chair. The scene is paced with unflinching deliberation.

Wilma's behavior here is part maternal, part sexual. She tucks Homer in like a child and kisses him good night like a lover. Though muted, the sexuality here is clear, but the maternal content is also quite explicit; Homer even admits that without his hooks he is "as dependent as a baby that doesn't know how to get anything except cry for it." Wilma has become his hands; his body has, in effect, merged with hers—not sexually, but functionally. They have achieved what amounts to a mother-child reunion.

Though Homer finally allows himself to surrender to Wilma and her ministrations, it is not surprising that he has resisted for so long, for union with Wilma carries the threat of assimilation by the feminine, a loss of adult masculinity. Notably, until now it has been Homer's father, not his mother, who has helped him each night, symbolically enabling him to stave off the threat of maternal domination.[31] In assuming the position of the maternal, Wilma displaces the father, reversing the oedipal direction—indeed, drawing Homer back to a preoedipal state.

The exaggerated normalcy of the wedding suggests, however, that Homer and Wilma's marriage will not remain at the level of regressive chastity, but that the sexual element of their relationship will be allowed to flower. True, the entire event has been (literally) orchestrated by Uncle Butch—Hoagy Carmichael, who appears (as he so often does in 1940s films) as an apparently celibate emotional gadfly. If Homer takes Butch as a model, the marriage will, indeed, be sexless. Butch, however,

---

[31]Kupper (n. 14 above) contends that mothers' attention to their veteran sons all too frequently slips into—or is perceived as—efforts to control them. Accordingly, he strongly advises mothers to hold back in their ministrations and expressions of affection (pp. 188–89).

has repeatedly pushed Homer (who would prefer to hang out with his service buddies) into the emotional fray, counseling him to open himself up to Wilma and the rest of his family. The image of the other two couples—Al and Millie, with their wise, beaming smiles, and Peggy and Fred, eyeing each other hungrily across the proceedings—has the effect of deepening the disjuncture between the whole bodies and the maimed one. At the same time, their presence suffuses the entire scene with sensuality, endorsing the sexual as well as the legal union between Wilma and Homer.

There is no organic, physical reason why Homer cannot function sexually. It is, finally, up to Wilma to accept him—to accept his hooks or his stumps upon her body—so that Homer can be resexualized and restored to his proper masculine place in society. Whether or not she finds this repulsive, neither Homer nor the film permits her to say. For her sexuality, her desire, is never fully articulated, but rather expressed through her demure, quasimaternal affection toward Homer. The denial of Wilma's desire allows Homer's to monopolize the sexual field. Insofar as the film imagines their sexual union at all, it is almost exclusively genital, for there is little indication of the possibility of oral sex—Homer's obvious alternative for giving Wilma pleasure, given the loss of his hands.[32]

Such a suggestion, even in the mid-1940s, would not have been completely farfetched. The most popular and explicit marriage manual of the day, Theodore Van de Velde's *Ideal Marriage* (1930), recommended the "genital kiss" as one of several techniques for conjugal sexual satisfaction. Moreover, according to Alfred Kinsey, oral sex was commonly practiced among the younger cohorts of married adults who were sexually active during this period.[33] True, the Production Code would have prohibited all but the most veiled reference to such a practice on screen. But *The Best Years* (like many "woman's films" of the period) takes other liberties with the code: the suggestive bedroom antics of Al and Millie; Fred and Peggy's passionate kisses, one of them while Fred is still married to Marie; and even the key scene between Homer and Wilma, in which two unmarried adults are shown together in a bedroom, and Homer's stumps are exposed. Why, then, does it stop short of suggesting the possibility of sexual satisfaction for Wilma?

[32]Some viewers have suggested that the film does visually indicate the possibility of oral sex when Wilma buttons up Homer's pajama jacket, moving toward his mouth, while the demure V-neckline of her crisp blouse points down to her breasts. But their kisses remain strictly above the neck, giving only the slightest hint of sexual ardor. In later films, as we shall see, references to oral sex become completely explicit; see the discussions of *Coming Home* and *Born on the Fourth of July* below.

[33]See D'Emilio and Freedman, pp. 267–69.

While the film must, as I argue above, allow Wilma to become both mother and sexual partner to Homer, it cannot allow her to play either role to excess. Like that of all women of the 1940s, Wilma's sexuality is threatening, even more so because of the fragility of Homer's masculinity. The film therefore seeks to contain her sexuality within conventional terms, rejecting any form of satisfaction that might require "special treatment" on Homer's part and thereby privilege Wilma's desire. Instead she must tailor her satisfaction to his psychological, as well as physical, limitations.

My reading of *The Best Years* differs significantly from another recent study by Kaja Silverman. In her essay "Historical Trauma and Male Subjectivity," Silverman contends that the film not only fails to reach resolution but is actually quite unusual, within the Hollywood canon, in its willingness to leave its male subjects exposed and vulnerable. It "not only . . . inverts classic cinema's scopic regime (a regime which turns upon woman's castration) but . . . openly eroticizes male lack. . . . *The Best Years of Our Lives* makes no attempt to contain the negativity which it unleashes, nor does it at any point facilitate a phallic identification on the part either of its male characters or its male viewers."[34] Silverman links the film's sexual inversion with its pessimistic view of the postwar social order, a view that dismisses the trappings of military victory (such as Fred's medal for distinguished flying) as "junk" and exposes the economic injustices many veterans had to face.

These critical elements are unquestionably present in the film, but in my view they become neutralized within its libidinal economy. Not only Wilma, but Millie and Peggy, too, must sacrifice their sexual and psychological autonomy in deference to their men. Millie yields her wartime place as head of the family to Al, though he is hardly up to the stress of the position. While her parents struggle to maintain the veneer of a conventional marriage, Peggy surrenders any hope for security she may have had in pursuing Fred. In the closing scene, he warns her, "You know what it'll be, don't you, Peggy? It'll take us years to get anywhere. We'll have no money, no place to live. We'll have to work . . . be kicked around." It is precisely this prospect that Marie has rejected, preferring to assert her independence and chance it on her own. Taking Marie's place, Peggy implicitly agrees to subordinate her own needs to Fred's and accept whatever he can offer.

Though acting with determination to win Fred—as does Wilma in pursuing Homer—Peggy ends up deferring to her man in order to prop up his sense of authority within the relationship. And she, along with Wilma and Millie, will learn to temper whatever sexual and emotional

[34]Silverman, p. 127.

autonomy they have managed to achieve during the war. The film makes it clear that no matter how vulnerable, how threatened their masculinity, Fred, Al, and Homer have nothing to fear from *their* women.[35]

The gender of recuperation is made explicit in the title of a 1950 film about a paraplegic veteran, *The Men*. Teresa Wright once again comes on the scene, this time as Helen, the fiancée of Lt. Bud Wilcheck (Marlon Brando), who is undergoing rehabilitation in a military hospital. As the opening flashback establishes, Bud had been a strong and active individual, boldly leading his men when he was struck down in action. When the film opens he is bitter and dejected, deeply pessimistic about his future. Helen assigns herself the task of helping him come to terms with his permanent injury so that he can rejoin society. Like Homer, Bud tries the patience of the woman he loves by alternately withdrawing and lashing out; he is sometimes fiercely independent, sometimes hypersensitive and paranoid. And, like Homer, Bud wants to cling to the familiarity of an all-male social group, in this case his comrades in the veterans' hospital, rather than face the difficult challenges of marriage and civilian life.

For Bud and other paraplegics, more so than for Homer, marriage implies surrender to the feminine, reunion with the maternal without the possibility of rescue through sexuality, for their disability—paralysis from the waist down—leaves little hope for genital sexual functionality. When another patient marries a nurse, one of Bud's wardmates comments, "It should work out—after all, she's a nurse. She knows what she's getting into." But the nurse/wife role cannot be separated from the maternal, with its connotations of incest. One of the veterans baldly draws the connections as he jibes at an older, plain-faced nurse: "If you wasn't so sexy, you'd remind me of my mother."[36]

The prospect of spending the rest of his life with a nurse/mother is

---

[35]One might also construct an interpretation of recuperated male power in this film by following the line of argument developed by Christopher Newfield in his ingenious analysis of *The Scarlet Letter*, "The Politics of Male Suffering: Masochism and Hegemony in the American Renaissance," *Differences* 1 (Fall 1989): 55–87.

[36]Male attitudes toward nurses differed markedly from nurses' own perceptions of their work and affect. In examining World War I texts, Gilbert and Gubar note, "This education in masculine functioning that the nurse experienced as a kind of elevation was often felt by her male patient as exploitation: her evolution into active, autonomous, transcendent subject was associated with his devolution into passive, dependent, immanent medical object" (*No Man's Land* [n. 4 above], 2:286–87). For a different interpretation of some of these texts that stresses the nurses' devastation (as opposed to "elevation") by what they saw, see Jane Marcus, "Corpus/Corps/Corpse: Writing the Body at War," in *Arms and the Woman: War, Gender, and Literary Representation,* ed. Helen M. Cooper, Adrienne Auslander Munich, and Susan Merrill Squier (Chapel Hill, NC, 1989), pp. 124–67.

precisely what Bud cannot tolerate. The nature of his disability compels him to depend upon others both physically and emotionally, but his needs are overdetermined by the fact that he is an orphan. His unmet desire for parental affection heightens his susceptibility to maternal love. Fearful of admitting this desire, he repeatedly denies it by rebuffing Helen's advances. Until he can find some way to restore his own sense of masculinity and autonomy, he cannot accept her love.

As in *The Best Years,* Bud's masculinity will be restored at the expense of Helen's sexuality. Again, the film never fully acknowledges the *woman's* sacrifice. In an early scene, the hospital's medical chief, Dr. Brock, lectures a group of veterans' wives, girlfriends, and mothers on the nature of paraplegia. He explains that most of the men will be "unable to have children"—the film's euphemistic synecdoche for sex. But what he fails to mention, either directly or by innuendo, is that it is still possible for the men *and their partners* to enjoy other forms of sexual pleasure; nongenital and female-genital sex lie outside his—and the film's—sexual imagination. The implication, then, is that if the man cannot function "normally," there will be no sex at all.

After the meeting, Helen approaches Brock and asks him to help her get through to Bud, who has been refusing to see her. The doctor parries, "Why don't you just leave it alone? It takes a pretty special kind of woman in a lot of ways." "Maybe I'm special," Helen retorts with spunk. Through persistence and strength of will, she earns the right to Bud's appreciation; by contrast, his resistance to coming to terms with his disability and accepting the responsibilities of marriage appear perverse and antisocial. But what gets lost in the momentum is Helen's sexuality—the fact that she is being consigned to a lifelong union that, however emotionally fulfilling (and even this is dubious), holds out little prospect of sexual satisfaction for her *or* Bud, at least within the erotic framework of the film.

Though unexpressed, sexual anxiety is the underlying cause of a quarrel on their wedding night, prompting Bud to retreat to the hospital. Taking cover once again behind his emotional wall, he rejects Helen's apology (a gesture that exposes her masochistic position within the relationship, since it was *he* who precipitated the quarrel). What finally breaks down Bud's resistance is not a recognition of Helen's sincerity (or her seemingly infinite supply of self-abnegation), but a conversation he has with Dr. Brock.

Brock is the focus of patriarchal power within the film. He gives orders to everyone, staff and patients alike, pronounces authoritatively on all medical questions, and even seems to hold the key to family happiness as he doles out prognoses to the veterans' loved ones. Throughout, his manner is inexplicably brusque and cynical; it is not until this conversation with Bud that we learn why. Years earlier, Brock's wife had become paraplegic as the result of a car accident. But medical science had not yet advanced to the point where such patients routinely could be saved, and she eventually died. Brock continues to mourn her, his sorrow the source of his unstinting devotion to his patients as well as his abrasive manner.

When Bud complains that Helen does not really love him but only married him out of pity, Brock dismisses his suspicion. "I'd give anything in the world to go home and find [my wife]," he tells Bud, "*in* a wheelchair." In effect, Brock offers Bud an acceptable model of *male* sacrifice—one that allows him to come to terms with his own disability and also to believe that Helen's motives are sincere. The film's closing dialogue suggests that this step brings him into some kind of mutuality with Helen. As he drives up to her parents' home, where she has been staying, she observes, "You've come a long way." He replies, "I had a flat tire—fixed it myself." "Do you want me to help you up the steps?" "Please." Helen seems to have the upper hand at this point (she is pushing his wheelchair), but it is clear that she will be continually challenged to uphold his masculinity at the cost of her own sexuality and ego. Once again, we are left with the image of a vibrant, healthy woman (intertextually, the same one who procreatively joined Dana Andrews in *The Best Years*) sacrificing herself for a disabled man.

These films are interested not simply in exploring the psychological subtleties and intrinsic drama of postwar readjustment, but in showing the possibility for alignment and mutual reinforcement between the gender and the political orders. To confirm the political rectitude of the Allied victory, gender relationships were to uphold, rather than undermine, preexisting gender arrangements. Throughout World War II, "the family" had served as the centerpiece of America's war goals—symbolic of all that was to be fought for and protected.[37] Accordingly, the family, with "proper" gender roles restored, became a centerpiece of postwar readjustment.[38] With their emotional as well as physical difficulties, disabled veterans potentially represented an ongoing affront to both familial and political normalcy. Through recourse to—and containment of—the maternal/sexual, these films manage the political as well as the physical and psychological recuperation of these men.

Films about disabled veterans underwent a renaissance during and after the Vietnam era. Though similar in some ways to the earlier ex-

[37]See Sonya Michel, "American Women and the Discourse of the Democratic Family in World War II," in Higonnet et al., eds. (n. 5 above), pp. 154–67.

[38]See Hartmann, "Prescriptions"; and May, especially ch. 6.

amples, the later films vary the pattern we have seen so far in ways that confirm the linkage between patriotism and the maternal/sexual. Two bear closer analysis, *Coming Home* (1978) and *Born on the Fourth of July* (1989). In both, paraplegic veterans refuse at first to accept their disabilities or to allow themselves to recuperate through the maternal. For both Luke (Jon Voigt) in *Coming Home* and Ron Kovic (Tom Cruise) in *Born on the Fourth of July,* coming to terms with their handicaps potentially means accepting the war and its politics. Renouncing the privileges of the returning hero, they instead begin to speak out against the war.

Both films open in Veterans Administration hospitals where, notably, conditions are depicted far less rosily than they were in *The Men.* Luke, face down on a gurney, is careening angrily around the ward, his bladder bag overflowing, when he meets Sally (Jane Fonda), who has come to volunteer as an aide. Reserved and conventional, Sally has just seen her husband, a marine officer, off to Vietnam. She is initially abashed by Luke's outburst but soon befriends him. Though Luke accepts her help, he fiercely attempts to be self-sufficient. He is also explicitly sexual, at first with a prostitute and then with Sally herself. Through cunnilingus, Sally even experiences orgasm with him, something she has been unable to do with her hypermacho—and hyperpatriotic—husband, Bob, played by Bruce Dern. In sharp contrast to the earlier films, *Coming Home* clearly indicates that disabled veterans can enjoy a range of sexual pleasures by looking at, touching, and satisfying their partners. In refusing to privilege (male) genital sexuality (though still unquestioningly heterosexual), the film opens onto a whole new realm of satisfactions for both the veterans and their female partners.

The sexual relationship between Sally and Luke is also an essential element of the film's political scheme, which traces the war to macho values and behavior while aligning antiwar politics with a new, *egalitarian* form of heterosexuality. Luke's willingness to speak out parallels his deepening relationship with Sally. Susan Jeffords reads Luke's behavior as "feminized," but I would contend that within the context of the film, his actions appear to be androgynous.[39] Though Luke repudiates his own behavior in Vietnam, he does so publicly; both this and his other

---

[39]According to Jeffords, "the price of [Luke's] release from the hospital was his gradual containment of . . . anger and violence, now effectively neutralized (feminized/castrated)"; she seems to regard his confession of guilt as "feminine" (pp. 146–47). The film's emphasis on Luke's sexuality and strength of character can hardly be read as his being castrated; moreover, when Bob threatens Sally and Luke with his M-1, it is Luke who disarms him, removing the symbol of his phallic power along with the weapon. If anyone is feminized in the film, it is Bob, who commits suicide by drowning, that most female of all methods.

antiwar acts of passive resistance demonstrate personal (but not explicitly heroic) courage. Luke's sexuality, demeanor, and politics all seem to carry the endorsement of feminism.

In linking antiwar politics to sexual and women's liberation, this late-1970s film indulges in a certain amount of hindsight, for it constructs associations that even movement activists were only dimly aware of during the Vietnam era itself. Though set in the late 1960s, the film reflects a mindset rooted in values that did not converge in American culture until the late 1970s. For it was not until then that the movement for sexual liberation began to incorporate *feminist* views of female sexuality. Along with its generally relaxed attitudes toward choice of partner and locale, prescriptive literature also began to expose the "myth of the vaginal orgasm" (a move dismissed a decade earlier as radical feminist screed), which established the principle that women's pleasure is centered in the clitoris, not in the vagina.[40] At the same time, many feminists' ideas were gaining mainstream political and intellectual legitimacy. *Coming Home* offers evidence that feminist values had not only begun to permeate left-wing interpretations of the Vietnam war but had even made their way to Hollywood.

By 1989, however, antiwar sentiment and feminist values had become uncoupled, as *Born on the Fourth of July* strikingly reveals. The film is rampantly misogynist. For example, in the retrospective prologue designed to expose the militaristic, competitive atmosphere of American boyhood in the 1950s, Kovic's mother is portrayed as the major source of his socialization. It is she, rather than his mild-mannered father, who eggs him on in high school athletic competitions, and who plants in him visions of patriotic service and fame. When he returns home in a wheelchair, she is depicted as being unable to accept his condition, and it is his father (like Homer's) who assumes responsibility for his physical care.[41]

The film literalizes and completes the madonna/whore split when Ron goes off to a seedy Mexican watering hole that is a favorite with disabled veterans. The men even have a special brothel to cater to their needs. "Charlie from Chicago" (Willem Dafoe), the self-appointed guide to the place, initiates Ron into local sexual customs by indicating, with a thrust of his tongue, that most of the men practice oral sex. (His exaggerated gesture reads as a vulgar caricature of the sensual, almost

---

[40]See Freedman and D'Emilio, pp. 330, 337. Sexual pleasure was condoned both inside and outside of marriage, and homosexuality was also gaining recognition and acceptance.

[41]The portrayal of Mrs. Kovic as villain seems to be largely director Oliver Stone's invention, for she is presented more sympathetically in Kovic's 1976 book of the same title, on which the film was based.

reverential love scene between Luke and Sally in *Coming Home*.) Refusing Charlie's cynicism, Ron falls for the first pretty prostitute who plies her art upon him. Predictably, he becomes disillusioned when he discovers her lavishing her charms on another customer (shades of Marie in *The Best Years of Our Lives*). Following a now familiar pattern, Ron seeks comfort with his male buddy, Charlie.

The two men set out into the desert, but they soon fall into a bizarre form of macho one-upmanship, arguing over who committed the most outrageous atrocities in Vietnam (and, by implication, who should be the most guilt-ridden). In a not so subtle homoerotic wrestling match that recalls a similar scene in the film version of D. H. Lawrence's *Women in Love,* the two wheelchair-bound men roll around in the sand for a while before eventually reconciling. They then decide to return to the States, where—somewhat inexplicably—they join the Vietnam Veterans against the War.

Ron soon becomes a leading spokesperson for the movement. Notably, his role is highly individualistic, not unlike that of the classic veteran-hero, and his reference group is prominently devoid of women, either as mothers (real or role-playing) or as lovers.[42] The film suggests that in the remasculinized culture of the 1980s, opposition to the war has found an acceptable niche, but women are once again viewed as threatening.[43] Wheeling his chair out onto a stage to face a cheering audience and the blinding lights of the national media, Ron is at once fulfilling and repudiating his mother's dream for him, and he does so surrounded by his fellow (male) veterans.

Taken together, these four films mark out a complex set of alignments between the maternal, the sexual, the patriotic, and the masculine. As a sacred national symbol, motherhood is something to be defended. But as maternal *power* (embodied in the bossy nurse or the overzealous mother) or when aligned with patriotism (mothers send men off to war—nurses repair them and send them back), motherhood is cast as a threat to masculinity.[44] In patriotic postwar films such as *The Best Years*

[42]Luke's style of sexuality apparently held no appeal for either the cinematic Ron or his actual counterpart; in his autobiography, Kovic remarks, "I gave my dead dick for John Wayne" (quoted in Holmes [n. 4 above], p. 182).

[43]Throughout her study, Jeffords, following the lead of Klaus Theweleit, argues that remasculinization requires the reestablishment of male bonds, almost always to the exclusion of women; see Theweleit, *Male Fantasies,* 2 vols. (Minneapolis, 1987, 1989).

[44]Here my argument diverges somewhat from Doane, who contends that the "strategy of imbricating the concept of the maternal with that of a nationalistic patriotism also succeeds in giving the woman a significant position in wartime which does not constitute a threat to the traditional patriarchal order" (*The Desire to Desire* [n. 23 above], p. 79).

and *The Men,* the maternal is tempered with sexuality, allowing for maculine recovery *and* resexualization. The *sexual*/maternal becomes a vehicle for political rectitude, as veterans resume full social participation and citizenship, now signified as masculinity. But, as I have tried to show, such films at the same time implicitly produce a recontainment of female sexuality and subjectivity.

The link between patriotism and the sexual/maternal is exposed and criticized in *Born on the Fourth of July,* which simultaneously manages to salvage a masculinity of sorts—homosocial, if not homoerotic—and link it to a specific kind of antiwar politics, which now falls within the political pale. But both masculinity and opposition to the war exist at the cost of marginalizing all women and specifically vilifying both mothers and prostitutes.

The only feminist film of this group, *Coming Home,* does not depend on the sexual/maternal for recuperation. Sally is caring but not caretaking, and her sensuality is fully acknowledged. Interestingly, this is the only one of the four films that pays more than token attention to women's caring activities or is willing to portray their reactions to injuries and disability honestly and uncritically. The film not only shows Sally's hospital work in some detail, but allows her to express tentativeness and even revulsion when she first approaches the patients. She is granted far more emotional latitude than her ever smiling predecessors, Wilma and Helen. By recognizing Sally's right to ambivalence, the film spares her both the self-denial and self-sacrifice that befell these earlier characters and the moral repudiation that would be Mrs. Kovic's fate.[45]

Indeed, *Coming Home* is as much about Sally's coming to personhood as it is about Luke's coming to terms with his disability and coming of age politically. The mutual respect that develops between them carries over into their sexual relationship, and this, in turn, allows Luke to oppose the war without becoming feminized. Neither his gender

---

[45]While rare in male-authored texts, the open-ended exploration of women's responses to pain, suffering, and dismemberment has been a central theme in women's wartime and postwar writing (especially those by and about nurses and ambulance drivers); female writers adopted several distinctive voices to express and contain their anguished perceptions, ranging from the heavily ironic to the unflinchingly frank. For excellent discussions of women's texts of caring, see Claire M. Tylee, *The Great War and Women's Consciousness* (Iowa City, IA, 1990), especially pp. 93–100, 190–97; and Marcus, pp. 124–67. In her study of fifty nurses who served in Vietnam, Elizabeth Norman observed that they tended to "insulate themselves, build up a shield that allowed them to work" (*Women at War: The Story of Fifty Military Nurses Who Served in Vietnam* [Philadelphia, 1990], p. 34). But neither irony nor emotional isolation was an option for the postwar cinematic wives of the 1940s and 1950s.

identity nor his politics wavers in the vicinity of women. Nor does the film require female sacrifice to achieve male recuperation.

The fact that *Coming Home* was succeeded by *Born on the Fourth of July* suggests that it is difficult to maintain such a delicate gender balance in modern American culture. Indeed, to Susan Jeffords, the cycle of "remasculinization" seems almost inexorable.[46] But the War in the Persian Gulf may have reshuffled the pack, dealing caring responsibilities to men and military duties—with all of their attendant risks—to women. As a result, this conflict has carried the usual wartime destabilization of gender roles to a new level. It will be interesting to see whether "the new world order" once again will bring back the old gender order—in new political clothing.

[46]See Jeffords (n. 5 above), especially the final chapter.

# Portraits of Three "Physicians of Conscience": Abortion before Legalization in the United States

CAROLE JOFFE

*Department of Sociology*
*University of California, Davis*

THE POLITICAL CLIMATE surrounding abortion today in the United States, especially the perceived fragility of legal abortion itself, has created renewed interest in the conditions that existed before the Supreme Court legalized abortion in 1973 with the *Roe v. Wade* decision. In particular, the prochoice movement has expended much effort to focus public attention on the untenable situation facing women with unwanted pregnancies in that period. The movement has used a strategy of promoting two symbols of that era: the coat hanger (seen on buttons and placards at demonstrations), which represents the desperate lengths to which women would go in attempts at self-abortion, and the "back alley butchers," those incompetent and exploitative abortionists to whom women were forced to resort, risking sexual abuse, injury, and death, repeatedly invoked in movement discourse.

The coat hanger and the butcher are certainly not invented symbols. Women in fact did try to self-abort using hangers (among many other similarly dangerous objects), and we have ample documentation of women's encounters with butchers, both physicians and laypersons.[1] But butchers

An earlier version of this paper was presented at the Berkshire Conference on the History of Women, Douglass College, Rutgers University, June 1990. I am deeply grateful to the Faculty Research Fund and the Changemaster Fund, both at Bryn Mawr College, a faculty research grant from the University of California, Davis, and the Louis Stott Foundation for the financial assistance that made this research possible. My thinking on this subject has benefited greatly from conversations with Jean Hunt of the Elizabeth Blackwell Center in Philadelphia. I also appreciate the help of Patricia Anderson, Terry Beresford, James Reed, and two anonymous reviewers for the *Journal of the History of Sexuality*.

[1] For a recent discussion of women's vulnerability to butchers in the pre-*Roe* era, see Ellen Messer and Kathryn May, *Back Room: Voices from the Illegal Abortion Era* (New York, 1988).

This essay originally appeared in the *Journal of the History of Sexuality* 1991, vol. 2, no. 1.

and coat hangers were only partial aspects of a more complex reality that formed the culture of illegal abortion before *Roe*. About one third of the approximately one million illegal abortions per year that are estimated to have occurred in the United States in the years immediately preceding *Roe* were performed by physicians,[2] and to view all of these physician providers as butchers, I argue, is both historically incorrect and politically costly to the current prochoice movement.

Rather, I suggest that we must further acknowledge another category of physicians active in the pre-*Roe* era, a group whom I call "physicians of conscience." In contrast to those of the butchers who had medical degrees, these physicians of conscience were not incompetent medically (and hence unable to function in mainstream medicine), did not appear to have performed abortions primarily for financial reasons, and were not exploitative of their patients. Like all physicians who offered abortions in that era, these physicians of conscience risked both imprisonment and loss of medical license, but given that these providers were already well-established in mainstream medical careers, they arguably risked more by their actions.

In this essay, I will describe the activities of three such physicians of conscience who offered abortions before legalization. First, however, in order for the reader to fully appreciate the significance of such activities, I will very briefly recapitulate the history of abortion in the United States before the key *Roe v. Wade* decision in 1973, focusing on the relationship between abortion and organized medicine.

## ABORTION BEFORE *ROE V. WADE*

Prior to the middle of the nineteenth century, abortion was only minimally regulated in the United States.[3] The prevailing standard was that abortions that occurred before "quickening" (generally occurring between the fourth and sixth months of pregnancy) were not regulated at all, and there was minimal attempt to police those abortions that occurred afterward. Abortion apparently was commonly practiced, and abortion services were freely advertised in newspapers, offered by a range of practitioners of widely varying degrees of medical training and credentials. Much of the

[2]Daniel Callahan, *Abortion: Law, Choice, and Morality* (New York, 1970), p. 131.

[3]This section draws on James Mohr, *Abortion in America: The Origins and Evolution of National Policy, 1800–1900* (New York, 1978); Carroll Smith-Rosenberg, "The Abortion Movement and the AMA, 1850–1880," in her *Disorderly Conduct: Visions of Gender in Victorian America* (New York, 1985), pp. 217–44; Kristin Luker, *Abortion and the Politics of Motherhood* (Berkeley, 1984); Rosalind Petchesky, *Abortion and Women's Choice: The State, Sexuality, and Reproductive Freedom* (Boston, 1990); and Leslie Reagan, "When Is Abortion Necessary to Save a Woman's Life? The Political Dimensions of Therapeutic Abortion during the Period of Criminalized Abortion in the U.S., 1880–1973" (paper presented at the Berkshire Conference on the History of Women, Wellesley, MA, June 19–21, 1987).

abortion activity of the period consisted of attempts at self-abortion using various herbs and drugs, either purchased from an apothecary or ordered through the mail. The drive to criminalize abortion, which started in mid-century and peaked by the early 1880s, when all the states had enacted antiabortion statutes, stemmed from a variety of motivations, including increasing societal anxiety about the declining birth rates of Anglo-Saxon women in comparison to those of newly arriving immigrants.[4] The campaign also included the participation of the Roman Catholic church and many Protestant clergy, which up to this point had been silent on the abortion question.

But as recent scholarship has demonstrated, the most important force in the campaign to criminalize abortion were the physicians. The American Medical Association (AMA), founded in 1847, made the abortion struggle one of the highest priorities of the new organization. The argument of these physicians, in brief, was that abortion was both an "immoral" act and a medically dangerous one, given the incompetence of many of those practitioners then providing abortion. The abortion campaign of the nineteenth century thus is most usefully understood as a key component of a larger battle then underway: the attempt of "regular" or "elite" physicians (that is, those who were university-trained) to attain professional dominance over the wide range of "irregular" medical practitioners—healers, homeopaths, and the like—who had flourished throughout the first part of the nineteenth century. Abortion was a particularly appropriate territory over which to stake such claims of professional monopoly, both because so much of the irregulars' activity apparently was abortion-based and because much abortion work was being done by laypeople with no claims whatsoever to medical credentials.

The objective of regular physicians was not simply to abolish all abortions, however. Rather, the AMA argument, which ultimately prevailed, was that physicians should control the terms under which "approved" abortions were performed—that is, "legal" abortions were now to be confined to those performed in a hospital, for "medically indicated" reasons. After criminalization, virtually all states passed legislation authorizing abortions if the pregnancy jeopardized the mother's life. Some, moreover, passed vague statutes permitting abortions if the health of the mother, in some

---

[4]Smith-Rosenberg, in her brilliant essay, offers a broad, highly complex view of the nine-teenth-century abortion struggle that transcends any one causal factor: "The endangered fetus, the physically and politically constrained woman have become condensed, emotionally charged symbols of social change, autonomy and power—legitimate and illegitimate. Viewed against a backdrop of economic, demographic and technological factors, the abortion issue can be seen as a political code. It functions as a sexual language through which divergent gender, economic, regional and religious groups discuss issues of social change and social conflict far broader than the fate of fetuses or even the sexual rights of adult women" (p. 218).

cases including mental health, were in jeopardy. Thus, beginning in the 1880s, there was established a pattern (which continued through to the *Roe* era) of an abortion climate that both was highly uncertain—how does one precisely define threats to the physical or mental "health" of the mother?—and saw enormous variations from state to state, and often even within states, as to which abortions could be considered legally permissible.[5] Organized medicine attempted to manage the problem of abortion by establishing "therapeutic abortion committees" within hospitals, which would act on petitions by individual doctors to obtain abortions for their patients. In many locales, these committees, fearful of attracting unwanted attention, inevitably acted in a highly cautious manner, developing informal—if not formal—quota systems.[6] In contrast, in some other states (especially in the period immediately before *Roe*), where abortion statutes permitted "mental health" considerations, abortions essentially became available to nearly anyone who could afford the price of a psychiatric evaluation.

The uneven, erratic, and highly insufficient supply of legal abortion after criminalization created a widespread system of illegal abortion in the near-century before legalization. A highly regarded study published by Frederick Taussig in 1936 estimated a half-million illegal abortions were taking place in the United States annually; the Kinsey Report in 1953 suggested that nine out of ten premarital pregnancies among its respondents were aborted, while over 20 percent of married women in the sample reported an abortion while married,[7] and, as already noted in this essay, estimates of illegal abortion in the immediate pre-*Roe* period range as high as 1.2 million. The enormous variations in the quality of illegal abortions that were available in the pre-*Roe* era posed a number of dilemmas for individual family physicians and obstetrician/gynecologists, who typically were the first practitioners approached by patients with unwanted pregnancies.

---

[5]The celebrated case of the "San Francisco Nine" in 1966 illustrates the enormous uncertainty under which the practice of legal abortion in the United States operated. In this case, nine highly respected obstetrician/gynecologists in San Francisco were abruptly threatened with the loss of their licenses because they had been performing hospital-based abortions on women infected with rubella, a practice that was increasingly common in a number of states by the 1960s (in New York, in 1964, over half of all hospital-performed abortions were rubella-indicated). The sudden decision to prosecute these physicians apparently came from one individual, the strongly antiabortion head of the California Board of Medical Examiners. The case gained national media attention and drew an unprecedented show of support from influential physicians (for example, more than 100 deans of medical schools) from across the country, thus helping to galvanize the abortion reform movement. Ultimately the charges against the nine were dropped. For an account, see Larry Lader, *Abortion II: Making the Revolution* (Boston, 1974), pp. 67–69.

[6]Luker, p. 57.

[7]Mohr, p. 254.

Those sympathetic to the patient's plight, but unwilling or unable to perform an illegal abortion themselves, scrambled to find reliable, medically competent referrals. For patients with sufficient means, this usually meant sending the patient out of the country, with Japan, Puerto Rico, England, and Mexico being chief points of referral in the 1960s. The referring physician then would offer postabortion care to the patient (and in this way be able to make some judgment about the skill of the abortionists and thus their suitability for further referrals). For patients without such means to travel, the doctor's options were more limited: in those cases where he or she knew of a reliable local underground abortionist, a referral could be made, an act which in itself put the referring doctor at some risk;[8] when the physician did not have reliable referrals, he or she was left with the task of either trying to discourage the patient herself from seeking out an abortionist who was probably incompetent or, in some small fraction of cases—typically in cases of longtime private patients—manipulating the system to obtain an abortion for the patient, in ways to be described later in this article.

In conclusion, we can see that the abortion climate within organized medicine in the decades pre-*Roe* was quite a contradictory one. On the one hand, there was the undeniable legacy of the highly negative image of the abortionist—a legacy that stemmed both from the nineteenth century when "quacks" were routinely providing abortion and from the illegal abortion market of the twentieth century, when some abortionists were incompetent, exploitative physicians whose abortion practice seemingly stemmed from their inability to earn a livelihood in mainstream medicine. On the other hand, the ever-increasing demand for abortion by women of all social classes—including doctors' wives and daughters and female doctors themselves—made it extremely difficult to sustain the notion of abortion as an immoral act, as organized medicine had argued in the nineteenth century. Similarly, the inevitability of women's resort to illegal abortions—and the sad results, to which many doctors were exposed in emergency rooms—made it increasingly clear to many physicians that denying women abortions constituted misguided medical practice. Thus, internal divisions over abortion became more and more evident within the medical profession, particularly as the demand for abortions rose in the 1960s. How extensive a training residents would receive in abortion techniques and what kinds of informal socialization about abortion their professors would impart was very much a function of the particular climate

[8]One physician interviewed for this study, in practice on the East Coast in the 1940s, recounted that while he was fearful of directly giving out the name of a reliable abortionist known to him, he taped the abortionist's phone number in a public phone booth in his office building and thus was able to suggest to abortion-seeking patients that they drop by that phone booth.

not only in a certain region, but often of the particular hospital in which residents happened to train.[9] This, then, was the confused and volatile climate wherein the subjects of this essay confronted the issue of abortion in their medical practice in the 1950s and 1960s.

## THREE PHYSICIANS OF CONSCIENCE

The following material is taken from an interview study of forty-four physicians who in various ways were involved in abortion before *Roe* (fifteen of this total interview group actually performed abortions).[10]

In what follows, I will describe three distinctive styles of abortion provision among this group. The very small size of the total sample precludes me from making claims of representativeness, and I readily acknowledge the methodological difficulties of selecting subjects who qualify as physicians of conscience. Nevertheless, I contend that a detailed look at those individuals who chose to provide abortion before *Roe* gives us a fuller understanding of the challenges of the post-*Webster* era.[11]

[9]All obstetrical/gynecological residents, in theory, were given training in the completion of a "spontaneous abortion" (miscarriage), which is similar, though not identical, to the commencing of an abortion procedure. Training in the latter, as well as training in the more technically challenging procedure of a later (second-trimester) abortion, was highly variable from program to program.

[10]The initial respondents for this study were located in various ways, including personal networks, inquiries at professional associations, and advertisements placed in medical journals. As the study progressed, one of the key ways of locating respondents was through the "snowball" technique—that is, those whom I interviewed would recommend colleagues whom they felt would be appropriate for this research. While I can make no claims about the representativeness of my sample, I do feel quite confident that those I ultimately interviewed and included in this study met the criteria of "conscience"—that is, because virtually all of these physicians apparently were launched on successful medical careers at the time of their involvement in abortion activity, it seems reasonable to conclude that this activity was not motivated primarily by financial considerations. Two of this subgroup of fifteen—David Bennett and Henry Morgantaler—did become, eventually, full-time abortion practitioners, but this is because they (unlike the others) made the decision to offer abortion services to all who sought them, and the volume of abortion seekers made any other medical practice impossible. A further indication of "conscience" that aided me in selecting this group was that although there was variation as to whether fees were routinely charged for abortion services, all of these physicians claimed to have offered abortions free to indigent women. The abortion-related activities of others in the sample, who did not provide illegal abortions themselves, included finding adequate referrals for patients needing abortions; offering back-up medical care for recipients of illegal abortions; participating in hospital committees that were established to approve guidelines for hospital-based abortions; and engaging in various forms of community education and political work to hasten the legalization of abortion.

[11]Here I am referring to the landmark Supreme Court case, Webster v. Reproductive Health Services, decided in July 1989, which gave states the right to impose severe new restrictions on abortion services. In the *Webster* case itself, the Court upheld a Missouri law that banned public employees from participating in any abortions not necessary to save a woman's

## Daniel Fieldstone: The Private Practitioner

Daniel Fieldstone's abortion practices were probably the most typical of physicians of conscience in the pre-*Roe* period. That is, he quietly provided abortions to certain private patients with whom he had a special relationship, but not to others.

Fieldstone (not his real name) came from the New York area. He trained at Mount Sinai Hospital in the 1950s under one of the most influential obstetrician/gynecologists of that era, Dr. Alan Guttmacher, and thus was exposed early in his training to innovation around the issues of reproduction, with abortion being only one of several controversial areas. Liberalized sterilization and birth control policies were also part of Guttmacher's agenda at Mount Sinai. As Fieldstone said:

> We were also looking at the whole question of fertility in the 1950s. The abortion issue is only one part of it, although it's been portrayed as a single issue. Mount Sinai was much more notorious for its sterilization regulations, which looking backwards were incredibly terrible, but at the time struck everyone as very liberal. There was the "rule of 30"—you had to have six kids, living, by the time you were 30, five by age 35, four by age 40, or have had three C-sections [births by cesarean section] and you had to have the permission of your husband, or if you were separated, he had to have been gone seven years. . . . Those were the most liberal set of regulations in the country for elective sterilization, and we were sterilizing hundreds of Hispanics, blacks, poor women, who up to that time were having children every year. So six under 30 seemed like a big deal, but we had a lot of people who qualified.

Fieldstone commented on birth control at Mount Sinai: "We had a contraceptive clinic, a jammed contraceptive clinic, at a time when it was illegal to provide contraceptives in municipal hospitals. We were fitting diaphragms when women could die in a municipal hospital over a lack of contraception. So it all sort of hung together. Guttmacher really was a descendant of Margaret Sanger in terms of his thinking. Which was of course that women had the right to control the number of children they wanted."

It was in this atmosphere that Fieldstone received training in the techniques of performing abortions, as well as a positive image of the abortion provider.

---

life, banned the performance of abortions in public hospitals, even if no public funds are expended (except, again, those abortions necessary to save a woman's life), and upheld viability testing for any fetus thought to be at least twenty weeks.

Mount Sinai was virtually the only hospital in New York City that had a therapeutic abortion committee at that time, and that allowed therapeutic abortions. Now in other places, you just died. . . .

"Abortion" was such a dirty word then . . . and "abortionist" was such a dirty word, it was just one step above a pervert, or child abuser. . . . It was incredible, to be called an abortionist in the 1950s, you were the scum of the earth. . . . And in fact, the only time you ever saw the word "abortionist," it would be something like, "Bits of body found in Queens sewer traced to abortionist's office, who said he panicked when she died and he chopped her up and threw her down the sewer."

Encouraged by Guttmacher and others at Mount Sinai, Fieldstone began what would become a career-long academic interest in abortion and undertook demographic research into the incidence of illegal abortion. This academic research soon became joined with political involvement in the movement to legalize abortion: "I had been working on this research for a number of years, it was part of the effort to assist the reform movement in getting a model abortion law passed. . . . But I was always more of a medical activist. . . . We had a great big meeting, in Hot Springs, it resulted in two volumes coming out on abortion, that really changed things. . . . They brought together what we knew about incidents and effects of criminal abortion, what the effects of legalization were, and what was known then about techniques." One of the most significant aspects of this conference, which was sponsored by the Association for the Study of Abortion in 1968, was that it introduced to an American audience the recently developed "vacuum suction" method of abortion.[12] Suction, which is now the standard technique for most first-trimester abortions, caused many fewer injuries than the previous method of sole reliance on a surgical curette.

In the early 1960s, Fieldstone for a time joined the private practice of his father, also an obstetrician/gynecologist, in the New York metropolitan area. There he gained his first experience in providing illegal abortions.

My father had always very quietly taken care of his own patients who had undesired pregnancies. He did do a few abortions. It was a very effective way, and you could get away with it unquestionably, as long as you didn't do it as a business. You would see them in the office, and

[12]The proceedings from this conference were published as *Abortion in a Changing World*, ed. Robert Hall, 2 vols. (New York, 1970). It is noteworthy that at this conference one of those invited to present a paper was Robert Spencer, M.D., of Ashland, PA, a well-known (and highly respected, medically) provider of illegal abortion.

use one of our biopsy instruments to create some bleeding and send them to the hospital as an incomplete abortion [where either of the Fieldstones then would complete the procedure]. So he took care of his own practice but he never took care of anybody else. I did the same.

We never said anything about it, and we didn't charge any more for it, we didn't announce it, and we didn't take care of anybody else. It was a quiet, not particularly courageous act.

Fieldstone went on to explain why he and his father were so selective: "I wasn't going to be on the receiving end of the underground, dealing with hundreds of women coming for abortions and throwing my career and my license up for grabs."

In this statement (which was echoed, incidentally, by many others in this study), the fear seems to be not only of the potential volume of the abortion seekers, but of their status as strangers:

Dad had been practicing in the same location in ——— since 1935. By the time I got there he was taking care of the daughters of the women he delivered in the 1930s. Before I left, he was taking care of their granddaughters. There really weren't too many strangers in that practice. So we didn't take much risk by dealing with people we didn't know. The biggest risk we took is we'd start one, and somehow or another they'd bleed to death or they'd get a super infection and get angry at us. It would have been a problem. But litigation wasn't as scary then as it is now.

"Risk management," then, for Fieldstone and his father was a function both of dealing only with trusted longtime patients and of keeping volume down. As Fieldstone said, "Spontaneous abortion was pretty common, it's always going to be about 15 percent of your practice, so if you raised it to 20 percent, who would know? Nobody sat there at the end of the year and said, 'Daniel Fieldstone did $x$ deliveries this year and $y$ abortions.' Now if we had made a business of it, that would have been different."

Finally, like virtually all other respondents in this study, Fieldstone commented on the unfairness of the prevailing abortion situation before the 1970s:

Basically, the wealthy woman had access to a legitimate doctor, occasionally she had to go overseas, but most of the time, if you had money, you'd find somebody. Somebody reputable. By the 1960s, it wasn't any great problem because I could call up two of my psychiatrist friends, and say to the patient, "You go over there and tell them you're going to commit suicide and for $100 apiece, they'll write you a letter and that's that"—we went to the committee in the hospital with those letters and that was it. Also, there was this handbook by Pat Maginnis, it taught you how to fake a suicide attempt . . . what you should say to a psychiatrist to convince him you're suicidal.[13]

If you had the money, you could do it. The catch was, if you were fifteen years old, you couldn't do it. If you were black and poor, you couldn't do it. They ended up in our hospital emergency rooms.

This disparity between the abortion outcomes of women of means and poor women has been graphically documented in a memoir by Bernard Nathanson, a physician very active in abortion reform in New York in the early 1970s (and who later became controversial for his turnabout on the abortion issue and his involvement in antiabortion activity):

> I would be informed at 2:00 A.M. or thereabouts that a clinic patient was bleeding in the Emergency Room. . . . There a petrified, shivering creature would be lying on the examining table, bleeding profusely from the vagina, and moaning softly to herself. Invariably, the patient would be black or Puerto Rican. A thermometer registering 103° or 104° would be taken from her mouth. . . . I would proceed immediately to the ordeal of vaginal examination, often fishing out sizable chunks of pregnancy tissue lying free among the huge clots. Another victim of a hack abortionist or of self-abortion. I would pass an hour or two mindlessly . . . until it was time to carry out the D & C [dilation and curettage], removing the rest of the tissue. If she were lucky, she would be returned to her room, be discharged 48 hours later. . . . If she were *not* lucky, she might:
>     —vomit under anesthesia, aspirate her vomitus and die of respiratory obstruction and cardiac arrest.
>     —continue to bleed from a perforation of the uterus that had been inflicted by the abortionist. Hysterectomy (removal of the uterus, causing lifelong sterility) would be carried out without delay.
>     —continue to spike high fever for days or weeks. In that era we had only a few antibiotics available. . . . In many cases the infection would be uncontrollable by means short of hysterectomy.
>     —Occasionally, even a hysterectomy would not slow the steady march of internal gangrene and the woman would die painfully, her vital organs filthy with the satellite abscesses of her disease. . . .

[13]Fieldstone is referring to *The Abortion Handbook for Responsible Women*, published in 1969 in San Francisco by Lana Phelan and Patricia Maginnis, two abortion rights activists on the West Coast. Besides informing readers how to simulate psychoses, the book also gave instructions in "do-it-yourself abortions" and in how to simulate a hemorrhage, so that a hospital-approved abortion would be granted. Portions of this handbook have been reprinted in a volume published by the National Women's Health Network, *Abortion Then and Now: Creative Responses to Restricted Access* (Washington, DC, 1990).

A little different story with the private patients. If you were the resident on the private service, the call would usually come at seven or eight in the evening, a short time after office hours. The private physician would be on the other end of the line advising you that he was sending in Mrs. Buggins with heavy vaginal bleeding, the diagnosis being incomplete abortion—that is, miscarriage. He wanted to do the D & C in a couple of hours, so would you please prepare her for the O.R. and inform the anesthesia people? . . .

She would invariably appear in an astonishingly blooming state of health and her sanitary pad would have a single dime-sized stain of blood on it. . . . She would be wheeled into the O.R. and coaxed gently to sleep by a solicitous anesthesiologist. . . . Then the private physician would appear to be ceremonially gowned and gloved for the operation.[14]

### David Bennett: The Politico

David Bennett is distinguished from the other respondents (except one) in the subsample of thirteen providers of illegal abortions in that he ultimately made the decision to offer an abortion to all who requested one. Although the very small numbers of respondents in this study necessitates caution in drawing conclusions, it is nonetheless intriguing that Bennett and the other provider of abortion on request, Henry Morgantaler, were the two interviewees who most explicitly tied their abortion involvement to prior involvement in progressive political movements.[15]

Bennett (not his real name) was born and raised in the rural Southwest. His first confrontation with the issues of abortion and unwanted pregnancy occurred when he was an adolescent:

Something happened when I was in high school, that's when I can trace back when I really began to accept the possibility of being involved in abortions in the future. . . . There was a young woman that was kept outside of the group, I came to find out that she had had a child and not been married, and before this event occurred, she had been popular and belonged to clubs, was a good singer. She was no longer allowed to participate in anything—she could come to class and that was it. This seemed very unfair to me . . . I knew other boys

[14]Bernard Nathanson, *Aborting America* (New York, 1979), pp. 19–22.

[15]Although I use fictional names for the other physicians discussed in this essay, Henry Morgantaler and Jane Hodgson—because of the public nature of their arrests and trials—will be identified as such. Morgantaler, a Holocaust survivor, went to Canada after World War II and spent the next forty years challenging Canada's abortion laws by openly providing abortions in his clinics. He experienced numerous arrests and received one jail sentence of several years.

and girls in the high school were engaging in sexual activities. It was rumored that there was someone who would do abortions for $500 (which in 1953 was a tremendous sum of money), so if you had enough money there would be a different outcome, but here she was. . . . It had a very profound effect on me.

In medical school in the early 1960s, Bennett received some training in abortion, which, typical for that period, centered on dealing with complications of illegal abortions as well as learning to complete spontaneous abortions (miscarriages). The message Bennett received from professors about abortion was unequivocally negative—both physicians who provided this service and women who sought it were to be condemned. Also, like many others interviewed for this study, Bennett was urged to report to the police any women who came to the emergency room suspected of having had an illegal abortion. "I was naive—once I reported someone who had an illegal abortion, the police came and questioned her, she reported who did it, and they went to arrest this person, the woman who induced the abortion, and filed charges against her. That was the last one I ever reported."

Bennett's actual involvement in abortion practice came several years later, in the mid-1960s, when he was just establishing a family practice in the small town in which he had been raised. Pressures to come to terms with the abortion issue came from two overlapping groups with which he was then involved. The first was the local Unitarian church, which ultimately put him in touch with the Clergy Consultation Service, a national network of clergy that made abortion referrals, both inside the United States and abroad, before *Roe v. Wade*.[16] The second factor was his immersion in "movement" activities (and corresponding personal networks) of that period: the civil rights movement, the antiwar movement, the emerging feminist movement.

Both of these groups began, in different ways, to put considerable pressure on Bennett to become involved in clandestine abortions. The clergy, sensing Bennett's sympathy with the issue, proposed that he offer illegal abortions, or, short of that, that he be willing to serve as a back-up physician for women who received abortions out of the country or from "underground" practitioners locally. Pressure from Bennett's political comrades, in the loosely organized "movement" circles in his region, were more intense and personal:

At that time, we would have many sessions where we would talk about, "What kind of world did we want?" And there were many

[16]For a memoir of the Clergy Consultation Service by its founders, see Arlene Carmen and Howard Moody, *Abortion Counseling and Social Change, from Illegal Act to Medical Practice: The Story of the Clergy Consultation Service on Abortion* (Valley Forge, PA, 1973).

women there. . . . It became obvious that many felt it wasn't a fair
world for women. . . . The consequences of sexual activity can be so
devastating to a woman, and to a man it could even be a source of
pride or prestige. . . . He could go right on with his college career,
and a pregnancy can interrupt her life. Her life is radically and drastically changed, which didn't apply to the man. If she should find
herself pregnant, for whatever reason, she should have the choice of
terminating that pregnancy. And once I came to that position, it became harder and harder for me to resist doing what I felt I could do.

After much soul-searching with his wife, clergy friends, lawyer, and
other close associates, Bennett made the decision to offer abortions to those
who sought them. Part of this soul-searching process involved confronting
the possibility of a prison sentence. "I was talking with a friend of mine,
who taught at a Baptist seminary. I said, 'Well, if I go to prison, there's a lot
of books I want to read.' You understand, this was very naive. In retrospect,
prison is not time off to go to the library. It was part of a lot of inner deception. I think it was one way of controlling some of the fear and apprehension I had."

Initially, Bennett proceeded in somewhat the same way Daniel Fieldstone did, as described above. That is, he started an abortion in his office by
inducing bleeding, then instructed the patient to go to a hospital and claim
that she was having a miscarriage. A key difference, though, was that Bennett's patients were coming from a wide geographical area, were not all
going to the same hospital, and, most crucially, were going to hospital
emergency rooms—and thus not being admitted as the private patients of a
solicitous physician. Bennett soon grew dissatisfied with this method of
operation:

These women are going to all kinds of hospitals. They are bleeding
and cramping, they may get infections, they've got all these potential
complications. They've got a big hospital bill. Sometimes they have
police hassling them. This is just no way to do this. There must be a
better way. That's when I decided I was going to order the instruments, I was going to do it [the entire procedure]. I was going to
complete the surgery in such a way that the woman could bear it. I
had already been entering the cervix, I knew I could go in with instruments and get into the uterus.

The decision to escalate his already illegal practice by offering complete
abortions brought further risks to Bennett, starting with the need to order
the instruments necessary to do a complete dilation and curettage: "I just
called and ordered the instruments. . . . I called the detail man who ser-
viced me, he brought over a pretty good instrument catalog, and I ordered

all these instruments, dilators, curettes, and all the instruments you need in the hospital. It was scary . . . this detail man, he knew by the order that you don't order these instruments . . . it was obvious why I was ordering them. But I did it." Bennett's abortion practice became much easier, technically, when suction machines became available around 1968, though, again, the actual act of ordering the machine was a nerve-wracking experience.

Predictably, Bennett's decision to offer illegal abortions created problems for him in a number of ways. First, though he had done some minimal abortion work in the hospital while a medical student and intern, he was now engaged in full-scale abortion work without any colleagues with whom he could consult. Recalling the isolation he felt during that period, and his reluctance to confer with peers, he said: "I had no one to talk to, because I didn't want to jeopardize them. . . . I had the feeling that if anything happened, I didn't want them to be in a position of testifying against me. Some of them were people I knew, if I told them, they'd have to lie under oath and I didn't want to put people in that position."

Reconciling the flow of abortion patients with the rest of his practice was another problem for Bennett. Although initially he intended to restrict abortion patients to those who came to him via the Clergy Consultation Service, this soon proved impossible as abortion seekers came to him from a variety of sources, and he felt incapable of turning them down. His abortion work grew in such volume that it overwhelmed other aspects of his medical practice, and with considerable wistfulness he gave up his family practice and began to do abortions on a full-time basis.

Security was of course a major concern for Bennett. Even before his involvement in abortion, he had been occupying a very visible, and ambiguous, position in his community. On the one hand, his father was a well-respected figure in local politics, and Bennett himself was active in a variety of mainstream community activities, such as the school board. On the other hand, as already indicated, he was also involved in various "movement" activities in this highly conservative area. Summing up his rather anomalous position in town, Bennett said, "I was the guy who wore the black armband [to protest the Vietnam War] when I had lunch at the Rotary Club."

Bennett's already tenuous relationship with the local authorities, especially the police, became intensified as his abortion traffic increasingly drew people from out of town. At one point, in fact, the local police suspected him of being a drug trafficker: "Cars and vans are coming into town, many with out-of-state plates. In this county people notice out-of-state plates. They [police] start following these cars. They think I'm in the drug business. . . . Most of these are young people. The boyfriend comes with them, they bring friends with them. . . . The young people in those days, they come in, they have the long hair, hippy clothes on, they're smoking marijuana and they come cruising into town for their abortion. The police just watch all this and pull them over." In one particularly harrowing incident, an abortion patient, whose boyfriend had been arrested by police as the couple were en route to the abortion, rushed into Bennett's office and proceeded to flush some marijuana down the toilet, leaving Bennett terrified of an imminent police raid.

Blackmail attempts by patients were one of the greatest threats facing Bennett during this period. As he put it, "I could have gone to the police and said, 'I'm going to do abortions today'—but unless someone were there to bring charges, they couldn't do a thing about it. But all you need is one patient unhappy, one bad outcome, and that's it. So every patient I saw in those days was a potential." In fact, out of the thousands of illegal abortions that Bennett performed before *Roe,* only one blackmail attempt was made (by the boyfriend of one patient). After considerable thought, Bennett decided he could not capitulate and simply refused to cooperate. "I told him to go to the police if he wanted. I said, 'The police know I'm doing abortions, sometimes they refer people to me.' I never heard from him again."

Given today's litigious climate and the overall atmosphere of distrust between many physicians and patients, it does seem remarkable that there were no more blackmail attempts against Bennett. Beyond the unquestionable factor of simple luck, other elements also help to explain this. First, most of Bennett's patients were prescreened by clergy working for the consultation service, where they were not only informed about the technical aspects of the abortion but also presumably socialized into a political understanding of the risks that the cooperating physicians were undertaking. Second, the policies that Bennett adopted himself for his abortion practice also were conducive to a relationship of trust: he reduced or waived the fee in cases of financial need, he informed all patients that he would refund their fees if not satisfied with his service, and if any patient needed hospitalization after the procedure, Bennett would pay her bill.

It is also clear, in retrospect, that the abortion service that Bennett offered was quite different from that of many other abortionists of that period (and indeed, of many practitioners today)—and this, too, may help to account for the enormous loyalty of so many patients. Basically, Bennett quite early in his abortion career became committed to making the abortion a "positive experience" for the recipient. Initially, this meant a focus on the ways to reduce the pain associated with the procedure: "It was the pain that bothered me. Women sometimes experienced excruciating pain. . . . I'm doing this for reasons of conscience and compassion and here I'm inflicting this terrible pain on women. They were good . . . they would bite their lips till they bled." Bennett was experimenting with various kinds of local anesthetics but felt constrained from too much experimentation, given that his operations were totally removed from a hospital setting. He soon came to observe that the patients who came to him through the clergy consultation network as a whole suffered less pain than those who came from other referrals. "I began to ask the women who went to the ministers why they had less pain. They were less scared, they were more confident. . . . They had some issues they had talked about. Well, that led me from the pain medication to get on with relaxation techniques and hypnosis. I certainly became aware that fear was a major contributor to your reaction to the procedure."

Bennett's interest in the related issues of pain management, relaxation techniques, and what would only later be known as "abortion counseling," developed in this pre-*Roe* period, would lead to a career-long interest in the abortion "experience" (as opposed to the more narrow medical focus on the abortion procedure). As he later reflected on his mind-set during his days as a provider of illegal abortions:

> I didn't want abortion to be simply the lesser of two evils. I wanted this to be a humane experience, but more than that . . . no matter how conflicted the woman might be, even feeling bad about herself . . . that she feel good about those providing the service . . . and perhaps we could facilitate her feeling better about herself . . . and this could be a growth experience for her, that out of this she would have a sense of her own worth. If we provided services in a dignified way, respecting her as an individual, involving her in the process, then she could feel her own strength. So that's how we went from thinking of this as the lesser of two evils to a life-enhancing experience.

While, as indicated above, Bennett received only one serious blackmail threat and was never formally charged by the police for performing abortions, his life nonetheless during the three years he offered abortions in his hometown was extremely stressful. Because of rumors about his abortion activity and also his involvement in other controversial political activities, he and his family (which included two young children) constantly were harassed and began to receive physical threats. He always felt the threat of possible arrest: "I got to this point, seeing a police car in my rearview mirror caused irrational fear." After three years of such pressure, he moved with his family to a large city, where he continued to perform illegal abortions for two years. He then moved to a nearby state, which by the early 1970s had considerably liberalized its abortion laws.

## Jane Hodgson: The Test Case

Jane Hodgson performed only one illegal abortion before *Roe v. Wade;* she did so openly in order to provoke a legal confrontation that she hoped would lead to the overturning of restrictive abortion laws in her home state of Minnesota and beyond. Her willingness to openly defy existing laws—and hence to magnify the risk of prison and the loss of her license—was certainly not typical of physicians of conscience in the pre-*Roe* era, but she does demonstrate, in extreme form, how physicians used legal, as well as medical, strategies to overcome barriers to safe abortion.

Hodgson was born in 1915 in rural Minnesota. She did not recall the abortion issue looming large in her childhood, even though her father was a country doctor. The connection she did draw, however, between her early years and later abortion activity was the humanistic character of her father's medical practice: "He was as kind to the prostitutes in the county jail as he was to his private patients."

In her medical school education at the University of Minnesota in the late 1930s and later in advanced obstetrical/gynecological training at the Mayo Clinic in the early 1940s, Hodgson received little training in abortion technique and much antiabortion propaganda: "I had been taught in medical school that to invade the uterus was the most dangerous thing you could do. We were taught that it was illegal and dangerous. We saw all the criminal cases with those horrible infections. You began to believe how dangerous it was. My whole experience, even at Mayo, we were never taught how to do a therapeutic abortion . . . all we did was learn to complete an abortion that had already been started. We always put a patient to sleep, it was a big deal."

Hodgson started a private practice in the Minneapolis/St. Paul area in 1947, some twenty-six years before *Roe.* Being one of the few women in private practice during that period, she was flooded with requests for abortions. The hospital in which she worked had a therapeutic abortion committee but approved abortions only in the face of life-threatening conditions. Even some medically indicated abortions seemingly beyond dispute were difficult to get through the committee: "I remember one abortion I did that caused a lot of discussion—a young woman who had two sons, she had breast cancer that had metasticized, her life expectancy was short. She got pregnant from a diaphragm failure. It was a matter of increasing her life expectancy to interrupt that pregnancy. I remember how heartless some of those people were when we were discussing that case."

Like other physicians during the 1950s and 1960s, Hodgson made use of several strategies to deal with unwanted pregnancies among her patients. In the 1950s, she made many referrals to "maternity homes" in the Midwest, institutions where young women would carry their pregnancies to term, put their babies up for adoption, and return to their communities with their "secret" intact. In the 1960s, with the help of the Clergy Consultation Service, she was able to refer those patients with resources to abortion providers outside the country. These options were inadequate to handle the demand, however. As she put it, "It got very wearing to always be turning people down."

In Hodgson's case, then, it was not—as it was for some others in this study—one particularly memorable case, but rather a variety of convergent factors that transformed her from someone only mildly involved with the abortion issue to an abortion activist. The combination of constant patient demands, seeing the recipients of botched abortions in the emergency rooms, the hypocrisy of her physician colleagues ("who would be publicly antiabortion but always asking me if I knew where their daughters or wives could get abortions"), as well as the lack of compassion expressed by those on her hospital's therapeutic abortion committee led her to an intense period of thinking and studying about the abortion issue. "My position on abortion evolved. I had been taught that abortion was immoral. I gradually came to change, I came to feel that the law was immoral, there were all these young women whose health was being ruined, whose lives were being ruined, whose plans had to be changed. From my point of view, it was poor medicine, it was poor public health policy. After much soul-searching, I realized that no one could make the decision, no other person could make that decision."

Hodgson was determined to take action against restrictive abortion laws, and, in 1970, she found a suitable test case. A young married woman, the mother of two children, had contracted rubella during her third pregnancy. Hodgson knew that ultimately this patient could have found a hospital-approved abortion in another state (by 1970, hospitals in a number of states approved abortion for rubella because of the likelihood of fetal deformity). But the patient "had a sense of justice" and was willing to serve as a test case. Hodgson then went to federal court in Minnesota, asked that the abortion law be overturned, and, when she was refused, went ahead and scheduled the patient for a D & C in Hodgson's home hospital in St. Paul.

As Hodgson had anticipated, the police were notified and, shortly after the procedure, came to her office and arrested her. The arrest set off a three-year period of legal activity, during which Hodgson's license to practice medicine in Minnesota was in question. After an initial conviction, she appealed to the Minnesota Supreme Court, and, while that case was still in process, the U.S. Supreme Court handed down the *Roe v. Wade* decision, thus overturning her earlier conviction.

Hodgson became intensely visible in the Twin Cities area, in the period immediately before the abortion (when she asked the federal court to overturn existing abortion laws) and especially in the period after the abortion, when she was arrested and went to trial. This period brought enormous changes to Hodgson's life, at professional, political, and social levels. She initially found herself professionally at a standstill, unable to practice medicine in her home state because of her suspended license, and became demoralized as her appeal dragged on. She decided to take a job in Washington, DC (where, in 1971, abortion was legal) at the recently founded Preterm clinic, one of the country's first models of a freestanding abortion clinic. She worked as Preterm's medical director for several years, flying back to her family in Minnesota on weekends.

Professionally, the Preterm experience was highly gratifying. The clinic was performing about sixty abortions per day, and Hodgson thus had the opportunity to initiate groundbreaking research on outpatient abortion procedures in a normal population. She wrote papers on complication rates ("they were remarkably low—20,000 abortions with no deaths and a 0.9 complication rate"). She collaborated on a study of the use of antibiotics after outpatient abortion, which helped to establish standard procedures for the many abortion clinics that in a few years would develop across the country. Also, during her stay in Washington, Hodgson increasingly took on a public role of medical spokesperson for the freestanding clinic, giving interviews and writing articles and letters to journals, which argued for the medical safety of outpatient abortion. Indeed, the Preterm experience was so compelling to Hodgson that she did not return to Minnesota in the immediate aftermath of the *Roe* decision in January 1973 but stayed in Washington for another nine months: "I thought that this was kind of important, not to come tearing right back. I thought if I did, it would kind of minimize the importance of what I had been doing out there. So I deliberately stayed . . . both for political reasons and because there was still work to be done. I hated to relinquish the platform of medical director of Preterm, I was doing a lot of speaking." After Hodgson's return to Minnesota, she became very involved in establishing abortion services, both in the Twin Cities area and in the rest of the state.[17]

Hodgson's professional immersion in abortion, which grew out of the test case experience, also transformed her politically. She became very vis-

[17]Hodgson was instrumental in founding the Women's Health Center in Duluth, which is currently the only place outside the Twin Cities area where women can obtain an abortion in Minnesota. However, no Duluth-based physician is willing to work in the clinic, and thus Hodgson today, at the age of seventy-five, commutes once a week to Duluth to perform abortions there, along with three other commuting physicians. See Lisa Belkin, "Women in Rural Areas Face Many Barriers to Abortions," *New York Times* (July 11, 1989); and Cynthia Gorney, "Hodgson's Choice: A Long, Cold Abortion Fight," *Washington Post* (November 29, 1989).

ible in the media as a spokesperson for abortion rights; she served as an expert witness in a number of cases involving accusations of abortion malpractice; she was involved, as plaintiff, in numerous court actions in Minnesota seeking to expand or protect existing abortion services.[18] In short, over the course of a few years, she went from being a conventionally successful obstetrician/gynecologist in private practice, prominent in mainstream medical politics (she served a term as president of the Minnesota Obstetrical Society), to being the most visible abortion activist in the medical community in her state. This transformation inevitably led her to rethink earlier assumptions about mainstream medicine and her place within it: "I think frankly I got turned off to the medical profession and with organized medicine. . . . Originally, I wanted respectability and to get to the top of things medically, and politically too, when I got out of med school, but I came to realize that's not for me. I don't admire organized medicine for many reasons—doctors have become too greedy, and many of them are too narrow in their perspective."

The events that flowed from her decision to perform the test case abortion also created enormous changes in Hodgson's social life. People who had been close friends and colleagues for years abruptly cut off ties with her—"My favorite nurse in the office, I had delivered all her kids, I haven't seen her since I did that abortion." Two particularly painful episodes occurred: she was shunned by some former classmates when Carleton College (her undergraduate institution) honored her, and then, after her return from Washington, she was accorded a cold reception when she gave a paper at the Minnesota Obstetrical Society—where she had been president only a few years previously. At the same time, her political/professional transformation brought a new set of social ties that have been immensely satisfying—"the pluses outweighed the losses—I have traveled in circles I wouldn't have traveled in, made friends I never would have made. If I hadn't gotten involved in this, I would have gone through life, probably being perfectly satisfied to go to the medical society parties. I would have been bored silly."

## CONCLUSION

In thinking about the relationship between the pre- and post-*Roe* phases of each of these physicians' careers, certain similarities emerge. Each of the three individuals described here found abortion work sufficiently compelling that it became a central focus of his or her lifetime work: Fieldstone, as

---

[18]One of the two major abortion cases before the Supreme Court in the 1990 session (argued but not announced as of this writing) is Hodgson v. State of Minnesota, a case about parental notification in cases of teenagers seeking abortion.

a professor of obstetrics/gynecology at a leading medical school, has put tremendous effort into training residents in abortion procedures and has continued his own research on abortion techniques; Hodgson, in addition to the activities mentioned above, has written an important textbook on abortion.[19] Bennett, while running two successful outpatient clinics, has continued his pioneering work in pain management and counseling in the abortion process. All three have been prominently involved in the activities of the National Abortion Federation (NAF), an association of abortion providers, since the organization's founding shortly after *Roe*.

Yet in spite of the undeniable successes of their individual careers and the affirmation and colleagueship they receive at groups such as NAF, all three of these respondents expressed considerable bitterness about the abortion climate in this country post-*Roe*. In part, it is because these physicians, who had experienced such stress before *Roe*, in no way anticipated the rise of the antiabortion movement that would soon become so disruptive. Bennett expressed this most poignantly: "I was working in a clinic the day when the news [of the *Roe v. Wade* decision] came over the radio. It was just an overwhelming feeling, I got tears in my eyes. . . . At last it was all over, finally. Never again will I have to fear the threats, the violence, the constant harassment, the fear of women not being able to get service. I was naive . . . in fact, it became more difficult, not easier. Since it's been legal I've had much more personal harassment."

Each of these physicians has been the target of antiabortion actions, both at home and at the workplace, with Bennett, as the operator of two private clinics, receiving the most violent treatment, including several fire-bombings at his office.[20] But beyond the stress caused by antiabortionists, all three also described with great bitterness the relationship of the medical establishment and abortion since *Roe*. In spite of legalization, these three physicians said, abortion never has been fully accepted by mainstream medicine, particularly by the most relevant specialty of obstetrics/gynecology, and those who provide abortion have had to pay a price. Each of these distinguished practitioners can point to a host of abortion-related incidents, some merely painful at the personal level, others more consequential: silent treatment or insults from colleagues, withheld promotions or honors that might otherwise be expected, a cold reception to abortion-related research

[19]Jane Hodgson, ed., *Abortion and Sterilization: Medical and Social Aspects* (New York, 1981).

[20]In 1989, there were 201 incidents of blockades at clinics and private offices offering abortion; 24 "invasions" of abortion facilities; 12 assault and battery incidents against clinic personnel and patients; and a total of 12,358 arrests in connection with clinic and office disruptions ("Incidents of Violence and Disruption against Abortion Providers" [National Abortion Federation, Washington, DC, 1990]).

by editors of important journals and organizers of sessions at professional meetings.[21]

The marginalization that these three abortion providers have experienced at the individual level is mirrored by the larger picture of abortion provision in the United States. Currently, only about one third of all practicing obstetrician/gynecologists provide abortions, and the number of residencies that routinely provide training in abortions is decreasing.[22] Eighty-two percent of all counties in the United States do not have abortion providers within them.[23] And in the wake of the *Webster* decision in 1989, which invited states to impose their own restrictions on abortion services, a new antiabortion strategy became apparent in some state legislatures—that is, to propose legislation that imposes severe penalties on physicians who provide abortions in certain contexts, while not penalizing women who obtain such abortions.

In starkest terms, then, women's right to legal abortion in the United States is threatened not only by the prospect of a direct overturning of *Roe v. Wade* but also by a growing crisis in the supply of abortion providers. There is no one simple solution to this complex problem, but clearly one important strategy the prochoice movement must develop is to confront the negative image that many people have of the abortionist (a negative image that stems, in part, from the political capital that the movement has gotten from dwelling on the butchers of the pre-*Roe* era). One element of such a strategy must be to broaden movement discourse about the pre-*Roe* era to encompass the genuine heroism that characterized some providers of illegal abortion.

[21]For an important discussion of the culture of abortion provision—and the sanctions against abortion providers—in a medium-sized community, see Jonathan Imber, *Abortion and the Private Practice of Medicine* (New Haven, CT, 1986). See also Gina Kolata, "Under Pressures and Stigma, More Doctors Shun Abortion," *New York Times* (January 8, 1990); Delia O'Hara, "Abortion: MDs Who Do Them and Those Who Won't," *American Medical News* (December 8, 1989), pp. 17, 27–29.

[22]Philip Darney et al., "Abortion Training in U.S. Obstetrics and Gynecology Residency Programs," *Family Planning Perspectives* 19 (1987): 158–62.

[23]"Hospitals Have Essential Role in Abortion Services," factsheet (National Abortion Federation, Washington, DC, 1989).

# Disclosure and Secrecy among Gay Men in the United States and Canada: A Shift in Views

ROY CAIN

*School of Social Work*
*McMaster University*

THE REDEFINITION of homosexuality as nonpathological is one of the more thoroughly explored examples of the normalization of a behavior that was once viewed as deviant. The decision of the American Psychiatric Association (APA) in 1974 to delete the diagnostic classification of homosexuality is cited as an example of "demedicalization," or the process by which a previously defined medical concern is reinterpreted in terms other than illness or pathology. Several studies have examined moves within the APA to redefine homosexuality as a nonpathological variation of sexual expression.[1] The focus of research on the demedicalization of homosexuality has, however, distracted attention from an accompanying process that pathologized a new aspect of gay sexuality. When homosexuality was considered pathological, secretiveness about one's homosexuality was widely viewed as normal and desirable; openness, conversely, was seen as an expression of personal and social pathology and as a political liability to gays in general. In contrast, when homosexuality was normalized, openness about one's homosexual preferences came to be viewed as desirable, while secretiveness came to be seen as problematic. Disclosing one's homosexual preferences, especially to nongay others, is now considered to be psycho-

An earlier version of this paper was presented at the annual meetings of the Society for the Study of Social Problems, Berkeley, August 1989. The author thanks Prue Rains, Dorothy Pawluch, Jane Aronson, and Eli Teram for their comments.

[1] Ronald Bayer, *Homosexuality and American Psychiatry: The Politics of Diagnosis*, 2d ed. (New York, 1982); Peter Conrad and Joseph Schneider, *Deviance and Medicalization: From Badness to Sickness* (Toronto, 1980), pp. 204–11; Judd Marmor, "Epilogue: Homosexuality and the Issue of Mental Illness," in *Homosexual Behavior: A Modern Reprisal*, ed. Judd Marmor (New York, 1980), pp. 391–401; Malcolm Spector, "Legitimizing Homosexuality," *Society* 14 (1977): 52–56.

This essay originally appeared in the *Journal of the History of Sexuality* 1991, vol. 2, no. 1.

logically advantageous to the individual gay person and politically advantageous to the gay community.

This essay examines the shift in how three groups in the United States and Canada have viewed disclosure and secrecy: mental health professionals, gay political activists, and sociologists. The essay describes the position taken by each group in the 1950s and 1960s on the question of whether gays should reveal their homosexuality to others and contrasts these earlier positions with more recent conceptualizations of how gays should manage personal information concerning their sexual preferences. The shift in views concerning disclosure and secrecy is then described in light of recent work on normalization and social control. The new views of disclosure of homosexuality may help to free gays from their oppressive social situation, but paradoxically they may contribute further to controlling them by individualizing and depoliticizing gay concerns. This article does not address disclosure and secrecy among lesbians because there are important gender-based differences in the regulation of sexual behavior and in its significance for the personal identity of men and women. A separate analysis is required to understand how these different expectations shape contemporary thinking on how lesbians should manage information relating to their sexual preferences.

## SECRECY AS NORMALITY: DISCLOSURE AS DEVIANCE

Until the late 1960s and early 1970s, mental health professionals, gay political activists, and sociologists valued secretiveness among gay men more than overtness. While authors from these three perspectives agreed that it was desirable for gays to exercise discretion in the expression of their homosexuality and to avoid making public disclosures about their sexual preferences, they had somewhat different rationales for their points of view.

The dominant clinical position on homosexuality during the 1950s and 1960s held that it was a psychopathological condition. As others have observed, most psychological research of this period examined questions relating to the etiology, classification, and treatment of homosexual preferences.[2] Homosexuality was listed as a "sociopathic personality disturbance" in the American Psychiatric Association's list of mental illnesses, the *Diagnostic and Statistical Manual of Mental Disorders,* or *DSM-I.*[3] When the second edition of the *Diagnostic and Statistical Manual (DSM-II)* was released in 1968, homosexuality was classified as a "sexual deviation" along

[2]Stephan Moran, "Heterosexual Bias in Psychological Research on Lesbianism and Male Homosexuality," *American Psychologist* 32 (1977): 629–37; Martin Weinberg and Alan Bell, eds., *Homosexuality: An Annotated Bibliography* (New York, 1972).

[3]American Psychiatric Association, *Diagnostic and Statistical Manual of Mental Disorders* (Washington, DC: 1952).

with fetishism, pedophilia, transvestitism, exhibitionism, voyeurism, sadism, and masochism.

Homosexuality was viewed during the late 1940s and early 1950s as hard to treat, with the result that homosexuals often were not accepted as patients. By the 1960s, American psychiatrists such as Edmund Bergler, Irving Bieber, and Charles Socarides argued that while homosexuality was a serious mental disturbance, it was often curable through psychoanalytic treatment.[4] These authors dominated the clinical perspective on homosexuality with their etiological view that a homosexual orientation in adulthood was the result of disordered psychosexual development in childhood. For instance, Bieber argued that the presence of a seductive or dominant mother and a detached and hostile father was an important cause of homosexuality in men. The goal of psychiatric treatment was to "cure" the individual by helping him resolve developmental conflicts and develop heterosexual interests.

The manner in which gays managed information about their homosexuality was not an important concern in the mental health literature. However, the dominant clinical position implied that revealing oneself as homosexual was undesirable. The subjective distress or guilt that kept the patient from divulging his homosexuality to others was seen as evidence of a promising degree of normality and, therefore, as a good prognostic indicator that heterosexuality might be achieved through psychotherapy. Guilt was seen as "the vehicle for therapeutic changes in psychiatric treatment."[5] Often speaking of his homosexual patients in derogatory and abusive terms, Bergler argued that homosexuals who were distressed by their sexual orientation suffered from neurotic homosexuality, while those who did not feel guilty about their sexual orientation—those who were more likely to tell others about it—suffered from perverted homosexuality. Perverted homosexuals were viewed as fixated at an earlier stage of psychosexual development and, therefore, were seen to suffer from a more profound form of psychological disturbance than neurotic homosexuals.[6] Their willingness to proclaim their homosexuality was not seen by Bergler to be an expression of self-acceptance, as it would be viewed by many clinicians today, but as an attempt on the part of perverted homosexuals to "satisfy neurotic pseudo-aggression."[7] The dominant clinical perspective would have regarded a homosexual patient's claim that his sexual preferences were

---

[4]Irving Bieber et al., *Homosexuality: A Psychoanalytic Study* (New York, 1962); Edmund Bergler, *Counterfeit Sex: Homosexuality, Frigidity, and Impotence* (New York, 1956), and *Homosexuality: Disease or Way of Life?* (New York, 1957); Charles Socarides, *The Overt Homosexual* (New York, 1968).

[5]Bergler, *Counterfeit Sex*, p. 25.

[6]Kenneth Lewes, *The Psychoanalytic Theory of Male Homosexuality* (New York, 1988), pp. 95–121.

[7]Bergler, *Homosexuality*, p. 281.

acceptable and healthy as symptomatic of his disturbed psychological condition; revealing these preferences would have been viewed as a further indication of the individual's degree of psychological disturbance.

Since the prevailing belief about homosexuality during the 1950s was that it was a mental illness, many of those involved in the development of the gay movement saw homosexuality as pathological.[8] Evidence challenging this view was provided in the Kinsey Report on male sexual behavior.[9] Alfred Kinsey, a biologist from Indiana University, reached celebrity status with the publication of his report on male sexuality and, later, with his report on female sexuality.[10] The work of Kinsey and his colleagues provided evidence that showed the prevalence of homosexual behavior to be much higher than previously imagined. The reports directly challenged the notion that homosexuality represented mental disorder. Kinsey stated that it was "difficult to maintain the view that psychosexual reactions between individuals of the same sex are rare and therefore abnormal or unnatural, or that they constitute within themselves evidence of neurosis or even psychosis."[11] Homosexuality, he argued, should be seen as a natural and nonpathological phenomenon.

Kinsey's research and the public debate it stirred in the United States helped to legitimate discussion of homosexuality and spur the growth of a gay political movement.[12] Other researchers also provided the new movement with the intellectual and rhetorical resources it needed to contest the dominant psychiatric view of homosexuality as pathology and to organize an effective political force.[13] The cross-cultural and cross-species research of Clellan Ford and Frank Beach showed that homosexual behavior occurred in most, if not all, mammals and in most societies,[14] and Evelyn Hooker demonstrated that projective tests used by psychologists could not differentiate homosexual men from heterosexual men.[15] Findings such as these challenged the conventional presumption of pathology and were employed as political resources by gay organizers.

[8] See Daniel Webster Cory, *The Homosexual in America: A Subjective Approach* (New York, 1951).

[9] Alfred Kinsey, Wardell Pomeroy, and Clyde Martin, *Sexual Behavior in the Human Male* (Philadelphia, 1948).

[10] Alfred Kinsey, Wardell Pomeroy, Clyde Martin, and Paul Gebhard, *Sexual Behavior in the Human Female* (Philadelphia, 1953).

[11] Kinsey, Pomeroy, and Martin, p. 659.

[12] Laud Humphreys, *Coming Out: The Sociology of Homosexual Liberation* (Englewood Cliffs, NJ, 1972), p. 59; Edward Sagarin, *Odd Man In: Societies of Deviants in America* (Chicago, 1969), p. 82.

[13] For an account of this period, see Bayer (n. 1 above), pp. 41–62.

[14] Clellan Ford and Frank Beach, *Patterns of Sexual Behavior* (New York, 1952), pp. 132–51.

[15] Evelyn Hooker, "The Adjustment of the Male Overt Homosexual," *Journal of Projective Techniques* 21 (1957): 18–31.

Gay political groups in the 1950s and 1960s advocated increased tolerance, acceptance, and the gradual integration of homosexual individuals into the society at large.[16] The homophile movement, as it was then called, shared many of the liberal assumptions of the early civil rights movements of blacks and women. The movement adopted a stance that stressed the similarities between homosexuals and heterosexuals and the importance of education in reducing discrimination and injustice. Toby Marotta, a historian of the American gay political movement, described the "basic homophile outlook" as "the belief that prejudice, stereotyping, and discrimination were the source of the homosexual's problems and that education, policy reform, and help for individual homosexuals would bring about the recognition of basic similarity, equality of treatment and integration that were tantamount to social progress."[17] Those involved in the homophile movement worked to eliminate discrimination and injustice, but their social and political activities were characteristically cautious and measured.

Disclosure of homosexuality to others was not often encouraged by those in the homophile movement. The first major national gay group in the United States, the Mattachine Society, founded in 1950 and named after the "medieval court jesters who told the truth to kings while hiding behind masks," stressed the importance of remaining secret about one's homosexuality.[18] The rather cryptic name of the organization was chosen to avoid being easily identified as a group for homosexual men, and, like other homophile groups, it denied that its membership was exclusively homosexual.[19] The Mattachine Society tried to keep a low public profile and to appear professional and nonpolitical. Emphasis was placed on the group's research and educational functions. Organizers were careful not to offend the public or government officials or to take any action that might attract undue publicity, fearing that this might jeopardize the organization or otherwise hamper its efforts to promote change. They felt that public confrontations and "flaunting one's sexuality" would hinder the movement's chances for promoting acceptance of gays.

The cautious stance of homophile groups reflected their concern about the safety of their members, as well as their own viability. Homosexual men faced real risks at this point in American history, even those who attempted to steer clear of overt political activity. They risked severe social sanctions such as rejection by nongays, arrest, termination of employment, or harassment. Many gays nevertheless involved themselves in homophile activities

[16]Toby Marotta, *The Politics of Homosexuality* (Boston, 1981); Bruce Voeller, "Society and the Gay Movement," in Marmor, ed. (n. 1 above), p. 232.

[17]Marotta, p. 11.

[18]Humphreys, *Coming Out,* p. 52.

[19]Dennis Altman, "What Changed in the Seventies?" in *Homosexuality: Power and Politics,* ed. Gay Left Collective (New York, 1980), p. 58; Marotta, p. 15.

and revealed themselves to selected others, but they typically were concerned with how nongays would perceive them and the movement as a whole. Disclosure was not generally seen as personally necessary or strategically important in this context. Indeed, for the most part, it represented a personal and political threat.

Sociologists in North America paid little attention to homosexuality before the 1960s. Maurice Leznoff and William Westley published one of the earliest sociological studies of homosexuality in 1956.[20] Their research was the first major ethnography of an urban homosexual community and the only study until the early 1970s to deal directly with the issue of secrecy and disclosure. Their analysis is of particular interest because it is organized around the distinction between "secret" and "overt" homosexual men. The authors viewed the Canadian homosexual community they studied as being composed of two distinct groups: men who kept their homosexuality secret from nongays and men who did not. This dichotomy today appears to be an oversimplification of how gays actually structure their lives, but it nonetheless represented an important step toward a greater appreciation of the complexities of gay communities.

Secret homosexuals were observed by Leznoff and Westley to hold higher status jobs; they found themselves compelled to conform to social demands, were conscious of their social position, and sought occupational mobility and prestige. Members of secret homosexual social groups were seen to hold diverse interests and occupations. There were informal standards of admission to the groups, and members exercised discretion in the manner in which homosexuality was practiced and took extensive precautions to conceal their homosexuality from others. Overt homosexuals, by contrast, were seen to "retreat from the demands of society and renounce societal goals."[21] They held lower status jobs than did secret homosexuals and were less concerned with occupational advancement. Members of overt homosexual social groups were described as spending their time "in endless gossip about the sexual affairs of [other] members." Leznoff and Westley also observed no standards of admission to the social groups of overt men and noted an "unselfconscious and unrestrained practice of homosexuality."[22] The sociological perspective thus viewed overtness as characteristic of the less occupationally successful and more marginal members of the homosexual world.

## DISCLOSURE AS NORMALITY: SECRECY AS DEVIANCE

The 1960s witnessed an increasing militancy on the part of many groups that previously had been defined as deviant. A number of those stigmatized

[20]Maurice Leznoff and William Westley, "The Homosexual Community," *Social Problems* 3 (1956): 257–63.
[21]Ibid., p. 260.
[22]Ibid., p. 262.

mobilized to "declare their presence openly and without apology to claim the rights of citizenship";[23] they rejected others' definitions of them and defined themselves as "oppressed" rather than "deviant." By the end of the decade many gay groups had also become more radical in their views. Rather than stressing the similarities between gays and nongays and requesting understanding and tolerance, as the earlier, liberally oriented homophile groups had done, new radical organizations demanded legal rights and social opportunities for gays and adopted an overtly political and confrontational orientation. Activists focused their attention on oppressive social institutions, rather than focusing primarily on the adjustment and assimilation of gay individuals. They rejected the idea that homosexuality was a mental illness and took aim at mental health professionals. Significant political differences existed among radical activists, but there was general agreement that gays should develop pride in themselves and assert their legitimacy, build a strong community, and demand greater political power. As Jeffrey Weeks observed in the British context during this period, "the axioms of 'gay pride,' 'coming out' and 'coming together' . . . reinforced each other as necessary components of a new homosexual identity."[24]

Disclosure became a central strategy of the gay movement. Confronting others with one's homosexuality came to be viewed as the principal way for gay individuals to bring about social change. Rather than representing a personal and political danger, self-revelation held out the promise of bringing about real change in the social situation of gays and of overcoming the self-hatred and shame they often feel. Secrecy, on the other hand, was no longer seen as a rational and justifiable choice. It was instead held up as an indicator of self-oppression and as one of the major reasons for the ongoing oppression of gays. The individual and the community both were seen by activists as benefiting from self-disclosure. On an individual level, disclosure was viewed as necessary to achieve a positive gay identity and as evidence that one no longer held ideas and attitudes that led to self-oppression. In their anthology from the *Body Politic*, a Canadian gay liberation journal published from 1971 until 1987, Ed Jackson and Stan Persky argued that "to come out of the closet was an affirmation that gay is good. It was the proud assumption of a homosexual identity. It has been, in many ways, the gay movement's central political act."[25] Gays were told not to concern themselves with respectability or with how others would react to the disclosure; they were urged to be nonapologetic and assertive. Reject-

---

[23]John Kitsuse, "Coming Out All Over," *Social Problems* 28 (1980): 3.

[24]Jeffrey Weeks, *Sex, Politics and Society: The Regulation of Sexuality since 1800*, Themes in British Social History (London, 1981), p. 286.

[25]Ed Jackson and Stan Persky, "Victories and Defeats: A Gay and Lesbian Chronology, 1964–1982," in *Flaunting It! A Decade of Gay Journalism from the Body Politic*, ed. Ed Jackson and Stan Persky (Toronto, 1982), p. 224.

ing the polite and deferent stance that characterized the homophile movement, activists advocated "public, indiscriminate, indiscreet self-disclosure."[26]

A link was thus made between individual action and political change; "the personal is political" was a popular slogan with gays, as it was with feminists and other groups on the political Left. The gay movement of this period also shared the militancy of the New Left. One activist stated that telling others of his homosexuality was "the aggressive statement of what I am and what I am fighting for. It is part of my refusal to be invisible."[27] Increased visibility through public disclosure was said to promote political change in three ways. First, it would demonstrate that gays were a sizable minority of the population; recognition of the large number of gays would help to undermine the belief that they were sick or immoral and would highlight their potential political power. Second, by revealing themselves as "ordinary" people, gays would break down the negative stereotypic images that perpetuated their oppression. Finally, increased visibility would help younger gays to more easily recognize and accept their own sexual preferences and feel less isolated.

Mental health professionals and their "treatment" of homosexuality became a key concern for radical activists in the late 1960s. The dominant view of homosexuality held by mental health professionals changed in the late 1960s and early 1970s. Although there was still considerable support for the conventional pathology-based view of homosexuality, particularly among psychoanalytically trained clinicians,[28] an increasing number of mental health professionals began to support the position that homosexuality was not a psychopathological condition.[29] Mounting pressure from gay activists coupled with political divisions within the American Psychiatric Association led to a debate within the organization over the official definition of homosexuality as a mental illness.[30]

---

[26]Andrew Hodges and David Hutter, *With Downcast Gays: Aspects of Homosexual Self-Oppression* (Toronto, 1974), p. 18.

[27]Gerald Hannon, "Throat-ramming," in Jackson and Persky, eds., p. 10.

[28]Irving Bieber, "Homosexuality: An Adaptive Consequence of Disorder in Psychosexual Development," *American Journal of Psychiatry* 130 (1973): 1209–11; Lawrence Hatterer, *Changing Homosexuality in the Male* (New York, 1970); Leon Ovesey, *Homosexuality and Pseudohomosexuality* (New York, 1969); Charles Socarides, *The Overt Homosexual* (n. 4 above), and *Beyond Sexual Freedom* (New York, 1974), pp. 81–112.

[29]Martin Hoffman, *The Gay World: Male Homosexuality and the Social Creation of Evil* (New York, 1968); Judd Marmor, "Homosexuality and Cultural Value Systems," *American Journal of Psychiatry* 130 (1973): 1209; C. A. Tripp, *The Homosexual Matrix* (New York, 1975); George Weinberg, *Society and the Healthy Homosexual* (New York, 1972).

[30]For a detailed description of this debate, see Bayer (n. 1 above), pp. 101–54; Conrad and Schneider (n. 1 above), pp. 204–9; Marmor, "Epilogue" (n. 1 above), pp. 391–401; Spector (n. 1 above), pp. 52–56.

Gay activists and some mental health professionals argued that homosexuality was a variation in human sexual expression and that it should not be considered as a pathological condition.[31] The opposing view was held by those psychiatrists who believed that homosexuality should continue to be considered and classified as a mental disorder.[32] A compromise position between the two groups was eventually reached: homosexuality was deleted as a diagnostic category and a new diagnostic classification, sexual orientation disturbance, was introduced.[33] Sexual orientation disturbance, which referred to individuals unhappy with their homosexual preference, was replaced by a new category, ego dystonic homosexuality, in the third edition of the APA's *Diagnostic and Statistical Manual of Mental Disorders (DSM-III)*, published in 1979. All reference to homosexuality was dropped in the 1986 revision of *DSM-III*, after gay-positive professionals and activists successfully argued that the retention of the classification of ego dystonic homosexuality stigmatized gays and served no clinical or research function.[34] The original inclusion of sexual orientation disturbance (and later, ego dystonic homosexuality) in *DSM* was widely viewed as a politically necessary compromise in the debate to declassify homosexuality.[35] At the same time, however, the categories reflected a growing acceptance among mental health professionals of the normative concept of a "healthy" gay identity.

As the diagnostic status of homosexuality was being debated in the early 1970s, some clinicians began to address explicitly the issue of disclosure.[36] Consistent with the position of gay activists, these professionals argued that the social and psychological problems that confronted many gay men stemmed from their covert existences, rather than from their sexual preferences per se. This assertion was fundamental to the argument that there was nothing inherently pathological about homosexuality. Alan Bell, a psychologist from the Kinsey Institute, stated that covertness led some gays to "compartmentalize their sexual lives in ways that do them little good. They

[31]Marmor, "Homosexuality and Cultural Value Systems," p. 1209; Ronald Gold, "Stop It, You're Making Me Sick," *American Journal of Psychiatry* 130 (1973): 1211–12.

[32]See, for example, Bieber, "Homosexuality: An Adaptive Consequence," p. 1209.

[33]American Psychiatric Association, "Position Statement on Homosexuality and Civil Rights," *American Journal of Psychiatry* 131 (1974): 497.

[34]Bayer, pp. 208–18.

[35]Ibid.; Socarides, *Beyond Sexual Freedom;* Robert Spitzer, "The Diagnostic Status of Homosexuality in DSM-III: A Reformulation of the Issues," *American Journal of Psychiatry* 138 (1981): 210–15.

[36]Alan Bell, "The Homosexual as Patient," in *Sex Research: Studies from the Kinsey Institute,* ed. Martin Weinberg (London, 1976); Evelyn Hooker, "The Homosexual Community," in *Sexual Deviance,* ed. John Gagnon and William Simon (New York, 1965), pp. 167–84; F. Myrich, "Homosexual Types: An Empirical Investigation," *Journal of Sex Research* 10 (1974): 226–37.

frequently experience a great deal of tension in pretending to be what they are not, a profound disparity between their inner and outer selves."[37] Clinicians argued that the inability of gays to tell their families and friends about their sexual orientation led to feelings of estrangement from others, a sense of alienation from society, and a tendency to isolate sex from emotional commitment and affection; covertness was associated with low self-esteem, social isolation, and a sense of powerlessness and incompetence. Healthy acceptance of one's gayness was now widely viewed as requiring self-revelation. One observer has noted, "Achieving a positive gay identity appears to be contingent upon disclosing one's sexual orientation to significant non-gay others."[38]

Several clinical models of identity development among gay men have been advanced since the APA reclassification decision.[39] These models aim to organize the major "milestone events" in a stage-sequential process. Most models include consideration of such issues as feelings on the part of young gays of being different from others, their growing awareness of an attraction to others of the same gender, self-labeling as homosexual, involvement in first gay relationships, and adoption of a gay life-style. While the various models differ on what events they include and their timing, they all view the revelation of one's sexuality to others as an important milestone event. Movement through the stages described by the models is assumed to be positive growth and, therefore, psychologically desirable: those gays who are at a more advanced stage of the process are more psychologically healthy than others. They are seen as being less likely to develop a "negative or self-hating identity."[40] Movement through the stages is seen to lead to "a healthier and more mature outlook."[41] Gays who complete the identity development process, in which disclosure to others is an important part, are clearly seen as more psychologically adjusted and socially skilled than those who do not.

Professional counselors are now advised by new gay-positive authors to help gay individuals decide whom to tell and how to make the revelation.[42] While recognizing the risks involved in making some disclosures, there is now general agreement in the literature that self-revelation should be encouraged to promote the development of a healthy gay identity. In Britain,

[37]Bell, p. 210.

[38]Gary McDonald, "Individual Differences in the Coming Out Process of Gay Men: Implication of Theoretical Models," *Journal of Homosexuality* 8 (1984): 54.

[39]See, for example, Raymond Berger, "What Is a Homosexual? A Definitional Model," *Social Work* 28 (1983): 132–41; Vivienne Cass, "Homosexual Identity Formation: A Theoretical Model," *Journal of Homosexuality* 4 (1979): 219–35; Eli Coleman, "Developmental Stages of the Coming-Out Process," *American Behavioral Scientist* 25 (1982): 469–82.

[40]Cass, p. 224.

[41]Coleman, p. 470.

[42]Natalie Woodman and Harry Lenna, *Counseling with Gay Men and Women* (New York, 1980).

clinical psychologists Glenys Parry and Ray Lightbown suggest that counselors discuss with covert gay clients the risks of overtness and the
advantages of developing an integrated self-concept. But they offer this
caution: "The gay person who says, 'I accept my homosexuality, but I don't
see why I should tell anyone else about it, it's my own business,' is likely, in
our experience, to be whistling in the dark. Such a statement may reflect
considerable uncertainty about whether one is deep down lovable, basically
OK."[43] Their position illustrates the degree to which disclosure has now
been associated with mental health and shows how secrecy can now be
viewed as a priori evidence of problems in psychological adjustment.

There are parallels here with the process that Donileen Loseke and
Spenser Cahill described in their sociological study of the new views of
domestic violence and the treatment of battered women.[44] They observed
that professional experts on battered women now encourage them to leave
their abusive spouses. The competence of women who choose to return to
their abusive home situations can be called into question. "In effect, experts discredit the ability of a category of persons to manage their own
affairs without interference. The actors in question are portrayed as incapable of either understanding or controlling the factors which govern their
behavior. In order for them to understand their experiences and gain control over their behavior, by implication, they require the assistance of
specialized experts."[45] Women who previously would have been encouraged to return home are now often advised to leave. Those who do not
leave may be seen as suffering from emotional overdependence or poor self-
image or as holding traditional ideas about relationships and, therefore, as
requiring some form of assistance.[46]

In a similar fashion, the new normative views of disclosure and secrecy
mean that gays' own explanations of their covertness now can be reinterpreted as evidence of a poor self-esteem or an internalized negative image
of homosexuality. Parry and Lightbown state, "The person whose self-
esteem is so fragile as to be threatened by the thought of others 'knowing' is
likely to be acting from a basis of self-depreciation, not trusting her or his
own experiences of her or himself."[47] Like most clinicians, they recognize
that secrecy can be a rational choice made by gays in difficult social situations; however, secrecy now can be associated with emotional problems in
a way that would not have been possible previously as a result of the re-

[43]Glenys Parry and Ray Lightbown, "Presenting Problems of Gay People Seeking Help,"
in *The Theory and Practice of Homosexuality*, ed. John Hart and Dianne Richardson (London,
1981), p. 162.

[44]Donileen Loseke and Spenser Cahill, "The Social Construction of Deviance: Experts
on Battered Women," *Social Problems* 31 (1984): 296–310.

[45]Ibid., p. 305.

[46]Ibid., p. 300.

[47]Parry and Lightbown, p. 162.

definition of homosexuality and the advent of the new models of gay identity development.[48]

The contemporary sociological position on disclosure differs markedly from that expressed by Leznoff and Westley in 1956. In the 1970s, sociologists began presenting overt homosexuality in positive terms and covert homosexuality in negative terms. Secrecy came to be associated with a range of personal and social problems. When compared to overt men, covert homosexual men were seen to have a lower self-concept, more health-related complaints and psychophysiological symptoms, a greater degree of social isolation, a greater likelihood of internalizing negative images of homosexuality, a greater degree of guilt and anxiety relating to their sexuality, and greater social awkwardness.[49] The contemporary sociological position on the disclosure of homosexuality now is consistent with the dominant mental health position, and, in fact, several sociologists have presented models of identity formation that are similar to the clinical models, which view disclosure as an important element of a positive gay identity.[50]

The new views of disclosure and secrecy are also reflected in the vocabulary employed by sociologists. Laud Humphreys, who played an important role in the development of the new gay-positive sociological views, used the term "closet queens," which reveals a negative evaluation of secrecy; closet queen is a derogatory term that implies that the covert individual is an outsider to the gay community.[51] The respondents he classified as closet queens were seen by Humphreys to experience higher degrees of psychophysiological symptoms, self-hatred, and loneliness than any of the other four types of gay men he described. Like Humphreys, Barry Dank also employed the term and suggested that these men were more likely to internalize negative images of homosexuality than were overt gays. British sociologist Kenneth Plummer clearly concurs with the association between covertness and personal and social problems when he states, "Coming-out to the straight world is often the first sign that the homosexual person has successfully navigated his own problems and has moved on to those of

[48]See Richard Isay, *Being Homosexual: Gay Men and Their Development* (New York, 1989), for an example of a more moderate viewpoint on disclosure.

[49]Barry Dank, "Coming Out in the Gay World," *Psychiatry* 34 (1971): 180–97; Laud Humphreys, *Tearoom Trade: Impersonal Sex in Public Places* (Chicago, 1970), pp. 125–29; Martin Weinberg and Colin Williams, *Male Homosexuals: Their Problems and Adaptations* (New York, 1974), pp. 248–61.

[50]Kenneth Plummer, *Sexual Stigma: An Interactionist Account* (London, 1975); Richard Troiden, "Becoming Homosexual: A Model of Gay Identity Acquisition," *Psychiatry* 42 (1979): 362–73; Thomas Weinberg, *Gay Men, Gay Selves: The Social Construction of Homosexual Identities* (New York, 1983).

[51]Humphreys, *Tearoom Trade*, p. 125; Carol Warren, *Identity and Community in the Gay World* (New York, 1974), p. 125.

others."[52] Interestingly, the manner in which disclosure and secrecy are portrayed has changed despite the sociological research that suggests that gay men continue to be covert in many of their social interactions.[53]

Homosexuality continues to be highly stigmatized and oppression continues to be a regular feature of the lives of gays, but the social context of gay activism has changed in important ways. The radicalism of the gay movement in the early 1970s was relatively short-lived, and by 1972 Humphreys had already noted that most of the radical groups had ceased to exist. Calls for gays to disclose their sexual preferences to others, however, continued. In 1982, Dennis Altman observed, "In one sense all gay politics remains a variant on the original theme of coming out, the public assertion of homosexuality."[54] He noted that those involved in the movement had become more concerned about appearing politically correct and respectable than they had been during the more radical period. The gay movement came to rely increasingly on nongay political and social institutions to promote change. Human rights legislation was enacted in many jurisdictions in Canada and the United States that, in addition to being symbolically important, provided gays some protection against overt discrimination. Recourse to the legal system for protection from physical aggression and discrimination increased and the movement came to depend on political lobbying and the national political parties to push for legislative change.

The advent of AIDS has had a major impact on the gay movement and on the degree to which many gay men are open with others. Some gays are more reluctant to reveal their sexual preferences, fearing an "antigay backlash" as a result of AIDS. Others find themselves compelled to acknowledge their sexuality to others when they discover they are HIV-positive, as the diagnosis of HIV infection may reveal a previously undisclosed history of homosexual activity. For many gays, the AIDS crisis underlines the importance of self-disclosure. Homophobia and the covertness it engenders is an important factor in the AIDS crisis in that secrecy may be correlated with unsafe sexual behavior.[55] Many men identify themselves as both gay and HIV-positive in an attempt to reduce discrimination and publicize the inadequacies of government responses to the epidemic. The ideology of "the personal is political" continues to be an important element of the gay political struggle, even in the context of AIDS.

[52]Kenneth Plummer, "Going Gay: Identities, Life Cycles, and Lifestyles in the Male Gay World," in Hart and Richardson, eds., pp. 102–3.

[53]Alan Bell and Martin Weinberg, *Homosexualities: A Study in Diversity* (New York, 1978), pp. 62–68; Weinberg and Williams, pp. 248–61.

[54]Dennis Altman, *The Homosexualization of America* (New York, 1982), p. 138.

[55]See Michael Fitzpatrick and Don Milligan, *The Truth about the AIDS Crisis* (London, 1987).

The HIV epidemic has become an important preoccupation for many gay activists, diverting energy and attention previously afforded to other political and social issues. At the same time, however, the success of AIDS activism in the United States and Canada, particularly the well-publicized activities of ACT UP (AIDS Coalition to Unleash Power), has rejuvenated a more radical orientation among many gay activists. By using tactics such as loud protests and "die-ins," where groups of activists block major intersections by falling to the ground in symbolic representation of the people who have died as a result of government inaction, ACT UP has been very successful in focusing governmental and scientific attention on the epidemic and in raising the public's awareness of the problems associated with AIDS.[56] Following on the successes of ACT UP, new direct action groups calling themselves Queer Nation have started in several major cities to combat homophobia and the invisibility of gays and lesbians. Queer Nation groups are organized as nonhierarchical and collective working groups, as is ACT UP, and borrow many of its strategies. "Visibility actions" such as zaps, kiss-ins, and queer-ins aim to shock people, forcing them to recognize the existence of gay men and women and to respond to their political concerns.[57] Politically moderate gays fear that the radical tactics of groups like Queer Nation, which they view as offensive and irresponsible, may serve to alienate many gays from the political movement and to increase the hostility of nongays toward the aims of the movement. They fear that by offending people, the activities of direct action groups like Queer Nation may ultimately impede the goals of the movement.

The recent radicalization also has led to debates among gay activists about the manner in which gays should identify themselves and their communities. In the past year, the use of the words "queer" and "faggot" (and, for women, "dyke") has been the subject of considerable controversy. Once a pejorative word that was used against gays, "queer" has been substituted for the word "gay" by many activists and gay journals. Queer Nation posters proclaiming "Queers Are Everywhere" and "Queers Are Here—Get Used to It" plaster downtown areas in several cities. A Vancouver-based group, the Front for Active Gay Socialism, recently renamed itself "Queer

---

[56]For a partial history of AIDS activism in the United States and Canada, see Douglas Crimp, *AIDS Demo Graphics* (Seattle, 1990); Josh Gamson, "Silence, Death and the Invisible Enemy: AIDS Activism and Social Movement Newness," *Social Problems* 36 (1989): 351–57; Cindy Patton, *Sex and Germs: The Politics of AIDS* (Montreal, 1986).

[57]Lynn Iding, "Toronto's Queers Come Out to Kiss In," *Rites* 7 (November 1990): 3; Mark Michaud, "Queer Nation in Toronto," *Rites* 7 (October 1990): 3; Chris Nealon, "Straight Bar Throws out Queer Nation Members," *Gay Community News* (October 14–20, 1990), p. 3; Deborah Schwartz, "Queers Bash Back," *Gay Community News* (June 24–30, 1990), p. 1. Also see the series of short articles on Queer Nation appearing in *Outlook* 11 (Winter 1991): 12–23.

Action." Many gay newspapers now use the word "queer" in their head-lines and stories to refer to politically active gays. Those who support the use of words like "queer" argue that gays must reclaim homophobic dis-course to undermine its power. The intent is not only to identify oneself and others as gay, but to shock people and to challenge the oppressive use of such words. More moderate activists oppose such terminology. In Vancouver, for instance, organizers of the Gay Games 1990, an interna-tional athletic competition for gays and lesbians, debated whether to allow a show called "Queers in Art" to be associated with the games because of objections to its name. Some gays find the recent acceptance of derogatory words offensive and politically counterproductive and believe it may actu-ally legitimize the homophobia that underlies their use by many nongays.

Increased radicalism in the way gay activists view disclosure is perhaps most clearly reflected in recent debates concerning "outing."[58] Outing re-fers to publicly revealing the sexual orientation of gays who would rather remain covert. The targets of outing tend to be public figures, generally prominent actors or politicians, particularly those who support causes that are viewed as harmful to gays and lesbians. Gay activists, such as Michael Bronski, argue that outing reveals the large number of hidden gays in influ-ential positions, brings together the personal and political dimensions of gays' lives, and challenges the hypocrisy of secretive and conservative gays in positions of influence.[59] Advocates of outing note that gays do not freely choose to be secretive but are forced into the closet by the stigmatization that surrounds homosexuality; in this context, they argue, it is meaningless to speak of free choice when it comes to being open or secretive. Support-ers of outing argue that nongays have used the tactic of publicly revealing the homosexuality of others and gays are simply reclaiming a strategy that has been used against them for decades.

Those opposed to outing insist that the decision to reveal one's sexuality must remain an individual choice because secrecy protects gays from their oppressive social situation. These liberationists claim that it is unethical to force someone out of the closet who might be harmed as a result. They also argue that all gays could be harmed by condoning any disregard for the right to privacy. Gays have been fighting for the privacy to live their lives as they choose; outing thus goes against one of the fundamental aims of the movement. Moreover, they question whether forcing reluctant gays out of the closet will foster gay pride; one commentator asked, "Who wants pub-

[58]David Gelman, "'Outing': An Unexpected Assault on Sexual Privacy," *Newsweek* (April 30, 1990), p. 66; William Henry, "Forcing Gays Out of the Closet," *Time* (January 29, 1990), p. 50; Randy Shilts, "Is 'Outing' Gays Ethical?" *New York Times* (April 12, 1990), p. A23.

[59]Michael Bronski, "Outing: Challenging the Power of the Closet," *Gay Community News* (June 3–9, 1990), pp. 15–18.

lic role models who are whining, wailing, and pulling their underwear back up as they try to crawl back in the closet?"[60]

Disclosure and secrecy are central issues in the revitalized radical gay politics that has grown out of AIDS activism. Controversies surrounding "visibility actions" and tactics such as outing or reclaiming the homophobic discourse of others rekindle old discussions and debates about the oppressive power of secrecy and the utility of disclosure, and the role of militant and confrontational strategies in promoting social change. The debates surrounding the new radical actions parallel those of the late 1960s and early 1970s, when many in the homophile movement expressed concern about the confrontational activities of radical gays. The AIDS crisis has served to heighten the anger of gays as well as demonstrate the effectiveness of more radical activities. This has again drawn attention to the utility of disclosure for the gay political agenda. In doing so, it underscores divisions between radical and moderate views of the desirability of openness and the best strategies to achieve it, divisions that have been largely dormant since the mid-1970s.

## SHIFTING DEFINITIONS AND SOCIAL CONTROL

The history of the normative views of disclosure and secrecy among gays points to some of the ironies of political activism. The gay political movement and the modern gay-positive psychologies it inspired are helpful and liberating in many ways. Homosexual preferences are now often viewed as nonpathological alternatives to heterosexuality by many professionals and nonprofessionals alike. Gays are not being studied and classified by outsiders to the degree they once were, and they are more likely to receive support and compassion from their counselors. Mental health theories can no longer be used to justify homophobic laws and policies. At the same time, however, the oppressive attitudes and behaviors of others continue to be everyday features of the lives of gays, particularly those who do not live in large urban centers. Furthermore, the social control role of mental health professionals, even gay-positive ones, has not disappeared; it has been transformed. Professionals continue to play a role in interpreting and regulating gay experiences, although often an unwitting one, by promoting the desirability of self-disclosure.

There has been a political realignment among gay activists, mental health professionals, and social scientists. Activists in the early homophile movement allied themselves with mental health professionals, even though homosexuality was viewed as psychopathological and undesirable. Later,

[60]E. J. Graff, "Outing Cannibalizes Our Community," *Gay Community News* (July 29–August 4, 1990), p. 5.

radical activists came to reject the professional and social scientific views of homosexuality and to actively challenge their dominance in the field. The radical gay movement rejected the liberal assumptions of their homophile predecessors, preferring to celebrate the differences between gays and non-gays, demand civil rights, assert the naturalness of homosexuality, and proudly declare their sexual preferences. They rejected both the professional beliefs concerning the nature of homosexual preferences and the professional ideology that focuses on individual pathology and that validates the power imbalance found within conventional counselor-client relationships. They established nonprofessional counseling centers that, among other things, stressed the importance of peer support and of helping gays understand their sexuality within a broad sociopolitical context.[61] Gay radicalism eventually gave way in the 1970s to a more moderate gay movement, where talk of "oppression" and "liberation" was replaced by talk of "discrimination" and "civil rights"[62] and where gay activists again allied themselves with professionals.

The redefinition of homosexuality as nonpathological and the integration of many activists' political ideas into the new clinical models of homosexuality, coupled with the increased number of openly gay professionals, has led contemporary activists to view the new psychological experts on homosexuality as allies, not enemies, in their struggle to improve the social situation of gays. Moreover, the recent professional portrayal of the maladjusted covert homosexual supports the political ideology of gay organizations. They receive professional support and legitimization of their view of homosexuality as a nonpathological variation of human sexuality and their belief that covert homosexuality is problematic and that gays should in fact come out. Contemporary activists thus have little to gain by challenging the new models of gay identity development or the related assumptions about disclosure; they would also risk losing the "psychological establishment" as an important political resource.

The radical movement that has grown in response to the AIDS crisis directly challenges many social institutions that are oppressive to those affected by HIV. AIDS activists have taken particular aim at health care professions and professional dominance in HIV-related concerns. Many community-based AIDS organizations provide nonprofessional counseling and support services, which are often run by gays and which help people affected by HIV to understand how many of their health-related problems are shaped by the stigma surrounding AIDS and homophobia. In this way, the AIDS movement provides at least some gays with alter-

---

[61]Françoise Castel, Robert Castel, and Anne Lovell, *La société psychiatrique avancée: Le modèle américain* (Paris, 1979); Charna Klein, *Counseling Our Own: The Lesbian/Gay Subculture Meets the Mental Health System* (Seattle, 1986).

[62]Altman, *The Homosexualization of America,* p. 125.

native and politically progressive mental health services. Despite these new AIDS organizations and the challenges they pose for mental health professionals, the psychological study of gays and interventions into their lives continue to be legitimized. Even though homosexuality is no longer defined as psychopathological, discussions of gay-related issues, such as how and when to reveal oneself to others, are framed in psychological terms. Since the dominant clinical perspective is one that tends to personalize problems, concerns again center primarily on individual adjustment.

To the extent that now many psychological professionals are themselves gay and are more sensitive to the everyday realities of living in a heterosexual world, progress has been made. However, because they were trained in traditional programs and institutions, the new gay experts may reproduce the conventional and typically heterosexist professional ideologies, which fail to take structural issues into account and which legitimate traditional power imbalances between counselor and client. Moreover, the clinical models contribute to the appearance of political neutrality. By focusing on identity development, self-disclosure, and individual integration into gay worlds, gay-positive professional intervention may depoliticize gay issues in much the same way that the previous pathology-based models did.[63] Gay activists were once sensitive to the dangers inherent in professionalization of gay concerns, but few now express concerns about recent clinical models and interventions of mental health professionals. The changes in normative beliefs relating to gay identity development and the disclosure of sexual preferences to others appear to be more liberating than controlling, which may help to explain why they are not often the subject of criticism by gay activists. The relative invisibility of the dangers inherent in the new gay psychologies makes it an unlikely issue for political mobilization. Social historian and philosopher Michel Foucault observed, "The obligation to confess is now relayed through so many different points, is so deeply ingrained in us, that we no longer perceive it as the effect of a power that constrains us."[64] In this sense, the contemporary gay-positive models and their positive evaluation of disclosure may represent more sophisticated and effective means of regulating gay identities and behavior than the obvious homophobia that characterized the views of earlier professionals.

The shift in views regarding the desirability of disclosure and secrecy and its justification in psychological terms reflect a broader historical shift in patterns of social control. The exercise of modern power through law and overt oppression is giving way to a process whereby power is deployed

[63]See Celia Kitzinger, *The Social Construction of Lesbianism* (London, 1987), pp. 178–82, for a similar critique of gay-positive research.

[64]Michel Foucault, *The History of Sexuality: An Introduction,* vol. 1 of *The History of Sexuality,* trans. Robert Hurley (New York, 1978), p. 60.

through normalization.[65] Institutional forms of oppression are being replaced by notions of health and pathology. The process of normalization results in an "invisible, abstract, disembodied, ubiquitous" form of control.[66] Modern power is thus more penetrating, less visible, and more pervasive than before. Sexual actions, thoughts, and identities are no longer kept in check by overt policing mechanisms of the state; they are defined by shared understandings of normal sexuality and monitored primarily through individual conscience. People are not controlled by others as much as they police themselves. "We are in the society of the teacher-judge, the doctor-judge, the educator-judge, the 'social worker'-judge; it is on them that the universal reign of the normative is based; and each individual where ever he may find himself, subjects to it his body, his gestures, his behavior, his aptitudes, his achievement."[67] Modern power is not simply repressive, it is productive. Rather than simply denying, prohibiting, censoring, or silencing, power creates behavior, identities, and desires that are then subjected to control.[68] Foucault's arguments about normalization are particularly relevant in this examination of shifts in the normative evaluations of disclosure and secrecy in regard to homosexuality and help explain why gays often turn to professional counselors when struggling with concerns about how to manage information about their sexuality. Modern power is "exercised through its invisibility; at the same time it imposes on those whom it subjects a principle of compulsory visibility."[69] The felt need to divulge one's sexual preference reflects the internalization of newly created personal norms—norms that are simultaneously liberating and restraining: the power that enables liberation is the same power that constrains and organizes behavior and identity.[70]

Political and professional theories and their normative assumptions are located in specific social and historical contexts. Gay activists, mental health professionals, and social scientists who have been involved in the process of redefining disclosure and secrecy have been predominantly white, middle-class, urban, and well-educated men. The current agreement about the desirability of disclosure, and indeed the very image of the independent, assertive, and self-accepting gay man, reflects the experiences and taken-for-granted norms of this particular segment of society at a specific

[65]Ibid., p. 149; Weeks, *Sex, Politics, and Society* (n. 24 above), pp. 6–11.

[66]Gamson (n. 56 above), p. 357.

[67]Foucault, *The History of Sexuality*, 1: 304.

[68]Michel Foucault, *Discipline and Punish: The Birth of the Prison*, trans. Alan Sheridan (New York, 1979).

[69]Ibid., p. 187.

[70]For a discussion of Foucault's views of power, see Nancy Fraser, "Foucault on Modern Power: Empirical Insights and Normative Confusions," in her *Unruly Practices: Power, Discourse, and Gender in Contemporary Social Theory* (Minneapolis, 1989).

point in time. Gays from other social and cultural backgrounds may not see themselves represented in the new psychological models. Cultural and social factors are important in shaping people's sense of identity, their sexuality, and how they manage personal information, but by stressing the importance of asserting one's sexuality and by viewing disclosure primarily in terms of identity development and individual adjustment, the new clinical views do not easily allow for consideration of how these social and cultural forces are experienced.

Likewise, much of contemporary gay politics in the United States and Canada reflects and universalizes the interests of white, middle-class gay men and fails to adequately account for other forms of structured inequality, such as gender, class, or race. Theories of gay subordination that more adequately allow for an analysis of race or cultural dominance would likely lead to a more complex understanding of the need to disclose one's sexual identity and how personal presentation is shaped by social context. Such theories might identify a different role for disclosure in shaping individual identities and in promoting social change. Different analyses might also point to different strategies for change, which could conceivably displace disclosure as the central political act of gays. Contemporary identity politics and the manner in which disclosure is constructed as a need are products of social, political, and historical circumstances, rather than the natural outcome of developing identities. Our notions of identity and disclosure would undoubtedly take other forms if they emerged from groups with a different social makeup and where different political analyses dominated.

In this sense, the history of the changing views of disclosure and secrecy is entangled in the debates concerning essentialist and social constructionist theories of sexuality. Normative evaluations of disclosure and secrecy have changed over the past two decades, but many of the essentialist assumptions underlying our conceptualization of homosexuality and sexual identity have not. The perceived need to disclose one's "true inner self" by declaring one's sexual preferences is essentializing: it portrays the individual as responding to some universal inner force. By accepting the existence of a gay identity and the need to proclaim it, the new gay-positive psychologies tend to treat sexuality and sexual identity as naturally occurring and biologically rooted entities. Dianne Richardson has observed that the recent conceptualizations of homosexuality and gay identities assume "that sexual self-awareness inevitably emerges through a process of maturation. The individual's sexual identity is merely a cognitive 'realization' of the 'true' sexual nature of the self."[71] The tendency for the new professional and political models to talk about healthy or unhealthy gay identities or the

---

[71]Dianne Richardson, "The Dilemma of Essentiality in Homosexual Theory," *Journal of Homosexuality* 9 (1983–84): 84.

"need" to disclose one's sexual identity reveals the same kind of essentialist assumptions found in earlier models that viewed homosexuality as a psychopathological condition.

To the extent that they derive from the similar essentialist assumptions, the new gay-positive approaches present many of the same problems as the previous pathology-based ones. Since our understanding of sex continues to be implicitly grounded in biology, it tends to separate sexual behavior and identities from their historical and social contexts. Largely deterministic in nature, essentialist theories create fixed and limited categories by which we can understand our behavior and experiences. Ultimately, they limit the range of questions we pose, our ability to define what is problematic, and our ability to envision alternative solutions.[72] Essentialist theories of homosexuality can be depoliticizing because they frame our understandings of sex and sexual identities as natural processes that take place within individuals, rather than as elements that are socially created and politically alterable. However, the essentialist concepts of gay identities or gay histories ironically provide a politically useful and personally liberating discourse and provide people with a sense of shared community and common history. In this sense, essentialist theories can be at once liberating and constraining. From the social constructionist perspective, notions of normal and abnormal sex or healthy and unhealthy identities result from the coming together of particular historical, social, and political forces. The history of how disclosure of homosexuality has come to be viewed as desirable illustrates the context-dependent and political nature of matters relating to sex and identity. By doing so, it may provide a vantage point from which to question the dominant professional and political positions and may point to new avenues for personal choice and social action.

This article illustrates some of the contradictions of the definitional shift concerning disclosure and secrecy among gay men. To the extent that the study suggests a transformation of one type of control to another, it may indicate that we are hopelessly trapped in a web of power relations. The new views of disclosure and secrecy are liberating to many, but they pose new challenges and political dangers. However, to identify their dangers is not to deny their utility for the gay movement or for gay individuals. On the whole, the redefinition of homosexuality and the shift in normative views of disclosure represent a significant advance for many gay men in the United States and Canada. The challenge lies in grabbing hold of the benefits, while being wary of the costs.

[72]More detailed discussions of the essentialist and social constructionist views can be found in Dianne Richardson, "Recent Challenges to Traditional Assumptions about Homosexuality: Some Implications for Practice," *Journal of Homosexuality* 13 (1987): 1–12; Carole Vance, "Social Construction Theory: Problems in the History of Sexuality," in *Homosexuality, Which Homosexuality?* ed. Dennis Altman et al. (London, 1989); Jeffrey Weeks, *Sexuality* (London, 1986), pp. 11–44, and *Sex, Politics, and Society*, pp. 1–6.

# Rubber Wars: Struggles over the Condom in the United States

JOSHUA GAMSON

*Department of Sociology*
*University of California, Berkeley*

In the early 1940s, Dr. Woodbridge Morris, general director of the Birth Control Federation of America, complained to the American Social Hygiene Association about its overwhelming silence on the matter of condoms. "I appeal to you to take a positive stand in this matter," he argued, "before the public finds out that you are, in fact, permitting the spread of venereal disease because the most effective method to control it *happens to be* a method of contraception."[1] Meanwhile, Catholics arguing against birth control continued to treat the condom exclusively as a contraceptive method, arguing that in using such devices to "positively frustrate the procreative purpose of sexual intercourse" couples "pervert the order of nature and thus directly oppose the designs of nature's Creator."[2]

Over forty years later, the condom is again being pushed and pulled, molded into a variety of meanings. Jerry Della Femina, chairman of the advertising agency hired in the mid-1980s to promote LifeStyles condoms, complained in 1986 of the network ban on condom advertising, echoing Dr. Morris: "What the networks are saying is, 'We don't care if people die. We have our policy.'"[3] Testifying before the House Subcom-

---

I am grateful for comments on an earlier version of this paper to Kristin Luker, William Gamson, and two anonymous reviewers.

[1] Quoted in Allan M. Brandt, *No Magic Bullet: A Social History of Venereal Disease in America since 1880* (New York, 1985), p. 159; my emphasis.

[2] Father Francis J. Connell, "Birth Control: The Case for the Catholic," *Atlantic Monthly* 164 (October 1935): 469.

[3] Quoted in Joanne Lipman, "Controversial Product Isn't an Easy Subject for Ad Copywriters," *Wall Street Journal* (December 8, 1986), p. 1.

This essay originally appeared in the *Journal of the History of Sexuality* 1990, vol. 1, no. 2.

mittee on Health and the Environment in 1987, Alfred Schneider, vice president for policy and standards at Capital Cities/ABC, argued for network policy on the grounds that "it is impossible to separate this product from the original and long-standing use of the product, which is for birth control purposes." Therefore, he argued, ABC could not advertise condoms without violating "standards of good taste and community acceptability."[4]

The condom, then, is a disease preventive that happens to also block conception and a conception preventive that happens to block viruses. Meanings proliferate in popular discourse: the condom is a sign of sexual license, a sign of sexual maturity, a sign of AIDS awareness, a cumbersome piece of rubber, and so on. Oddly, bitter fights are and have been waged—in courts, in congressional hearing rooms, on television, in scientific journals, and presumably in bedrooms as well—to make the condom mean certain things and not others, to associate it with some uses and behaviors and dissociate it from others. It is given a power afforded few inanimate objects.

Why and how do people fight so hard to make their meaning of the condom dominate? Two heated periods in the public history of the condom in the United States (court cases of the 1930s and 1940s and publicity debates of the 1980s) provide an interesting base from which to formulate an answer. In the process of examining the theoretical and historical aspects of condom disputes in the United States, I hope to raise and suggest answers to more general questions: How do objects become endowed with meaning? How do meanings shift? What conditions underlie and affect the construction of these meanings? What difference does an object's uses—for example, a sexual use—make for this process?

## THEORETICAL ISSUES

The theoretical issues with which this essay begins and ends rest in the realm of cultural theory. The assumption of a "social construction" of the condom obviously defines the approach taken here. I am clearly opposed to an approach that treats the meaning of an object as inherent in the object itself. Among those who do argue that cultural meanings are actively constructed, though, the question of *who* in fact does the constructing is too often avoided.

On the one hand, many theorists of culture operate under a model in which texts and artifacts are read as "mirrors" of collective sentiment or values, symptoms of the goings-on in a society's "psyche." Here, by relying

[4]U.S. Congress, House, Committee on Energy and Commerce, Subcommittee on Health and the Environment, *Condom Advertising and AIDS,* 100th Cong., 1st sess., February 10, 1987, pp. 48–49.

on the notion of a homogeneous national psyche—itself an ideological assertion—"reflection theory" generally sidesteps the agents of meaning construction.[5]

A competing model sets ideology and those constructing it at the center. Here, the audience becomes largely irrelevant, injected with the repressive ideology of powerful leaders and cultural producers. (Theodor Adorno and Max Horkheimer, and the subsequent writings from the Frankfurt School, articulated this "hypodermic" model in its purest form.)[6] A more sophisticated version of this view, in discussions of ideological hegemony, conceives of cultural products not as unproblematically imposed but as constantly renewed through the incorporation of challenges. Still, cultural products within this model are generally analyzed to reveal the successful operation of "ruling-class" hegemony.[7]

Overemphasizing unity, then, a model of cultural artifacts-as-mirrors underemphasizes the concrete actions taken to *produce* them as pieces of culture, to infuse them with particular meanings. Overemphasizing ideological production, the model of a hegemonic culture is ill equipped to explain when and how certain pieces of a culture become *disputed:* it does not take seriously the possibility of cultural construction by a wide variety of interested groups, nor does it go far in explaining how new agents might enter the game and under what conditions, nor when and how interests collide and align.

The approach taken in this paper is nearer to this second model in that it pays close attention to the mobilization of particular meanings to serve particular political and material interests; however, it sees the construction process as at times a more open one than "hegemony" implies. The evidence presented here suggests that the process does involve a wide range of players, that new players and new strategies and new constraints arise, and that shifts in meaning occur in a process more complex than an inevitable incorporation of subversive alternatives.

Examining the condom at disputed moments means recognizing that

[5]For an early examination of "reflection theory," see Milton Albrecht, "The Relationship between Literature and Society," *American Journal of Sociology* 59 (March 1954): 425–36. For examples of this sort of argument, see Leslie Fiedler, *Love and Death in the American Novel* (New York, 1966); Martha Wolfenstein and Nathan Leites, *Movies: A Psychological Study* (New York, 1970); or nearly any popular magazine analysis of cultural trends. For a helpful review of sociological approaches to culture, see Richard Peterson, "Revitalizing the Culture Concept," *Annual Review of Sociology* 5 (1979): 137–66.

[6]Theodor Adorno and Max Horkheimer, "The Culture Industry: Enlightenment as Mass Deception," in *Mass Communication and Society,* ed. James Curran et al. (Beverly Hills, CA, 1977), pp. 349–83.

[7] For further discussions of this model, see Raymond Williams, "Base and Superstructure in Marxist Cultural Theory," *New Left Review* 82 (November–December 1973): 3–16; Todd Gitlin, "Prime Time Ideology," *Social Problems* 26 (February 1979): 251–66.

asserting what the condom "is"—the meaning of these pieces of latex or skin—becomes a central part of actors' strategies to affect the distribution and use behaviors surrounding it. Drawing from recent studies of social movements, it seems most fruitful to view these battles as "framing contests," in which actors "assign meaning to and interpret relevant events and conditions"—and, I would add, relevant *objects*—"in ways that are intended to mobilize potential adherents and constituents, to garner bystander support, and to demobilize antagonists."[8] Viewed as definitional disputes, debates over the condom can illuminate the process of cultural construction, its dynamics and limits, and its link to concrete actors.[9]

## THE OBJECT ITSELF: THE MALLEABLE CONDOM

Condom-like sheaths are known to have been used for disease prevention as early as the sixteenth century (some writers date their origins as early as ancient Egypt) when the Italian anatomist Gabriello Falloppio recommended lubricated linen condoms as protection against venereal disease. Condoms are first known to have been used against conception in the eighteenth century; by then, sheaths were widespread.[10] With the vulcanization of rubber in 1844 came a major boost, the mass production and distribution of condoms (they had previously been made from animal skins). With the introduction of latex in the early 1930s came a second revolution. Sales increased enormously, and prices dropped. By the mid-1930s, the fifteen major condom manufacturers were producing one and a half million a day at an average price of a dollar per dozen.[11]

The naming of the condom is somewhat more mysterious, attributed variously to Daniel Turner but—revealingly—called the "French letter" by the English and "la capote anglaise" ("the English cape") by the French.[12]

Built into this history is a malleability born of the condom's dual function. This distinguishes it from other contraceptives and allows it to more easily become the focal point of framing debates. Most contraceptives have

[8]David Snow and Robert Benford, "Ideology, Frame Resonance, and Participant Mobilization," *International Social Movement Research* 1 (1988): 198. See also William Gamson and Andre Modigliani, "Media Discourse and Public Opinion on Nuclear Power: A Constructionist Approach," *American Journal of Sociology* 95 (July 1989): 1–37.

[9]Jerome Himmelstein has examined *The Strange Career of Marihuana* (Westport, CT, 1983) from "killer weed" to "drop-out drug" through a similar lens, tracing "how the public discussion of marihuana has been framed or structured; how this conceptual framework has been socially shaped by moral entrepreneurs, the social locus of use, and broader social conflicts; and how it in turn has helped to determine the nature of marihuana laws" (p. 146).

[10]Linda Gordon, *Woman's Body, Woman's Right: A Social History of Birth Control* (New York, 1976), p. 44.

[11]Ibid., p. 317.

[12]Norman E. Himes, *Medical History of Contraception* (New York, 1936), pp. 187, 192.

a "fixed" overall meaning—they are used before or during sexual intercourse to block conception—and disputes have generally involved groups asserting individual "rights" opposed to groups asserting the need for state involvement in the regulation of "morality." Disputes over distribution of and access to contraceptives do not generally revolve around definitions of the objects themselves.[13] Because condoms have been used to serve an additional prophylactic function, however, the *definition* of the condom itself becomes a tool.

Definitional strategies center primarily around these two possible meanings: actors first of all attempt to push the condom toward the end of a contraceptive-prophylactic continuum that serves their needs. They push it along a second continuum, as well. The condom, as an external barrier method, always carries with it—even more strongly than do other devices, such as the birth control pill—some connotation of sexual intercourse. Thus, running alongside and intersecting with the contraceptive-prophylactic dimension is a sexual one: actors try to push the condom toward or away from its place in sexual intercourse—wrapping it, for example, in medicinal garb or playing up its image as the friend of the prostitute. At times, the usefulness of locations on these continua conflict, and putting together a successful definition is especially tricky: a group may want to define the condom as a prophylactic, for example, while denying an association of condom use with disease itself.

How do these fights over meaning play themselves out? Who are the actors in the struggles and what are their interests? The condom has brought together institutions and actors guided largely by political interests (increasing or limiting women's collective power and individual control, increasing or limiting the group's power, furthering political careers) and material interests (building and defending professional expertise, expanding and controlling a market share). These actors in turn operate within a state for which two self-defined interests are triggered by the condom: (1) an interest in monitoring and protecting public health; and (2) an interest in monitoring and regulating the sexual "morality" of its citizens.[14] During two periods in this century, to which we turn now, these actors have been especially visible fighting over the condom.

[13]See, for example, the October 1935 arguments in *Atlantic Monthly* (pp. 463–73); the arguments of the Supreme Court justices in Griswold et al. v. Connecticut, 381 U.S. (1965); David M. Kennedy, *Birth Control in America* (New Haven, CT, 1970); John D'Emilio and Estelle B. Freedman, *Intimate Matters: A History of Sexuality in America* (New York, 1988); and Gordon.

[14]Much has been written recently about state involvement in the regulation of sexuality and sexual behavior, and the (mostly economic) interests guiding this regulation. See, for example, many of the essays in *Powers of Desire: The Politics of Sexuality,* ed. Ann Snitow, Christine Stansell, and Sharon Thompson (New York, 1983); and Catherine MacKinnon, "Feminism, Marxism, Method and the State," *Signs* 7 (Spring 1982): 515–44.

## CONDITIONS OF THE EARLY DEBATES

In the first three-quarters of the nineteenth century, information about contraceptive devices circulated widely in the United States, through journals and advertisements in newspapers and almanacs. In 1873, however, the federal government became heavily involved in the regulation of contraceptive information and devices through the Comstock Act, which forbade the mailing, interstate transportation, and importation of contraceptive materials and information. Many state legislatures followed suit with their own "little Comstocks."[15]

It was not until the 1930s and 1940s that successful battles to revise state control over access to contraception and contraceptive information were waged. Even then, it was not through direct industry confrontation of the laws themselves that reforms were achieved, but indirectly, through court rulings on issues in which definitions of the condom—which assumed a central place in liberalization of the Comstock statutes—were necessary.

Why did the industry or others fail to confront the laws directly? There is little direct data available to explain inaction; when we look closely at the actions taken, though, clues begin to surface.[16] In the 1920s, birth control activist Margaret Sanger became convinced by a New York ruling to shift her strategy from repeal to reform of birth control legislation; a limited attack was necessary. New York Judge Frederick Crane had construed a state law to allow physicians the right to prescribe contraception "for the cure and prevention of disease," while birth control in general would continue to be classified as obscene and unlawful. Sanger, convinced "that her best prospect lay in a legislative amendment that would keep control in medical hands,"[17] spent nearly a decade pursuing "doctors-only" bills, with no success. This pursuit of an amendment allowed Sanger to gather medical support behind her and "appealed also to the cautiously limited liberalism emerging in the Protestant churches." She failed, David Kennedy argues, because she had to settle for "impotent political allies" in her fight: "Birth control, in spite of quietly growing public acceptance, was still such an explosive subject that most politicians preferred to avoid it."[18]

Sanger's activity, however, set the stage for understanding the activity of the 1930s and 1940s: it highlights both the constraints and the key ac-

[15]D'Emilio and Freedman, pp. 159–60.

[16]And why did change take so long? Here, although I do not examine the period between the 1870s and the 1930s, one again finds clues by noticing key actors in the later activities. The rise of women's activism, birth control activism in particular (see Gordon), and the solidification of medical professionalism (see Peter Conrad and Joseph Schneider, *Deviance and Medicalization* [St. Louis, 1980]) may have been necessary conditions for a challenge to the state's control.

[17]Kennedy, p. 220.

[18]Ibid., pp. 227, 231.

tors. What was apparently necessary was a battle in which the interests of "most politicians," who depend in their careers on "public acceptance," were not central. Moreover, a strategy was necessary that would not provoke mobilization on the part of the strongest opponent of birth control, the Catholic church. Contraception had long been opposed by religious leaders, and a "vigorous campaign" against it had been conducted by the Catholic hierarchy since the end of the nineteenth century, reaching its climax in Pope Pius XI's 1930 statement that those who used contraception violated "the law of God and nature" and were "stained by a grave and mortal flaw."[19] The context was such that direct changes through the legislature were unlikely and politically unfeasible. The site of activity necessarily became the judiciary, and the route for change paralleled Sanger's attempts: limited reforms through an embracing of the medical profession.[20]

CONDOMS IN COURTS: THE DEBATES OF THE 1930S AND 1940S

In the court cases of the 1930s and 1940s, the condom was consistently treated as an *exemption* from a state regulation of sexual behavior, which itself went unchallenged. This exemption turned on a *reframing* of the condom in medical terms.

Interestingly, the series of court cases surrounding condoms began with an internal industry dispute: in 1930 the Youngs Rubber Corporation charged C. I. Lee and Company with a trademark infringement in interstate commerce. In resolving the dispute, the Court of Appeals essentially redefined federal statutes. Condoms, the judge argued, "may be used for

[19]Quoted in J. T. Noonan, "Contraception," in *New Catholic Encyclopedia*, 16 vols. (New York, 1967), 4:274. We see examples of a strategy that does not take the Catholic hierarchy and constituency into account later: birth control advocates in Massachusetts twice forced a referendum amending state statutes, in 1942 and 1948. Both cases aroused "bitter campaigns in which the Protestant and Catholic Churches aligned against each other," and in both cases the referendum lost by approximately a seven to five margin (see Jack Hudson, "Birth Control Legislation," *Cleveland-Marshall Law Review* 9 [May 1960]: 248).

[20]The medical profession, it should be noted, was particularly well-positioned for this alliance. Since the mid-nineteenth century, groups of physicians had been working to professionalize medicine, striving for both prestige and "for exclusive professional and economic rights to the medical turf," which had until then been quite open. Much of the striving involved "medical crusading," assertions of expertise and calls for licensing and regulation, the translation of "social goals of cultural and professional dominance into moral and medical language." As a contraceptive, control of the condom would appear to be in the domain of the state; as a medical device, control would switch to medical professionals (see Conrad and Schneider, pp. 10–14). The strategy by doctors of avoiding the sexual dimension in their public actions, and sticking close to disease, is illustrated nicely by the American Medical Association. The AMA, "seeking not to appear to sanction promiscuity," refused to discuss condoms as preventive techniques in their 1960s campaign for the control of syphilis and gonorrhea (see Brandt, *No Magic Bullet* [n. 1 above], p. 176).

either legal or illegal purposes. If, for example, they are prescribed by a physician for the prevention of disease . . . their use may be legitimate; but, if they are used to promote illicit sexual intercourse, the reverse is true. . . . A manufacturer of drugs or instruments for medical use may in good faith sell them to druggists or other reputable dealers in medical supplies, or to jobbers for distribution to such trade."[21] Here, federal law is reinterpreted through the lens of medicine and the condom exempted as a legitimate medical instrument—that is, as a prophylactic. The "legitimate use" argument, and the Youngs Rubber case itself, became central in later rulings.[22] In 1936, the liberalization of federal birth control law was solidified in the One Package case, in which the Second Circuit Court of Appeals literally defined the federal statutes to allow "the importation, sale or carriage by mail of things which might intelligently be employed by conscientious and competent physicians for the purpose of saving life and promoting the well being of their patients."[23] State rulings followed this path; the Massachusetts Supreme Court (which two years earlier had upheld state regulations under the "police powers of the state to control the morals of its people") ruled that "where an appliance, in this case a sheath-type rubber condom, had the *dual capacity* of being a contraceptive and at the same time preventing venereal disease, the *prosecution must show that the seller is aware that the buyer intends to use the device for a contraceptive purpose.*"[24] In this case, the court explicitly directed condom advocates toward the disease frame.

It is important to notice that, while the liberalization of state regulation of birth control information and distribution came about through a definition of a legitimate (that is, medical) use of *any* device, the cases themselves all involved condoms. The dual function of the condom provided openings allowed few other sexual objects. By activating the disease-prevention meaning to which condoms lend themselves and disassociating them from sex, manufacturers could align with the medical profession and the pharmacists to exempt themselves from federal statutes. Moreover, the conflicting interests of the state are themselves triggered. On the one hand, the state has a long history of protecting the institution of monogamous marriage and reproduction via sanctions on sexual behaviors that depart from it; on the other hand, the state is institutionally invested in protecting the public health of its citizens.[25] In the condom, these two interests conflict— a conflict on which interested groups, quite literally, capitalize.

[21]Youngs Rubber Corporation v. C. I. Lee & Co., 45 F.2d 103 (1930).
[22]In, for example, Davis et al. v. United States, 62 F.2d 473 (1933).
[23]United States v. One Package of Japanese Pessaries, 86 F.2d 737 (1936).
[24]Hudson, p. 247; my emphasis.
[25]The tug of different state interests may have become especially acute during the world wars, when protecting soldiers from venereal disease through condom distribution became

Just how important the disease frame was—and how important its distance from the contraception frame—becomes apparent in a test case brought by a licensed physician in Connecticut in 1942. In this case, it was to be determined if a physician would be exempted from the prohibition of the right to disseminate contraceptive advice or prescribe a device when another pregnancy would likely result in the death of the mother. The court upheld the statute, arguing that "sexual abstinence might be practiced where life was endangered."[26] For disease prevention, information about and provision of devices tends to be allowed, and this is a function exclusive to condoms; for the prevention of conception, even to save a life, abstinence is recommended.

It is clear that change took place here in the judicial arena, and I have suggested why this was the necessary site and why a limited strategy in which the condom was central was necessary. What was gained by the alliances that produced the changes? Birth control activists, who were not in fact actively involved in the court battles, saw some of their goals achieved: the Comstock Act and many of the "little Comstocks" suffered a partial defeat. Doctors, also involved peripherally, won a certain symbolic victory, a furthering of their status as professionals, in that exceptions read into the statutes often turn on insuring that control of information and dissemination was in the hands of medical professionals. The greatest material gains, though, were for manufacturers (who could now expand marketing so long as it was for "legitimate use") and pharmacists (who took their places as the main gatekeepers of disease-preventative condom distribution).

In part the gains for manufacturers and pharmacists were a result of their ability to mobilize around the disease frame, which allowed them to defuse active resistance (by moving the condom away from "religious"—that is, intercourse-related—issues) and call up alliances (from birth control reformers and professional doctors). These strategies were taken within the limits set by state interests. In part, I would add, they also benefited from a situation set up by the state regulation they opposed. Given that *dissemination* of condoms (rather than use or publicity) was the focus of state regulation, and that the judiciary was the logical site of dispute, manufacturers and pharmacists became the key actors directly involved and arguing their cases in the judicial process. Other actors—condom users or activists for or against—were essentially excluded from direct participation.

---

policy. The success of the disease frame may well have been strengthened not only by the fact that the government had actually positively sanctioned condom use but also by the interest of the state in dissociating this policy from a positive sanctioning of sexual promiscuity (see Brandt, *No Magic Bullet*).

[26]Tileston v. Ullman, 129 Conn. 84 (1942).

## CHANGED CONDITIONS

Between the 1940s and the 1980s, several major developments significantly altered the context in which discussions over the condom took place. Building on the legal openings provided by earlier condom disputes and supported by a strong and growing women's movement, birth control activists continued to challenge the legal status of contraceptives. In 1965, with the Supreme Court ruling in *Griswold et al. v. Connecticut* removing the ban on contraceptive use by married persons, the government effectively withdrew from this area of moral policing. And in 1977, the Supreme Court ruled that the advertisement and display of contraceptives could no longer be prohibited and that the arguments that "advertisements of contraceptive products would offend and embarrass those exposed to them" and would "legitimize sexual activity of young people" were not cause for restricting First Amendment rights to expression.[27]

While the state was withdrawing from regulation, the condom was withdrawing from popularity. With the introduction of the birth control pill in 1960 and the broadened use of both the pill and the intrauterine device (IUD) in the 1960s and 1970s, the condom went into a dramatic decline. Between 1965 and 1970, condom use declined 22 percent.[28] From the mid-1970s to the mid-1980s, U.S. condom sales fell by half.[29] This all changed, of course, with the spread of AIDS from the early 1980s onward and the discovery that the use of latex condoms helps prevent the transmission of the HIV virus. The promotion of "safer sex" through condom use, diligently pursued by former Surgeon General C. Everett Koop, other public health officials, and AIDS activists,[30] had immediate effects on the condom industry. Retail condom sales in the United States rose 25 percent from 1982 to 1984.[31] In 1986 alone, sales increased by 10 percent, and stock prices in Carter-Wallace, Incorporated (the manufacturer of Trojans, which has over half of the U.S. market share) shot up by 55 percent. From 1987 to 1989, sales increased by more than 60 percent.[32]

These changes have meant a shift in the site of disputes over the condom. The condom has very rarely appeared as a subject of judicial or

[27]Carey, Governor of New York, et al. v. Population Services International et al., 431 U.S. 678 (June 9, 1977).

[28]Charles F. Westoff and Norman B. Ryder, *The Contraceptive Revolution* (Princeton, NJ, 1977), pp. 21–22.

[29]Colin Leinster, "The Rubber Barons," *Fortune* 114 (November 24, 1986): 106.

[30]For a well-documented, and overly sensationalist, history of the epidemiological and political history of AIDS, see Randy Shilts, *And the Band Played On* (New York, 1987). For a representative activist response to AIDS and sex—a response consistently ignored in Shilts's writing—see Douglas Crimp, "How to Have Promiscuity in an Epidemic," in *AIDS: Cultural Analysis/Cultural Activism*, ed. Douglas Crimp (Cambridge, MA, 1987), pp. 237–71.

[31]Robert Hatcher et al., eds., *Contraceptive Technology, 1988–1989* (Atlanta, 1989), p. 345.

[32]"Can You Rely on Condoms?" *Consumer Reports* 54 (March 1989): 135–42.

legislative inquiry since the 1960s. Instead, interested parties take to the realm of publicity, as witnessed in the continuing debate over condom advertising. Condom use declined, one physician lamented in a medical journal in 1979, due to "bad press" during the 1960s and 1970s. The solution he proposed to revive use was revealing: "Persuading the National Association of Broadcasters to allow condom advertising on radio and television and . . . convincing the copy-review boards of newspapers and magazines in general circulation to do the same. . . . Organized medicine and public health can take the lead here by bringing their collective weight to bear on the media to reverse this policy. . . . Medical journals can also help by encouraging condom manufacturers to advertise their products . . . in their pages."[33] In the contemporary site of condom dispute, different constraints and some new actors operate. Essentially, it is media practices that determine the rules, and new alliances are forged, now with the advertising industry.

## CONDOMS IN THE MASS MEDIA: THE DEBATES OF THE 1980s

The sudden boom in sales provided by the "free publicity" of AIDS—tastelessly appearing as one of *Adweek's* "Hottest Markets of 1987"[34]—has triggered a marketing war between the established manufacturers. (Two manufacturers, Carter-Wallace and Schmid's, which makes Ramses and Sheik, account for approximately 90 percent of the market.)[35] It has also triggered the entry of a number of new contenders. In 1986, Carter-Wallace launched a multimillion-dollar advertising campaign, the largest expenditure on a single advertising campaign ever undertaken in the industry, and a new company planned to spend between two and three million dollars marketing its Mentor condoms.[36] In this war, manufacturers have faced two related problems: first, how to break down media-industry opposition to condom advertising; and second, how to target condoms to particular markets. In both cases, not surprisingly, condom manufacturers have steered away from contraception and toward prophylactic use.

Until recently, condom advertising was found only in heterosexual men's sex magazines. In 1985, the first billboard condom advertisements

[33]Yehudi Felman, "A Plea for the Condom," *Journal of the American Medical Association* 241 (June 8, 1979): 2517–18.

[34]"The Business of AIDS," *Adweek* 37 (April 16, 1987): 4–11.

[35]The division of the market share has changed little in recent years, with Carter-Wallace at 56 percent and Schmid's at 34 percent, and the remaining 10 percent divided about equally between Circle Rubber and Ansell-Americas (see Leinster).

[36]Gail Appleson, "Women Taking Condom Initiative," *Oakland Tribune* (October 19, 1986).

appeared (for Ramses, in Atlanta). By 1986, many mainstream magazines—including women's magazines such as *Modern Bride, Vogue,* and *Family Circle*—had dropped their long-standing bans on contraceptive advertising and accepted condom ads. Over the course of 1987, nearly all bans were dropped, including those by holdouts such as *Newsweek, U.S. News and World Report,* and the publications of Time, Incorporated.[37]

How has such a dramatic change come about? Primarily, it is a result of aggressive and careful marketing shifts on the part of manufacturers. The underlying factor is the revision by advertisers of what it is that is being sold, so that publications (like the courts in the 1930s) can essentially *maintain* their ban on contraception: condoms are simply not contraceptives. Manufacturers and their marketers do not attempt to repeal mass media "policy" but accept its logic and work around it.

Companies actively target new markets with new marketing strategies. The key here is the basic logic of marketing: try to determine the tastes, desires, and fears of the audience in order to play to them. "We're not going after the *Playboy* and *Penthouse* market," says Mentor vice president Al Mannino. Instead, they are going after (heterosexual) women, who, according to an industry spokesperson, now make up 40 percent of the condom market, and in particular after unmarried women who, according to a recent study, used almost twice as many condoms in 1987 as they did in 1982.[38] To reach women, as well as the non-*Playboy* male markets, strategies have been adapted to give the condom a makeover, from sleazy to "smart."

A major part of this strategy involves desexualizing the condom. Advertising, says *Family Circle*'s advertising director, is "more clinical, nonsuggestive, and informative," a "service" to readers, as opposed to the earlier "suggestive" ads, with their "emphasis on the *pleasure* of the product."[39] The condom, Mentor's health-care products manager asserts, "is a personal hygiene item."[40] Manufacturers and advertisers link themselves directly to public health. "I say God bless him," said John Silverman, the president of Ansell-Americas, makers of LifeStyles, after the surgeon general announced that using condoms is the best protection against HIV-infection

[37] Patricia Winters, "TV Stations Embrace Condom Spots," *Advertising Age* 58 (February 2, 1987): 4.

[38] See "Packing Protection in a Purse," *Time* 132 (August 15, 1988): 65. Another major new market is the gay male population. Carter-Wallace recently decided against advertising in gay media, after "reviewing a cross section of the regional and national gay publications," arguing that "we advertise in a lot of general media and feel gay men aren't excluded as readers" (quoted in *Adweek* [December 14, 1987], p. 26)—a logic belied by its selective application. Here, again, the minimum-risk decision-making process seems to lead companies to avoid associating their products too closely with controversial activities and populations.

[39] Quoted in Leinster; my emphasis.

[40] Quoted in Patricia Winters, "Condom Ads Aim at AIDS," *Advertising Age* 57 (December 1, 1986): 99.

barring abstinence. Silverman quickly called for adjusting advertisements to "support [the surgeon general's statements] with public information advertising" and wrote to drugstores that "Ansell has accepted the challenge and responsibility for taking this message to the public."[41] The LifeStyles ads made no mention of contraception.

Packaging has been similarly adapted both to reach women and to detach the condom from its sexual-player meaning. Schmid's Koromex brand uses a simple box with a businesslike holder. Mentor condoms are sold in individually wrapped, small plastic cups. Carter-Wallace's Trojans for Women are sold in pink and lavender boxes picturing a woman; according to the company's vice president of marketing, this will help the product make the move to "display space in the feminine hygiene section of stores."[42]

In a variety of ways, then, the condom has now been marketed as not-a-contraceptive: it is a beauty aid, a personal hygiene item, a public service—all, however euphemistically, based on the prevention-of-disease frame and a desexualization of the condom.

None of this, however, has yet broken the ban by the three major television networks. (Many local affiliates have broken over the last three years with network policies, agreeing to air the commercials, usually under the conditions that they not run during children's hours, not promote condoms as birth control, and are in "good taste." In addition, many cable stations accept the ads.)[43] The code of the National Association of Broadcasters has held that broadcasters should refuse any advertisement "which the station has good reason to believe would be objectionable to a substantial and responsible segment of the community."[44] This is, of course, the same basic logic guiding newspapers and magazines: do not endanger your sales by offending your audience.

Since 1986, industry outsiders have stepped up pressure on television advertising. Planned Parenthood placed coupons addressed to network executives in print ads in 1986 and in 1987 charged that the networks were "out of step with the great majority of the American people," producing a Harris survey showing support for condom advertising.[45] House subcommittee hearings in February 1987, including testimony by Surgeon

[41]Lipman (n. 3 above), p. 19.

[42]Quoted in "Condom Makers Aim at Women Buyers," *Wall Street Journal* (June 21, 1988), p. 41.

[43]See the testimony in U.S. Congress, House, Committee on Energy and Commerce (n. 4 above).

[44]Myron Redford, Gordon Duncan, and Denis Prager, eds., *The Condom* (San Francisco, 1974), p. 152.

[45]"Harris Survey Shows Viewers Think Contraceptive Ads OK," *Broadcasting* 112 (March 30, 1987): 178.

General Koop, other public health officials, and network executives, focused directly on condom advertising. The outcome was a nonbinding "urging" of network cooperation. Despite charges of "media malpractice" and pointed arguments between congressmen, the hearings give testimony to the recognition that the networks, not the government, determine their own policy. Again, it becomes clear that the arena of dispute, and those setting the rules in that arena, has shifted.

Ralph Daniels, NBC's vice president of broadcast standards, defended NBC's policy of refusing condom commercials at Congressional hearings: "Our network television standards reflect the fact that we provide program service to over 200 individual television stations serving local communities across the nation. The audience served by these stations includes a wide range of religious beliefs, social attitudes and mores, as well as local and regional concepts of propriety and acceptability. . . . *Broadcast network or local stations cannot ignore the fact that condoms are also contraceptive devices.*"[46] While noting that broadcast standards "evolve," Daniels and other network representatives argued that, despite its function as a disease preventative, the condom continues to be seen as a contraceptive and thus to trigger antagonistic beliefs, mores, and concepts of propriety that the networks literally cannot afford to arouse. "At some point," said an NBC spokesperson after the hearings, "there may be such a health problem that we would have to overlook the morality question."[47] Here, like the courts before them, the change-makers instruct interested parties in how to become exempt from the rules under which they operate: define the product in terms of "health problems" (disease) rather than "morality questions" (contraception).

## OLD AND NEW VOICES

It is not entirely clear why the networks are so resistant, though one might speculate that their gradual decline in the television market with the advent of cable television and video cassette recorders leaves them in a position particularly disposed against taking advertising risks. The fear of offense and backlash is not unreasonable. Once again, arousing the Catholic church and the religious Right, which hold that "it is not responsible action to use the devastating disease of AIDS as an excuse to promote artificial birth control,"[48] does pose a threat.

[46]U.S. Congress, House, Committee on Energy and Commerce, pp. 36–37; my emphasis.

[47]Quoted in Steven Colford, "Nets Take Flak on Condom Ads, but Congress Won't Force Change," *Advertising Age* 58 (February 16, 1987): 79.

[48]Bishop Bevilacqua, "The Questions Raised by School-based Health Clinics," *Origins* 17 (September 3, 1987): 188.

The Catholic discussion of AIDS itself pushes those wishing Catholic support or fearing Catholic opposition toward a birth control version of the condom. In 1987, the U.S. Catholic Administrative Board stated that AIDS educational efforts "could include accurate information about pro-phylactic devices or other practices proposed by some medical experts as potential means of preventing AIDS. . . . Such a factual presentation should indicate that abstinence outside of marriage and fidelity within mar-riage as well as the avoidance of intravenous drug abuse are the only morally correct and medically sure ways to prevent the spread of AIDS."[49] This qualified approval, briefly ratifying the disease-only approach, set off im-mediate controversy within the church. Bishops responded that "it is never morally permissible to employ an intrinsically evil means to achieve a good purpose"[50]—that is, they reasserted the contraception frame to reinforce, in the pope's phrasing, the church as "sole interpreter of the law of God and 'expert in humanity.'"[51]

This controversy led American bishops to develop a further document in November 1989, which emphasized abstinence and insisted more ex-plicitly that "it is not condom use that is the solution to this health problem," reunifying in a 219–4 vote in favor of the new statement.[52] What is important to note in this controversy is more than how the bishops reasserted the contraceptive frame in the service of moral arguments, a clue to those needing their support. Significantly, their action was also heavily focused on *publicity*: Archbishop John May of St. Louis complained of "a misunderstanding in media reports" of the original document; Archbishop Roger Mahony of Los Angeles complained that "many media headlines and stories have seriously confused our Catholic people." Not to address the issue, May argued, "would leave people to learn of them from factually misleading campaigns designed to sell certain products or to advocate safe sex without reference to a moral perspective."[53]

Opponents of *any* condom publicity also enter the debate on occasion, again articulating the limits of mass media risk-taking. Representing an or-ganization called the Committee on the Status of Women on an ABC "Nightline" report devoted to condom advertising, Kathleen Sullivan ar-gued for abstinence publicity rather than condom publicity: "I'm really appalled at you gentlemen," she said to liberal San Francisco supervisor

[49]U.S. Catholic Conference Administrative Board, "The Many Faces of AIDS," *Origins* 17 (December 24, 1987): 482–89.

[50]"Reaction to AIDS Statement," *Origins* 17 (December 24, 1987): 489–92.

[51]Pope John Paul II, "Address to Vatican AIDS Conference," *Origins* 19 (November 30, 1989): 435.

[52]U.S. Bishops' Meeting, "Called to Compassion and Responsibility: A Response to the HIV/AIDS Crisis," *Origins* 19 (November 30, 1989): 429.

[53]"Reaction to AIDS Statement," pp. 490, 491.

Harry Britt (arguing for condom ads) and WCVB-Boston general manager Jim Coppersmith (arguing for television's autonomy). "You ought to be really debating how much you are going to stress the how and why of abstinence. . . . [Children] want to know the reasons how and why it's healthier for them not to be sexually active."[54] Coppersmith quickly responded that his station "would never do anything . . . that would encourage promiscuity. I recognize clearly that abstinence is the very best defense against AIDS."[55] This exchange captures these two players' acknowledgment of each other's power: the conservative moralist recognizing that television is a key to achieving her goals and the station manager recognizing that the conservative constituency must be reassured of television's conservatism.

Condoms also take a place in the actions of the AIDS activist movement, which, while not powerful enough to set severe limits on the actions of policymakers, does add a grassroots voice to condom debates.[56] AIDS activists make explicit attempts to "campaign and organize in order to enter the amphitheater of AIDS commentary effectively and unapologetically on our own terms."[57] The position taken by groups such as the AIDS Coalition to Unleash Power (ACT UP), and other predominantly gay-run AIDS organizations, is similar to the public health position but broadened to include larger goals and strategies than safer sex education. For these groups, of course, the condom almost never appears as a contraceptive and is instead entirely a life-saving protection against HIV transmission. It becomes a symbol not only of *safe* sex, though, but of safe *sex:* ACT UP, for example, calls for "explicit" sex education[58] that recognizes sexual diversity. Condoms take their place within an overall strategy that includes, for example, same-sex "kiss-ins" and "fuck me safe" T-shirts. These groups, while sharing the disease frame with public health officials and mainstream AIDS service organizations, *resexualize* the condom to bring it into a broader challenge to sexual norms. Implicit in this is a recognition that AIDS, like venereal disease,[59] often serves to stigmatize; since much discourse associates AIDS with "immoral" behavior, the condom method of prevention is also tied into questions of morality. Their strategy for waging

---

[54]"Nightline," ABC News (January 21, 1987). Representative William Dannemeyer took a similar position during the Congressional hearings. See U.S. Congress, House, Committee on Energy and Commerce.

[55]"Nightline," ABC News (January 21, 1987).

[56]See Josh Gamson, "Silence, Death, and the Invisible Enemy: AIDS Activism and Social Movement 'Newness,'" *Social Problems* 36 (October 1989): 351–67.

[57]Simon Watney, *Policing Desire: Pornography, AIDS and the Media* (Minneapolis, 1987), p. 54.

[58]ACT UP/San Francisco, "Our Goals and Demands" (1988, informational flyer).

[59]See Allan Brandt, "AIDS: From Social History to Social Policy," in *AIDS: The Burdens of History,* ed. Elizabeth Fee and Daniel M. Fox (Berkeley, 1988), pp. 147–71.

a challenge to stigmatization and sexual hierarchy aims directly for "the amphitheater," largely through events staged for the media—and through the free publicity of street postering.[60] (See fig. 1.)

In the case of current condom advertising, then, the shift in the site of activity has brought new players (advertisers, marketers) to the forefront and others more deeply into the game. Significantly, the essential definitional strategy remains the same and has had a similar effect: by defining the condom as a health *exception* to an overall accepted "morality," those who stand to benefit achieve a liberalization of (in this case informal) policy surrounding it. Obviously, the manufacturer-advertiser alliances most successful at breaking down barriers stand to gain the most financially, through access to targeted markets, and this is the crux of the battle. The limits of their strategies are set primarily by media practices—guided by low-risk decision making—which, in turn, are limited by the threat of backlash from organized religious and conservative groups, on the one hand, and pressure from public health officials and birth control and AIDS activists on the other.

## CONTINUITIES AND DISCONTINUITIES

A number of continuities are visible through these two moments of contestation over the condom. First of all, what remains at the center of both contests are the material interests of condom manufacturers; what shifts are the alliances made by manufacturers and the constraints on their tactics. (Among these constraints, the fear of religious-group backlash also seems to remain constant.) Second, both periods clearly involve a liberalization of regulation of the condom: in the earlier period, a liberalization of laws regulating distribution and access; in the later one, a liberalization of publicity policies. These changes were achieved through the successful placement of the condom in a "disease and prevention" interpretive package. This package, moreover, involves in both cases a desexualization of the condom, a disassociation of the condom from pleasure (through its centralization in medical hands in the 1940s and through a pulling-back from the "pleasure sell" in the 1980s) and, of course, from reproduction (through its severing from contraceptive functions).

The fundamental use of "meaning" in these cases has a certain irony: actors whose primary interest is in increasing profits liberalize policies and democratize access to condoms by distancing themselves from liberal mod-

---

[60]See J. Gamson. For a discussion of the relationship of social movements to the mass media, see Todd Gitlin, *The Whole World Is Watching* (Berkeley, 1980).

Prevent AIDS. **Practice safer sex.** Use a condom. **It could save your life.**

# JUST SAY KNOW

FIG. 1 "Just Say Know": Poster produced by Boy With Arms Akimbo, an anonymous group of "cultural activists," for an ACT UP–sponsored benefit, San Francisco, January 1990. According to a recent flyer (March 1990), Boy With Arms Akimbo approaches social change through "intellectual subversion and visual intervention," the appropriation and reappropriation of images to challenge conventional discourse; thus, when asked for permission to reproduce this poster, one member responded, "Appropriate away. That's our point."

els (that is, models involving individual choice in contraception), claiming instead an exemption from the conservative model (that is, sexual behavior can and should be state-regulated), thereby affirming that model.

Even more instructive, though, are the discontinuities. The most important shift is in the *site* of activity from the courts to the media, from legality to publicity. Additionally, state involvement has become much less central and the marketplace much more central. This shift brings with it a change in agents of control: the gatekeepers are no longer judges but media executives. New actors are also thus brought onto the scene. Publicity battles are in fact more open to a broad range of actors than are legal ones. Second, the *point of intervention*—that is, at what stage control is attempted and contested—has shifted. In the 1930s and 1940s, availability was at issue (through the control of actual distribution by the state); in the 1980s, visibility and knowledge are at stake.

How do we make sense of these shifts? Clearly, accidents of history (the rise of diseases such as venereal disease and AIDS) provide opportunities for the mobilization of certain interpretive frames. But this does not explain a shift in site, the entry of new actors, and a shift in the point of intervention.

Broadly put, it seems that recognizing the increased centrality of consumption, and a rise in the industry of publicity, are necessary for understanding these changes. Consumerism, the "mass participation in the values of the mass-industrial market," argues Stuart Ewen, developed from the 1920s on as "an aggressive device of corporate survival"—essentially to educate a nation of buyers to fit the needs of growing mass production. Advertising, whose impulse was one of "actively channeling social impulses towards a support of corporation capitalism and its productive and distributive priorities," became the "key apparatus for the stimulation and creation of mass consumption."[61] In this context, it is a shaping of consciousness, the shaping of a particular relationship toward goods and buying, that becomes central.

Without delving into the complex history of mass culture and advertising (and the growth of radio and television technologies immediately drafted into commercial services), I would suggest that this historical shift, while not altering the strategy of frame construction, accounts for the shift in site and the balance of opportunities and constraints. "A consumption economy," argues Daniel Bell, ". . . finds its reality in appearances."[62] In a market- and publicity-centered society, spreading or restricting public knowledge of the condom, controlling its *image,* becomes more central

---

[61]Stuart Ewen, *Captains of Consciousness: Advertising and the Social Roots of the Consumer Culture* (New York, 1976), pp. 54, 81.

[62]Daniel Bell, *The Cultural Contradictions of Capitalism* (New York, 1976), p. 68.

than opening or restricting manufacture and distribution of condoms; *knowledge* of sexual behavior logically becomes a focal point of attempts to control that behavior. This in turn means that more players can enter the dispute—witness, for example, the use of the media by AIDS activists and others to publicize condoms for safe-sex use. Finally, it means that the constraints on manipulating the condom's definition turn on media rather than judicial processes, dependent on perceptions of "public sentiments," the maximum profits with the minimum risk. This opens up new avenues for those attempting to effect change: by showing through polling, for example, or through social movement activity that the public does or does not accept a particular interpretive package. At the same time, it sets financial considerations firmly at the center of the struggle over the meaning of the condom.

## CONCLUSION: WHAT ABOUT THE REST OF US?

I have argued that the condom has been made to mean many different things; that its meaning is in fact determined by the actions taken by interested parties involved in "framing" the condom to help achieve their interests; that broad historical shifts have changed the arena of these debates from legality to publicity; and that, despite a continuity in overall strategies, these shifts provide different opportunities and constraints for actors and, thus, changes in what the condom may come to mean. This is not a process particular to the condom, although the condom is particularly easy to manipulate, but a model for understanding how cultural artifacts are generally imbued with meanings.

Questions remain, however. What does "the public" actually think? And what is the relationship between their interpretation of what the condom is and their use of the object? These are questions that examining attempts to frame the condom in particular ways do not answer. Even superficial evidence suggests that, while different framing strategies explain how it has been possible to open access to condoms and knowledge about them, the shifts in public meaning do not translate into shifts in private understandings. The source of most people's definitions—and the control over their knowledge—may be influenced very little by maneuverings in courts and advertising boardrooms. Cultural understandings differ across social groupings (race, class, gender, age) as well as across time—clearly subject to other influences.[63] Lee Rainwater, for example, found in the

---

[63]For discussions of the complexities of audience reception, see Fred Fejes, "Critical Mass Communications Research and Media Effects: The Problem of the Disappearing Audience," *Mass Communications Review Yearbook* 5 (1985): 517–30; David Morley, *The "Nationwide" Audience* (London, 1980); and Janice Radway, *Reading the Romance* (Chapel Hill, NC, 1984).

early 1960s that "working class women. . . generally have less information about sex and contraception than do the men . . . [and] have learned what they do know (usually about condoms) from their husbands since their marriage."[64] Similar discrepancies between the definitional packages discussed in this paper and the attitudes toward the condom by young men and teenagers are readily seen.[65] Even if one does assume reception by the public of the condom in the public frame that dominates, it is not at all clear that "knowledge" of "what it is" translates into use behaviors. Other considerations and definitions (comfort, who the partner is, and so on) may very well override the publicly asserted definitions of the condom.

This, of course, has implications for the theoretical issues with which I began. Asking in whose interest certain definitions of the condom serve and how these interested parties achieve particular arrangements is necessary for understanding the operation of cultural "meaning" and its relation to access both to the condom itself and to knowledge about it. The approach, though, suggests its own limitations. Looking at the framing process alone also leaves many key questions unanswered—in particular, the reception of interpretive packages by individuals and groups of condom users. How similar are public frame and private? How are they linked? Without explaining discrepancies between construction and reception— the relationship between interest groups shaping public definitions of the condom and the privately held definitions of citizens—questions of impact on everyday lives are left blurry.

[64]Lee Rainwater, *And the Poor Get Children* (Chicago, 1960), p. 64.
[65]Redford, Duncan, and Prager, eds. (n. 44 above), pp. 182, 172.

# The Return of Butch and Femme:
# A Phenomenon in Lesbian Sexuality of the
# 1980s and 1990s

LILLIAN FADERMAN
*Women's Studies*
*California State University, Fresno*

I got to thinkin'... about how I was s'posed to be so damn butchy—
with my denim, and leather, and studs, and my ducktail; and you with
your heels, your make-up, and skirts ... you, so very much the smoldering
woman.... Thinkin' 'bout the time when we didn't have no money and
needed gas, and you tore out the station with the nozzle in the tank. ...
Thinkin' how you *made* me git out on the floor an' dance with you at the
Sweetheart Dance—didn't care *who* saw we was two women.... Got to
thinkin', maybe this butch/femme stuff wasn't quite rule of thumb—
maybe leather didn't make you a tough broad, or silk a sissy; got to
realizin' that *maybe* I was always on top 'cause you let me be, and how soft
and warm you made me feel, like sometimes I wanted to wear long,
flowin' skirts, and look pretty just for you.... Then I reached for the keys
in my cowboy jacket pocket... and said, "This time—you drive."
[Charlene S. Henderson, "Texas '52," in *Sinister Wisdom,* 1988]

THE CLICHÉ ABOUT the 1980s is that it was a far more conservative
period than the 1970s for a whole complex of reasons, not the least of
which was the fearful connection between sexual pleasure and danger
that the AIDS virus brought to public consciousness. It is true that the
1980s ushered into the parent culture a more cautious sexuality, which
even rubbed off somewhat on the lesbian culture. For example, the non-
monogamy that radical lesbian-feminism encouraged in the 1970s is
out and commitment is in in many lesbian circles (although the retreat
from open sexuality on the part of both heterosexuals and homosexuals
has not yet resulted in an ethos anywhere near as rigid as that of the

This essay originally appeared in the *Journal of the History of Sexuality* 1992, vol. 2, no. 4.

1950s). Some lesbian social critics see the contemporary impulse to revive butch and femme relationships as being one more lesbian manifestation of the contemporary right-wing backlash. They have associated it
with a 1950s nostalgia à la "Happy Days," a desire for the security of
what is naively imagined to have been better times, perhaps a fantasy created out of exhaustion from the battles lesbian-feminists had to fight in
the 1970s. But it would be inaccurate to attribute the resurgence of
butch/femme roles and relationships in the 1980s to the relative conservatism of the period. Neo-butch/femme may be seen instead as a reaction against the sexual conformity that lesbian-feminism ironically
mandated in the course of a radical era. Women who stifled such role
identifications in the 1970s dared to examine them and even flaunt
them in the next decade. Women who never thought about them in the
1970s began exploring them with curiosity.[1]

Neo-butch/femme may also be related to an attempt to resist cultural
assimilation. In the 1970s not only did heterosexual women dress much
like the most blatant lesbians of earlier eras, but even the taboos against
lesbian sexuality were largely relaxed. What was there to distinguish the
radical lesbian—who often wanted to be distinguished—from the run-
of-the-mill liberated woman? The resurgence of butch/femme coun-
tered such assimilation.

Although a few women who identified as butch or femme in the
1980s (or at present) did so with the same deadly seriousness that
characterized the women of the 1950s, many others did it out of a
sense of adventure, a historical curiosity, a longing to push at the limits. For them neo-butch/femme roles and relationships often maintain
the lessons of feminism that lesbians learned from the 1970s. They are
more subtle, complex, flexible. There are few contemporary butches
who would entertain the notion that they are men trapped in women's
bodies. For these reasons, the meaning of butch and femme over the
past decade was very different from what it had been thirty or forty
years earlier.

[1] I wrote an initial version of this essay intending it to be a chapter in *Odd Girls and Twilight Lovers: A History of Lesbian Life in Twentieth-Century America* (New York, 1991).
However, in the course of numerous revisions I cut much of the material, finally using
only a fraction of it in the chapter entitled "Lesbian Sex Wars in the 1980s." This essay in-
corporates most of the material of my original draft for a separate chapter on contemporary
butch and femme relationships. My research for *Odd Girls and Twilight Lovers* included
186 unstructured interviews with women from seven states, ranging in age from seventeen
to eighty-six, of various socioeconomic and racial backgrounds. I also made use of several
excellent archives, especially the Lesbian Herstory Archive in New York and the June
Mazer Lesbian Collection in Los Angeles.

## BUTCH/FEMME AS "POLITICALLY INCORRECT" IN THE 1970s

At the height of radical lesbian-feminism, what was seen as an imitation of heterosexuality was officially frowned upon by the most vocal elements of the subculture. Lesbian-feminists of the 1970s believed that lesbianism was not simply a bedroom issue but also a political issue, and that the personal was political. They regarded butch/femme as roles in which the players were acting out with each other the oppression they had learned from the parent culture. It was a corruption to be eschewed. They had no doubt that butches were trying to mimic men, and their typical response to that was, "I'm not interested in a man *manqué*—in being one or knowing any. I'm not into lesbianism because I like men."[2]

For many women who came to lesbianism through feminism, butch/femme looked like nothing so much as a repetition of that which they left heterosexuality to avoid. Those roles seemed to place a limit on their free growth and expansion, which to them was the most exciting part of feminism. They refused to believe that butch or femme roles came naturally to any women and explained their prevalence in some lesbian communities as resulting from socialization: lesbians had been well brainwashed by the parent culture so that they acquiesced into making their subculture a carbon copy of heterosexuality. Abbott and Love suggested in their popular 1972 book, *Sappho Was a Right-On Woman: A Liberated View of Lesbianism,* that lesbians often came to accept mimicking the roles of heterosexuals through the lesbian bars, which were their entry into "the life." There, a young woman who initially only wanted to find ways to express her love for other women was forced to take on the stereotype of "the Lesbian," whether or not it had anything to do with who she was: "Whereas [before entering the subculture] she has been impersonating a heterosexual woman, now she is impersonating a Lesbian. She gives herself over to a new image, also defined by central casting. The stereotype of the Lesbian becomes self-fulfilling."[3]

Because butch/femme came to be seen as contrary to feminism and "unnatural" to the free woman, lesbian-feminists considered those who assumed the roles "politically incorrect." Such women were accused of shutting themselves off from the benefits women had accrued through feminism, which included not only the recognition that both partners in a relationship could and should be equal but also the freedom to love

[2]Questionnaire respondent in Dolores Klaich, *Woman + Woman: Attitudes towards Lesbianism* (New York, 1974), p. 117.

[3]Sidney Abbott and Barbara Love, *Sappho Was a Right-On Woman: A Liberated View of Lesbianism* (New York, 1972), p. 95.

homogenderally, since feminists challenged the pervasive 1950s belief that only opposites attract.

Lesbian-feminists insisted that while the choice to be butch was understandable in previous years, there was no longer any excuse for it. Some saw that earlier choice as having to do with dress restrictions: women had been drawn to dressing as men because they believed that in men's garb they could do anything that a man could do. But, as one writer for a lesbian journal observed in 1975, dress codes had changed since the 1950s and roles had naturally changed along with them— when women and men are wearing basically the same attire, the roles become less clearly defined. "Men have less power over women; women become less vulnerable." Just as heterosexuals were ostensibly rejecting role divisions, even in their unisex dress, this writer said, so were lesbians, so that butch/femme was bound eventually to be "abolished."[4]

Others blamed the earlier butch/femme divisions on monogamy, which was now a major taboo among lesbian radicals. They argued that the dyad relationship encouraged roles because roles permitted more "efficiency": for example, one person would take care of the house, while the other would go out to work. Radicals saw such efficiency as "part of the whole capitalist trip. A form of social programming." They protested that its purpose was to keep "the old marriage machine going." And their verdict was that it was "boring."[5]

Still others rejected roles because what was most attractive to them about lesbianism were the possibilities they believed it opened for androgyny. They saw themselves as desiring the best elements of what traditionally was defined both as male and as female, and they were attracted to other women who also strove for both elements. Not only was their own favorite attire jeans and a shirt, but they also preferred their partners in the same outfit.[6]

In the 1950s the most readily identifiable lesbians were the butches and the femmes who accompanied them. Consequently, they were the ones who created the dominant lesbian image of the era. In the 1970s the "dyke" was dominant. The dyke image consisted of boots, jeans, "men's" shirts, short hair—and, ideally, aggressive behavior. In effect, it meant that everyone within the radical community looked like what had previously been called butch, but the concept of butch was redefined: a dyke did not look for a femme as a love partner; she looked for another

[4]Victoria Brownworth, "Butch/Femme: Myth/Reality, or More of the Same," *Wicce* 4 (Summer 1975): 7–9.

[5]Interview with Marty, in Brownworth, p. 9.

[6]Personal interview with Paula, age fifty-one, Boston, December 29, 1987; personal interview with Dot, age thirty-seven, Fresno, CA, October 8, 1987.

dyke. She did not consider her behavior masculine; rather, it was femi-nist. According to some critics, sexual expression was often prescribed in dykedom almost as severely as it had been in some areas of butchdom in the 1950s, when the butch had to be the aggressor and could seldom allow herself to be "flipped." Susie Bright, who proclaims herself a femme today, remembers that in the late 1970s dyke relationships had to be heavy on the romance and light on the sex because women were terrified of using each other as sexual objects: "Inserting your fingers into your lover's vagina was considered heterosexual," she says. "Touch-ing her breasts meant that you were just objectifying her. The only thing that was all right was oral sex, and you had to be sure that you both got it for an equal time."[7]

## The 1970s Butch/Femme Underground

Although the most vocal lesbians had no interest in butch/femme roles and relationships during the 1970s, some women clearly did. Apoliti-cal women who felt that feminism had little to do with them and who had never even heard of lesbian-feminism, with its precept that roles were politically incorrect, continued to live as they always had. In some ethnic-minority lesbian communities the pressure to adhere to roles was exerted as strongly as it was in earlier decades. H. O., a Chicana woman, says that in Merced, California, where she came out in 1970, all the Chicana lesbians in her small community were into roles. Since she was having a relationship with a woman who "wore lots of make-up, false eyelashes, and had her boobs showing," she felt an obligation during the seven years they were together to project a "macho image," to wear pants and tee shirts, and to be a stone butch (one who does not let herself be touched sexually by her partner), de-spite what she says was her deep preference for mutuality in a sexual re-lationship. She explains that both she and her lover "fell into those roles because that's all we knew."[8]

In some black communities as well, butch/femme roles often re-mained rigid, even throughout the "liberated" 1970s. A study of "lower-lower-class" black lesbians in central Harlem during the mid-1970s observed that only 17 percent of the women in the sample would not identify themselves as either butch or femme, and that while the butch character was considered an anathema outside the area of the

---

[7]Personal interview with Susie Bright, age twenty-nine, San Francisco, August 11, 1987.

[8]Personal interview with H. O., age thirty-six, Merced, CA, October 28, 1987.

study (that is, in middle-class or non-ghetto lesbian life), she was "a fixture on the ghetto scene."[9]

Some black women complained that when they moved outside the ghetto into integrated lesbian communities in certain areas, even in the 1970s, white women sometimes automatically assumed that black women would be butch in a sexual relationship or even manipulated them into being butch. As Iris, a black lesbian from Omaha, Nebraska, remembers, "They didn't like you to wear make-up. They wanted you in masculine dress, but they wanted to be real 'fou-fou' themselves." She attributes the predilection to a covert racism that is blind to femininity in black females.[10]

Among lesbians in prison, the butch/femme division was also strictly maintained throughout the 1970s. Any attempt to diverge from the "mom" and "pop" roles, as they were often called, was met with the same disdain and discomfort that such unorthodoxy elicited among certain groups in the 1950s. As one black lesbian convict described the situation: "I like both parts. They say I'm a faggot because I don't treat any woman the way a butch should. I share with her and do her clothes when she's busy. Sometimes I'm passive and let her be the aggressive one. Both the butches and the femmes get mad."[11]

Some women outside ghettos and prisons also insisted, even in the face of powerful lesbian-feminist opposition, that one or the other of the roles was simply natural to them. In a 1979 interview in *Lesbian Tide* one woman declared that, from her own observations, 80 percent of all lesbians had behavior patterns that could be seen as butch or femme. She admitted that for some years she pretended not to be a butch because it was politically incorrect, but she discovered that she "could just not get it together emotionally" with women who were not femmes. She concluded that although she had had affairs with lesbians who covered the entire spectrum of masculinity and femininity, deep down she always remained a butch: "If I was celibate for the rest of my life, I would still be butch."[12]

Her firm role identification was sometimes echoed in print by other women during the 1970s, despite the fact that that position was generally unpopular with the most vocal of the lesbian community. In another interview for a 1970s lesbian-feminist magazine, a twenty-four-

---

[9]William A. Fitzgerald, "Pseudo-Heterosexuality in Prison and Out: A Study of Lower-Class Black Lesbians" (Ph.D. diss., City University of New York, 1977), pp. 117, 151.

[10]Personal interview with Iris, age thirty-three, Lincoln, NE, October 13, 1988.

[11]Fitzgerald, p. 98.

[12]Interview with Susan in "Are Roles Really Dead?" *Lesbian Tide* (September/October 1979), p. 10.

year-old woman named Mickey discussed her own views of butch and femme, which at the height of the lesbian-feminist movement were no different from many of her counterparts twenty years earlier. Relationships, for Mickey, had to be not only heterogenderal but extreme in their divisions. She associated her own butch role with independence, control, "shutting off my emotions when I have to and knocking someone out in the street if I have to." And, she believed, "being a butch you have to be the boss. Most femmes want that. They want you to make the decisions."[13] Not all women who continued to adhere to roles during radical feminism's apogee were so stereotypical in their thinking. Some explained, under the partial influence of feminism, that it was necessary to share powers and privileges in a relationship, regardless of who wore the make-up or the short hair, but that it was unfair of the community to impose a uniform style of behavior on individuals. They protested that pressures to conform had gone from one extreme to the other. In the 1950s one had to be butch or femme in order to be accepted into certain communities. In the 1970s one dared not be butch or femme if she wanted to be accepted in certain communities.

Because the prescriptions, ironically, were so heavy against butch/femme behavior—which had had its own very heavy prescriptions in the past—many of those who would have preferred the roles believed they had to mask their inclinations. Honey Lee, a San Francisco woman who identifies herself as a working-class butch, remembers that in the early 1970s she realized that the rules were changing and that, although she had never needed to defend her behavior before, suddenly she was open to criticism for being butch: "In the parlance of the '70s I was male-identified, but I socialized with people who assumed I was just a feminist. I had to hide my stuff," she says. "I really felt bad when I learned that what I liked was looked down upon." She explains that she was able to retain her butch self-image, even in the midst of a women's movement that denigrated it, because she always saw herself "as a maverick—never really part of women's lib or gay lib."[14] Such a perception, thinking of oneself as essentially separate from a group, permitted some women to hold out against prescriptions during an era of lesbian-feminist tyranny.

Working-class women in particular, who had identified as butches or femmes and then became genuinely involved in feminism, were often alienated by feminism's attitude toward roles. They perceived that

---

[13]Interview with Mickey in Brownworth, p. 7. Antoinette Azolakov's character Lester (Celeste) in *Cass and the Stone Butch* (Austin, TX, 1987) is a good fictional portrait of lesbians like Mickey who continue to exist in the 1980s and 1990s.

[14]Personal interview with Honey Lee, age forty-one, San Francisco, August 6, 1987.

feminists wanted them to repress a large part of themselves for the sake of a political image. Joan Nestle, who, like Honey Lee, identifies herself as being from a working-class background, complained in 1982 that feminism put her in an unconscionable position: if she dressed as a femme to please herself and her lover she would be called a traitor "by many of my own people" because she would be seen as wearing the clothes of the enemy. But if she wore "movement" clothes because she was afraid of the judgment of those same people, she would still be a traitor—to her femme sense of personal style. Her anger was reiterated by many other working-class lesbians who had identified as butch or femme before feminism.[15]

Some women saw the conflict as a class war, fought on the battle-ground of feminism. It was a war butches and femmes were destined to lose throughout the 1970s, but their convictions often persisted. Sarah, a Boston woman, talks about the battles at the Cambridge Women's Center that took place among the feminists, lesbians, and lesbian-feminists. Wearing make-up, she remembers, was considered "horri-ble," but being butch was also out of the question: "It made me angry. Who were these people to come out of their middle class and tell us what being lesbian was supposed to mean? They even took over the term 'dyke.' Here they were from their rich, sheltered backgrounds wearing their dyke buttons. They didn't have to go through the name-calling we suffered through. Their version of being a lesbian was 'fashionable.' How could they understand what butch meant to those of us who had lived it?"[16]

Those committed butches who did not want to fight a class war and were tired of going against the grain not only in the heterosexual world but in their own lesbian world sometimes chose to opt out of lesbianism altogether, not by developing an interest in men but by becoming men themselves. In San Francisco during the mid-1970s, older masculine women were flocking to the Langley Porter Clinic, asking for sex change operations because, as Phyllis Lyon, codirector of the National Sex Forum, observed, "Lesbians were saying butch was out."[17] If a lesbian was no longer supposed to want to be butch, they reasoned, and yet they themselves still felt butch, it must be because they were really men trapped in women's bodies.

[15]Joan Nestle, "The Fem Question; or, We Will Not Go Away" (paper presented at "The Scholar and the Feminist: Toward a Politics of Sexuality" conference, Barnard College, April 24, 1982).

[16]Personal interview with Sarah, age thirty-nine, Boston, July 14, 1987.

[17]Personal interview with Phyllis Lyon and Del Martin, San Francisco, August 14, 1987.

The division between women who saw their lesbianism in images that were popularized in the 1950s and the "new gay" lesbian-feminists led occasionally to heated jockeying for control of the public manifestations of lesbian culture. In one Southern California bar, for example, there was a running battle between old gays and new gays over the issue of playing the song "Under My Thumb" on the jukebox, which to lesbian-feminists was a particularly offensive specimen of male chauvinist piggery and to old gays only a lively expression of dominance and submission in a love relationship. One researcher observed in her study of Albuquerque lesbians and their bars in the 1960s and 1970s that the split was even spatial: "Old dykes would stand on one side, feminists on the other."[18]

## BATTLEGROUND IN THE 1980S

The 1980s gave birth to new attitudes toward butch/femme relationships among many lesbian radicals. The midwife to this new view was Joan Nestle, whose poignant articles during the early 1980s pinpointed what came to be seen as the arrogance of lesbian-feminism in trivializing butch/femme in lesbian history. Nestle romanticized 1950s butches and femmes, depicting their open expression of nonconventional sexuality in an antisexual era as a rebellion of a colonized people. The appeal of that heroic image has been tremendous among many lesbians who not only want to honor that aspect of history, as Nestle did, but to live it, though filtered through their own time.

Their enthusiastic romanticizing has sometimes promoted an ahistoricity. Judy Grahn, for example, associates butches with the core members of a minority community who keep the "old ways." She sees them as "its true historians and 'true' practitioners, its fundamentalists, traditionalists, and old timers [who] retain the culture in a continuous line from one century to another." Unfortunately, in this reading of lesbian history romantic friendship, Boston marriage, the lesbian aristocracy of expatriate Paris, and much of middle-class lesbian life as it was lived in twentieth-century America are inadvertently eradicated.[19]

Those who claimed butch or femme identities in the 1980s (or presently, in the 1990s) often see themselves as taboo-smashers and iconoclasts. They are no longer primarily working-class women, as they were

[18]Bright (n. 7 above); Patricia Franzen, "The Transition Years: Researching the Albuquerque Lesbian Community" (paper presented at the Berkshire Women's History Conference, Wellesley College, June 20, 1987).

[19]Judy Grahn, *Another Mother Tongue: Gay Words, Gay Worlds* (Boston, 1984), p. 85. I discuss romantic friendship and Boston marriage in *Surpassing the Love of Men: Romantic Friendship and Love between Women from the Renaissance to the Present* (New York, 1981).

in the 1950s and 1960s—they are just as likely in the 1980s and 1990s to be intellectuals whose roots were in the middle class. They see their open role choices as being a defiant proclamation of their lesbianism. To them it is much more honorable than being a lesbian who can "pass for straight" among heterosexuals through her own appearance and that of her lover. As writer Pat Suncircle declares in a lesbian short story: "To love a bulldagger is to be unable to lie."[20]

Some lesbians say they were fed up with the doctrines of lesbian-feminism that wanted to mold all women into a single image. In their view, the lesbian-feminist creation of political propriety that swept into women's bedrooms was far more damaging to lesbian liberty and pursuit of happiness than the rigidity of butch/femme roles in the 1950s and 1960s. In reaction to that propriety they proudly proclaimed, "I like being a butch. I like being with other butches with our nicknames and ballgames—women with muscles and pretty faces," and "When I wear flowing dresses on a hot summer day I believe it is a femme choice coming from my authentic lesbian self. . . . That real self was denied by a lesbian-feminist analysis fearful . . . that possibly we were imitating heterosexual roles." The newly proclaimed femmes were now resentful that they had had to "trade in our pretty clothes for the nondescript uniform of that decade." "Let's face it," they said disdainfully of the 1970s style, "feminism is not sexy."[21] Many were furious that the 1970s had forced them into androgyny, which alone became the accepted norm for dress and behavior in the radical feminist community. They see themselves now as virtually doing battle with the lesbian-feminist dragons of conformity.

But confusion has abounded because the usual definition of butch-dom in the past decade has been not very different from that of 1970s dykedom or even feminism. Not unlike the early sexologists who explained "aggressive" female behavior not as a challenge to the restrictive concept of woman (as it was believed to be in the 1970s) but as a sign of the invert, in the 1980s and 1990s such behavior has been explained as a sign of the butch. A butch is "the woman who doesn't automatically smile and shuffle for every man she encounters. The woman who walks for her own purpose and not for other people's entertainment. The woman who looks both capable of defending herself and ready to do so.

---

[20]Pat Suncircle, "Miriam," in *Lesbian Fiction,* ed. Elly Bulkin (Watertown, MA, 1981).

[21]Donna Allegra, "Butch on the Streets," in *Fight Back: Feminist Resistance to Male Violence,* ed. Frederique Delacoste and Felice Newman (Pittsburgh, PA, 1981), pp. 44–45; Paula Mariedaughter, "Too Butch for Straights, Too Femme for Dykes," *Lesbian Ethics* 2 (Spring 1986): 96–100; Norma, "Butch/Fem Relationships Revisited," *Hartford Women's Center Newsletter* 5 (December 1982): 1–2.

The woman who does not obey. The woman who is in revolt against enforced femininity, who claims for herself the right not to dress and act and talk 'like a woman' (meaning like a toy)." Another lesbian declares that "competence and dignity . . . are, for me, at the heart of butchdom." But Julia Penelope, who adamantly rejects butch roles, defines the dyke in terms very similar to those in the above definitions of the butch: for example, the dyke is "a woman who resists feminization."[22] And not many feminists, dyke or otherwise, would disagree that women should be subjects instead of objects, or that they should be serious and competent individuals.

The current confusion regarding the butch label may stem from an impatience and disillusionment that some self-identified butches feel with the failure to spread feminist goals quickly and widely enough: if there are still women who shuffle for men and obey them and let themselves be made into toys, then those who resist must be something other than mere women—born-and-bred butches. The historical figure of the butch has thus been metamorphosed into the prime warrior against male chauvinism, replacing for some radicals the feminist and the dyke of the 1970s.

The confusion is compounded by the fact that since the butch image has been presented in such politically attractive terms, not many women are prepared to call themselves femmes. One woman reports having taken an informal head count in a lesbian bar in San Francisco, finding that "butch" was sometimes being used in the 1980s as a substitute for the term "dyke": "One table of eight responded with eight enthusiastic butches, though some were in couple relationships with each other," she reported. As much as many radical femmes have insisted the contrary, it seems that in many lesbians' minds "femme" is associated with feminine, connoting "weak" and "vulnerable"—qualities that women often became lesbians in order to reject. They are too familiar with the stereotype of femininity to be able to believe in the image of femme strength suggested by Charlene Henderson in the passage quoted at the beginning of this essay.[23]

While the 1980s and 1990s consensus among many lesbians seems to be that one should have the freedom of self-definition, the very diversity of homosexual women guarantees that there would be some dissidents from such liberalism. At the one extreme is a group that echoed the 1950s, insisting that all women fall naturally into either butch or femme

[22]Julia Penelope, "Whose Past Are We Reclaiming?" *Common Lives/Lesbian Lives* 13 (Autumn 1984): 16–36.

[23]Grahn, p. 158; Charlene S. Henderson, "Texas '52," *Sinister Wisdom* 35 (Summer/Fall 1988): 43–45.

roles and that the refusal to choose is due to ignorance of self or coward-ice or sheer perversity. At the other extreme is a group that maintains the stance of the 1970s, arguing that butches and femmes are backsliders who are demolishing all the sacred tenets of lesbian-feminism. They insist that there is no such thing as an innate butch or femme identity, and they ridicule role divisions by calling themselves "futches" and "bems."[24]

Although butch/femme reemerged in the 1980s essentially as a pro-test against the doctrinaire conformity and sexual monotony of radical lesbian-feminism, it appears to be gradually bringing with it its own pressures. Perhaps such constant shifts are inevitable in any minority group that is tied together by one factor in the members' identity but fragmented by all the other variables in their personalities. Those who are the most enthusiastic in their newfound butch/femme freedom seem determined to fix one or the other label on all lesbians, insisting that one cannot escape the butch/femme model if one is being honest. They claim, with some homage to Freud, that butch and femme personalities are formed at an early age (generally in response to or reaction against heterosexual indoctrination into feminization) and that they are un-changeable. Judy Grahn suggests that all women fall naturally into one or the other category, even if they try to deny it:

> Among middle-class American Lesbians, extreme butch-femme polarities are tempered. The dykes simply disguise both members of their relationship in a modified drag known as "Lesbian," with perhaps one haircut a little shorter, one voice thrown a little lower, or some other distinguishing butch mark. The couple probably makes a few jokes about it now and then, meanwhile following feminist movement rhetoric by maintaining the "roles" are "patri-archal" and beneath our advanced consciousness.[25]

Some women say that butch or femme has less to do with the behav-ior and appearances that were so intrinsic to those roles in the earlier era than with what they feel in themselves and in other women, what they mystically describe as "the essence of butch" or "the essence of femme." They tell of party conversations in which it was possible to get a consen-sus among a half-dozen women about who was butch and who was femme in their town, not through dress but rather through what was sensed about the person. In the course of a presentation on lesbian art

[24]Isabel Andrews, in "Femme and Butch: A Readers' Forum," *Lesbian Ethics* 2 (Fall 1986): 96–99; personal interview with Paula, age thirty-four, Omaha, NE, October 13, 1988.
[25]Grahn, p. 160.

before 1930, which I attended at the 1987 Berkshire Women's History Conference, the presenters as well as some women in the audience speculated with varying degrees of seriousness on whether the subjects in the paintings had a butch aura or a femme aura. Such mystical knowledge seems to deny refutation. One writer has not so facetiously compared the significance of butch/femme for lesbians today with that of astrology for flower children in the 1960s.[26]

However, the issue of butch/femme has created the most heat among radical lesbian-feminists, who have charged butches and their femmes with being "morally regressive" in their refusal to "think seriously about the meaning of life, the value of developing real human potentials, and the responsibility we each share to enhance the growth of the human community." Some women tell horror stories of their butch/femme encounters, seeing them as insidiously dangerous. Pauline Bart, in a 1986 article entitled "My Brief Career as a Femme," complained that the norms governing femme behavior in the subculture as she experienced it made her life as a Culver City housewife in the 1950s seem like Lesbian Nation. She claims that she soon realized that if she followed those norms, "within a few weeks [many of] the skills I had developed as a woman functioning in the world without a man would be lost." She finds butch/femme relationships irresponsible because dependence on another individual to take care of her leads the lesbian into the same learned helplessness, lack of autonomy, and low self-esteem that is endemic among heterosexual women.[27]

Radical feminists insisted that even the labels butch and femme are dangerous because they form perceptions, limit actions, and perpetuate certain behaviors that are women-oppressing and macho-glorifying. The issue of butch/femme became so heated in the 1980s that it even led to public confrontations and protests, such as the one at Barnard College in 1982. At a conference on "The Scholar and the Feminist," women

[26]Noretta Koertge, "Gender Stereotypes and Lesbian Lifestyles" (paper presented at the International Scientific Conference on Gay and Lesbian Studies, Free University, Amsterdam, December 15–18, 1987), p. 11; De Clarke, in "Femme and Butch: A Readers' Forum"; Lois Anne A., "Butch/Femme; or, I'm Glad I Went to TALF," *Triangle Newsletter,* May 1985, pp. 4–6; Pat Califia, *Sapphistry: The Book of Lesbian Sexuality,* 2d rev. ed. (Tallahassee, FL, 1983), p. 58; Nancy A. F. Langer, "The New Butch/Femme: The '80s Answer to Astrology," *New York Native,* July 29–August 11, 1985. See also Karen Lutzen, "The Return of Butch and Femme," *Hvad Hjertet Begaerer: Kvinders Kaerlighed til Kvinder 1825–1985* (Copenhagen, 1986), pp. 306–9. I am grateful to Karen Lutzen for a translation of this material.

[27]Julia Penelope, "Heteropatriarchal Semantics: Just Two Kinds of People in the World," *Lesbian Ethics* 2 (Fall 1986): 58–80; Mary Crane, letter to the editor, *Lesbian Ethics* 2 (Spring 1986): 102–3; Pauline Bart, "My Brief Career as a Femme," *Lesbian Ethics* 2 (Fall 1986): 92–95.

who identified themselves as "a coalition of radical feminists and lesbian-feminists" handed out leaflets protesting that butch/femme women and those who rally around them constitute a backlash against radical feminism. The feminists accused butches and femmes of internalizing patriarchal messages and advocating those very sex roles that are the psychological foundation of patriarchy.[28] The radical feminists continue to promote the 1970s notion that the personal is political and that even bedroom behavior needs to conform to what is politically correct.

## NEO-BUTCH/FEMME

For many of the women who identify as butch or femme today, the concept has little actual connection with the lived experience of those labels in the 1950s. Butch/femme relationships are perhaps more complex now than they were in the earlier era, reflecting the complexity of sexual relationships in the parent culture as well. Heterosexual roles, through the influence of feminism, are no longer universally simple but may legitimately take on all manner of androgynous nuances; so too lesbians who want to identify as butch or femme today have the choice of expressing themselves in an unprecedented variety of images: aggressive butch, passive butch, baby butch, stone butch, clone butch, old-fashioned femme, aggressive femme, and so on. While distinctions in dress between modern butch/femme couples are not unusual, it is also common for both women in the couple to dress in a unisex style.

The more egalitarian day-to-day living arrangements that feminism has brought to the parent culture also seem to be reflected in butch/femme relationships, so that butch/femme may be reduced to who makes the first move sexually (and sometimes not even that). One 1985 study of lesbian couples showed that while almost 70 percent maintained role divisions in sexual relations, in that one or the other woman in the relationship would almost always initiate sex, in other aspects of their lives, such as household responsibility or decisionmaking, there were no clear divisions along traditional lines. Even if sexual initiation or receptivity does indicate butch/femme roles in sexual relations, there seems not to be much left of gender stereotyping in any other area among most lesbian couples.[29]

A few women continue to use stereotypical gender descriptions in

[28]Penelope, "Whose Past Are We Reclaiming?"; "We Protest," leaflet distributed by the Coalition for a Feminist Sexuality, New York, April 1982.

[29]Jean Lynch and Mary Ellen Reilly, "Role Relationships: Lesbian Perspectives," *Journal of Homosexuality* 12 (Winter 1985/86): 53–69.

talking about their butch/femme relationships, such as Kendall, who identifies as a femme: "I could do all the things my lover does and still not be butch. It has to do with receptivity and vulnerability; femmes also tend to be more manipulative, willing to express emotions, more concerned with relationships. The butch is the push; the femme is the pull."[30] But too much has happened for history simply to repeat itself. The male hippies of the 1960s challenged the old concept of the masculine: a man could wear his hair to his shoulders and be opposed to violence and wear jewelry. The feminists of the 1970s challenged the old concept of the feminine: a woman could be efficient and forceful and demand a place in the world. Except to the most recalcitrant, there is little that remains of the simplistic ideas of gender-appropriate appearance and behavior. And lesbians, who historically have been at the forefront of feminism (in their choice to lead independent lives, if nothing else), cannot easily return to the old fashions in images and behaviors. Most would have a hard time taking such a return seriously. For that reason, butch and femme exists best today in the sexual arena, which invites fantasy and the tension of polarities.

Not even the old fashions in dress could have the same function today: butches who wore pants in the 1950s because it was their symbolic statement of rebellion against the limitations placed on them as women, who were claiming the prerogatives men had reserved for themselves and refusing to be objects and victims, were the mid-century forerunners in the struggle that other women took up in the 1970s. However, the gesture has lost its greatest significance as a political protest, since not only have many of those battles been won, but also heterosexual women who do not consider themselves rebels at all wear pants as much as lesbians do. Yet while there is frequently little distinction in attire between women who identify as butch and women who identify as femme, in the 1980s and 1990s femmes have felt much freer to wear dresses and even extreme feminine garb than they would have in the radical 1970s. It represents play and style, as does the extreme masculine garb that some latter-day butches wear.

Butch/femme roles, styles, and relationships today often appear to be conducted with a sense of lightness and flexibility. As Phyllis Lyon characterizes contemporary butch/femme, "Women 'play at it' rather than 'being it.'" Other lesbians testify to that sense of play. One woman says that she (a butch) and her femme lover complement each other in the roles they play, but they recognize it as play, as a pleasurable game: "She really can find a spark plug, she just prefers not to. Feeling that I have to protect her is an illusion that I enjoy. She allows me my illusion for she

[30]Personal interview with Kendall, age twenty-five, Berkeley, CA, August 15, 1987.

enjoys being taken care of like this."[31] Such an awareness of the "game" of roles would have been unlikely in the serious 1950s.

Therefore, for most lesbians the roles are not the life-or-death identity they often were in the 1950s, but rather an enjoyable erotic statement and an escape from the boring "vanilla sex" that they associated with lesbian-feminism. Their purpose is to create erotic tension in a relationship instead of the merging that is being held responsible for what lesbian sexologist Joann Lulan has called lesbian "bed death" (the statistically frequent fading of erotic interest in lesbian relationships after a couple of years).

The resurgence of butch/femme in the 1980s may also reflect reaction to the "drab stylelessness" of lesbian-feminists, as one woman describes the radical group she belonged to in the 1970s. Her friends, she recalls, were philosophically appealing, but they created "the unsexiest environment": "Everyone was doctrinaire about how you should look and act: short hair, no make-up, denim overalls, flannel shirts, hiking boots. It was 'hippy masculine.' I compared it to Mao's China. Plain and sexless. I'd love to see what they're wearing now."[32] As expressed today, butch/femme roles open to lesbians the possibility of wearing fashions that are signals for the erotic in the heterosexual western world in which they grew up, and which would have been ridiculed by lesbian-feminists in the 1970s: high heels, leather, lace, delicate lingerie.

In an only somewhat tongue-in-cheek article, "The Anguished Cry of an '80s Fem: I Want to Be a Drag Queen," Lisa Duggan talks about her last summer at Cherry Grove, where gay male and lesbian positions had been reversed. While gay males came to see drag as a dinosaur—an apolitical holdover, boring and dying—the lesbians at the Grove "were going to Drag Search every Sunday night. We planned our schedules around the drag teas at Cherry's, . . . and the fems had taken to borrowing boas from the boys to go dancing on Saturday night." Duggan suggests the sense of play in the new femme style when she concludes, with an insouciant verbal pout, "We didn't see why the guys had to be so goddamned serious."[33]

This sense of play and flexibility is also reflected in sexual object choice, even among many butches and femmes. The old sexual dynamic is far from clear in a modern butch/femme relationship. The stone

[31]Personal interview with Phyllis Lyon, San Francisco, August 14, 1987; Karen Cameron, in "Femme and Butch: A Readers' Forum"; Norma, "Butch/Fem Relationships Revisited."

[32]Bright (n. 7 above).

[33]Lisa Duggan, "The Anguished Cry of an '80s Fem: I Want to Be a Drag Queen," Out/Look 1 (Spring 1988): 63–65.

butch, who was common in the 1950s and 1960s, is a rare figure, perhaps because a woman who does not want to be reminded of her femaleness by having another woman make love to her has the option today (more easily than she would have had earlier) of eradicating her femaleness through a sex change operation. One lesbian who characterizes herself as a "possible femme" admits that she picks "butchy" women (those who flaunt their unfemininity) as sexual partners, but, she adds, "I cannot stereotype my lovemaking. There, more perhaps than anywhere else, I feel unrestricted enough to do what seems natural to me—and I will not limit myself to *anyone's* code of behavior." She asks that lesbians make no assumptions about what "butchness" and "femmeness" mean to other lesbians, but rather that each woman allow herself to explore and act out unforced role behavior that feels comfortable to her. A Lincoln, Nebraska, woman who says she identifies as a butch admits that she also likes to wear long dresses occasionally, and she does most of the cooking and cleaning chores in the home she shares with a woman who calls herself a femme but is very career-oriented. This "butch's" flexibility is suggested by her attire at a recent function in the lesbian community: "a tuxedo with a matching shade of eye shadow, and a necklace along with a bow tie." Butch and femme today can mean whatever one wants those terms to mean. A woman is a butch or a femme simply because she says she is. The 1966 *Random House Dictionary of the English Language* definition of "butch" as "the one who takes the part of a man" in a lesbian relationship has lost whatever inevitable truth it may have once had.[34]

Lesbian sexual roles have loosened in other ways as well. Just as in recent years it has become easier for a heterosexual to admit homosexual interests, so has it become permissible for a butch to admit interest in another butch, or a femme in another femme. Since the kiki taboo (in which 1950s butches and femmes characterized lesbians who were neither butch nor femme as "confused") no longer exists, women have no external pressure to conform in their selection of partners, although some may be confused over the apparent contradiction in their self-definition. If they can adjust to that ambiguity, there is little to prevent them from identifying however they wish, changing that identity when they wish, and choosing a partner who is either heterogenderal or homogenderal.

But some lesbians even today do not feel such flexibility in their sexual self-image. They are sometimes defensive about their role choice,

[34]Laura Rose DancingFire, "Meditations of a Possible Femme," *Common Lives/Lesbian Lives* 14 (Winter 1984): 10–19; personal interview with Neva, age forty-six, Lincoln, NE, October 12, 1988.

and in areas as diverse as New York City and Lawrence, Kansas, they have considered it necessary to establish "butch support groups" and "femme support groups" to help them counter what they perceive as hostility from those lesbians who continue to reject roles. They define their preference for butch sexuality or femme sexuality as "a drive that comes from the very deepest core of sexual necessity," having little to do with learned behavior. Amber Hollibaugh, who calls herself a femme, says that her own sexual fantasy life is entirely involved in a butch/femme exchange: "I never come together with a woman sexually outside of those roles. I'm saying to my partner, 'Love me enough to let me go where I need to go and take me there. . . . You map it out. You are in control.'" She hints that perhaps her interest in that kind of dynamic comes from much richer territory than simply that of roles, but like many other women today, she uses the vocabulary that has been revived from the 1950s to explain it.[35]

One woman, who also identifies as a femme although she says she has been butch with inexperienced women, finds that being a femme sexually means playing off feminine stereotypes—the little girl, the bitch, the queen, the sex pot—and making those images into your sexual language. For her it is primarily camp and fantasy, and it does not necessarily have to do with other aspects of personality. Nor are those roles limited in themselves, she explains. One can, for example, be a femme "top" (that is, the sexual dominator) or a butch "bottom."[36]

The roles are often sexually charged in a way that would have been unthinkable in the sexually tame 1970s, when erotic seduction was considered a corrupt imitation of heterosexuality; but the actors who indulge in these roles, femme as well as butch, are now frequently cognizant of the feminist image of the strong woman. The femme fantasy ideal may now be a lesbian Carmen rather than a Camille. One woman, for example, dares to write in a radical lesbian journal of her favorite sexual fantasy, in which she would appear at a lesbian dance in a "sleazy" black silk, low-cut dress with hot pink flowers on it:

> I would come in, not, I repeat, *not* like a helpless femme-bot [= robot], but like a bad-ass-no-games-knows-her-own-mind-and-will-tell-you-too femme. First I would stand there and let my lover wonder. Maybe I would just stand there altogether and let her come to me. Or maybe, while all the heads were turning . . . I would stride across the dance floor in a bee-line for that green-eyed

[35]Amber Hollibaugh and Cherríe Moraga, "What We're Rollin' around in Bed With," in *Powers of Desire: The Politics of Sexuality,* ed. Ann Snitow et al. (New York, 1983), p. 398.

[36]Personal interview with S. B., age twenty-nine, San Francisco, September 12, 1987.

womon [*sic*] I love, so that everyone could see who the one in the black dress was going to fuck tonight.[37]

As expressed in the 1980s and 1990s, the roles have become both a reflection and a feminist expansion of the early inculcation by the parent culture, and women are using them largely for their own pleasurable aims.

The erotic play that is at the center of neo-butch/femme mirrors Michael Bronski's definition of "gay lib" as it related to gay men: "At its most basic, [it] offers the possibility of freedom of pleasure for its own sake."[38] During the early years of the movement, when lesbians were busy defining the very serious tenets of lesbian-feminism and living by them, the concept of pleasure for its own sake was alien, and the AIDS crisis in the gay male community has now made that definition problematic for men as well as for many lesbians who sympathize with them. Yet in neo-butch/femme as an area of sexual play, a good number of lesbians in the 1980s felt entitled to claim pleasure for its own sake.

It is also a reflection of the current era that even among those lesbians who are mindful of themselves within a lesbian community there is less concern about the strictures of the movement and the group than there was in the 1970s and more interest in self-fulfillment. They claim the liberty to define themselves with fewer references to the expectations of either the parent culture or their immediate society. If butch or femme is part of that self-definition, for whatever reason, they are now likely to claim it. Political correctness is mostly out and individual expression is mostly in.

[37]Jess Wells, "The Dress," *Common Lives/Lesbian Lives* 8 (Summer 1983).
[38]Michael Bronski, *Culture Clash: The Making of Gay Sensibility* (Boston, 1984), p. 214.

# Of Purebreds and Hybrids: The Politics of Teaching AIDS in the United States

KATHERINE CUMMINGS

*Department of English*
*University of Washington*

Nothing could be more meaningless than a virus. It has no point, no purpose, no plan; it is part of no scheme, carries no inherent significance. And yet nothing is harder for us to confront than the complete absence of meaning. . . . [For] the end of meaning . . . threatens the fragile structures by which we make sense of the world. [Judith Williamson, "Every Virus Tells a Story," in *Taking Liberties*]

Language is itself a metaphor, and we can no more "purify" it in discussing disease than in describing a beautiful day. . . . Constructing less devastating ways of regarding an illness . . . [always depends upon] what's available metaphorically, what the implications of current metaphors may be for various audiences, and who benefits from those conceits most commonly at work in media, medicine, politics, and public health. [Jan Zita Grover, "Constitutional Symptoms," in *Taking Liberties*]

AIDS IS A DEVASTATING illness with real physical, emotional, and institutional effects. AIDS is also a metaphor that replaces the private language of human bodies with a public language whose purpose is to explain human suffering and death. These metaphors have real consequences. Representations of AIDS determine how people living with AIDS experience their illness, how scientists proceed in their research, how health care workers treat AIDS patients, how governments react to the AIDS pandemic, and how people without AIDS respond to those who have AIDS, who have tested positive for the human immunodeficiency virus (HIV) believed to cause it, or who have been classified as being "at risk."

Representations of AIDS are frequently strung together within a narrative whose explicit aims include making illness meaningful and/or

This essay originally appeared in the *Journal of the History of Sexuality* 1991, vol. 2, no. 1.

teaching subjects how to behave. For that reason, AIDS narratives might equally be called pedagogies. One of the lessons they teach is the distinction between "us" and "them." This distinction is fundamental to narratives that return to the origins of organisms (subjects, communities, nations) in the attempt to make sense of AIDS. An overview of scholarly literature on the subject illustrates.

In the early 1980s, numerous publications in medical journals cited the "gay lifestyle," and specifically the hypersexuality of gay males, as the cause of pneumocystis *Carinii* pneumonia and Kaposi's sarcoma (two opportunistic diseases subsequently linked to the immune deficiency disorder now known as AIDS).[1] Other essays located the source of AIDS in the gay environment, zeroing in on the sexual use of poppers (amyl nitrates) by gay men.[2] Subsequent journal articles retained an originary focus while shifting the terrain; they found HIV to be *the* cause of AIDS.[3] Before HIV had been isolated and the syndrome named AIDS, the illness was defined in

[1]See, for instance, Michael S. Gottlieb et al., "Pneumocystis *Carinii* Pneumonia and Mucosas Candidiasis in Previously Healthy Homosexual Men," *New England Journal of Medicine* 305 (1981): 1425–30; Carlos Navarro and Jack W. C. Hagstrom, "Correspondence on Opportunistic Infections and Kaposi's Sarcoma in Gay Men," *New England Journal of Medicine* 306 (1982): 933; and James L. Fletcher, "Homosexuality: Kick and Kickback," *Southern Medical Journal* 77 (1984): 149–50, from which I quote: "Of magnetic interest is the rather select group of individuals afflicted by this syndrome. Male homosexuals (or bisexuals) have comprised more than 75% of those affected. . . . Could it be that a causal relationship exists between their behavior and their disease? Might we be witnessing, in fact, in the form of a modern communicable disorder, a fulfillment of St. Paul's pronouncement: 'the due penalty of their error'? . . . Indeed, from an empirical medical perspective alone, current scientific observation seems to require the conclusion that homosexuality is a pathogenic condition" (p. 150).

[2]See "Epidemiological Aspects of the Current Outbreak of Kaposi's Sarcoma and Opportunistic Infections," Report of the Centers for Disease Control, *New England Journal of Medicine* 306 (1982): 248–52; Jeffrey Ratner and Allen Thomas, "Opportunistic Infections in Gay Men," *Southern Medical Journal* 77 (1984): 227–28; and Ronald W. Wood, "Correspondence on Opportunistic Infections and Kaposi's Sarcoma in Gay Men," *New England Journal of Medicine* 306 (1982): 932–33, which, after advancing the hypothesis that the inhaling of amyl nitrates lies behind the gay epidemic, concludes: "Enhancement of the orgasm and relaxation of the sphincter muscles by nitrates may contribute to their popularity with this group" (p. 932). For an alternative reading of the so-called gay environment, see Hans H. Neumann, "Correspondence on the Use of Steroid Creams as a Possible Cause of Immunosuppression in Homosexuals," *New England Journal of Medicine* 306 (1982): 935, which argues: "Promiscuity . . . and recreational drugs are not new and do not explain the recent epidemic. . . . A link is missing. There is a remarkable coincidence in time between the upsurge in cases and the over-the-counter availability of cortisone creams."

[3]See *Science* 220 (1983): 806–7, 859–70, especially "Isolation of a T-Lymphotropic Virus from a Patient at Risk for Acquired Immune Deficiency Syndrome (AIDS)," pp. 868–70; and *Science* 224 (1984): 475–77, 497–508. For popular versions of the same story, see Robert Gallo, "The AIDS Virus," *Scientific American* (January 1987), pp. 47–56; and *AIDS: Chapter One,* NOVA no. 1205, originally broadcast on PBS on February 12, 1985.

relation to the first reported cases and thus recorded under the name "gay immune deficiency syndrome" (GRID). All such originary narratives of immunodeficiency affixed and continue to affix blame on gay men. Proliferating stories of monkey "carriers," Africans, and Haitians (the three of which often occur within the same frame) employ an identical logic.[4] As a group, such narratives construct a homogeneous organism that is alien, exotic, and primitive; all three traits clearly separate the AIDS-ridden organism from a clean-minded collective of familiar, ordinary, and civilized folk.

My assumption is that AIDS stories of organisms and their origins reflect "what's available metaphorically."[5] That is, they occur as frequently as they do partly because they are underwritten by an originary metanarrative whose sustaining oppositions Jacques Derrida and others have identified as constitutive of Western metaphysics. In the first section of my essay I map the contours of the West's metanarrative while addressing the work of narrativity in producing and policing subjects. A critical review of *Thinking AIDS: The Social Response to the Biological Threat*, a science book, then illustrates how such originary narratives are put together and what effects they have upon students of the text. A reading of Donna Haraway's article, "A Manifesto for Cyborgs: Science, Technology, and Socialist Feminism in the 1980s," ends the first section; in it I consider how Haraway's cyborg subjects and politics encourage alternative responses to AIDS. The second section of the essay brings the workings of both organic and cybernetic narratives into the university classroom, where they inform my reading of educational videos distributed by national and municipal departments of public health for the purpose of teaching college and high school students the "facts" about AIDS. In essence, both sections argue that narratives are sites of hermeneutic contestation and political struggle; they "can be both

---

[4]See "New Human T-Lymphotropic Retrovirus Related to Simian T-Lymphotropic Virus Type III (STLV-III)," *Science* 232 (1986): 238–43; John Langone, "AIDS in Africa and Haiti," in *AIDS: The Facts* (Boston, 1988), pp. 107–24; and Alexander Moore and Ronald D. Le Baron, "The Case for a Haitian Origin of the AIDS Epidemic," in *The Social Dimensions of AIDS: Method and Theory*, ed. Douglas A. Feldman and Thomas M. Johnson (New York, 1986), pp. 77–90, whose thesis is that the viral "agent" causing AIDS found "its way into human hosts in Haiti and in equatorial Africa, through the regular ingestion of uncooked animal blood sacrificed in spirit possession ceremonies. . . . Moreover, in the 1970s tourism to the Third World took place in the context of the sexual liberation of North Atlantic countries. Thus, AIDS may well be the first of a number of strange and lethal new maladies borne by sexually active [gay male] tourists. It is also one carried by that new traveler, the elite Third World native" (pp. 77, 84). But see also June Osborne, "The AIDS Epidemic: An Overview of the Science," *Issues in Science and Technology* 2 (1986): 40–55, which reproduces all of the origin plots I have mentioned within the framework of a detective story.

[5]Jan Zita Grover, "Constitutional Symptoms," in *Taking Liberties: AIDS and Cultural Politics*, ed. Erica Carter and Simon Watney (London, 1989), p. 152.

an instrument and an effect of power," as Foucault has observed, "but also a hindrance, a stumbling-block, a point of resistance and a starting point for an opposing strategy."[6] Thus, while all narratives attempt to seduce their readers into thinking and desiring in textually specified ways, no narrative is finally capable of determining its reading subjects or of controlling precisely how it will be read—and certainly not those narratives which would compel us to confront the imminence of our own mortality under the acronym of "AIDS."

## ORGANISMS AND CYBORGS

Narratives are technologies for making meaning. They impose sense on subjects and events by emplotting them in purposeful sequences; and they re-present material phenomena in metaphors, which are historically specific and ideologically loaded. Because metaphors enforce distinctions by arranging subjects so that their differences from each other become apparent, and because they predispose us to see phenomena in particular ways, it might be said that the function of metaphoricity, language, is to impose discriminating (differential and pre-judicial) names.

Both the classificatory and emplotment functions of narrative presuppose that some kind of detective work is occurring or, in fact, has already occurred. This is probably why analogies between detecting and narrating are frequently made. Each activity can be represented as a high stakes investigation, the point of which is to decipher signs, read riddles, and compel subjects to speak their secrets in order that the detective/narrative might name what has not yet been named. Not only do detection and narration share many of the same techniques; at least one order of narrative and detective work rests on identical postulates.

The narrative I have in mind is a Western saga of individuation. This story, a narrative of origin, informs the writing of nineteenth-century historicism, science, psychoanalysis. Indeed, it is widely remarked that the hunt for the organism's origins animates the so-called master-narratives of the West. Again and again, Western writers take up the search for some originary moment in which the subject will stand revealed in his or her truth. Peter Brooks has suggested that master-narratives thus resemble arch-detectives in their assumption that "we can explain who we are only by finding out how we got that way, through plotting that story which traces effects to origins and enchains events along the way."[7] Here, Brooks speaks

[6]Michel Foucault, *The History of Sexuality: An Introduction,* vol. 1 of *The History of Sexuality,* trans. Robert Hurley (New York, 1978), p. 101.

[7]Peter Brooks, "Fictions of the Wolfman: Freud and Narrative Understanding," *Diacritics* 9 (1979): 74.

directly to what is arguably the most powerful work of *all* narrativity—the production of human subjects. These subjects explain "who we are in stories." Yet we need not conclude that we explain ourselves solely in relation to an origin, unless we assume that we are textual purebreds, hapless offspring of a single narrative strain. A more credible assumption would leave a space for textual mongrels, whose explanatory myths bear the markings of different narrative pedigrees.

In *Alice Doesn't,* Teresa de Lauretis implicitly takes up Brooks's thesis. Arguing that "the very work of narrativity is the engagement of the subject in certain positionalities of meaning and desire," she implies that stories are pedagogies that teach reading subjects how to think, feel, behave.[8] To conclude that narratives teach "certain" lessons is not to conclude that lessons are passively received, however, or that reading subjects learn exactly what a "certain" narrative would have them learn. My dictionary includes the following entry under "certain": "definite or particular, but not named [beforehand] or specified [originally]." Reading "certain" as "particular" has an obvious advantage. It enables us to recognize how any narrative makes available "definite" subject positions, with which its readers are encouraged to identify, without our having to assume that these positions are fixed. Another definition of "certain" opens up the domain of narrativity, inviting us to compare "some" narratives—myths of origins, for instance—to others whose existence "certain" presumes. Both definitions suppose that narrativity and its correlative, subjectivity, are multiple: subject to modification, negotiation, change.

Neither definition is given much play by de Lauretis, however. On the contrary, in *Alice Doesn't* "certain" assumes the meaning of "destined"; it functions the same way that "only" does in Brooks's exposition of narrative work. Thus, de Lauretis's subjects are all bred from a single narrative; they find their meaning in the logic of sexual difference and their desire in the reenactment of oedipal dramas. Her explanatory myth of origins inscribes more clearly than Brooks's does, however, the determinations of subjects in their truth. From de Lauretis we learn that the very being of any subject depends upon not being an other; thus, men are precisely not-women and women, conversely, not-men. Oedipal is similarly defined against pre-oedipal so that everywhere we look we discover cohesive little categories. While each is in need of an opposing category for its definition, each is cut off from any commerce with the other, so that every subject remains essentially self-enclosed: impermeable, but by no means impervious to an alien other, whose existence is perceived to threaten its own integrity. That the outside(r) be kept out and the inside(r) in is, in brief, the central operation

[8]Teresa de Lauretis, *Alice Doesn't: Feminism, Semiotics, Cinema* (Bloomington, IN, 1984), p. 106.

in narratives of origin, which is why they are called dramas of individuation or histories of the One.

Two of the "biggest" AIDS stories that appeared during the fall of 1990 are patterned on the same narrative scheme. In October, the front cover of *People Magazine* featured a young, white, female virgin whose gay male dentist gave her AIDS. In December, television reporter Connie Chung aired the story of another white woman who had been raped by an "AIDS-infested" black, heterosexual, male drug addict.[9] Both stories explicitly pit "monstrous others" against "innocent ones" (hence, the emphasis on virginity and violation in the first story); in representing the commerce between each couple as deadly, they imply the need for quarantine.

Donna Haraway makes use of an alternative narrative. A self-styled "science fiction," her "Manifesto for Cyborgs" attempts to reimagine "lived social and bodily realities" in a cybernetic age. Haraway's cyborg does not "mark time on an Oedipal calendar," nor has the cyborg "an origin story in the Western sense." There is no "myth of original unity here," or drama of individuation. Although the organism survives, it is no longer whole; the subjects Haraway calls cyborgs are, rather, hybridic mixtures of organism and machine. Unlike the subjects of origin stories, cyborgs have "permanently partial identities"; they—we—are decidedly *not* self-contained.[10]

To situate Haraway's cyborg-netic history and address its applications to AIDS, it will be necessary to introduce a second science text, which belongs to the older genre of originary narratives and with which the "Manifesto" might usefully be compared. By usefully, I mean structurally and politically, since the structures of both narratives give shape to their separate subjects, while these subjects in turn affect how we, their readers, will respond to the material reality of AIDS.

My representative story of organisms and their origins comes from a recently published biomedical book called *Thinking AIDS*.[11] The text has been widely praised for its lucidity, scope, and sensitivity; it recognizes that the body has multiple zones of pleasure, alludes to the cultural constructedness of human sexualities, explicitly condemns AIDS discrimination, opposes mandatory diagnostic testing and screening for HIV, and devotes much of its space to talking about the immune system in a language that laypersons can readily understand. With recommendations such as these, *Thinking AIDS* asks to be adopted for use by educators in what I imagine might be advanced high school and lower-level college classrooms.

[9]*Face to Face,* with Connie Chung, originally broadcast on CBS on December 10, 1990.

[10]Donna Haraway, "A Manifesto for Cyborgs: Science, Technology and Socialist Feminism in the 1980s," in *Coming to Terms: Feminism, Theory, Politics,* ed. Elizabeth Weed (New York, 1989), pp. 175, 179.

[11]Mary Catherine Bateson and Richard Goldsby, *Thinking AIDS: The Social Response to the Biological Threat* (Reading, MA, 1988).

A modest master-narrative, the text does not feature detectives hot upon the trail of a virus; its authors are not out to crack the genetic code of HIV or to pin down the virus's source. Still, when Bateson and Goldsby tell the story of AIDS, they speak of organisms as being originally coherent and self-possessed; in detail, they describe the organism's dissolution and dis-possession, and they talk the talk of contamination, defense. Hence, in *Thinking AIDS*, we learn: "The body, like a fortress, is designed to keep things out."[12]

"The body" is not just any body, of course. On the contrary, the enclosed body is a recognizable synecdoche for male bodies in a society where bodily impenetrability, integrity, has been systematically enlisted to signify "male" and penetrability its opposite, "not-male." This cultural definition of male-ness informs heterosexual readings of gay male sexuality as "a deliberate [and petrifying] renunciation of the signs and privileges of the masculine role."[13] The equation of maleness and impenetrability also helps to explain why "passive anal sex" is regularly represented in male heterosexual fan-tasies of gay men. As Ana Maria Alonso and Maria Teresa Koreck have argued, "a being who is born with a closed male body but who subjects him/her-self to being opened and penetrated like a woman" forfeits his title to manhood; "she" enters the category of "other," culturally defined as "not-men."[14] No doubt, this naming of gay males marks an attempt to shore up the category of maleness; motivated by the dread of "leakage" or "contamination," nomination thus replicates the logic and function rou-tinely identified with bodily quarantines.[15] Once named "not-men," gay men are simultaneously isolated from "real men"; the threat they pose to the continuance of a cohesive masculinity, an organic maleness, is thereby contained.

[12]Ibid., p. 26.

[13]Michel Foucault, *The Use of Pleasure*, vol. 2 of *The History of Sexuality*, trans. Robert Hurley (New York, 1986), p. 19.

[14]Ana Maria Alonso and Maria Teresa Koreck, "Silences: 'Hispanics,' AIDS and Sexual Practices," *Differences* 1 (1988): 101.

[15]On "the ideology of leakage," see especially Jan Zita Grover, "AIDS: Keywords," in *AIDS: Cultural Analysis, Cultural Activism*, ed. Douglas Crimp (Cambridge, MA, 1988), pp. 17–30; and Simon Watney, *Policing Desire: Pornography, AIDS, and the Media*, 2d ed. (Min-neapolis, 1989), and "Taking Liberties: An Introduction," in Carter and Watney, eds. (n. 5 above), pp. 11–57. Grover tracks the representation of leakage in the mass media to its fan-tasmatic ground in the heterosexual imagination of "gay male sexual practices and social haunts" ("AIDS: Keywords," p. 28). In *Policing Desire*, Watney deconstructs mass media pro-ductions of the British "family" as a unified organism that must be mobilized against the threat of AIDS. In the current "crisis," mobilization consists in closing ranks against those perceived as "other"; its manifest aim is impermeability and, more precisely, a (national) fami-ly kept safe from foreign influence, noxious fluids—leaks. He returns to the same subject in "Taking Liberties" when discussing "disciplinary based" pedagogies (pp. 28–44).

Returning to Bateson and Goldsby, we read: the "first line of defense" to bodily "integrity" is the exterior epithelium. When the skin "is breached or compromised by whatever means, the inner space of the body becomes available for colonization."[16] This configuration of the body, permanently arrested within the imaginary, sustains a series of textual oppositions between self and other.[17] Acting as a point of origin, in other words, the fortress body imposes a specious sort of sense on subsequent subjects and events.

Two translations of the fortress body haunt *Thinking AIDS*. The first is the "living cell" within the organism; the second is the social cell, variously represented by the family, the nation, or the body politic. Taking their cue from the fortified body, both cells stand on enemy alert. Enter HIV.

In the story of the organism, the virus wears the look of the exotic and primitive. Though it can pass as living, the virus lacks autonomy and so falls short of "genuine" life. Like other parasites, that is, HIV "can reproduce only by gaining entry into an appropriate type of living cell and exploiting its life processes. Once inside a cell, the virus's library of genetic instructions . . . [fabricates] new virus particles so that the cell is metabolically tricked into becoming a molecular factory for the reproduction" of anti-life.[18] Among the cells infected by HIV are T-cells and macrophages; their fates are diametrically opposed. Thus, where T-cells are killed in the course of producing HIV, macrophages "are not destroyed in the process." Hidden in blood and semen, these "free virus particles" may, in combination with "already infected cells, . . . become agents for the export of the disease to someone else." If the "inner space of the body" is indeed colonized territory, then the free virus particles would appear to be liberated natives on the move.[19] If so, then they are very like the infamous "Third World traveler" who carried AIDS to the West.[20]

With metaphors of infectious agents and Third World migrants we have entered the body of the socius. Moreover, we have entered it along a route

[16]Bateson and Goldsby, p. 27.

[17]The fortress trope is a stand-in for the ego, the product of the self's bodywork; as such, it belongs to the repertoire of the Lacanian imaginary. Indeed, Lacan has spoken precisely of coherent bodies—I's—being regularly "symbolized in dreams by a fortress, or a stadium" (Jacques Lacan, "The Mirror Stage," in *Ecrits: A Selection,* trans. Alan Sheridan [New York, 1977], p. 5). The Lacanian trope asks to be read against an other fortress implicit in representations of colonized peoples and places. The second fortress is decidedly more pregnable than the first; always already feminized, its defenses are simply there to be overcome. Within the West, refigurations of the faulty fortress have defined "woman," "Third World," and "native," all of whom have been imagined as there for the taking by subjects who are strong enough, civilized enough—man enough—to lay claim.

[18]Bateson and Goldsby, pp. 52–53.

[19]Ibid., pp. 56, 27.

[20]Moore and Le Baron (n. 4 above), p. 84.

that will carry us in a direction very nearly the opposite of the authors' avowedly nondiscriminatory aim. By way of explaining how this conflict of interest occurs, let me review the organism's story and its foundational trope of the besieged body once again. In reviewing, my purpose, apart from noting internal incoherencies, will be to interrogate the narrative's potential impact upon its readers by asking how the bodywork represented in *Thinking AIDS* disciplines subjects—that is, prescribes or suggests certain readings—thereby producing students of the text. The answer to how bodywork functions is related to where it occurs.

Basically, bodywork goes on in two locations, one of which is the text and the other its social context or margins. Textual margins are repositories of other discourses specific to the time and place of the text's production; operating much like a computer database, they ensure that "the messages most likely to reach . . . [readers] are messages already there."[21] Hence we have the reading of "Third World traveler" in the inscription of a once colonized and now emigrating macrophage. Because my immediate subject is the making of messages—and thus the positions of intelligibility afforded by *Thinking AIDS* as opposed to actual readers of the book—I will be speaking initially of the student body as if it were a well-disciplined organism programmed to respond to downloaded texts. The differences among actual readers and the resistances they enact in reading punctuate my review.

First, we students of the narrative are directly encouraged to conflate the migrations of HIV-infected macrophages inside the body with the potential wanderings (movements and malpractices) of viral "agents" or carriers within the body politic (more on this conflation momentarily). Second, we are asked, however indirectly, to see the virus as the ancestor of those who are "not-us." In the latter instance, it bears pointing out that Bateson and Goldsby do not do the asking. Instead, the ancestral question is posed by the cultural narrative embedded in the writers' allegedly scientific scripting of the immune system. The immune system's cultural subtext of exotic and primitive parasites has its own history in the discriminations of the West. The subjects of "other" sagas within the Occident include Third World peoples, homosexuals and intravenous drug users in toto, prostitutes of

---

[21]Leo Bersani, "Is the Rectum a Grave?" in Crimp, ed. (n. 15 above), p. 210. For a more complete discussion of the relation between text and context, see Paula Treichler's "AIDS, Gender, and Biomedical Discourse: Current Contests for Meaning," in *AIDS: The Burdens of History,* ed. Elizabeth Fee and Daniel M. Fox (Berkeley, 1988), pp. 190–266; and Donna Haraway's "The Biopolitics of Postmodern Bodies: Determinations of Self in Immune System Discourse," *Differences* 1 (1988): 3–43. Treichler's essay addresses the intrication of scientific writing in cultural mythology at some length; Haraway's essay specifically argues that biomedical discourses are "lumpy"—that is, packed with scientific and extrascientific narratives whose condensed meanings they both contain and contest (p. 4).

both sexes and all nations, promiscuous women of any color and every nation, and nonwhite Westerners in general, all of whom are imagined to engage in infantile pleasures without restraint—their libido misdirecting their ego, insinuating "other" messages into the information system of the organism, which will lead it on an improper and self-destructive course. At the same time, these peoples are routinely imaged as social parasites, preying upon healthy members of society, while sapping the life blood of the body politic. (For the first set of vampires read "homosexuals," "prostitutes," "Third World terrorists," and "militants"; for the second read presumably nonproductive "intravenous drug users," "nonwhite Westerners," and "Third World peoples" in general.) Because "other" subjects are fantasmatically intersubstitutable over and beyond their particular modes of address, and because the "other" always remains on call, awaiting the moment when the self feels threatened and acts to allay its anxiety by naming, isolating, and thus containing the so-called threat, it seems likely that Bateson and Goldsby's life-endangering virus will be read as a kind of genome for the replication of dangerous "others" in the West.[22] Consider the profile of the migrating macrophage, for example, and the colonized scene of its birth. Were it not for the reference to colonialism, the figure I have identified as "Third World traveler" could just as easily be represented by various other unsavory denizens of the West. One of them is the "mobile gay man" or "pleasure-seeking tourist"; another is the "woman who walks the streets." Both figures are as much a part of Western mythos as they are a part of pedagogies on AIDS.

The likelihood that the virus will be read as an archetype for those already perceived as other is increased by the structure of Bateson and Goldsby's book. Though explicit critiques of homophobia, racism, and anti-sex ideology are interspersed throughout the text, these critiques are fundamentally informational, and while Western ethics occasionally supplement facticity, desire is not substantially engaged. Unlike the chapters on the immune system, that is, the mini-critiques have no characters with which to solicit our identification or aversion and no storyline made up of compelling events. Structured along the lines of docudrama, *Thinking AIDS* marshals morality and documentation to end discrimination; drama

[22]Critiques of the us–them dichotomy and processes of othering are salient features in exposés of dominant AIDS discourse. See, for instance, Treichler on the " 'us'–'them' divide" as "a form of semantic imperialism" (p. 197); Leo Bersani on the equation of female prostitutes and gay males under the sign of promiscuity (pp. 211–12); Richard Goldstein on the association of gay men and intravenous drug users under "an act of penetration deemed illicit" ("AIDS and the Social Contract," in Carter and Watney, eds. [n. 5 above], p. 90); and Simon Watney on the identification of "unhygienic Africans" and gay men under the rubric of contamination or contagious agency ("Missionary Positions: AIDS, 'Africa,' and Race," *Differences* 1 (1988): 95, and "Taking Liberties," p. 37).

is reserved for the cast of "living cells," viral "agents" and their human replicants; it is here in the staging of immunology that desire itself is engaged.

On the immunological set, aversion and identification become the poles of desire. Self-preservation, which implicitly depends upon adapting the technology of cellular sorting to the demands of the social domain, represents the crux of desire, or what is otherwise termed the organism's "aim." The objects of immunological desire remain relatively uncertain in comparison to the organism's well-defined poles and aim. Clearly, "self" and "other" are imprecise sorts of objects, which (whatever their unconscious appeal) are of no material value to individual organisms in achieving their aim. Bateson and Goldsby thus purport to come to their students' aid; while they are careful not to mention a culturally specific "other," they do drop a cautionary name.

Anxiety is allayed, but only momentarily. Students focus on the nominal object placed before them and realize it "contains" no one in particular. This vacuum is simply intolerable. Someone must be put there to make good the deficit; likely candidates include members of so-called risk groups ("others"), but in any event definite objects will be chosen to inhabit Bateson and Goldsby's empty name. Here, however, I overstate the case; though the given name lacks a definite object, it is by no means without an affective charge. You will recognize the affect and the name.

The objects of subjects' aversion are to be "carriers." We have already learned that "carriers" are viral "agents"; we are about to learn that "they" are the "guilty ones." These peripatetic pollutants are the moral antitheses of well-rooted, hygienic organisms called "us." Hence, on ethical grounds, Bateson and Goldsby conclude: "A supportive and caring attitude towards afflicted individuals, whatever their lifestyle or personal history, in no way conflicts with a clear condemnation of continuing irresponsibility" in the face of AIDS. On grounds of "self"-preservation, they continue: "The body of an AIDS carrier is potentially a weapon of slow death, and putting sanctions on the negligent or even deliberate use of that weapon is not an unwarranted invasion of privacy," which liberalism must protect. And in the language of egoistic interest, they conclude: "If healthy people respond with compassion to those who have AIDS, . . . [the 'sick'] will be more likely to respond with the effort to protect society from the further spread of the disease."[23]

[23]Bateson and Goldsby, pp. 114–16. In another critique of cellular politics, Watney has noted how "AIDS is increasingly being used to underwrite a widespread ambition to erase the distinction between the public and the 'private' and to establish in their place a monolithic and legally binding category—'the family'—understood as the central term in which the world and self are henceforth to be rendered intelligible" ("The Spectacle of AIDS," in Crimp, ed. [n. 15 above], p. 86).

"Compassion," it would seem, is another technology; rightly applied, it seduces potential miscreants into behaving responsibly, thereby recruiting "others" into the ranks of our "selves." Although recruitment may win over some foreigners, it does not abolish the " 'us'–'them' divide." On the contrary, the very act of recruiting highlights division and emphasizes conflict. In the context of *Thinking AIDS*, recruitment says quite clearly, the enemy is out there along our borders; it is time to hoist the drawbridge and "man" the fortress walls.

We are encouraged to identify with this fortress body, but there is no guarantee that the interpellation will work. Failure is always possible because each interpellation "has to encounter, accommodate, and be accommodated by a whole history of remembered and colligated subject positions. . . . What always stands between the text's potential or preferred effect and an actual effect is a reader who has a history of his/her own."[24] This personal history is neither self-engendered nor self-contained but is infused with the metaphors and informed by the plot lines of master-narratives, cultural mythologies particular to the historian's location. Personal histories are not necessarily at one with dominant histories, however; alternative histories, local narratives, and "counter-memories" too may have their place in subjects' explanations of peoples and events.

Here, in brief, are three personal histories that interfere with the disciplinary work of interpellation in *Thinking AIDS*. None of these histories need be thought of as exclusive, I should add; indeed, any or all of them may be operative in actual readers of the text. Take, for instance, a history of political struggle. Individuals currently engaged in AIDS activism or popular alliances against racism, homophobia, and sexism may well resist the pedagogy of the text. At the very least, my hypothetical readers will need to alter or forget their own histories in order to assume a subject position based upon excluding an "other" who may well be themselves and whom in any case their politics would include. Take again the history of individuals infected with HIV. How are they to inhabit the fortress body subject? By definition, they already have been invaded, and by implication they have become body invaders. Finally, take the configuration of a desire that is other than a defense mechanism of the ego; with it, take the history of desiring subjects for whom "life is a window of vulnerability" and the "perfection of the fully defended 'victorious' self . . . a chilling fantasy."[25] Take these subjects and you have taken Donna Haraway's cyborgs for whom the fort-ified body is an object of aversion. This is not to say that cyborgs (reactively) identify with the text's viral agent, any more than the

---

[24]Paul Smith, *Discerning the Subject* (Minneapolis, 1988), pp. 34, 37.
[25]Haraway, "The Biopolitics of Postmodern Bodies," p. 30.

subjects of my previous histories do. It is to say that, from a cyborgean per-spective, the "one is too few and [the] two too many." Both subject positions are inextricably caught in the oppositional logic of the imaginary, and cyborgs are as antipathetic to the body politics of entrenchment as they are different from the unified organisms (monads) such politics presup-pose. Indeed, "far from signaling a walling off of people from other living beings, cyborgs signal disturbingly and pleasurably tight coupling." From one perspective, the cyborg world is about the imposition of governmental control, a telecommunications industry (command center), one of whose tasks is the production of educational programs aimed at teaching the "general public" (my organism) the "facts" of AIDS. From another per-spective, the cyborg world is about interference, static, cultural activism, and alternative information systems. "The political struggle," Haraway says, "is to see from both perspectives at once, because each reveals both dominations and possibilities unimaginable from the other vantage point."[26]

Cyborg signals solicit our attention as we undertake the task of renarrat-ing/rethinking "AIDS." In beginning, we are encouraged to identify with the subjects of Haraway's manifesto and so to speculate on the kinds of cou-plings—sexual and political—that might be possible, pleasurable, and socially productive in the context of the HIV epidemic. Speculating, we hazard new fantasies and rediscover forgotten zones of pleasure. Because we realize coupling can be dangerous, we learn how to practice bodily dis-cretion. Allison Fraiberg explains: "Condoms, dental dams, clean needles, and reserved blood manifest a surface awareness, a consciousness focused clearly on delineating the boundaries of bodies. The traditional, tenuous limits of the body dissolved into fused networks, into open circuits of inter-connectedness produce an ontological recognition that, from an AIDS related perspective, urges the body into discretion. . . . A [bounded body thus] resurfaces from within the integrated network . . . as a condition of cyborg systematicity."[27] However conscious of boundaries, we cyborgs do not give up the pleasure of penetrating or being penetrated, nor do we imagine penetration to be what "males" do to "not-males." On the con-trary, we refuse to be engendered as exclusively male or female; while trying on different positions, we maintain sexual fluidity and so are loath to take permanent sides. Hybrids ourselves, we displace "identity politics" with "affinity politics"; and thus, while holding on to the goal of a "united front," we conceptualize unity on inclusive as opposed to exclusive terms. Because we are fabulists and not idle dreamers, we understand that inclu-sion demands hard work.

[26]Haraway, "A Manifesto for Cyborgs" (n. 10 above), pp. 201, 176, 179.
[27]Allison Fraiberg, "Of AIDS, Cyborgs, and Other Indiscretions" (seminar paper, 1990).

We recognize that AIDS is a syndrome, for instance, and a syndrome does not wear one face. Understanding that the opportunistic infections of HIV are multiple and the sequences in which infections occur variable, we realize that the virus will assume various forms and permutations within particular individuals, communities, nations. Part of our knowledge includes the fact that women commonly present a variety of gynecological symptoms that may be early signs of HIV infection. These women-specific symptoms include chronic pelvic inflammatory disease, vaginal candidiasis, and neoplasia (for example, cancers in the cervix and vagina).[28] We also know that M.A.I. tuberculosis (another AIDS-related opportunistic infection) is prevalent among the world's poor and that Kaposi's sarcoma (an opportunistic cancer) has manifested itself disproportionately among gay men.

Discovering and procuring humane treatment for the opportunistic infections associated with AIDS is itself a herculean task. In the United States, AIDS activists face a number of institutional roadblocks, one of the biggest being the health care system. Today, the United States and South Africa are the only industrialized nations in the world without some form of nationalized health care. Faced with a federal government that allocates the largest portion of national resources to defense spending, lobbyists for AIDS research and treatment monies are forced to compete with other health interest groups for scarce dollars. To date, 80 percent of the clinical trials researching the effects of experimental treatments on AIDS patients have been devoted to testing the efficacy of antiviral drugs inhibiting the replication of HIV.[29] A mere 20 percent of AIDS clinical trials involve experimental drugs treating the opportunistic infections from which people with AIDS die. Impoverished, nonwhite, and non-English-speaking, the majority of women with AIDS are unable to procure primary health care or AIDS-related treatments. In consequence, women die from AIDS-related disorders even faster than men. Epidemiological studies in New York City indicate that on the average a white woman diagnosed with AIDS lives six months after diagnosis; a black woman lives fifty-four days, and a Latina woman thirty-six.[30] These figures teach us that AIDS can no more be separated from institutionalized poverty, racism, and sexism than science or health can be divorced from politics.

Finally, we know that different people have different histories, material concerns, political investments; we are convinced that these differences matter and must therefore be recognized in any united front that "we," the

[28]Risa Denenberg, "Unique Aspects of HIV Infection in Women," in *Women, AIDS, and Activism*, ed. ACT UP/New York Women and AIDS Book Group (Boston, 1990), cited in an ACT UP/Seattle factsheet, "Women and AIDS: Background" (November 23, 1990), p. 2.

[29]The most common of these drugs is AZT (Azidothymidine).

[30]"Women and AIDS," p. 1.

culturally diverse members of an affinity group, make. In practice, a united front means combating racism, sexism, homophobia, and militarism (any one of which may or may not immediately oppress one of us) at the same time that we fight to procure treatment for people living with the acquired immune deficiency syndrome to which these social illnesses are systemically related. Our alternative to the "walled-in organism" is thus the "network," an avowedly "ideological image," as Haraway employs it, "suggesting the profusion of spaces and identities and the [always risky] permeability of boundaries in the personal body and in the body politic."[31]

## Screening in the Classroom:
## Pedagogical Work on "AIDS"

Cyborgs meet organisms in the classroom. From each position and those which fall between them, teacher and students view educational videos on "AIDS." Initial positions are revised in watching, as viewers set about re-making their separate histories in order to accommodate what they have "learned." Accommodation is never one-directional, however. Rather, in the act of viewing, videos also undergo a species of "secondary revision." That is, the positionalities they make available to spectators are consistently modified or otherwise challenged by the semantic and affective invest-ments actual viewers have already made. This silent exchange between video and viewer is punctuated by a class discussion in which students and teacher reproduce what they have seen and heard. In the process, the mean-ings and politics of each video are further contested; additional config-urations of desire emerge. Generally, one's ability to read a video critically depends partly upon having read others of its kind. In deciding to screen a variety of "AIDS" videos in their classrooms, educators encourage stu-dents to notice the differences in filmic productions, to see who is invisible and to hear what is unspoken.

In my classroom, I show three types of videos, representing politically distinct yet temporally overlapping moments in the history of AIDS edu-cation. Their production dates are 1985–87, 1987–89, and 1989–90, respectively.[32] The first generation of videos is addressed to an audience imagined as homogeneous; in most cases, its members are white middle-class heterosexuals, who are assumed to be free of HIV but in danger of

[31]Haraway, "A Manifesto for Cyborgs," p. 194.

[32]The videos I will be discussing are: *A Letter from Brian,* produced by George Chitty and Carol Susman (American National Red Cross, 1987; 30 mins.); *AIDS-Wise, No Lies,* written by Ann Downer (Current/Routledge, 1989; 22:30 mins.); *All of Us and AIDS,* directed by John Fenn and Kathleen Laughlin (Peer Health Education Resources, 1988; 30 mins.); *Seriously Fresh,* directed by Regge Life, produced by John Hoffman (Select Media, 1989; 22 mins.); and *Vida,* directed by Lourdes Portillo, produced by John Hoffman (Select Media, 1990; 18 mins.).

"getting it."[33] The videos' educators are invariably adults, most of whom appear in scientific segments that have been spliced into the films' story-lines. Science and fiction here rest upon an identical postulate. Their premise is that the "facts about AIDS" will change student behavior—facts, along with scare tactics that are doubly rooted in appeals to self-preservation and a desire responding solely to the name of "fear." With some significant modifications, the first videos thus repeat the history of the organism. Both the second and third generation of videos are more cyborg-netic in type; committed to networking, their keyword is "affinity" and not "identity." The second type of video addresses a heterogeneous audience, made up of different races, ethnicities, classes, and sexualities. To some degree, the differences among video subjects are neutralized by their "common language"—a language that is recognizably white. Class and cultural diversity are conspicuously absent from representations of gay males, who are annoyingly stereotyped as sensitive middle-class whites. In contrast to their educational precursors, second-generation videos feature youthful educators who are either students or "nonexperts" whose relative lack of formal training renders them student-like. The old reception model of education is thus replaced by a production model, in which students (far from receiving the knowledge of "experts") generate knowledge themselves. The pedagogical techniques of second-generation videos are also quite different from those that were deployed in the first. Hence, there are no segments of "pure" information; sexual desire is given more play than fear; and while the dangers of unprotected intercourse are recognized, so too are the pleasures of safe penetration. The third generation of videos replicates the educational model and pedagogical techniques of the second. Significantly, neither their audience nor their language is common; rather, these videos are produced by and for local communities of blacks and Latinas, whose idiolects they employ and whose diverse sexual practices and politics they represent. Unlike the videos that immediately precede them, third-generation videos are careful to represent sex between men of color without necessarily invoking the culturally dominant definitions "gay" and "bisexual."

The students who will be responding to these videos represent the combined populations of three English studies classes at the University of Washington. Predominantly they are white middle-class heterosexuals in their mid-twenties. Approximately 65 percent are women; 15 percent are people of color; and 30 percent self-identify as lesbian, gay, or bisexual. Most are English students; about half are graduates and the rest undergraduates.[34]

[33]A notable exception is *Don't Forget Sherry*, whose audience is exclusively composed of middle-class black heterosexuals.

[34]The above is simply demographic information for which two qualifications are in order. First, I make no empirical claims about college students' reception of AIDS videos based on

While all of the videos play to viewers in their late teens and twenties, none (with the exception of *All of Us and AIDS*) explicitly targets a college audience. One, *A Letter from Brian,* is obviously intended for high school students. Moreover, it is the standard video for public high school seniors in the state of Washington, where AIDS education is mandated in the public schools for grades five through twelve.[35] In viewing *A Letter from Brian,* numbers of Washington undergraduates actually will be engaged in rewatching a video they have seen and in rethinking the position from which they had viewed it.

Produced in 1987, *A Letter from Brian* encapsulates the best and worst features of first-generation videos. My review of it implies (without exhaustively reproducing) a generic relation to Bateson and Goldsby's science book. Considering their relation demands both attending to the texts' common reliance upon originary structures and organic metaphors and also recognizing where and how the two diverge. Evidently, the video's sexual politics are pronouncedly more conservative than the book's. First, gays and lesbians are invisible (but not unheard of) in a film where the narrative interest turns solely upon the culturally admissible romance of Beth and Scott. On one occasion, Michael Warren, who takes the voice of sexual liberation as far as it goes in the documentary portion of the video, looks earnestly into his viewers' eyes and says: "Remember, the deadly AIDS virus doesn't care what color we are, what sex we are, or if we're straight

---

my classroom experience. Second, I am troubled by the classification of students according to demographic criteria, since it risks masking as many differences as it reveals. For whatever their sociological utility, such classifications contribute to constructions of *the* white heterosexual, *the* person of color, etc. In my classroom, those I have grouped together on paper tend to be a diverse lot.

[35] A number of factors contribute to the popularity of *A Letter from Brian.* To begin, the leads are rural white students, as are the majority of those in the state's public schools. (Exceptions include districts in Seattle, Tacoma, and Yakima where this particular video is not regularly shown.) Given the supply of largely white and/or innocuous multicultural AIDS videos, however, it must answer other needs as well. These needs are essentially ideological and can be formalized under two postulates. One insists "Just say 'no' to sex and drugs," which the video says repeatedly in just these words. Another asserts school and community-based public health education must submit to parental authority; the same hierarchy of power–knowledge is made explicit in the opening frame of the video and might be recast in the complementary slogan "Just say 'yes' to familialism." Both postulates have since been incorporated into *Guidelines for Effective School Health Education to Prevent the Spread of AIDS* released by the Centers for Disease Control (CDC) in 1988. These guidelines stipulate: "Any health information developed by the Federal Government that will be used for education should encourage responsible sexual behavior—based on fidelity, commitment, and maturity, placing sexuality within the context of marriage. Any health information provided by the Federal Government that might be used in schools should teach that children should not engage in sex and should be used with the consent and involvement of parents" (*Morbidity and Mortality Weekly* [January 1988], p. 10).

or gay."[36] Second, all forms of sexuality—apart from platonic kissing, hugging, and hand-holding—are banished from the visuals of the set. Admittedly, we do hear about intercourse indirectly in the voice-over, when Warren mentions the possibility of using condoms for safer sex. The condom option is not given much play, however, since Warren immediately suggests that students discuss any sexual decision with their parents, while offering the advice that it is probably wise to wait. Warren's configuration of parent-child relations as a chain of command in which the head of the (social) body rules its lesser parts reproduces the hierarchical structure of the organism once again.

Despite its relentlessly white narrative, the racial politics of the video are somewhat more progressive than the book's. For unlike *Thinking AIDS, A Letter from Brian* dramatically contests the assumption that "real knowledge"—science—is "naturally" produced by Western white men (and perhaps a few white women), for the edification of "others" who are incapable of authentic knowledge production themselves. With one notable exception, the video's "experts" thus flaunt the cultural expectations of its implied viewers. Indeed, the film's initial authority is a middle-aged black biology teacher known as Mrs. Winston. She gives Scott and Beth their introductory lesson on the "facts" of AIDS. Because the narrative is interrupted by the first of the video's "hard science" segments at the moment when Winston says "We need to talk," we do not actually hear the woman's words. We are privy to the speech of a middle-aged black man, however, who introduces himself as Michael Warren. A real-life public health official, he obviously has greater authority than the video's female biology teacher. Soon after Warren concludes his lecture, the video cuts to an older white man, C. Everett Koop, who extrapolates on the findings of the black man and whose position as Surgeon General of the United States accredits what the other has said. In grounding the lesson of Warren in the pronouncements of Koop, the video operates as do all narratives of origin.

I want to point out two more instances of origination in *A Letter from Brian* before mentioning how its meanings and politics are challenged by students in the classroom. I have already suggested that the video's opening frame of familialism represents its origin in the epistemological sense. Let me now review the semiotics of the frame. The background is black; in the foreground of the frame is a message from the American Red Cross, which has been printed in blocked white letters. The contrasting color scheme and plainly lettered graphic produce at least two expectations in the audience. One is that the film's language will be simple and straightforward, its AIDS

---

[36]Although "gay" refers to gay males as well as lesbians, the reference to lesbians is manifestly indirect. Moreover, because their sexuality is never spoken of directly in *A Letter from Brian,* lesbians are unlikely to feel addressed by Warren's text.

metaphors less than obvious, therefore, and harder to spot than the troped "fortress body" was, for instance. Another, more particular, assumption is that the presentation of AIDS will be categorical or clear-cut; reading into the stark contrast of black and white, we might well suppose that facts will in time be set against fictions, behavioral "do's" distinguished from "don'ts," "good" (healthy/moral) folks isolated from "bad" (unhealthy/immoral) ones, and so on. In all of these suppositions about plain talk and binary address, we will have been substantially correct.

Colors are not all we have to go on, however. Here is the first message of the text: "For a variety of health, social, and economic reasons, saying 'no' to sexual activity is highly recommended behavior for young single teenagers." Young is narratively defined as seventeen to eighteen, the approximate ages of Beth and Scott. When the story opens, the couple is about to have sex. A letter arrives from Brian, Beth's summertime boyfriend, with the news that he had experimented with drugs and now has AIDS. (Incidentally, it is consonant with the video's politics of isolationism/quarantine that Brian himself never appears on set. Because the AIDS body presumptively threatens to contaminate the healthy, it must be displaced by a letter, safely distanced through the mediations of a text.) The immediate effect of the AIDS news is to estrange Scott from Beth. Once the two learn the "facts," they get back together, but not, by any means, on the same terms. Beth and Scott have learned that loving means abstinence; to their lesson, the viewer adds sex = death, at least as a possibility, for that is how she or he is constructed by the text. For women viewers, there is an additional sexual message. Before Scott and Beth are reconciled, Beth talks privately with two girlfriends, one of whom speaks for safer sex. The girl's speech and looks lock her into the role of a "dizzy blonde" who, in her own words, gets "pretty out of control sometimes." In thus typing its only female advocate for condoms, *A Letter from Brian* separates smart girls from silly ones, further implying that safe sex is ridiculous and that women who have sex are fools at best.

Another originary moment occurs in Mrs. Winston's biology classroom, where a lesson in anatomy is taking place. Today's subjects are frogs, whom the students are to dissect. These amphibians are clearly reservoirs of knowledge, but just as clearly they cannot articulate their truth. The pedagogical task is to discover a language that will bring the amphibians' secret to light. What is demanded, in other words, is a translation/transformation of frog bodies into scientific discourse. Shortly after the biology lesson, we are introduced to Al, the intravenous drug user, whom we are encouraged to examine as a subject of AIDS. Like the amphibian, the white working-class Al is a source of scientific truth, whose habit and body are proof that HIV is transmissible through intravenous drug use. Although Al can speak, as the frog cannot, his speech departs from his body's truth. In talking about personal cleanliness and clean needles, Al only succeeds in introducing misinformation; hence, we are in need of a second-order discourse that can represent the subject's truth as he cannot. That discourse is again science, which discovers *the* effect of "the AIDS virus" in Al's body and *an* origin of "the disease" in his addiction. "AIDS virus" and "disease," it must be said, are sloppy scientific language at best. For as AIDS activists have often repeated, "AIDS" is not a disease but a syndrome.[37] The actual virus does not name AIDS, which is neither contagious nor infectious, but is a shortened form of HIV, which cannot be caught but is transmissible through certain practices, as the video rightly says.

There is another way in which the amphibian sets the stage for Al and through him for the subject of AIDS. Because amphibians are routinely dissected in high school biology classes, whatever qualms students feel about dissecting frog bodies, nonetheless they know their engagement is part of the curriculum—as conventional as it is safe. *A Letter from Brian* makes use of its viewers' prior understanding both to allay expected AIDS anxiety and to credential AIDS education.[38] It too will be seen as part of the high school curriculum, where it will be read in a context that says, Because it is safe and conventional to dissect frogs in biology class, it is safe and conventional to dissect Al in AIDS education class.[39]

Predictably enough, college students are overtly critical of the romance scenario in *A Letter from Brian*. A number utter loud boos at the closing sequence in which Scott and Beth (visually bathed in a romantic blue wash) look soulfully into each other's eyes while vowing to wait. A handful call out, "How long?" In discussion, some read the overdeterminations of the closing score, "Don't Dream It's Over," suggesting that not only does the song romanticize chastity, but the lyrics and title tacitly equate the alternative, sex, with the final "overness" of death. Despite their sexual histories, which vary, most argue that high school students are not that different from college students; because both are and continue to be sexually active, telling them to "just say 'no'" does not work. At the very least, they ask that equal time and equal weight be given to the use of condoms. By the end of the discussion, all seem to agree that *A Letter from Brian* is a

[37]See, for instance, Simon Watney, "Taking Liberties," pp. 16–19, 34; and his "The Subject of AIDS," *Copyright* 1 (1987): 126.

[38]I am indebted to Helen Tartar for this observation.

[39]The message on safety is addressed as much to parents as it is to students. Although parents are not my subject, their responses to AIDS videos merit consideration since they determine what videos precollege students are likely to see. Not only do parents sit on local school boards that decide upon the specific content of AIDS education in public schools, they preview—or are allowed to preview—all AIDS educational materials used to teach their children. In the state of Washington parents have the right to remove their children from AIDS education classes if they object to the material being taught.

white wash, though a few admit that they had not particularly noticed the narrative absence of people of color at first. Students also concur that the video presupposes a homogeneous audience of heterosexuals, while implicitly denying both the presence of gays and lesbians in the audience and the reality of HIV infection in the gay community. They further agree that the history of Brian's needle use, coupled with the summertime romance between him and Beth, effectively block the entry of gay males into the video. Once again, consensus on each point is reached through negotiation, many students having failed to notice the sexual politics of the video while viewing it. If students' preconceptions are unsettled by anything in the video, it would be by the presence of Al, which challenges what they have learned from popular fictions (newspapers, television, conversation, and so on) linking intravenous drug use with nonwhites.[40]

*All of Us and AIDS* (1988) and *AIDS-Wise, No Lies* (1989) are two second-generation videos. The subjects of both films are culturally diverse and their representations of desire as various as the social meanings they make of "AIDS." I have elected to read *All of Us* in some detail, limiting my discussion of *AIDS-Wise* to that footage which complements, reworks, or contests the lessons of its precursor.

*All of Us* explicitly thematizes the production of meaning and desire in a video whose subject is the making of an educational docudrama on AIDS. The docudrama's producers are nine middle-class college students—black, Latina, and white—who are collaborating on a film in fulfillment of a course requirement. All are friends, and six are heterosexually coupled.

One couple, Karen and Robert, is black. Somewhat contrary to viewers' gender expectations (though congruent with white stereotyping of black women as "jezebels"), Karen is the sexual aggressor. Her position is rendered doubly problematic by the opening frames of the video in which Robert plays an intravenous drug user and Karen a prostitute.[41] Where Robert's subsequent behavior distances him from the stereotypical addict, Karen's performance remains unchallenged, as does the tacit equation of black woman = slut. Of equal importance, Karen lacks sexual imagination, or so the video would have us suppose. Her proposal to "have sex" is met with Robert's response, "Let's wait"; there are "other ways of making each other feel good," such as "touching everywhere," he explains. Under

---

[40]For a critique of the systematic equation of HIV-infected drug users and people of color within the media, see Evelynn Hammonds, "Race, Sex, AIDS: The Construction of 'Other,'" *Radical America* 20 (1987): 35; and Alonso and Koreck (n. 14 above), pp. 104–5. Students remember Al in watching a later video production entitled *AIDS-Wise, No Lies,* in his name contesting the second film's stereotypic representation of HIV-infected intravenous drug users as Latino males.

[41]Both frames are voted down by the producers, who decide that *All of Us* will avoid stereotypes by focusing on AIDS, realistically, in relation to themselves.

Robert's tutelage, we and Karen learn that the body's erogenous zones are multiple; all kinds of couplings are feasible; and—most significant—orgasms are possible without penetration and the risk of HIV infection. Robert's message is later reinforced by a white couple, John and Becky, who, at John's prompting, discover the mutual pleasures of giving and receiving body massages. In this episode, we are taught that "the largest organ of the human body" is the skin, whose "millions of nerves" are simply there "to feel pleasure." The erotic practices of the two couples remain in tension with the penetrative sexuality of George and Wendy, both of whom have a history of promiscuity and are sexually active with each other in the present. Their sexuality is initially represented for the viewer in a shot of preliminary petting that is interrupted when Wendy proposes, "We should use a condom." In the petting frame, which remains unqualified by an alternative scene emphasizing male sexual responsibility, Wendy gives heterosexually active women and men a traditional lesson in the law of gender: namely, women are responsible for safe sex. At her suggestion, she and George go on to film a condom buy. In addition to providing us with information on using condoms with spermicide for destroying HIV-infected sperm, the episode makes a number of affective appeals. One is simply to "lighten up"—buying and using condoms can be fun. Another recaps the other couples' lessons, again stressing the importance of mobilizing fantasy, while safely sexualizing the body within "an erotics of protection, succor and support."[42] For all three couples, AIDS represents what Richard Ledes calls "a rallying point with the potential of acknowledging bodies and pleasure rather than isolating them," as in the earlier case of Brian.[43] The rally appeal returns in a sexy song-and-dance sequence performed in the studio as the film's finale. Black, white, and Latina women shake it up while singing, "All of us can get it together," simultaneously punning upon the material reality of a global HIV epidemic, the strategic necessity of forming new alliances across cultural and political divides, and the human need to imagine sexual alternatives that admit the pleasures of coupling while recognizing the risks.

Shortly before the finale, Mark screens a video clip of Wendy and George's entitled "How to Put on a Condom." The clip begins; the lights are cut; student viewers are left in the dark, listening to voices constructing "condoms as new stage props in the theatre of . . . desiring fantasies" and libidinal practices.[44] Some of the couple's cohorts raise immediate objections to the condom clip on the grounds that penetrative sex is risky and

[42]Watney, *Policing Desire* (n. 15 above), p. 132.

[43]Richard C. Ledes with the assistance of Martin G. Koloski, "AIDS and the Ninjas," *Copyright* 1 (1987): 140.

[44]Watney, *Policing Desire,* p. 133.

should therefore be displaced by other footage that discusses (Robert and Karen) and represents (Becky and John) safe pleasures. But if there is disagreement over what constitutes an appropriate sexual "message," there is agreement that conflict is fundamental to education. In the end, the students opt to include all of their clips in the completed video, making contestation an integral part of pedagogies on AIDS. Contestation carries over into the classroom, as student viewers, who have disparately identified with the subject positions of the video, continue to argue sexual politics off-screen.

*All of Us* would not seem to be "all of us," of course, without the obligatory inclusion of *the* representative gay male. As with any instance of typing, the video's synecdochical presentation of gay males distorts. Not only does the representative portrait mask real differences among gay men, but it arrests the fluidity of gay male desire within "a stable object," thereby suggesting the existence of one and only one gay male sexuality.[45] When applied specifically to gay subjects, in other words, "all" only feigns to be "the many"; in actuality, it is a metaphor for "one." Such distortions and dangers are compounded by the fact that lesbians have no place—neither here, nor in any other governmentally sponsored AIDS education video. Rather, they—we—continue to inhabit the space of "not-us," our very absence and the exceptionally "safe" status our omission implies effectively jeopardizing the lives of lesbian viewers.[46]

The one gay male in *All of Us* has a history of attraction to other men but no sexual experience, with the presumable exception of fantasies (about which we do not hear). The omission of Stephen's fantasies in a video where heterosexual pleasures are emphatically pronounced itself marks the gay male as different from—less than—the filmic "us." Stephen's dif-

[45]Watney, "The Spectacle of AIDS" (n. 23 above), p. 79.

[46]That lesbians are not addressed by AIDS videos or, indeed, by mainstream AIDS education in the United States is a direct consequence of how AIDS is reported by the CDC. Homosexual/bisexual males, intravenous drug users, male homosexual intravenous drug users, heterosexuals, and children born to mothers with or at risk for AIDS/HIV infection are included in the CDC's table of AIDS cases according to transmission category. These are tidy boxes—organisms by another name. People, I have been arguing, are much sloppier; neither their identifications nor their practices are so readily contained. For example, intravenous drug users are also sexual. Some users are women who have sex with other women. But nowhere are these people and practices sexually named. The refusal to name women in relation to women or to speak of a woman as such is hardly a lesbian issue only. In studies of transmission, as in popular coverage of AIDS, we find "infected" mothers in relation to fetuses (that is, breeders of AIDS babies), "infected" women in sexual relation to men (that is, breeders of AIDS), and "clean" women in relation to dirty men (that is, receptacles for AIDS). All of these findings deny women's subjectivity by defining them in relation to what they are not. In my first and second examples, specifically, all we can gather of the woman is that she is a creature of "no account."

ference from his straight friends is remarked by the staging of the video.[47] Whereas others appear in couples and tight groups, Stephen usually stands on the fringes, speaking from a distance that is at once hermeneutic (his assigned interviewer in the film is frankly puzzled by Stephen's sexuality), libidinal, and spatial. In effect, the gay male is almost but not quite alone.

In *AIDS-Wise,* where "AIDS is . . . made to rationalize the impossibility of the 'homosexual body,'" quarantine is total.[48] Briefly, the video juxtaposes nine distinct mini-narratives, whose subjects represent different ages, genders, classes, interests, occupations, ethnicities, races, and sexualities. With one exception, all speakers are introduced by a direct camera shot that brings them face to face with the audience, bridging the distance between viewer and viewed. The exception is Richard, the video's representative gay male.[49] Richard's segment opens with prolonged shots of two painted figures, rendered in an expressionist style, exteriorizing affect. The signature "Rick" appears on the screen, followed by a short medium-distance shot of a man's upper torso. The camera then pans across a white interior, pausing momentarily at medical paraphernalia and art objects in its path. The art objects range from the familiar to the foreign; among them are framed personal photographs, which appear to have been shot by the room's inhabitant, an expressionist self-portrait in which Rick is represented as the double of van Gogh, some "cultured" reading material, and exotic African masks. More than any other object in the room, the masks bear the burden of announcing the "other"; they are, then, functionally related to the portrait of an American Indian woman we later see on the wall. After tracking various artifacts of alterity, the camera halts before a mirror. Only now does the reflected image of a bedridden man appear. The shot is held just long enough to record a living death; then, as if animated by aversion, the camera pulls back. It tracks to a close-up of pill bottles, with which the "stricken man" is surrounded. While medical and art objects speak for the AIDS subject, they do not speak in place of him. Indeed, *AIDS-Wise, No Lies* needs the gay man's confession for the "truth" it purports to tell. Thus, we learn about a phone call he had placed to a friend, Kathy, who now hates gay men for what they have done to Richard

[47] I am indebted to Andy Barker for pointing out to me Stephen's physical separation from the other producers of *All of Us.* Andy Barker and Robin Reid, "What Isn't 'Normal' and 'Ordinary,' or What Most People Do Not Do and Do Not Approve of Other People Doing" (seminar paper, 1990).

[48] Watney, "The Spectacle of AIDS," p. 79.

[49] Although Richard represents gay male sexuality, he does not appear to be the video's only gay male. Wayne, another white male, who is also HIV-infected, addresses us as the loving father of a young son; we infer that he is gay from what he says about the AIDS-related death of a male friend. Inference is all we have, however, in a film where Wayne's identity is centrally defined as Ethan's dad.

and will not—cannot—visit. Kathy is the only "friend" of Richard's identified, and she is no friend at all. Unlike Stephen in *All of Us* and the four other people with AIDS in *AIDS-Wise*, who are represented among family or friends or simply with other people, Richard is utterly isolated. He is alone in a room and alone in a video where others are living with, as he is dying from, AIDS.

Class discussions of *AIDS-Wise* often begin with Richard; just as often, discussion accelerates into open conflict. Some students argue that the video moved them to "feel for" Richard, which they cite as a "good" in itself. More important, they add, by prohibiting identification with Kathy, *AIDS-Wise* encourages maintaining close ties with HIV-infected friends. Respondents are quick to sieze upon "feeling for" as distinct from "feeling with." The first, they argue, equals "pity," and pity demands an object who is less than the feeling subject. While they concur that the video blocked their identification with Kathy, they note that the only positionality made available is that of the implicitly straight female or male friend. Not only is it impossible to identify with Richard, they conclude, but the film is fundamentally homophobic. Targeted at an audience assumed to view gays as foreign, exotic, isolated, and sick, the video imagines a homogeneous group of viewers who have had little or no contact with homosexuals (so far as they know) and who are heterosexuals themselves. "Sick," a few point out, refers to more than physical debilitation, which is simply the most obvious sickness in the film. They argue that while Richard himself seems lucid ("unsick"), words are only part of his construction. Of equal importance is the self-portrait of the gay man as the "crazy" expressionist. "What do you say about a man who would cut off his own ear?" is their reply to the representation of Richard as van Gogh. Sickness, exoticism, isolation—homophobia—are arguments that ask to be accommodated; and few adhere to the "pity" perspective by the end of the class.

Students invariably compare Stephen favorably to Richard, as well they might; given the differential function of comparison, however, it is difficult to dislodge a general conviction that Stephen is depicted as anything other than one of "us." In one respect, *AIDS-Wise* is judged to improve upon *All of Us* in its diverse representations of HIV-infected subjects. Briefly, the population here is constructed, in Watney's terms, "as a complex matrix of overlapping and interlocking social constituencies, all of which contain infected members."[50] This cyborg-netic representation of the public is formalized in the video's opening and closing frames, as they splice in other subjects whose histories are represented in the middle frames.

*Seriously Fresh* (1989) and *Vida* (1990) are third-generation videos whose immediate audiences are black males and Latina women, particularly those

[50]Watney, "Taking Liberties" (n. 15 above), p. 29.

whose ages fall roughly between eighteen and thirty and whose communities are urban. Both videos teach us that national definitions of
heterosexuality, bisexuality, and homosexuality are "socio-culturally and
historically produced categories which cannot be presumed to be appli-
cable to U.S. minority groups or to other societies."[51]

In *Vida*, mainstream definitions of sexuality are challenged by the mention of Ophelia's male lover, who "goes both ways." He neither defines
himself nor is he locally defined in relation to hegemonic sexual categories;
as one woman puts it, "He ain't gay; he don't even think he's gay." The operative identification here is culturally specific; its name is "machismo."

Black macho generally identifies the male subjects of *Seriously Fresh*, who
in their own ways are distinctly "down brothers." All are outstanding
hoopsters and linguistic pros, who signify on each other with finesse. Sexual experience is a central part of their self-definition; fluidity of sexual
practices and heterogeneity of sexual identities are underscored by the film.
The star of *Seriously Fresh* is Dollar Bill; an unconventional pedagogue, he
gives his brothers (and us) some lessons on sexual diversity and AIDS.
Bill's own teacher is his friend Kenny, a college basketball star from the proj-
ects, who has returned home after being diagnosed with AIDS. In an
interview between the two, Kenny traces his illness to needle use—a social
habit he shares with one of the brothers on the project's basketball team.
Kenny talks about AIDS phobia in the black community and worries
about his old friends "dissing" him once they hear the news. AIDS phobia
sets the stage for homophobia, as Bill comes out to Kenny in turn. It is clear
that Kenny can "understand" the other's sexuality only because his personal
history has forced him into rethinking his old position on gays. Under Bill's
tutelage, the brothers overcome their AIDS phobia, but apart from Kenny,
who alone knows Bill's secret, collective thinking on homosexuals remains
the same.[52] Sexual identity seems less recalcitrant than ideology, in that
one brother, Daryl, is the subject of potential change. This self-styled
"Super-fly" makes a point of his heterosexual conquests, while voicing the
"anti-faggot" politics of the brothers. In the video's penultimate frame, he
sits alone thinking things over; in the final frame, he takes off at a run after
his main man, Bill. Whether or not Daryl is moving in a gay direction is left
up to viewers, whose personal histories will determine their respective
readings of the film. Sexual practices are obviously more subject to negotiation than identities, and the erotic use of condoms— "putting the cap on
jimmy"—is the most significant sexual behavior change in *Seriously Fresh*.

*Vida* confronts cultural taboos on condom use within the Puerto Rican
community in New York City where, in the words of Dooley Worth and

---

[51] Alonso and Koreck (n. 14 above), p. 107.

[52] Bill also mentions having a girlfriend; in the context, she appears to be less an object of
desire, however, than a useful sexual screen.

Ruth Rodriguez, "'Machismo' and its feminine counterpart, 'Marianismo,' require the . . . Latina female to defer to the male, making it difficult for her to introduce the idea of protected sex or to resist the efforts of the male to have sex without condoms."[53] In *Vida*, these cultural roles are enacted by Elsie and Luis. Elsie's "instinctive" impulse is to protect herself by saying "no" to sex, but desire destabilizes her position; at the urging of her mentor-friend Lucie, she determines to ask Luis to use a condom despite her fear of rejection. Luis follows the machismo script to the letter; thinking only of his own sexual pleasure and manhood, he is threatened by a woman who will not submit her desire to his. The episode closes with Elsie walking out, while Luis is left alone in his room to think. Her potential sexual loss (which appears slight given the unsympathetic character of Luis) is more than offset by gains in self-confidence and self-worth. These lessons are substantiated by the final frame of the video in which Elsie teaches her mother about caring for those with AIDS.

Where both videos challenge the ethnocentric definitions of sexuality to which earlier videos subscribe, *Vida* alone contests dominant definitions of feminism. Faced with Elsie, Western white feminists are compelled to rethink the meaning of feminist politics on AIDS. Rethinking means discovering that there is nothing inherently feminist in women's insistence that men assume responsibility for safe sex; in fact, depending upon the historical situation, feminist practice may be better represented by women taking the sexual initiative. Screening *Vida* in combination with *All of Us* thus enables students to recognize that feminist politics are culturally specific—as particular as the local meanings given to subjects, (sexual) behaviors, AIDS.

Apart from their specific messages, second- and third-generation videos model effective pedagogy for educators. Their screening and discussion teaches us how "the production of meaning is tied to emotional investments and the production of pleasure." It is the two productions—of meaning and of pleasure—that "are mutually constitutive of who students are" and the futures they envision.[54] Of more immediate importance, the introduction of AIDS videos, coupled with the contestation of AIDS pedagogies in the classroom, promotes a hermeneutics of suspicion, while opening a space for alternative politics and desires to speak their names. In "the struggle for language and the struggle against . . . the *one* code that translates all meaning perfectly," students and educators abandon the coherent language of organisms and origins.[55] We practice "cyborg politics" in the face of AIDS.

[53]Dooley Worth and Ruth Rodriguez, "Latina Women and AIDS," *Radical America* 20 (1987): 66.

[54]Henry A. Giroux and Roger I. Simon, "Critical Pedagogy and the Politics of Popular Culture," *Cultural Studies* 8 (1988): 296.

[55]Haraway, "A Manifesto for Cyborgs" (n. 10 above), p. 199 (my emphasis).

# "Black Gay Male" Discourse: Reading Race and Sexuality between the Lines

ARTHUR FLANNIGAN-SAINT-AUBIN

*Department of Romance Languages and Literatures*
*Occidental College*

> Respect yourself, my brother
> for we are so many wondrous things
>
> Like a black rose
> you are a rarity to be found.
> Our leaves intertwine as I reach out to you
> After the release of a gentle rain.
>
> You precious gem,
> black pearl that warms the heart,
> symbol of ageless wisdom
> I derive strength
> from the touch of your hand.
>
> Our lives blend together
> like rays of light;
> adorned in shades of tan, red,
> beige, black, and brown.
>
> Brothers born from the same earth womb.
> Brothers reaching for the same star.
>
> Love me as your equal
> Love me, brother to brother.
> [Lloyd Vega, "Brothers Loving Brothers"]

LLOYD VEGA'S POEM, from which Essex Hemphill might have culled the title of his anthology, *Brother to Brother: New Writings by*

This essay originally appeared in the *Journal of the History of Sexuality* 1993, vol. 3, no. 3.

*Black Gay Men,* is located quite precisely in the very center of the book.[1] It is difficult to read this as a mere fortuity of editing. The poem appears to encapsulate the celebration of black gay men and the call to arms that are the seeming hallmarks of this collection of writings. *Brother to Brother* constitutes experiential writing in the sense that it emanates from experience, the lived and the imagined experiences of African American gay men. It is personal writing, simultaneously documentary, biography, autobiography, fiction, and poetry. The volume constitutes in effect an attempt to erase the boundary between life and literature.

*Brother to Brother* constitutes also experimental writing to the extent that it attempts exigently to articulate the inarticulate or to utter the unutterable: black gay male desire. When reading these texts, one has the presentiment that the ultimate question posed is one of identity—to the extent at least that it can be posed and understood separately from the question of desire. Even more so than desire, identity is implicitly at the heart of every poem, every essay, every short story. Moreover, from one text to the next, in every case, the question is posed or reposed in the same way: How is the black gay male to forge his own idiom, to speak, and to represent himself in an ethnocentric, racist, homophobic culture? How is he to resist the subjecthood imposed by the dominant culture(s)? How is he to negotiate the double bind of contradictions presented to him as both black and gay? How might he poeticize that negotiation while explicitly politicizing his resistance? How might he then inscribe his resistance in texts? These remain, for the most part, implicit questions in *Brother to Brother*; they begin to become evident as one begins to read between the lines of the poems and the fiction.

Black gay male subjecthood or subjectivity is necessarily a political and poetic enterprise. And writing, as Teresa de Lauretis poses it, is necessarily "constant disclosure, exposure, composure through which self-knowing and the knowing self are (in)formed."[2] In this case in particular, writing is a technology of sexuality and ethnicity. One might indeed expect an anthology subtitled *New Writings by Black Gay Men* to explore and thematize a number of issues: the interplay between racism and sexuality, the decolonization of desire, and the poetics and politics of minority identity. And on most of these points, *Brother to Brother* ac-

---

[1] *Brother to Brother: New Writings by Black Gay Men,* ed. Essex Hemphill (Boston, 1991), p. 106. All citations to works in the anthology will be included in parentheses in the text.

[2] See, in particular, Teresa de Lauretis, "The Essence of the Triangle; or, Taking the Risk of Essentialism Seriously: Feminist Theory in Italy, the U.S., and Britain," *Differences* 1 (1989): 3–37. See also Nancy K. Miller, "Changing the Subject: Authorship, Writing, and the Reader," in *Feminist Studies/Critical Studies,* ed. Teresa de Lauretis (Bloomington, IN, 1986), pp. 102–20.

quiesces. In this present essay, I shall direct my attention to the poetics of the volume, placing politics—to the extraordinarily difficult extent that this may be possible—somewhat in parentheses. However, I do not wish to suggest that one should or even can separate poetics and politics; I am suggesting rather that one can explicate a particular readerly reaction by attempting to deconstruct the poetics of these writings. I do this simply because it is in its poetics that the anthology, in my estimation, fails or at least disappoints.

One way to read this failure or to understand this disappointment is by the sexualization and the ethnicization of the reading process itself, which consists in posing certain questions pertaining to the relationship between the writers and their texts, between the writers and the presumed reader(s) of these texts, and between the presumed and actual reader(s) and these textual productions. Who is the presumed reader of these texts? That is to say, to whom do the writers implicitly and explicitly address these poems, short stories, and essays? Is—and how is—the reader encoded within the texts? How do the texts orchestrate and determine their own meaning, and how does the reader participate in the production of meaning? Is there an underlying theoretical framework that subtends and collates the collection of writings in *Brother to Brother* and that allows the reader to attribute meaning to these signifiers? My own reading has necessarily been interstitial and extratextual; that is, I have been able to make sense of the divergent and sometimes seemingly conflicting claims of these writings only by reading between the lines and by filling in those spaces between the lines of a particular text and between different texts in such a way that each individual piece emits an autonomous, singular meaning while remaining within a plural, coherent, unified (if not seamless) whole. I contend that the nature and scope of this anthology necessarily open up spaces within and between texts for the reader to enter and to participate in the production of meaning. I contend further that there is an underlying set of basic assumptions upon which these texts are built—which must be reconstructed during the process of an interstitial reading.

Given the explicit intent of the volume, as expressed in the preface to the anthology, for example, the answer to the question "To whom do the writers address these texts?" is a surprising one. This group of black gay male writers create no real space—that is to say, no exclusive, safe place—for the black gay male reader. Although some of these texts explicitly invoke and apostrophize a black gay male reader, implicitly they are addressed to and articulated for the white gay male and the black heterosexual male readers. This is prefigured in Hemphill's introduction: "In our fiction, prose, and poetry there is a need to reveal more of our beauty in all its diversity. We need more honest pictures of ourselves that are not the stereotypical six-foot, dark-skinned man with a big dick. . . . Ours should be a vision willing to exceed all that attempts to confine and intimidate us" (p. xxvii).

Counterpoised already between the lines here are both the black heterosexual male reader and the white gay male reader for, as subsequent pieces in the anthology seem to bear out, they are the ones to be convinced of "our beauty in all its diversity." They, more than the black gay male reader, need the corrective of "more honest pictures." And when Charles I. Nero writes in the final section of the anthology, in an essay entitled "Toward a Black Gay Aesthetic: Signifying in Contemporary Black Gay Literature," that "because of heterosexism among African American intellectuals and the racism in the white gay community, black gay men have been an invisible population" (p. 229), he confirms in fact that black gay male entry into literary discourse will be predicated upon first countermanding this invisibility effectively. It might very well be that not only the texts in this collection but any attempt at black gay male textuality must necessarily be programmed, at least implicitly, for the very readers that attempt "to confine and intimidate." Although, as I shall specify later, this is most obvious in Marlon Riggs's poem "Tongues Untied" (pp. 200–205), it is equally clear—at least in terms of addressing the black heterosexual male reader—in, among others, the first three texts in the volume (two poems: "Sacrifice" by Adrian Stanford [p. 2] and "Daddy Lied" by Rory Buchanan [p. 7]; and a short story, "The Jazz Singer" by Charles Henry Fuller [pp. 3–6]), in which a heterosexual father motivates the utterances of his gay son. Therein heterosexual fathers in general become the ideal readers for these works.

In "The Jazz Singer," for example, what begins ostensibly as a possibly safe, exclusive space for the black gay male reader—"a very special space," writes Fuller, far away from "the confining roles of family misfit and neighborhood oddity" (p. 3)—transforms itself into a noxious space dominated by a solicitous discourse addressed initially to the menacing but disembodied voice of the father who calls up to the attic to his son, who is furtively playing drag by transforming himself into Lena Horne and Sarah Vaughan.

> "What are you doing up here? Dressed like that?" my father spat out from the top of the stairs.
> If he'd slapped me in the face, I couldn't have been more startled. Oh God, I thought, oh dear God. I tried to speak, but my stammering was so bad the words were incoherent gibberish. . . .
> I remember that he avoided looking directly at me. . . .
> My father was a big man. Though he never hit me more than once or twice at a time, I suddenly felt menaced by him, so I called

out: "Daddy, I'm sorry. Please don't hit me anymore. I'm sorry."
[pp. 4–5]

Subsequently, when the father appears physically before the son, the narrative confirms that what had begun as a powerful, eloquent locution by (and to) a gay son—to all gay sons—modulates not so much into *tongue-tied* "stammering" and "incoherent gibberish" as into total aphonia and aphasia. That is, at this point the imagined (ideal) reader envisioned for this narrative is the one whose primary identification is with the father and not with the protagonist. The text ceases, in my opinion, to be the narrative *of* the son to become a narrative to and *of* the father; the most distinctive feature of the son's voice, its gay-affirmative timbre and inflection, is silenced:

"Daddy, I can explain."
"No, you can't," he cut me off. "There is no way on God's green earth that you can explain why you're dressed up like that. Don't even bother to put some story together, because I don't want to hear it." [p. 4]

Indeed the real reader of this text is precluded from hearing the "story" because the narrative focus shifts from the pleasure of the son to the anguish and anger of the father. In essence, the discourse of the father first subordinates and then appears to occlude the discourse of the son, since one must henceforth read the story as fathers of gay sons would read it: with anguish and anger. The narrative must be read ultimately as a plea to fathers and symbolic fathers; that is, one can best understand the story as an attempt to persuade the (heterosexual) reader not foremost of the son's beauty but rather of the father's solicitude while simultaneously marginalizing his injustice:

"Are you deaf?" he shouted, rushing at me. "I said take this shit off!"
He snatched the wig off so quickly, I felt my heart jump in my chest. The air was cool as it licked the back of my neck and head where the wig had been. I put my hand up to cover my—what—shame? My dad read this as a sign of protest and struck me with such force that I slammed into a box of clothing. [p. 5]

Finally, in fact, the father emerges at the conclusion of "The Jazz Singer" as a loving, nurturing parent whose anger is justifiable and whose violence becomes curative:

"Christopher, I'm sorry." His voice was so awkward and soft, it pained me to hear it.... My mouth opened and closed, soundlessly, again and again, until a thread of saliva streamed down and caught in the folds of the dress. I didn't wipe it away. My dad, seeing this, knelt down very close beside me and dabbed at it with his dinner napkin. [pp. 5–6]

In many of the other essays, poems, and stories in *Brother to Brother*—for example, Reginald T. Jackson's "The Absence of Fear: An Open Letter to a Brother" (pp. 206–10), Ron Simmons's "Some Thoughts on the Challenges Facing Black Gay Intellectuals" (pp. 211–28), and Essex Hemphill's "In an Afternoon Light" (pp. 258–60)—the black heterosexual father, uncle, brother, homeboy, intellectual colleague, or political leader provides the tone and determines the ultimate meaning encoded within the text. These texts, like "The Jazz Singer," create a heterosexual space for the reader to enter, a heterosexual readerly position from which meaning can be produced. The reader, in other words, must play the role of a black heterosexual reader because he is the one who is encoded and dramatized within the text and he is the one, therefore, who gives the text coherence.[3]

As for the female reader, these writings operate on a double silence or erasure: on the one hand, they make no attempt to address the female reader; on the other hand, the writers do not address the important issue of how black gay men are oppressors of certain women. In other words, these black gay male writings make clear the extent to which they are "black"—they resist white subjectivity—and they make clear the extent to which they are "gay"—they resist heterosexual hegemony. They are quite often conspicuously silent on the extent to which they are "male" and therein complicitous with the machinations of patriarchal culture—though this too emerges intermittently between the lines of certain texts, as in the short story "Obi's Story" by Cary Alan Johnson (p. 90) and as in Melvin Dixon's poem "Aunt Ida Pieces a Quilt" (p. 145). This is, however, most evident in the essays in the anthology. When Ron Simmons concludes, for example, that "there are three basic challenges facing black gay intellectuals. First, we must develop an analysis and understanding of homosexuality in the African American community that is affirming and constructive. Second, we must correct the bias and misinformation put forth by black homophobic and heterosexist scholars. Third, we must not allow the hurt and anger we may feel toward such scholars to cause us to dismiss them or their ideas on other issues that we may agree on" (p. 212), he expediently erases women and

---

[3]Of course, there is always the possibility of reading a text against the codes, that is, consciously or instinctively reading against the grain or *mis*reading a text. See, for example, the theories of reading in Judith Fetterley, *The Resisting Reader: A Feminist Approach to American Fiction* (Bloomington, IN, 1978), and in Jonathan Culler, *On Deconstruction: Theory and Criticism after Structuralism* (Ithaca, NY, 1982).

the centrality of women in the lived and imagined experiences of gay black men from the agenda, although he, like some of the other essayists, parenthesizes a disclaimer in a footnote concerning black lesbians: "This essay focuses on black gay males. It does not address the experiences of black lesbians" (p. 226). However, beyond the important issue of the homology and therefore the contingent alliance with black lesbians, the reality of middle-class, black, gay men as contributing to the oppression of some women and working-class or poor men surely must be included in any strategy for "liberation" and "survival." The one essay in this collection that comes closest to addressing the issue of the black man as oppressor is Isaac Julien and Kobena Mercer's "True Confessions: A Discourse on Images of Black Male Sexuality" (pp. 167–73)—though it too fails to speak specifically to how and why *gay* black men in particular ally themselves with heterosexual black men and with men of the dominant culture.

Precisely because the female is absent as author, central theme, or reader in this collection of writings by black gay men, it would be informative to address the issue of the man/woman, male/female relationship. I am suggesting here a future reading of *Brother to Brother* formed and informed by feminist theory. Moreover, feminist writers and readers have taught us, among other things, that all textual dichotomies can ultimately be reduced to the man/woman opposition so that black/white and homo/hetero might be illuminated by an interrogation of the gendered opposition.

By structuring a discourse to and for the white homosexual reader and to and for the black heterosexual reader in two distinctive voices or modes, these writings imply that the two oppressions are separate or can be easily separated. Furthermore, they imply that these oppressions are symmetrical and that "black" and "gay" on the one hand have nothing to do with "male" on the other. The question that remains unexplored then is the following: How do different forms of oppression connect and intermingle and yet remain distinct? And how can one complex identity (which I call blackgaymale) be both oppressed (black/gay) and oppressor (male/middle-class)? "That one is *either* oppressed or an oppressor . . . or if one happens to be both, that the two are not likely to have much to do with each other still seems to be a common assumption in . . . male gay writing and activism."[4] On this point blackgaymale writing has much to learn from feminist thought, both black and white on the one hand and lesbian and heterosexual on the other. Some black feminist writings have addressed, for example, the issue of how being

[4]Eve Kosofsky Sedgwick, "Across Gender, across Sexuality: Willa Cather and Others," *South Atlantic Quarterly* 88 (1989): 54.

oppressed both as black and as female does not constitute symmetrical oppressions even if they interface in many complex ways; and some white feminist writings have concluded, sometimes reluctantly, that being oppressed as a woman does not erase one's prerogative as white oppressor. Whereas most of the poetry and fiction in *Brother to Brother* interrogates those places and those instances where black and gay oppressions are separate, it would have been equally informative to interrogate where they interlock, as indeed Hemphill's own words in the introduction would seem to mandate: "I *tried* to separate my sexuality from my negritude only to discover, in my particular instance, that they are inextricably woven together" (p. xvi, emphasis added).

## THEORIZING DIFFERENCES: BLACK/WHITE, HOMOSEXUAL/HETEROSEXUAL

One of the assumptions of *Brother to Brother* that remains unquestioned is that a person occupies one of two binary and homologous terms: black/white; homosexual/heterosexual. The anthology explicitly posits "black" before "gay" in its subtitle of *New Writings by Black Gay Men* (as opposed to writings by gay black men); and thereby it would seem that it wishes to privilege the black/white distinction. Implicitly and perhaps ironically and unconsciously, these texts privilege in actuality the homosexual/heterosexual distinction, as seen, for example, in the first three works in the anthology discussed above. Implicitly then and counter to many of the textual cues posited in Nero's essay on a black gay aesthetic when he writes that black gay men do write and must write "partly as a reaction to racism in the gay culture, but mostly in response to the heterosexism of black intellectuals and writers" (p. 235), the assumption of *Brother to Brother* is that there is an essential difference and homology, first, between (black) *homosexual* and (black) *heterosexual,* and, second, between *black* (homosexual) and *white* (homosexual). What precisely is the nature of this difference? The creative and expository texts here do not respond, nor do they attempt to theorize this difference. And why this particular hierarchy of difference? Why does sexuality (and, more precisely, the gender of object choice) supersede race and ethnicity? Does homosexual culture marginalize or erase race and ethnicity? Or does the community of blacks coalesce in such a way that the homo/hetero difference is marginal? One could postulate an essential "gayness" common to all gays suppressed or repressed by heterosexist institutions, just as easily as one could postulate an essential "blackness" common to all blacks oppressed by racist institutions. Finally, even if one accepts black/white as oppositional and homologous, one is inclined today, in light of recent articulations of "Queer Theory," not to accept homosexual/heterosexual as such.[5]

Is the intermixture of black and gay somehow sufficiently distinct from both categories to warrant an anthology that could not simply be a black or gay anthology? The editors and writers here certainly think so, though they fail to substantiate such a claim. Is there a distinctive black-gaymale conception of the world? Is there an imagination, a discourse, a subjective process, a historical consciousness that we can identify as blackgaymale? And would this authorize the category of blackgaymale speech or texts? In other words, does a blackgaymale imagination engender a particular kind of thinking, a particular mode of knowledge production, a particular way or practice of speaking and writing (or reading and listening)? What is black about it, gay about it, male about it, textual about it? Is there, for example, an essential difference between a blackgaymale understanding and, say, a white straight female understanding of the self and its relations to eurocentric, patriarchal cultural institutions?

These are, of course, challenging and far-reaching questions. This essay does not and cannot propose to attempt to answer them. To do so would mean more than the mere assumption of a blackgaymale identity; it would mean an in-depth analysis of its historical specificity—"the particular conditions of its emergence and development, . . . its assumptions and forms of addresses; the constraints that have attended its conceptual and methodological struggles; the erotic component of its political self-awareness; the absolute novelty of its radical challenge to social life itself."[6]

However, one might challenge first the logic and the validity of the homo/hetero distinction by posing what might seem to be a hostile and blasphemous question: Within African American communities, why should the homosexual/heterosexual distinction be privileged? Why privilege in general the gender of object choice in attempting to identify and classify human beings? As Eve Kosofsky Sedgwick has remarked, "It is rather amazing that, of the very many dimensions along which the genital activity of one person can be differentiated from that of another (dimensions that include preference for certain acts, certain zones or sensations, certain physical types, a certain frequency, certain symbolic investments, certain relations of age or power, a certain species, a certain number of participants, etc., etc., etc.), precisely one, the gender of ob-

---

[5]See, for instance, Teresa de Lauretis, "Queer Theory: Lesbian and Gay Sexualities, An Introduction," *Differences* 3 (1991): iii–xviii.

[6]De Lauretis, "The Essence of the Triangle," p. 4. Although de Lauretis is writing here of feminism, her formulation could apply as well to blackgaymale identity.

ject choice, emerged from the turn of the century, and has remained, as *the* dimension denoted by the now ubiquitous category of 'sexual orientation.'"[7] Yet, the gender of object choice emerges indeed in *Brother to Brother* as a diacritical mark for identifying a certain kind of black man. When it comes to the sexuality of black men, however, the assumption that the gender of object choice supersedes all other differences ignores and erases important differences among gay black men and creates a myth that gay black men are, in the final analysis, indistinguishable and monolithic. Sexual orientation in general and blackgaymale orientation in particular encompass so much variation that the gender of object choice does not begin to describe. These dimensions include differences of and preferences for acts or erotic techniques that may be implicit in gender object choice but not coherently so. "Other dimensions of sexuality, however, distinguish object choice quite differently (for example, human/animal, adult/child, singular/plural, autoerotic/alloerotic) or [they] are not even about object choice (e.g., orgasmic/nonorgasmic, noncommercial/commercial, using bodies only/using manufactured objects, in private/in public, spontaneous/scripted)."[8] It seems clear that reducing sexual orientation to the gender of object choice might well hamper or skew one's ability to understand the dynamics of sexuality and how it intersects with race to construct a particular and historically unique identity, which is precisely the stated objective of *Brother to Brother,* at least as Hemphill articulates it in the introduction to the collection.

Even if we accept orientation to mean gender of object choice and even allowing for distinctions of race, class, and gender, this would not deny that within the category of "black men who choose men" there are still significant differences. There might be more significant (for instance, political or psychological) similarities between black men and black *women* who choose *nonblack* objects than between black men who choose men. In other words, the race (or class, age, number, and so on) of object choice may be as important as gender or even more determinant. Or why should there necessarily be any meaningful similarity between black men who choose black men and black men who choose white men, for example? "To assume the distinctiveness of the *intimacy* between sexuality and gender [of object choice] might well risk assum-

[7]Eve Kosofsky Sedgwick, *Epistemology of the Closet* (Los Angeles, 1990), p. 8. I am aware, of course, that *Brother to Brother* was not conceived or produced, nor will it be consumed, in a vacuum; it exists within a larger Western discourse on sexuality. I am attempting to suggest here precisely that such a discourse might be especially fraught with incoherence when superimposed with the consideration of race.

[8]Sedgwick, "Across Gender, across Sexuality," p. 57.

ing too much about the definitional *separability* of either of them from determinations of, say, class or race."⁹ I suspect that, in this culture at least, race and class can no more unproblematically be extricated from sexuality than can gender. In fact, there are compelling historical and social reasons to believe that the racial difference (even if not as singular) is at least as significant as the gender difference. Most people are assigned at birth into categories of race and gender, and the classifications are unalterable. The gender of object choice or sexual orientation has a greater potential to be altered. One could argue quite persuasively indeed that since race and gender are usually public, unequivocal, and fixed whereas sexual orientation is more likely to be private, equivocal, and mutable, the latter would take priority in the construction and the experience of identity and subjectivity. However, as Sedgwick indicates, "an essentialism of sexual object choice is far less easy to maintain, far more visibly incoherent, more visibly stressed and challenged at every point in culture, than any essentialism of gender" or race.¹⁰ I do realize, of course, as others have noted, that there was a historical shift from the consideration of same-gender sexuality as proscribed and isolated genital acts—which anyone could perform—to a consideration of same-gender sexuality as an index of immutable identity to the point that one's attire, speech, or associates could identify one as homosexual, irrespective of one's genital activity.

There are black men who choose men but for whom this choice has no implications whatsoever for self-identity, because it does not and cannot inscribe, circumscribe, or describe the construction or the experience of their own sexuality and identity. Moreover, black men who engage in identical genital acts interpret these acts in different ways. To some black men, sexual orientation is circumscribed completely by genital acts; to others, it includes these acts in an ill-defined way or is completely independent of them. Although psychoanalysis informs us that there is a connection between sexuality and identity, for some black men it has a central role, for others a peripheral one. Some black men "have their richest mental/emotional involvement with sexual acts they don't do, or even don't *want* to do. . . . For some people the preference for a certain sexual object, act, role, zone, or scenario is so immemorial and durable that it can only be experienced as innate; for others, it appears to come late or to feel aleatory or discretionary."¹¹

So, again, to isolate and ascribe meaning to black men who choose men is ultimately arbitrary since some of these men, like people in gen-

⁹Sedgwick, *Epistemology of the Closet,* p. 31.
¹⁰Sedgwick, "Across Gender, across Sexuality," p. 56.
¹¹Sedgwick, *Epistemology of the Closet,* p. 25.

eral, whether they are heterosexual, homosexual, or bisexual, do not necessarily fantasize or experience sexuality as intimately wedded to gender, the meaning of gender, or the differences in gender. Perhaps, we are inclined to isolate and to valorize gender of object choice because it is easily knowable, whereas the other distinctions depend on a level of introspection that is difficult, if not impossible, to attain. Although the reduction of sexual orientation to gender of object choice might appear to us to be natural and self-evident, it is clearly the result of history, of culture, and not of nature.

## RESISTANCE TO BLACK HETEROSEXUAL PRACTICE: TONGUE-TIED

When a number of the poetic and narrative texts in *Brother to Brother* explicitly engage the black heterosexual reader the tone appears solicitous, tentative, or tongue-tied, as in "The Jazz Singer"; yet when the essays in the anthology explicitly engage the black heterosexual reader the tone, on the contrary, is unswerving, proud, and often contentious, as is Essex Hemphill when he writes elsewhere that "open and proud black gay men and lesbians must take an assertive stand against the blatant homophobia expressed by members of the black intellectual and political community who consider themselves custodians of the revolution."[12] The impulse is understandable: the first section of the book is subtitled "When I Think of Home." These writings, as well as those in other sections, justifiably acclaim and proclaim the desire and the right of black gay men to "go home," to participate fully in their communities. They suggest that any institution or ideology that estranges and pits blacks against blacks must be understood as a tool of racist domination. In an attempt to deconstruct and understand homophobia, the essays in particular are trenchant in explicating how blacks ground their homophobia and heterosexism. In the final section of the book, for example, Ron Simmons, in the essay cited above, is both incisive and insightful in his critiques of Molefi Keke Asante, Amiri Baraka, and Louis Farrakhan, among others. When appealing to the black heterosexual community and the heterosexual man in particular, Simmons's essay and other texts, both fictional and nonfictional, appeal to his sense of solidarity by indicating that homophobia denies him a potentially committed and politically astute ally in his fight against the oppressor.

Though significant space is devoted to addressing explicitly the black heterosexual reader, he is not, in my reading and understanding of these

[12]Essex Hemphill, "If Freud Had Been a Neurotic Colored Woman," *Outlook* 13 (1991): 55.

texts, the principal interlocutor or reader envisioned. The principal interlocutor is rarely addressed directly, appears at times barely visible, yet in some respects dominates the discourse. Though frequently absent, he appears between the lines of these poems, stories, and essays and seems to haunt every word and image. He is the white homosexual reader. When addressing this reader, these texts are still proud; now, however, they do not seem so contentious; they appear rather plaintive. Perhaps one can best understand this not as a specific feature of *Brother to Brother* but rather as inevitably characteristic of any and every attempt at black-gaymale textuality—indeed a minority inflection within a minority literary corpus—given the particular modes of literary production and dissemination and the particular patterns of literary consumption in this culture: Who publishes? What gets published? Who reads? In order for this collection to constitute a commercial and political success, it must engage the white gay male reader even if it does not explicitly or consciously attempt to do so.

Even a poem like Lloyd Vega's "Brothers Loving Brothers"—quoted in the epigraph to this essay—which, on the surface at least, is addressed exclusively to another "brother," makes an obligatory if barely perceptible nod to the white (gay male) majority. The explicit message of the poem counters in fact the absent but unrelenting message of the dominant culture in general and of the dominant gay culture in particular, which wounds and devalues the blackgaymale. When one reads between the lines of the poem—by asking what motivates the poem—one perceives and understands the voice of the majority: "You are not 'wondrous' nor 'rare' nor 'wise.'" The message of the poem therefore replicates that of virtually every African-American parent in this culture: in spite of the ubiquitous images to the contrary and in spite of the inexorable efforts to devalue, to defame, and to deter you, "Respect yourself, . . . for we are so many wondrous things" (p. 106). Finally, even if one assumes that the (reading) "brother" has indeed internalized the dominant message, one has to conclude that he is not envisioned as the sole target of the poem's message. Vega's poem constitutes indirectly a plea (to the nonbrother) to cease and desist the regrettable defacement of a natural beauty ("black rose," "black pearl," "rays of light").

Although "Brothers Loving Brothers" constitutes the paginal center of *Brother to Brother,* it is nevertheless Marlon Riggs's "Tongues Untied" that orbits closer to its ideological and aesthetic centers. Although within the poem's thematic a black gay male is the protagonist, the poem, ostensibly written for a "brother," is in actuality addressed to a white reader. That is to say, although the poet and the editors of the anthology presume that a black gay man will read the work and thus he (a black gay man) may be the explicit presumed reader, implicitly the poem is constructed for and addressed to a white reader. This silent interlocutor hovers between the lines and in the parentheses throughout.

> I'd heard my calling by age 6
> We had a word for boys like me.
> (Punk)
> Punk not because I played sex with other boys—
> everybody on the block did that.
> (Punk)
> But because I didn't mind giving it away.
> (Punk)
> Other boys traded—"you can have my booty
> if you gimme yours"—
> But I gave it up,
> free,
> (Punk)
>
> At age 11 we moved to Georgia.
> I graduated to new knowledge.
> (Homo)
> "Don't you know how to kiss?"
> my new best friend asked,
> (Homo)
> . . . . . . . . . . . . . . . . . . . . . . . . . . . . . . . . . . . . .
> "No," I answered
> "I'll show you how," he said,
> his brown eyes inviting.
> (Homo)
> We practiced kissing for weeks,
> dry, wet, French.
> (Homo)
> 'Til his older brother called us a name.
> (Homo)
> "What's a 'homo'?" I asked.
> "Punk, faggot, freak."
> I understood.
> We stopped kissing.
> Best friend became
> worst enemy.

[pp. 200–201]

"Tongues Untied" is a narrative, lyrical poem in which the first two stanzas recount the protagonist's boyhood and prepubescent experi-

ences of sexuality.[13] Moreover, they recount the construction of an identity, first assumed ("Punk") and then imposed ("Homo," "Faggot,"
"Freak") within a black community. One can suppose that the identity is
first assumed from the assertion that "We [as opposed to "they," which
appears subsequently] had a word for boys like me." For the first two
stanzas then, race is not an issue; only desire emerges as problematic.
What surfaces here as significant is that not all same-gender desire is
proscribed—merely certain (public) manifestations of it. One must assume that these words were uttered for the black heterosexual reader, for
the message is: I was initially no different from you; you were the object
of my desire, as I was yours; but finally, you alienated me from my natural desire for another (just like me: black male).

Although there are no textual cues in these first two stanzas to indicate that they envision a reader of a race different from that of the poetic
voice, this becomes evident as one continues to read and to understand
that the first three stanzas in fact constitute part of the preamble to a
plaintive discourse found in the fourth stanza. This plaintive discourse,
which occupies the center of the poem, is again implicitly addressed to a
white gay reader.[14]

There is, however, a third stanza before one arrives at the center of
this poem. This third stanza begins parenthetically with the invective of
nameless and faceless whites:

> (Muthafuckin coon)
> Age 12, they bused me to Hepzibah Junior High
> on the outskirts of Augusta.
> (Muthafuckin coon)
> A spray-painted sign greeted me on the wall.
> (Niggers Go Home)
> (Muthafuckin coon)
> Rednecks hated me
> because I was one of only two blacks
> placed in 8A, the class for Hepzibah's

[13]I should note that I am using "stanza" to denote syntactic and semantic groupings
and divisions and not necessarily typographic divisions or how the poem is displayed on
the page.

[14]I realize that reading is a complicated process and that my postulation of "the gay
reader"—black or white—as a "self" with definable characteristics and practices is theoretically problematic. Outside one's own personal and idiosyncratic reading, one can postulate the gay reader only as an ideal; no two people read in exactly the same manner; there
can exist only degrees and instances of gay reading. See, for example, Arthur Flannigan-
Saint-Aubin, "The Mark of Sexual Preference in the Interpretation of Texts: Preface to a
Homosexual Reading," *Journal of Homosexuality* (forthcoming).

best and brightest.
(Muthafuckin Coon Nigger Go Home)

[p. 201]

Here, as opposed to the first two stanzas, it is race and not sexuality or desire that is at issue. One understands that this particular assault and insult are experienced as more insidious and more hurtful because whereas previously the protagonist is merely labeled—almost benignly ("Punk," "Homo")—and whereas he remains a part of the collective ("we"), here the labels are modalized and modified ("*Muthafuckin* Coon") and are launched by an absolute "Other." The implication is that the protagonist is more profoundly threatened, not merely or simply now in his public identity but equally in his self-identity and in his very person, his physicality. Here, the labels evolve into menacing imperatives: "Muthafuckin Coon Nigger Go Home."

As the third stanza continues, race and class appear to fuse as the protagonist becomes both "Uncle Tom" and "Coon"; then, race, sexuality, *and* class appear to collide:

The blacks hated me
because they assumed my class status made me uppity,
assumed my silence as superiority.
(Uncle Tom)
I was shy.
(Uncle Tom Muthafuckin Coon)
I was confused.
(Uncle Tom Muthafuckin Coon Nigger Go Home)
I was afraid and alone.

(Uncle Tom Muthafuckin Coon Punk
Faggot Freak Nigger Go Home)

[p. 201]

And yet the imperative ("Uncle Tom Muthafuckin Coon Punk/Faggot Freak Nigger Go Home") must be read as less threatening and debilitating than the purely racial one because it represents a vacuous (tenuous, at best) alliance of black and white heterosexuals. The poem offers no basis for such a collusion: what would motivate the "rednecks" of the third stanza to join the "blacks" of the first or second to negate the protagonist? In actuality, race and class on the one hand and sexuality on the other do not logically join forces as the surface structure of the poem might suggest. In fact, the invective "Uncle Tom Muthafuckin Coon Nigger Go Home" defies logic, since the black voice uttering "Uncle Tom" could not possibly excoriate the protagonist to "Go Home." Although, on the contrary, one could surely read (or misread) this as the poetic voice's attempt precisely to invoke the illogic of an alliance whose forces nevertheless converge in devastating ways, the poem itself does not facilitate such a reading. The second part of this stanza, which catalogs the attempts of the protagonist to escape by withdrawing within the self, concludes the preamble:

> Cornered
> by identities I never wanted to claim,
> I ran.
> Fast.
> Hard
> Deep
> inside myself
> Where it was still.
> Silent.
> Safe:
>
> Deception.
>
> [pp. 201–2]

The body of the poem (as specified also by the poet's own divisions and schema), which is the shortest section of the poem and is composed of only one (semantic) stanza, provides the emotional and thematic center of the work. Here, the protagonist realizes and experiences a true, almost divine, uncomplicated, and uncompromising jouissance:

> A whiteboy came to my rescue.
> Beckoned with gray/green eyes, a soft Tennessee drawl.
> Seduced me out of my adolescent silence.
>
> He called me friend.
> I fell in love.
> We never touched, never kissed,
> But he left his imprint.
> What a blessing
> his immaculate seduction.
> To feel the beat of life,
> to trust passion again.
> What a joy.
> That it should come from a whiteboy
> with gray/green eyes,
> what a curse.
>
> [p. 202]

The remainder of the poem, like the protagonist's life—the protagonist who now occupies the metaphoric space of the Virgin Mother impregnated with life by the Holy Spirit—is indelibly imprinted with the presence and the muted locution of the whiteboy savior.

## RESISTANCE TO WHITE HOMOSEXUAL THEORY: TONGUES UNTIED

*Brother to Brother* would lead us to believe, as Charles Nero indicates, that "some African American brothers become 'black gay men' while others become 'gay black men' [and that this] . . . often underscores painful decisions to have primary identities either in the black or in the gay community" (p. 244). And the texts in *Brother to Brother* devote substantial space in order to articulate, both implicitly and explicitly, the differences and the grievances with the dominant gay culture. One could cite here any one of the eleven or so essays in the collection, for which indeed this constitutes an important if not always exclusive theme, or any number of the poems in the anthology (such as Adrian Stanford's "Psalm for the Ghetto" [p. 166]); but return for a moment to "Tongues Untied," for example, where the theme resonates uncannily:

> In California,
> I learned the touch and taste of snow.
> Cruising whiteboys, I played out
> adolescent dreams deferred.
> Patterns of black upon white upon black upon white
> mesmerized me. I focused hard, concentrated deep.
>
> Maybe from time to time
> a brother glanced my way.
> I never noticed.
> I was immersed in vanilla.
> I savored this single flavor,
> one deliberately not my own.
>
> I avoided the question, why?
>
> Pretended not to notice
> the absence of black images
> in this new gay life,
> in bookstores
> poster shops,
> film festivals,
> my own fantasies.

Tried not to notice
the few images of blacks
that were most popular:
joke
fetish
cartoon caricature
or disco diva adored
from a distance.

Something in Oz, in me, was amiss,
but I tried not to notice.

I was intent on the search
for love, affirmation, my reflection
in eyes of blue, gray, green.

Searching, I found something I didn't expect,
something decades of determined assimilation
could not blind me to:

In this great gay mecca,
I was an invisible man, still
I had no shadow, no substance.
No history, no place.
No reflection.

I was an alien, unseen, and seen, unwanted.
Here, as in Hepzibah,
I was a nigga, still.

I quit the Castro
no longer my home, my mecca
(never was, in fact),
and went in search of something better.

                                        [pp. 202–3]

This impulse too, like the one to "go home," which surfaces frequently
in *Brother to Brother,* is understandable: it constitutes an attempt to
demarginalize the black gay male who, within the larger gay imagination, has been reduced to that "ubiquitous, forever big, forever hung,
sexy, dominant, aggressive Black top" that one encounters so frequently
in personal ads.[15] Within gay fantasy, the black male is highly coveted,

[15]Lyle Ashton Harris, "Revenge of a Snow Queen," *Outlook* 13 (1991): 9.

yet invisible—forever desired, yet never embraced. He is a sign, an index, and even an emblem. Dominant gay men's identification as gay men does not entrain their identification with gay men differently positioned within the power structure. Moreover, white gay male theory and practice pose themselves as universal, the essence of gay. They create a space for the "nigger," give him a voice, a language that is not his own. Much of the writing in *Brother to Brother* is an attempt to make the black gay male not only the center of desire but the subject of his own text. It re-presents and represents the black gay male occupying the position of subject instead of that of object. It attempts to give him an authentic and authenticating voice. These texts, in resisting so eloquently and so vehemently this racialized desire and objectification, ironically fail to acknowledge and explore what the photographer Lyle Ashton Harris calls the contradictory feelings provoked by the image of the black male as seen in personal ads for black men found in the white gay press: "I am intrigued by the blatantly spoken racialized desire in such voices, yet torn by this type of objectification of black men and the feeling of alienation and estrangement this objectification engenders in me."[16]

*Brother to Brother* refuses to accept the racialized space created for the black gay man in the dominant gay language and community. In this very refusal, it fails to undertake a systematic scrutiny of this space. On the contrary, one needs to inhabit this space because, although it is enslaving, it is potentially liberating: it is there that race and gender and sexuality collide in illuminating ways. It is by going to that very space that the black man can begin to reclaim and articulate his "decolonized sexual subjectivity." It is by reappropriating and playing on dominant racial and sexual myths about the black male, as Harris would insist, that black men can begin to engage one another in a personally liberating discourse and in a political discourse of liberation: "Claiming a radical black gay subjectivity through the process of self-interrogation . . . and the interrogation of *location*, . . . transgression begins not by going beyond but by inhabiting that racially and sexually fetishized space, and by exploring our relationship to it."[17] I am suggesting here a blackgaymale entry into literary discourse that explicitly and presciently engages the white gay male reader by judiciously encoding him within the text; I am suggesting further a blackgaymale entry into literary discourse that, unabashedly and without self-deprecation, inhabits, explores, and thematizes the imposed role of the "ubiquitous, forever big, forever hung, sexy, dominant, aggressive" sexual object. It is presumptively noble and instructive perhaps to resist the role with its requisite images,

16Ibid., p. 8.
17Ibid., p. 13.

as *Brother to Brother* does; it would be preemptive, more disruptive, utterly revolutionary to call them into play, to play on them.

Following Harris's example with the visual arts, these writings might have explored both the exterior *and* inner space of blackgaymale sexuality by questioning specifically how the black gay male internalizes and experiences the value placed on the black male body within the homosexual community. None of the writings here attempt to do that. Although they critique racism, these texts fail to interrogate the contradictory spaces of pain *and* pleasure engendered by this racism. These texts, with the possible exception of Riggs's poem, ignore or at least underestimate (and at what price?) the private hurt and public humiliation caused by the blatant racism of individuals and institutions within the homosexual community *and* the double sting caused by the indifference of progressive white gays and lesbians who nevertheless refuse to aggressively engage the community in a dialogue on the role of race in sexual politics. Black gay subjectivity is complex and contradictory; it behooves one then to explore it in all of its complexity and contradictions.

*Brother to Brother* posits quite effectively the differences (or at least the perceived differences) between black and white on the one hand and homosexual and heterosexual on the other. With few exceptions, as I have already stated, these writings do not attempt to theorize these differences. The poetic and narrative texts might have provoked the reader by contesting the implicit homology and by "transgressing the boundaries imposed by the binary structures of sexuality and race, [by] exploring the possibilities of fluid and multiple identities and relationships."[18] They do give voice to and represent primarily black-to-black and man-to-man experiences. These texts, in effect, accomplish an extraordinary task simply by naming these experiences in fiction, poetry, biography, autobiography, and essay. They legitimize ways of being and speaking blackgaymale. Ultimately, though, the anthology attempts to inscribe the blackgaymale into already existing homosexual and African American traditions. Occasionally and understandably, given the pull of dominant discourses, it attempts to translate blackgaymale into the language of white gay men or black straight men. Yet *Brother to Brother,* invariably and in spite of itself, indexes ways of being blackgaymale within this particular culture; and, in this way, these stories, poems, and essays present the words, thoughts, and knowledge of black gay men as a road map for other "brothers." In reading these texts, one has a profound sense of process, of an emerging identity, of learning to be blackgaymale. One

[18]Ibid., p. 11.

has the sense of a self-portrait, a black self-image, a coming out, a celebration.

The creative texts in particular are used in this anthology as a way to posit and to expound lived and fantasied experience. Poetry, for example, can be and is here "a way to interrogate the construction of . . . identity as well as [to explore] the multi-faceted relationship [that one has] towards that construction."[19] *Brother to Brother* does lay claim to a metaphoric space for black gay men; it does explore many of the dimensions of constructing and experiencing a blackgaymale identity—the dangers, the fears, the playfulness, the pleasures. One needs to go further. The next logical step is to deduce from these texts a blackgaymale theory, defined not merely as critiques of eurocentric and heterosexist culture and institutions but also as critical elaborations of blackgaymale sensibility and perspective, of its difference and specificity.[20] It is now time to proceed from a narrowly focused political critique and analysis of white gay male culture and black heterosexual culture to a broader critique and analysis of society and culture in general and of patriarchal domination in particular. It is time too to call into question and perhaps to break with some aspects of the dominant aesthetic—including the privileging of the written word, the separation of the arts (music from literature from sculpture, and so on), and the prevailing Western valorization of "self" at the expense of the group. It is perhaps time to leave the homosexual plantation, and, without exaggerating the importance or denying the existence of former enslavers and masters, to turn one's locution completely and unapologetically to fellow travelers. Black gay men might counter the impulse of the poetic voice in Riggs's poem by ceasing to feel constrained or compelled to immerge themselves or their writings "in vanilla." Moreover, they must cease to feel compelled to learn the alienating and wounding language of their heterosexual fathers.

Race and sexuality are ideal spaces from which to articulate a politics and a poetics, a theory of social, political, and aesthetic practice. What does it mean to be blackgaymale? Is it merely a politically assumed identity? Is it an identity at all? Does there exist an essential blackgaymale? Even if one rejects the notion of an essential "gayness" or an essential "blackness," one can still claim the complex of sexuality and ethnicity as a locus of difference from which to think, to act, and to create. In fact, one could postulate blackgaymale theory as positionality—a position,

---

[19]Ibid., p. 9.

[20]De Lauretis, "The Essence of the Triangle," p. 10. Again, the author is writing specifically about feminist theory; but one can see how this might be expanded to apply to blackgaymale theory as well.

within the academy or within the arts, for example, from which a black-gaymale politics and poetics can emerge. Being and thinking blackgaymale means assuming "a position, a point of perspective, from which to interpret, to construct, or to reconstruct values and meanings."[21] It is from this perspective that the transformation of the poetic voice in Riggs's poem—which might otherwise be read as rhapsody and fortuity—must be read as ineluctable logos and catharsis:

> I was blind to my brother's beauty/my own
> but now I see.
> Deaf to the voice that believed
> We were worth wanting/loving
> each other.
> Now I hear.
> I was mute,
> tongue-tied,
> burdened by shadows and silence.
> Now I speak
> and my burden is lightened
> lifted
> free.
>
> [p. 205]

[21]Ibid., p. 11.

# Notes on Contributors

JESSE F. BATTAN is associate professor of American studies at California State University, Fullerton. He has published "The 'New Narcissism' in Twentieth-Century America: The Shadow and Substance of Social Change" (*Journal of Social History*, vol. 17 [1983]) and is currently working on a book entitled "The Politics of Eros: Sexual Radicalism and Social Reform in Nineteenth-Century America."

ROY CAIN is associate professor of social work at McMaster University in Hamilton, Ontario. His research interests have focused on secrecy and disclosure among gay men and related counseling concerns. His current research examines community-based AIDS organizations in Canada and the social forces that shape their development.

KATHERINE CUMMINGS is associate professor of English at the University of Washington. She is the author of *Telling Tales: The Hysteric's Seduction in Fiction and Theory* and is currently writing a critical history of AIDS discourses in the United States from 1981 through 1992.

ANN DUCILLE is associate professor of English and women's studies at Wesleyan University. She is the author of *Coupling and Convention: Black Women Novelists and the Marriage Plot, 1853–1948* (Oxford University Press, forthcoming, 1993) and is currently working on two other forthcoming books: *Inconspicuous Consumption: Labor, Leisure, and the Production of African American Culture, 1850–1930*, and, with Indra Karamcheti, *Black Feminist Criticism in Theory and Practice*, a critical study of some of the debates that have defined the field of black feminist literary studies over the past twenty years.

LILLIAN FADERMAN is professor of English and director of women's studies at California State University, Fresno. She is the author of *Surpassing the Love of Men: Romantic Friendship and Love between Women from the Renaissance to the Present* and *Scotch Verdict*, as well as numerous articles on lesbian life and literature. Her most recent book is *Odd Girls and Twilight Lovers: A History of Lesbian Life in Twentieth-Century America*. She is presently working on a book-length critical study, *Love between Women in Drag: Decoding Lesbian Literature*, to be published by Viking Penguin.

ARTHUR FLANNIGAN-SAINT-AUBIN is chair of Romance languages and associate professor of French at Occidental College. He has published several articles on race, gender, and sexuality in francophone literature in the *French Review* and in *Callaloo*; he is the author of *Mme de Villedieu's Les Desordres de L'Amour: History, Literature, and the Nouvelle Historique*.

JOHN C. FOUT is professor of history at Bard College. He is the editor of two books on European women's history. Currently completing an anthology on "Male Homosexuals, Lesbians, and Homosexuality in Germany, 1871–1945," he is also writing a book-length study entitled "The Moral Purity Movement in Wilhelmine Germany: The Male Gender Crisis and the Concern about the Regulation of Masculinity." His archival research is currently focused on documentary materials on working-class and middle-class men, both rural and urban, arrested for same-sex sexual behavior in Nazi Germany. He is the founding editor of the *Journal of the History of Sexuality* and general editor of the Chicago Series on Sexuality, History, and Society.

JOSHUA GAMSON is a doctoral student in sociology at the University of California, Berkeley, and was a 1990–91 fellow at the Townsend Center for the Humanities at the University of California. His most recent article, "Silence, Death, and the Invisible Enemy: AIDS Activism and Social Movement 'Newness,'" was published in *Social Problems*.

PAMELA S. HAAG is a doctoral student in American history at Yale University. She has published "Commerce in Souls: Vice, Virtue, and Women's Waged Work in Baltimore, 1900–1915" (*Maryland Historical Magazine*, vol. 36 [October 1991]) and "The Ill Use of a Wife: Patterns of Working-Class Violence in Domestic and Public New York City, 1860–1880" (*Journal of Social History*, vol. 26 [March 1992]).

MARTHA HODES is assistant professor of history at the University of California, Santa Cruz. She is the author of "Wartime Dialogues on Illicit Sex: White Women and Black Men," in *Divided Houses: Gender and the Civil War* (Oxford University Press, 1992). Her dissertation on sexual liaisons between white women and black men in the nineteenth-century South won the Alan Nevins Prize of the Society of American Historians; she is currently preparing the manuscript for publication.

JOAN SMYTH IVERSEN is professor of history at the State University of New York College at Oneonta and founding member of the Women's Studies Committee. Her published articles include "Feminist Implications of Mormon Polygyny" (*Feminist Studies*, vol. 10 [1984]); "Living the Suffrage Relationship: Personal and Political Quandaries" (*Frontiers: A Journal of Women's Studies*, vol. 11 [1990]).

CAROLE JOFFE is professor of sociology and women's studies at the University of California, Davis. She is the author of *The Regulation of Sexuality: Experiences of Family Planning Workers*. Her current research includes the preparation of a book-length study on physician involvement in abortion before legalization, as well as the politics of teenage pregnancy prevention efforts.

ANGUS MCLAREN is professor of history at the University of Victoria. His books include *Sexuality and Social Order: The Debate over the Fertility of Women and Workers in France, 1770–1920; A History of Contraception: From Antiquity to the Present Day*; and *Our Own Master Race: Eugenics in Canada, 1885–1945*. A new volume, *A Prescription for Murder: Late Nineteenth-Century Sexual Tensions and the Serial Killer*, is forthcoming from the University of Chicago Press.

SONYA MICHEL is assistant professor of history at the University of Illinois at Urbana-Champaign. She often writes on gender, sexuality, and film in historical perspective. She is also a coeditor of *Behind the Lines: Gender and the Two World Wars* (1987) and *Mothers of a New World: Maternalist Politics and the Origins of Welfare States* (forthcoming, 1993).

KEVIN J. MUMFORD writes on race and sexuality in American cultural history and is at work on a dissertation, "From Vice to Vogue: Black/White Sexual Relations in the North, 1890–1930."

ANTHONY S. PARENT, JR., is assistant professor of history at Wake Forest University. He has completed a book-length manuscript on the formulation of slaveowning society. He and his coauthor Susan Brown Wallace are collaborating on a collective biography entitled "Chattel's Children: A History of Childhood under Slavery."

SUSAN BROWN WALLACE is a psychologist in the Fairfax County, Virginia, Public School District. As a child psychologist and educator, Dr. Wallace is concerned with issues of childhood identity development. She and her coauthor Anthony S. Parent, Jr., are writing an article on the relationship between childhood experiences, including those of a sexual nature, and later religious conversion experiences.

ROBYN WIEGMAN is assistant professor of English and women's studies at Indiana University. She is presently working on a book entitled "Economies of Visibility: Race and Gender in U.S. Culture." Her work has appeared in *American Literary History, Cultural Critique,* and *Bucknell Review*, and she is coeditor, with Judith Roof, of the forthcoming anthology *Who Can Speak? Authority and Critical Identity in Feminist Thought.*

# Index